Woman of Valor

Ellen Chesler

ANCHOR BOOKS
DOUBLEDAY
NEW YORK LONDON TORONTO SYDNEY AUCKLAND

Woman of Valor

Margaret Sanger and the Birth Control Movement in America

AN ANCHOR BOOK
PUBLISHED BY DOUBLEDAY
a division of Bantam Doubleday Dell Publishing Group, Inc.
1540 Broadway, New York, New York 10036

Woman of Valor was originally published in hardcover by Simon & Schuster in 1992. The Anchor Books edition is published by arrangement with Simon & Schuster.

Designed by Carla Weise/Levavi & Levavi

Library of Congress Cataloging-in-Publication Data

Chesler, Ellen.
Woman of valor : Margaret Sanger and the birth control movement in America / [Ellen Chesler]. — 1st Anchor Books ed.
p. cm.
Originally published: New York : Simon & Schuster, 1992.
Includes bibliographical references and index.
1. Sanger, Margaret, 1879–1966. 2. Birth control—United States —Biography. 3. Women social reformers—United States—Biography.
I. Title.
HQ764.S3C44 1993
613.94′092—dc20
[B] 93-16110
CIP

ISBN 0-385-46980-2

PRINTED IN THE UNITED STATES OF AMERICA
FIRST ANCHOR BOOKS EDITION: JUNE 1993
10 9 8 7 6 5 4 3 2 1

For Matt

She Deserves It

Mrs. Margaret Sanger, founder of the Birth Control League, has been awarded the annual medal of the American Woman's Association, which cites her for the qualities of "vision, integrity and valor." Mrs. Sanger deserves this honor; she deserves more honors than a world against whose darkness of mind she has fought bravely and consistently for twenty years is ever likely to give her. Mrs. Sanger has carved, almost single-handed and in the face of every variety of persecution, a trail through the densest jungle of human ignorance and helplessness. She has been many times arrested, assailed and covered with mud—which remains perhaps the most substantial tribute to her pioneering genius. Pretty nearly everything and everyone has been against her—pulpits and legislatures and newspapers, public men and private citizens, and whole regiments of the prejudices, fears, bogeys and dragons that still infest the mind of civilized man.

But such is the common sense of what she has been saying, and so great the courage and conviction of her way of saying it, that people have at last begun to listen and believe. Her victory is not by any means complete, but the dragons are on the run.

—The *New York Herald Tribune,* November 13, 1931

Contents

Introduction

Margaret Sanger went to jail in 1917 for distributing contraceptives to immigrant women from a makeshift clinic in a tenement storefront in the Brownsville section of Brooklyn, New York. When she died fifty years later, the cause for which she defiantly broke the law had achieved international stature. Though still a magnet for controversy, she was widely eulogized as one of the great emancipators of her time.

For more than half a century, Sanger dedicated herself to the deceptively simple proposition that access to a safe and reliable means of preventing pregnancy is a necessary condition of women's liberation and, in turn, of human progress. Her most exquisite triumphs were her last. She was past seventy when the world finally began to heed her concern for unchecked population growth, past eighty when the team of doctors and scientists she had long encouraged first marketed the oral, anovulant birth control pill. She lived to see the realization of her repeated efforts as a litigant and a lobbyist through the landmark 1965 ruling of the Supreme Court of the United States in *Griswold v. Connecticut*, which guaranteed constitutional protection to the private use of contraceptives. She died just as Lyndon Johnson incorporated family planning into America's public health and social welfare programs and committed at least a fraction of the nation's foreign policy resources to it, fulfilling her singular vision of how best to achieve peace and prosperity at home and abroad.

Since her death the rebirth of a vigorous feminist movement has given new resonance to her original claim that women have a fundamental right to control their own bodies. Her direct legacy endures in the far-reaching international family planning movement that descends from her pioneering organizational efforts. She has become an occasional scapegoat of extremists opposed to abortion or of black militants, who insist that family planning is genocidal in intent. But by and large, she shares the ignoble fate of so many iconoclasts like her who have lived to see the routine acceptance of ideas once considered disturbing. She has been forgotten.

Every woman in the world today who takes her sexual and reproductive autonomy for granted should venerate Margaret Sanger. With the full promise of scientific contraception still unfulfilled—with the right to legal abortion now compromised for those who cannot pay, and again at risk for all American women regardless of means—her courageous and determined career merits renewed consideration.

This new biography aims to recapture Sanger's vitality and the intensity of her long struggle to establish the legitimacy of her concerns. It examines both the personal and public dimensions of her life much as she experienced them, layering complicated private struggles and intimate relationships upon larger intellectual and political pursuits. Though she encountered enormous resistance in her own lifetime and still invites criticism, Sanger popularized ideas and built institutions that have widespread influence today. Her leadership, while often quixotic, helped create enduring changes in the beliefs and behavior of men and women who perceive themselves as modern, not only in America but throughout the world. Birth control has fundamentally altered private life and public policy in the twentieth century. No other issue has for so long captivated our attention or so dramatically polarized our thinking. As the psychologist Erik Erikson once provocatively suggested, no idea of modern times, save perhaps for arms control, more directly challenges human destiny, which may account for the profound psychic dissonance and social conflict it tends to inspire. This study necessarily incorporates some of the history of these sweeping developments. It veers away at points in the narrative from the woman herself, and the reader is appropriately cautioned.

Yet the force of Sanger's personality asserts itself, even when she is not at center stage, and the life she uniquely defined for herself as an independent woman develops on its own as a subject worthy of interest, quite apart from the content of her work. Many aspects of her character were admirable. Some were not. Under close scrutiny, she does not always occasion sympathy or seem worthy of praise, but her weaknesses as well as her strengths ought to be more clearly understood. Knowing her better can only help to illumine the history of her times and yield insights into the tensions of our own, when so many of us struggle to complete her still unfinished journey as feminist and reformer.

The middle child of a large and poor Victorian family, Margaret Higgins Sanger learned to dream at an early age from a magnetic Irish father who squandered away his talents and his humane social vision on too much talk and drink. From an overburdened but resourceful mother, however, she was lucky to absorb a powerful motivation to improve her own lot and the essential habits of self-discipline that made it possible to do so. One parent taught her to defy, the other to comport. She always warred between the two but took away from both a distinctive resolve to invent a better life for herself and for others.

She emerged on the American scene in those halcyon days at the turn of this century, when it was easy to believe in the potential of individual and social renewal—in the inevitability of human progress. The country seemed wide open with possibility. Frustrated by her work as a visiting nurse in New York City's bleak immigrant slums—her young marriage turned sour—she first teamed up with labor radicals and bohemians to organize strikes and pickets and pageants in the hope of achieving wholesale economic and social justice. "No Gods, No Masters," the rallying cry of the Industrial Workers of the World, became her personal and political manifesto. But like so many of the callow youth of her generation, this joyous faith in revolution served only as a way station to a more sober confidence in the ability of science and education to shape human conduct. She soon jettisoned Socialism in favor of an alliance with progressives, confident that capitalism might reform itself voluntarily and that bold public initiatives could be planned for human betterment.

At the heart of this political conversion was the maturing of her consciousness as a feminist. Sanger lost confidence in the power of working people to unite for change but decided to invest in the collective potential of women. Chided at one point for taking herself too seriously, she responded deadpan: "I am the partisan of women who have nothing to laugh at." She openly rebelled against conventional gender arrangements that confined men and women to separate spheres but also insisted that the price women pay for achieving equality should not be their sexuality or personal fulfillment. Following in the footsteps of a generation of suffragists and female reformers who had proudly forgone marriage and sacrificed themselves at the altar of professional advancement and political gain, she became the standardbearer of a far less ascetic breed, intent on a broader range of satisfactions. Far from subverting the political or economic advancement of women, she saw nothing wrong in wanting them to have it all, or in establishing birth control as the necessary condition to the resolution of their often conflicting needs. And just as she took issue with traditional images of respectability for women, so she also rejected the equally confining determinism of Sigmund Freud. A disciple of the social theorist Havelock Ellis, she believed optimistically in the power to liberate human sexuality, even from the yoke of the unconscious.

Sanger envisioned a united front of women who would claim the legalization of contraception, along with greater public candor about sexuality, as a fundamental right. The nation's birthrate was already declining as the result of largely private contraceptive arrangements, but birth control remained illegal and underground, and it was she who first recognized the far-reaching consequences of bringing the issue of reproductive freedom out into the open. Birth control, she argued, would enhance the opportunities of women beyond the promises of economic reformers, on the one hand, and of suffragists on the other. It would be a tool for redistributing power fundamentally, in the bedroom, the home, and the larger community. Women would achieve personal freedom by experiencing their sexuality free of consequence, just as men have always done, but in taking control of the forces of reproduction they would also lower birthrates, alter the balance of supply and demand for labor, and therein accomplish the revolutionary goals of workers without the social upheaval of class warfare. Bonds of gender would transcend divisions of ethnicity, race, or class. Not the dictates of Karl Marx, but the refusal of women to bear children indiscriminately, would alter the course of history.

Through the 1920s and '30s, Sanger divorced herself from her radical past, bested her competitors for leadership, and made her name virtually synonymous with the birth control cause. With an uncanny feel for the power of a well-communicated idea in a democracy, she wrote best-selling books, published a widely read journal, held conferences, gave lectures, and built a thriving voluntary social organization. Her intent was nothing less than to construct an international network of clinics where women would receive a full range of preventive health care services. To this end, she had no choice but to mobilize men of influence in business, government, labor, the emerging professions and academic sciences, but her most active recruits always remained women, many of them veterans of the American and British suffrage movements, or daughters of former volunteers, who had learned to do political battle. Her pioneering facilities provided contraception, preventive gynecology, sex education, marriage counseling, and infertility services to poor women and to many who could afford private doctors but simply preferred a sympathetic female environment. Under the best circumstances they became laboratories for her idealism, but, as often as not, the experiment failed, and even Sanger herself grew disillusioned.

The birth control movement stalled during the long years of Depression and World War II, stymied by the cost and complexity of the task of reaching women most in need, engulfed by internal dissension and overwhelmed by the barrage of opposition it provoked. Timid politicians shied away from sexual controversy and refused to reform anachronistic obscenity laws. Many women feared compromising hard-won political gains, especially as birthrates plummeted in the face of economic crisis, precipitating a backlash against their increasing independence. In the social sciences, biological explanations for human behavior lost favor. Eugenic ideas about manipulating heredity, at first the province of progressive proponents of social reform, quickly deteriorated into an excuse for the control of undesirables on the straightforward basis of race and class. Margaret Sanger was never herself a racist, but she lived in a profoundly bigoted society, and her failure to repudiate prejudice unequivocally—especially when it was manifest among proponents of her cause—has haunted her ever since. Intent in her view of contraception as a tool of liberation, she always carefully distinguished between voluntary and coercive applications of her ideas, but this task proved no less daunting for her than it has been for advocates and policymakers since, who have struggled to balance the rights of individuals against a larger vision of the collective social good.

Above all, Sanger more than met her match in the powerful political opposition that was mounted against her by the American Catholic Church. For the first time in its history in this country, the church created a national mechanism for lobbying and for mobilizing its core constituency of faithful women. Sanger was identified as a dangerous subversive, intent on destroying the family and limiting the fertility of the very people she was trying to help. The alliance she forged with the country's establishment came to haunt her as the votes of urban Catholics and rural Southerners became critical to the Presidential ambitions of Franklin Roosevelt. And birth control was denied a place in the social welfare and public health agenda of the triumphant New Deal, tragically distinguishing the American experience from those of Western European nations.

Embittered by her failure to win support at home, Sanger grew personally irritable, politically conservative, and rabidly anti-Catholic as she grew older. Disenchanted with the increasing pronatalism of postwar Americans after years of deferred fertility, she turned her attention abroad and struggled valiantly, though never with complete success, to secure her stature among a new generation of international population policymakers, and to imbue population programs in the developing nations of the world with her never-wavering concern for the precarious status of women.

Margaret Sanger was an immensely attractive woman, small but lithe and trim. Her green eyes were flecked with amber, her hair a shiny auburn hue, her smile always warm and charming, her hands perpetually in motion, beckoning even to strangers. As H. G. Wells once described her, she also had a quick Irish wit, high spirits, and radiant common sense. Men adored her. She married twice and enjoyed the affection and esteem of men and women alike, who provided her a lifelong network of emotional, financial, and organizational support. At the same time, she could be impossibly difficult and was known to make enemies. She was not easily scorned, and those who dared to disagree with her quickly discovered her explosive temper.

Yet it was probably less temperament than sheer tenacity and doggedness of purpose that made her so controversial. She may simply have claimed too much for birth control, antagonizing supporters on the left for whom the dialectic of class remained a central determinant of economic and social change, confounding more bourgeois followers with her disdain for incremental politics, and yet, at the same time, provoking conservatives whom she sometimes courted despite an underlying contempt for convention and conformity. Always a pragmatist, perhaps at times even an opportunist, she deliberately shifted her tactics and strategies to accommodate changing political or economic currents and left herself open to the accusation that she was trying to be all things to all people.

These traits have made her especially controversial with biographers. An image problem actually developed with the two autobiographies she wrote during the 1930s, both self-aggrandizing books filled with petty deceits and outright duplicity. Neither attempts to explain her intriguing personal and political odyssey, for the risk of doing so while she was still alive might have been to ignite even more controversy. With the help of ghostwriters, she wrote entertaining, superficial books of the sort that inspire disbelief, and readers have been appropriately skeptical.

In 1955, the journalist Lawrence Lader tried to present a more balanced and candid portrait in *The Margaret Sanger Story*, but Sanger herself edited the final manuscript, and it tends to recapitulate the many myths she created about her life. In 1970, Emily Taft

Douglas in *Margaret Sanger: Pioneer of the Future* wrote a posthumous celebration of her accomplishments that makes almost no attempt to analyze motivation or explain conflict, while the historian David Kennedy, in *Birth Control in America: The Career of Margaret Sanger*, presented an interpretive study that is marred by his unexplained animus and patronizing attitude toward his subject. Kennedy belittles Sanger's importance, berates her intelligence, and argues that a persistent emotionalism compromised her effectiveness. Yet, contradictorily, he gives her credit for having undermined the accomplishments of the suffragists by offering women a more palatable personal life that provided them a false sense of liberation. Finally, Madeline Gray, in *Margaret Sanger: A Biography of the Champion of Birth Control* (1978), offers little more than a voyeuristic examination of her private life, reducing a remarkable journey of self-discovery to the level of soap opera and riddling it with factual errors. All of these books are now out of print. Only two current monographs address Sanger's career. Linda Gordon, in *Woman's Body, Woman's Right* (1976), condemns her retreat from the left and portrays her unfairly as an unredeemed conservative who became the pawn of the social and professional elites with whom she tried to work. James Reed in *The Birth Control Movement and American Society: From Private Vice to Public Virtue* (1983) refutes this reading of Sanger's relationships with the physicians, social scientists, and philanthropists who joined her cause, but his emphasis is really more on those individuals than on her.

None of these works utilized the full range of archival materials Margaret Sanger carefully assembled and left behind. Though increasingly cautious and personally discreet during her lifetime, she preserved a personal and professional record of both rare intimacy and enormous scope. Her own life was in many respects a monument to the vision of freedom for women she embraced, and she wanted it known after her death that she had lived more or less contentedly by rules of her own devising. Hundreds of boxes of papers available in the archives of the Library of Congress and Smith College form the basis of the research for this project, along with many more examples of her spirited correspondence that have been uncovered in the papers of friends and colleagues throughout the world. Family and friends have also been generous with their reminiscences.

Out of this inquiry an arresting figure emerges. She incorporates emotional and intellectual tensions that make her intensely human and familiar, yet curiously difficult to assess. She was an idealist who devoted herself to achieving concrete reform. A reformer who believed in the determining influence of both biology and culture. A bohemian who loved money and things material. A confirmed sexual materialist who remained an incurable romantic. An adoring mother who abandoned her children. A Socialist who became a registered Republican. An internationalist who was always wary of cultural and political imperialism.

She was sometimes practical, sometimes impetuous, alternately irreverent and amusing, or pompous and boring. She could be strategic and savvy, or obdurate and implacable. She was occasionally a cynic, but more often an optimist. Laughter was always her best defense against despair.

She often surprises, and yet there is a poignant, painful pattern to her life. So much of what Margaret Sanger became seems to have been there right from the start.

The Woman Rebel

CHAPTER ONE

Ghosts

She remembered herself first as a child of three who was crying. The house, ominously silent. A somber neighbor hovering over her mother. She was sent outside, kicking and screaming, but managed to drag a crate beneath the window of the room from which she was forbidden. She hoisted herself up and peered under the drawn shade at her mother lying in bed, white and still, braided hair falling gently at her shoulders—the neighbor now bent in prayer. She stood there until her father entered, and she was reassured that her mother would not die.

Nearly half a century had passed when she committed this memory to writing, and there is of course no way of knowing how much of it was true, how much of it pure invention. Autobiography was for Margaret Sanger a wholly self-conscious gesture. By nature, she was not deeply introspective, always in far too great a hurry to engage in anything more than the most elementary analytic exercise. From her father she had learned to externalize her demons, to subordinate personal malaise to political doctrine and find comfort in the championing of a good cause. From her mother, perhaps, came a rare facility for turning her back on remorse completely, an extraordinary capacity for denial. Yes, she shared the enthusiasm of her generation for the new psychology of Sigmund Freud, but she was never one to get bogged down by the details. She had patience for the particulars of her own past only to the extent that they formed a pattern and offered a compelling explanation for her life's work. To this end, the stories she told about herself may be more reliable as myth than as fact—facts were there for embellishment.

Beyond published autobiography, however, she also left traces of herself in journals, letters, conversations, and photographs where, in Virginia Woolf's memorable phrase, submerged truths invariably do rise to the top. A child emerges needing the love and attention of her mother. The mother is ill and unavailable, presumably from the complications of multiple pregnancies. The child invests her father with the power to resolve this predicament but learns instead of his complicity in the matter. She grows up to proclaim that women must own and control their own bodies, if ever they are to call themselves truly free. The symbolism is palpable, whether or not she ever really stood there at the window.[1]

She was born Margaret Louisa Higgins in Corning, New York, on September 14, 1879, the sixth child and third daughter of Michael Higgins, an Irish stonecutter by trade, and his wife, Anne Purcell. For years she lied about her age and claimed the birth date of a favored younger sister as her own. She even hastily wrote over her mother's inscription in the family Bible, which she deposited with her papers at Smith College, but the ink of the original record is clear, and a handwritten Steuben County census for 1880 confirms the date.[2]

Anne Higgins recovered from the crisis that determined her daughter's most enduring sensibility, and though she remained frail, there were, incredibly enough, five more babies after Margaret, each "without a blotch or blemish," a point of considerable, and often remarked-upon, family pride. As the middle child, Margaret felt the full measure of this large family's difficult circumstances and knew each of her siblings as rivals for parental affections and resources that were never adequate. Yet, they also provided much of the joy she experienced in childhood, and she remained devoted to them throughout her life. She took special pride in the physical prowess and exuberance of the ruddy boys and was particularly fond of the youngest, Bob, later an All-American football hero and a celebrated college coach, whose gratitude to his four older sisters knew no bounds. The Higgins girls, by contrast, were red-headed, delicate, and fair, with a distinctive, wholesome Celtic beauty celebrated by Yeats, the favored poet of their ancestral homeland. They were not, however, blessed with the quiet nature Yeats also willed for his women, and Margaret saw in this predicament the seeds of her own mature discontent.[3]

Their father, Michael Hennessy Higgins, was a first generation Irish-American uprooted by the great famine that ravaged his homeland and sent him across the sea in search of opportunity. Born in 1846, he found his way to Canada as a boy with a widowed mother and a younger brother but left home in his teens and never saw his family again. Margaret's autobiographies say her father answered Lincoln's call for volunteers in the fight against slavery, but too young for active duty, then joined the Union Army as a drummer boy, claiming an adolescent adventure that forever after inspired the awe of his children. Margaret, though she became a committed pacifist and recoiled from human death and suffering, named her second son Grant after her father's revered Yankee general.

Official military records confirm only part of this story. They reveal that Michael enlisted as a private in the New York Cavalry in December of 1863, claiming to be a twenty-year-old laborer in New York City. For reasons that remain obscure, but may have been intended to conceal his age or something else in his past, he called himself by the name of "Michael Hennessy." Margaret goes on to say that Michael marched with General Sherman's troops across Georgia and was cited for bravery. But, in truth, he seems to have escaped the glory and the carnage of that campaign. Assigned to New York's 12th Regiment in January of 1864, he was recorded as absent and sick with tonsillitis on the company's first muster roll. For the remainder of the year, he served daily duty uneventfully at Bachelor's Creek, North Carolina, and, through the war's end in April of the following year, was listed as missing in action. In June, he was honorably discharged. Years later, when pressed to recount his military mettle in a pension application, the single incident he could identify must have been the one that accounted for the MIA designation, a reconnaissance mission that took him behind enemy lines, where he captured a lone Confederate soldier on a mule.[4]

Still, Higgins left the Union Army as a decorated veteran and returned with a fellow soldier after the war to Flemington, New Jersey, then a small but prosperous farming community about forty-five miles from New York City. There, in 1869, he found his Irish bride, the twenty-one-year-old daughter of a day laborer named Joseph Purcell, who also traced his roots back to County Cork. An enterprising family, the Purcells owned real estate valued on the 1870 census at a very respectable $3,500. Having succeeded far better than most of their kinsmen, despite humble origins and illiteracy, they apparently resented Higgins's independent mind, his contempt for religious authority, his sharp tongue and high spirits. They were understandably worried about his prospects.

The newlyweds moved almost immediately to Queens County, New York, where Higgins apprenticed himself to a stonemason. They tried their luck next in Brooklyn and then went west to Massillon, Ohio, but were back in Flemington in 1875, already by then the parents of four small children. Two years later they settled permanently in Corning, where the town's renowned glassworks provided jobs for a large and devout Irish Catholic community, whose fancy cemetery monuments were a visible symbol of its heavenly devotions and earthly rewards. According to local lore, the irreverent Higgins bartered a gravestone adorned with angels and saints for the rental of the house in the river flats where his daughter Margaret was born. It was a ramshackle structure owned by a small local railroad company whose trains ran on tracks just beyond the front door. Cut off from the more densely populated immigrant districts in town, it was transformed in her published memoirs from a simple shanty to an idealized cottage in the woods surrounded by pine trees.[5]

Michael opened a marble and stonecutting business in Corning, but he was an artisan, not a businessman, a talker, not a doer, and as his wife's family had predicted, he never knew material success. While American craftsmen and manufacturers made a historic transition to the structured, time-disciplined habits of the modern workplace, he lagged behind, always mingling work with conversation and drink. He claimed at one point to have been the victim of an embezzlement, but his sons offered a different interpretation of these reverses, blaming them on their father's own improvidence and remembering that often when a customer appeared in his shop, they would have to haul him out of some heated argument, so he could make a sale. Others shared their assessment and thought him at worst a worthless drunk, at best, a foolish spouter. Few respected his principled advocacy of the rights of labor and other advanced social causes of the day. Yet, as success in business eluded him, he seems to have depended all the more for self-esteem on his political convictions. His granddaughter, Olive Byrne Richard, remembers him fondly in the early years of this century as an energetic old man with carrot red hair, freckled face, and twinkling blue eyes, standing at the factory gate, exhorting the glassworkers to organize in pursuit of economic justice and individual freedom. By Margaret's account, his heroes were the legendary single-tax advocate, Henry George, the free-thinker, anticleric and notable early feminist, Robert Ingersoll, and the Socialist Party organizer, Eugene V. Debs, whom she also came to revere.[6]

Higgins got started in politics as a member of the Knights of Labor, a fraternal association that predated the movement for trade unionism by craft in this country and espoused a utopian brand of Socialism. What made this affiliation most unusual was the Knights' strident opposition to America's open-door immigration policy, even to Michael's fellow Irishmen, on the grounds that a steady stream of imported labor would only further erode domestic wages. The Catholic Church was especially suspicious of this sentiment and of the Knights' anticlerical tendencies.

Corning's glass industry prospered in the late 1880s, and substantial support did develop for some form of worker organization. By 1887, local tensions erupted in the wake of the national labor unrest that produced the American Federation of Labor. The glassblowers organized a strike and demanded shorter hours and better wages in the first of what would be many confrontations with the tightly knit family that still retains control of Corning Industries today. The well-publicized imprisonments of the organizers of Chicago's landmark Haymarket labor uprisings that same year fueled local passions, but the union went down to defeat after a train crash killed a number of strikers who were returning home from temporary jobs they had found in Ohio while they were out of work. The glassworks was not successfully organized until the 1930s.[7]

The town's highly skilled craftsmen were a proud and yet, in many respects, a conservative lot, who labored by hand over the dangerous molten substance they molded and blew into glass. Their industry was startlingly slow to mechanize. All the men really wanted from a union was more money and safer working conditions, not the drastically altered industrial and social arrangements of which Michael Higgins dreamed. What is more, Higgins directed his ire not only at the town's economic establishment, but at a diffident, local parish hierarchy that sided with management during the glass strike and appeared to subvert the interests of its own constituents.*

This vocal apostasy won him few friends in any quarter and cost him dearly in work for church cemeteries. His livelihood never transcended these indiscretions, and the situation only deteriorated fur-

* It was not until the 1890s that Pope Leo XIII sanctioned enlightened principles of labor reform and encouraged his bishops to cooperate with emerging trade unions in Europe and America.

ther after he identified himself publicly with the infamous atheist, Robert Ingersoll, an incident that Margaret later claimed as another of her clearest memories.

Ingersoll was a prominent and widely published tribune of rationalism and freedom from superstition, as well as an enthusiastic advocate of human liberty and the rights of women. He was also an early proponent of artificial contraception. To the faithful, of course, he was seen as a symbol of evil incarnate. Ingersoll, according to his own biographer, toured the towns of upstate New York in 1894. Margaret's account of his visit to Corning is unclear in many details but does recall vividly that tomatoes, apples, and cabbage stumps began to fly as supporters of the church prevented the infidel lecturer from using the town's major meeting hall. While there is no corroboration of these facts, she claims he spoke instead from an outdoor field and provided her a first lesson in the value of free speech and free thought. And, at the same time, she openly links the event to the social ostracism and deprivation that followed in its wake. The Higgins children were branded as "children of the devil," their names shouted and scorned by schoolmates.[8]

Margaret always harbored a distinct ambivalence toward her father's political beliefs. On the one hand, she admired his convictions deeply and identified his radicalism as "the spring" from which she drank. She often quoted his admonition that the only obligation of his children was to "leave the world a better place," but the emotional price of this iconoclasm also left a strong imprint. A compulsion to make something concrete of Michael's well-meaning but largely empty political gestures surely underlay her own enthusiasm for reform. Yet with his experience in mind, perhaps, she could never tolerate a losing cause and, after a brief infatuation with radicalism of her own, adopted a strategy of political accommodation and tried to secure herself against the potential public censure of her ideas by aligning herself with individuals of recognized social and professional standing. When they came her way, she thrived unabashedly on acceptance and acclaim. Her style in a curious way mirrored Ingersoll's, an embattled public figure, who, quite unlike her father, had carefully secured himself an education, wealth, and impeccable social credentials, all of which helped insulate him from popular disapproval.[9]

With the decline in Michael's fortunes, the Higgins family was evicted from its cottage in the river flats and moved for a time to makeshift quarters above his failing monument shop. The oldest brothers—Joseph, John, and Thomas—then successively left school and found jobs for a time in the glass factory, while the older girls, Mary and Nan, took positions respectively as maid and governess in local Corning homes. Their salaries allowed the family to rent a succession of houses in the more established Irish and Italian districts on Corning's western hills. By a neighbor's recollection, Anne Higgins also took in washing to help earn money, and the parish priests supplied baskets of food. Years later, Margaret and her younger sister, Ethel, still recalled having walked miles to a milk station to save a penny on the retail price of a five cent quart, so money would be left for candy.[10]

After losing his own business, Michael worked occasionally for the two surviving stonemasons in town, but his love of talk and drink kept him from steady employment, and the sharp deterioration in his circumstances steadily undermined his authority at home. He was finally forced to rely on his sons to get him a job in the glass factory. This domestic crisis may help explain one of the most chilling of Margaret's autobiographical passages—a transparent allegory of oedipal tensions—that conveys her hopeless confusion when the barriers that normally separated men and women, parents and children, were broken down in her own household.

The year was 1892, and Margaret's four-year-old brother had died from pneumonia. Henry George McGlynn was named for two of his father's heroes, the tax reformer, whose wholesale contempt for the perquisites of private property made him anathema to the church, and a maverick Catholic priest, Father McGlynn, who had supported the Corning glassworkers. The little boy had never been baptized, and Anne feared for his damnation, her grief inconsolable for days following the burial. Believing with the phrenologists popular in his day that the human face is a reflection of a transcendent soul, Michael determined to fashion a mask of the dead child. Enlisting Margaret's assistance, he apparently set off late on a pitch-black night on the long walk to the cemetery, pushing a wheelbarrow filled with tools and plaster of paris. Her job was to stand guard and give warning if anyone approached, while her father, in flagrant violation of laws of church and state, uncovered his son's coffin and made a cast of the dead boy's head and shoulders. The two worked in secret for several nights and then presented the sculpture to a tearful but appreciative mother.

Real or invented, the story characterizes Margaret as the child chosen to conspire in an audacious and illicit act, quite beyond the more narrowly circumscribed universe of her mother and sisters. This was an initiation into her father's independent, even reckless, world, and as his accomplice, she was made to sanction Michael's impetuosity, his emotional extravagance, his contempt for authority. Many years later when she wrote about the incident, she could still recall the remorse she had felt on discovering a lock of human hair stuck in the plaster model. She had found it perfectly lifeless and of no comfort whatsoever. Her father may until then have inspired absolute fealty, but no more.[11]

Her autobiography also reports an explicitly erotic recollection from this time in her life, which may even more clearly reveal the overladen nature of her emotions. The rather innocently told story of a first "sex awakening" recalls her terror at waking on a cold winter night from a feverish, typhoid-induced sleep to find Michael in the bed beside her. An advocate of homeopathic medical remedies, he almost always served as his family's doctor and had apparently fallen asleep on the sickbed watch. His heavy breathing alarmed her, and she dreaded that he might awaken before she could summon her mother to the rescue. But instead he rolled over in his sleep taking the covers with him and leaving her in the cold, feeling at peril—as she put it so many years later—as though she were "falling," the sensation Freud often discovered in dreams of women and associated with anxiety about sexual defilement.[12]

Michael had given Margaret morphine to reduce her pain and fever, and the then commonly prescribed drug may have accounted in part for the intensity of her memories when she awoke and when she wrote about the incident so many years later. Exactly how old she was and what weight attached to her father's actual seductions or her subliminal fantasy can never be clear. We do know, however, that he was indisputably a lusty man, and that he openly lavished affection on his wife, who seems herself to have been responsive to his advances. Even as an aging widower, he still enjoyed chasing "a gray haired lassie" every now and then, or so he wrote in an unabashed letter to his eldest daughter, Mary. A dandy fellow by the standards of his day, he dressed in starched white shirt, coat, and tie, even when pictured at work engraving a monument, and Margaret, for all her reservations about aspects of his behavior, seems to have been genuinely drawn to him. She also took from him a positive and strong sensuality of her own, recognizing in herself the inherent attractiveness that only a daughter who has felt herself especially beloved by her father may ever be capable of feeling. This response certainly distinguished her from her sisters, two of whom never married, while the third, Ethel, after a teenage marriage and divorce, lived with a man but openly disdained the oppressiveness of marriage and placed little value in romance.

Still, no matter how deeply Margaret may have been drawn to her father, she never learned to trust him, and this surely was Michael's most enduring legacy. However much he beguiled her, he failed her miserably as a parent—as a reliable model of male industry and authority. She would eventually learn to satisfy her own erotic strivings and court the seductions of men, but she would never allow herself to be defined by them, as women of her generation were expected to do. She would fall in love and marry twice, yet never be beholden to these relationships. She would, indeed, maintain the goal of empowering women to live independent, self-fulfilled lives as her social mission for half a century.[13]

Michael Higgins's rather pathetic decline placed a heavy burden of self-reliance on his oldest children, whose labors, in turn, rescued his family. The price they demanded for assuming this premature responsibility, however, was a high degree of industry and ambition and some measure of conformity to prevailing standards of social behavior and religious belief.

Corning's hillside community of industrious Irish immigrants provided the Higgins children with their first real friendships and role models outside the home. In Margaret's memory, the girls she met there were especially intelligent and fun-loving. They ridiculed the frocked parish priests, even as they went to Mass every Sunday and provided her a model of adolescent comportment far more acceptable than her father's peculiar extremism. The registry of St. Mary's Catholic Church in Corning records the baptism of thirteen-year-old Margaret Higgins on March 26, 1893, little more than a year after the extraordinary grave-digging incident, but the latter event never found its way into her autobiographies.

With this conversion Margaret also attended the parish school in the Corning hills and was confirmed there a year later. When she returned to Corning in 1943 as the academy's most infamous graduate, a God-fearing former classmate remembered that she had been an extremely quiet and intelligent student, absolutely ignorant of the "heretical" ways of thought for which she subsequently became known.[14]

The eighth grade at St. Mary's must also have been the scene of the contretemps reported in her autobiographies with a teacher who ridiculed her for arriving late to school one day, wearing a pair of kid gloves that had been a present from her older sisters. Margaret used this event to illustrate the punitive nature of her schooling in Corning, but it may more clearly identify the humiliation she suffered over an obvious rebuke to the pretentious behavior of a child whose family history was so notorious. The incident, and its proximity to Robert Ingersoll's appearance in Corning, also helps explain the decision to have her complete her secondary education at the Claverack College and Hudson River Institute, a boarding school located across the state in Hudson County, a comfortable distance away from the distractions and tensions at home.[15]

Founded by Dutch Protestants in the 1830s, Claverack was distinguished by its commitment to offer a special course of instruction for women and by its willingness to make "special arrangements" for children who could not afford to pay the full costs. Mary and Nan Higgins pooled meager resources to cover Margaret's tuition, while she worked in the school kitchen to earn room and board. The total cost was $225 a year—far from inconsequential—but the only real option available to anyone who wished to continue her education beyond the eighth grade when local public and parochial schooling ended.[16]

The curriculum at Claverack included English, mathematics, natural science, classics, and the arts, along with special preparation for careers in either teaching or commerce. Margaret reveled in this introduction to a rich secular education and, perhaps still under her father's influence, found herself especially drawn to the social sciences, where she presented speeches on women's suffrage, free silver, and other advanced political issues of the day. Her later accounts of this experience are surprisingly sparse, however, for its significance may have been as much social as intellectual. Gradations of class and family background gave way in the leveling atmosphere of the rambling white clapboard dormitory of the boarding school, and for the first time she experienced a confident sense of belonging. She was becoming an extremely pretty adolescent woman, with a soft, charming smile and a slight, well-proportioned figure, and her good looks combined with high spirits and prankish inclinations to win her instant popularity.

Her published recollections and the letters she shared with Claverack alumnae through the rest of her life describe a gay and spirited crowd of students who self-consciously rebelled against the formality and restraint they so strongly identified with the bourgeois culture of Victorian America. Margaret formed intense attachments to several

New York City girls, whose sophistication she especially admired, and she later defended the innocence of these infatuations as important steps in her own emotional development. She had several significant male suitors as well—one of them a particularly handsome beau from Long Island by the name of Corey Albertson, with whom she posed for a formal portrait on the school lawn one beautiful spring day.

By the testimony of her closest friend at Claverack, Amelia Stuart, Margaret practically never spoke of home during these years, or later, when the two trained as nurses together. If she rarely talked of her family, however, she remained very much in its debt. Surviving letters to Mary from boarding school, for example, are filled with girlish prattle about vacations and clothes and a boy who sent her bouquets of violets and roses. At one point Margaret enlivened the rather dreary world of her devoted sister and mentor by enlisting her in the fantasy that one day she would become an actress. The two of them even assembled a portfolio of captivating portraits, but when a casting agency requested a record of Margaret's bust and hip measurements, she was rudely awakened to the life of the vaudeville stage in its coarse, practical aspects and abandoned the pursuit. No letters to her parents from Claverack remain, however, and though she later claimed to have maintained a lively correspondence about the curriculum with her father, it seems more likely that, even if distance helped resolve some of the tensions between them, her pampered situation as a student also brought further estrangement.[17]

By this time Mary Higgins had gone to work in the home of a Corning family named Abbott, wealthy relations of the Houghtons, who owned Corning Glass. There she developed a taste for the habits and affectations of her employers and a secure belief in the virtues of frugality, hard work, and self-reliance. She kept a diary of her work, and occasional entries offer poignant testimony to her fierce determination to dream her dreams, while taking care to observe the proprieties demanded of servants in such a setting. From her entries we also learn that Margaret visited with her when she came home from school and shared in these preoccupations. On one occasion the two girls ate so much food that poor Mary began to worry whether the mistress of the house would return and punish them. Mary spent the rest of her life as a servant without apparent resentment of her station, but Margaret seems never to have lost the hidden injury of this predicament.[18]

The Abbott home was just up the hill from the town's immigrant community, but with the ascent came more sunshine and space and for Margaret the appearance of a life of leisure and freedom to which the working-class girls down below might aspire. She learned to admire the stylish young mothers of the town's emerging middle-class, who in her memory walked hand in hand with their children on daytime shopping expeditions and in the evenings played croquet with their husbands on the manicured lawns beside their homes. Like many young people raised in poverty, she associated wealth and social status unequivocally with personal fulfillment. She came to believe that money must necessarily bring happiness. Having never felt real solidarity with the working class in which she grew up, no doubt because of her father's eccentricity and unpopular ideas, she was never able to attach real dignity to life within it.[19]

Still, however far Michael strayed from conventional expectations as a provider for his family, he remained solicitous of his wife's affection, and she of his. Estranged from extended family and community, he made a haven of his home. By Margaret's recollection, her parents' marriage was rich in mutual respect and unusually intimate for its day. She could remember only one occasion on which Anne had rebelled openly at her husband's tendency toward self-absorbed behavior and foolish profligacy—when he allegedly took money his oldest son had earned to buy the family's winter coal and spent it on a dinner to honor Henry George. Yet even then, by her recollection, he was quickly able to woo the light back into his wife's emerald eyes.

Margaret would come to see this willingness to barter strongly held principles for the security of a man's affections as a sign of tremendous weakness in a woman, but, at the same time, her mother remained a powerful presence in her memory, whose quiet indulgence had demonstrated fortitude and resilience in the face of few other options. For Anne Higgins to have admitted disappointment in her husband openly would have been a concession of victory to her parents who had spurned him, her neighbors who censured him, and her children who resented him. And she was apparently far too proud to admit such defeat openly.[20]

Two portraits survive. The first, a miniature hand-colored photograph, reveals an attractive, rather ethereal, young woman in an elegant costume of satin and lace, an ivory brooch at her collar, her long hair beautifully curled and piled high. The pose is captivating and wonderfully romantic. The second, a sepia photograph, shows a matronly woman dressed in black and much sobered by age and circumstance, her aquiline features broadened and hardened, her beauty lost, but her will still strong and determined. In Margaret's memory, her mother never grew stout and always carried herself perfectly erect, without a hint of the slouch to which so many working women of her era succumbed. And then there were the wild flowers she used to decorate the family table, because there was never money or leisure to plant a garden. She possessed a simple grace with nature.[21]

Family legend traced the Purcell lineage to the Norman conquerors of England and Ireland and maintained that ancestors had ruled over County Cork as squires and country gentlemen since the twelfth century, leaving their mark in war and politics. The Purcells even claimed a distant kinship with the distinguished Victorian man of letters, Edward FitzGerald, author of the popular *Rubaiyat of Omar Khayyam*, whose hapless crises of religious conviction made him a cultural icon. The friend of Tennyson, Thackeray and Carlyle, FitzGerald was actually born a Purcell and only later assumed the noble patronym of his mother's family. The stories were probably nothing more than the fabulation of aspiring Irish immigrants who felt a need to distinguish themselves from more common brethren, but they provided a romantic and powerful legacy.[22]

Grand as they were, however, Anne's affectations could not undo the harsh conditions of her life. Michael, by his daughter's recollection, read the children fables and fairy tales and *Gulliver's Travels* and later engaged them in discourse on history, phrenology, and science, but it was Anne who fetched the water from the outdoor pump that cooled a child's feverish lips on cold and dark winter nights. She routed the vagrants from the kitchen floor when her husband left the door unlatched as his way of defying the exclusionary prerogatives of private property rights, and she faced up to the schoolteachers who lashed her sons for asserting the irreverent opinions their father had taught them at home. Moments of shared intimacy and repose between mother and child were obviously cherished, and even as an old woman herself, Margaret remembered how her mother had gently rinsed her hair in pure rainwater captured in a barrel, so it would retain its natural luster. Through all the years, Margaret kept the thick auburn braid of hair that she had first cut off when bobbing became the fashion of the 1920s, the relic of an innocence that, however remote, could still totally absorb her.[23]

Anne Higgins served her family with selfless strength even as her health deteriorated from a chronic tuberculosis that more than once threatened her life. By her daughter's reckoning, she always had a cough so severe she would have to brace herself against a wall to regain composure. The therapeutic regimen that sent wealthy Victorian consumptives to sanitaria in search of rest and fresh air was not available to her, and she seems to have wasted slowly from the disease and from the constant pregnancies that weakened her resistance to it. Whatever homage Margaret later paid her father, she could never forgive him for this. She could never reconcile his ardent embrace of the advanced political and social thinking of his day with the indulgence that in her mind so obviously left the promise of her mother's life unfulfilled. In her autobiographies Margaret blamed this predicament on her parents' ignorance of birth control. What she chose not to acknowledge openly were her mother's deeply felt religious convictions in the face of contraceptive knowledge that circulated widely at the time.[24]

Americans devised a clear pattern of fertility control in the nineteenth century. Though there were variations by social class, geographic region, race, and ethnicity, each generation after 1800 reduced the number of its children, so that by century's end the nation's birthrate had been cut in half, from an average family size of more than seven children to fewer than four. Contraceptive tracts and instrumentalities disseminated widely. But while options were abundant, they remained essentially primitive and often unreliable, so that no agreement ever developed about their utility, safety, or moral efficacy. Instead, religious, social, and scientific taboos against contraception gained currency as the century progressed and eroded confidence in commonplace behavior. Attitudes toward contraception incorporated the larger sexual and social tensions of the culture, and private strategies for limiting fertility became more problematic, rather than less.

What were the most common arrangements of the era?

There was, first, coitus interruptus or withdrawal, a self-evident, autonomous and cost-free procedure.* The New Testament clearly

* The practice is explained in the Bible in a fragmentary account of the origins of the Hebrew tribe of Judah which appears in the Book of Genesis: When Judah's eldest son, Er, is slain, he commands the second-born, Onan, to go to his brother's wife and "raise up seed for your brother." Onan, however, refuses to father children in his brother's name, so whenever he has relations with his brother's wife, he "lets [his seed] be lost on the ground." This is seen as a defiant and egotistical act, and God punishes Onan with death. The Hebrew Talmudists who first interpreted this text, however, encouraged sentimentality and sexuality within marriage, and claimed that Onan was not punished for his contraceptive act per se, but for his insubordination. They did not condemn the practice in all instances, but the early Christian disciples, reacting to the rampant pagan practices of a Roman citizenry they were either eager to convert or to defend themselves against, used Onan's misdeeds to enforce a ban on all contraception and the dedication of conjugal sexuality to childbearing exclusively. In Christian doctrine the narcissistic Onan came to symbolize the wantonness of all nonprocreative sexual acts, including

enjoins withdrawal, and the prohibition is mentioned occasionally in eighteenth-century religious texts, but it only became a public controversy when European thinkers began to link the size of individual families to an emerging concern for the larger economic and social well-being. In 1798, an Anglican clergyman in London by the name of Thomas Malthus, soon to make his reputation as demographer and economist, first published postulates on the potential conflict between unrestrained population growth and what he believed to be the finite nature of the world's food supply. A devout man, Malthus only recommended postponing the age of marriage as a voluntary check on the birthrate. In 1821, however, the British liberal James Mill wrote in the Encyclopedia Britannica of the need to find a more practical means of preventing conception. The British reformer, Jeremy Bentham, arguing that withdrawal diminishes sexual pleasure, then advocated contraception through the use of "certain sponges," as a utilitarian remedy for poverty. And in 1822, the self-educated London tailor, Francis Place, who became another leading spokesman of British liberalism, circulated an anonymous pamphlet—the Diabolical Handbill, as it came to be known—identifying both withdrawal and sponges as procedures already well-established in France. In his widely read *Everywoman's Book* of 1826, the reformer Richard Carlile then presented condoms as a third option.

These ideas first found their way to America in the hands of Robert Dale Owen, son of the utopian social reformer of New Harmony, Indiana, who in 1831 wrote *Moral Physiology; or A Brief and Plain Treatise on the Population Question*. The younger Owen advocated contraception, not only as an economic benefit, but also as an in-

masturbation and withdrawal, both commonly referred to as Onanism and condemned as sins in theological texts. The basis for both a moral and legal argument against contraception was established in the reading of divine authority into a natural order that sanctifies marriage solely for the purpose of placing women in the home with an injunction to bear children.

At the same time, the Apostles further devalued sexuality by insisting that Mary had been a virgin and by demanding celibacy of her son and his spiritual disciples, the latter practice, of course, remaining unchallenged until the Protestant reformation. By that time, however, Christian asceticism had been strongly reenforced by what proved to be the extraordinarily enduring teachings of Augustine of Hippo, who lived during the third century. Repenting of his own youthful infatuation with the dissolute and promiscuous Manicheans, Augustine achieved Christian sainthood by bequeathing Western culture a doctrine of original sin that has long since provided intellectual justification not only for religious repression and persecution, but also for political intolerance. By transforming the Biblical story of Adam and Eve from a hopeful affirmation of human desire and free will into a somber warning of man's bondage to the temptations of lust, Saint Augustine inspired generations of conservative thinkers and institutions whose mission has been to protect humankind from this inherent vulnerability to evil.

strument to promote the right of women to self-determination and to advance his own perfectionist social ideas. His pamphlet, in turn, influenced a free-thinking Boston physician by the name of Charles Knowlton whose *Fruits of Philosophy; or, The Private Companion of Young Married People* became, in 1839, the first known tract on the subject published in this country by a physician. Knowlton recommended the superior contraceptive utility of postcoital douching to flood the vagina with water and evacuate the sperm. Though prosecuted for his views under common law obscenity statutes in the Commonwealth of Massachusetts, he became a respected member of his profession and his community. The pamphlet sold thousands of copies, was widely plagiarized, and as late as the 1870s, was still being referred to in popular advice books on marriage. Numbers of different "sanitive" powders or suppositories were marketed, from the relatively harmless bicarbonate of soda to such potential toxins as carbolic acid and borax. Fountain syringes were also widely distributed among women and became staples of mail order houses such as Lydia Pinkham's.

Charles Knowlton also influenced a well-known writer and traveling lecturer on marriage and sexuality by the name of Frederick Hollick, who popularized douching and in subsequent years advanced a rhythm system of contraception to use in tandem with withdrawal, and in place of barrier methods, which physicians were beginning to blame for vaginal infection and disease. Hollick's proposal was based on a crude but substantially accurate calculation of the woman's menstrual cycle, the precision of which was subsequently challenged by several established medical authorities, but then, contradictorily, endorsed by others. (Medical confusion on the matter was finally ended in the 1930s, when definitive research on ovulation was made available.)

In 1837, the Connecticut inventor, Charles Goodyear, had successfully vulcanized rubber in his laboratory, subsequent refinements of which made possible the manufacture of a flexible new material with thin and delicate properties. A domestic industry then developed in rubber condoms. Male sheaths had been used since ancient times, but had been made previously from the internal membranes of sheep or other animals. Manufactured in small quantities in France, they were imported to the United States at great expense. With Goodyear's discovery, condoms could be mass marketed cheaply and became a staple of prostitutes and so notorious in reputation that the inventor never dared take any credit.

Among the hundreds of products listed in his published inventories of the 1850s, however, were rubber devices known as pessaries and commonly sold to married women in pharmacies, to be inserted into the vagina in order to support or medicate the uterus. Pessaries became something of a gynecological fad, and a Philadelphia physician and sexual liberal named Edward Bliss Foote soon described their contraceptive potential. Foote actually invented a "womb veil" made of India rubber and marketed it to married women to insert before intercourse. He was considered a bit of a kook, however, and though his device had similar properties to the modern vaginal diaphragm or cervical cap, it did not enjoy a terribly wide circulation. By contrast, devices of this nature, invented around the same time in Germany and Holland, earned the confidence of established physicians there and were widely recommended.

Information was flawed, and almost every idea had its detractors, yet by the middle of the century, knowledge of coitus interruptus and various proposals for periodic abstinence, spermicidal douches, condoms, sponges, and other occlusives, along with emmenagogues believed to bring on menstruation and other nostrums of varying degrees of effectiveness, was widely circulated in America by midwives, physicians, popular health lecturers, phrenologists, freethinkers, and pharmaceutical salesmen. Abortifacient properties were attached to chemicals like morphine and tannin, and to such plants as tulips, yarrow, milkweed, or rosemary, whose capacity to alter the estrogen and progesterone levels necessary to female reproduction has since been scientifically confirmed. Until obscenity statutes were passed in the 1870s, contraception was also openly advertised in the highly competitive tabloid newspapers and penny presses of the day, in almanacs and mail-order catalogs, and thereafter a covert trade prospered. Young women whose marriages were announced in local newspapers commonly received advertisements and circulars in the mail—often for pharmaceutical products sold under the euphemism of "feminine hygiene," or simply given a "French" label, but widely recognized as contraceptives.[25]

Who used these products and who did not is less clearly understood. Little is known for certain, apart from what has become a much analyzed and often quoted survey of female behavior—a questionnaire of fifty wives of Stanford University professors distributed in the 1890s by a female physician in Palo Alto named Clelia Mosher. Dr. Mosher's questionnaire uncovered nearly universal sexual activity and contraceptive practice, and this among a sampling of married women said to be demographically representative of a larger middle-class population.*

The accepted motivation for contraceptive use was the simple desire to get ahead in a world where a large family was no longer a necessary asset, but success also demanded discipline over personal gratification. The cost of artificial preventives may have been a factor, as well. Prices declined over time but remained high relative to family income. A dozen reusable condoms of allegedly high quality was advertised at $9.00 by the health writer Frederick Hollick in 1847, at $5.00 by his competitor Edward Bliss Foote in 1865, and at $1.50 in a Chicago mail order catalog from the 1880s. Yet, the average annual income of a working man in midcentury was only $600. Fertility thus correlated inversely with income, education, and job status, Margaret's own experience being exemplary.[26]

Until the 1870s, in fact, American birthrates declined steadily, and the commercial trade in contraception prospered, with remarkably little accountability or controversy, and with virtually no resistance from organized religion. The silent complicity of the nation's clergy reflected the ascendence of a liberal theology and utilitarian moral theory in the Protestant churches, where the dark legacy of Saint Augustine gave way to a more popular romantic optimism about human nature and to increasing confidence in the possibility of scientific improvement on divine intention. This new relativism admitted the possibility of reasonable differences of individual conscience and behavior in such matters as family size, and contraception was tolerated within marriage, because it promoted the desirable ends of smaller families, improved standards of living, and human happiness. Tolerance, however, never meant outright endorsement. American Protestants made no official statements on birth control until well into the twentieth century, and even then, only over the protest of conservative and fundamentalist elements among them.

By contrast, the Catholic Church closed ranks around a traditional morality rooted in ancient canons demanding individual discipline and self-sacrifice. The Vatican's theological orthodoxy demanded that personal considerations never justify deviation from absolute, revealed standards of good and evil, right and wrong. Pope Leo XIII,

* Of forty-three women responding to the survey, all but four admitted having used some form of artificial family limitation. Douching was most popular, followed by the safe period, withdrawal, the condom, pessary, and sponge. Methods were consciously distinguished by gender, with women identified as responsible for the douche and pessary, and men for the condom and withdrawal.

in an encyclical issued in 1880, dwelt at length on the danger of interpreting marriage as a mere human arrangement subject to individual whim and fancy. Instead, he emphasized the sacramental character of the wedding contract and its significance as a symbol of the inviolable union of Christ and his church. His message expressly enjoined divorce on these grounds, but, surprisingly, it did not explicitly mention or prohibit contraception, despite the fact that decrees issued in the 1850s by the Holy Office in Rome had declared Onanism as intrinsically evil and forbidden by natural law.

The Pope may have been reticent to dignify the subject by addressing it directly. Earlier, the Vatican had cautioned its priests not to inquire openly into the private practices of their confessees, even when illicit behavior was suspected. Church fathers unwilling to challenge long-standing patriarchal principles also advised that absolution be granted women who confessed sexual submission to husbands engaging in Onanistic practice. But gradually this modest, laissez-faire attitude was abandoned at the urging of officials in Belgium, France, and Germany, who were increasingly alarmed about precipitous population declines and the growing challenge to their authority from secular doctrines. In the 1890s, even as the Vatican embraced a more liberal social activism, it was formally instructing priests to confront penitents with a rigorous inquiry into their sexual lives.

Concern about Catholic fertility in America, moreover, had distinct political overtones. Still an embattled minority in 1850, with only a million and a half constituents and one bishop, the "Church of Rome," as it was derisively known, confronted outspoken suspicion and prejudice here and had no choice but to shy away from organization and controversy. Only as a consequence of internal population growth and vast ethnic migrations from Central and Eastern Europe would the Catholic population in this country reach 12 million by 1900 and more than 33 million by 1950, making it the largest single denomination nationwide, and one capable of asserting moral authority and political influence.[27]

A freethinker like Michael Higgins would then have most certainly known about contraception, but Anne Higgins remained a pious Catholic whose religious faith helped sustain her tenuous hold on life and provided an important social bond—as the woman who ministered at her sickbed and the parish priests who helped feed her children so well illustrate. Through the many years of Michael's apostasy, she kept her devotion to her church, never flagrantly disobeying his wishes by baptizing the children or attending mass, but instead, saying her prayers in private. Her fecundity, however, offered one indisputable, public testimony to her moral rectitude, and in the gilded Higgins family Bible, she dutifully recorded the birth of each child in a bold and confident script, beneath the papal injunction, "Lo children are an heritage of the Lord." When she died, these private devotions were recognized by the parish priest who administered the sacraments and buried her inside the consecrated grounds of St. Joseph's Church cemetery in Corning, where years later Michael was laid to rest nearby in a grave unmarked and unblessed.[28]

It is also apparent that Anne's childbearing redeemed her aspirations for this world, as well as for the next. By the industry of her older children, the larger opportunities of her young ones were secured. An identical pattern of mobility had, in fact, existed in her own family. Her youngest brothers, William and Richard Purcell, left jobs as potters in New Jersey in the 1880s, went to law school, and then headed west to the Dakota territories, where they made their fortunes as lawyers and wheat ranchers. In 1887, William Purcell was appointed United States attorney for the region by Pres. Grover Cleveland. In 1906, he was elected to the legislature of the new state of North Dakota as a Democrat, and in 1911, was designated by a new governor to fill a vacancy in the United States Senate. Though he was not reelected and served for only three years, he was able to help out Michael Higgins, then an aging widower living in a veteran's retirement home in Bath, New York. Margaret and her sister Nan documented the well-worn saga of their father's capture of rebel soldier and mule, and their uncle filed a private pension bill on his behalf, securing him an increase in the meager income he collected as a disabled Civil War Veteran. Margaret never mentioned this lineage in her autobiographies. She may have hesitated to acknowledge an uncle who was a proud and practicing Catholic. Even more important, perhaps, she might not have dared give credence to the notion that all those Higgins children had provided her poor mother with what little fulfillment she found in life. It was the deprivation of that life, and of her own childhood, that governed her mature thoughts and feelings.[29]

In Margaret's memory, her mother was forever cooking, cleaning, or sewing, in a futile attempt to bring order to her chaotic household. But constrained by poverty and poor health, she did little more than exacerbate her children's sense of material and emotional deprivation. A Corning neighbor once recalled the chagrin of a Higgins brother made to wear girls' clothes while his mother mended his only pair of pants. By contrast, a serene photograph survives from what were obviously better times, when the four sisters assembled in elegant dresses, each fashioned by hand with loving and meticulous attention to the details of the pleated bodices and mutton sleeves.[30]

From the fragments we have, we can only presume the quality of young Margaret's emotional life. Yet it hardly seems too much to say that the woman whose earliest memory was of a mother who might die—the woman who held on to the knotted braid of her youth—was telling us something important about the bond that is the essential foundation of personality. Though on most occasions Margaret would identify her iconoclastic father as her most significant influence, children depend on the approval and affection of both parents. And the child who early on senses her mother at risk, and never experiences this first attachment as secure and uncompromised, may be especially burdened. Margaret remembered herself as a toddler beset by fears of wandering away and getting lost, of sleeping in the dark, of descending unlit cellar stairs, all commonly understood anxieties of separation, intensified, no doubt, in her own experience by her mother's actual, precarious situation. Her autobiographies also recall that this pattern of insecurity carried forward into later childhood when she felt compelled to test herself in dangerous and forbidden situations, such as crossing a harrowing railroad bridge, where a single misstep would have sent her plunging into a ravine below. They admit, as well, to her intense jealousy of Ethel, her younger sister, who as the winsome baby girl of the family became their mother's favorite. Margaret claimed that in triumphing over such childish phobias and rivalries, she had secured and prepared herself for the risk and adventure of her adult experience, but it is just as likely that her continued preoccupation with this behavior was evidence of its sustained irresolution. Never secure in the embrace of her own mother, she seems never to have known herself with a reflected contentment. And this emotional residue of childhood most certainly compelled her toward public exposure and her historic role as a social reformer.[31]

Anne Higgins died of consumption on March 31, 1899, at the age of fifty, worn-out and emaciated, her only solace, perhaps, that it was Good Friday, one of the holiest days of the year. Mary and Nan had not been able to come up with enough money to support Margaret through the third year of Claverack required for a diploma, and, instead of finishing school, she had somehow (perhaps, with the help of her mother's family) located a position in an elementary school in New Jersey, where she spent an exhausting half-year trying to teach English to foreign-born first graders. However trying this experience, teaching was a coveted avenue of upward mobility, and she could only have come home reluctantly in midcourse to nurse her dying mother through the final stages of her illness. She was herself just nineteen years old.[32]

The ever-obliging Mary recorded in her diary that she had just finished baking an angel-food cake for the parish bazaar when a boy came hurrying up the hill with the news. She ran home to find her father sitting dazed and despondent by the corpse. He removed Anne's gold wedding band and gave it to her, a gift of which she thought herself unworthy. The assistant pastor of St. Mary's Church administered last rites and years later claimed that Margaret had stood at the foot of her mother's bed and looked on coldly, refusing to kneel and join in the prayers, but he seems to have confused her with Ethel or Nan, for Margaret had been invited to spend the Easter weekend with a boarding school friend from Buffalo and returned hastily only when she received a telegram of the news. The dependable Mrs. Abbott, for whom Mary still worked, got out black dresses, hats and trimmings, veils and gloves, so there would be proper mourning attire. And Mary herself took care of the casket and all other arrangements, a responsibility that left her with a terrible headache, the only sign of emotion she let slip into her record of the day's events.[33]

Margaret's autobiographies treat the event with a suspicious economy, a single, if resonant, sentence recalling the mournful howl of her family's beloved dog, Toss, as he stood guard over the body. The event was years away, of course, yet the absence of the barest mention of grief is in stark contrast to the intensity of many of her other memories and of the one reaction she did acknowledge in this instance. She was enraged by the necessary reallocation of household drudgery after Anne was gone. With the older girls off working, the care of a bereft father and three young boys still at home fell to her and to Ethel. They had to wash and scrub and mend the trousers.

Margaret may have resented and belittled her father's mourning, because it seemed so hypocritical. She had lived away from home for almost three years and was eager for independence when her mother died, though still very uncertain of what to do with her life. In this fragile moment of emotional and physical separation from her own youth, she was probably not disposed to feel her sorrow deeply, or dwell on her loss. She seems instead to have experienced her mother's death as an unwelcome inconvenience and imposition, behavior that is commonly observed among adolescents who lose a parent while still absorbed in the challenge of resolving identity conflicts of their own.

She immediately enrolled herself in a school of nursing. Yet for years thereafter her mother remained a distinct if unresolved presence. In 1920, two decades after Anne died and in the same year that American women finally won the right to vote, Margaret published her first book, a manifesto that demands the democratic dissemination of birth control as a fundamental right of women. The book proposes that political and economic enfranchisement will not alone guarantee an end to discrimination—that medicine and science must also be harnessed to secure women an equal right to experience the full range of human possibility. It bears a simple but powerful dedication to the memory of a mother "who gave birth to eleven living children."[34]

CHAPTER TWO

Love and Work

Eager to leave Corning, Margaret arranged through Claverack connections to be placed as a probationer in the nurse's training program at the White Plains Hospital downstate in Westchester County. Michael Higgins's behavior deteriorated markedly in his wife's absence. He suddenly became an "irritable, aggravating tyrant," by his daughter's recollection, interfering with her ambitions and social life, on which he placed rigid curfews. The family scattered, the four oldest having already established themselves in jobs. Mary's employer moved to Buffalo, and Nan followed her there as a commercial secretary, later moving to New York City. Joseph and Thomas remained in the glass factory. The fifth in line, John, left home in 1895 never to be heard from again, and was subsequently presumed dead in a drowning accident. The younger ones got caught up in their father's fury. Ethel eloped with a high school sweetheart in an ill-fated marriage that produced two children before it broke up. Richard, only twelve years old in 1901, had a run-in with the local police and was booked for willful injury to local property. With an older brother, Lawrence, he eventually left home, wandered around and with Nan's help found his way to Lehigh University and then into the navy during World War I. Robert, the baby brother who became a football star, was also sent away to school by his older sisters.[1]

Margaret settled on training as a nurse, an occupation considered far more menial and unworthy than teaching. Before the formalization of nursing education in the late nineteenth century, the line between nursing and domestic service was not clearly delineated, and old stereotypes were hard to overcome. Overworked and underpaid, nurses traditionally ministered to the most elementary needs of their patients, emptying bedpans, changing soiled linens, cleaning and even cooking, their status elevated beyond servant only by what little patina derived from their association with emerging medical professionalism. What Margaret really wanted was to become a doctor, a highly considered profession for educated girls of the Victorian middle class, because medical ministrations seemed a natural extension of inherently female sympathies, but the aspiration was far beyond her own economic reach. Nursing was in this sense a disappointment. The hours were too long and the work too arduous, but by her own acknowledgment, the experience left her with a discipline and an endurance she depended upon for the rest of her life.

Two trends would converge by the turn of the century to revolutionize the delivery of health care in this country and dramatically alter its professional and social status. First, scientific advances in bacteriology allowed physicians to understand the etiology of disease, a critical step in the development of modern diagnostic and therapeutic procedures. Second, a specialization of medical practice logically followed these advances. Doctors, once concerned with the patient's overall well-being, were transformed into specialists in the cure of isolated illness, and hospitals, until then institutions of last resort serving mainly the poor, became more sterile and disciplined bureaucracies providing training for physicians and nurses and treatment for all social classes.[2]

This transformation undermined the traditional holistic approaches that had first attracted Margaret to medicine as a career option. The ratio of women doctors actually began to decline by the early decades of this century, as medical schools and hospitals began to practice sex discrimination under the guise of professional standardization. Yet these developments, in turn, had precisely the opposite effect on nursing, where the number of professionals began to increase dramatically, from some 15,000 in 1880 to 120,000 in 1900. Formal schools of nursing and professional associations were organized on the model developed by Florence Nightingale in England, and leaders in the field made insistent arguments claiming nursing as women's work on the same grounds that women doctors had done before them. Since no secondary degree was then prerequisite, nursing also became more accessible than medical school to women in circumstances like Margaret's.[3]

Preparation for nursing differed widely in length and intensity, from elite, hospital-based programs to short-term correspondence courses. New York State took the lead in formulating legislation to register nurses and to regulate their training through standardized three-year courses, while also continuing to permit those without this formal preparation to work as "practical" nurses.

At White Plains, Margaret entered into an accredited two-year program that combined textbook instruction with experience on the wards and in homes nearby. Completion of this course would have qualified her for the additional, specialized year of training soon to be required for certification as a registered nurse. The conditions of nursing in what was still a rural setting were essentially primitive and harsh. The original twelve-bed hospital was housed in a converted and inefficient three-story mansion and left her with vivid memories of climbing dark and drafty stairwells, where every step echoed with strange sounds that conjured up her worst childhood phobias. There was no central heating or plumbing. A new wing in 1900 added modernized facilities, but with no resident physicians on staff, responsibility for maintaining the ill fell solely to the probationary nurses. By Margaret's recollection, the nurses were often prey to the nighttime entreaties and assaults of drugged and delirious patients, a daunting assignment under any circumstances, and a particularly harsh burden, perhaps, to a young woman wary of a hard-drinking and temperamental father.[4]

Margaret went about her duties, presided at births and deaths, assisted in surgery, and earned enough respect to be appointed head nurse of the women's ward. In a letter to Mary, she described one case where she served on "special" duty during the surgical removal of a cancerous growth in a patient's intestine. "I am nearly dead," she admitted. There were also many more routine assignments, and when she became a celebrity years later, she would still receive letters from women who remembered her fondly as their own nurse-midwife.

Through all this, however, her own health deteriorated, and after experiencing loss of weight, low-fever, and constant fatigue, she underwent the first of a number of surgical procedures for what was diagnosed as tuberculosis in the cervical lymph nodes, a highly communicable form of the disease which she may have contracted from her mother. Conditions at White Plains depleted her resistance to infection, and this first breakdown established an associative pattern of stress, overwork, and illness that would repeat itself throughout her life. Small pockets of tubercular infection remained in her neck, and the operation left her with a draining sinus that opened and closed repeatedly over the next twenty years, causing sporadic incidences of acute illness and interim fever and weakness.[5]

Despite this situation she was photographed in the candy-striped uniform of the training nurse, looking frail but cheerful. She lived in a local boarding house with her dear friend, Amelia, and other new classmates who provided sororal support, exchanging gifts of books, photographs, and bedroom slippers at Christmas and other holidays. Her sister Mary, and Nan, who had moved to New York City and found work as a private secretary, sent small amounts of expense money and welcome gifts, which she vowed to repay in other ways, as she put it, "when I get rich." There were also occasional outings with suitors, including a weekend visit in June of 1902 from the handsome and devoted Corey Albertson of Claverack, whom she described elusively in a letter to Mary as "the same old boy." The two young people apparently had a secret agreement to marry, but Margaret wanted her nursing degree first, and she may have been troubled as well by her perception of the deep social chasm that existed between them outside the egalitarian setting of the boarding school. Albertson was from a middle-class family, and she apparently never brought him to Corning or introduced him to her family.[6]

Margaret was completing her training and planning on entering the third-year degree program, when she traveled to New York City over the summer for a special clinical course at the Manhattan Eye and Ear Infirmary. She had missed a month of school because of her operation, and the summer session provided an opportunity to make up the lost credits. She welcomed the chance to serve in a modern, scientific facility and to enjoy a more leisurely schedule. The few letters that survive from this experience communicate a rare self-esteem born, perhaps, of this first opportunity to experience herself as a competent and accomplished professional. Her newfound independence may also explain her extremely erratic response to a romance that suddenly altered the course of the plans she had charted.

There are several conflicting stories about how she met William Sanger. One suggests that he dropped by a hospital dance in White Plains one evening to deliver a set of architectural drawings to a doctor who was his client, another, that he came in to the hospital in Manhattan to have a fragment of construction glass removed from his eye. Whatever the exact circumstances, he pursued her from the moment they met with a torrent of emotional and romantic gestures including daily letters and phone calls, books and flowers, a gold watch and chain and the promise of a diamond ring. Her longtime suitor, Corey Albertson, dropped inexplicably from the picture, and she quickly agreed to marry Bill instead, as soon as she finished the nursing degree, which remained, unequivocally, her primary goal.

In 1902, a woman in Margaret's situation could not have expected to combine a profession with a husband and family, and the prospect of marriage probably evoked deep feelings of vulnerability within her. She was, after all, her mother's daughter.[7]

Margaret Higgins and William Sanger married on August 18, 1902, having known each other for less than six months. The decision was impulsive, the ceremony impromptu, and it took weeks for the bride to recover her emotional balance. Earlier she had written plaintively to Mary: "When I think of all the hard work—the bitter tears I shed night after night for the old training—the lonesome nights I passed waiting for some old tramp to die—then when it is finished, without a laurel to get married—then I want to stop it all. I would love one year of private nursing—and get some money—and then if anyone wants me all right—but Wm Lad does not care about waiting longer than six months—he is working like mad—he adores father already—both socialists—oh heavens—the conversations they will hold!" She also worried that without her own earnings to pay for a wedding, none of her Claverack friends could attend, because her family was too poor to mount a proper spread. She thought about eloping, as Ethel had done, but dismissed the idea and proposed to her sister that "a good way to save expense would be to have him [William] on the verge of death, and I can nurse him & insist on a deathbed marriage." In a more serious vein, she then suggested a small wedding at home: "Have we a house or a barn—it was somewhat of a barn when I last saw it," she concluded, this time probably only half in jest.[8]

The dilemma resolved itself when Bill showed up with marriage license in hand at the hospital in Manhattan on a sultry summer afternoon and demanded her immediate assent. As she later described the scene to Mary and Nan, the two drove around in a carriage for several hours debating the matter and finally found the house of a local minister, a Rev. Dr. Norris, where a witness was waiting, along with a young boy to hold the horse. The formalities took place in haste, so she could return for the 4:30 nursing shift. She was wearing an old blue dress and looked horrid.

When the deed was done, she found herself overcome by doubt and confusion. Refusing at first to even see her new husband, she vowed in the letters to her sisters that she could not live with "such a beast of a man" and would not give up her training. "He was selfish," she added, "afraid the precious article would be lost to him." Since nursing students were prohibited from marrying, she at first determined to keep the event secret and remain in the hospital residence in lieu of setting up housekeeping until the following year. She begged forgiveness from the sisters who had forsworn marriage for themselves and done so much to help her, yet sheepishly explained that while she was sorry to have eloped without their knowledge, she could not have "a better husband—he is my ideal in many ways."[9]

Bill took the view that however serious the matter of marrying before her training was complete, and without the authority of her family, it was a question of "then or never." Well aware of Margaret's professional aspirations, he had promised Mary enthusiastically in July that "I shall do my utmost to make her sojourn at WP [White Plains] less difficult. Then she will ride triumphant in Corning with her dress suit and cane in one hand and diploma in the other. . . . She is sunshine, true joy and happiness." Yet, at the same time, he feared that she would be wooed away by her Claverack suitor or by one of the doctors with whom she worked. As to the degree question, he professed after the fact, "I didn't realize it would loom in such prodigious proportions. . . . I have persuaded Margaret to change her mind and she will send in her resignation in the next few days."[10]

In Bill's view, Margaret's choice was to have a husband take care of her or waste the best years of her life as a nurse standing on her feet all night. He promised to establish himself on a solid financial footing as quickly as possible, so she could give up the strenuous life. His marital idyll was a "a real home" with his "Margaret dearest" as "Presiding Queen," and "love the necessary household utensil," or so he put it in one of his many impassioned letters, his ardor and his good intentions not always matched by the felicity of his prose. His expectations of marriage were entirely conventional. He hoped to provide economic security and professional status in exchange for physical and spiritual intimacy with a woman. However strong Margaret's reservations—her sense of obligation to her sisters for their support, and her recognition of an independent impulse—she yielded to this prospect of security and companionship and, no doubt, to the drama of an impetuous, impassioned romance.[11]

Bill was twenty-eight years old at his marriage, a dashingly handsome young architect who had earned a degree at the tuition-free Cooper Union in New York, while supporting himself by working as an artisan in the fashionable stained-glass trade. By Margaret's account, he then worked for a time at the prestigious firm of McKim, Mead & White, and the legendary Stanford White identified him as one of the best young draftsmen in New York. Thoroughly absorbed in his work, he was overwhelmed by the depth of his response to this first love affair. Margaret, on the other hand, had as a basis of comparison the experience of what she later identified in the quaint fashion of the times as a "trial marriage" with Corey Albertson, but her apparent sexual experience seemed only to intensify Bill's desire. Many years later he could still summon the passion of their first encounter and insist that she had filled him "with the purest longing I ever experienced."

For her own part, however unconsciously, Margaret may have been driven to find a man like her father in temperament and enthusiasm, who would also provide the emotional and economic security that had long eluded her. To be sure, she would find her marriage tolerable only so long as it rewarded her on these grounds.[12]

Similarities between husband and father were striking. Both were virile and emotionally effusive men—aesthetes and romantics—given to favor sentimental gestures over practical considerations. Both were idealists, intellectually and politically committed to doctrines of economic reform and social justice. Both were Socialists and rebels against religious orthodoxy. But Bill came from an observant Jewish family, a potentially complicating circumstance that may itself have accounted for some of the impulse and mystery surrounding the wedding. Only several weeks earlier, in confiding a concern to Mary about how her in-laws would look and behave, Margaret had, in fact, resorted to conventional ethnic stereotypes. The Sangers were preparing to have an "at home" for her, she wrote in a letter that reflected her immaturity and small-town insularity, but also outright prejudice. "Ye Gods I dread to meet them," she continued, "I wonder if they will have long noses and own flashy diamonds—by the way, I am to have one."[13]

The elder Sangers were Jewish immigrants who had come to New York with their two young children, William and Cecilia, from northeast Germany in 1878. Bill's father, listed variously on immigration and naturalization records and in city directories as "Edward Elias" or "Ely," established himself in the city's burgeoning garment trades. He identified himself on two separate occasions as either a wool manufacturer or a yarn merchant. Margaret's autobiographies, instead, distinguish him as an English merchant, who was once deeded large tracts of land in Australia and met his wife, the daughter of the educated mayor of Konensburg, a small town in Germany, when he was traveling. While there is the possibility that Edward Sanger traveled before marrying and coming to America, the story seems at least in large part invented. Stuart Sanger, Margaret and Bill's first son, says that the only evidence of any exotic past was the pistol his grandfather left when he died at the age of sixty-eight in 1903. At his death, he was listed as resident with his wife, the former Henrietta Wolfberg, in a Bronx tenement.[14]

Yet the ethnicity Margaret perceived as a social disadvantage may initially have provided an important bond in her marriage. Marrying a Jew seems to have redressed her own sense of class and ethnic inferiority and perhaps explains why Bill, unlike Corey Albertson, was quickly introduced to her father, with whom he apparently got along quite well. And, apart from her youthful confidences to her sister, there is no evidence that Margaret was ever again overtly anti-Semitic, even in private. To the contrary, she found ethnic prejudice offensive, and when bigotry was virulent and even fashionable in some of the circles she frequented during the 1920s and '30s, she surrounded herself with Jewish colleagues and friends and displayed no apparent prejudice of her own. As she achieved public prominence, however, she went out of her way to disguise the truth about Bill's background and apparently never spoke to her children or grandchildren about it. At a time when informal Jewish quotas still existed, she also wrote a letter supporting the college application of Joan Sanger, Bill's daughter by a second marriage, identifying the girl as "a Protestant born of a long line of American citizens."[15]

Chaotic from the start, the Sanger marriage came under further strain within six months of the wedding when Margaret became pregnant. She still suffered from tuberculosis, and like her mother before her, the physical stress of carrying a child aggravated the illness. But quite unlike Anne, she was immediately packed off to the Adirondacks to spend her confinement at the well-established Trudeau sanitarium at Saranac Lake and returned to the city only in time to give birth. The labor and the delivery were difficult. Stuart Sanger was born on November 18, 1903, and given the family name of her friend, Amelia. Years later, the attending physician would write to inquire "just what bearing my lack of knowledge of obstetrics may have had upon this profound movement that is so essentially yours," and admit: "It was a hard night for both of us."

Sent back upstate with her baby, Margaret installed herself in a farmhouse near the sanitarium and resumed a rigid regimen of sleep and fresh air and the prescribed daily diet of tuberculars: a dozen eggs, four quarts of milk, meat, vegetables, and creosote, a toxin thought to be effective in destroying the infection. When months passed and her health had not improved, she lapsed into what she subsequently described as a severe depression. She refused to eat at all and was advised again to enter the sanitarium.[16]

Saranac in the early years of this century reported "cure rates" for 70 percent of its patients, but often what was billed as a cure was only a remission of the disease. Before antibiotics, surgical procedures excising the infected tissue, of the kind performed on Margaret at White Plains, and again in England in the 1920s, offered the only hope of controlling local tubercular infections. Bedrest and nutrition, at best, only gave the body's natural immune system a chance to regenerate and contain the disease, while the thin air of high altitudes was supposed to provide less of the oxygen on which the germ depends for active growth. At its worst the community of the sanitarium provided fertile ground for contagion, and the incidence of patient death, though not advertised of course, was high. By her own account, Margaret refused hospitalization, defied medical orders, and returned to New York. Freed from her enforced isolation in the mountains, her outlook and appetite improved, and her condition again stabilized, but the recovery was slow, and she did not chance another pregnancy until five years after Stuart's birth.

Romantically inclined, the Sangers could not have been immune to a prevailing mythology of their culture that tuberculosis was at once a disease of body and soul, infusing its sufferers with a special dimension of spirituality and passion, even as it ravaged them physically. The wasting nature of the illness also served to reinforce a prevailing assumption of male culture—to which Bill certainly appeared sympathetic—that delicate, ethereal and dependent women were all the more alluring. Yet if tuberculosis in some measure infantalized women, it also, however paradoxically, gave them license to be sexual and seductive. The prospect of being cut off from life's experience encouraged defiance of established social and moral sanctions, and, indeed, it was not only in the sanitaria of literary invention that high altitudes gave way to giddy behavior.[17]

Many years later Margaret spoke privately to her sons, and with uncharacteristic reverence, of the young love she had shared with their father. She once told another confidant, as well, that she had learned everything she ever knew about romantic love from Bill Sanger. In an age of still imperfect contraception, however, this coupling of passion with the prohibition on pregnancy advised as a result of Margaret's illness could only have been a strain. It most certainly made reliable birth control a condition of marital satisfaction, and in her subsequent disdain of popular but imperfect contraceptive practices such as condoms and withdrawal, she undoubtedly spoke with authority born of personal experience.[18]

The young couple had rented a house in Hastings-on-Hudson, a newly developing community of families like their own just up the river from New York City, but Margaret's contentment with the security and status of this environment proved to be short-lived. She later blamed her growing sense of futility in this setting on her prior experiences as a nurse "in the midst of life," but the turmoil of her childhood did not predispose her to domesticity or suburban complacency, and her illness may have also intensified her unrest. She exhibited behavior commonly associated with chronic tuberculosis. Having tarried for so long with a disease believed to be terminal, she could never seem to settle down, and in the eyes of Olive Byrne Richard, who remembered her from these years, seemed literally to "float" from one activity to another, as though she were impatient with tameness and eager for an adventure comparable to the challenge of standing up to death.

This accelerated behavior left her strangely indifferent to the responsibilities of mothering, and despite a conscious effort to compensate for the deprivations of her own childhood, she never gave her children the sustained attention they demanded and deserved. There were the requisite shopping expeditions and trips into the city and summer outings to the Rockaway Beach on Long Island, but Margaret was always just "sort of patting little children on the head in passing," according to Olive, who also observed: "I remember (strange that I should remember) she always burned the cocoa."[19]

In 1908, Margaret gave birth to a second son, Grant, and only twenty months later, a daughter was born and given the same name as her mother. Bill Sanger called them both by the affectionate diminutive Peggy. Though Margaret later remembered that she had reveled in having babies to tend, she also feared they would contract her illness and therefore approached them with reluctance. She hired wet nurses and nannies to supervise their nurture, and with this rationale seems to have related to her children with what was perhaps a predictable distance and self-absorption. Understandably, she also found the incessant demands and petty rivalries of three young children increasingly provoking. She worried about Grant, who by contrast to his older, more assertive brother, seemed especially sensitive and hungry for affection, and she may have unwittingly intensified this middle child's discomforts by delighting in the carefree and vivacious personality of his adored baby sister.

There is also evidence that despite Bill's enormous devotion to his children, the question of his help with the housework and the "kiddies," as he called them, became a recurring source of friction. Life in a white house with a rolling lawn did not turn out to be as carefree as Margaret expected. Intensely disdainful of housework, she employed a maid for as long as she could afford to do so, but years later admitted having neglected her children to the point that the "thrifty, good housekeeping neighbors took them into their laps, removed the safety pins that held their clothes together and sewed on a proper button." She also discovered that routine household cooking was a loathsome burden, though she liked to cook occasionally as a form of recreation. What is more, Bill sometimes consented to wash the supper dishes when he came home from the city, but only after he drew the shades, so as not to be seen in a compromising assignment.[20]

Early in 1908, the Sangers finished building the house in Hastings that Bill had lovingly designed for his young family. Thoroughly modern by the standards of the day in its structural simplicity and white stucco facade, it was billed in a local newspaper as one of the town's "showplaces." With a large nursery opening onto a veranda overlooking the Hudson, and a yard shaded by graceful catalpa and locust trees, the structure embraced his most sentimental vision of life. For months he returned from his job in the city each night to labor with Margaret over its most spectacular adornment, an intricate rose window of lead and stained-glass that illumined the staircase. This personal detail was intended to represent the stability of the life they were building together, but as though it were an augur of the future, the faulty installation of a furnace caused a fire only days after the Sangers moved in, destroying the window and almost all of the interior furnishings. The house was restored without the window, and along with the symbolism, the family did not survive intact. With land and construction costs exceeding $12,000, Bill found himself considerably overextended financially, an impracticality Margaret could never forgive. The sad experience, she later claimed, convinced her forever of the futility of material possessions.[21]

Never resigned to the ravages of the fire, and desperately short of cash, Bill sold this suburban property in 1910 and plunged back into the faster pace of urban life. He took a railroad flat uptown in New York City's Washington Heights section with just enough room for his widowed mother, who came to board and help care for the children, while Margaret found work as a visiting nurse and midwife in order to help make ends meet. The motivation behind this move was money, not ideology, but the transition liberated her to pursue an independent and self-fulfilling life. For Bill, however, it was a different matter altogether. Many years later, he would still regret the sale of the only real estate he ever owned. More than just a home, it was the expression of a confidence in himself and an enthusiasm for life he never recaptured.[22]

CHAPTER THREE

Seeds of Rebellion

The Sangers arrived in New York in 1910 at a golden moment of political, intellectual, and cultural ferment. "The fiddles are tuning up all over America," wrote the young critic, Van Wyck Brooks, capturing the spirit of a generation that had come of age in a new century and was convinced of its obligation to redefine the basic tenets of life in a manner coincident with the much ballyhooed significance of the calendar change. Nothing established was sacred any longer. In Washington, the "new nationalism" of Teddy Roosevelt and the "new freedom" of Woodrow Wilson distilled the nation's uncompromising faith in progress—in its ability to unite democratic aspirations with modern tools of management, to make government a force for the dissolution of unjust concentrations of wealth and capital and for the eradication of poverty. In cities across the country, reformers came to power to weed out decades of municipal corruption and graft, and politics only reflected a sweeping cultural rebellion against virtually all expressions of Victorian formality in thought, feeling, and behavior.

The century's turn inaugurated an era of innovation in the arts that produced such pioneer modernists as Theodore Dreiser, Eugene O'Neill, Isadora Duncan, T. S. Eliot, Georgia O'Keeffe, Alfred Stieglitz, and many more. Influenced by European movements away from the rigidly structured conventions of the nineteenth century, they, in turn, created an aesthetic tradition of their own that celebrated America's uniqueness as a haven for freedom of expression and identified wholesale cultural transformation as the necessary condition of the nation's continued social and political progress. Theirs was the credo of the favored philosopher of the day, William James—the pragmatist's faith in man's role as creator of his own future.

"We are living and will live all our lives in a revolutionary age, and nothing is so important as to be aware of it," wrote the young Walter Lippmann. "The dynamics for a splendid human civilization are all about us." With characteristic dispassion, a mature Lippman later recalled these years as a happy time: "The air was soft, and it was easy for a young man to believe in the inevitability of progress, in the perfectibility of man and of society, and in the sublimation of evil." It was an innocent era, a "glorious intellectual playtime," as the writer Floyd Dell remembered it—before war, revolution, and repression created the more sober reality of the century.[1]

Having dabbled in Socialist politics, and even as suburbanites attended party meetings in Yonkers, the Sangers joined New York City's active Socialist Party Local 5. In 1911, Bill ran for municipal alderman and received 352 votes, his candidacy serving as a vehicle to build party recognition and strength. Following the tragic fire that year at the Triangle Shirtwaist Factory, he put his professional skills to work for the cause by documenting the building code violations that contributed to the deaths of the young seamstresses who could not escape. Margaret was quickly recruited for the party's women's committee, but unsure of herself and uncertain of the strength of her comrades' interest in women's issues, she deferred to her husband. She later recalled that whenever she had an idea at a meeting, she would lean over and whisper it to him first, and then he would wave his hand enthusiastically, saying, "Have you heard Margaret? Margaret has something to say."[2]

The attractive young couple became favored comrades, and to their uptown parlor flocked the leading young rebels and scoffers of the day, distinctions among them counting far less for the moment than their common vision of a better world for all. As Margaret remembered the scene, progressives working for protective labor legislation came together with parliamentarian Socialists looking to redress their grievances at the ballot box. New York trade unionists took on activists of the Industrial Workers of the World, or Wobblies as they were better known, who advocated direct action to subvert production as a means of controlling wages and conditions of labor, rather than await orderly and peaceful unionization by craft. Impassioned anarchists heralded the coming of a day when the individual would reign supreme over all governments and laws.

The Sanger house was filled with powerful presences: Big Bill Haywood, the bullish IWW organizer who honed his political skills in the lumber mills and copper mines of the West; John Reed, the young reporter, like his classmate, Lippmann, just out of Harvard, and intent in his sympathies for direct action; Jessie Ashley, a young woman lawyer who gave her professional expertise and considerable family wealth to the cause, and made an incongruous pair with the coarse and flamboyant Haywood, her lover; the determined but gentle-natured anarchist, Alexander Berkman, only recently released from a fourteen-year prison sentence for his attempt on the life of industrialist Henry Clay Frick; and his more outspoken cohort, the indomitable Emma Goldman, whose brash manners Margaret never forgave, even as she absorbed her forceful doctrines of radicalism and feminism. As a measure of her own diffidence in those years, however, Margaret recalled that these people really came to see her husband, while she fixed the coffee and poured the cocoa.[3]

The Sangers became active Socialists in the movement's heyday, when, under the elegiac national leadership of Eugene Debs, the party contended for serious electoral status. In 1912, it polled almost 6 percent of the total vote and, Bill's experience aside, elected more than 1,000 Socialists to office, including hundreds of aldermen and councilmen, fifty-six mayors, and a United States Congressman, Victor Berger. For a brief time, at least, Socialism shared in the prevailing optimism of the times and fostered heterogeneity within its ranks.

What is more, Debs had long been known for his sentimental veneration of women and his ardent support of women's rights, and under his continued leadership the party initiated a self-conscious effort to mobilize women members in their own right. In 1908, what had long been a tradition of independent Socialist women's clubs was incorporated by edict directly into the national party machinery. During the next five years, millions of promotional pamphlets were distributed with individualized appeals to homemakers, laboring and professional women—from the recently unionized workers of the garment industry to department store salesgirls, teachers, and farmwives. The party embraced the cause of women's suffrage as an organizing tool, and Margaret was hired to promote the vote for women. Socialist Party letterbooks from 1911 record her compliant distribution of meeting notices and leaflets, but this experience was also short-lived. She quickly came to view the effort as a low priority in the larger struggle of working women for economic and social justice.[4]

The formal movement for women's rights in this country had been founded years earlier, in 1848, at a convention held in the tranquil village of Seneca Falls, New York, where a broad and radical declaration of feminist principles was drawn with the nation's own Declaration of Independence as a model. Until 1920, when American women were finally enfranchised, they were granted little more than the most basic legal guarantees of personhood and property, their virtues tolerated only as symbols—their stewardship bounded by home and church—while a privileged fraternity guided the nation's advancement through an age of industrial development and geographic expansion.

The women who assembled as delegates at Seneca Falls had demanded equality of opportunity for men and women in affairs of state, church, and family. Elizabeth Cady Stanton, the organizing force and intelligence behind this historic conclave, was an advanced and innovative thinker on women's issues, who understood the complex sources of sexual subordination and, in addition to the vote for women, advocated domestic reforms including the right of women to affirm their sexuality if they chose to do so, or contrarily, to refuse sexual relations altogether when necessary to avoid pregnancy. Stanton also supported cooperative child rearing, rights of property, child custody, and divorce. Though venerated within her own small circle, she came to be viewed by more traditional supporters as a source of potential controversy and embarrassment.[5]

Having achieved little progress in more than fifty years of lobbying, a new generation of women's rights advocates consciously altered its strategy by incorporating expedient, conciliatory arguments into the abstract, egalitarian rhetoric of the movement. The ballot for women was marketed as a logical extension of the obligations of wife and motherhood and inevitably the vote was won, not just as an inalienable right, but also as a practical tool for protecting and serving the family in a world where government and politics had taken on traditional responsibilities of the home, such as education and social welfare.[6]

The architects of that victory, women such as Stanton's more decorous colleague, Susan B. Anthony, or the considerably younger Carrie Chapman Catt, were made to confront the efforts of progressive Americans who were eager to translate their growing concern for the moral and social well-being of families into a broad public obligation. The family had come to be seen as nothing less than a guarantor of the basic understanding of authority and community that develops citizens for democratic self-rule. Viewed as a kind of school for civic life itself, it ranked as a social question of first importance—in the words of Teddy Roosevelt's annual message to Congress in 1905. The new President endorsed a ground-breaking government activism in the arena of social welfare on the theory that the modern industrial state might justifiably assume the role of "over-parent," supplying housing, schooling, health and welfare services in the interest of stabilizing and securing family life. He carefully distinguished this rationale from the collectivist social goals advanced by more left-leaning thinkers of the day.

If the state were to protect the family, however, so the family would serve the state. Roosevelt roundly condemned the increasingly low birthrates of Americans, blaming the phenomenon on rampant egotism and selfishness. He especially deplored women who dared place individual aspirations over their paramount obligation to the perpetuation of family, class, and nation. A popular and voluble leader, he effectively translated these deeply held convictions into a national alarm about racial suicide and decline and gave credibility to supremacist social theory and to anti-immigrant prejudice, which fed on the differential fertility rates, however temporary, between native and foreign born. At the same time, he put women's rights advocates on the defensive and developed a political lobby to counter their efforts through such pronatalist measures as the celebration of Mother's Day and the promulgation of a federal income-tax deduction for children. As a result they had little interest in confusing the suffrage message with too much talk about what was going on in the nation's bedrooms. What possible value could be derived from calling more attention to sexuality and fertility as the critical matrix for defining gender relations?[7]

Even so advanced a feminist thinker as Charlotte Perkins Gilman, while disputing the suffragists' pragmatic strategies, shared their reticence of sex. Gilman's pioneering turn-of-the-century feminist tract, *Women and Economics,* condemned Victorian patriarchy and demanded that women move beyond the family as a principal source of identity. Her vision of social and economic parity, however, did not incorporate any explicit concern for sexuality and childbirth but instead condemned women to bear these private burdens in silence.

This was a strategic consideration. Twice married and the mother of one child, Gilman would later become a strong public advocate of birth control and an ally of Margaret Sanger. For many feminists well into the middle decades of this century, however, sexual control would remain an obligation of personal conduct and of public expression. They would simply never talk about sex. Indeed, in large numbers they would forgo marriage altogether, rather than risk losing their independence to husbands and children. They would listen to Charlotte Gilman condemn matrimony for denying women the opportunity of self-realization and watch the legendary social reformer, Jane Addams, show the world just how much good an unmarried, self-reliant woman might do. As teachers, physicians, social workers, writers, and artists, many would eschew personal fulfillment in favor of social commitment. Their androgynous vision would claim sexuality and family life as the price women must pay for equality, and they would remain silent in the debate over what contraception was doing to the nation's fertility. Indeed, the situation might have remained this way had Margaret, and others of her comrades on the political left, not experienced a growing estrangement from these priorities.[8]

Margaret's disenchantment with suffrage as a tool of empowerment for Socialist women also reflected her dramatically altered personal circumstances. Bill Sanger's new enthusiasm for left-wing politics apparently cost him his job in architecture, a notoriously conservative profession at this time, where a young man who was Jewish would have had little opportunity for advancement through traditional channels under any circumstances. Bill began to devote more and more of his time to painting, a personal interest of longstanding, and this pursuit of a purer aesthetic ideal left his family with no secure means of support. Margaret was forced to find paid work.

Beyond three children and a live-in mother-in-law, the Sangers were also helping Ethel Higgins, who had abandoned her husband

and children in Corning and enrolled in nursing school at Mt. Sinai Hospital in New York. When she emerged with a coveted degree and tried to reclaim the children, she was taken to court by disapproving in-laws and lost permanent custody. Bill and Margaret helped with the legal expenses, and Ethel tried to repay her debt by finding her sister assignments as a relief nurse, which became more and more critical to everyone's well-being. Years later, Ethel's daughter, Olive, still remembered the affection Margaret extended to her during a visit to Corning in those lonely years: "I always thought of her as Christmas. She had red hair and sparkling green eyes, and she opened her arms to me and hugged me. Nobody had done that in a long time."[9]

Working part-time with Lillian Wald's Visiting Nurses Association in the immigrant districts of New York's Lower East Side, Margaret was exposed to the social pathos of a poverty hauntingly familiar to her from her own youth in its victimization of women and children.* Unlike Wald and the legions of economically secure men and women who swelled the ranks of the social settlement houses and reform associations of the era, however, she never found working among the poor a personally redeeming experience. She could never understand the rich and colorful "Spirit of the Ghetto," portrayed in the classic book of that title by her contemporary, Hutchins Hapgood, and immortalized in the compelling photographs of Jacob Riis. Where they saw hope and possibility, she saw only the degradation and despair wrought of ignorance, poverty, pregnancy, abortion, child abandonment, and child labor.[10]

These contrasting viewpoints derived from differences of background and personality and from the simple fact that where others brought pencil or camera to their work in the tenements, she carried the instruments of the midwife and a strong identification with her clients' plight. An inherent sympathy for the sufferings of poor women—intensified, perhaps, by an unspent grief for her mother and increasing anxiety about her own uncertain prospects—gave coherence to her political indignation. The intimate community she discovered with the women of the Lower East Side became the avenue of her social concern. As she watched groups of fifty women, shawls over their heads, line up outside the office of a $5.00 abortionist,

* The Visiting Nurses of Henry Street Settlement employed single unmarried women on a full-time basis, and after May 6, 1912, also required that all staff be registered. Married nurses and nurses with practical training were only permitted to work on relief and at night. Not all part-timers were accounted for, however, and Sanger's name does not appear on available ledgers for 1910 and 1911.

even the small comforts of her own marriage and family life seemed a reproach to her.

What she came to think of as an "awakening" allegedly occurred in the service of a young Jewish immigrant woman named Sadie Sachs, whom Margaret nursed in a Hester Street tenement through the complications of a self-induced septic abortion. Countless times through her fifty-year career, she would repeat the saga of Mrs. Sachs's broken plea for reliable contraception and the doctor's callous rejoinder that she tell her husband, Jake, "to sleep on the roof." As Margaret always told the story, she had volunteered her personal knowledge of condoms and coitus interruptus, the commonplace contraceptives of the day which she found unacceptable, because they placed a heavy burden of control on men. Three months later she returned to find Mrs. Sachs dying of septicemia and resolved to abandon "the palliative career of nursing in pursuit of fundamental social change."[11]

Sadie Sachs may have existed in fact or may have emerged as an imaginative, dramatic composite of Margaret's experience, but the prevalence of maternal mortality and morbidity in the urban ghetto she confronted is indisputable, a situation directly attributable to the absence of effective public health programs that offered prenatal care and to a high incidence of criminal abortion among the poor.

The practice of abortion had been well-established in New York and in other of the nation's cities since the middle decades of the nineteenth century. Commercial abortionists first began advertising their services in the 1830s, when the elimination of fetal life before the perception of movement by the mother—or "quickening" as it was then known—was still considered legal under prevailing common law statutes. Soon thereafter the procedure was criminalized in England, where prohibitions were ostensibly necessary to protect women from medical malpractice, but Americans remained more permissive than the British, with most states here first promulgating statutes that regulated intervention only after quickening. The physical or chemical interruption of fetal development early in pregnancy continued to be widely regarded as a "natural cessation of the menses" and, as such, a relatively safe recourse for married women wishing to terminate a pregnancy. By the 1850s, it was estimated that one out of every five to six pregnancies in America was willfully terminated. So bold and competitive was the market for abortion that journalists began to question, not so much its morality, as its independence from any regulation whatsoever in terms of price, quality and availability to the unwed.*

Journalistic attention to the abortion phenomenon in turn succeeded in arousing the concern of an expanding community of university-trained physicians, who expressed alarm about the potential dangers to women. Fundamental scientific developments were steadily increasing scientific understanding of human physiology and of the etiology of disease, and with these advances, doctors with formal training began to enjoy a professional advantage over allopathic, homeopathic, and other irregular medical practitioners. The physician's status still remained insecure, however, in such routine matters as childbirth, where the benefits of their intervention were not always realized—in fact, where they often did unintended damage—until reliable antiseptic and anesthetic procedures were introduced late in the century. Obstetrics and gynecology thus became an early testing ground for the introduction of professional medical standards and the hegemony of physicians over midwives.

The American Medical Association was founded in 1847 and within a decade began undermining practices widely identified with their less-educated, and in many instances, female, medical competitors. For the next thirty years, it launched a virulent and determined campaign against abortion, which advanced a moral argument for the protection of fetal life at all stages of development from barbaric, primitive interventions and also played upon the class, race, and gender tensions developing as a consequence of the steady erosion of fertility among native white American women. The reputation of abortion—if not its actual practice—was considerably undermined by this campaign and the legislative prohibitions it produced. Abortion nonetheless remained prevalent, especially among the waves of non-English speaking immigrants, who had trouble gaining information and access to contraceptive supplies. A small sampling of immigrants on New York's Lower East Side in 1917 would determine that about a third knew of no birth control methods at all, other than abortion, the practice on which many of them relied. The remainder had used unspecified forms of prevention, but with limited success.[12]

A 1916 study of more than 160,000 female policy holders in New York by the Metropolitan Health and Life Insurance Company then revealed that one fourth of its claims were puerperal related. More-

* In what emerged at this time as a highly competitive metropolitan newspaper environment in New York and other cities, abortion investigations drew readers by sensationalizing sex and crime, and, at the same time, by providing them practical consumer protection from fraud and, in the worst cases, from outright danger.

over, of these, at least another quarter did not result from normal pregnancies but, instead, involved the complications of admitted abortions, of septicemia probably related to attempted abortion, or of unspecified "acute diseases and conditions." These bleak numbers propelled the company to sponsor preventive medical programs, including the Visiting Nurses for which Margaret worked, and these private gestures paved the way for an organized campaign for publicly assisted preventive health care programs. For years, it became common practice to display comparative national statistics that showed the United States near the bottom of the chart with a maternal mortality rate of approximately seven deaths per 1,000 live births, a figure comparable to that of developing nations with notoriously low medical standards, and far below that of countries like England and Holland, where urban health and social welfare programs were more advanced. No progress would be made until the 1920s, however, when a national public policy of maternal and infant welfare through the Sheppard-Towner Act briefly funded public health clinics for poor women and children, the only comprehensive federal health program of this nature that existed until the 1960s.[13]

Lecturing before Socialist Party women in New York in 1910 and 1911, Margaret dramatically evoked the pathos of the lives of poor immigrant women and condemned public prudery for prohibiting open discussion of sexuality and reproduction, leaving them the innocent victims of their own ignorance. Her popularity resulted in an invitation from John and Anita Block, editors of *The Call*, New York's popular Socialist daily, to write on sex education and health for the Sunday supplement's women's page, which was read by Socialist audiences throughout the country.

Though they may appear cautious by contemporary standards, Margaret's graphic descriptions of the reproductive process and of sexuality in childhood, adolescence, and adulthood, presented in 1912 and 1913 under the column head "What Every Girl Should Know," aroused a furor among many reticent *Call* readers. Journalistic restraint about sexual subjects was still the norm. The pioneering case studies of British sexologist Havelock Ellis had been published here only in limited-circulation medical texts. Freud had just recently made his first visit, and his work was just being translated, but his ideas were only beginning to permeate the public consciousness. For a woman to write about sex was especially provocative. To tackle such subjects as pregnancy and abortion, masturbation, menstruation, and defloration, the material of Margaret's first forays as a columnist, demanded considerable courage, even though she took a traditionally Victorian and conservative view of sexual excess, especially with respect to masturbation, which she condemned as harmful on the grounds that it made the experience of sexual gratification in conventional intercourse more difficult.

In fact, the series provoked a full page of letters in response, ranging from the one reader who said she "blushed" but found the articles "indicative of a higher, purer morality than whole libraries full of hypocritical cant about modesty," to another who canceled her subscription to the paper, taking offense over Margaret's candor and her incendiary ideas. In a coda to the series, Margaret insisted that existing economic and social arrangements fundamentally compromised and degraded women by forcing them to rely on men for support. She set forth a rudimentary but nonetheless radical argument demanding economic and social freedom for women so as to permit greater autonomy in choosing a mate and bearing children.

It took several articles that dealt explicitly with the subject of venereal disease, however, to provoke a direct confrontation with the still vigilant public censor, Anthony Comstock. Comstock banned the column early in 1913, and the following week the paper ran an empty box in its place headlined "What Every Girl Should Know—Nothing; by order of the U.S. Post Office." The action provoked another round of more sympathetic responses from readers, who defended Margaret on First Amendment grounds. *The Call* challenged the post office action, and following machinations with local officials that are not documented, the censored column on syphilis was published several weeks later.[14]

In an interview in *Harper's Weekly* in 1915, Comstock would boast that in his long career he had convicted enough people of sexual misconduct to fill a sixty-car passenger train and had destroyed hundreds of tons of obscene materials. The lore of his censorship was surely enormous, even if his bold claims vastly overstated the truth.[15]

Born in rural New England in 1844, Comstock first developed his appetite for righteous moral indignation as a Yankee soldier in the fight against slavery. He then found employment as a dry goods salesman in New York City, where an increasing alarm over the temptation put in his way by local merchants of drink, gambling, prostitution, and vice led him to the Young Men's Christian Association, an organization founded to provide wholesome recreational alternatives for the city's similarly rootless and disaffected. Even after his marriage, however, obscenity remained something of an obsession for him, and with the YMCA's backing, he quit his job to devote himself full-time to saving America's youth from the devil's temptations. "Satan lays the snares and children are his victims," he wrote. "His traps, like all others, are baited to lure the human soul."[16]

Comstock's campaign prospered as a result of a conservative social backlash that followed the Civil War, and its intensity reflected the deep distresses that had been unleashed by the dislocations of that bloody conflict. During the 1870s, native white Americans concerned about the apparent threat to their hegemony from European immigrants and free blacks took refuge under a banner of social purity and religious orthodoxy. They were joined by religious fundamentalists, physicians looking to secure their status, and self-proclaimed feminists who believed they were promoting their own autonomy by regulating sexual behavior and by attacking pornography, alcohol, and vice. Class and gender tensions were thinly disguised in these crusades, which saw zealous reformers calling for the wholesale transformation of culture and baldly associating drinking and vice with poverty, ethnicity, and race.[17]

Obscenity until this time had not been an indictable offense under common law, but in England in 1868, criminal sanctions were introduced with the provision that the "tendency of the matter charged as obscene was to deprave and corrupt those whose minds are open to immoral influences." A year later, Anthony Comstock helped secure a similar measure in New York State, one that expressly prohibited traffic in contraception and abortion, and soon he was able to bring federal legislation to bear on the moral pollution that had become his personal demon. With evangelical fervor he committed himself to root out sin wherever he could find it, and to reassert the virtue of biblical imperatives about sexuality and social conduct. So prestigious was the backing of the YMCA, and so effective were his lobbying efforts, that he prevailed on Congress in 1873 to pass the broad but vaguely defined federal obscenity statute, which thereafter informally carried his name. The act vastly expanded existing legislation that narrowly prohibited the transport of obscene literature via the public mails. Comstock cleverly displayed piles of pornographic literature, contraceptive and abortifacient devices, and other allegedly "vile" materials at committee hearings on his new proposal, and without establishing any real evidence, linked them to hysterical allegations of rampant immorality in the nation that no politician risked disputing. His bill was passed by voice vote, with only two Senators and one Congressman objecting to the absence of any floor debate whatsoever.[18]

In the last-minute rush of the session of 1873, Congress amended the United States criminal code to prohibit the transport by public mail of materials including the following:

> Every obscene, lewd, or lascivious, and every filthy book, pamphlet, picture, paper, letter, writing, print, or other publication of an indecent character, and every article or thing designed, adapted, or intended for preventing conception or producing abortion, or for any indecent or immoral use; and every article, instrument, substance, drug, medicine, or thing which is advertised or described in a manner calculated to lead another to use or apply it for preventing conception or producing abortion, or for any indecent or immoral purpose.*

Yet, if Congress had overreached its intentions, it made no effort to correct them. In 1878, a group calling itself the National Liberal League petitioned Washington with 60,000 signatures demanding modification or repeal of the statute, but Comstock again confronted a committee hearing on the matter with his piles of smut, and no further Congressional action was again attempted until the 1920s. Meanwhile, the original statute had triggered an immediate impact at the state level, and every state but New Mexico took some form of action. Twenty-four of them passed conforming legislation prohibiting not only the transport of obscene materials, contraceptives, and abortifacients, but also their circulation by any means of publication or advertising. Most, nonetheless, did exempt licensed physicians, and some of them even pharmacists as well. Yet, fourteen state statutes also enjoined speech on the subjects at hand, and the Connecticut legislature outlawed contraceptive practice outright, though it provided no effective means of enforcing its will.

Next door in New York, however, state representatives chartered

* The act also set fines for such offenses of $5,000, or imprisonment of five years, or both. Its sweeping inclusivity, and the absence of sustained dissent, served as indications to subsequent advocates of reform that the full implications of the prohibition were not fully considered by the legislators—that their intent was never to inhibit the behavior of lawfully wed adults. Enforcement of the law was always selective and its impact on private marital practice tangential. Earlier drafts of the bill clearly excluded "physicians in good standing" from its prohibitions, but this exemption was deliberately struck from the final version by a particularly vigilant and God-fearing Senator from Connecticut.

the YMCA's Committee for the Suppression of Vice as a publicly sponsored vehicle for legal enforcement of its prohibitions. Comstock himself was authorized by the United States Post Office and by the State of New York to work as a "special agent," with the power to undertake searches and seizures and to make arrests. Only under more sober circumstances in 1881 would Albany legislators respond to pressure brought by the medical profession and amend the statute to curb Comstock's jurisdiction and allow physicians to prescribe contraception for use in combating the spread of syphilis and other diseases. "An article or instrument used or applied by physicians lawfully practicing, or by their direction or prescription, for the cure or prevention of disease," was thereafter declared exempt from definition as "immoral or indecent," but this was the extent of the alteration.[19]

Prohibited from interfering with doctors in his home state, Comstock remained free to persecute nonprofessionals who dared challenge him, and his particular penchant for hounding sexually flamboyant women suggests that his entrapment anxiety may not have extended only to *merchants* of vice. His first demonstrable victory came when an infamous but well-established New York abortionist, who practiced under the French name of "Madame Restell" (though in reality she was a British-born commoner named Ann Lohman) committed suicide after Comstock indicted her for criminal negligence in connection with the death of a client. Following soon upon this incident, Comstock staged a major press event by appearing at the sensational trial of radical feminist Victoria Woodhull and her sister, Tennessee Claflin, who distinguished themselves nationally in the 1870s with an outspoken candor about sexuality. The two women stood accused of libeling the prominent Brooklyn minister, Henry Ward Beecher, by exposing his alleged extramarital escapades in one of the unorthodox feminist newspapers they published. Comstock testified on Beecher's behalf, and the result was a hung jury, but Woodhull found herself persecuted for her views and ultimately left the country, abandoning women's rights to those more cautious about speaking out on sex. Several years later, Comstock enjoyed an unequivocal success in the Massachusetts prosecution of an outspoken sex radical there, named Ezra Heywood, for distributing an underground journal that advocated free love and advertised contraceptives.

However flamboyant these encounters, the larger effect of Comstock's zealotry is hard to measure. Not a single reputable physician was actually prosecuted during his tenure, and medical supplies were regularly mailed without interference, as were limited circulation textbooks incorporating contraceptive information. Comstock himself publicly denied that the laws bearing his name had ever been intended to handicap physicians in private practice, though, at the same time, he called all nonprocreative sexuality, even in marriage, "bestial and base." In place of artificial contraception, he counseled self-restraint and refused to admit the possibility of a distinction between moral and immoral uses of preventives. Even if his obscenity laws did not technically circumscribe physicians, this bald identification of contraceptive practices as criminal and immoral seems to have discouraged their intervention in all aspects of the matter. Physicians in private practice who counseled their patients on contraception did so quietly. The subject was all but banned from public discourse on the subject, records of medical symposia reflecting only occasional interest. It was not until 1912 that the American Medical Association again debated contraception openly at the encouragement of its outgoing president Abraham Jacobi, husband of the outspoken female physician, Mary Putnam Jacobi, and himself the proponent of a more socially responsive medicine.[20]

If Comstock never succeeded in suppressing sex radicalism or the popular culture's brisk trade in contraception and abortion, however, he did manage to push them farther underground into the hands of quacks and charlatans. Reputable publishers banned the subject altogether from popular editions, and this left only paperbound pocketbooks, printed in remote areas of states like Texas and Kansas, where they were out of the reach of censors. Respectable farm journals, women's magazines, and most mail-order catalogs accepted only advertisements disguised under such euphemisms as the ubiquitous "feminine hygiene." Patent medicine manufacturers became multimillionaires, but they cautiously coded announcements for contraceptives. Lydia Pinkham, for example, made a fortune selling emmenagogues to dispel "stomach tumors." Edward Bliss Foote, the proponent of womb veils and a popular health writer, was convicted by Comstock and forced to reissue his advice book on contraception in a truncated version that only advertised douching. As to the manufacture of commercial contraceptives, standardization and regulation of quality and price became virtually impossible, and in these nebulous circumstances the contraceptive market expanded out of the reach of the law, until some federal policing of merchandise was undertaken in the 1930s.[21]

Yet these constraints on public discussion of sexuality had no apparent impact on behavior. Indeed, as birthrates continued to plummet, patterns of sexual behavior grew more permissive rather than less. There is little reliable survey data from this era on sexual behavior, but the same Dr. Clelia Mosher of Stanford University, who questioned the wives of professors about contraception in 1895 also asked about sexual responsiveness, and on this matter, her data has been variously interpreted. She reported nearly universal sexual activity, but still a sizable incidence of orgasmic deficiency and rather low levels of desire on the part of women, at least by more recent standards. Only a third of the women claimed they usually reached orgasm—a few more said "sometimes"—and the majority said they were interested in sex only about once a month. Lack of enthusiasm for sex, not surprisingly, correlated directly with reports of ineffective use of contraception.

By contrast, Alfred Kinsey's pioneering studies of women who came of age in the earlier years of this century found that they experienced greater frequency of intercourse in marriage, nearly universal contraceptive use, and higher levels of sexual satisfaction. Moreover, they did not confine sexuality to marriage but instead engaged in permissive premarital sex-play, which for most stopped short of intercourse, though fully a third of Kinsey's respondents also admitted having consummated these relationships, most often with the partners they subsequently married, Margaret's own personal experience in this respect once again being instructive.

This closer accommodation to a single standard of sexuality for men and women also paralleled the decline of prostitution as a sexual outlet for men. The availability of commercial sex had long enforced a double standard and provided a semilicit physical outlet for men, but progressive efforts in public health and social hygiene increased awareness of the high risk of contracting venereal disease from prostitutes and of the unfortunate consequences of sexual vice in a world without antibiotics or any other assured cure. Even as physicians and scientists developed new regimens for treating syphilis and gonorrhea, it remained apparent that the best deterrent to the spread of disease was outright prohibition. The campaign to regulate prostitution actually produced a more liberal sexual doctrine in this country, its hallmark a new egalitarianism in personal conduct that licensed middle-class women to be sexual, so men would not need to find relief away from home.[22]

Most important, birthrates continued to decline as a result of private contraceptive arrangements made quietly among networks of women or by husband and wife. Small families became increasingly fashionable by the turn of the century, especially among the most prosperous families, where one and two children were not uncommon. And fertility declined steadily, if still more slowly, among women of the working classes as well.*

By the early 1900s, indeed, the venerable Anthony Comstock's reputation had declined. He became something of an eccentric symbol of old-fashioned values—"a four square granite monument to the Puritan tradition"—in the description of one of his biographers. His celebrated 1905 injunction against the American production of Bernard Shaw's *Mrs. Warren's Profession,* a comedy of manners with prostitution as its theme, was never enforced in court, though it earned the country an international reputation for philistinism. Comstock still achieved notoriety with the confiscation of nude female drawings in a pamphlet of the Art Student's League in New York City in 1914, but again there were no legal repercussions. A cartoon in *The Masses*, then a popular journal of the left, parodied Comstockery by showing a man dragging a woman's body before a judge with a caption that read, "Your honor, this woman gave birth to a *naked child.*" Several months later, in fact, he lost his official status as a government agent, which left him with only the institutional support of like-minded fanatics whose voluntary commitment to vice suppression had long helped support his activities.[23]

Yet if the intemperate zeal of old age eroded Comstock's personal credibility, his legislative legacy continued to resist change. Obscenity laws lent themselves well to selective enforcement and provided a

* A statistical survey of 1,000 married women, all of them college-educated and/or women's club members, published by the reformer Katherine B. Davis in 1920, would find that 75 percent reported effective use of contraception. Well into the 1920s, however, Robert and Helen Lynd in *Middletown*, their historic, sociological portrait of Muncie, Indiana, continued to find differentials in the contraceptive practices of the working and business classes. The demographer Raymond Pearl, who studied the contraceptive practices of more than 5,000 black and white women in eleven major cities in the early 1930s, would also find similar differentials by class and race and an overall contraceptive use rate of only 46 percent, but Pearl's sampling had an unusually high concentration of Catholic women, and his estimates were considered overly-conservative. By contrast, information then being gathered at Margaret Sanger's pioneering birth control clinic in New York established a nearly universal desire, if still limited success, in contraceptive practice among working-class women who had the motivation to seek out services. This data would later be corroborated by survey research on contraceptive practice conducted by Alfred Kinsey at the Institute for Sex Research in Bloomington, Indiana.

See Katherine B. Davis, "A Study of the Sex Life of the Normal Married Woman: The Use of Contraceptives, *Journal of Social Hygiene* 8 (1929), pp. 173–89; Robert and Helen Lynd, *Middletown* (New York: 1928); Raymond Pearl, "Contraception and Fertility in 4,945 Married Women," *Milbank Memorial Fund Quarterly*, 12 (July 1934), pp. 355–401; Marie E. Kopp, *Birth Control in Practice: An Analysis of Ten Thousand Case Histories of the Birth Control Clinical Research Bureau* (New York: 1934), pp. 19–21.

convenient tool for government suppression of social deviants and, as Margaret would soon discover, of political radicals as well. Male politicians were hardly more anxious to debate sexual subjects openly than advocates of women's rights were, and this curious but unmovable constellation of elements sustained Comstock's anachronistic laws, even long after the old man himself was gone.[24]

Margaret breached a well-established social and political contract when she took on Anthony Comstock in the columns of *The Call*. She did not invent a freer sexuality for women or discover contraception, but by insisting on raising both as public issues, she did fundamentally alter the social discourse of her times and of our own.

For the moment, however, her principal heresy was in becoming as much a political radical as she was a social libertarian.

CHAPTER FOUR

The Personal Is Political

Margaret had used the Socialist Party to establish herself within a community in New York and to find her voice as a journalist, but to her dismay the issues she began to write about, and feel so deeply, attracted little attention from party leaders. Within a year she openly shared in a growing resentment that only lip service was being paid the real concerns of women. Jessie Ashley, whom Margaret greatly admired, withheld a $500 contribution to the New York City locals for women's work in 1912, because she could secure no agreement from the governing body on how the money would be spent.[1]

In the preceding twenty years, the number of women in the labor force had doubled from 4 to 8 million. Yet, despite the extraordinary success of the Women's Trade Union League in leading the strike of 1909–10 that invigorated the International Ladies Garment Workers' Union, the Socialist Party and the male-dominated trade unions made little further effort to organize women workers, whose labor was stereotyped as marginal and impermanent. As a result, many women were frustrated by internal squabbles and began to break ranks.[2]

Despairing of conventional political processes, Margaret drifted toward the party's left wing and radical tactics of direct action in support of labor. Her *Autobiography* admits that she first found herself in "absolute rapture" at a laundry strike in New York City in 1911, while listening to the IWW's favored female agitator, Elizabeth Gurley Flynn. Flynn was known, among activists, affectionately but with respect, as "girlie," and in tabloid headlines of the day as the "Rebel Girl." That day she advised the workers not to surrender their pay envelopes in a walkout, but instead to engage in a form of quiet sabotage of their employers by deliberately mixing up orders of socks and shirts. The two women next had the chance to talk at the Sangers' uptown flat, while bathing Peggy in the sink. Then came the strike at Lawrence.

The Wobblies had moved East to organize immigrant textile workers and for this decidedly unpolished but committed band of organizers. Margaret, who was native-born, well-spoken, and quietly attractive, became an especially valuable recruit. When the IWW struck the Lawrence textile mills in Massachusetts early in 1912, she was asked to lead a well-staged and highly publicized evacuation of workers' children from the strife-torn Massachusetts town to New York City, an action intended as much to call attention to the strike and to arouse sympathy, as it was to protect the children from extreme conditions. The bitter job action had put 22,000 people out of work, most of them foreign-born, and the humanitarian tactic played brilliantly as sympathetic families in New York took in the forlorn immigrant children. The favorable publicity so enraged local authorities that they used billy clubs to prevent a second contingent of children led by Flynn from leaving town.

The violence provoked Congressman Victor Berger to call an investigation, and in March Margaret traveled to Washington with several young women strikers to condemn the textile industry for its assault on women, children, and families. Helen Taft, the President's wife, and Alice Roosevelt, the former President's daughter, came to hear the testimony of the "nurse from New York," as she was billed, and her moving portrayal of the children of wool workers, who in the cold of winter were without warm clothes, made national headlines as a "remarkable exposition of capitalist brutality." Within two weeks the strike was settled, and the workers won raises of 5 to 25 percent, gains which had a ripple effect throughout the New England textile industry. The results were not as positive, however, in Hazelton, Pennsylvania, where Margaret was twice arrested a month later for trying to prevent workers from entering a silk plant the Wobblies did not successfully organize.[3]

Lawrence brought her overnight recognition and a valuable initiation in political organization, promotion, and lobbying. She also took away from the experience enduring friendships with strike organizers Bill Haywood, Carlo Tresca, and the charismatic, silver-tongued Flynn, friendships that would transcend her own later retreat from radical activism.

She strongly identified with the engaging but fiercely committed Flynn. The two attractive and spirited Irish women both traced the roots of their political activism to well-intentioned but domineering fathers, who had disappointed them for being so "long on talk and short on work," as Margaret once caustically described them. They also had in common strong-willed mothers, who had encouraged independence in their daughters. Most important, perhaps, they shared the experience and responsibility of being mothers themselves, since Flynn had a child from a brief teenage marriage, who lived with her family in the Bronx. Here the similarities stopped, however, for while Margaret was struggling over responsibilities to a young family, Flynn was riding the IWW strike circuit from coast to coast, lending her flaming oratory to the cause of labor from the mills of the East to the mines out West. When they met, Flynn had also just become involved in a tempestuous love affair with the mysterious and daring Tresca, whose abandoned Italian wife and daughter lived just blocks away in New York.*

* There is, in fact, no evidence that Flynn, who remained a committed radical and later became America's most prominent female Communist, ever begrudged Margaret her subsequent defection from the left or her comfortable life-style. Margaret's name was included on the dinner committee that honored Flynn in 1926 on the occasion of her twentieth year in the labor movement. And there is surely no apparent sign of estrangement or bitterness in a letter that survives from the years Elizabeth spent in self-imposed exile in Oregon, which shares personal confidences and requests a loan of $2,500, a substantial sum of money at the time, for an investment in a Brooklyn movie house by her mercurial and alcoholic brother, Tom. Margaret's political moderation was apparently less distressing to her old radical friend than the simple fact that she had stayed so beautifully thin. Elizabeth gained seventy pounds during her years in Portland and what she wanted, along with the loan, was approval of a new and trendy "California diet," on which she claimed to have already lost weight. During Flynn's occasional trips to New York, the two women dined together, reminisced and celebrated old times, and Margaret maintained the friendship and support even after Flynn returned East permanently, publicly avowed her Communism, and was ostracized by many old friends on the left. It was not until anti-Communist hysteria led to Flynn's imprisonment in the 1950s that contact between the two old friends appears to have come to an end. And even then Flynn was careful to credit Margaret's "long hard struggle" in her historical accounting of the legacy of women in American Socialism. See E. G. Flynn to M.S., Jan. 22, 1930, MS-LC. (She

Late in 1912, Flynn and Tresca led a strike of restaurant and hotel workers in New York, which caused a riot they did not condone but, at the same time, refused to condemn. On this occasion the workers rebuked the call for nonviolence and rather than simply adulterate the food they prepared and served, they left their jobs, smashed the plate glass windows of Delmonico's and other elite establishments, and wildly attacked scab workers. Circumstances quickly overtook ideology.[4]

The publicity generated by these events gave the Wobbly leadership, and the philosophy of syndicalism which it endorsed, an increasing celebrity outside radical circles, especially among an East Coast intelligentsia that had long heralded the rights of labor. The French philosopher Henri Bergson developed his doctrine of the pri-

already owed her $1,700.) Sanger's description of the fathers is in *Autobiography,* p. 79; Flynn-Tresca relationship in Tresca, "Autobiography," CT-NYPL, pp. 141–52, 112, 180, 208; he uses the phrase "silver-tongued" to describe her. The Flynn Dinner Committee announcement and reference to a July 2, 1942, telegram congratulating Flynn on a Communist Party rally at Madison Square Garden are in Margaret Sanger's file at the U.S. Department of Justice, Federal Bureau of Investigation, made available in response to a request by the author under the Freedom of Information Act on May 13, 1985. The quote from Flynn's *Women in American Socialist Struggles* (1960) is taken from Rosalyn Fraad Baxandall, *Words on Fire: The Life and Writing of Elizabeth Gurley Flynn* (New Brunswick and London: 1987), p. 171. Also see Flynn, *Rebel Girl,* pp. 86–89, 109, 224–25.

Margaret also never got back the money she gave Tresca in the late twenties to support his Italian labor news weekly, *Il Martello,* and to open a radical bookstore, a project he abandoned when the Depression hit. The loan was her way of repaying an obligation she felt she had incurred in 1925, when Tresca was sentenced to a year in the federal penitentiary in Atlanta for publishing a two-line advertisement in his paper for a book on birth control. His conviction under the obscenity statutes was widely viewed as a contrivance for silencing his political viewpoints. Margaret visited him in Atlanta and then used her influence with a large number of prominent Republican women, who prevailed on President Calvin Coolidge to commute his sentence. For years thereafter, whenever she traveled through the South to lecture on birth control, she sent him postcards in New York from what she mockingly called his "country farm." Through the 1930s, as Tresca became an increasingly controversial Italian-American opponent of Mussolini, he wrote to her about the dangers of the Fascist promotion of childbirth and race building. After he was assassinated on a New York City street corner in 1943, allegedly by Fascist agents, she sent money to his widow and helped to establish a memorial fund, to which she contributed for at least another decade. Harold Hersey, "Margaret Sanger. The Biography of the Birth Control Pioneer," New York (1938), p. 129, talks about a dinner arranged by Tresca, with Sanger, Flynn, Joe Ettor, the hero of Lawrence, and others. Tresca to Sanger, Feb. 6, 1932, MS-LC, says he wants to set up a dinner celebrating the publication of her latest book. Also see M.S. to J. Noah H. Slee, Dec. 10, 1924; E. G. Flynn to "Dear Friend," Nov. 24, 1924; Mrs. Oakes Ames to Pres. Calvin Coolidge, Dec. 15, 1924; M.S. to Hon. Calvin Coolidge, Dec. 18, 1924; M.S. to Carlo Tresca, Jan. 7, 1925; Tresca to Sanger, "Dear Margherita," n.d. (1925); Tresca to Sanger, March 17, 1925, from Atlanta; Tresca to Sanger, "Dear Margaret," n.d. (late 1920s), "My Dear Margaret," n.d. (1931), and Feb. 6, 1932; Sanger to Mrs. Carlo Tresca, Jan 15, 1943, all in MS-LC. The FBI kept files on Tresca's contact with Sanger, see reports for Jan. 9, Jan. 19, and Mar. 11, 1924, in the FBI file. Finally see additional Tresca-Sanger correspondence in MS-SS, and the letter about her contribution, Dec. 22, 1955, in the Carlo Tresca Memorial Committee Papers, Manuscript Division, NYPL.

macy of immediate subjective experience—his *elan vital*—and gave intellectual respectability to grass-roots labor confrontation. He was invited to lecture at Columbia in 1913 and was also profiled in the Sunday magazine of *The New York Times*. But if university scholars and Greenwich Village literati were suddenly engaged by the new unrest, established Socialists and trade unionists in this country were not so easily romanced. The success at Lawrence had been made possible by an effective coalition of IWW organization and Socialist Party money and public relations. Virtually on its heels, war broke out between the party's reform faction and those willing to condone violence. The reformers held control and, singling out Haywood, voted to expel any member who opposed electoral participation and advocated direct action. Margaret, along with most of the left wing, resigned her party affiliations, and the rift never healed. So too, the American Federation of Labor disavowed the New York cooks and waiters who had followed Flynn and Tresca, splitting the local into warring factions.[5]

Differences of strategy that had been tolerated only a year earlier became open fissures on the landscape of the left, and the debate over tactics and goals intensified in 1913 during the long and disruptive silk workers' strike in Paterson, New Jersey. As with Lawrence, the practical short-term goals were a minimum wage, an eight-hour day, extra pay for overtime, and other minor workplace reforms. But a zealous IWW leadership, inspired by its victories in New England and ever conscious that Paterson was within range of the nation's communications hub in New York City, also attempted to convert the thousands of strikers there into true believers in the righteousness of their cause and the inevitability of class conflict. Flynn took charge of the strike along with Haywood and Tresca, and the goal, in her words, was to create "a feeling of solidarity" out of the diverse religious, ethnic, and political constituencies in Paterson—to instill a unified "class spirit, class respect, class consciousness." To this end the Wobblies did more than organize picket lines. They deluged Paterson with forums, rallies, marches, and parades, and on Sundays sponsored mass picnics, which were meant to keep the strikers' spirits high and ward off the likelihood of a break in ranks. In this effort they enlisted the money, sympathy, and skills of New York's bohemia just across the Hudson River, providing a critical opportunity of politicization for many of its young rebels, most notably the romantic John Reed, who first went to jail in Paterson when local authorities tried to rid the town of outside agitators.[6]

The Paterson strike reached an impasse by midyear as the repression and sheer mayhem instigated by company management and local officials escalated, while the strike funds and emergency relief needed to maintain discipline among the strikers began to run out. Looking for a publicity vehicle on the order of the Lawrence children's crusade, a group of Greenwich Village supporters met with Haywood at Mabel Dodge's famous salon and came up with the idea of staging an enormous pageant in New York's old Madison Square Garden that would feature the silk workers themselves in a vivid dramatization of their plight. Margaret had been traveling back and forth to Paterson to lecture striking women as part of the IWW educational strategy, and to organize an evacuation of children comparable to the one she led at Lawrence. She was apparently at the Dodge evening that launched the pageant, and subsequent organizational meetings were held at her apartment. John Reed threw himself into staging the event with customary zeal, and on June 7, 1913, it became part of history. Thousands of spectators broke into revolutionary chants and song as 1,000 strikers reenacted their struggles, and Wobbly leaders shouted out their standard fare with an immense IWW sign and a flaming red stage set as their backdrop.

Yet for all its dramatic intensity, the event was a fiasco. Intended to raise money and support for the cause, it wound up with virtually no profit at all. The strike was lost, and after five months of poverty and unemployment, the workers returned to the factory with no gains. Some blamed defeat on the fractioning of worker unity along ethnic and gender lines, as new immigrant labor replaced the old, and women took jobs once reserved at higher pay for men. But others were quick to criticize the IWW leadership for condescending to local organizers and diverting attention from discipline and organization to symbolic but empty gestures of pageantry and song. When it was all over, Reed sailed for Florence with the new lover he found in pageant coorganizer, Mabel Dodge. Haywood followed with Jessie Ashley shortly thereafter. Flynn was left to pick up the pieces in Paterson, and Margaret found herself in utter despair.[7]

When she later wrote her autobiographies, at the height of a still precarious professional achievement in the 1930s, Margaret deliberately glossed over this youthful radicalism and the profound personal alienation that gave resonance to her early political activism. Like the mature author who disowns her early work as a youthful apprenticeship, she undermined the seriousness of her intentions in this period. From her own superficial accounts, it is tempting to dismiss her radicalism as faddish and suggest that she embraced labor activism because it was daring and fashionable and a good deal less boring than the children's expeditions and women's literary groups that had occupied her time in the suburbs. In this context, she would seem more at home in the bohemian haunts of prewar Greenwich Village than on the barricades of Lawrence and Paterson. We can picture her savoring a meal at Polly's Restaurant, or having a drink at Paddy Halliday's, the fabled watering hole, where rebellion was fomented in work and politics, culture and family. The Village crowd was, of course, even more notorious for flaunting conventional marital and domestic arrangements than for advancing economic radicalism. Its apparent contempt for the moral constraints of bourgeois life was so intense that Max Eastman, intemperate editor of *The Masses*, the fashionable intellectual journal of the left, used to refer to these years as the "adolescence" of the new century.[8]

Margaret was clearly intoxicated by bohemia's warm and welcoming community with its adventuresome and carefree spirit. The Village she knew was vigorous and alive with unconventional ideas—many of which have retained an intellectual allure well into our own time. Its meandering streets with quaint and historic houses for rent, cafés brimming with people and conversation, and shops stuffed with books and prints and bric-a-brac, offered a welcome respite from the affluent but culturally sterile suburbs she had left. The jumbled intensity of life there more closely resembled the rejected household of her childhood than the well-ordered, middle-class life she had inevitably found wanting. She felt a sentimental affinity to legions of similarly alienated young people who flocked to New York in search of kindred community. Positive associations to her youth positioned her well to embrace her generation's ethical concern for the collective welfare. The emotional conflicts and burdens of that past, however, also left her willing prey to its passion for unbridled personal liberation. For many of her contemporaries, however, including her own husband as it turned out, pursuing the twin goals of individual freedom and disciplined social renewal seemed inherently contradictory, and the failure to resolve this conflict in his own life was to leave him a defeated and dispirited man.[9]

Yet bohemia did not define the boundaries of Margaret's experience in these years. She was not, after all, one of the groping and sensitive young writers or artists for which the era is legendary, who wandered into New York with responsibility to nothing but their own substantial talents. She had to care for a husband and three children still under the age of ten, while she also met the obligations of at least part-time paid employment. Still, it does not undermine the significance of her disenchantment with the short-term rewards of bread-and-butter Socialism, and the increasing chaos of IWW syndicalism, to say that the lure of personal freedom also engaged her. This gradual orientation toward a more intimate and personally felt politics raised her consciousness as a feminist and wrought havoc on her marriage and home life.

Bill grew increasingly jealous of Margaret's time away from home and intensely suspicious of her collegiality with such free spirits as Haywood, Tresca, and Reed. One of her early articles in *The Call* betrayed growing problems in their marriage with its utter contempt for any man who championed the liberation of an entire class, while his own wife remained enchained to a domestic servitude. "Most radicals are stirred by the Socialist call to the workers to revolt from wage-slavery, but they are unmoved by the Socialist call to women to revolt from sex slavery," she wrote with an abrupt and startling authority in her prose. "They are still too oversexed, too tainted with the sins of their fathers, to be able to look upon women's claims as their own." She soon discovered, however, that most of her new political associates were hardly less chauvinistic in their attitudes toward women than her own husband. Joining Haywood at a rally in Paterson, for example, she spoke passionately about a woman's right to limit her family, yet he followed with a rosy picture of the "economic commonwealth of the future" where women "could have without fear of want all the babies they pleased." A sister organizer in the audience remembered feeling totally insulted.[10]

Deeply moved by the physical hardship endured by the women and children of the Lower East Side and in Lawrence and Paterson, Margaret came to resent what she saw as the narrow focus of the radicals on economic gains for a predominantly male work force. If Socialists and unionists had failed to organize women workers, the Wobblies were compounding the error by ignoring the special needs of mothers and homemakers. "They were failing to consider the quality of life itself," she later recalled. The theme, of course, recapitulated the drama of her own childhood with a father whose lofty principles never translated into comforts for his own wife and children.[11]

Yet however personally she felt these grievances, Margaret quite clearly adopted her feminist ideology, and much of the rhetoric she later claimed as her own, from Emma Goldman. Disenchantment with masculine reasoning and with the organized initiatives of male radicals and labor activists drew both women inexorably to an anarchist faith in individual renewal, but it was Goldman who first fused a concern for economic and social justice with bold issues of personal liberation. In a sweeping vision that freed working people from cultural conformity as well as from economic tyranny, she made enemies of both capitalism and Comstockery. Unlike the far more publicly demure Elizabeth Gurley Flynn, Goldman never felt compelled to hide her own personal flamboyance, in deference to the traditional social and religious beliefs of her still largely foreign-born constituency. Instead, she openly challenged more conventional comrades, who argued that the emancipation of women would have to await the coming of a totally new economic order, while, at the same time, she deliberately courted audiences of middle-class women whose lives may have been better endowed in a material sense, but were no less alienated in other respects.[12]

Emma Goldman, perhaps more than any other prominent woman of her times, understood the perplexing psychological and sexual dimension of women's subordination in modern industrial culture. Until the early nineteenth century in Europe and America, households had typically been economic constellations, centered around the production of goods or services and often encompassing workers and servants. Men worked at home as farmers, artisans, and tradesmen, while women birthed and nurtured large numbers of children well into the final years of life. These were hardly asexual and emotionally austere environments, to be sure. Love and personal affection were valued, yet marriage, as often as not, was made to serve collective needs over individual ones, and personal behavior deferred to fundamental religious convictions—to the twin fears of divine retribution and community sanction that defined the prevailing world view.

By 1800, however, these cloistered worlds had begun to come apart. The revolutionary pamphlets of British freethinkers, French encyclopedists, and American nationalists had challenged not only the sovereignty of kings, but also the dictates of ministers and priests, and, along with them, the immutability of nature itself. Enlightened thinkers, whose ideas had achieved wide circulation, encouraged a higher level of achievement and control in all dimensions of human behavior. And the sudden shift in the demographic data of the period reflected that marriages were increasingly serving the objective of individual happiness over the traditional obligations of procreation and patronage. The custom of arranged couplings declined. Rates of premarital pregnancy and illegitimacy increased dramatically, and contraceptive information began to circulate, as a more democratic philosophy of family life encouraged the voluntary limitation of family size.* Traditional avenues for transmitting values and enforcing social discipline weakened further as established patterns gave way to the distinguishing features of modern life—the emergence of large-scale manufacturing, the commercialization of agriculture, the expansion of markets, the beginnings of mass migrations from Europe to America and from town to city. Universal public schooling brought widespread literacy, and along with it the possibility that reasoned, utilitarian arguments about social conduct could prevail over religious jeremiads. A buoyant commerce developed in secular tracts offering moral and practical advice on marriage and family life. Husband and wife were to marry on the basis of affection, rather than convenience or arrangement, and subject their relationships to the tension of heightened romantic expectation, he becoming the household's sole provider, she, governing at home with a scientifically disciplined attention to domestic organization, individual hygiene, nutrition, and psychology. Emphasis was to shift from the child's value as a producer of labor and lineage for his parents, to the parent's—and especially, the mother's—responsibility for the enrichment of the child. And with fewer children, the experience of parental love and discipline would shape individual expectations of social interaction and authority—the very attributes that inspired Friedrich Engels's derisive commentary on the bourgeois personality in London in 1848 and, later in the century, shaped Freud's disquieting ruminations on family dynamics.[13]

This new ideology never challenged traditional assumptions of patriarchy, but in pursuing a goal of mutuality in marriage, it sanctified a separate, private sphere of influence for women and enhanced their status within it. Husband and wife were intended to serve complementary roles, he retaining authority for the family's economic life, she, protecting its heart and its soul, he moving ahead in the public world, she guarding the intimate and the private. Men were to be coarse, competitive, and aggressive, women, by contrast, pure, obedient, and passive, a dichotomy that rigorously barred women from politics and public life and explains why organized campaigns for women's rights and suffrage met with such formidable opposition.[14]

* These dislocations also explain the widespread spiritual malaise and reactive waves of religious revivalism that were characteristic of the early decades of the nineteenth century. For most Americans, however, the evangelical promise of redemption through a retreat to enforced values provided no more of an enduring solution to their problems then than it does today.

These arrangements also fostered the unusually high degree of emotional anxiety and tension with which the middle-class Victorian cultures of England and America are so often identified. Small, closely knit families became economically sensible and socially desirable in environments that did not suit all temperaments or provide universal economic opportunity, as the experience of Michael and Anne Higgins so well demonstrates. And fewer children became an asset while contraceptive technology remained essentially primitive and unreliable, and while pregnancy still posed the possibility of an ordeal of pain and suffering. Under the circumstances, it became necessary to devalue sex itself and instead extol the superior virtues of metaphysical, romantic expressions of love and sentiment. Traditional stereotypes that viewed women as innately and powerfully sexual were abandoned in favor of more refined and delicate representations of femininity. Women were encouraged to be emotional and affectionate, but not physically passionate, a prescription for behavior that became heavily invested with the weighty authority of biological science, as physicians increased their control over popular beliefs and behavior and assigned to themselves, and to all men for that matter, the more powerful sex drive.[15]

Few could live contentedly by these rules. Moral and social standards constitute ideals of conduct, not accurate descriptions of behavior. No culture can be expected to produce unanimous agreement on what constitutes the correct relationship between men and women, no less between personal aspiration and sexual expression, and the nineteenth century obviously produced its share of individuals unwilling or just unable to subscribe to the rigidities and repression that its children, long since Margaret Sanger, have so casually ascribed to the era.*

* It has, in fact, recently become fashionable among scholars to search out nineteenth-century tracts that contradict these stereotypes and endorse sexuality enthusiastically, along with titillating diaries and letters offering indisputable testimony that pleasure in sexual experience sometimes resisted negative prescription and remained a powerful component of life within marriage and outside it. Human desire can and did, in fact, triumph over the dictates of culture, and the culture itself was never monolithic. Yet, however eager the lust of a few sexually charged individuals who confessed their transgressions in diaries, however compelling the personal affections that controlled a simple couple like Anne and Michael Higgins, these recent findings hardly dispute the underlying tension in Victorian sexual behavior or discourse. Peter Gay is the most extreme of the revisionists, see *The Bourgeois Experience, Victoria to Freud*, Vol 1: *Education of the Senses* (New York: 1984), esp. pp. 71–168. He makes Mabel Loomis Todd of Amherst, Mass., a woman previously known for helping publish the poetry of Emily Dickinson, into a new symbol of Victorian wantonness, because she carried on an extensive extramarital affair with Dickinson's brother Austin and left an intimate diary of her vivid sexual responses. For a respectful criticism of Gay, see Noel Annan's review of Gay's second volume, *The Tender Passion* (New York: 1986), "In Bed with the Victorians,"

Yet women, with rare exception, were expected to remain chaste outside marriage, and even within it, to practice a degree of restraint sufficient to realize the generally agreed-upon objectives of smaller families, emotional cohesion, and economic mobility. And as a result, many who could afford to do so simply took to bed, finding refuge from their discontents in the neurasthenic ailments and other hysterical complaints that doctors of the era widely condoned as reasonable behavior. Others rid themselves of tension at the sanitaria, water cure establishments, and other such retreats that proliferated in this era. Still more stayed home and got high on the opiates that circulated freely as the principal ingredients of household tonics sold by mail order and in neighborhood pharmacies. Many educated women also began to reject marriage outright, refusing to subject themselves to its potential degradation. In larger numbers than ever before or since, they remained single and worked as servants or secretaries, like Margaret's own sisters or, in the more fortunate circumstances of many of the reformers and suffragists, pursued professional openings to women in fields such as education, medicine, and social work. Poor women, meanwhile, who had neither the chance to conform to middle-class habits of discipline, nor the luxury to reject them, often taught their children bourgeois manners nevertheless, and in the process, as Margaret's story again so poignantly demonstrates, subverted the legitimate economic grievances of their fathers. Many of those children then themselves rebelled.[16]

Foremost among the rebels was Goldman, a Russian-Jewish immigrant. Despairing of the possibility of collective political action to achieve social change, Goldman narrowed her strategy to the elusive realm of the personal and individual will to act. By 1910, she had proclaimed herself an anarchist, declaring that true emancipation for women would only begin in achieving liberation from within, not in breaking down institutional barriers to achievement, such as suffrage. "[Woman's] development, her freedom, her independence, must come from and through herself," she later wrote. "First, by asserting herself as a personality, and not as a sex commodity. Second, by refusing to bear children, unless she wants them, by refusing

The New York Review of Books, Nov. 20, 1986, pp. 8–14. Carl Degler takes a more balanced view of the subject in *At Odds: Women and the Family in America from the Revolution to the Present* (New York: 1980), esp. pp. 249–78. All of this work is indebted to the pioneering study of the underworld of Victorian England by Steven Marcus, *The Other Victorians: A Study of Sexuality and Pornography in Mid-Nineteenth Century England* (New York: 1964).

to be a servant to God, the State, society, the husband, the family etc., by making her life simpler, but deeper and richer."[17]

Considerably gifted as a speaker and writer, Goldman disseminated her revolutionary ideas on politics, sexuality, and culture through lectures, articles, and books. Her well-read journal, *Mother Earth,* along with *Anarchism and Other Essays,* a distillation of her best lectures published in 1910, provided a rationale for the libertarian attitudes toward love and marriage that became so fashionable in bohemia. In reality, Goldman was personally tormented by her own subordination to her lover and manager, the exploitative and philandering Ben Reitman. But as a philosophical matter, she stood firmly against any relationship that compromised a woman's independence, and she condemned repressive traditions of marriage and motherhood, institutions that existed, in her view, only to "subdue women's innate and powerful sexual cravings . . . undermine her health . . . make her dull . . . break her spirit . . . stunt her vision." She demanded a thorough transformation of social and moral values—one that would transcend what she saw as the "artificial stiffness and narrow respectabilities" of issues of political and economic independence for women, extolled, on the one hand, by leading male radicals and, on the other, by such prominent advocates for women's rights as Susan B. Anthony and Charlotte Perkins Gilman. Goldman's thinking gave intellectual weight to the confusion and self-doubt born of Margaret's own experience.[18]

Just as important, Goldman introduced Margaret to a neo-Malthusian ideology then fashionable among European Socialists, who disputed Marxist orthodoxies that condemned contraception as hopelessly bourgeois and encouraged a high proletarian birthrate. They argued instead that women's control over reproduction was no less essential to the goals of a revolutionary class struggle than control over conditions of employment. After attending the historic meetings of the Socialist International in Paris at the turn of the century, where this ideology became conventional wisdom among the Europeans, Goldman returned to the United States and began to promote contraception in her own lectures. With only a handful of lesser known dissidents in this country, she dared to advance what were still considered socially incendiary ideas. She supported "voluntary motherhood," for example, to serve the revolutionary goal of a "birth strike," which would at once liberate women from the bondage of maternity and, at the same time, withhold the steady supply of human labor that fuels the industrial machine.

When the first scholarly history of contraception was published in

1938, it paid homage to Margaret Sanger's pioneering efforts in the field but never even mentioned Goldman. Ben Reitman immediately wrote the author, Norman Himes, and reminded him in mock epic verse:

> Emma Goldman
> More than any one person in America
> Popularized B.C. . . .
> She was Margaret Sanger's INSPIRATION
> No that ain't the word.
> Margaret imitated her and denied her
> . . . GET THIS INTO YOUR HEAD
> This was all done as part of the radical propaganda
> ANTI WAR
> ANTI MARRIAGE
> ANTI CHILDREN BY ACCIDENT.[19]

By this time Goldman herself was out of the country, having fallen victim to the red purges of World War I. Deported in 1919, she lived in exile in the south of France and later in Canada, where she died in 1940. There she wrote a long and reasonably candid memoir under the careful editorial eye of Alexander Berkman, who challenged her to treat other women's accomplishments fairly. The book acknowledged Margaret's achievement in distributing practical birth control information to women, but its somewhat gratuitous flattery was never reciprocated. Margaret continued to popularize Goldman's claim for the revolutionary potential of women's control over their own bodies but never admitted any debt to her. She would deliberately disparage Goldman in her own memoirs and lie outright about their association in a 1935 letter to a new supporter of birth control. As she courted establishment money during the 1930s, she may have felt the need to be prudent about advertising her early association with industrial radicalism and violence, but since she never disassociated herself from Flynn or Tresca, the Goldman disavowal must also have been personally motivated. Margaret's deceit was testimony to the intense rivalry that had developed over the years between two women who both thrived on public attention and acclaim. "She never liked me personally and has belittled my work in her book, to say nothing of the manner in which she greeted me the other night when I went up to give her a word of welcome," Margaret claimed in refusing to support Goldman's efforts to reinstate her United States citizenship in 1934. "One can get slapped just once too often, and I am through."[20]

Margaret recognized that the extraordinary publicity she first generated for birth control had been, in some measure, at Goldman's expense. Emma had long advocated the principle of family limitation in her lectures and had actually supplied practical knowledge to many women during clandestine encounters that followed her speeches, when she sometimes distributed a leaflet describing condoms and womb veils. Yet it was also true that she would only dare to challenge the Comstock laws publicly after Margaret was first arrested for doing so, and she would then infuriate the Sangers by advising that Margaret had insufficient public recognition or experience to carry the cause on her own.

This slight would rankle even more as Margaret's reputation grew, and as she came to identify Goldman with the stormy sentiments of these prewar years when she herself abandoned her husband and children, ostensibly in pursuit of a greater good for all women. Having paid the price of her former friend's theories in deeds, not just in words, Margaret would simply claim them as her own.[21]

CHAPTER FIVE

Bohemia and Beyond

The political and cultural ferment of 1913 effectively destroyed the Sanger marriage. Bill's roots in Socialist politics were deeper than Margaret's, and though he too flirted for a time with the IWW, he tired of its extremism more quickly than she and retreated from the confusion of politics to the subjective, interior world of his art. By quitting his job, he staged his own personal revolt against the "wage slavery" that had become a fashionable object of scorn on the left. Margaret never forgave him for this decision—as she never excused the insolvency of his earlier real estate dealings in Hastings. Though the romantic side of his nature had once seemed so attractive, she thought he was selfish to pursue the purity of artistic expression and leave his family without a secure means of support. He argued, in reasonable defense, that he had subordinated himself and his art to her needs for long enough, but these were not the terms on which their marriage had been premised. The lesson Margaret took from childhood was that men were worthy only as providers, and she seems to have quickly punished her husband's profligacy with sexual infidelity, the only real weapon she had available to her.

It is impossible to determine exactly whose indiscretions came first—or which were more significant to the ultimate dissolution of the relationship—but it is clear that the marriage would not survive. Whatever her inclinations, Michael Higgins's daughter was fundamentally unsuited to be the wife of an artist, and she may have finally defeated her father, as well as Bill, when she abandoned the husband who had come to resemble him in so many ways.[1]

Bill Sanger virtually unraveled under the pressure of the radical assault on his family life, his politics, and even more critically, perhaps, on his art. Though it had failed miserably as a labor tactic, the Paterson Pageant of 1913 represented the ascendancy of rebellion as a cultural fad. Its effect on New York's intellectual and artistic life was much like that of the historic Armory Show that preceded it by just a few months, showcasing Post-Impressionist, Cubist and other Abstract painters, and permanently changing the way we look at art today. In the most fashionable haunts of the Village, a link was drawn between the two. One evening at Mabel Dodge's celebrated salon, John Reed compared the disintegrative effects of both Cubism and the I.W.W., while Bill Haywood antagonized many of the assembled professionals from the art world by celebrating a future when the energies of workers would be released to develop a people's art, free of formality and restraint.[2]

Bill could scarcely conceal his contempt for this sort of reductionism. Nor was he ever really comfortable with the dissonant clashing of forms and colors of now well-known Modernists who frequented the Dodge evenings, such as John Marin, Marsden Hartley, Andrew Dasburg, Max Weber, Arthur Davies, and Charles Demuth. He continued to paint in two distinct styles, without a great deal of critical acclaim or financial success. One was an intense, schooled realism that captured the pathos of urbanism and industrialism and reflected the influence of George Bellows and the emerging Ashcan school of painters, the other, by contrast, an appealing Impressionist mode that offered a safe, romanticized retreat from the discordance of contemporary life. If he sheltered his work from the influence of the new iconoclasm, however, he could not safeguard his marriage.[3]

In Dodge's drawing room discussion strayed from the more familiar terrain of politics to art, literature, education, and psychology. As a measure of what some have called bohemia's eclecticism, and others have dismissed bitterly as its sheer confusion of principle, the fortunes of this eccentric, industrial heiress underwrote much of the era's rhetoric of rebellion. Here Margaret encountered a world of new and unconventional ideas. There was discussion of Nietzsche, whose attack on established religion and morality had just been translated and was embraced uncritically, while his less tasteful views about racial supremacy and female inferiority were apparently ignored. There was talk of the new psychoanalytic theory, with the pioneering New York analyst and translator, A. A. Brill, elaborating on the unconscious and licensing a libertarian conduct, despite Freud's contrary views on the inevitability of human sexual repression and restraint. And there were lectures by the young Will Durant on the pathbreaking research of the British sexual psychologist, Havelock Ellis, into the diversity and range of human sexual expression. In sum, there was an unapologetic celebration of freedom in love.

Mabel Dodge, by her own admission, gathered ideas and people with the intense determination of a society matron accustomed to collecting fine furniture or porcelains. She became a "species of head hunter," as she put it, and the heads she brought together in conversation in her lower Fifth Avenue apartment presaged many issues that have since been central to this country's political, intellectual, and cultural life. Still, while some of the evenings were devoted to disciplined exposition and debate of new ways of thinking and communicating, they were, at the same time, a spirited bacchanalia. Her sumptuous salon featured the latest in painting and decoration assembled amid elegant, if eccentric for the time, white furnishings and draperies. There was always a lavish buffet of fine food and wine, and for Margaret, this constellation of rebellious sentiment and bourgeois comfort proved a thoroughly seductive experience. But not for Bill: "Madame Pompadeau Dodge's—her salon—Oh! Gosh! how nauseating!" he wrote her frantically. "The I.W.W. in the parlor! . . . Parlor Discussion, Parlor Artists, Parlor Socialists, Parlor Revolutionists, Parlor Anarchists—I know where art & revolution is . . . you bet."[4]

He also began to rave over the duplicity of once trusted comrades, whom he now suspected of embracing their revolutionary ideas only to justify stealing away his wife. Away from New York, trying to paint in peace, he insisted: "You don't need their intellectual dope. . . . You are a salon all by yourself." The Village became for him nothing more than a "hellhole of free love, promiscuity and prostitution masquerading under the mantle of revolution," or, as he put it in another letter, a "saturnalia of sexualism, deceit, fraud and Jesuitism let loose." Elsewhere he added: "If Revolution means promiscuity, they can call me a conservative and make the most of it." He was willing to embrace the concept of Margaret's right to independence as an abstraction, and he soberly paraphrased the Swedish feminist Ellen Key and the French writer George Sand in his increasingly frantic letters. But understandably, perhaps, he only saw his wife's sudden interest in new personal experiences as a rejection of him, not as a positive affirmation of herself, a response which provoked her added resentments.

Bill destroyed all of Margaret's letters to him, so we must intuit her thoughts from his long and vitriolic responses, which she gathered together and saved, but they make clear that the avant-garde of the Dodge salon provided her a sympathetic forum for challenging established patterns of submissiveness in her marriage. Long-stored resentments apparently tumbled forth about money, child care, household management, and what in one case she referred to directly as Bill's "overbearing" personality. By the time she assembled these complaints, however, she also had ample reason to be defensive about her own behavior. Bill either discovered on his own, or she herself told him about, the one love affair from this period of her life that is clearly documented—a liaison with a man by the name of Walter Roberts, who was for a time an editor at *American Parade*. It began during the summer of 1913, while she was vacationing with her children in the still quaint fishing village of Provincetown, Massachusetts, where New York artists and literati escaped the city heat. Bill was commuting back and forth from New York, and the writer Hutchins Hapgood later remembered him from that summer as "a sweet gentle painter who lacked ego and ambition," and to whom his "pretty wife . . . seemed to grant little value."

By Margaret's published recollection, her Provincetown holiday that year was memorable only because she spent much of it brooding over the specter of Sadie Sachs and the dilemma of Comstock's censorship of her articles in *The Call*. Leaving the children in Ethel's care, she crossed the harbor to Boston to continue research she had begun in New York on contraceptive technology. She consulted all available medical texts, but owing to the profession's continued reticence on the subject, found virtually no agreement on a preferred method. Indeed, the array of options discussed and debated by physicians confirmed her view that the dissemination of simple but reliable information was desperately needed.[5]

Neither of these accounts, however, reveals a third unhappy development that obviously consumed at least some of her time that summer and exhausted her emotional energy. According to Grant

Sanger, his adored baby sister Peggy had come down with polio during the hot summer of 1910 and been left with a weakened and foreshortened leg. Grant remembered clearly that the rambunctious child walked with a limp, but Margaret resolutely refused to acknowledge the severity of her daughter's condition. During their summer at Provincetown, it became apparent that Peggy would have to be fitted with a brace, yet nothing was done, and in a frenzied letter the following year, Bill admonished Margaret to pay attention to the "little limb," implying that she was being negligent.[6]

In the meanwhile, the unexpected death of Henrietta Sanger from cancer in September of 1913 seems to have effected a brief rapprochement in her son's marriage. Desperate to hold on to all he valued, and free of obligations to the elderly mother who had been helping to care for the children, Bill prevailed upon Margaret to accompany him to Paris, where he hoped to restore their relationship and pursue his painting in an atmosphere free of the corrosive immorality of New York. The trip was financed with the final payments on the mortgage they still held from the sale of the Hastings house. "I want to help you in your work loved one—you must help me to help you," he wrote poignantly, though with a condescension that may well have infuriated her by this time. "Sidestep New York. . . . The reaction for you was inevitable, as you admitted. Your *finer* sensibilities only escaped its ravages in time. If you can cut out the *Nirvana bunk* . . . you might cast your sunshine once again."[7]

The Sangers traveled to the Continent via Scotland, where Margaret had an assignment to report for *The Call* on municipal ownership of housing and utilities in Glasgow, a city which, despite this commendable experiment, she found squalid and unappealing. In Paris she apparently continued her research on contraception. Through Bill Haywood and Jessie Ashley, who were also traveling there, she met the French syndicalists, long known to her through Emma Goldman, and learned firsthand of their theories in favor of state-supported policies of family limitation. Victor Dave, a prominent French Socialist and lone survivor of the nineteenth century Communards, argued in favor of scientific fertility regulation as a dimension of social reconstruction. Margaret believed that his enthusiasm derived from a long-established tradition of contraceptive use among the French peasantry, which took root in the anticlerical fervor of the Revolution and was then sustained by Napoleonic codes mandating equal division of property among children. To keep their family holdings together as much as possible, French women defied church edict and passed along birth control secrets from one generation to another. The syndicalist desire to shape peasant economy and ingenuity into official state policy suddenly seemed a more practical solution to the disturbing problems of poverty and unemployment than the besieged efforts of labor activists in the United States. Here, moreover, was a program that identified women as principal agents of social and economic change.

"A whole year had been given over to inactive incoherent brooding. . . . With this background I had practically reached the exploding point. I could not contain my ideas, I wanted to get on with what I had to do in the world," she later wrote. By the eve of the new year, she and the children were back on a steamship headed for home, while Bill stayed behind, alone, to find himself as a painter.[8]

"I shall never forget the expression in your face when I threw the last kiss. I'm sure I mean something in your life," he wrote immediately upon her departure. "I feel now that nobody can take you away from me." Yet, the same letter acknowledged his emerging recognition that they had been torn irreparably asunder. He groped for words:

> I have had a lot of queer thoughts in my mind—I just wonder if I made myself clear on one of the vital things in our lives. That thing of sex gratification with a woman. Most men seem to violate confidence as regards their relations with the opposite sex—it always ends by the disparaging of the character of the woman. . . . Its the double standard of morals. I've been thinking whether we have considered this vital part enough. I would not have a finger ever pointed at you. In the quiet of my studio—one thought seems to crowd out all others. Oh well—dear heart—sometime I'll tell you—my heart is too full. I shall always love you with all the power of my being whatever *you do*.[9]

Back in New York Margaret assured him that she was "settling down to systematic work," and he accommodated to their predicament and to his loneliness by convincing himself that she needed "seclusion" to work out her "lines of intellectual development." He encouraged her to hire a nursemaid while she went to work herself and somehow also found time to begin her intended writing on contraception and women's issues, and he promised to work hard in Paris, in return, "to make the future more secure." But the only exchange of money between them appears to have come from either her salary or the mortgage installments from the Hastings house. As she continued to support her husband, the inherent contradiction between his prattle about her independence and his continued insistence that she remain faithful to him began to annoy her. He insisted:

> Dear Heart I would want you to stand on *your* own feet as a professional woman without obligating yourself to anyone except with the circle of the immediate family. I must repeat you are the mother of my children. I would not have the finger pointed at you. Propagate an idea—no matter how revolutionary. I would not care what the world might think—but unless a relation is based on love. . . .

And there he drifted off into another thought, only to write again, even more pathetically, in March:

> Yes, I pray for you to be the *big* woman of our generation, and I know you're right that you must be relieved from the family care. . . . I have adapted myself to your wish as you grew. I shall always be with you in everything you do . . . indeed, I shall always consider it a marvelous privilege to sit beside you obediently that you might express the best that is you.[10]

There followed a staggering twelve-page letter filled with suggestions for her writing, but it was too late. His next letter made clear that she had finally told him in "clear and unmistakable language" that on returning to New York she had renewed her love affair with Walter Roberts and demanded to be released "physically and spiritually," from her wedding vows. Bill's tragic response admitted that he was "staggered" by the weight of the "struggle—the soul combat" that they had begun at Provincetown.

As her own commitment to the new relationship developed, Margaret tried to enlist Bill's understanding and encourage his own sexual experimentation in the belief that their marriage might actually survive, if their infidelities were mutual. She told him that their future together depended upon the shattering of old habits, but the more consumed she became with issues of her own autonomy and satisfaction, the more intensely he communicated a paramount sense of emotional obligation to their shared past and to their children's future. He literally begged her to consider the children. Refusing to believe that she was responsible for her own actions, he attacked the men who preyed upon her, and identifying Walter Roberts by the initial "R," viciously accused him of trying to break up the Sanger family. Bill's letters deteriorated steadily as it became clear to him that Margaret felt empowered by her new relationships, while he was growing despondent and weak, unable to work, to love other women, or even to care for his children, behavior which she could not tolerate and only further diminished her respect for him. "I am essentially a monogamist, and that's why women don't understand me," he acknowledged. "I cannot adapt to new personalities. . . . I live for you, I strive for you." Without her, he admitted to losing conviction in himself and in his painting, for she had long provided his inspiration. Divorce was never mentioned, but the marriage was over.*[11]

Though Margaret actually shared some of Bill's disdain for the radical chic, her commitment to the free-love ideal would endure long after others of the Village crowd had retreated in confusion and unhappiness to a monogamy that became more acceptable simply with the maturity of age or, in many instances, as the result of intensive psychoanalysis. She, by contrast, would find apparent satisfaction through intimacies with many other men who were eager to indulge her independence, as her bereaved husband could not. She came to believe that she had simply grown beyond Bill—that he had somehow failed her. For years he tried to salve his wounds by hurting her with accusations of selfish and licentious conduct, but the attacks seemed only to solidify her resolve, and she made a political platform out of her own experience, brazenly proclaiming a woman's right to rebel against established religious, moral, and legal codes.

Mabel Dodge recalled in her typically flamboyant prose that Margaret was "the first person I ever knew who was openly an ardent propagandist for the joys of the flesh." Margaret believed that traditional sexual attitudes were "infantile, archaic, and ignorant, and that mature manhood meant accepting the life in the cells, developing it, experiencing it, and enjoying it with a conscious attainment of its possibilities that would make previous relationships between men and women with their associations of smirking shame and secretive lubricities, seem ignoble in their limitations and stupid beyond words in their awkward ignorance." An enthusiastic Dodge remembered a private encounter when Margaret "told us all about the possibilities in the body for 'sex expression'; and as she sat there, serene and quiet, and unfolded the mysteries and mightiness of physical love it seemed to us we had never known it before as a sacred and at the same time a scientific reality."[12]

No better testimony to this new enthusiasm for an intense and passionate sexuality exists than in the vividly erotic poem written for Margaret by Walter Roberts sometime in the spring of 1914:

* At the turn of the century, there were only twenty divorces per 10,000 marriages in America, and though the rate of divorce was increasing at what was considered an alarming 3 percent per year, the legal dissolution of a marriage remained a serious and unusual action.

Marvelous lover, give me leave to sing,
Your body's beauty in keen words lay bare
Your breasts for burning kisses, and declare
The glory of your eyes unfaltering. . . .
Forbid me not that I should call you fair.
Behold I am entangled in your hair,
And at your mouth have found the whole sweet Spring![13]

* * *

When Margaret later wrote her autobiographies, she wanted the world to believe that she had abandoned Europe and a marriage of twelve years with a confident eye on the issue and movement that would assure her future success and celebrity. Perhaps, she wanted to believe it herself. With emotional and sexual conflicts long buried, she looked back from the comfortable distance of two decades and said simply that personal feelings were a necessary sacrifice to "ideals that take possession of the mind." Even in Bill's letters from the winter of 1914, clearly she had already invented a calling out of her work, which rationalized her disobedience as a wife and mother.

Yet the predominating turmoil of her personal life was readily apparent when she arrived back in New York during the unusually bleak and cold winter of 1914. Aboard the ship from France, she conceived the idea of a magazine to be called *The Woman Rebel*, dedicated to working women and intended to challenge Comstock's prohibition of information about sexuality and contraception. She gathered a group of radicals one evening in the cheap flat she had rented way uptown, and on that historic occasion a young friend by the name of Otto Bobsein coined the term "birth control" to identify the social and economic objectives of the campaign Margaret planned to launch. All agreed that it was a simple term, with greater public appeal than such awkward phrases as "family limitation" or "voluntary motherhood," which remained in standard usage.[14]

Disenchanted with the factionalism of the left, and still smarting over the discrimination she had experienced as a woman organizer, Margaret then presented her ideas before a feminist group called Heterodoxy, whose elite membership included Charlotte Perkins Gilman, Crystal Eastman, and Henrietta Rodman. These women shared her disdain for the narrow focus of suffragists on political instruments and goals, and some of them were also Socialists. In the cause of birth control, she hoped to effect a united front of women across class lines on the model that had succeeded so well for women garment workers, but the women of Heterodoxy apparently turned her down, perhaps reluctant to associate with her avowed radicalism in politics and social behavior, perhaps skeptical of her lack of education and her erratic emotional behavior. Advertisements in radical journals instead produced the several hundred advance subscriptions that got her going and cemented an alliance with the politics of the extreme left. By March, *The Woman Rebel* had been launched from her dining room table, under the provocative Wobbly banner that first antagonized God-fearing workers at Lawrence and Paterson by proclaiming "No Gods, No Masters."[15]

Why *The Woman Rebel*? Margaret asked in the inaugural issue:

> Because I believe that woman is enslaved by the world machine, by sex conventions, by motherhood and its present necessary childrearing, by wage-slavery, by middle-class morality, by customs, laws and superstitions.

The manifesto went on to trumpet an anarchist faith in the potential of individual action. It celebrated a passion for freedom best represented by the nation's immigrant and working classes and ended with a revealing rhetorical flourish that summoned all women:

> To look the whole world in the face with a go-to-hell look in the eyes; to have an ideal; to speak and act in defiance of convention.

In an accompanying article Emma Goldman then raised the Malthusian banner:

> The defenders of authority dread the advent of a free motherhood lest it rob them of their prey. Who would fight wars? Who would create wealth? Who would make the policeman, the jailer, if women were to refuse the indiscriminate breeding of children? The race, the race, shouts the king, the president, the capitalist, the priest. The race must be preserved, though woman be degraded to a mere machine.

But Margaret's intention was to look beyond economic and political arguments to an autonomy for women founded on wholesale change in attitudes and behavior. In a signed editorial she lamented the criminal sanctions then imposed on contraception, abortion, and illegitimacy and attacked the deeply rooted conventions of marriage and motherhood that governed the behavior of women and limited their opportunity. She called on working women to reject the standards and values of the upper classes and promised to provide them practical contraceptive advice in the columns of her papers as a first step toward their liberation. But before taking on a certain legal battle, she intended to raise the consciousness and belligerency of her readers and to assure herself widespread financial and moral support among women on the left. Mocking an absence of "vitality" among American bourgeois feminists, she praised the militancy of British suffragists instead and proclaimed:

> What rebel women claim . . . is the right to be lazy. The right to be an unmarried mother. The right to destroy. The right to create. The right to live. The right to love.

She wrote in a breathless plea for moral autonomy, and it was this boast that made its way beyond her small audience into stories that appeared about her in the daily newspapers.[16]

Filled with anger and bombast, and lacking intellectual depth or literary grace, the paper was not terribly well-received. Writing in *The Masses* Max Eastman regretted its extremism and absence of "poise" and with apparent condescension accused Margaret of falling into "that most unfeminine of errors—the tendency to cry out when a quiet and contained utterance is indispensable." "*The Woman Rebel* seems to give a little more strength to the business of shocking the bourgeois than the bourgeois really are worth," he wrote, chiding her especially for attacking the suffragists and other more moderate feminists, but still endorsing and promising to support her legal efforts to challenge the Comstock laws. Goldman herself wrote from Chicago that even the IWW women were "up in arms" over Margaret's brazen methods. "But, of course, they are women liberated only on paper and not in reality," she added, and later said that the paper was, nonetheless, "the best seller we've got."[17]

According to Margaret, thousands of women also wrote encouraging her provocation and requesting the practical birth control advice. But long before she got down to the technicalities of contraception, she was indicted simply for sending "indecent" materials through the mail and on other unanticipated grounds. The Post Office confiscated her first issue with notice that she would be subject to criminal prosecution if she continued to publish. She continued nonetheless, and in syndicalist style, dropped discreet bundles of the paper into mailboxes throughout the city in an attempt to avoid detection. In August of 1914, the authorities finally arrested her and charged her on four criminal counts carrying a maximum sentence of forty-five years.[18]

* * *

The Comstock laws proved an effective device for rounding up radicals, and the company Margaret kept, as much as anything she actually wrote, explains the severity of the indictments brought against her. The nation's economy had plummeted into depression in the early months of the year. With an estimated 300,000 unemployed in New York City alone, labor demonstrations and marches had grown larger and more militant, and even the city's more enlightened establishment feared the potential of widespread violence and disruption. Local newspapers in New York began calling for a crackdown on dissent, and the newly elected reform administration of Mayor George Purroy Mitchell complied.

The principal victim of this headline-driven hysteria was a young man named Frank Tannenbaum, who initiated an effort to dramatize the plight of New York's unemployed and homeless. Tannenbaum would later become a distinguished professor of history at Columbia University, but at this point of his life he looked to experienced IWW insurgents for support and for the kind of public relations gimmicks they had made their specialty. Early in February, Carlo Tresca, for example, discovered that the Childs' Restaurant chain was giving away special reduced-price meal tickets as a promotion. He had them reprinted in large numbers and persuaded Margaret to lead a delegation of stylishly attired ladies in fancy cars down to the Bowery, where they distributed them to the assembled hordes of street people.[19]

The incident made the tabloids, but then Tresca and Tannenbaum came up with an even more controversial tactic. On a snowy winter night, they organized bands of homeless into roving street "armies" that demanded shelter in churches throughout the city. Tannenbaum was arrested for breaking and entering a church, and his subsequent imprisonment for a year made him a martyr for the left, the kind Margaret had no desire to be. His associate, Becky Edelsohn, was also jailed and began a well-publicized hunger strike, to which Margaret gave extensive publicity in *The Woman Rebel.* It seems only logical that their fate influenced her own subsequent legal strategy.[20]

The institution most closely identified with Tannenbaum's activities was the Ferrer Center Association, or the Modern School as it was also known. It was founded in 1910 by anarchists and other radicals in New York to commemorate Francisco Ferrer, the freethinker and educational reformer, whose execution at the hands of Spanish monarchists in a Barcelona prison a year earlier had provoked an international outcry. Ferrer had set out to free Spanish peasantry from the yoke of illiteracy and blind faith by setting up a network of schools in the countryside whose goal was to educate the masses for participatory, democratic rule. With his death he became a martyr to free thought. Established as his legacy, the International Modern School Movement emphasized improvisation, experimentation, and social awareness in the classroom, intending to prepare a new generation for leadership roles in a free and cooperative society. With its roots in political, economic, and anticlerical insurgency, however, it quickly became more than an educational experiment in keeping with such contemporary innovators as Montessori, Piaget, and Dewey.

In New York especially, the Ferrer Center established itself as a local forum for labor and cultural radicalism. In addition to its program for children, the school featured evening courses for adults with Goldman and Berkman, Tresca and Flynn, Jack London, Upton Sinclair, and Rose Pastor Stokes speaking on Socialist theory. The realist painter George Bellows and the young modernist Man Ray gave art lessons. Eugene O'Neill and Theodore Dreiser taught writing, and Margaret lectured on sexuality and family limitation. Long active in the Ferrer movement, the Sangers had enrolled their son Stuart in Will Durant's class at the day school in 1911. By 1913, the center had relocated from Greenwich Village to East 107th Street, a neighborhood that was home to many immigrant laborers and radicals, and it again provided a community for Margaret and the children when they returned from Paris and lived briefly uptown.[21]

The imprisonment of Frank Tannenbaum and the harassment of labor militants in New York, however, shattered the millennial spirit of the Ferrer Center just as it began to destroy the golden age of rebellion in a larger sense. In March, the second of two Union Square rallies coordinated by a Ferrer committee to defend Tannenbaum was disrupted by police brutality and arrests. The following month came the massacre of thirteen women and children at Ludlow, Colorado, when a fire erupted after National Guardsmen clashed with striking miners. The human toll grew to 74 before the strikers finally gave up in December of 1914. The stock of the company involved was controlled by a publicly callous and indifferent John D. Rockefeller, Jr., and the smoldering remains of the historic struggle would haunt his family for decades to come. In May, the Ferrer Center sponsored a protest in Tarrytown, New York, home of the Rockefeller estate at Pocantico Hills, which again ended in a confrontation with the police and more arrests for disorderly conduct. And through the spring continued demonstrations and threats in front of the Standard Oil headquarters at 26 Broadway foreshadowed the later street protests of the Depression and of the civil rights and antiwar movements of the 1960s.

Sometime in June at the Ferrer Center, a conspiracy was launched by Alexander Berkman and a group of young militants to blow up the Rockefeller home in retaliation for Ludlow. On July 4, while the association was holding its annual Independence Day picnic in New Jersey, a bomb accidentally exploded in a Harlem tenement, killing three young men and a woman. The dead were immediately identified with the Ferrer movement, and the plot on the Rockefellers was uncovered. A dramatic memorial service in Union Square the following week attracted an estimated crowd of 15,000 to 20,000, many of them wearing red and black revolutionary armbands and singing the Internationale. But as newspapers sensationalized the story throughout the summer, those in the movement who disavowed violence became alarmed and began to break ranks. The Ferrer Center and other radical gathering places came under continuous police and press surveillance. Within a year, the resignations of prominent moderates and financial supporters, together with internal divisions believed to have been spawned by government agents and spies, resulted in a decision by the Ferrer leadership to abandon New York altogether and establish a utopian residential colony and school called Stelton in rural New Jersey.[22]

Writing in *The Woman Rebel,* Margaret called the deaths of the young bomb makers an act of "courage, determination, conviction, a spirit of defiance." The greater tragedy for the revolutionary movement, she claimed, was "the cowardice and the poisonous respectability" of those leaders who apologized for the incident. An article defending the assassination of industrial or political tyrants accompanied her militant commentary, and the paper carried an admonition to "Remember Ludlow." Only three of the four criminal counts brought against her had to do with Anthony Comstock's obscenity statutes. The fourth accused her of using the mails to "incite murder and assassination," but in later years, when questioned directly about this charge by a reporter for the *New Yorker,* she deliberately tried to cover it up.[23]

Margaret was arraigned in August and given six weeks to prepare herself for trial. Instead, she sat down and wrote *Family Limitation,* an unassuming pamphlet which, in straightforward language and with the aid of diagrams, explained the common forms of birth preventives employed furtively but often without confidence by millions of American women, and still unknown to many more. The pamphlet soberly weighed the relative merits and drawbacks of withdrawal, condoms, douches, suppositories, sponges, and plugs, and recommended as most trustworthy a rubber pessary widely used in Europe to block the cervical passage. It also presented women with political arguments for using contraception. Embracing the rhetoric of revolution, Margaret argued the economic benefit to the worker of small families. Finally, she made a special plea to women for the virtue of mutually satisfying sexual union consummated without awkwardness or haste. "Birth control must not be set back by the false cry of obscenity," she wrote dramatically. "There must be no sentimentality in this important phase of sexual hygiene. Women must learn to know their own bodies."[24]

At first Margaret refused to hire a lawyer, and friends and family alike expressed their alarm. Michael Higgins, she later claimed, encouraged her to flee with him for a "rest cure" upstate, while the free-speech advocate, Theodore Shroeder, recommended a psychoanalytic consultation. She was reminded that she had little experience as a propagandist, nor the money or social influence to arouse public support for her acquittal. What is more, news of the impending war in Europe was making headlines; public attention, if not prosecutorial interest, was turning away from the radicals.

When her trial came up in October, she did retain counsel but spurned his advice to plead guilty and negotiate her sentence and fine. Instead, she requested a further postponement, and when it was denied, decided to flee, prepared to live abroad until the political climate at home improved, in the style of the exiled British suffragist, Christabel Pankhurst, whom she admired. Stuart, already ten years old, was away at boarding school. Bill had returned to New York on hearing the news of her arrest and could be expected to watch over Grant and Peggy, who were temporarily lodged with friends in the Village. Fearing that an emotional farewell would break her resolve, Margaret apparently never even said good-bye to them.

Instead she boarded a midnight train for Canada, where contacts in the radical community falsified papers that provided her passage to Europe under an alias. From aboard the R. M. S. *Virginian*, the ship that carried her out of Montreal Harbor to the Atlantic, securely outside U.S. legal jurisdiction, she cabled Bill Shatoff, a radical New Jersey printer who was waiting to release 100,000 copies of *Family Limitation*, already addressed and bundled and awaiting distribution through IWW locals and other sympathetic groups. They were the first of thousands more that in subsequent editions circulated clandestinely for more than twenty years.[25]

Alone in her stateroom, Margaret speculated about the opposing pulls of reason and emotion in her life, a debate that she had carried on with herself since childhood. From as early as she could remember, she had felt herself torn between competing temperaments—"the two Me's," she called them in her first autobiography, one deliberate and thoughtful, the other, intrepid and daring. The one cautioned restraint, the other urged her on to action and adventure. The one seemed weak, the other strong. The one she identified with her head, the other with her heart. The head told her to conform, the heart to rebel. Reason she now wrote, "is the accumulated knowledge of past acts of consequence. Emotion is that which urges from within without consciousness of fear or consequence—together they make up the perfect man."

The focus of her concern then shifted to reveal more clearly what was on her mind. "The man who shouts loud about his liberal ideas finds the servile submission of his wife charming and womanly," she continued, paraphrasing the manifesto she had made public in *The Woman Rebel.* "Virtue, marriage, respectability, they are all alike . . . the whole sickly business of society today is a sham. One feels like leaving it entirely and going about shocking it terribly."

Yet, if she was rid of marriage, however strong the social sanctions against divorce remained, she could not so impetuously cast motherhood aside. "Dear Peggy," she wrote, "how my heart goes out to you. I could weep from loneliness for you—just to touch your soft chubby hands—but work is to be done dear—work to make your path easier—and those who come after you."[26]

CHAPTER SIX

A European Education

When Margaret posed for a passport photograph in 1914, her face was thin, her features finely chiseled, her eyes wide and soulful, her mouth full and alluring. A black rimmed cloche sat at a stylish angle on her head, framing a complexion striking in its purity. She wore a tweed woolen coat with a tattered fur collar that gave an unmistakably fashionable, if slightly bohemian, effect. She seemed pensive and disarmingly vulnerable. Charged with a felony, she was subject to extradition under federal law, and so she traveled under an alias, Bertha Watson, a coarse and rather unappealing name meant to convey a demeanor totally at odds with her own. She regretted the choice almost as soon as she had made it.[1]

The transatlantic passage to Europe in 1914 took a week or more, and as her ship steamed through rough and seasonably cold seas, she amused herself in innocent flirtation with a handsome businessman aboard, whose attentions she courted even as she mocked his bourgeois presumptions and condescending manner. An unaccompanied young woman, shrouded in mystery but still charming and undisputedly sensual, made unusual company on such a journey. Margaret, in fact, was so startled by the attention and admiration she received as a single American woman roaming around Europe that she drafted an engaging article about her experiences but never published it. When she went ashore at Liverpool on a bleak, rain-swept November day, she took full advantage of the situation and anxiously passed through customs with her counterfeit documents, assisted by her worldly shipboard companion.[2]

Once settled in a small hotel, loneliness overwhelmed her as she had not felt it since her first homesick days at boarding school some twenty years earlier. She had to deal with the full force of the personal predicament she had created by fleeing and leaving her family behind. Toward Bill she felt surprisingly little remorse and, indeed, within a month's time, wrote him unequivocally ending their relationship and asking for a divorce. But the effort left her feeling "disconnected," as she put it, a response she associated with the emotion of separating herself from other past involvements, like the church of her youth or later her faith in Socialism. This speculation conveys strangely little sentiment for a woman who was ending a marriage of twelve years at a time when divorce was rare, but it does reveal the surprisingly sober understanding that being a wife had provided an anchor for her own identity, not essentially different from the many other ways of defining herself that she had pursued intensely and then cast aside. She was now, once again, adrift.

By contrast, Bill wrote her with tender passion of his suffering, of wanting still to have her in his arms, to love and caress her. Christmas passed, and as he tried to entertain three bereft children in his painting studio, he longed for the warmth and festivity she had created on holidays past. "You are all the world to me," he insisted in a letter that apparently crossed hers at sea.[3]

Of the children, however, she wondered often and anxiously in her diary. Young Grant and Peggy were left temporarily in Greenwich Village in the care of Caroline Pratt, the progressive educator and founder of the City and Country School, and her companion, Helen Marot, who had recently resigned as executive director of the National Women's Trade Union League, where she had organized the historic dressmakers' strike of 1909-10 in the New York garment industry. Bill wrote Margaret that Peggy, confused and vulnerable in the wake of her mother's abrupt and incomprehensible departure, cried each time he visited and then had to leave again to go off to work. Weighted down by the new cast he had fitted for her leg, despite Margaret's protests that any action await her return, the unhappy little girl wanted to know if she could "fly to her mother on wings." To ease her distress, Bill then took the children back, and their Aunt Ethel moved in temporarily to do the cooking.

There were occasional, stoic notes from young Grant in a self-conscious scrawl, assuring her not to worry about him, asking dutifully when she would be coming home. Stuart, alone at boarding school and uncertain of what the future held, betrayed an unmistakable sadness with his simple request for a photograph of his mother to hold on to in her absence. Earlier he wrote that he had mailed his Aunt Nan a bunch of flowers from the school garden. "I would have sent you some," he added wistfully, "but you are so far away."

Margaret saved the letters, starved for the children's affection and for news from home, but the outbreak of war in Europe only served to complicate communications that were not always reliable in the best of times. Mail took weeks, and sometimes months, to reach her. "How lonely it all is," she wrote. "Could any prison be more isolated—any confinement more solitary—than wandering around the world separated from the little ones you love, from their childish prattle, caresses, whisperings and quarrels?" Yet, at the same time, she took delight in her newfound freedom, in having the time to "get acquainted with myself, to reflect, meditate and dream."[4]

She spent the better part of her first days alone as a conventional tourist, finding solace in the tranquillity of Liverpool's well-ordered neighborhoods with their quaint brick row houses and small, well-kept business establishments, a respite from the disarray of Manhattan's teeming residential and commercial districts. In the evenings she sought out companions at the Clarion Café, a local gathering place for activists and intellectuals. Leafing through the register there, she was delighted to discover Bill Haywood's familiar signature along with the names of such prominent British freethinkers as George Bernard Shaw and H. G. Wells. Indeed, she arrived at the Clarion, on the evening of her first day in Europe, just in time for an informative Fabian lecture on the war. An enthusiastic rendering of Nietzsche later restored her own rebellious conviction and purpose. She reveled in the poetry, if not in the often elusive meaning of the text, and copied down the aphorism since recited by legions of kindred rebel spirits: "Men and women must be Gods unto themselves and stop worshipping at the shrine of other egos."[5]

At the Clarion she made the acquaintance of a courtly Spaniard who was teaching at the University in Liverpool and living in exile, because of a long association with the legendary Francisco Ferrer. The man was Lorenzo Portet, and on Ferrer's death he had been named executor of all international literary rights associated with publications of the Modern School. Margaret made only casual reference to Portet in her diary, but the few characteristics she noted about him dramatically changed the course of her European sojourn. He was "vigorous, full of confidence and quick to understand," she wrote, exactly the qualities she had found wanting in her husband. He also happened to be married, but that did not for the moment concern her.[6]

Lorenzo Portet was, by Margaret's description, a dignified man of middle height and weight, "a born teacher and natural protestor whose spirit flames in protest at every injustice. . . . There is an alertness about his glance which sums one up with an accuracy that is not always pleasant." He was born in 1871 in a village just outside Barcelona, the only surviving son of Catalan farmers who sent him to the university to become a barrister. Swept up as a student by Spanish republican enthusiasms, he rebelled against family, church, and monarch, and struck out in search of the more open society of Argentina. Returning from Buenos Aires after five years, he found himself a target of the wholesale arrest of radicals that followed nationalist uprisings in Spain in 1896. He fled to Paris and there met Ferrer, who was also living in exile, making his living teaching Spanish while also feeding stories about the various atrocities of the Spanish monarchy to the foreign press. Portet traveled back and forth to Spain, carrying Ferrer's message that the nation's political regeneration depended first upon education and social organization. When Ferrer was executed in 1909, Portet organized the formal demonstration in France that sparked an international protest. Portet was arrested during a demonstration in front of the Spanish embassy in Paris and expelled again, this time fleeing to England.[7]

He and Margaret apparently became lovers immediately. She extended her stay in Liverpool, and there was a romantic sightseeing trip to a rural village in Wales. Portet followed her to London, and they met again in Paris, where he ran the Ferrer-inspired publishing venture that exported the literature of Spain's political and cultural revolution and, in turn, translated censored titles from other countries and smuggled them into Madrid. In the spring of 1915, he was permitted to return temporarily to Spain, and they spent seven weeks together touring Rationalist schools in the countryside that held on tenuously as legacies to Ferrer's resistance to government and church.

Margaret's *Autobiography* recounts their Spanish escapade with a transparent innocence. She also kept a journal of the trip, and so we know that they sipped wine in cafés, took in the drama of a bullfight, the charm of a whitewashed mountain village, and the romantic splendor of a seaside Mediterranean vista—all the while tracked by government agents who followed Portet whenever he set foot on Spanish soil and amused her with their dignified manners and solicitousness, even as they carried out their surveillance. When it rained, these shadows took out umbrellas to shield her; when her hat blew away in the wind, they ran after it; when some petty thieves saw her cash a check at a local American Express office and threatened to rob her, they intervened and arrested them. She laughed at the absurdity of this situation even as she deplored so flagrant an invasion of her rights and privacy. In May, she returned to London with the intention of reclaiming her children in Canada and then rejoining Portet and working in Paris.[8]

If she needed an excuse for wandering about Europe with a lover, she found it in the one communication from Bill that had managed to reach her expeditiously. The letter carried news that he had been framed by a government agent and was subsequently arrested in his New York studio for handing out a copy of his wife's *Family Limitation* pamphlet. His arraignment was attended by Anthony Comstock himself. Bill was angry that Margaret had been writing him at the studio, and claimed that her letters led to his entrapment, but as always his hopeful affections modulated his tone. He encouraged her to remain abroad and leave the murky *Woman Rebel* indictments unresolved until he stood trial on what now presented itself as a clear-cut challenge to the constitutionality of the Comstock prohibition on birth control.[9]

This was not entirely a welcome development. Margaret could not be confident that public attention to Bill's defense would necessarily carry over to her own, though it would most certainly absorb financial support from the New York radical network, which she was counting on to sustain her in exile. For a time, in fact, she tided herself over by waiting on tables in a London tearoom. Moreover, she felt considerable personal frustration, for by becoming involved in her work, Bill seemed to believe that he had found a way to heal the divisions between them. He begged not to be "excommunicated" from her life. When his trial was set for April, she went off to await the outcome in Spain and learned only on her return to London in May that procedural appeals of the judge's decision to deny a verdict by jury were causing continued postponements. "Bill had to get mixed up in my work and make it harder," she complained to her sister Nan from Barcelona.[10]

In a series of articles for the magazine of the Modern School in

New York, Margaret described how the church suppressed the imagination and initiative inherent in native Spanish character. In this juxtaposition of nationalist and anticlerical sentiment, she sounded much like an exuberant Michael Higgins talking about the Irish. Though she made no effort to conceal her public association with Portet in her writing, she did go to some lengths to keep its private dimension discreet, assuring Nan in a letter from Spain that she was the guest of Mr. Portet *and* his wife. Margaret lived a profoundly unconventional life, but unlike the more comfortably flamboyant Emma Goldman, traditional social sanctions always governed the public image she projected, if not her actual behavior. Beyond a small group of intimates that did not include her family, she carefully cultivated an appearance of propriety. She was particularly sensitive about her conduct in Europe, because letters from New York gave her the impression that Bill was accusing her of deserting her children. Once she became a celebrity, this deliberate subterfuge about her personal relations also kept open doors to public acceptance and acclaim. Nelle Dick, an English woman who was active in the Ferrer Movement and knew Portet when she was young, recalls that he too masked a revolutionary temperament with fastidious manners, much as he concealed his gun beneath an impeccably tailored suit. Still, she says, everyone in the Ferrer circle knew about his love affair with Sanger.[11]

Only a few telegrams survive as evidence of a sustained affection after Margaret returned to the United States in 1916, but they clearly indicate that an ever-devoted Portet anticipated her immediate return, a development precluded by World War I. In Paris during the summer of the following year, Portet died suddenly of tuberculosis, a disease he had apparently long endured, since Margaret had visited him in a sanitarium while in Europe. The common ailment may have been an additional bond between them. In 1919, well after there had been other admirers, she confided her continued preoccupation with him in sorrowful diary entries, and several years thereafter, when she finally returned to Europe, she recalled him longingly in personal letters. For years she could not bring herself to return to Paris, the city with which her memories of him were most intimately bound.[12]

After Portet's death, Margaret struggled to extricate herself from haunting associations of the past. As her own politics moderated after World War I, moreover, she had ample cause to hide the depth of her feelings for the dynamic, radical Spaniard. In his place, she wove a myth around the relationship she had formed with another mentor from her year of exile in Europe—Henry Havelock Ellis, the

British sex psychologist, whom she had heard so much about at Mabel Dodge's salon.

On her arrival in London in late November 1914, Margaret had contacted Dr. Charles Vickery Drysdale, an heir by family lineage to the mantle of British Malthusian doctrine. Drysdale's parents, Charles Robert and Alice Vickery, both physicians and feminists, together with his uncle, Dr. George Drysdale, a prominent pamphleteer for birth control in the 1860s, had been founders of London's Neo-Malthusian League (so-called because it added "prevention" to Malthus's original argument). The Drysdales defended Annie Besant and Charles Bradlaugh during their widely publicized trial in 1878 for distributing *Fruits of Philosophy*, the birth control tract by the American Charles Knowlton, an event to which Margaret's recent indictment in New York was being compared. Though reversed on appeal, the famous case had won Neo-Malthusianism the support of such prominent late nineteenth century British liberals as John Stuart Mill.[13]

By the century's close, however, British liberals, preoccupied on the one hand with the practical agenda of trade unionism and on the other with the growing popularity of millennial Socialist doctrine, were suspicious of Malthus's ideas as economic theory. Many were willing to support the idea of population control as an economic and personal benefit but not as a solution to poverty. In 1896, the Manchester Labour Press did publish Edward Carpenter's *Love's Coming of Age*, a historic and widely circulated series of papers on the relations between the sexes, which advocated greater freedom in love and bemoaned the absence of a foolproof system of birth prevention. As an official matter, however, the Labourites stayed clear of these issues well into the 1920s. The widowed Alice Vickery and her son were lonely voices for their cause and understandably, therefore, gave enthusiastic welcome to a beleaguered American convert. They helped Margaret find lodgings, arranged a lecture opportunity at London's Fabian Hall, and secured her an invitation to tea with Ellis, who was their most prominent advocate.[14]

When Henry Havelock Ellis opened the door of his Brixton flat to Margaret Sanger on December 22, 1914, she saw in the soft glow of the candlelit room a "tall, lovely simple man with the most wonderful head and face and smile," whose shock of white hair and flowing white beard gave him the look of a seer. He was fifty-six years old and looked more than his years. She was just thirty-five but already claiming to be less, a fiction that easily deceived because, indeed, she appeared young and cultivated an earnest demeanor. She found Ellis open and easy in intimate conversation, which was a relief to her. They talked of their respective legal battles, for the volume of his *Studies in the Psychology of Sex* that dealt with sexual inversion, the then-standard label for homosexuality, had recently been censored. They also discussed the virtues of various birth control methods. Ellis extolled *Tokology*, a pamphlet written by the nineteenth century American spiritualist and sex radical, Alice Stockham, which encourages husbands to withhold orgasm until their wives have been sexually satisfied and then ejaculate outside the vagina, a practice labeled "karezza."

Margaret was overwhelmed to have conversed with "the one man who has done more than anyone in this century toward giving women and men a clear and sane understanding of their sex lives and of all life." Ellis, for his part, though he found her "quicker, more daring and impulsive" than was his temper and strongly disapproved of her radical politics, had rarely known a more charming companion and never found one so quickly.[15]

It is virtually impossible to overestimate the impact Ellis would have on Margaret. She met him when he was at the height of his influence, having established an international professional reputation with the completion in 1910 of his path-breaking *Studies*, an iconoclastic, multivolume taxonomy of the range and diversity of human sexual expression. The son of a wandering sea captain, he was raised by a deeply pious and moralistic mother and four sisters, none of whom married. His earliest remembered sexual encounter came aboard his father's ship when he traveled around the world as a handsome youth of eight and witnessed the autoerotic—and probably the homosexual—behavior of sailors. Nevertheless, he long associated his first consciousness of sexual excitement with memories of watching his mother stand and urinate in a park, claiming that this urolagnia "never developed into a real perversion" but "became in some degree attached to my feelings of tenderness toward women." An extremely shy adolescent, he was troubled by the experience of "wet dreams," and since masturbation was then rigidly circumscribed, he resolved out of his own confusion to train as a doctor and study sexuality.[16]

In America before World War I, while Freud still remained relatively obscure, Ellis enjoyed enormous intellectual and even popular prestige as a scientist who wrote about sexual psychology with rare literary accessibility and grace. His reformulated theories of hygienic conduct gave immense stature to the emerging revolt against what was perceived as a pervasive Victorian fear and discipline of unlicensed sexual behavior. His sheer enthusiasm for sexuality and his inherent disdain of reticence and duplicity made him the undisputed prophet of a modernist tradition that has been confident and optimistic in its conviction that a freer sexual life is essential to individual and social well-being, a tradition that has since been given further credibility by the empirical sex research of men like Alfred Kinsey. Ellis's capacity to write sympathetically and without moral sanction about an endless variety of sexual predilections as they were reported to him by patients—including homosexuality and autoeroticism, the subjects of his first two volumes—stood in sharp contrast to dominant standards of propriety. Even Margaret was for a time disturbed by his frankness, claiming that an initial reading of his case studies gave her "psychic indigestion."[17]

At first, Ellis's stature in America increased along with Freud's. He was one of the earliest writers in English to appreciate the significance of the psychoanalytic argument for the fundamental relationship between sexuality and neurosis. But as Freud veered away from the relative optimism of his early writings and began to emphasize the inherent conflict between sexual drives and internalized restraints and moral sanctions, Ellis countered with a more liberal and humane approach to the subject. He eschewed the rigidity of orthodox psychoanalytic imperatives, which in his view were problematically concerned with the danger of an unchanneled sexual instinct. In a rather sweeping indictment, he challenged Freud's dogmatic views about the necessary course of childhood development and sublimation, of adult social behavior and coital performance. He especially despaired of a therapeutic model that sought to enforce strict norms, and at one point called Freud's published views on the interpretation of dreams and other symbols nothing more than "didacticism and divine revelation." He once identified Freud as "an extravagant genius—the greatest figure in psychology who was almost always wrong." But since Ellis himself failed to produce an alternative theory of personality and behavior, or a therapeutic model anywhere near the scope or complexity of Freud's, his reputation did not survive the psychoanalytic revolution unscathed.*[18]

* Freud himself kept an inscribed photogrtaph of Ellis on his examination room wall and admired his early case histories immensely, but claimed that he tended to "lose himself in abstractions" and paid him the dubious compliment of praising his literary gifts over his scientific ones. He judged Ellis superficial because his kindly tolerance of individual sexual variation failed to delve below the surface of memory.

Ellis viewed sexuality as an inborn drive that could only become repressed or distorted by culture. He argued that more liberal social attitudes would necessarily breed contentment by setting men and women free from inherited taboos and letting them do whatever seemed natural and right. This optimism was born of his faith, at least before World War I, in the educability and malleability of the human personality—a viewpoint that rejected both traditional, Christian doctrines of man's fall from grace and Freud's secular reformulations on the subject. Ellis endorsed any number of reforms, including universal coeducation and a program of sex education for children, so as to permit boys and girls from the start to feel comfortable with themselves and with each other. He was supportive as well of organized feminism, because the woman's movement promised to shatter the traditional formality and distance between men and women that fostered the inhibition and misunderstanding on which he believed most heterosexual dissatisfaction rested. Though he found Freud's linkages between disturbances of the unconscious and hysteria quite fascinating, he insisted that individual mechanisms for repression and denial could be easily penetrated in the kind of patient therapy he practiced, where simply talking about anxiety and bringing it to the surface often acted as its own cure.[19]

Unlike Freud, Ellis did not demand that his patients change their habits, whatever they might be, only that they accept them. His standards for what ought to fit within a reasonable spectrum of normal sexual activity accommodated not only conventional practices, but many that were then commonly labeled perverse, and often still are. Ellis, in fact, celebrated deviation from conventional coital sexuality as a laudable, inventive and distinctively human phenomenon.* His sexual theory was premised on a willingness to under-

* Ellis categorized and attempted to explain away abnormal practices as a form of "erotic symbolism," which unites the higher imaginative capacity of human beings with the basic reproductive impulse seen in even the lowest forms of life. He argued that the sexual variation he uncovered in his case studies was neither degenerate nor psychologically anomalous, as Freud labeled much of it, but instead, evidenced a unique and constructive ability on the part of the individual to create what he once called "man's own paradise." Elsewhere Ellis identified fetishism as "the supreme triumph of human idealism"—though he admitted somewhat paradoxically that the erotic practices some find satisfying may seem absurd, disgusting, or even criminal to others.

For example, he validated even such behavioral extremes as sadism and masochism by explaining, albeit quixotically, that the seeming contradiction of the capacity to derive sexual pleasure from the experience of pain is the distillation in human lovemaking of atavistic tendencies. By his biologically determined reasoning, just as males in the animal world fight over and subdue their female sexual prey, so primitive man reenacts this courtship drama in the practice of bride capture, while men and women in civilized society seek to intensify the emotion of the sexual encounter by introducing emotions of

stand and tolerate sexual diversity as a dimension of what he simply called "nature's balance." He believed in complete sexual freedom, apart from society's interest in protecting innocent individuals from behavior to which they do not consent, though he never spelled out exactly how this enforcement should work. He also believed women should be left alone to do as they please until they become pregnant, at which point society might reasonably assert its legitimate interest in the welfare of the child. In almost all these respects, Margaret deferred to his erudition and endorsed his scholarship wholeheartedly, accepting his theories as validation of her own experience, and making them the intellectual foundation for her subsequent work.[20]

Margaret found Ellis's formulations on female sexuality especially congenial. His writings celebrated the emancipation of an independent, self-defined woman whom she liked to think she resembled. He defended passion in both sexes as one of life's great driving forces but made a special plea for female eroticism, claiming in contradiction to established Victorian views on female sexual weakness and to Freudian confusion on the subject, that what women want is the fulfillment of their strong sensual nature. Ellis linked sexual desire to instinctual reproductive requirements and understood the sexual encounter as an intense courtship ritual—an extension of the primitive mating game. Yet, he argued that emphasis on reproduction at the expense of gratification had brought an unnatural and repressive influence to bear on human sexuality, especially for women. He instead legitimized the stimulation of desire through complicated patterns of arousal that for some might countenance sexual excess, for others, long periods of abstinence—all depending on levels of sexual energy,

fear and anger derived from physical stress. In similar, if rather reductive fashion, he also rationalized other sexual anomalies.

Perhaps most significantly, Ellis produced the first clinical studies of male homosexuals and endured ridicule and censorship of his work, because he explained sexual inversion as a genetic predisposition and demanded its legal and political protection. With respect to lesbianism, however, he was on less secure ground, defending women whom he believed to be biologically determined cases, but arguing that for many impressionable young girls, the inclination to love other women was simply an abnormal, acquired response to the fear of being subordinated by men. He insisted that this manifestation could be prevented or cured, if only Victorian social standards were relaxed, providing opportunities for greater collegiality and equality between the sexes. While he offered his observations in the hope of promoting tolerance, he left himself vulnerable to criticism for both his biological determinism and his apparent heterosexual bias. Margaret, too, believed that many women were impelled to "seek the society of Sappho," as she later wrote, out of sheer disgust with the drudgery and routine of women's lives in a man's world.

which he maintained were highly individualized. He advanced a view of orgasm emphasizing the similarity of male and female response and directly challenged Freud's dicta on the subject, claiming instead that orgasmic deficiency in most women is simply the result of male ineptitude. At the same time, he argued—somewhat contradictorily, in the view of some of his critics—that the process of sexual arousal and gratification in women ("tumescence and detumescence," as he called them) is generally more complicated and time-consuming than in men. He meant no criticism by this—indeed, virtually all of his writings condemn male, phallic-centered notions of gratification and endorse a more imaginative and creative sexual regimen on the grounds that response patterns in both sexes are better when made more diffuse. Nonetheless, this preoccupation limited the revolutionary implications of his thinking. He encouraged men to play upon women as they would upon delicate and finely tuned instruments and left himself open to misrepresentation and misunderstanding as an apologist for traditional gender arrangements. His views must have substantiated Margaret's own quite clearly, however, for she too never saw any hazard for women in greater male solicitude of their sexual desires and needs.

Though his sexual theory was grounded in biology and anthropology, Ellis was at the same time an aesthete and romantic by temperament. He believed that the sex drive is instinctual but also argued that the emergence of self-conscious human beings allows for the integration of sex and love—for a union of physical and spiritual impulses.* This peculiar blend of a modernist temperament with respect to rights of sexual expression and a conventional, romantic outlook about relationships (however many he might countenance at a single time) made him an ideal mentor for Margaret. His writings on love and on freedom in marriage, even more than his explicit thinking about sexual practices, confirmed her own viewpoints and

* To this end, he cultivated a grand and complex art of lovemaking emphasizing intimacy, foreplay, and noncoital stimulation by and for both sexual partners, a routine considered iconoclastic and liberating in its own time, though criticized by many since for becoming the standard of a sexual revolution that has dramatically raised expectations about performance and created its own form of tyranny. However explicit Ellis's sexual materialism then, its intent was clearly idealistic. He advocated a better understanding of sexual functioning only as an avenue toward what he called a higher, "spiritual" transcendence of the physical experience, which he saw as the supreme objective of human intimacy and love. He endorsed premarital and extramarital sexuality, for example, on the grounds that most couples would benefit from a diversity of experience. But in attempting to free sex from exclusivity, jealousy, and guilt, he did not intend to divorce it from affection and intimacy, and he deplored the common tendency of many men of his day to do so. He hated the unabashed materialism of prostitution, for example, and refused to encourage its legalization.

quickly formed a new catechism for her own unorthodox behavior and beliefs.[21]

The historian Paul Robinson, in a thoughtful essay, points out that in praising both naturalism and romanticism, Ellis raised to the level of debate, but did not resolve, the most vexing problem of human sexual psychology—"the paradoxical need for both companionship and variety in erotic life."* Ellis might have agreed with this assessment, but he would have us believe that he accommodated the dilemma in his own life by remaining intensely devoted to his wife, whom he doted on emotionally and intellectually, while both had sexual relations with other women. The arrangement seemed satisfactory to all parties concerned until Margaret Sanger became the other woman in his life.[22]

Ellis's first love affair had been with Olive Schreiner, the distinguished South African feminist and author of *Woman and Labor* and *The Story of an African Farm,* but she rejected him when she found that he could not sustain an erection and experience normal coitus. Instead, he married Edith Lees, a highly neurotic and self-absorbed essayist and novelist of considerably less repute, who as a self-avowed lesbian found an occasional diffuse intimacy with her husband satisfactory, this situation accounting, perhaps, for some of Ellis's irresolution on the subject. Edith described the unusual nature of their rapport in a thinly veiled gothic romance about a coal miner's wife who takes a lusty lover after her husband is paralyzed in an accident, but then returns to him in recognition of the virtue of their higher "spiritual" union.[23]

By contrast, the lover of Ellis's mature years, Françoise Lafitte Cyon, a French schoolmistress and translator in London, with whom at least one of his biographers claims he eventually achieved conventional sexual compatibility, explained in her memoir how her first intimacy with Ellis brought her a gratification she had never experienced despite two earlier marriages:

> On the first day I foolishly expected the marital act I had so far known, but now with a man I truly loved. There was, therefore, a slight dread when this did not happen. . . . But instantly came the astounding assurance—as a stroke of lightning before he had touched me—that when true love abides everything is perfect. This "travail" of my soul

* This tension continues to burden modern sexology and sex therapy, such as the laboratory work of Masters and Johnson, who reject psychoanalytic approaches to marriage counseling in favor of a program of practical sex instruction and behavior modification. They encourage their patients to diversify their sexual practices, however, only within the context of conventional, monogamous partnerships.

> proved the birth of my new being: Woman at last, woman in soul. On that bed, in broad daylight, his hands and his kisses, never jerking me with fear, tenderly brought me to this delight. My body, husbandless, yet spontaneously acclaimed its true rule at the guidance of another soul: Love, and do what you like.[24]

Within a week of meeting Margaret, Ellis was guiding her reading at the British Museum, flattering her skills as a writer and encouraging her to visit him at home again and again. After an intimate New Year's Eve together, he was writing love letters, admitting that he "sensed something" happening most unusual for him, a "reserved, slow, undemonstrative person." The body of these notes invariably followed endearing, boyish salutations to "My little rebel," "My darling woman," "You wicked woman," or "Dear twin." In one he teases her about his fear of being "gobbled up," an obviously erotic reference, and in another compliments the hat she was wearing, and then tantalizes her with the certainty that "if you wore nothing I should think that costume also suited you just perfectly."[25]

Some fifty communications of this nature survive, all dated between December 1914 and September 1915, and what is at once remarkable and yet rather pathetic about them is that for much of this period Margaret was out of London and frequently traveling with Portet. Ellis may have agreed in a letter to Margaret dated January 13 that "passion is mostly a disastrous thing," but only two days later he was writing anxiously wondering why he hadn't heard from her in a week, though he'd already written twice and been several times to the library to try to find her. When in mid-February she went off to Amsterdam and the Hague to investigate contraception in Holland's pioneering state-supported maternity clinics, he admitted that he had begun to miss her before she left and had rushed down to Victoria Station in anticipation of catching her before her departure. He then acknowledged some suspicion about her whereabouts in a reference to her "mysterious seclusion in some unknown spot with the unknown comrade," which he hoped would not keep her away too long. When subsequently he learned she was in Barcelona and later in Montserrat, destinations he had extolled in a popular book called *The Soul of Spain,* he wrote that he often thought of her and tried to imagine what she was doing, regretting that he was not the one to introduce her to those lovely spots. As she kept delaying her return, he began to grow impatient and wrote salaciously that "it is all very well to send me your thoughts to eat . . . but when you do arrive I shall be eating you up, if you aren't careful, I shall be so hungry." There are allusions as well to his urolagnia, of which she was apparently aware.[26]

Margaret's letters to Ellis from this period were, for the most part, either lost or deliberately destroyed, so it is impossible for us to know how she responded to these overtures. She did continue writing, though never as often as he would have liked, and she did lead him on flirtatiously—at one point explicitly encouraging him to go on missing her. She was, nonetheless, never duplicitous with Ellis about her whereabouts or her divided loyalties. One of his early letters, in fact, playfully accuses her of "already unwinding her scarf to wave to someone else." In mid-March, he cautions her never to do anything brash in matters of the heart, and a month later offers only the weakest acknowledgment that her expeditions on the Continent would be profitable to her future work. When she finally returned to London in May, she appeared to be avoiding him, but he frantically searched her out again at the British Museum and other haunts, only to be disturbed that she was "shy" at their reunion. Clearly disappointed, he conceded in a letter to his wife that Margaret was "quite nice and a very pleasant companion, but she has no power to help or comfort me; I should never dream of telling her I *needed* help or comfort. . . . Mneme means much more to me [referring to a young girl with whom he had long carried on one of his trysts, a girl who was also, coincidentally, about to break off with him in order to marry another man]. And you know, or you never will know, the only *one* person has really hold of my heart strings, for good or evil."[27]

Edith Ellis had ample need for reassurance. She had been traveling in the United States when Margaret first appeared at her husband's door, delivering lectures under the billing of "Mrs. Havelock Ellis," an affront to feminist proprieties that always rankled in Margaret, who accused her of living off her husband's reputation. Ellis was too reserved and retiring to speak in public himself, and the fact that his wife delivered his lectures sheds considerable light on the depth of their intellectual congress and perhaps explains why the relationship endured despite its apparent sexual anomalies. For several weeks, however, Ellis neglected to mention his new friendship at all in letters to Edith but then began writing about it with a frequency and an enthusiasm that did not elude her. The terms of their marriage had accommodated past involvements confined to the physical sphere, but here the competition of a notorious, reputedly attractive, and gifted young woman suddenly presented itself. Fragile and anxious by nature, and accustomed to monopolizing her husband's emotional and intellectual life, Edith suddenly grew paranoid and wrote him of her intense feelings of abandonment and thoughts of death. She mentioned that she had heard many nice things about Margaret in America—that she was "sweet and deep and good"—but also cautioned that a few people, by contrast, had described her as "fanatical and unbalanced." When a newspaper story appeared in New York saying Margaret was in London "studying" with Havelock Ellis, he, in turn, wrote to Spain and anxiously cautioned that Margaret not mention him again in her letters home.[28]

Ellis, in fact, quite quickly abandoned Edith for Margaret when the two returned to London in May within a day of one another, and despite contrary assurances to his wife, his letters testify that he remained in a frenzied emotional state until Margaret, feeling ill, fled England's damp climate in August and rejoined Portet at a French sanitarium. Edith herself was exhausted and depressed when she returned from her American trip aboard a ship that anxiously left New York only hours after the Germans had torpedoed the *Lusitania*, killing more than a thousand passengers and escalating American involvement in the war. Thereafter, her mental and physical health deteriorated dramatically, and within the year she was dead of a diabetic condition complicated by neurasthenia and at least one suicide attempt. In a deathbed letter to her husband, she pledged "love, forgiveness and eternal comradeship." Though other women would more successfully arouse him sexually, none proved worthy of a comparable spiritual bond.[29]

When she deposited Ellis's letters in the Library of Congress to be opened after her death, Margaret apparently saw no reason to expurgate the details of their intimate relations. Until then she had been considerably more circumspect, though her response to a biographer's inquiry in 1953 admitted that when she first knew Ellis "he was alive (and) alert to all physical impulses and delights, as his relationship with two other women testified." On the matter of his potency, she admonished her correspondent not to confuse premature ejaculation and impotence since "then about 65% of *American* men could be called sexually impotent." (On the basis of personal experience, she subscribed to the popular stereotype that European men tend to be more satisfying lovers than Americans, though she never explained why this cultural variation should be so.) This testimony could mean that she had aroused Ellis beyond his customary habit, which would have accounted for his unusual infatuation. It could also mean that, along with Françoise Cyon, she wished to protect his reputation from further damage, for she also admitted, somewhat contradictorily, that Ellis felt himself to be an unsatisfactory lover in conventional terms. And she claimed to join with Ellis and Cyon in the belief that "there are various means of receiving physical satisfaction . . . the important thing to make the union perfect or satisfactory is not alone the physical method, but the reverence and the spiritual oneness created through the physical contact."[30]

After the failure of her first marriage, Margaret never again demanded that any one man be all things to her, or she to him. In this regard her own oedipal disappointments may have cast a shadow, but she used Ellis's teachings to license her behavior. Often she went to bed with men like Ellis who enriched her thinking and advanced her work. She perceived herself as fully liberated in her personal and sexual life and never willingly tolerated control by any man. If she ever again yearned for the integrity of a single, enduring relationship with one individual, she did not admit it.[31]

Margaret's intimacy with Ellis may never have been entirely satisfying, but there is no doubt of the profound intellectual impression he made. She did not always welcome his advances, but she became nonetheless one of his most devoted disciples, and through the essays and commentaries he produced with remarkable frequency for the remainder of his life, he continued to shape and educate her mature world view.[32]

On the completion of his empirical studies in 1910, Ellis turned his attention to theoretical work and attempted to extract new premises for social policy from his liberal formulations about human sexuality and behavior. He set out to prove that the rationalization of sexuality would advance, not only individual human happiness but, even more important, the interests of society as a whole. When he met Margaret, he had just published *The Task of Social Hygiene,* a series of papers that addressed significant issues of contemporary social discourse, including sexual emancipation and the family, women's rights and family limitation, as birth control was still commonly known.

Ellis had never exhibited a sustained interest in politics, though as a young man he had been a founding member of the progressive society called the Fellowship of the New Life, a faction of which later split off under George Bernard Shaw to form the more practically oriented Fabian Society. By his own claim, Ellis expressed a theoretical concern for "the socialization of all material necessaries of life as the only means of obtaining freedom for individual development."

Though never active as a Fabian, he believed in the value of educating a cadre of enlightened, scientifically minded men and women to foment change. These elites would overcome the emotions and prejudices of the masses, which stood in the way of their effecting revolution from the bottom up, as orthodox Marxist theory prescribed.

In the fractious years before World War I, as many on the British left despaired of doctrine altogether, Ellis offered an alternative to conventional social theory. Taking into account the combined influences of biology, heredity, and environment on human behavior, he advocated that conventional strategies for reform be supplanted by a program of "social hygiene" that addressed itself to the systematic prevention of social ills before they became problems in need of solution. In this respect, he endorsed eugenics, the movement founded in England in the late nineteenth century by Francis Galton, a cousin of Charles Darwin. Taking its name from the Greek *eugenes*, meaning "well-born," eugenicism called for the regulation of human reproduction to improve the biological characteristics of humanity, much as enthusiasts of horses or dogs, for example, might dedicate themselves to the production of a better species of thoroughbreds. At the turn of the century, eugenic theories of hereditary selection and improvement were provided a putative rationale when the botanist Gregor Mendel experimented with his peas and promulgated what were then perceived to be hard, scientific principles of genetic transfer. If, as Darwin said first and Mendel then confirmed, only the fittest were to survive, surely it was in society's best interest to improve the quality of humans, as well as plants.

Though its darker potential was always clear to some skeptics, eugenicism enjoyed a surprisingly large intellectual following well into the 1930s among liberals and progressives in the United States and Europe, who simply assumed that hereditarian principles were compatible with a commitment to egalitarianism and to social welfare initiatives in education, health, and labor, much as an enriched soil mixture made possible the propagation of Mendel's bigger and better pea. Even the prominent theorist of moderate Socialism, Peter Kropotkin, endorsed eugenicism, though he warned against arbitrary imposition of eugenic theory,[33] and Kropotkin, in turn, influenced Emma Goldman.

Knowing of the reactionary and inhumane objectives that scientific theories of human improvement have since served, it is difficult to recapture this naive confidence in the possibilities of doing good through the rational application of medical and scientific advances to human life. The ugly and tragic link of eugenicism with the intolerance and prejudice that produced Naziism has undermined its earlier association with scientific progress meant to promote the welfare of the individual and the public. Also lost is the fact that eugenicists were largely responsible for having introduced explicitly sexual topics into the boundaries of acceptable scientific discourse.*

Ellis always considered himself both a eugenicist and a Socialist and convinced Margaret of the coherence of this viewpoint. A pioneering advocate for the socialization of medicine as a public responsibility, he never tackled difficult moral or practical considerations about the implementation of eugenic policy, instead assuming, as she also would, that its benefits would be universally understood, because all human beings desire self-improvement. Medical and scientific advances would be available to all and welcomed by all; they would never need to be imposed. As the naïveté of this viewpoint became apparent with the rise of Fascism, Ellis shied away from the subject altogether, claiming to be bewildered, and refusing to hold himself in any way responsible for what he believed was a total perversion of eugenic theory.[34]

Ellis made his most important contribution to eugenic doctrine, at least from the standpoint of Margaret's interest, when he assigned women to act as its chief enforcers. Women are critical agents of civilization's progress, he argued, because as individuals they alone have the power to produce and nurture fewer, fitter babies, while, collectively, they can exercise the will to reduce substantially the pressure of population on the environment and the competition of labor in the marketplace. Increased sex expression and wider use of birth control were thus significant tools in the eugenic program, and accordingly, he condemned eugenicists who refused to endorse birth control because they wanted more children for the better classes. Though he never saw birth control alone as a panacea for social ills, and often encouraged Margaret to diversify her interests, he assumed a necessary equation among women's emancipation, contraception, and human betterment.

This linkage evolved logically from his views about gender differ-

* Although only the most conservative faction of the eugenics movement engaged in explicit racial stereotyping, it is nonetheless true that few of its proponents were entirely lacking in prejudice by modern standards. Ellis, for example, once defended his program of social hygiene with a metaphorical salvo that betrayed his obvious, if in its day widely condoned, elitism: "The duty of purifying, ordering, and consolidating the banks of the stream must still remain," he wrote. "But when we are able to control the stream at its source we are able to some extent to prevent the contamination of that stream by filth, and ensure that its muddy floods shall not sweep away the results of the laborious work on the banks." Yet at the same time, he never endorsed eugenics as a tool for selective breeding, but only as an obvious opportunity to emphasize qualitative over quantitative principles of behavior—to provide smaller numbers of people with a more abundant life.

ence and women's instinctive mothering nature. With his professional roots in biology, Ellis saw no value in a feminist agenda that strictly imitates men. Despite his efforts to break down barriers between the sexes, he, in fact, never questioned conventional stereotypes of men as aggressors and women as nurturers. By perpetuating these distinctions, however, he did not intend to relegate women to an inferior status. To the contrary, he believed that the assertion of woman's biologically determined responsibility for fertility would automatically empower her in a larger scientifically minded culture. Moreover, he celebrated the ascendence of feminine values of community and cooperation in the public polity and deplored traditionally male-associated traits of self-assertion and dominance. He once wrote aphoristically: "Charm is a woman's strength, as strength is a man's charm. . . . Civilization involves the substitution of women's methods for man's."

Ellis's ideas in this regard engaged not only Margaret but also such outspoken feminists of the era as Emma Goldman, Olive Schreiner, and Ellen Key, all of whom also treasured his friendship and quoted his writings extensively in their own work. They looked to him as inspiration for a philosophy that argued for the recognition of a different voice, and for the accommodation of woman's special needs and values, in the making of social and political policy. They brought his concerns to bear on the popular thinking of their generation by debating the relative merit of an agenda that emphasizes absolute equality of opportunity for men and women, over one that takes stock of fundamental differences in biology. With Schreiner, Ellis shared the view that a modern industrial and consumer society allows men productive economic roles and participation in marriage and family life, but forces women to choose between the two. He supported a feminist doctrine which encouraged meaningful work and economic independence for women. On the other hand, he also agreed with the Swedish-born Key that a collective family life, which frees women of domestic responsibilities and enables them to work—an idea then advocated by many radicals—fosters a fearsome social conformity and robs children of the psychological nourishment and individual enrichment of the independent home. Key's solution to the problem was to advocate state support of mothers with young children, so women would neither have to work or be financially dependent on a man during the period of their maternal responsibility, and it is her legacy that informs the program of compensatory maternal and child care benefits for which the Scandinavian countries today are duly praised. She offered no resolution, however, to the dilemma of woman's enforced absence from the labor market while she mothers or to the difficulties of reentry and retraining when she wishes to return.

Ellis wrote lavish introductions to the English translations of Key's books, condemning the dogmatism of a first generation of feminists in their fixation on work and their reticence about sexuality and family life, and arguing for a "new phase" of the woman's movement, which would begin to understand the rights of women "to be unlike men." He never resolved the question of whether a social philosophy recognizing and protecting the reality of biological difference between men and women is logically and legally compatible with egalitarian principles that must also govern a society where opportunities for women are unbounded, but he did raise consciousness about it. Along with Ellis, Schreiner and Key were beginning to be read in America, and Margaret herself had already incorporated some of their ideas into *The Woman Rebel*.[35]

Havelock Ellis would thus provide Margaret an empowering philosophy in the years following World War I, as she steered the birth control movement away from radicalism. It is a mistake, however, to believe that his moderating influence immediately eroded her prior commitment to fundamental economic change, and it is important to emphasize again the competing influence of Portet, who as a follower of Ferrer may have preferred education to violence as a vehicle of social change, but nonetheless always carried a gun.

Indeed, when Margaret addressed London's Fabian Society on July 5, 1915, she faced an audience that was not sympathetic to the extremism of her own economic and social philosophies, but still she refused to accommodate. The speech she wrote out in longhand recounted the struggle of American labor against an industrial giant dependent on the sweat of women and children and explained her defiant advocacy of family limitation, not as a "panacea," but as a first step in breaking the cycle of the "present economic enslavement." A month later in a letter addressed from London to her American "Comrades and Friends," she made no claim for herself as a pioneer for birth control: "The industrial and economic conditions had done all the pioneering which was done in America, and especially among the working people; but as soon as I was convinced that the information to prevent conception was a necessity of woman's as well as man's emancipation, I set to work at once to do my part in giving it." For the time being, at least, birth control remained subordinate to the larger concerns of the working class.[36]

Throughout the summer she learned of a growing interest in her cause from her radical friends at home. Leonard Abbott first wrote that the Free Speech League had appealed for $500 to fight Bill's case and raised considerably more. He enclosed a $100 check but cautioned that despite the growing sentiment in her favor, she was likely to receive a long prison sentence if she returned. She would have to decide for herself whether she was willing to "face the music." Only a month later, however, he advised that the situation was changing for the better and told her to come home. Elizabeth Gurley Flynn also warmly urged her to overcome her distaste for public speaking and undertake a national lecture tour, with the support of IWW locals and other groups, as a means of generating interest in her trial. From Washington, D.C., and from as far away as Texas and California, letters came commending her courage and daring and asking for more copies of the revised editions of *Family Limitation* she was sending home from Europe with new information on the rubber spring diaphragm, the favored contraceptive method of the Dutch clinics she had visited. The only breach of solidarity she felt was from Goldman, who neglected to write anything at all about *The Woman Rebel* convictions in *Mother Earth* until after Margaret left the country, and then never even mentioned Bill's subsequent arrest. Ironically, given her more determined radicalism, Goldman was annoyed that Margaret's defense of assassination in *The Woman Rebel* had compromised the integrity of her legal challenge to the contraception statutes. There was a public apology after Margaret wrote a long letter to *Mother Earth* from London defending her actions, and the journal gave better coverage to William Sanger's trial that September, but again Goldman implied that Margaret lacked sufficient experience and judgment to operate independently. The rift between the two strong-willed women never really healed.[37]

Bill Sanger, meanwhile, stood alone before three judges of the Court of Special Sessions in New York City on September 10, 1915. After months of haggling over procedural technicalities without success, he gave up all hope of justice and dismissed his lawyer. In a statement reflecting the impassioned turmoil of his private life, he identified emotionally with his wife's work and called Anthony Comstock the victim of an "incurable sexphobia" who lacked "the intelligence to distinguish between pornography and scientific information." He was offered the alternative of a $150 fine or a thirty-day prison sentence, and he chose jail without appeal.

Ironically, the judge's opinion actually intensified interest in the case. It defined the issue unequivocally as a dispute not about obscenity, but about women's role, and therein set the terms for a public debate on birth control that continues to this day: "Your crime is not only a violation of the laws of man, but of the law of God as well, in your scheme to prevent motherhood," it read. "Too many persons have the ideas that it is wrong to have children. Some women are so selfish that they do not want to be bothered with them. If some persons would go around and urge Christian women to bear children, instead of wasting their time on woman suffrage, this city and society would be better off." One hundred supporters who had crowded into the courtroom, and an equal number waiting restively outside, broke into a raucous protest. Two weeks after the trial, however, there was cause for renewed celebration, because Anthony Comstock caught a cold and died of pneumonia at the age of seventy-one.[38]

When Margaret learned of these events, she immediately decided to return and stand trial herself. She either felt she owed Bill a sacrifice comparable to his own, found herself jealous of his sudden notoriety, or thought that with Comstock gone, she would receive a fairer trial. Perhaps she also took her loneliness for the children as a guide. She was desperate to see them, and for weeks, in fact, had been plagued by dreams about Peggy, a pattern that betrayed anxiety and perhaps some guilt as well, about her long and in part self-indulgent absence, though she explained it away simply as a premonition of trouble at home, a premonition bound, inexplicably, to the number six.[39]

CHAPTER SEVEN

The Frenzy of Renown

Margaret left her ship in lower Manhattan in October of 1915 and stopped immediately at a newsstand. There, by her own account, the words "birth control" stared back at her from the headlines of the popular weekly, *Pictorial Review.* Ever the gifted storyteller, she may well have invented this incident too, or encapsulated several experiences into one for dramatic effect, but a substantial shift in public consciousness on the issue had, indeed, occurred during her absence. Newspapers and magazines had quite suddenly turned their attention to the birth control controversy. As Bill Sanger languished in a New York City jail, the prosecutors who had hoped to check birth control propaganda with his conviction achieved exactly the opposite effect. They unleashed the most widespread, outspoken, and sympathetic public discussion since the Bradlaugh-Besant trial in London years before.[1]

Margaret had fled indictment in order to buy herself time and sympathy, and the strategy born in panic actually began to show results during her ten month exile. None of New York's mainstream papers or periodicals at first carried news of her situation. The only coverage had come from such predictable supporters on the left as *The Call* and *The Masses*. Early in 1915, however, the infant *New Republic* also took up her cause. In March, that new but suddenly fashionable journal featured an emphatic defense of contraceptive advocacy. Its brash young editors wrote with zest and confidence:

> Birth by physiological accident, birth by necessity, birth by the mere action of an over-powerful, unchallenged sexual impulse, will give way increasingly to birth by human design. . . . We are done with the irresponsible stork. We are done with the taboo which forbids discussion of the subject. We are done with the theory that babies, like sunshine and rain, are the gifts and visitations of God, to be accepted submissively and with a grateful heart.

The endorsement constituted a striking dissent from the emphatic pronatalist sentiments of the Teddy Roosevelt brand of Progressivism with which the magazine was politically allied.[2]

Between April and November of 1915, *Harper's Weekly*, then the country's foremost popular intellectual forum, carried an exhaustive series on what it still decorously labeled as the question of "family limitation." These soberly reported articles differed immeasurably in tone from Margaret's polemics, only mentioned her by indirection, and surely did not embrace her radical politics. Yet they marshaled similar medical, social, and economic arguments to those she had employed. They defined contraception for the first time as a scientific, rather than a moral issue, and in its defense assembled data on maternal and infant welfare, income, education, and fertility patterns. They thoughtfully summarized current arguments identifying smaller families with racial betterment and women's rights, and most important, perhaps, gave currency to birth control as a subject fit for responsible public debate.

The emerging legitimacy of the issue can also be traced in *The New York Times*'s coverage of the Sanger story during 1915. Margaret's arrest and exile had apparently not been considered newsworthy, but within months the situation changed. Bill's confrontation with Comstock did get a small story on the inside pages, followed by several subsequent articles during the summer on efforts to organize for his defense. His trial in September received still more sustained attention from the *Times* and other dailies, and by November even the popular national news digest, *Current Opinion*, featured "The Debate over Birth Control." Reticent editors at the *Times*, however, covered the story without ever using the words "prevention of conception," which forced John Reed to intervene with friends on the paper's editorial page in the hope of placing a more candid piece of writing there.

In 1914 there had been only three articles in the *Times* on birth control, and only fourteen in 1915, but in the following two years, there were a total of ninety. An identical pattern existed for national news magazines, though popular women's periodicals, such as *Ladies' Home Journal* and *Good Housekeeping*, remained timid about the subject well into the 1930s. Small-town newspapers also gave little coverage.[3]

The media breakthrough Margaret observed not only helped stimulate, but probably also reflected, the public support of birth control by a coalition of women far broader in its economic and political viewpoints than the radical labor community. The birth control controversy erupted at a critical juncture in the larger debate on women that still engaged the country. The woman's suffrage campaign suffered its last major defeat in the New York State referendum of November 1915, just as Margaret returned home. A national coalition of support then developed for a constitutional amendment in Congress, where victory was finally achieved in 1920. By martyring herself and creating a dramatic new public controversy, Margaret compelled women who were already politically mobilized to deal frankly and openly with the issues of sexuality and contraception for the first time. She gave them a new cause.

In Margaret's absence several of the feminists who had originally heard her at Heterodoxy had organized a committee called the National Birth Control League. She returned to the United States to find that a new audience had rallied against the accusation by Bill's angry judge that all women were to blame for daring to assert selfish personal considerations over their obligations as wives and mothers. Contraception had become a public controversy, not as an instrument for the redress of class grievance, but as a dimension of the much larger and more elusive debate on the "woman question."

The National Birth Control League established itself as a coalition of activists dedicated to reforming the federal and state Comstock statutes. Its moving force was Mary Ware Dennett, a Boston Brahmin who was divorced, coincidentally, from an architect and had left behind her own career in interior design to hone political skills in the suffrage movement. Having served as an officer of the American Women's Suffrage Association for four years, Dennett believed in the efficacy of persistent legislative reform and rejected the direct action tactics Margaret advocated. Other prominent founding members of the group included Helen Marot, the labor activist who had cared for Peggy and Grant, Lucy Sprague Mitchell, the progressive educator, Rose Pastor Stokes, the Socialist benefactor, and Lincoln Steffens, the journalist.

If more conservative than Margaret by temperament, the committee's membership nonetheless rallied around her. The full import of this support was illustrated at a dinner in her honor in January of 1916, when the anthropologist Elsie Clew Parsons stood up and asked fifty married women in the audience to sign a manifesto demanding that information about birth control be made public and admitting that they used it themselves. Only six agreed to sign the first part of the statement; only three signed the second. For some, birth control advocacy remained tainted by Margaret's political radicalism, but many others, as Parsons herself observed, were simply reluctant to acknowledge a social problem by laying bare their own lives. By shrinking from public identification with birth control, they also objected to what Parsons had once condemned as "the domination of personality by sex."*[4]

Margaret's first challenge then was to teach this audience to speak out in public. To broaden her constituency, she had to extend the ongoing debate about the relations between men and women beyond issues of work and suffrage, just as she had first tried to do among radicals. To this end, she ingeniously courted the attention of the popular media, displaying her sophisticated understanding of the value of public relations over conventional political organization. Between 1916 and 1918, she produced an extraordinary volume of newspaper and periodical coverage, which helped destroy old taboos.

Returning to the United States under the influence of the rationalism and optimism of Ferrerists and Fabians alike—and empowered by Havelock Ellis's formulation of the elements of a new social hygiene—she created a constituency for the view that only women in control of their fertility hold the key to personal fulfillment through marriage, motherhood, and independent self-realization. Abandoning the class antagonisms of *The Woman Rebel,* she argued for solidarity of gender. Women would make themselves the instruments of

* In 1920, in a private letter to Margaret, Carrie Chapman Catt would still insist: "When the advocacy of contraceptives is combined with as strong a propaganda for continence, (not to prevent conception but in the interest of common decency), it will find me a more willing sponsor. That is, a million years of male control over the sustenance of women has made them sex slaves, which has produced two results, an over-sexualizing of woman and an over-sexualizing of men. No animal is so uncontrolled as is the mass of men. Now, merely to make indulgence safe doesn't do enough."

a social regeneration of far greater consequence than what might be achieved simply by winning the vote or getting a job. They would reconstitute the family, that fundamental unit of collective life, in a manner consistent with the rigor and discipline the modern world demanded in all dimensions of human activity. Only with the individual thus remade might a more complete social agenda move forward.[5]

Margaret also had a compelling practical motivation for suddenly courting support from women of more comfortable circumstances. She returned from Europe with no income apart from occasional revenues from the sale of her pamphlets, *What Every Girl Should Know* and *Family Limitation*, along with small direct contributions from the national radical network. She needed to reach into deeper pockets to support herself and her children. During her year in Europe, Bill and Leonard Abbott, the free-speech advocate, had collected money from Mabel Dodge and other radical patrons, but these contributions were not sufficient to meet mounting obligations. "It's so funny how many people have told me what they either *would like* to do or will *do,*" Bill wrote her dejectedly from jail. "When it came to a show down nobody takes a chance for fear of arrest! Can you *beat that*—somehow it all ends in swindle. You stand alone dear heart in doing the yeoman work."

This disillusion could only have intensified after an editorial in *The Call*, signed by Anita Block, expressed admiration for Bill but challenged his tactics, saying collective action was needed more than individual martyrdom. To save his family from indebtedness to the radicals he had come to distrust, he accepted checks from the philanthropist Gertrude Pinchot, of the family of Amos and Gifford Pinchot, both prominent progressive Republicans, and her sister Grace Sargeant Crane. This money covered the costs of tuition and board at the Stelton School for Grant and Peggy. Stuart, who had never been able to learn to read in Stelton's chaotic atmosphere, was attending a small boarding school on Long Island selected and paid for by Nan Higgins, because it was run by Christian Scientists whose unequivocal faith in self-reliance she admired and had herself embraced.[6]

Margaret worried constantly about money and conveyed a deep resentment of her dependence on charity, while Bill began to deflect his grievances toward her. Had she not been indicted, he might have remained in Paris, happily painting and suffering no adverse political exposure, or so he insisted in a letter to Mabel Dodge. During the dreary month of his jail sentence, however, he tried to overcome these regrets by reveling in memories of happier times when he had frolicked on Westchester hillsides with his adored young family. He filled his prison letters to Margaret with a sentimental longing for this past, and even wrote her a poem entitled "My Beloved." Weak in its imagery and difficult to follow, the poem communicates a tragic and alarming deterioration in his mental and emotional state. He began:

> *Accuse me not, beseech thee that I wear*
> *Too calm and sad a face in front of thine!*
> *For we two look two ways and cannot shine*
> *With the same sunlight on our brow and hair.*
> *On me thou lookest with no doubting care*
> *As on a bee shut in a crystalline.*
> *For sorrow hath shut me safe in lives divine*
> *And to spread wing and fly to the outer air*
> *Were most impossible failure.*

The remaining stanzas wander on almost incoherently. Even before the ordeal of his trial and conviction, he had repeatedly written Margaret of his despair, claiming that he could not live without her. "I live, or exist now, because I was too cowardly to die," he told her after receiving her first request for a divorce, and this may again have been his intended meaning in his sweet but rather enfeebled verse.

Margaret never bothered to visit the Tombs, the squalid jail where Bill was imprisoned, and he only learned of her return to New York from Leonard Abbott. When they were finally reunited, and he faced the reality of a callous and indifferent woman whose affections so evidently lay elsewhere, his enormous disappointment spilled over into the vindictive and insulting behavior that characterized their relations for years thereafter. Both behaved so poorly that Margaret later wrote to say she wished she could return his name to him, but did not see how that might be accomplished.[7]

What finally made this bitter estrangement irreparable was young Peggy Sanger's sudden death on November 6, 1915, the date that had inexplicably haunted Margaret in Paris and would continue to cast its shadow over the rest of her life. The engaging child took ill at Stelton and within a week died of pneumonia at Mt. Sinai Hospital in New York, cradled in the arms of her mother and her devoted Aunt Ethel, then a nurse on the staff. The death left a long legacy of resentment and remorse in the Sanger family. Young Grant revealed his essential feelings by repeating over and over again that, if their mother had only been there, Peggy would have never become so sick and died, and this drove Stuart to even deeper despair. Bill was totally distraught and, in an eerie recapitulation of Michael Higgins's behavior, sculpted a plaster cast of his daughter, which he kept in broken pieces for years, until his second wife insisted that he finally rid himself of his ties to the past in preparation for the birth of their own child. [8]

There is no way to know whether Margaret commissioned or even condoned the sculpture, though her grief was nonetheless intense. Overcome with emotion, she retreated from friends and family for days, a time for which there is little documentation. Peggy's body was cremated, and her ashes were later interred at the beachfront cottage on Cape Cod that Margaret purchased with the first money she ever made as a lecturer. The gesture at least gave her the comfort that the child's remains would forever overlook the seashore she had so loved.

Margaret never fully stopped mourning Peggy or exorcised the guilt over having been absent during the final year of her brief life. For years after, she could not sit across from another mother and daughter on a train, or in any other public setting, without losing control. She wrote in her journal of recurrent sleeplessness, reporting that images of a child slipping away from her haunted her dreams, and left her to awaken in tears. On a trip to Chicago in 1923, she dreamed that she was standing in the rear yard of a New York building when suddenly she heard roofs crashing down around her. In the commotion she began to worry about her little girl, but realized that she had been neglecting her for years and did not know where she was. She found herself running through the streets cradling a sweet-faced infant, thinking of her lost child, weeping, crying aloud, and pulling her hair, and only then did she wake up. For years thereafter dreams of babies remained as a persistent anxiety pattern. She was often disturbed during sleep by these dreams, which she recorded in letters and journals in the honest belief that the images were portents of developments in the birth control movement, happy babies promising good news, and sad ones bad. But more likely they were haunting reminders of the more fundamental sense of vulnerability she carried with her after Peggy's death.

Even as she achieved public prominence, Margaret carefully maintained a private space for herself, an "imaginary landscape," as she once described it, set apart from the rest of the world, where her daughter grew to maturity "untouched by harsh actuality and disillusion." Every year on the anniversaries of Peggy's birth and death, she canceled her public appointments and mourned. Grant, who could barely remember the sister who had been the lone friend and reliable companion of his youth, regularly wrote or phoned his mother to share in this ritual.[9]

By sustaining this private and intensely spiritual bond with her daughter, Margaret was able over time to shape her anguish into something she could bear. As she told the story many years later, this curious accommodation began when she awoke from a bedside vigil in the hospital on the eve of the child's death, convinced that she saw an astral figure of Peggy, bathed in light, rise from the actual body and disappear out the door in a trail of smoke. Margaret's anxiety heightened in the following months as she found herself overcome by the certainty that the dead child's pattering footsteps continued to follow her around. Seeking comfort, she embraced a set of mystical beliefs that provided spiritual solace and emotional relief without tying her to any of the conventional religious doctrines that she had since rejected. Though she had long considered herself an atheist, she never completely abandoned the quest for absolutism that Catholicism instilled in her as a child and that Socialism briefly supplanted. Peggy's death may have only intensified it.[10]

Desperate to hold on to some dimension of the child, Margaret began to study Rosicrucianism, then a fashionable mystical cult among British intellectuals to which Havelock Ellis had first introduced her in London. The Rosicrucians advanced an oriental regimen of private meditation intended to connect the individual to powers within the self that derive from a supreme higher force, a "god within," as she interpreted it, paraphrasing Nietzsche. Moreover, they counseled that successful practitioners of their faith would come away with healing powers of their own and become "a force for good among men." This compelling practical rationale served Margaret's professional needs as well as her personal ones, and helped overcome the void left by her increasing disenchantment with radical politics. Never troubling herself with intricacies of theological speculation, she simply accepted uncritically the Rosicrucian notion that every individual possesses "a spark of divinity," which determines the potential to express oneself in a constructive and meaningful way. This gave a spiritual dimension to the doctrine of self-reliance she absorbed from such icons of secular American culture as Ralph Waldo Emerson and her father's hero, Robert Ingersoll—the same credo, perhaps, that her older sister practiced as a Christian Scientist. The power to believe in individual renewal may have rescued her from the loss of a collective Socialist ideology.

With Havelock Ellis, moreover, Margaret believed that science and mysticism could coexist without conflict since they both served essential, if distinct, human needs for self-understanding. Quiet meditation offered a kind of emotional crutch that enhanced her self-esteem and provided communion with her lost daughter, even though she never really believed that talking to the dead was more than a useful fabrication. Margaret rejected much of the dogmatism of the Rosicrucians and never accepted anything as eccentric as their belief in reincarnation. From this point on, however, her dabbling in spiritualism helped strengthen private doubts and misgivings for which neither political ideology, nor the objective world of science and medicine, provided meaningful solutions. She sometimes "talked" to Peggy and encouraged close friends to do the same with deceased loved ones of their own.[11]

Much unlike her husband and sons, Margaret thus emerged from Peggy's death with the intent of achieving something concrete and important in her life. She seems to have shed some of the disabling confusion and self-doubt that had long been troubling her, not only about her marriage, but also perhaps about the mother she had long ago refused to mourn and the father she had summarily rejected. A distinctive maturity and personal coherence followed, yielding a new determination and practical orientation to her continuing efforts as a social reformer. Through her work for birth control, she would translate painful, personal circumstances into public achievements, and no one would stop her.

The tragedy of Peggy's death may have tied Margaret emotionally to her daughter, but it left her little more attentive to the practical care of her surviving sons than she had been before. To the contrary, she could now satisfy a sense of maternal obligation without deviating from her chosen path, since Peggy remained with her—in effect, if not in reality—as the justification for her own professional preoccupations.

Margaret blamed the unruly Ferrerist colony for letting Peggy get sick, and many of her associates there believed that her growing disaffection from the left also derived from an irrational association of the radical life-style with her child's death. There was also the precedent of Stuart's unsatisfactory academic progress, and with both in mind, she immediately yanked Grant out of Stelton and placed him with his brother on Long Island, where she could count on more careful monitoring of his activities and thus be assured of continued freedom from routine domestic responsibilities. Thereafter she spurned progressive environments in favor of order and discipline in her sons' education. Later, the boys transferred to the Peddie School in New Jersey, where their young uncle, Bob Higgins, had been a scholarship student. By way of compensation for her usual absence, she hovered over them on holidays, occasionally took them with her on trips, or joined them at seashore.[12]

Yet often, she didn't even manage to meet these meager obligations. Letters from ten-year-old Grant in 1918 cried out for her attention. "It is getting near Spring. The birds are coming from the South. I know you are very busy or you would come see me," he wrote in February, and, then, several weeks later, "Am I coming home Easter? Write and tell me so, please." Just before Thanksgiving, he implored her: "Mother will you come down. . . . Now you put down in your engagement book, Nov. 28, Go down to see Grant!" Many years later Stuart Sanger recounted to his own children the story of how he had once walked twenty miles along the Cape Cod beach on a hot day to greet his mother at the station, only to find that she wasn't on the train and hadn't bothered to wire ahead with an explanation.

When they did reunite, however, Margaret was a spirited, energetic, and thoroughly modern mother by the standards of her day, eager to join her sons in ocean bathing, horseback riding, and other active sports, which gained their respect and admiration. The family's humble cottage on the sublime beach at Truro, Massachusetts, had special sentiment for her, because of Peggy, and because she bought it for $500 in 1917 from John Reed, who needed the money to help pay for his legendary expedition to cover the Russian Revolution. It was there that she most often retreated with her boys, and primitive home movies from the 1920s show them relaxed and cavorting in the rough Atlantic surf.

Occasional family letters also survive and are generally chatty and affectionate. Yet the emotional duress she imposed upon Stuart and Grant when they were young seems to have erected a permanent barrier to meaningful, sustained intimacy. To cope with their apparent unhappiness, the boys in turn learned to hide their true feelings, bury resentments, and never question their mother's motivations. They became good students, competent athletes, and eventually reasonably successful professionals with families of their own. But this resilience never disguised an unappeased hunger for the love and approval of a mother at once appealing and seductive, yet fundamentally elusive—a mother who lavished her exuberance on other people and causes but never found enough time for them.[13]

What may be most essential about Margaret's wholesale neglect of her boys at this time, however, is that she did not consciously hold herself accountable for it. She rationalized the situation by arguing that she was driven to work in order to support and educate them, since their father had abdicated all financial responsibility, an argument that was certainly true. Her first priority was to shelter them from the economic deprivation she had experienced as a child and equated foremost with emotional stress. Once she achieved stature as a reformer, however, her work became its own justification and reward. Yet, she relished telling friends of the joy she found in those hours she was able to spend in her "maternal corner," as she called it, and she became something of a heroine to women colleagues who had consciously forfeited children for a career. A typically envious response came from the British suffragist and birth control advocate Edith How-Martyn, who wrote: "You make me wonder if I have made a mistake in not having any babies, but if I had I could not have done the little bits of public work I do, and we cannot have it all ways of life."[14]

Early in 1916, Margaret's friend and personal doctor, Morris Kahn, certified in a letter that she had suffered a disabling emotional breakdown after Peggy's death and could not possibly stand trial on *The Woman Rebel* charges. Just who requested the document is unclear, but she refused to use it and went ahead with preparations for a courtroom defense on January 18, the date set for disposition of her case. She consulted the New York law firm of Guggenheimer, Untermyer, & Marshall, then prominent for its handling of First Amendment cases, but refused to heed the advice that she plead guilty to reduced charges, promise never to break the law again, and pay a small fine. This obstinacy provoked derogatory comments about her mental state from some supporters, while others defended her determination to plead innocent and, if necessary, go to jail in protest. The young Socialist Bolton Hall pointed out that a fight would command more attention, and Emma Goldman, on a national speaking tour, wrote that she was suddenly finding substantially greater interest in birth control than in any of her other lectures. She even pledged to help raise money.[15]

As the appointed day of trial approached, Margaret, together with supporters among radicals and feminists alike, orchestrated a forceful lobbying and publicity campaign. Hundreds of sympathetic letters deluged judges, legislators, and other prominent political figures, none more newsworthy perhaps than Pres. Woodrow Wilson, who heard from a distinguished list of British intellectuals, including the internationally acclaimed H. G. Wells. Before leaving London, Margaret had arranged with Marie Stopes that a petition be sent to Washington. Stopes was a biologist whose emotional excesses would soon lead her away from the laboratory to a career as Britain's foremost sex reformer, and her cover letter to the quiet and reflective American President got a bit carried away in its visceral imagery:

> Have you, Sir, visualized, what it means to be a woman whose every fibre, whose every muscle and blood capillary is subtly poisoned by the secret, ever growing horror, more penetrating, more long drawn than any nightmare, of an unwanted embryo developing beneath her heart? While men stand proudly and face the sun, boasting that they have quenched the wickedness of slavery, what chains of slavery are, have been or ever could be so intimate a horror as the shackles on every limb—on every thought—on the very soul of an unwilling pregnant woman?

Probably with good fortune, this letter was never made public, and instead, more genuinely felt stories of Margaret's personal tragedy served to enhance public interest. At the urging of John Reed, Margaret wore a delicate lace-collared dress and posed with her young and winsome sons in a publicity photograph brilliantly calculated to undermine the notion that the support of birth control was a radical or immoral act. She had planned to dress in the costume of white shirt, black skirt, and tie that was then commonly worn as an emblem of suffragists, but the softer approach met with great success in newspapers throughout the country. The response produced the anomalous situation of a "prosecutor loath to prosecute and a defendant anxious to be tried," as she herself later described it.[16]

A support dinner was held under the auspices of the National Birth Control League at the Hotel Brevoort in New York City on the eve of the scheduled trial, and newspaper coverage focused on the broad range of endorsements she had suddenly drawn from establishment women's rights advocates, writers, physicians, and other professionals. The presence that night of such notables as the writer Charlotte Perkins Gilman and *The New Republic* editor, Herbert Croly, was considered especially newsworthy, as was a request by suffrage leader, Harriet Stanton Blatch, the daughter of Elizabeth Cady Stanton, that Margaret Sanger be guaranteed a trial by a jury composed of *equal* numbers of women and men.

Though still identified in the newspapers as a "Socialist leader," Margaret was clearly courting an elite constituency, undoubtedly hoping to avoid prosecution. Conscious of the broadening of her support she said in her speech at the Brevoort:

> I realize that many . . . cannot sympathize with or countenance the methods I have followed in my attempt to arouse working women to the fact that bringing a child into the world is the greatest responsibility. They tell me that *The Woman Rebel* was badly written; that it was crude; that it was emotional and hysterical; that it mixed issues; that it was defiant, and too radical. Well, to all of these indictments I plead guilty.

But she quickly defended herself, proclaiming that, "there is nothing new, nothing radical in birth control. Aristotle advocated it; Plato advocated it; all our great modern thinkers have advocated it!"[17]

Margaret's prosecutors had never been any more confident than she about structuring a case around the elusive *Woman Rebel* charges, and the tremendous public exposure given the subject of birth control in the year since the initial indictments against her substantially strengthened the rationale of her defense on free speech grounds. Who would be willing to punish her for initiating a debate that had since been discussed with impunity in major newspapers and magazines throughout the country? Uncertain of just how to proceed, the prosecutor, Harold Content, foolishly arranged to have the trial date postponed twice, allowing each adjournment to enhance Sanger's public profile and add more suspense to the drama of her persecution. She became a celebrity, with newspapers interested not only in what she said but in what she wore. "The accused was dressed in modish attire, a close-fitting suit of black broadcloth, patent leather pumps, white spats and an English walking hat," the *Evening Mail* in New York and the *Washington Post* both reported. Finally, having failed to structure a settlement, Content, on February 18, 1916, dropped all charges against her. Margaret Sanger, fugutive from the law for more than a year, was once again free.[18]

She received "a jubilee accorded a victor," in the description of one New York reporter, who covered a birth control rally held several nights later in a Broadway theater. And in the course of the year that followed, she took the opportunity to capitalize on her sudden fame by booking speaking engagements throughout the country. One exhausting itinerary took her by train from Rochester to Buffalo and then on to Detroit, Chicago, and San Francisco in the course of ten days. She also visited Boston, Pittsburgh, Washington, D.C., Cleveland, Milwaukee, Indianapolis, St. Louis, Denver, Los Angeles, Portland, Seattle, and Spokane, delivering her inaugural birth control lecture 119 times, always before packed and enthusiastic crowds of either working class dissidents, bourgeois feminists, or sympathetic establishment figures—and sometimes an unlikely mix of all three. In St. Louis, an attempt by local authorities to deny her the right to speak inspired a young settlement house worker named Roger Baldwin to the first of what would become a lifetime of civil libertarian protests. In Chicago, she addressed an audience of 1,500 people, assembled by local free speech advocates in a hall in the poor districts near the stockyards, but professors from the nearby University of Chicago and other civic leaders from the city also attended.

Margaret's handwritten notations on the original typewritten text of her speech suggest that she may have modified her arguments to address concerns specific to each of these various constituencies. The speech blended elements of the standard soapbox provocation she had learned from the radicals with a quieter approach based on scientific and sentimental arguments—a mix that was to become her own oratorical trademark. To all she recounted in measured cadence her conviction that basic ignorance of sexuality and contraception bred large families, disease, and poverty. To all she repeated the history of the government's suppression of her efforts to stimulate popular awareness of these issues. Groups made up predominantly of radicals and labor activists, however, heard her condemn an oppressive class structure and deplore the disparity of access to reliable contraception between rich and poor, while middle-class women received a substantially toned-down version, which identified birth control as a guarantee of their freedoms and made villains not of capitalists, but of the repressive authorities of church and state who dared to keep them in bondage. Margaret's success put to rest any lingering self-doubt over her ability as a speaker, though it would be years before she fully overcame her anxieties about performing in public.[19]

Wherever she spoke, she left a trail of ad hoc advocacy organizations behind her, many of them supported by well-to-do and socially prominent women drawn to the birth control cause on feminist and free speech grounds. Yet at the same time, praise for her from important voices within the radical community continued to be warm and enthusiastic. The ever-devoted Alexander Berkman, writing from

San Francisco, where he was publishing a national newspaper called *The Blast* and fomenting local anarchist activity, claimed that whenever a cynic bemoaned the forces of "economic determinism," he would cite Margaret as a "striking example of what *one* individual of brains, energy and determination can accomplish."

There is reason to speculate, though no proof, that Berkman was also a lover of Margaret's in these years, because he wrote passionately on this occasion and others of how taken he was by her "beauty and simplicity." The fact of an intimacy between them might provide another explanation for the rivalry with Emma Goldman. Still, the support Margaret received from radicals at this time extended well beyond personal relationships. When Margaret was subsequently jailed in Portland, Oregon, for distributing copies of *Family Limitation*, and then released by a judge who emphatically condemned prudery and supported her work, Anita Block changed her earlier view and lauded her progress in *The Call,* encouraging all Socialists to support her. Marie Equi, a well-known radical physician and lesbian-feminist in Portland, affectionately called her "a little bunch of hellfire." Later, she wrote intimately: "My Sweet, sweet girl. I love you with an ecstasy and understanding of Spirit that you alone have imparted to me thru the very brightness & flow of your intellect. . . . My arms are around you. I kiss your sweet mouth in absolute surrender."[20]

Back in New York, however, Emma Goldman was clearly unhappy about her disciple's sudden prominence. Charges brought for the first time against Goldman for giving birth control information in a lecture in New York were still pending, yet the reporter from the *New York Herald* who covered the first Sanger victory rally in January took the trouble to note in his story that all the enthusiasm left the normally voluble Goldman standing in the wings of the theater with no opportunity to speak. Even before this public slight, Goldman was snidely complaining that birth control was getting "*too* respectable for decent folk," and soon Ben Reitman was reminding the readers of *Mother Earth* that Margaret Sanger owed a debt to Emma's pioneering lectures on sexual subjects. The festering rivalry between the two women exploded again in April when Goldman defiantly went to jail for fifteen days. She never mentioned Sanger in the extensive coverage she devoted to her martyrdom in *Mother Earth*, and Margaret, in turn, was notably absent as a sponsor of the dinner called in protest, though she did send a telegram of support. Nor did she turn up at a Carnegie Hall rally held on Goldman's release, though again she prepared a message claiming illness as her excuse and affirming her strong concern. The rally made headlines when Rose Pastor Stokes defiantly promised to distribute slips of paper containing a birth control formula, but then reneged after she was pushed from the stage by a throng of rowdy women eager to have the information.[21]

The competition abated only as Goldman became consumed by the question of American involvement in World War I and lost interest in other causes. Though also a pacifist, Margaret made a strategic decision at this juncture to commit herself to birth control as a single issue. She was appalled when a young friend responded to the draft and showed up at her apartment in uniform but told him that others had made the mistake of diluting their effectiveness by embracing every worthy cause—that she would not risk the same fate.[22]

As American radicals turned their attentions abroad, Margaret had no choice but to broaden her constituency. Yet she did not abandon her dedication to civil disobedience as a means of direct action for social change, nor lose her disdain for progressive do-gooders and "pink-tea ladies," as she often privately described the new audiences she began to court. Her sense of distance derived, in part, from the intimidation she felt as a result of the money, social sophistication, and superior education—not to speak of the aristocratic bearing—of many of the women who became her followers. In her *Autobiography* she wrote of how much she admired these "robust, vital" daughters of the country's establishment and regretted that she did not give the same impression. "If I were in a room with ten people and somebody came in who expected me to be present, she invariably approached the *biggest* woman and addressed her," she said, admitting that for a time she tried to effect a more imposing appearance by wearing severe, mannish suits, until she recognized the futility and foolish expense of this contrivance.[23]

At the same time she had a distinct sense of superiority over women whose social position, stature, and self-confidence she may sometimes have coveted. In this respect, she never lost the ambivalence toward wealth and privilege she first experienced as a child. As an adult she led what was incontrovertibly an unconventional and independent personal life, and her experiences only bred more contempt in her for individuals, and especially for women, who had indulged and sheltered backgrounds.

She harbored a special grudge against Mary Ware Dennett and the National Birth Control League, resenting the fact that Dennett, like

Emma Goldman, did not initially show confidence in her own potential for leadership. She thought Dennett looked down on her. In their brief competition for control of the nascent birth control movement, each woman would filter her response to the other through the lens of her own insecurity.

Dennett did come from an elite Boston family, but her professional fortitude masked the enormous upset she had experienced when left with two children by a disaffected husband who ran off with one of his architectural clients. Dennett would later claim that the conflicts in her marriage had been ideological—that her commitment to suffrage had destroyed it—but this was apparently only part of the story. In private correspondence she would also acknowledge that while grieving the death of an infant daughter, she had stopped having sexual relations with her husband and felt in part responsibile for losing him. Much like Margaret, she was toughened by personal tragedy.[24]

Still, a more fundamental disagreement kept the two women permanently at odds. The National Birth Control League was not terribly effective in 1916 and 1917, in part because Margaret's continued militancy divided the membership. Dennett believed firmly in organizing to change the law, not in acting to break it, and she openly rejected blatant propagandistic tactics. Seasoned by her experience in the suffrage movement, she was certain that the time was coming when legislators would recognize the absurdity of maintaining an anachronistic prohibition of birth control.

In 1916, she had bills drafted to amend both the federal and the New York State obscenity statutes, and for the following two years she carried her campaign a step further by lobbying in Albany to repeal the words "preventing conception" wherever they appeared in the law and to add a new clause affirming that contraception was not per se obscene or indecent. Only two legislators, one a Socialist, the other a liberal New York City Democrat, would agree to submit her bill, however, and under those circumstances it surely had no chance of success with a Republican majority desperately frightened of radicals, or with a Democratic minority that remained wholly subservient to the social conservatism and religious orthodoxy of Tammany Hall bosses.[25]

Margaret remained skeptical of these legislative initiatives and refused to endorse Dennett's efforts, out of resentment, in part, but also because she continued to view elected politicians as conformists who at best reflected established shifts in "expressed public sentiment," as she put it, but rarely themselves initiated change. To explain her preferred mode of action, she paraphrased the familiar cry of labor activists of the day, "agitate, educate, organize, and legislate," and when she finally came around to supporting reform of the Comstock statutes, she did so only for publicity, not because she had any real expectation of winning.[26]

Paradoxically, the more conservative Dennett held out adamantly for total repeal of the obscenity statutes on free speech grounds. In so doing, she also rejected Margaret's conviction that the most appropriate system of delivery for contraception was the clinical, medical model pioneered in Holland. Margaret had begun to promote a bold vision of a democratic network of birth control facilities staffed by doctors and nurses who would guarantee the health, well-being, and solidarity of working-class women. When she finally framed her own legislative initiative, she took the position that reforming the statutes to allow doctors (at first, she also included midwives) the right to prescribe contraceptives not only made sense as public policy, but also had a better chance of winning support than a bill for total repeal. Dennett, to the contrary, insisted that such a compromise would only perpetuate an existing medical monopoly over contraception and serve established special interests. She could never reconcile deference to medicine with Margaret's political and social radicalism.[27]

In fact, Margaret's position derived from the larger vision of a socialized public health system she took from Ellis in England and from her own observations in the Netherlands. When she first visited there in 1915, the imperious Dr. Aletta Jacobs, who had founded the country's network of birth control clinics, would not deign to meet her, because even though she traveled with Ellis's introduction, she was not herself a doctor. She was received respectfully, however, by Dr. Johannes Rutgers, the second in command at the clinic in The Hague, whom she impressed in turn. Rutgers called *Family Limitation* "a brilliant pamphlet" and applauded her success in awakening American public opinion in favor of birth control.

What Margaret learned from him left an indelible impression, if little sense of the potential conflicts she would encounter trying to work with American doctors. By Rutgers's account, a committee of Dutch Neo-Malthusians had enlisted a "democratic" membership of 6,376 people in their organization. They then divided their small country of some 5 million inhabitants into twenty-four local subdivisions and, where they did not have a physical presence, identified individuals as "correspondents" who dispensed birth control and other gynecological and obstetrical information to women. They employed forty-eight trained nurses who, even with the distraction of war in 1917, were able to fit some 1,700 first-time users with diaphragms. However small this operation, it constituted a substantial health presence in the gynecological and obstetrical fields and was widely credited for the country's superior maternal and infant mortality statistics. In Margaret's view, it offered a useful paradigm for health-care delivery at home.[28] As she traveled the country she kept repeating:

> In my opinion the proper authorities to give advice on Birth Control are the DOCTORS and NURSES. No other class of men or women are so AWARE of the NEED of this knowledge among working people as they. YET THEY HAVE REMAINED SILENT! The time has come when they MUST TAKE THEIR STAND in the progressive movement. For though the subject is largely *social* and *economic* yet it is in the main *physical* and *medical,* and the object of those advancing the cause is to open the doors of the medical profession, who in turn will force open the doors of the laboratories where our chemists will give the women of the twentieth century reliable and scientific means of contraception hitherto unknown.

Following her lectures she was often sought out in her hotel room by women eager to know of more effective birth control methods, and their intense hunger for personal communication and instruction also convinced her of the superiority of a clinical distribution mechanism under scientific supervision. She soon discovered what contemporary family planning workers generally acknowledge—that individual counseling helps to establish client rapport and results in more successful use of contraceptive technology.[29]

Through her travels in the United States, she also found substantial interest in birth control on the part of a public health constituency that was gaining influence in most of the country's major cities. With advances in bacteriological science in the late nineteenth century, public officials came to recognize that they could intervene to stop the spread of diseases communicated by unsanitary conditions and human contact. This led, in turn, to the development by many states and municipalities of an urban health apparatus intended to educate in matters of personal and social hygiene, as well as to treat disease preventively. The more progressive communities took on the additional obligation of providing medical and nursing services to those too poor to afford the cost, through dispensaries or clinics paid out of the municipal treasury or by voluntary charities.

By 1915, there were 500 tuberculosis clinics in the United States and an equal number of facilities serving infants and children. Many areas of the country, especially in the South and West, offered only the most rudimentary services, but New York City's public health machinery was internationally acclaimed. Still, a survey on the city's Lower East Side found more than half of the population in need was getting no treatment. This tremendous overburdening of services, coupled perhaps with the virtual obsession of progressive social hygiene reformers about the problems of prostitution and rampant venereal disease, had turned professional and public attention to the issue of contraception. One of the most prominent physicians who endorsed Margaret's victory in *The Woman Rebel* case, in fact, was Herman Biggs, the widely esteemed commissioner of the New York State Board of Health.[30]

As a result of these gestures of support, the possibility of building a network of clinics to serve the health and contraceptive needs of women in this country was not altogether unthinkable. To that end, indeed, S. Adolphus Knopf, M.D., the leading private physician in New York City's public health efforts, addressed the American Public Health Association in October of 1916 on the "medical, social, economic and moral aspects" of birth control, citing the Dutch example and endorsing Margaret's recent victory against her federal prosecutors.

Knopf's remarks were considered of such significance that they were immediately reprinted in *The New York Medical Journal* and in *The Survey*, a magazine prominent in the progressive social welfare community. Attention was also called to the recent publication in the United States of books endorsing the public benefit of contraception and small families by C. V. Drysdale, the British Neo-Malthusian who had so warmly received Margaret, and by Dr. William J. Robinson, a popular writer on health who had long advocated birth control. The Drysdale book was featured in a full page story in the Sunday *New York Times Magazine*, and the Robinson book included an introduction by his friend, Abraham Jacobi, the physician and venerated former president of the American Medical Association who had first raised the issue of contraception without any visible fanfare in his annual address to that body back in 1912. After Margaret's indictment called attention to the issue, however, Jacobi's continued support of scientific contraception received ample press attention, and in 1915, while she was in exile, a committee of the New York Academy of Medicine actually met at his urging to consider the birth control problem, though without any visible result.[31]

There was then legitimate cause for optimism about doctors, yet

Margaret either did not understand, or chose to ignore, parallel developments in the medical profession that certainly did not bode well. The machinery of public health had, in fact, grown significantly, but the major professional thrust of the times was toward narrow scientific and technological developments. Orthodox physicians were consolidating their authority through reforms that improved the quality of medical education, reduced the number of doctors, and fostered specialization in practice areas, and these putative advances were producing a conservative professional elite intent on maintaining its own scientific hegemony, wealth, and social status. The stature of the public health component of American medicine would actually diminish after 1920, and support would erode for the kind of comprehensive clinical health facilities serving the working class and the poor that Margaret so optimistically envisioned. Public confidence in social solutions to health problems would actually decline, and the sovereignty of private practitioners would be institutionalized.

In this respect, the situation recapitulated the experience of the 1870s. In 1916, a committee of the New York County Medical Society again condemned the commercial sale of contraceptive products, because they were "absurd, frequently dangerous, filthy and usually unsatisfactory," and also suggested that licensing such practices would undermine "personal morality and national strength." At the same time, Dr. Robert Latou Dickinson, who would later be elected president of the American Gynecological Society and would ultimately become the most prominent medical ally of the birth control movement, advised a group of his colleagues in Chicago that same year to take hold of the matter of contraception, "not let it go to the radicals, and not let it receive harm by being pushed in any undignified or improper manner."[32]

Dickinson flatly turned Margaret down when she approached him with an offer of cooperation shortly thereafter, but this did not stand in the way of her determination to open a birth control clinic modeled on the Dutch facilities. She had first thought of getting started in a western state, where local law did not prohibit contraception, where a more hospitable attitude toward suffrage and women's rights had been demonstrated, and where there was less of a threat of religious opposition from politically influential Catholics. She had fewer contacts out West, however, and she recognized that no other location had the publicity potential of New York. What is more, Dr. Robinson advised her in a private letter that the local medical society would be unlikely to interfere if she staffed her facility with a licensed physician. Suggesting that she make a direct challenge on First Amendment grounds to the state's Comstock prohibitions on contraception, he reminded her of New York's "venereal disease" clause, the amendment to the state's original Comstock act that exempted doctors from prosecution for prescribing condoms to prevent the spread of disease. This, in his view, presented the possibility of a judicial reinterpretation that would sanction the prescription of contraception on broader medical grounds.

With a $50 contribution from a woman who had heard her lecture in California, Margaret found a sympathetic landlord in Brooklyn and rented space for a clinic. She later claimed to have first written the local district attorney advising him of what she proposed to do, but then never received any response. She moved ahead anyway and in so doing unilaterally determined the future course of the birth control movement in this century. Independent, not-for-profit medical facilities became the model for the distribution of contraception in the United States and throughout the free world, a development that occurred, not with the further cooperation of leaders in American medicine, but largely in spite of them.[33]

CHAPTER EIGHT

The Company She Kept

On October 16, 1916, Margaret Sanger opened the first birth control clinic in America, behind the curtained windows of a storefront tenement on Amboy Street near the corner of Pitkin Avenue in the Brownsville district of Brooklyn. Handbills, advertising the location in English, Yiddish, and Italian, promoted the benefits of contraception over abortion:

> MOTHERS! Can you afford to have a large family? Do you want any more children? If not, why do you have them? DO NOT KILL, DO NOT TAKE LIFE, BUT PREVENT.

The women of Brownsville patiently stood in line for service—there were 464 recorded clients during the several weeks the facility remained open. Surviving photographs show them handsomely attired in shirtwaists and billowing skirts. Draped in a shawl to protect against the autumn chill, one young mother hovers over a graceful wicker baby carriage in a romantic tableau that conceals the full dimension of the neighborhood's dispiriting poverty.[1]

Margaret had been advised "to proceed slowly and carefully in the matter of the clinic" and "avoid all unnecessary antagonisms." She may have intended to follow Dr. Robinson's advice and staff the clinic with a doctor, but failing to find a willing recruit, gave authority to her sister, Ethel Byrne, who was still working as a registered nurse at Mt. Sinai Hospital. Assisting with client intake and record keeping were Fania Mindell, a volunteer from Chicago who spoke three languages, and Elizabeth Stuyvesant, a social worker with Associated Charities of New York, who was apparently acting without institutional endorsement. That the presence of a doctor would have saved the clinic from attack was not clear, but in the interests of caution, Margaret and Ethel ostensibly agreed to provide only contraceptive information and sex education, rather than themselves dispense condoms and suppositories or fit the cervical appliances they advocated as a preferred birth control method. They charged 10 cents for each consultation. A device called the Mizpah Pessary was available at local pharmacies as a womb support for multiparous women who suffered from the then commonly diagnosed condition of prolapsed or distended uterus, which results when multiple or strenuous pregnancies weaken the vaginal muscles that hold the uterus in place. This pessary could also be effective as a contraceptive, and boxes of them were part of the clinic's inventory.[2]

On day nine of the clinic's operation, a modishly attired woman, identifying herself as a "Mrs. Whitehurst," arrived and immediately aroused suspicion. When she left, according to Margaret, the $2 bill she had paid for a 10-cent sex education pamphlet was pinned to the wall with a note that read "received from Mrs. Whitehurst of the Police Department as her contribution." The following day she returned with three plainclothesmen from the department's vice squad and arrested Margaret and Fania Mindell. The police impounded pamphlets, furnishings, and supplies, along with the case histories that had been compiled as a record of the clinic's activities.[3]

Provoked by this confrontation, Margaret threw all caution to the winds, betraying her radical roots. The afternoon edition of the *Brooklyn Daily Eagle* on October 26, 1916, described the scene:

> Mrs. Whitehurst placed Mrs. Sanger under arrest. The little woman was at first taken aback but in an instant she was in a towering rage. "You dirty thing," she shrieked. "You are not a woman. You are a dog." "Tell that to the judge in the morning," calmly responded Mrs. Whitehurst. "No. I'll tell it to you, now. You dog, and you have two ears to hear me too!"

According to the story, Sanger and Mindell were then "half-dragged, half carried" to a patrol wagon. With a gaggle of Brownsville mothers defiantly following behind them, they were taken to the local station house, where they were arraigned and released on $500 bail. But they chose to reap the publicity value of remaining overnight in a cold, vermin-infested jail. Several weeks later Margaret reopened the clinic, pending action by the courts, but it was closed down once again, and she was charged this time with maintaining a public nuisance.[4]

Though Margaret managed the publicity surrounding her arrest much like an old-fashioned Wobbly, her choice of counsel reflected a new and determined political savvy. Jonah J. Goldstein was a young liberal Democrat, who had grown up on the Lower East Side under the tutelage of Lillian Wald and Mary Simkovitch, progressive reformers in the local settlement houses. He became a lawyer in private practice and began his political life as an aide to Al Smith, then majority leader of the New York State Assembly. Later he would become a distinguished judge and family law theorist. He clearly knew his way around the courts and, through a variety of preliminary legal maneuverings, was able to keep postponing the case until January, allowing for an orderly preparation of his defense and giving Margaret plenty of time to pursue her own public relations strategy. Though he failed to win her the jury trial she desired, he did manage—after impassioned testimony from Margaret herself during the pre-trial hearings—to remove from the three-man panel that heard the case in Brooklyn's Court of Special Sessions the judge who had convicted her husband and was known for his extreme bias on the birth control issue.[5]

Goldstein's actual courtroom strategy, however, was not so successful. Ethel Byrne had not been there when the clinic was raided, but she was arrested shortly thereafter, and the charges brought against her came up first, on the court calendar of January 4, 1917. In pretrial arguments he had argued for dismissal on the grounds that the Comstock statutes were unconstitutional because they interfered with the free exercise of conscience and the pursuit of happiness; that they were arbitrary and unduly oppressive, because they allowed for no exceptions; that they failed to promote the health, welfare, and morals of the community; that they were so unreasonable as to place the life of women in jeopardy, thereby violating the equal protection provisions of the Fourteenth Amendment. His various entreaties failed, however, and during the trial itself, he took still a different approach, telling the judges that Section 1145 of New York's Comstock law, which provided a medical exception, infringed the constitutional rights of the poor, denying them the right to choose how many children they would have, a right enjoyed by middle-class citizens who could afford the services of private physicians.

Goldstein had intended to introduce the testimony of an expert medical witness, Margaret's own doctor, Morris Kahn, who was to explain the compelling medical, social, and economic indications for birth control use. Criminal defendants are normally allowed wide latitude in introducing evidence, and there was also some precedent at this time for judicial rulings that relied on socioeconomic arguments. The Brooklyn judges, however, allowed Goldstein only fifteen minutes for his presentation and ruled Kahn's remarks inadmissable, though they did not interrupt when any number of wild and unsupported extralegal charges were brought by witnesses for the prosecution. In the kind of racist accusation that would continue to haunt her sister, Ethel Byrne was accused by the prosecution of intending "to do away with the Jews" by dispensing contraception in an immigrant ghetto, and of hoping to make money in the process, because she had charged a small fee. She was found guilty of violating the statutory prohibition on giving birth control information and was sentenced to one month's imprisonment in the workhouse on Blackwell's Island. Goldstein applied to the State Supreme Court and to the Federal District Court to void her sentence pending an appeal, but he was denied by both.[6]

Disappointed by the failure of their legal strategy but emboldened by the sudden spate of publicity they were receiving, Sanger and Byrne embarked on an audacious course. They announced that Mrs. Byrne would undertake a hunger strike in jail in the manner of the British suffragists. Newspapers throughout the country bannered her vow to "die, if need be, for my sex." A farewell dinner of turkey and "plenty of ice cream" sustained the theatrics on the eve of her incarceration, and for the entire week that followed, news from prison of her deteriorating physical and emotional status vied for front-page headlines with stories of German belligerence against American ships in the seas of Europe. Ethel kept her fast for four days, giving rise to allegations, which were later denied, that she was drinking water when not observed. When the New York City corrections commissioner announced that forcible feeding of the prisoner through a tube inserted into the esophagus would begin, for the first time in United States penal history, the national wire services literally went wild. Even the normally sensation-shy *New York Times* carried the story on its front page for four days in a row, alternating reports from prison officials that Mrs. Byrne's response was "passive" to her thrice-daily feedings of a mixture of milk, brandy, and eggs, with overstated claims from Sanger that her sister could not resist because she was extremely weak and near death.[7]

Throughout this ordeal, Ethel and Margaret enjoyed the support of a group of women from the National Birth Control League, who called themselves the Committee of 100 and included Mary Ware Dennett, Rose Stokes, Jessie Ashley, Crystal Eastman, and Elsie Clews Parsons, along with others willing to associate themselves with Sanger's direct action. Their chairwoman was Gertrude Pinchot, who had earlier given the Sangers the money to keep their children in school, and their official credo was drafted by the prepossessing Juliet Barrett Rublee, an heiress from Chicago who would become Margaret's intimate friend and whose husband, George, served on the Federal Trade Commission as a Wilson appointee. The document, though not elegantly phrased, emphatically announced their purpose:

> We maintain that it is no more indecent to discuss sexual anatomy, physiology and hygiene in a scientific spirit than it is to discuss the functions of the stomach, the heart and the liver. We believe that the question as to whether or not, and when, a woman should have a child, is not a question for the doctors to decide, except in cases where the woman's life is endangered, or for the state legislators to decide, but a question for the woman herself to decide.

Margaret had impressed these women when she first appeared at one of what they called their "parlor meetings," and by dominating the media after the clinic raid, she persuaded them to support her activities along with their preferred legislative solution to the birth control problem. As a measure of their effectiveness and power, moreover, they raised $700 for birth control work by just informally passing around a hat, and pledged part of it for her legal expenses.[8]

When Ethel was sentenced, the Committee of 100 called a protest rally at Carnegie Hall. Falling right in the middle of her sensationalized hunger strike, the event attracted 3,000 supporters, most of them women, and raised another $1,000. Admission to the upper galleries was only 25 cents, and according to the newspapers, the seats were filled with poor working women, offering a sharp contrast to the "richly dressed" society types who adorned the boxes below. Margaret was, of course, the featured speaker of the evening, and her impassioned oratory elicited sustained cheers. She began:

> I come to you from a crowded courtroom, from a vortex of persecution. I come not from the stake of Salem where women were tried for blasphemy, but from the shadow of Blackwell's Island where women are tortured for obscenity.

At her suggestion, a group of Brownsville mothers were given "places of honor" on the platform behind her "to let everybody see what kind of women we are fighting for," and by all accounts this dramatic touch was extremely effective. One observer likened the spirit of the evening to that of the abolition days.[9]

Several days after the event, a well-connected delegation of the Committee of 100, upset that Ethel's militancy was getting out of hand and truly endangering her life, took Margaret to meet with New York Gov. Charles Whitman. Their intent was to win commutation of Ethel's sentence and to secure a pledge from the governor to appoint a commission to investigate birth control. Whitman was willing to pardon Byrne only if she pledged never to break the law again, a condition Margaret declared unacceptable, and no investigation ever took place. Through his intervention, however, Margaret was granted a pass to visit her sister in jail, which she had previously been denied. On discovering what appeared to be a genuinely alarming physical deterioration, she decided to accept the terms of the pardon on her sister's behalf. Given the extraordinary public interest in the situation, prison officials were only too happy to be rid of their charge, and Ethel was carried prostrate from the workhouse, wrapped in the fur coat of one her rich new benefactors.[10]

Once recovered, Ethel told Margaret that "I couldn't have lived or fought through anything if I hadn't known and loved you," and Margaret assured her in response that she had fought "the finest fight ever made by any woman in the U.S.A." Later, Margaret would gallantly identify the hunger strike as the most significant act of "self-sacrifice in the history of the birth control movement." Yet it effectively ended Ethel's participation in birth control activities and regrettably cast a permanent pall on relations between the two sisters. An undercurrent of rivalry had long festered beneath their deep and abiding affection, and these extraordinary events brought it to the surface. Ethel greatly resented Margaret's ambitious pursuit of the new social and political connections their sudden celebrity had wrought. They argued as well over Ethel's apparent sympathy for Bill Sanger, with which Margaret had little patience.

"Ethel was a smoldering fire, Margaret a blazing fire," as Olive Byrne Richard later distinguished them, saying elsewhere of her mother that "she liked to experience things but she had no endurance." Yet, the differences were about politics as well as character. As a hardworking nurse for the remainder of her life, Ethel would cleave to simple values. She could never countenance the deal that had been struck with authorities on her behalf or tolerate the aristocratic men and women who were being welcomed into the birth control cause. She had, indeed, confided to Margaret from jail: "I saw Mrs. Grace [Sargeant Crane] for a minute and she expressed her *pride*! in knowing the Birth Control Sisters! And I thought when I looked at her all done up in her thousand dollars worth of elegance, You should worry; ain't it a fact." But Margaret's view of the ability of upper class women to make things happen had by then dramatically changed from the unbridled contempt of her *Woman Rebel* days. "It is true that the fashionable seem far removed from the cause and its necessity," she wrote back. "But we cannot doubt that they and they alone dominate when they get an interest in a thing. So little can be done without them."[11]

The trials of Margaret Sanger and Fania Mindell got underway on January 29, 1917, while Ethel was still imprisoned and making headlines. Thirty Brownsville mothers who had been clients of the clinic were subpoenaed by the prosecution, and they filled the courtroom laden with bags of bread and fruit to eat, and with pacifiers and extra diapers to service the infants they held at their breasts. Newspaper reporters described a courtroom configuration of those who could barely afford the carfare to bring them to downtown Brooklyn seated beside the fashionable, formidable representatives of the Committee of 100, whose chauffeurs waited outside to drive them back to Manhattan. These accounts created an indelible impression of the birth control movement as a respectable alliance of wealthy and powerful women helping their less fortunate sisters, distinctions of class giving way to the common bond of gender.[12]

The prosecution called Mindell first, and she was summarily charged with selling Margaret's pamphlet, *What Every Girl Should Know*. Her case was adjourned until the judges had time to read the disputed copy, at which time she was found guilty on obscenity charges and given a $50 fine, which Gertrude Pinchot graciously agreed to pay. (This decision was subsequently reversed on appeal, essentially disposing of the definition of birth control literature as "obscene" under New York State law and providing the basis for Goldstein's later defenses of Sanger and others on charges brought against them in 1919 for distributing birth control propaganda.)[13]

Margaret's own trial began after additional technical objections by Jonah Goldstein were overruled. The policewoman, Mrs. Whitehurst, took the stand first as a witness for the prosecution. She testified that she had found Mrs. Sanger in the clinic's back room holding a box of suppositories and a rubber birth control appliance. A second witness also claimed to have heard her make abusive comments about the Jewish people, a canard that a third witness disputed, but the tactic, alas, had already done its damage.

Since Margaret openly admitted that she had given out birth control information, the question of her guilt under the state Comstock law was never in question. Most of the trial testimony, however, centered on the narrower issue of whether she had gone beyond verbal instruction to actually fit her clients with cervical devices. To the prosecutor this seemed an even more heinous crime. Boxes of confiscated pessaries, condoms and douching solutions were introduced as evidence, and one Brownsville mother did testify that Margaret had not only explained the contraceptive utility of the pessary when properly fitted but also offered to "adjust it myself," yet it was never clear that she, in fact, had done so. Margaret only admitted that she had "lectured" women on sexual physiology and hygiene, because they often did not themselves understand the reproductive functions and could not, therefore, comprehend how contraception worked. "Their gratitude was touching," she had earlier told one newspaper reporter. "Some of them sought to kiss our hands because we had taken an interest in them."[14]

The discrepancy between the prosecutor's allegations and the testimony of witnesses evidently troubled the three presiding judges. Indeed the most sympathetic among them, Judge Freschi, then specifically raised the basic question Margaret set out to test—whether the statute's Section 1145 medical exemption did countenance contraception when prescribed for the prevention of disease. This was an important breakthrough in the legal proceedings, because Margaret as a nurse did not have technical standing in court to demand clarification of physicians' rights under the existing statutes. Goldstein seized on the opening, and recognizing that the court had not been willing to hear expert medical witnesses, he had the Brownsville mothers tell their own tragic stories about multiparity, miscarriage, infant death, poverty, hunger, and disease.

Their testimony may have been compelling, but it had little to do with the question of Margaret's guilt or innocence under the law. Goldstein therefore tried to strike a deal in the judge's chambers, requesting a suspended sentence for his client in exchange for her promise not to violate the law again, while he appealed to higher courts on the larger issue of the clear intent of the state's Comstock laws with respect to physicians' rights to prescribe contraception on medical grounds. The court, however, would only comply if she promised to obey the law without limit of time, an agreement she refused to make. "I cannot promise to obey a law I do not respect," she calmly responded to clapping and shouting in the courtroom. When order was restored, Goldstein asked for leniency on his client's behalf, but she was found guilty and given the choice of paying a $5,000 fine or being sentenced. She chose prison and was given thirty days in the workhouse. By the newspaper accounts of the trial, a single word was then uttered loudly from a far corner of the room. The word was "Shame!"[15]

Margaret vowed publicly to repeat her sister's hunger strike in jail, and with that threat the women's facility on Blackwell's Island refused to have anything to do with her. She was instead sent to a quieter, more commodious penitentiary for women in Queens. Sobered by having seen Ethel's condition, and recognizing the diminished news value of a repeat performance, especially during a week when the Germans were sinking more American battleships and diplomatic relations between the two countries had been broken, she spent her incarceration compliantly in a private cell. She actually welcomed the rare opportunity to rest and be alone, and told her supporters in a published letter that their "loving thoughts pouring into her" protected her from sadness. She found that what she most resented was the poor quality of the prison food and, desperately hungry, wrote lightheartedly to Ethel questioning which fate was worse, slow starvation over thirty days or "getting the job done quick." In subsequent years, she would support movements for penal reform and prisoners' rights.[16]

By her own account, she passed her time reading to the illiterate women on her corridor, most of whom were convicted drug addicts and prostitutes. She even lectured them on sex and birth control over the protest of a resident matron who claimed they knew "bad enough already." She wrote compassionately of these women to Theodore Debs, the brother of Socialist Party leader Eugene, describing them as innocent victims of childhood poverty, large families, and neglect. "I wish I could wrap them all up in my arms and love them back to life again," he responded. "But the same beastly system which ruined them will pursue them implacably to the morgue and the potters field." Of Margaret's own situation he said heatedly: "when I think of you caged like a beast, my blood boils with bitter indignation."[17]

The only drama in Margaret's prison sentence came as she was about to be released on the bright but cold morning of March 6, 1917. For a month she had flatly refused on civil libertarian principles to submit to the indignity of the routine fingerprinting of prisoners. As the hour of her departure approached, several prison guards attempted to force her hands down on an ink pad, but she resisted and finally emerged the victor to a welcoming party of friends and supporters.

Ethel was there, along with Jonah Goldstein, Anna Lifschiz, Margaret's secretary, and Kitty Marion, a veteran of British suffrage militancy. The civic-minded Women's City Club of New York, which had recently appointed a birth control committee, was also represented, and the Committee of 100 sent the social worker, Helen Todd, chairwoman of the successful Carnegie Hall rally, as its standard bearer. A Russian Jewish immigrant by the name of Rose Halpern carried a bouquet of flowers from the mothers of Brownsville, and just before she died at the age of ninety-three, nearly sixty years later, she spoke to her daughter of her delight in having been present on this historic occasion.[18]

Margaret's *Autobiography* reports that when she finally appeared after her unexpected delay, the group began to sing the *Marseillaise*—"Ye sons of freedom wake to glory"—while the women prisoners, assembled at the windows of their cells inside, looked on. The French national anthem, then known to Americans as a favored marching song of Allied troops in Europe, made a curious refrain of welcome for a woman of Socialist and pacifist convictions. But it was no less odd than the composition of the assembled group, whose class-consciousness may have been keenly reflected in the manner one of its patrician representatives referred to the occasion. She called it Margaret's "coming out party."[19]

An appeal was filed, even though Margaret was self-evidently guilty and had already served her jail sentence. The saga of the Brownsville clinic continued through January 8, 1918, when a verdict was rendered by Judge Frederick Crane of the Court of Appeals of the State of New York. Crane upheld Sanger's conviction under Section 1142 of the state's obscenity law and thereby affirmed the state's right to prohibit laymen and women from distributing contraceptive information. His opinion, however, offered an interpretation of Section 1145 of the law that granted specific license to physicians to prescribe contraception not just to prevent or cure venereal disease, but on more broadly defined medical grounds. The decision offered protection from the risk of prosecution to doctors and to pharmacists acting on medical orders.

Just as Margaret's friend Dr. William Robinson had anticipated, the court provided a legal rationale for building a system of contraceptive service delivery with doctors in charge, the constraint under which Margaret subsequently built the birth control movement. She would have preferred a broader decision, licensing nurses as well, so she had Goldstein petition the U.S. Supreme Court to hear the case. Louis Brandeis, who had achieved distinction as a lawyer through his briefs grounded in social and economic arguments, was newly appointed to the court. He signed Goldstein's petition for a Writ of Error, which was docketed and scheduled for oral argument. America's entry into the world war caused postponements, however, and a hearing was not held until November of 1919. At that time, the court without explanation refused to accept jurisdiction.

While still in jail in February 1917, Margaret had received a frustrated letter from Ethel complaining: "I haven't heard from JJ [Jonah Goldstein]. I have felt just a bit peeved over this law business, which is about the way I imagine you feel too." But Margaret wrote back that it was foolish to think that Goldstein could "have saved us." "To me he did everything in his power to clear the issue and to keep it clean," she continued, "free of the commercial taint the enemy tried hardest to put in." Twenty-five years later, on the occasion of an anniversary celebration, she was even more effusive with praise for his lawyering: "Your genius got the decision out of the clinic raid for the 'DOCS', she wrote Goldstein. "You should be thanked and praised, not I, but you are used to that system, I know."[20]

America's entry into World War I in the spring of 1917 unleashed a shameful assault on political dissent in this country, a hysteria that only intensified after the success of the Bolshevik Revolution in Russia later that year, whose early stages most Socialists and radicals supported. The nation's residual intolerance of nonconformists and troublemakers was whipped into a frenzy of officially sponsored hatred and persecution by Woodrow Wilson's infamous propaganda machinery. Anyone who dared to remain unconvinced of the virtue of "the war to make the world safe for democracy," was put at substantial risk. Congress passed Federal Espionage and Seditions Acts threatening all speech, press, and assembly believed to obstruct the war effort with substantial fines, imprisonment, and even deportation, when the perpetrators were foreign born. The Wilson administration proudly announced that it had put a virtual police state into effect by instituting military surveillance of all internal radical activity, and states and municipalities quickly followed suit with local ordinances empowering police and investigatory apparatus of their own.

In the year and a half of official military engagement and during the "red scare" that followed the armistice of November 1918, American radicals were made scapegoats of this nationalist and militarist fever. The IWW became a permanent casualty of the mania when its meeting halls throughout the country were raided and plundered, and hundreds of its leaders, including Bill Haywood, were convicted of criminal activity. Seventy-five different magazines and journals on the left were enjoined from publication in a single year, and *The Masses* closed down forever. Five members who had been lawfully elected to the New York State Assembly as Socialists were summarily expelled. In the most celebrated incidences of repression, Eugene Debs received a ten-year prison sentence for delivering standard Socialist rhetoric linking the war effort to capitalist imperialism at a rally in Canton, Ohio, while Emma Goldman and Alexander Berkman were imprisoned and then forced to leave the country as convicted traitors. Even Elizabeth Gurley Flynn and Carlo Tresca, who had for the moment broken all formal ties to the IWW and other radical organizations, were harassed and arrested by federal agents, though never convicted, in both New York and Chicago.[21]

Margaret's cautious decision to focus on birth control provided her partial shelter from the perverse politics of the war. She was never personally victimized, although her continued association with many radicals did bring her under the surveillance of the Lusk Commission, which was authorized by the New York State Legislature to clamp down on local subversives. This may explain why, in revised editions of *Family Limitation*, she deleted all references to birth control as a radical tool of direct action or as a dimension of women's sexual liberation. The toned-down pamphlet managed to remain in circulation and, according to a newspaper clipping from Rochester, New York, could be purchased at any reputable bookstore.

Once Margaret joined the League for Amnesty of Political Prisoners that mobilized to protest the Berkman and Goldman arrests, she was also tracked by federal intelligence agents, who recommended that she again be prosecuted under the Comstock Act for endorsing birth control in a promotional mailing. They were overruled by the local United States attorney, because he did not think he could obtain a conviction. But from this point on, Margaret remained under the watchful eye of the Federal Bureau of Investigation, which emerged as a permanent legacy of these wartime surveillance efforts. The ever vigilant J. Edgar Hoover kept a file on her associations with Communists, civil libertarians, and other alleged subversives until her death nearly fifty years later. The file remained intermittently active, if rather innocuous, even as she steered the birth control movement away from partisanship and from any public association with the left.[22]

Margaret's conversion to political pragmatism also had deeper roots in a temperamental disdain for the ideological abstractions and sheer sentimentality that held together what remained of America's revolutionary fraternity after the war. Although she continued to venerate old heroes and solicit their support, she had little interest in elusive, wide-eyed dreams about the coming of a better world. She would write faithfully to Eugene Debs and Bill Haywood in prison and vote for Debs in the Presidential election of 1920 when he mounted a candidacy from the federal penitentiary in Atlanta. For the rest of her life, she would cast her Presidential ballots for Socialist Norman Thomas, probably one of the few votes he received in the Republican precincts where she subsequently made her home. Yet along with the small financial contributions she sometimes remembered to send, these votes were little more than private, sentimental gestures. She would never speak about national political issues or contests in public, except on the two occasions, in 1928 and in 1960, when Catholics ran for President, and by keeping quiet, she, in effect, chose her sides and made her statement. Following the war, she would deliberately court a constituency for birth control among the nation's elites in business, the professions, and academia, never forgetting the lesson of her earlier experiences as a radical—that she would be judged by the company she kept.[23]

By the war's end, in any event, few of Margaret's old friends on the left remained in positions of national leadership or authority, and those who did disdained her priorities, as much as she abandoned theirs. Though repression had taken a heavy toll on radicalism at home, the successes of political and economic insurgents in Russia, parts of Europe, and South America heralded the promise of the long-awaited triumph of revolutionary Socialism abroad. For a brief moment before this progress gave way to the harsh realities of counter-revolution and repression, impetuous dreams of global advances replaced the narrower, practical objectives that had occupied many radicals before the war. To many of them, the concerns of American working women for economic and social autonomy seemed trivial by comparison.

In 1919, Bill Haywood enthusiastically wrote Margaret from his Kansas prison cell that "the glorious Red Dawn" was breaking and asked her to send him a copy of John Reed's recently published report on his arrival at Leningrad's Finland Station in *Ten Days That Shook the World.* No response survives, but it is clear that she maintained her interest in revolutionary movements abroad only insofar as they provided greater opportunities for women. "We are interested in the freedom of women, not in the power of the state," she wrote in a subsequent issue of *The Call,* celebrating International Women's Day.

> Upon that freedom depends the power and endurance of the state, as well as the health of the women and children. Upon that freedom depends the revolutionizing of man's inherent attitude toward women, whether they be Russian men under the Soviets, or men in America. Without that freedom for women—not only economic, but personal freedom as well—the right kind of state cannot exist and will not exist. . . . What women desire is the knowledge which will enable them to have as few children as they themselves consider consistent with their health, their desires, their opportunities for development, their economic resources, their ability to rear and educate. Unless women understand this they are likely to find themselves under a co-operative commonwealth, a Socialist republic or a Soviet government, being fatted and fed and kept in excellent condition for breeding purposes, in order to maintain a particular form of society for masculine needs. A recognition of this fact is the fundamental basis of the birth control movement today.

Some years later, Margaret solicited a short message from Rose Pastor Stokes for an international birth control conference she was mounting in New York. Stokes wrote back testily that the goals they had once shared could only be achieved "by working for the abolition of capitalism and for the establishment of Soviet Governments." Margaret herself had long since abandoned that objective, yet she loyally included the statement in the published proceedings of the conference.[24]

Cautioned by Jonah Goldstein to keep a low profile pending the outcome of his appeal in the Brownsville case, and finding it increasingly difficult to compete with the war for attention, Margaret mounted only a few publicity initiatives in the months following her release from prison. She did realize long dormant theatrical aspirations, however, by playing herself in a silent film dramatizing her work among the women of the Lower East Side, which was produced with support from the women of the National Birth Control League. Arrangements were made for her to tour the country with the moving picture, until officials in New York City threatened to revoke the license of any local theater that showed it on the grounds that there was no "medical" justification for such propaganda. Local newspapers reported that "thousands" were turned away from the Park Theatre in Brooklyn, where a scheduled opening was canceled after an association of theater owners then officially banned the film as "unpatriotic." Goldstein again went to court and won an injunction against these actions, but they were sustained on appeal.[25]

A second opportunity for national exposure occurred in October of that year when *Metropolitan Magazine*, a tony New York publication which featured such prominent writers as Sinclair Lewis and Edna Ferber, published a new attack on the birth control propagandists by its regular political columnist, Theodore Roosevelt. The former President was distressed over a recent study that had been made of the birthrates of Harvard and Yale men and opined that the country's best stock was dying out, because with an average of only 2.3 children, Harvard graduates like himself were not reproducing themselves in *sons*. (That daughters might carry forward the Crimson banner was apparently unthinkable.) He reiterated his standard lament that the kind of individuals who ought to replenish the American breed already had more than enough access to contraception, while the "submerged" 10 percent of the population who really needed it were not being reached.

As a sure measure of her enhanced public profile, Margaret was given space in the magazine to respond. Her speeches in those days often alluded to Roosevelt by referring to the large number of requests for birth control information she had received from women in his hometown of Oyster Bay, New York, an audience teaser that would invariably provoke laughter and applause. Colloquy with the former President in a prestigious magazine, however, demanded a more reasoned response, and in the pages of *Metropolitan* she soberly disputed his low estimate of the nation's levels of poverty and gently encouraged him to consider the merits of quality over quantity as a general principle of family and social life. She seemed uncharacteristically tentative in her arguments, also venturing a rather contorted argument, which harkened back to Emma Goldman, about the adverse effect of the "social and economic complexities of modern life" on the ability of women to bear and raise children.[26]

Through the year she also devoted herself quietly to the business of publishing the *Birth Control Review*. Wary of all the squabbling and divisiveness she had experienced in radical politics, she conceived the magazine as an alternative to a national birth control organization. She would maintain it as her forum and leave the tedium of recruiting support, building programs, and raising funds to the twenty or so local birth control leagues that had been established in response to her 1916 tours, some by radicals, some by middle-class women and reformers, others an amalgam of the two that was only possible in the years before World War I heightened class tensions.

Ideological neutrality became impossible in these changed times, however, and in its first issue of January 1917, the *Review* evidenced Margaret's lingering radical orientation. During an appearance in Cleveland the year before, she had met an enthusiastic young charity worker and Socialist by the name of Frederick Blossom, who followed her to New York and took charge of putting out the magazine while she devoted herself to her clinic defense. Blossom addressed a cover letter enclosing the inaugural number of the *Review* to our "Dear Comrades," and after pledging to challenge "jesuitical bigotry and Comstockian prudery," closed with the provocative salutation: "Yours for more freedom—for everybody." A manifesto in the February number, signed by Sanger, Blossom, and Elizabeth Stuyvesant, the social worker who had also worked in the clinic, read in part as follows:

> Birth control is the most vital issue before the country today. . . . The men and women of America are demanding this vitally needed knowledge be no longer withheld from them, that the doors to health, happiness, and liberty be thrown open and they be allowed to mould their lives, not at the arbitrary command of church or state, but as conscience and judgment may dictate. But those to whose advantage it is that the people breed abundantly, well entrenched in our social and political order, are not going to surrender easily to the popular will. Already they are organizing their resistance and preparing their mighty engines of repression to stop the march of progress while it is yet time. The spirit of the Inquisition is abroad in the land.

Subsequent issues also reneged on Margaret's promise of political neutrality by defending pacifism and mocking the war effort. She couldn't seem to contain herself. When she published an editorial defense of pacifism, imploring women to protest conscription in order to demonstrate they would not be made "handmaidens of militarism," copies of the paper were confiscated by government censors, though without apparent follow-up. A cartoon lampooning the war machine for encouraging the breeding of more soldiers escaped the censors' eyes, as did another showing two young children greeting a veteran with the caption "Judge Returning Home After Sentencing a Birth Control Speaker to Six Months Is Met by His Two Children, Ages Three and Six."[27]

Frederick Blossom possessed an intelligence, sophistication, and charm that Margaret admired, but he did not remain in her employ for very long. They disagreed immediately over the war, with Blossom taking the position that the United States was obliged to defend England and France. Margaret also resented Blossom's interest in self-promotion. When she came out of jail, she was frankly unwilling to share what limelight remained for the birth control issue. Believing that she and her sister had made incomparable sacrifices for the cause, she demanded strict deference. By June of 1917, Blossom had moved on to work full-time as a Socialist Party organizer.

Subsequently, Margaret also accused him of deceit in connection with *Birth Control Review* revenues, for which he could not account. Funds intended to cover a year of publication were expended on the first three issues, and for the remainder of the year, she pursued him with cordial determination to explain discrepancies in the books. He politely put her off, and in exasperation she asked Jonah Goldstein to take the matter quietly to the district attorney, a move that was seen by party comrades as an unforgivable breach of solidarity. Claiming that she only took this step to give Blossom a scare and force him to respond, she dropped the charges when he asked a committee of Socialists to intervene and arbitrate the controversy. It turned out that about $1,000 was in dispute, not an inconsiderable amount for the time. When the committee exonerated Blossom (admitting, nonetheless, that the financial records he had kept were insufficient and unclear), Margaret called the investigation a whitewash and disassociated herself from all who supported it. Her only vindication was that Blossom himself broke with the Socialists shortly thereafter and later came under suspicion of the IWW for being a government agent, charges that were never proved.

Billy Williams, a Socialist and former Kansas City reporter who had come East to pursue a passion for radical causes, offered her a $500 contribution to replace the Blossom losses and promised to try to raise ten times that amount or more. Still other party activists, such as Cerise Carman Jack, the wife of a prominent Harvard University professor, publicly defended her actions. Yet, there is no doubt that the incident was a sign of her developing disillusion with the left and of her increased dependence on others for support.[28]

There were two competing birth control organizations in New York City in 1917, the National Birth Control League and the New York Birth Control League, which Blossom had organized. Margaret officially belonged to neither but worked with both until her dispute with Blossom. Mary Ware Dennett asked her to serve on the executive committee of the NBCL in 1916, and then again in 1919, when the name of the organization was changed to the Voluntary Parenthood League, but she refused both times, though Dennett did agree to write for the *Birth Control Review.* [29]

Margaret instead tried to maintain her own leadership and autonomy by keeping the *Birth Control Review* afloat on income from its several thousand subscribers, newsstand sales, and generous individual benefactors. The latter included a still devoted Gertrude Pinchot, Dorothy Whitney Straight, the activist philanthropist who with her husband Willard published *The New Republic*, and, most significantly, Juliet Rublee, who anonymously paid Margaret's office rent on lower Fifth Avenue, frequently sent money for her personal needs, and established her legitimacy with a large network of powerful and wealthy individuals in New York, Washington, and Chicago.[30]

Margaret could not have sustained her celebrity status or consolidated her leadership during these years without this friend's assistance, and for the rest of her life her devotion to Rublee remained unshakable. Having inherited a Chicago industrial fortune, Rublee had substantial sums of money to use at Margaret's discretion. She also happened to be married to the Harvard-educated lawyer, George Rublee, who served as a Wilson appointee on the Federal Trade Commission and whose personality was as reserved and cautious as hers was extravagant and wild. The marriage apparently did not satisfy the full extent of Juliet's energies or passions, and there were no children, because she was infertile as the result of overzealous surgery for pelvic complaints when she was young. Through her association with Margaret, this eccentric, if well-intentioned, woman would experience political engagement and personal adventure for which she was more than happy to exchange her money and contacts. More than any other figure in the country's social establishment, she would be responsible for subsequent changes in the orientation of the birth control movement.[31]

A personal rapport was well-established by the time Rublee went off to France in 1918 to work as a Red Cross nurse. Margaret sent her to meet Havelock Ellis and wrote often to inform her of developments in the birth control movement taking place beneath the facade of official accounts. Margaret confessed that she was using her office as an informal clinic to instruct from twenty-five to forty women a week in the use of pessaries, implying that this had been the procedure at Brownsville as well. Juliet, in turn, delighted in flouting the law and enthusiastically endorsed this work. Juliet also supported further distribution of *Family Limitation* among women workers in factories, mills, and mines. A concerted educational outreach was being made in several small towns in Pennsylvania and upstate New York. During the summer, an Italian woman in Pittsburgh had been sentenced to nine months in jail for giving the pamphlet to a miner's wife, and Margaret was trying to secure her pardon, while also printing and distributing an additional 20,000 copies of the pamphlet translated into Lithuanian and Polish with funds donated by Gertrude Pinchot.[32]

Before leaving New York, Juliet had also set the *Birth Control Review* on solid financial footing, following Blossom's abrupt departure, by helping to incorporate the New York Women's Publishing Company as a parent venture for the magazine. She sold $10,000 worth of stock in shares of $10 each, though it was never likely to be a money-making proposition. Several of Rublee's friends became officers of the parent company, and directorships were also offered to Jessie Ashley, Ethel Byrne, and Mary Ware Dennett, even as editorial control mostly remained with people from the left. Margaret's old beau, Walter Roberts, took over as managing editor. And an impressive range of writers and thinkers joined the editorial board, including Eugene Debs, Crystal Eastman, the lawyer and social reformer, and Florence Guertin Tuttle, a prize-winning journalist who had recently published a much-acclaimed book on world peace and would soon become a lobbyist for the League of Nations. From Europe came Havelock Ellis, C. V. Drysdale, Johannes Rutgers, Marie Stopes, and Stella Browne, a spirited young Socialist in London.[33]

For the moment the belligerent tone of the publication under Blossom disappeared. Gone was the bombast linking birth control to social revolution, replaced by reasoned arguments, setting forth poverty, maternal and infant mortality, child labor, tuberculosis, birth defects, and other generally agreed-upon objectives of the liberal social welfare agenda as a sufficient rationale. By the early months of 1919, however, Margaret was under pressure to earn money and embarked on an extended lecture tour through the South. Not feeling well, she then extended her leave of absence to write her book, *Woman and the New Race* and placed another old friend in charge, the rebellious journalist and self-styled revolutionary, Agnes Smedley.

Smedley was newly released from jail, where she had been held until the war's end, charged under the Sedition Act with abetting the Germans as a result of her association with underground Indian Nationalists accused of working in New York and London to undermine America's British allies. She was still under indictment when Margaret brought her to work at the *Review*, and the prospect of renewed militancy under her stewardship must have irritated some directors because a formal statement of editorial policy was adopted on June 17, 1919, limiting the magazine's interests to "Birth Control pure and simple. No other propaganda work of any kind."[34]

Margaret was not in town when the vote was taken, yet she was not herself immune from controversy. Only months later, Mary Ware Dennett resigned from the board to protest a front-page article urging women, regardless of their circumstances, to unite in a "birth-strike" for five years. The byline was not Smedley's, but Margaret's own. The country's attention was riveted on strikes in the steel industry in Pennsylvania, and she used the occasion to argue that at issue was not just worker exploitation, but the unchecked reproduction of a "future crop of wage slaves." Dennett objected on the grounds that this constituted endorsement of "a militantly feministic policy" and, even worse, employed the "terminology of the labor struggle." She had recently transferred her campaign for legislative reform from the statehouses to the Federal government and was concerned that Margaret's tactics would antagonize potential supporters of reform and discredit her efforts. Privately, she also condemned what she called Margaret's emphasis on "sex antagonisms," believing that birth controllers should adopt a more conciliatory tone toward men.[35]

Dennett argued with some merit for more soothing messages, but despite her promise of moderation Margaret was never so disposed. She took the view that confrontation in and of itself can be valuable. At least it kept her in the news. During the war, for example, when birth control had been able to achieve little conventional press exposure, she sent advocates to the city streets to sell their magazine at busy intersections. Her most effective salesperson was Kitty Marion, who had learned to hawk papers as a militant British suffragist.

Beginning in 1918, and for more than a decade thereafter, Marion stood almost every day during the afternoon and early evening at a familiar post on Times Square or outside Macy's Department Store at 34th Street, once claiming to have sold 90,000 copies of the *Birth Control Review* at 10 to 20 cents apiece. She called it a "liberty bond" for women's freedom and endured the frequent heckling of patriots who objected to what they perceived as her mockery of the war finance effort. She was repeatedly arrested by police officers who tried to interrupt her activities by enforcing local peddling restrictions.

In November of 1918, Marion landed in the Tombs on a thirty-day charge, until Jonah Goldstein could secure her acquittal on First Amendment grounds. She found herself in jail with Agnes Smedley, who was there because of her underground political work, and by Smedley's account in a letter to Margaret, they also shared their accommodations with cockroaches, bedbugs, and all kinds of other "very active human and animal life." Smedley complained of their mistreatment by a police detective, who told her he wished he had arrested her down South, where "she would be strung up to the first lamppost." She then reported that Kitty had turned the prison into a forum for birth control agitation. "Kitty came clattering down the stone corridors every morning with her scrub pail in her hand. 'Three cheers for birth control,' she greeted the prisoners and matrons. And 'three cheers for birth control,' the prisoners answered back." Years later Marion would sentimentally recall the incident: "If I have helped to diminish unnecessary suffering, I have received a very liberal education in return," she acknowledged, as she prepared to return to England, having outlived her usefulness to a professionalized birth control organization which by then wanted nothing more to do with sidewalk agitators.[36]

Margaret nurtured these activists, and they returned an enduring devotion and loyalty, because of a shared resentment over their subordination as women living in a world governed by men. The bonds among them transcended conventional boundaries of politics and class and unsettled women who were less disaffected, such as Mary Ware Dennett. Yet, at the same time, Margaret could also move comfortably in conventional circles and was remarkably successful at observing social amenities when the situation demanded. Unlike her sister Ethel, she bore the stamp of her bourgeois education in etiquette. She alternated between propriety and seething resentment—between the comportment she had learned at her mother's knee and the iconoclasm she both relished and resented in her father.

Margaret's unusual inspirational skills before a broad audience of men and women in these years may have been as important to her success as any specific message she communicated. Blanche Ames, the formidable, talented, and wealthy daughter of another Boston Brahmin family, who had left women's suffrage to embrace the birth control cause in her state, first heard Sanger in a 1916 speech before a frenzied meeting in Boston called to protest the arrest of a young college student by the name of Van Kleek Allison for distributing birth control pamphlets to unmarried factory girls. Ames later remembered:

> The impression she made on us was one of a gentle, beautiful woman of unusual force of character. She appeared frail at first, but then her spirit and eloquence seemed to increase her stature as she molded us into an integrated group. We were radicals and conservatives, anarchists and socialists, Republicans and Democrats, men and women of many religions—we all fell under her spell.[37]

Viewed as impetuous and somewhat neurotic even by his supporters, the young Allison made an unlikely martyr, but when he was tried and convicted, a conservative Boston judge handed him an outrageous three-year prison sentence, which was only later reduced on appeal to several months. These events provided birth control in Massachusetts with an effective organizing tool and pitted local Catholics against the Protestant elite. Blanche Ames was vilified for her activities, with one newspaper reporting that she was denounced in local Catholic churches as a menace to society—as a "woman of the idle rich, who prefers poodles to babies!"

In other states a similar pattern of conservative overreaction to birth control agitation also helped build a following for the movement. In 1918, in Pennsylvania, birth control advocates mobilized to defeat legislative prohibitions, which were passed where there had previously been none at all. So too, a citizens' coalition organized by several University of Chicago professors and Hull House physicians, Alice Hamilton and Rachelle Yarros, in response to Margaret's 1916 appearance, was able to kill a similar measure in the Illinois legislature. This, despite the fact the more prominent, but increasingly cautious, Jane Addams refused to lend her name to the still controversial cause.

Where there were no such confrontations, birth control activism simply foundered. Coalitions of radicals and reformers became untenable, and much of the nation turned its attention away from domestic political and social causes altogether. Many of the endorsements Margaret had won through her perspicacity as a publicist and by the sheer force of her personality proved ephemeral, as was the limited progress of Mary Ware Dennett's plodding legislative efforts. Neither woman, for the time being, was able to create a strong institutional legacy behind her. The tide turned against them. By 1920, most of the state and local committees that had organized to defend Margaret and carry forward her agenda were either quiescent or had ceased to exist altogether, though many would regroup in middecade around the concrete objective of organizing birth control clinics.[38]

Margaret found herself overcome by despondency and depression, unable to impose direction on her professional commitments. In 1919, she had begun writing again in a diary, and often inserted a line or two of philosophical reflection into her record of the day's correspondence, work obligations, and evening engagements. At the heart of her malaise was despair over the red scare and the deteriorating political climate, but she was confused and uncertain as well about her health and about her personal life. She was also ill with the familiar symptoms of fever, weight loss, and a persistent lump in her neck that she believed were signs of recurring tuberculosis. Assured by her physician that she was suffering only from "nervous fatigue," she went off to rest at Truro with her sons. When the conditions persisted, however, she seized the opportunity presented by the advance she received to write a book and decided to work in the restorative climate of Southern California.[39]

In February of 1919, she took Grant out of boarding school, and they traveled across country by train, observing with sadness the arrests and deportations of IWW activists along the way. She rented a cottage in Coronado, near San Diego, where she turned out a steady stream of chapters, which she then sent back to New York for editing. Her diary records her delight in the bright sun, the exquisite beach, the enchanting birds, the orange trees, and the graceful palms of the California coast. She traveled north to Los Angeles and San Francisco to visit her old IWW friends, Marie Equi and Caroline Nelson, but neither the natural beauty of the landscape, nor the progress of her work, nor old political enthusiasms—not even the Theosophists whose spiritual counsel she sought out en route—could cure her of a deepening despair. "It is a most awful anguish one suffers . . ." she confided in her journal, "a great aching void of loneliness takes hold in different places." California reminded her of Spain, and the ghost of Lorenzo Portet, she wrote in her diary, loomed up beside that of her beloved little Peggy "like a nightmare."

It seems certain that, had Portet lived, Margaret would have made an effort to reunite with him after the war. She had written Bill Sanger early in 1917, threatening to leave the country immediately if he refused to give her a legal divorce. "Won't you let go that straw of hope that you have clutched so long, and let me have freedom and a future happiness which I think is my right," she pleaded. "There is nothing I have to give you in love, there is nothing to be repaired, there is no way we can go on together. The kindest and most human thing is for us to cut the bond at once." Two years later, as she prepared to turn forty, the divorce was still not accomplished, Portet was dead, and she could not have been less pleased about her uncertain prospects.[40]

Although she often felt lonely and insecure, she seems nonetheless to have rarely been alone. In the bleak days that followed her return from Europe—then Peggy's death and later Portet's—she had resumed her affair with the ardent poet and journalist Walter Roberts. Through 1918, the two also worked together on the *Birth Control Review*, but despite Roberts's devotion to her personally and to her cause, she firmly resisted his desire for a permanent commitment. The relationship ended without any visible rancor, and years later, as with many of her old friends, she was still in touch and sometimes lent him money.[41]

Billy Williams, who helped raise funds for the *Review*, soon replaced Roberts as lover and coworker, and it was to him that she sent the chapters of her book for editing. During the war Williams had drifted from one cause to another—the Socialist Party, the Rand School, the birth control movement—lending his talents as a publicist. He was revered in Greenwich Village coffeehouse circles as a gentle, introspective sort who could sit for hours through an evening discussing politics and philosophy. Neither handsome nor terribly adventuresome, he seemed an unlikely candidate for Margaret's affections, as though in the wake of Portet's death she turned to someone completely different. The common thread was that all were passionate in temperament. Williams, as had Bill Sanger and Walter Roberts before him, wrote her almost embarrassingly plaintive love letters, and like Portet, he also died suddenly and tragically—of kidney disease in 1920, while Margaret was away in London, his last hours apparently soothed by her frantic telegram promising that she would return and nurse him back to health. He and John Reed died on the same day, and the two were memorialized together on the front page of *The Call.*[42]

There were apparently other romantic attachments as well. Though no clear record of any intimacy exists, Margaret wrote in her diary of dinners, operas, and assorted social engagements with the lawyer Jonah Goldstein, whom Stuart Sanger also recalls fondly as a personal presence in their lives, but she also seemed genuinely relieved when Goldstein married someone else. Herbert Simonds, whom Margaret later solicited to manufacture diaphragms and other contraceptive pharmaceuticals, once recalled that his life had been changed when they met at a resort shortly before America entered the war and discovered a shared enthusiasm for dancing and for each other. Harold Hersey, another rejected suitor from these years, had still not unburdened himself of his infatuation with Margaret when he attempted to write her biography twenty years later.

She seems to have completely fulfilled these men, but she did not fall in love with any of them, and she contemplated her situation in the privacy of her diary. Describing Williams, she wrote of "a man so big and generous and devoted . . . who offers his all . . . strength—talents—love . . . and though it's appreciated and valued, these essential qualities in and of themselves do not bring out of us the love they should." Goldstein was "fascinating" and "very keen of intellect" but "underdeveloped emotionally." Of both men, she wondered what exactly determined the "chemical side" of love and why it "has a big part in life." She later confided to Juliet Rublee that at least one problem with all these men was that as soon as they became involved in the birth control movement, they assumed their right to dictate policy. "The kind of man [we] have in mind has not been born dear," she concluded.[43]

She could only have been emotionally confused, as well, by the faithful attentions she continued to receive during these years from Havelock Ellis. Following his wife's death, Ellis first became involved with the Frenchwoman Françoise Cyon, who remained the permanent companion of his later years. Even so, he encouraged Margaret's affections, writing her on the occasion of one lovely spring day, for example, that "I most want you here and recklessly want to wander about with you to Ireland and anywhere. There is no danger of the Irishwoman you speak of being driven out of my heart by any French woman . . . for I always love to think of her, and it always thrills one to think, as I often do, of her first kiss."

Alone and perplexed in December of 1919, Margaret took herself to an exhibition of Bill Sanger's paintings. She found them powerfully drawn but filled with sadness, and the experience occasioned the only known apology she ever made to her husband for the pain she had caused him. The letter, though admitting her remorse, is fraught with self-justification. She wrote:

> My marriage to you and our love and the coming of the children, the saving for a home, the building of the house, the seeking, shifting, changing interesting life, all today have meaning & full value to me in this cause of humanity to which my life is dedicated. Often I have felt your loneliness & sorrow. Often I would like to seek you & fling my arms about you & hold your aching head to my heart and tell you of my tenderness for you and my love, but forces stronger than physical desire, stronger than personal love, hold me to my task, to the work I have undertaken to do. But I want you to know this, for I have told it to many, that you are to me the lover of all the world. Your love for me beautified my life and made possible the outlook on love & passion & sex, which have given me the courage & strength to go forth.

Margaret never sent the letter but instead tucked it away in her personal papers, with a notation that it be given to Bill after her death. Thereafter, still feeling weary and ill, she consulted the physician and scientist Robert Morris, author of the best-selling *Microbes and Men,* and he diagnosed a lingering tuberculosis. She entered the hospital where her infected thyroid was partially removed, and then prepared to recuperate over the summer in England. The manuscript of her book was finally complete, and she left for London with the expectation of returning to the United States in the fall when it was scheduled for publication.

"More than ever [I have] decided that one must make and direct one's life," she had written in the last entry of her diary for 1919. "Drifting cannot be the way." To renew the focus of her life and work, she again sought inspiration abroad.[44]

The Lady Reformer

CHAPTER NINE

New Woman, New World

Margaret remained in London from May through October of 1920, first letting a room in the central city and then moving to the garden suburbs, where she hoped the sunshine and fresh air would help cure her persistent tubercular cough. No journal of her trip survives, only an appointment book and a handful of letters to her new friend, Juliet Rublee. She lectured frequently—thirty specific bookings are identified—but she preached principally to the already converted. For that reason she was most enthusiastic about arrangements made for her to speak through the Women's Cooperative Guild, a voluntary association of 75,000 working women, whom she described as representing "the best and most advanced women of the working class." She looked to them to carry her message to even poorer and less educated women of their districts, and more important, to arrange opportunities for her to speak before men in Labour and Socialist circles who remained overtly hostile to birth control on the grounds that only income disparity, and not family size, was the cause of poverty. "The thought here is masculine and difficult to raise," she wrote home somewhat dejectedly, but her spirits revived a month later after a tour of what she described as some of the country's most "godforsaken" districts. "Oh, Juliet," she implored, "never was there such a cause. Poor, pale-faced, wretched wives. Men beat them. They cringe before their blows, but pick up the baby, dirty and unkempt, and return to serve him." Margaret was again driven forward by the conflicting strains of compassion and contempt she felt for the misery of poor women who capitulated to autocratic male authority—by the unresolved anger of her own childhood that never failed to move her. She also believed that the rank and file in the working classes were entirely open to birth control, despite leadership's resistance, because the wives of younger workers tended to be better educated, more independent, and determined to better their own lives and those of their children.

The Cooperative Guild did arrange audiences for her as far away as Ireland and Scotland, and years later, she described to an interviewer the exultant sight of what she estimated as nearly 2,000 shipyard workers who turned out on Glasgow Green to hear her. As in the United States, however, British political lines had hardened during the war, forcing supporters of birth control to take sides. The Neo-Malthusians, led by the Drysdales and Marie Stopes, had become virulently antilabor. Margaret privately deplored their "materialism," yet she knew that with the organized left unwilling to take a stand, she had nowhere else to go for support.[1]

Since coming to Margaret's assistance in 1915, Stopes had made herself something of a celebrity among England's middle and upper classes with the publication of a controversial and wildly successful book called *Married Love*. Stopes was a paleontologist by training but drew the inspiration for her new career from an unhappy experience with an impotent husband. After the marriage was annulled, she sat down at her writing desk to ensure that no women would again suffer as she had from sexual ignorance and inhibition. What she said about sex was hardly more advanced than Ellis's writings, and, indeed, her florid prose today seems more than a little quaint. She turned sexual orgasm into a marital sacrament, claiming: "The half swooning sense of flux which overtakes the spirit in that eternal moment at the apex of rapture sweeps into its flaming tides the whole essence of the man and woman." Tucked in among such profusions of sentiment, however, were more prosaic descriptions of coital positions and technique that a decade later became the standard fare of marriage manuals but seemed terribly shocking in this first instance. The book caused a public outcry in 1918 and became a runaway sensation, selling out six editions in a year and ultimately more than 1 million copies in a dozen languages.

Margaret had gone to some length to secure Stopes's book an American publisher. Turned down by the large commercial firms, she finally arranged for it to be printed by *The Critic and Guide,* the popular medical magazine run by her friend and mentor Dr. William Robinson, but the book was then censored in the United States. While Margaret expected the favor of her efforts to be returned in England, she was not quite prepared for the degree of enthusiasm with which Stopes embraced the birth control cause there in her own name, rather than Margaret's. By 1920, Stopes had married again, this time to a wealthy manufacturer who fathered her only child and was prepared to back her efforts to open a birth control clinic and marital advice center in England, where no laws existed to prohibit her effort. She also had a second book ready for press called *Wise Parenthood*, which promoted the individual and eugenic benefits of scientific contraception and small families, a book Margaret reviewed favorably in the *Birth Control Review.* In the opinion of Ellis and several of Margaret's other English correspondents, however, Stopes was a blustering and egotistical woman—class bound, politically conservative, blatantly anti-Semitic—and intent on dominating the new field she had staked out. No shrinking violet herself, Margaret refused to accommodate to someone she thought vulgar, and whose competitive instincts, though not wholly unlike her own, she found distasteful. She spent a weekend at Stopes's country home early in the summer of 1920 but thereafter always found some excuse for not seeing her when she was in London.

Within two years Stopes had, indeed, preempted Margaret by opening up the first birth control clinic in London, where instruction was given by midwives to women who could prove they already had at least one child, a regulation Margaret openly deplored. At about the same time, she accused Stopes of having breached an obligation and a trust by telling Mary Ware Dennett of Margaret's disregard for her, an opinion that had been shared in confidence. Stopes then allied herself with Dennett in opposition to Margaret's leadership in the United States, forcing a permanent estrangement. This was, to be sure, a contest of strong and fiercely ambitious personalities, but as with Dennett, substantive issues also bred antagonisms. Both women disparaged any action or pronouncement by Margaret that they could possibly interpret as evidence of a lingering political and sexual radicalism. By taking her to task for her confrontational postures in public, they effectively pushed her toward their own more accommodating political and organizational strategies. Yet personal relations among them were permanently damaged. Margaret, for her part, did her very best to pit such significant potential supporters as Havelock Ellis against Stopes, which was not difficult since he seemed little inclined toward her anyway. The Drysdales and others of the Neo-Malthusian group also split off and established a competing clinic in London, the Walworth Center, staffed by doctors and placing no restrictions on its clientele. Still, the name of Marie Stopes in England, like that of Margaret Sanger in America, became synonymous with birth control. London schoolchildren in the 1920s skipped rope to the chant:

Jeanie, Jeanie, full of hopes,
Read a book by Marie Stopes,
Now to judge by her condition,
She must have read the wrong edition.[2]

* * *

The principal purpose of Margaret's 1920 trip to England was to visit Ellis, and, in fact, the two spent much of their free time in London that summer together. Absorbed in a new relationship with Françoise Cyon, Ellis nonetheless seemed to make time for Margaret whenever she wanted. They reserved Sundays to be together at leisure, and her diary records lunches, teas, and long walks in the park. One such encounter is characterized with a simple but emphatic inscription: "glorious."

In July, she finally scheduled their long-anticipated outing to the Irish countryside, but with this opportunity for a sustained intimacy, things did not work out satisfactorily. The two of them rode about County Cork in an open carriage, searching through parish registers for confirmation of the exalted Purcell lineage Margaret heard so much about as a child, but their genealogical expeditions produced nothing. She must have apologized at some point for being "nervous, impatient and horrid" during the trip, for Ellis wrote later to excuse her from such behavior and to assure her in his typically salacious language that he still savored his "delicious memories" of their time together. She, by contrast, was absorbed wholly by material concerns, having borrowed a week's rent from Ellis, which she was anxious to repay. She seemed in no hurry to see him again and managed to find time for only "a brief glimpse" before she left England shortly thereafter to tour maternal health clinics on the Continent, and to inquire about recent developments in contraceptive technology. She traveled once again with his professional introductions and on this trip learned from physicians in Germany of the formula for the chemical jelly which, with some subsequent modification, became the substance she would recommend for use with the rubber spring diaphragm she had discovered in Holland.[3]

Ellis and Margaret were never lovers after that summer. She, in fact, rejoiced in the increasing satisfaction he derived from his relationship with Françoise, whom she sometimes disparaged, but with whom she quickly forged an intimate friendship. Effusive letters during the 1920s and '30s repeatedly conveyed appreciation for the sexual gratification and domestic tranquillity Françoise was able to provide Ellis—in Margaret's own words, for giving him renewed "youth and life." Yet these letters never seem totally candid. At one point, for example, Margaret wrote that she wished she was the one "cleaning his [Ellis's] flat," but given her antipathy to housework, this would seem a backhanded compliment. However grateful she was on Ellis's behalf, she probably viewed Françoise's situation somewhat dimly.[4]

As in the past, Margaret also found in London a far more conventionally satisfying physical relationship than she was able to enjoy with Ellis, who was himself responsible for the liaison, having introduced her to Hugh de Selincourt, a handsome patrician and novelist and a devotee of Ellis's philosophies. De Selincourt seduced the women of the Ellis circle by invoking a common reverence for their mentor's teachings and then performing for them with the technique and competence that Ellis himself could not achieve. This virility only called attention to Ellis's limitations and may have accounted for his subsequent disdain of men he identified as mere "sexual athletes." In fact, Ellis came to loathe de Selincourt, not so much because of Margaret, but because he also carried on an extended affair with Françoise Cyon, until Ellis objected and, setting his theoretical objections to sexual jealousy aside, insisted that she choose between them. Margaret, who seemed confident of her own relationship with de Selincourt, never minded sharing him, but Ellis, obviously hurt, rationalized that de Selincourt's intense hunger for personal conquests was compensation for intellectual deficiencies and professional failures.[5]

Within days of their first meeting, de Selincourt was wooing Margaret for a weekend at Wantley, his sublime countryside estate, "the loveliest spot in England," as he described it. "Here you could rest two, three or four days—a pianist would play to you; a novelist would laugh with you; a child would dance to you; and all the gods in the garden would welcome you—and you would return to lectures and public life so strong that no one could possibly resist you." The pianist was de Selincourt's aristocratic wife, Janet, with whom he no longer had any sexual relations, the child, their sprightly and talented daughter, Bridgette. The arcadian retreat, a sixteenth century house of stone surrounded by orchards and gardens, had once belonged to the father of Britain's celebrated romantic poet Percy Bysshe Shelley. The liberated de Selincourts were committed to re-creating in its midst the morally unconstrained universe that Shelley and his soulmate Lord Byron had pursued in exile in Italy some 100 years earlier, when fear of sexual scandal drove them from England. Like the free lovers of the Byron-Shelley circle, they were devoted to sensuous living—to music, poetry, and nature, and in this setting far removed from the surviving sanctions of Edwardian society, to an unfettered expression of physical love as a dimension of friendships formed within their group. They shared the house on a permanent basis with Harold Child, a well-known editorial writer and critic at *The Times* of London, who was for a time Janet's lover and later also became a lover of Margaret's. Other participants apparently came and went more or less casually, though Ellis himself, on whose theories it rested, never visited until late in the 1920s. Years later Margaret still remembered it as an atmosphere that would always "radiate beauty, stimulate mental and spiritual growth, utter kindness, unselfishness, and entirely do away with the pettinesses of jealousy, which so often occurs in the regular marriage."[6]

Margaret spent a weekend there in June of 1920. She returned for a full week in September, and tried to visit again at least once, whenever she returned to England. It was a place where she could unburden herself of worldly concerns, a "house of childhood"—as she once described its hold on her—where she always felt "young and happy." Yet the lure of the place and of the estate called Sand Pit, to which the de Selincourts subsequently moved, was hardly innocent.

Ellis was probably correct that sports and women were ways for the debonair de Selincourt to compensate for his failure as a serious writer. He vented his frustrations as an unsuccessful commercial novelist by playing a good deal of cricket, and he even earned a modest living by writing about his passion for the game. Margaret liked to think of him as someone removed from material drives and ambitions altogether—as a pure poet and aesthete. She was not entirely unaware of his questionable talent, and in an introduction to a 1924 novel he wrote about adolescent sexual awakening called *One Little Boy,* she praised his perceptiveness and candor about human nature but implicitly questioned the book's merit as a work of fiction.

Yet, for a brief time she was clearly infatuated by him. De Selincourt, in the effete and hapless essentials of his personality, was not unlike other men she had loved, including her father and her husband, but this relationship never offered any threat of responsibility. Uncompromised by any option of really serious involvement, it stayed lighthearted for its duration. Seeming to recognize the juvenile quality of her feelings for Hugh, Margaret once wrote that he was one of her "adolescent dreams—the man I looked for in books, on the stage—but never found."

Terribly self-absorbed, and perhaps stuck in a perpetual pubescence himself, de Selincourt always seemed grateful for Margaret's attentions. She was, after all, an attractive and high-spirited woman of international accomplishment and prominence, and he flattered her shamelessly, appealing in a puerile transatlantic correspondence to what he called the "spiritual" side of her nature, though it was probably her vanity he captured. Ellis snidely characterized this capacity for pandering when he wrote to Margaret that de Selincourt had been down to see him, and was reveling in one of her letters and "purring like a cat before the fire." On another occasion he told her that Hugh was "disconsolate" because he was not able "to kiss your darling feet for an hour or two."

The bond between Margaret and Hugh was unabashedly physical. His letters to her were hopelessly saccharine. He remembered her variously with words like "tender," "sweet," "saintly," "sensitive," "delicate," and "lovely," but his prose did achieve greater authenticity when he wrote explicitly of their sexual encounters—as on the one occasion he described her in down-to-earth fashion as "so gorgeously free." Whatever the two may actually have thought of each other, they seemed to have been genuinely ravished by their sexual dynamic. Margaret had at last found the accomplished and indefatigable lover she had been looking for—the "chemistry" that had eluded her—and her memories of him apparently nourished her during the long periods between their brief encounters. The letters she wrote Hugh over a decade's time, across vast distances, and often from the bed she shared with a second husband, were gushy and graphically sexual. She wrote of reaching out to hug and hold his "adorable head," of desiring his kisses in precisely "two places," of "the joys and delights a certain English old thing has given me"—often having not seen him for months or even years and with no expectation or demand of anything more tangible in the immediate future than more of his fawning responses. In the early 1930s, she tried to arrange for him to come to America on a lecture tour, but she was unsuccessful, and once the Depression and World War II intervened, they scarcely ever saw each other again.

"Our American husbands are everything but lovers. It seems to be a lost sense in the American male," she confided to him in 1932, entreating him, at the same time, to see Juliet Rublee, who was en route to London and had also long been availing herself of his services. Margaret first introduced the sexually unsophisticated Rublee to de Selincourt in 1921, and while the two of them were preoccupied with one another, she willingly turned her own attentions to Harold Child. "She needs you too," Margaret was still telling de Selincourt eleven years later, and on Rublee's return from that trip, she added: "She says you attracted her as no man has. She adores you now like I do, and we love each other all the more because of you."[7]

The Wantley experiment may have been plainly and simply a narcissistic exercise, however grandly conceived. Its devotees were almost certainly preoccupied with momentary self-gratification and probably incapable of sustained intimacy. At the same time, their rebellion was genuinely felt. They experienced their commitment to liberation from conventional moral and sexual behavior and from common, petty jealousies as a serious political act. Child may have best embodied the group's philosophy when he wrote in 1921 that the main source of human strength, activity, and happiness is love, and then defined love as neither "comfort nor contentment—not a negative measure of shutting out—but a positive measure of taking in more and more."

The various and complicated couplings of the Wantley circle were apparently never concealed from the larger group, and some of these sexual encounters may have involved more than two at a time, in configurations that joined the women, as well as the men. At one point in 1924, in a breathless letter to Juliet, Margaret confided that Hugh had spent the night, that Harold and Janet had also come to celebrate her return, and that she and Janet had "an embrace beyond any earthly experience." Still, it is clear that these unusual arrangements were best maintained without conflict when the parties kept at least an ocean's distance between them.[8]

Margaret also began a second affair during the summer of 1920, this time with someone she not only found endearing in bed but also embraced for his luminosity as a man of letters and of influence. H. G. Wells, novelist and essayist, had at that moment reached the pinnacle of his career and was quite possibly the best known writer in the Western world. If his reputation was preeminent, however, it was by no means conventional. He too was a dedicated free lover who had already been married twice and created a small scandal with two affairs that produced children out-of-wedlock, a daughter by one woman and a son by another, the aspiring critic and writer Rebecca West.

Wells had risen from humble Cockney origins. As a young author of science fiction, popular romances, short stories, and criticism, he churned out copy with an astonishing grace and speed. His extraordinary early successes encouraged him to try his hand at more complex literary works, and in the early years of this century he produced several critically acclaimed and enduring novels about Edwardian social conventions. He also began writing about politics. As a principal architect of Fabian Socialism, with its preference for incremental reform over revolution, he had a profound influence on progressive political philosophy in America and was so highly considered by Herbert Croly, Walter Weyl, and Walter Lippmann that they took the name for *The New Republic* from his writings. Following World War I, he emerged as a leading internationalist and exponent of the idea of the League of Nations. In despair over the power of demagogues to influence public opinion, he set out to raise the level of popular intelligence by writing a comprehensive outline of human history. With its wide circulation in the English speaking world and in translation, the book made him both a world figure and a man of considerable personal wealth.

Wells's reputation with the intelligentsia would decline during the 1930s, when his virulent contempt for Stalin provoked what many in England and in America judged to be a reactive, sentimental celebration of the virtues of democratic capitalism. Still, when he died in 1946 he had published more than one hundred books and was, in the view of a biographer, "the most popular of the serious writers of his time, and the most serious of the popular."[9]

Before World War I, Wells was well known as a prophet of liberation. Though a relatively small circle was privy to his personal escapades, his 1909 novel, *Ann Veronica*, created a widespread furor with its affectionate portrait of an emancipated modern woman who flaunted her independence and her sexuality. In a more serious vein, he promoted a Socialist theory that repudiated the patriarchal private ownership of women and children in favor of state support of mothers. He envisioned a utopian society that guaranteed the practical equality, economic independence, and personal freedom of men and women in and out of marriage. He was an avid proponent of scientific birth control as a sine qua non of domestic reform and had lent his name to the letter of support for Margaret Sanger that went to Woodrow Wilson.[10]

Wells and Sanger shared striking similarities of background and temperament. He wrote of them himself in a delightfully funny novel begun in the fall of 1920 when they first met, and then published two years later, after he had gotten to know her even better. *The Secret Places of the Heart* tells the transparently autobiographical story of a man caught in the turmoil of an emotionally satisfying marriage that provides him no sexual fulfillment, and a turbulent extramarital affair that gives him sex but not happiness. The situation recapitulated his own arrangement with Catherine (Jane) Wells, who then shared his home, family, business, and social affairs but sent him off to bed with other women, including West, with whom his longstanding illicit relationship was just then becoming tempestuous.

In the hope that a change of scene would help him resolve the dilemmas of his personal life, the protagonist of Wells's novel, who is called Sir Richmond Hardy (the name apparently an allusion to his sexual appetites) motors off to the English countryside on a fine summer day in the company of a medical doctor. The doctor serves as a vehicle for poking fun at Freudian paradigms, which were becoming much the rage in literary London. No sooner do the two men reach their destination, than Hardy becomes distracted by a woman named Miss Grammont, a "finely-featured, frank-minded but soft-spoken" American who is touring England for the summer with a friend. They strike up a conversation. She is a supporter of birth control and world population planning. She dresses smartly for dinner and wears a silver band with deep red stones in her hair. Hardy confesses that he is not good at judging a woman's age but guesses her to be somewhere in her twenties. He finds her charming and clever, yet he is most impressed by the depth of her experience in matters of love and of life.

> She has been shocked out of the first confidence of youth. She has ceased to take the world for granted. . . . It hasn't broken her but it has matured her. . . . That I think is why history has become real to her. Which so attracts you to her. History, for her, has ceased to be a fabric of picturesque incidents; it is the study of a tragic struggle that still goes on. She sees history as you and I see it. She is a very grown up young woman. . . .[11]

There are many thin disguises, some of them attributing facts clearly drawn from Juliet Rublee's life and not from Margaret's, but many details are exact, down to the way Margaret managed her evening coiffure at the time. Wells was even sensitive to her vanity about age. Of the meaning of the name "Miss Grammont," one can only speculate. Perhaps some reference was intended to the intelligent but licentious lover of Lord Byron, "Miss Clairmont," the clue resting in the deliberately formal identification of the two heroines only by their surnames.

Margaret Sanger was in many ways the embodiment of Wells's vision of the new woman: smart and sassy (though never really quite as articulate as he makes her in the book), attractive and sexual, and, above all, reconciled to the notion that love need not compel obligation. In the novel, he seems smitten by her. *The Secret Places of the Heart* was hardly a major literary achievement, but Wells was a lucid writer, and much of what he wrote undoubtedly described Margaret as he saw her.

> Their ways of thought harmonized. They talked at first chiefly about the history of the world, and the extraordinary situation of aimlessness in a phase of ruin to which the Great War had brought all Europe, if not mankind. The world excited them both in the same way, as a crisis in which they were called upon to do something—they did not yet clearly know what. Into this topic they peered as into some deep pool, side by side, and in it they saw each other reflected.

A few pages later the conversation becomes somewhat less exalted but no less compelling:

> He found that she was very much better read than he was in the recent literature of socialism, and that she had what he considered to be a most unfeminine grasp of economic ideas. He thought her attitude towards socialism a very sane one because it was also his own. So far as socialism involved the idea of a scientific control of natural resources as a common property administered in the common interest, she and he were very greatly attracted by it, but so far as it served as a form of expression for the merely insubordinate discontent of the many with the few, under any conditions, so long as it was a formula for class jealousy and warfare, they were both repelled by it. If she had had any illusions about the working class possessing as a class any profounder political wisdom or more generous public impulses than any other class, those illusions had long since departed. People were much the same, she thought, in every class; there was no stratification of either rightness or righteousness.

The characters continue their intense conversations as they tour the sights, share elegant meals, and then retire to a lovemaking that is only inferred. Anthony West, Wells's son by Rebecca, maintains in his vivid and controversial memoir of his father that Wells omitted graphic love scenes from his novels not only to avoid the censors, but also because he was inept at writing them. In *The Secret Places of the Heart,* the plucky Miss Grammont, after several romantic weeks, boards the train that will take her to Southampton and her return ship to America. She and Hardy make arrangements to write chatty letters to one another about political matters and common interests, but never about their affair. She says:

> In the New Age all lovers will have to be accustomed to meeting and parting. We women will not be tied very much by domestic needs. Unless we see fit to have children. We shall be coming and going about our business like men—we shall have world-wide businesses—many of us—just as men will. . . . It will be a world full of lovers' meetings. Some day—somewhere—we two will certainly meet again.[12]

And so they did. West also acknowledges that his father was never really as successful as he wished to appear at keeping his love affairs short and casual. Margaret, by the son's recollection, was "more genuinely pagan." Wells went off to Russia in the fall of 1920 to interview Lenin for a sympathetic newspaper series he wrote on the Bolsheviks and to spend time with his friend and intellectual mentor, Maxim Gorky. He and Margaret did not meet again until the following summer in London, and then later that year when Wells came to America to cover the Washington Naval Disarmament Conference, a major postwar diplomatic initiative. Margaret was clearly on his mind at that time. From London he wrote that she was "the most refreshing little human I've met for years" but then bemoaned that "We're like 2 busdrivers each very busy on his route who never get much nearer than lifting a hand as we pass." And later he wrote: "My plans in New York are ruled entirely by the wish to be with you as much as possible, *as much as possible without other people about.*" He wanted "sure sweet access" to her, and, recognizing that as two prominent individuals they had to be discreet, he suggested she rent him an apartment for the week, rather than a hotel room, so that he might "visit a lot with you in the costume of tropical island."

They apparently saw each other privately only on occasion thereafter, in London in 1922 and 1924, for example, when brief visits were commemorated by cards from Wells bearing such straightforward messages as "Wonderful! Unforgettable" or "Monday—Way out," the latter decorated with squiggles of ink that were meant to convey electricity, a characteristic of the funny drawings that often accompanied his letters. Beyond these intimacies, they would sustain a warm friendship, which accommodated weekend visits with each other's spouses and, in Wells's case, with subsequent lovers, as well. They saw each other in New York and London many more times and also crossed paths in Russia in 1934, when Wells was there to interview Stalin and Sanger toured Soviet birth control and abortion facilities. One of Wells's biographers argues that a neurotic search for perfect passion motivated his long series of sexual infidelities. He had many affairs beyond West and Sanger, each of which ended in bitterness as he tired of the women he possessed. The relationship with Margaret, however, was intermittent, casual, and without visible discord. When their physical intimacy ended, they remained correspondents until Wells died, and they seemed to maintain affection for one another in their old age, as former lovers and longtime friends. Few of Margaret's letters to Wells survive, but her *Autobiography* recalls that there was "no aloofness or coldness in approaching him, no barriers to break down as with most Englishmen; his twinkling eyes were like those of a mischievous boy. . . . He could be amusing, witty sarcastic, brilliant, flirtatious, and yet profound all at once, all in his thin, small voice. . . ."[13]

Wells came along and enhanced Margaret's self-esteem at a point when it was flagging. She was especially proud of their friendship and of the fact that he identified her as a woman with "a scientific quality of mind," a description she often repeated when she grew older, as though she needed to remind herself and others who thought less of her. Wells, like Ellis before him, also provided a secure intellectual rationale for changing her political posture from rebellion to reform. Indeed, he may even have been the more significant mentor in this regard because of his eminence as a Fabian thinker, despite Lenin's reasonably accurate description of him after their meeting in 1920 as an "unreconstructed bourgeois."

As aspiring children of the working class, Margaret and H. G., as he was called, shared a common inability to romanticize poverty. And once they enjoyed material comforts and rewards, they seemed reluctant to condemn the maldistribution of wealth, goods, and services that gave rise to widespread discontent in the economies of the West. These blinders, along with their disdain of violence, especially as manifest in early Bolshevik, and subsequently in Stalinist, terrorism, may best explain why in the end they wholly capitulated to liberal arguments that scientific advances and industrial organization offered a surer and safer route to social and economic reform than changing the political system or the means of industrial and commercial ownership altogether.[14]

Margaret returned from London to New York in the fall of 1920 to confront the glare of publicity that issued from publication of her first book, *Woman and the New Race.* Conceived during the postwar frenzy over dissent, and edited by the fervidly idealistic Billy Williams, it was written in the extreme, exhortatory style characteristic of the radicals. Probably because of this, the manuscript, first titled "The Modern Woman Movement" was rejected by the Macmillan publishing house and resold to Brentano's, which gave it the new title, an allusion not to distinctions of color but to "race" in its generic sense, as in "the human race."

The book tells women to give up on the solutions that men had proposed to alleviate their misery—to believe in themselves, instead, and their own ability to effect change. "The basic freedom of the world is woman's freedom," Margaret wrote, her prose polished by the gifted Williams's pen:

> A free race cannot be born of slave mothers. A woman enchained cannot choose but give a measure of that bondage to her sons and daughters. No woman can call herself free who does not own and control her body. No woman can call herself free until she can choose consciously whether she will or will not be a mother.[15]

Some years earlier Havelock Ellis had cautioned Margaret against the recklessness of the writing in *The Woman Rebel.* "It is no use . . . smashing your head against a brick wall, for not one rebel, or even many rebels, can crush law by force," he told her. "It needs *skill* even more than strength." *Woman and the New Race* was a self-conscious attempt to shape herself in her mentor's image—to take a more instrumental approach to social change. Essentially it wed Ellis's own formulations from *The Task of Social Hygiene* to feminist theory and to the practical goal of establishing a network of scientific birth control clinics, which would empower women in their own right.

Woman and the New Race maintains that through all of recorded history women had exhibited an "elemental" claim to freedom through their defiant, clandestine use of contraception, abortion and infanticide. The universality of these practices demonstrated a recognition that uncontrolled fertility is not only a personal burden, but also the root of widespread social pathology. The intelligent judgments of women, however, were rarely reflected in the laws of church and state, institutions where men traditionally dominate and subordinate women, so as to increase the size of the population. By this reasoning, Margaret argued, men suppress the expression of an innate "feminine spirit." Antagonisms of gender, as much as conflicts of class, were the root of social malaise.[16]

Margaret acknowledged that women themselves often became victims of masculine thinking. "War, poverty and oppression of the workers will continue while woman makes life cheap," she wrote. "They will cease only when she limits her reproductivity and human life is no longer a thing to be wasted." The availability of modern, scientific birth control, in her view, had suddenly presented women an unavoidable challenge to protect and promote their own freedom and to advance society's well-being by propagating individuals capable of meeting the rigorous demands of modern life.

Margaret attempted to reconcile her new vision of a society purified by the efforts of women with the social ideals that had fueled her energies as a radical. She did not intend birth control to replace "any of the idealistic movements and philosophies of the workers. . . . It is not a substitute—it precedes. . . . It can and it must be the foundation upon which any permanently successful improvement in condition is attained." Yet she could not have it both ways. By identifying birth control as a panacea, she certainly undermined the objectives of the revolutionary labor struggle, and by housing her abstract arguments in a practical political framework focused wholly on one issue, she implicitly challenged the value of even a more moderate agenda of progressive social reform.

As a result the book is abundant in contradiction. At one point it dogmatically attributes virtually all distinctions between native-born and immigrant Americans to their differential fertility rates and seems to implicate the victims of poverty and despair in their own oppression. Only pages later, however, it celebrates the ethnic and racial diversity of America and roundly condemns the intolerable conditions under which immigrants were made to live and work in this country, blaming their deficiencies on such environmental factors as slum housing, low wages, and inadequate health insurance, rather than simply on fertility. In Margaret's defense, however, this kind of intellectual tension was emblematic of the times. Her failure to resolve the relative importance of individual initiative and social renewal at once reflected, and also helped advance, a growing postwar disenchantment with collectivist solutions to social problems.[17]

Yet the book's political framework probably had little to do with its popular success. More important than Margaret's bold claims for birth control as a social tonic was her romantic paean to a new sexual morality. The book closes with a peroration in behalf of woman's freedom from the bonds of pregnancy and the release of her long dormant "physical and psychic nature." It celebrates the right of women to make love, as well as to do good, and this dimension of its argument, far more than its politics, underlay its commercial and critical appeal. Sales may also have been helped by a deceptive advertising campaign implying that the book contained technical birth control advice. The hardcover edition sold out immediately, and after several new printings, it was reissued by Truth Publishing, a soft-cover trade house that was also marketing Margaret's *Family Limitation* pamphlet.

The book did not entirely please Ellis, who wrote a rather tepid introduction, applauding Margaret's attempt to link the goals of the contemporary movements for women and for labor, but expressing some wariness about the boldness of her larger vision. In private, he urged her to adopt a still more cautious tone in the future, one that reflected the disillusion of a generation of European intellectuals whose confidence in the human condition, and in the possibility of any measure of reform, had been shattered by the chaos and devastation of World War I. He accused her of identifying birth control as "the sole guardian of civilisation," when he had meant it at most as "a condition of progress."[18]

This criticism may have prompted her decision to embark almost immediately on a second book. *The Pivot of Civilization* makes a more concerted effort to abandon dogmatism in favor of a dispassionate approach to the birth control question. In so doing, it reflects not only Ellis's critique, but the clear influence of Wells, whom Margaret had met in the interim, and who lent her a great deal of both intellectual and commercial credibility by writing a flattering introduction.

Able books had been written justifying birth control from the woman's point of view, Wells suggested, but this one offered the larger perspective of what birth control meant to "the public good." Indeed, *Pivot* presents a Wellsian world where a better life can be had for all without the necessity of violence and class warfare, because the great proletarian masses achieve self-direction and self-control by limiting their fertility voluntarily. On the grounds that labor servitude springs from numbers, Margaret characterized her ideas as an extension of the principles of trade unionists, who were seeking to limit the number of workers in any given industry. Marxism is too "flattering" a doctrine, she wrote, because "it teaches the laborer that all the fault is with someone else, that he is the victim of circumstances, and not even a partner in the creation of his own and his children's misery."

Still searching for a catechism, whatever her disillusion with Marxist orthodoxy—whatever her lip service to a new intellectual rigor—she argued once more for the fundamental relationship of sex and reproduction to the economic organization of society. Birth control would not simply promise fewer children and the potential of a higher standard of living. It was, in her newest phrase, an "entering wedge" for educating humanity in matters of long-term health and hygiene, which would totally transform their lives.[19]

Most important, Margaret attempted to further refine her argument for the essential compatibility of a progressive vision embracing both social reform and eugenics. Again paraphrasing Ellis, she took issue with conventional opposition to contraception on the part of conservatives worried about the reproduction of the "fitter" classes. There would be no "cradle-competition" between the haves and the have-nots, she insisted, because all women, rich and poor alike, would voluntarily limit their childbearing when presented with the option to do so. The one exception—the one population for whom enforced contraception might be necessary—were the physically or mentally incompetent, who could not themselves understand the benefits of smaller families. She declared her support for "negative" eugenics, or the weeding out of this "unfit" population, though she disdained the idea of promoting fertility, or "positive" eugenics.

The woman whose own autobiography so tellingly advertises the births of her ten siblings "without a blotch or a blemish" thus refused to consider that the handicapped may also be worthy, that the rights of the individual, in any event, must reign supreme in a truly democratic society. Nor did she question the reliability and objectivity of standardized methods of determining mental capacity, which were then just becoming much the rage. She was, of course, not alone in these oversights, nor in her willingness to sacrifice the individual rights of the most defenseless to what was being widely touted as the greater social good. Eugenics, for the moment, remained popular with a wide range of progressive thinkers who simply failed to anticipate that the enforcement of hereditarian reforms was likely to foster the very discrimination by ethnicity, race, and class that they denounced and worked elsewhere to combat. Like Ellis, Margaret was intent that biology be incorporated into social reform as a theoretical matter, but never really came to terms with how to do so in practice.

In *The Pivot of Civilization* she condemned the class bias of many eugenic writings and claimed that beyond "gross" examples of mental deficiency, there is no way of deciding the question of fitness in a democratic society. She maintained instead that birth control is where a true eugenic approach to social change must begin—that only controlled fertility can bring about the education and economic opportunity for women through which responsible motherhood is achieved. The initiative for individual and racial regeneration must "come from within. . . ." she wrote; "it must be autonomous, self-directive, and not imposed from without." She argued that the great majority of women, once given the opportunity to control their fertility, would willingly accept the responsibility to do so—that the fecundity of the uneducated and impoverished most often resulted from a lack of access to reliable contraception, not from poor motivation or self-control. And she maintained this conviction throughout her life.

Indeed, her idealism may help explain why she so blithely invited the support of powerful eugenicists, whose underlying assumptions were a good deal more offensive than her own. It is also important to remember that eugenicism remained, for the moment, still a well-established intellectual enterprise and actually gave birth control a patina of respectability. It also helped diffuse the widespread sensitivity among scientists to the more directly sexual dimension of Margaret's message. Beyond this expedience, she also seemed comfortable with the premise that the application of "intelligent guidance over reproduction" must be substituted for "the blind play of instinct," as she herself wrote. The fierceness of her attachment to the superiority of a sexual ethic governed by science, rather than by ignorance and fear, blinded her to troubling questions about the rights of the individual to reject the behavior she prescribed.[20]

As always, she was driven by the conviction that women bear the unfair burden of social laws and customs, which enforced childbearing on moral grounds. *The Pivot of Civilization* concludes with an eloquent plea for a new morality expressing the powers and responsibilities of women, not only in refusing to bring unwanted children into the world but in refusing to remain "passive instruments of sensual self-gratification on the part of men. . . . In increasing and elevating her love demands, woman must elevate sex into another sphere, whereby it may subserve and enhance the possibility of individual and human expression," Margaret wrote. "Man will gain in this no less than woman."[21]

The Pivot of Civilization embodies more a change of emphasis than of message, an effort to move birth control toward the political center with respect to both class and gender politics. Beyond Ellis and Wells, responsibility for its somewhat more even tone may have been due to Robert Parker, an editor and occasional critic at magazines like *The Literary Digest* and *Theatre Arts,* who became Ethel Higgins's live-in companion, and Margaret's longtime ghost writer. Beginning with *Pivot,* Margaret drafted ideas for books, articles, and some speeches, and Parker then polished them up for publication.

Ellis privately called the new book her "best and most mature work." Wells was publicly enthusiastic but protected himself in his introduction with the caveat that if not fully justified in calling birth control "the pivot or cornerstone of progressive society," Margaret correctly understood that it had become a test issue between two wholly distinct interpretations of the world—"of what is good in life and conduct." Where a person stood on the birth control controversy, he said, could tell you more about that person's general intellectual bent than just about anything else.

Independent critics remained more skeptical. Some doubted Margaret's optimism about the motivation of even the educable population to use birth control and effectively improve their lives. They worried about how fitness for marriage and responsible parenthood would be decided. Others condemned her refusal to consider the likelihood of continued inequality of opportunity and of resource allocation, even in a more scientifically disciplined society where birthrates had been brought under control. But, in fact, most reviewers emphasized the moral implications of the birth control issue over its political or eugenic dimension. *The New Republic* paired its Sanger review with coverage of a new book of essays on birth control by a conservative physician who argued that contraception contravened the true nature of women and was, in fact, causing them decay of a serious consequence—from fibroid tumors and sterility to rampant immorality and neurosis! As Wells himself had written, the issue was weighted down by symbolism. Even if divorced from the stigma of economic radicalism, it remained locked in larger, postwar cultural conflicts that aligned traditionalism against modernism—social orthodoxy against freedom and experimentation—and, in some cases, men against women. No matter how broadly Margaret framed her arguments, birth control served as a symbol of the social consequences of allowing women greater sexual opportunity.

"Mrs. Sanger, like a true propagandist, claims too much for birth control," wrote *The New Republic*'s reviewer, the psychologist and feminist Leta Hollingworth. "Education for birth control will not cure every ill from which we suffer in the body politic." Still, Hollingworth acknowledged that Sanger gave dignity to what had for too long been a private issue. "She proclaims aloud what women have been taught they must smother to whispers." That on its own was a credible achievement, or, as another supporter put it, "yesterday's criminal" has become "today's heroine."

Margaret's two books made effective propaganda and together sold 567,000 copies between 1920 and 1926. She earned respectable amounts of money for the first time in her life, but more than anything else, she accomplished her desire to reshape the objectives of the birth control movement for a mainstream American audience. Whatever their deficiencies, the intellectual foundations and political principles on which she built the modern birth control movement took shape in these books. She would organize women to advance themselves in the best interests of society. She would cast her lot against the backward forces of reaction in favor of the liberating potential of medicine and science. As she had redefined herself and the personal relationships in her life, so she would help shape a new woman for a new world.[22]

But first there were personal hurdles to overcome. Margaret had to confront the overwhelming obstacle of declining health and spirits. New X rays uncovered yet another spot of tuberculosis in her neck, and her doctors were again insisting that she rest. She was physically exhausted, temperamentally erratic, and suddenly fearing the worst possible outcomes, her despair intensified by personal loneliness in New York and by her recollection that her beloved Lorenzo Portet had finally succumbed to the disease when it spread to his throat.

During the summer of 1921, she reembarked for England with the ostensible goal of securing prominent supporters and speakers for a birth control conference scheduled for New York in the fall. She also welcomed the opportunity to recuperate in the comforting embrace of the Wantley circle, and to spend at least several weeks at a sanitarium in Switzerland, where she worked in seclusion on early drafts of *The Pivot of Civilization*. She then traveled on to Amsterdam to participate in a meeting being held there on birth control methods.

Still quite sick when she made her way back to London in September, she consented to see a physician whom Havelock Ellis recommended.

By Margaret's account, this doctor discovered a pocket of tubercular contamination that had lodged beneath her tonsils. It was the slow but steady draining of this infection into her sinus passages that had weakened her for so many years. He immediately put her in a local hospital, and surgical excision of the infected tissue quite remarkably cured her after twenty-one years of suffering from the persistence of a dreaded disease. She returned to New York and the conference that would launch the American Birth Control League, inspired by restored energy and health to new heights of ambition and resolve.[23]

CHAPTER TEN

The Conditions of Reform

The First American Birth Control Conference convened at the Plaza Hotel in New York City in November of 1921, heralding Margaret's bid for bourgeois approbation. An assortment of prominent social scientists, physicians, and reformers participated beside the former suffragists and society women who had long rallied to her support. Even a handful of her old Socialist sympathizers attended, though none of their names was included on an official list of sponsors, which instead featured such international luminaries as the accomplished member of the British Parliament, Winston Churchill, and the distinguished American novelist, Theodore Dreiser. Margaret invited members of the American Public Health Association, which was meeting concurrently in New York. She also scoured the list of participants in the Washington Naval Disarmament Conference for potential supporters and sent an official communiqué to the international delegates assembled there, who, with the possible exception of Wells, were more specifically concerned with limiting the number of warships in the Pacific Ocean than with her abstract pronouncements on the relationship of population and peace. Prepared with the assistance of the staff still publishing the *Birth Control Review*, her promotional literature linked "reckless procreation" to nothing less than the problems of worldwide unemployment, poverty, criminality, disease, famine, overpopulation, emigration, competitive armament, and war. She condemned established remedies, such as charity and legislation, as "paternalistic and superficial" and called for new organizational approaches and scientific solutions to these problems.[1]

The conference reestablished Margaret as the country's preeminent spokeswoman for birth control. During the many months she had spent abroad, substantial organizational gains had been made by her rival, Mary Ware Dennett, who had changed the focus of her legislative initiatives from the states to the federal government. Dennett achieved an undeniable breakthrough when the New York State Federation of Women's Clubs endorsed birth control after a contentious floor fight at its convention in October of 1920. Nationally, the General Federation was the largest organization of American women to emerge in the aftermath of the suffrage effort. Until mid-decade, when dissension split its ranks and politics was shelved from its agenda, it served as a bellwether among women on significant public issues.

Other groups that grew out of suffrage, however, such as the National Woman's Party or the League of Women Voters, had not yet consented to study or debate the birth control issue. Nor had Dennett met with any success on Capitol Hill. More than half the members of Congress at the time had two children or fewer, and few had more than three, yet they were still reluctant to confront birth control as a public policy or public health issue. Perhaps they needed no better deterrent than the political ordeal Pres. Warren Gamaliel Harding endured. As a member of the Senate's Public Health Committee in 1920, the Presidential aspirant had told Dennett in writing of his inclination to support a birth control bill, but when this commitment was made public in the campaign later that year, he was hounded by the Democrats and withdrew it. Harding, whose reputation as a ladies man was well known, may have been particularly sensitive to any association with a sexual subject, but even politicians of more pristine reputation remained timid.[2]

Skeptical of Dennett's strategy and riding the not inconsequential success of *Woman and the New Race*, Margaret immediately decided to reinvigorate the alternative organizational and lobbying strategy she had long espoused—to establish a network of birth control clinics on the medical model established in Holland. Six hundred people attended a 1920 luncheon in her honor, and they cheered her proposal to pursue state legislation. This legislation, in place of outright repeal, would codify the judicial ruling she had won through the appeal of her Brownsville clinic case, affirmatively license physicians to prescribe contraception, and ostensibly assure their willingness to serve in her proposed facilities.

She then put Juliet Rublee to work on her impeccable personal contacts among clubwomen and other potential supporters of a birth control organization Margaret might unilaterally control. For more than a year, Rublee reached out to a large personal network, including many of the prominent officials of women's organizations and also physicians, academics, journalists, and reformers, such as the settlement house leader Lillian Wald. On the legislative front, Rublee established contact with Belle Moskowitz, the Albany political operative who was a principal adviser to New York State Governor Al Smith, though no evidence survives of what transpired at their meeting. Efforts to find a sponsor for a New York bill failed, as did subsequent attempts in neighboring New Jersey and Connecticut. The Connecticut effort, however, produced an important alliance with local birth control activist Katharine Houghton Hepburn, mother of the soon-to-be-famous actress.

In 1921, Margaret also sent out a mailing to 31,000 individuals, most of them women, whose names she had put together over the years. She included a contribution card and a questionnaire on birth control practices. The reply rate was a respectable 18 percent, with more than 5,000 individuals writing back. Many simply requested further information, but some made small contributions, and 1,250 women took the time to describe their own birth control practices in detail. The majority said they were motivated to use birth control by considerations of economics, personal preference, health, or a combination of all three, and that they relied either on condoms or pessaries. The sample obviously had no statistical validity, but Margaret pointed to the sober and intelligent responses as evidence that women wanted the aura of mystery and immorality lifted from public discussion of birth control—that they wanted it out in the open.[3]

When all of these efforts culminated in an actual agenda and program, a new harmony of purpose and spirit prevailed. Only the participation of several conservative eugenicists provoked controversy and augured future problems. Antoinette Konikow, a Boston physician and Socialist who had years earlier broken with Margaret over the Blossom incident, objected testily to their presence and reminded the audience that she represented working class mothers—

"people that are often considered to be not fit." Even stronger resistance was raised when an equivocally phrased resolution was adopted advocating "a decrease in the world birth rate in general, but, at the same time, a recognition of the necessity of reproduction by those of unusual racial value." Margaret, who had elsewhere opposed "cradle-competition," remained silent in this forum, and the motion carried.[4]

The conference had been scheduled to conclude with a mass public meeting at New York City's Town Hall on Sunday, November 13, 1921. Margaret had arranged for Harold Cox, a former member of the British Parliament, editor of the erudite *Edinburgh Review,* and an accomplished speaker, to address this convocation. Cox was to follow the inspirational Mary Shaw, a popular Broadway actress and prominent supporter of women's causes, but before he even got to speak, he was forcibly removed from the stage by a band of New York City policemen, who claimed to be acting at the behest of the redoubtable Archbishop Patrick Hayes of nearby St. Patrick's Cathedral. Margaret, remaining serene and composed, and carrying a bouquet of long-stemmed red roses, was hauled away along with him, as the assembled crowd jostled the police, shouted in protest, and then broke into a mock patriotic rendition of "My Country 'Tis of Thee." A considerable fracas ensued, and she was booked on disorderly conduct charges and then released on her own recognizance. Police reserves were called in to control the crowds of protesters and onlookers who had followed her from Town Hall to the local precinct house. The confrontation received front-page newspaper coverage.

An official inquiry was undertaken by the mayor's office in response to protests brought on her behalf by a coalition of representatives of the American Civil Liberties Union and such pillars of New York's legal and financial establishment as Paul D. Cravath, Lewis Delafield, Paul M. Warburg, and Henry Morgenthau. Procedural disputes between municipal authorities and the birth controllers sustained the headlines for days on end. The investigators finally issued a report that placed sole responsibility for the raid on a local police precinct captain, who had impulsively sent in his troops. The Catholic Church was never formally linked to the event, but in the interim reporters were able to quote a spokesman for the archbishop as saying that "decent and clean-minded people would not discuss a subject such as birth control in public," and Hayes himself issued a ponderous statement in opposition to birth control, as the press kept hounding him to admit that he had, indeed, provoked the police action.[5]

According to the newspapers, when the suppressed forum was rescheduled on November 18, 1,500 people crammed into the Park Theater, and another 3,000 were turned away. This time the police provided protection and sent official stenographers to keep a record of any illicit activities. Young women from Barnard College, with fresh faces and bobbed heads, volunteered as ushers and kept order in the audience. From the podium, Harold Cox soberly challenged the prevailing religious conviction that sexuality without procreation was unnatural, immoral, and biblically enjoined. He formulated an alternative set of ethical principles for family life which, he argued, would condone family limitation, advance human health, welfare, and happiness, and also promote peace. He even cited biblical chapter and verse, quoting from *Ecclesiasticus*: "Desire not a multitude of unprofitable children, neither delight in ungodly sons. Though they multiply, rejoice not in them for one that is just is better than a thousand."

Margaret was a model of restraint, though she staked out her position in response to the appearance of an escalation of Catholic opposition to her activities. Noting that the hierarchy resolutely opposed women's suffrage, as well as birth control, she argued that church doctrine, though intended to sanctify the home, succeeded only by keeping women in ignorance and fear. She demanded a higher and truer moral code grounded in scientific knowledge and guaranteeing a motherhood of "dignity and choice, not ignorance and chance." She called on physicians to support women, announced her intention to raise funds for a birth control clinic under medical supervision, and lined herself up with the forces of enlightenment in what she saw as the decade's emblematic battle between reason and faith. What she said may have troubled some of the police department agents in the audience, but no one could reasonably call her conduct either disorderly or obscene.[6]

The extensive national press attention taught her a valuable lesson. By remaining calm and poised in the face of what was undeniably an abrogation of her rights, she regained the offensive against her opponents. Virtually every major newspaper in New York and several national magazines condemned the Town Hall raid. By surrounding herself with the socially powerful, she was also able to deflect attempts to tar her with her past radical affiliations. During hearings in December, *The New York Times* headlined an investigator's inquiry into "Leader's Birth Control Past," but the subsequent arrest of Juliet Rublee, when she tried to protest on Margaret's behalf during the proceedings, shifted the emphasis of the coverage and aroused another sustained round of public indignation. Once again efforts to muzzle the birth control propagandists produced exactly the opposite effect. This time, however, the papers promoted a movement that enjoyed the respect, not only of radicals or feminists, but of many of the most prominent men in New York's intellectual, professional, and business communities. Continued political and religious persecution only served to push Margaret more firmly into their orbit.[7]

Margaret's success as an activist and organizer in the 1920s would rest on her capacity to alternatively inspire and provoke the three constituencies that accounted for all the attention given to the First American Birth Control Conference—feminists, eugenicists and Catholics. She motivated a new generation of feminists, cajoled eugenicists, and then relied on the support of both groups, first, to escape her own past and, second, to neutralize increasingly virulent attacks mounted against her by religious opponents.

First, and most important to her, was the large population of women oriented to activism and looking for new challenges in the wake of the women's suffrage victory. Suffrage leaders had put forth an instrumental rationale for allowing women to vote, and success presented both leadership and rank and file with the complicated task of choosing a political strategy that would maximize the effect of their participation as franchised members of the body politic. By 1921, dissension surfaced within the National Woman's Party over the question of a constitutional amendment guaranteeing women equal rights. With this as its focus, the party removed itself altogether from the birth control debate, causing Margaret considerable consternation when she spoke before its national convention. The vast majority of former suffrage activists and more broadly focused feminists, however, opposed an equal rights strategy on the grounds that it would undermine long-term gains for women and children, which had been achieved through the promulgation of protective labor legislation and other progressive, social welfare initiatives. This fragmentation of interests and efforts meant that women did not exert a collective influence on the politics of the new decade, but instead tended to express and to vote their differences, just like men.

Yet, the novelty of their presence as voters and the effectiveness of their voluntarism did assure that issues of particular interest to women achieved prominence. Largely through their efforts, for example, the historic Sheppard-Towner Act was adopted by Congress that year, for the first time providing federal funding for state-administered maternal and infant care clinics. Although she made no attempt to discredit this legislation, Margaret did express misgivings about the wisdom of a welfare program designed to underwrite childbirth, but not to discourage it. The Sheppard-Towner clinics offered no contraceptive service but did provide a successful example of the kind of health network for women she wanted to build. They were a product of the new social feminist tradition in which she now hoped to locate birth control.[8]

If the political prerequisites for a birth control organization were in place, despite the continued reservations of some feminist leaders, so too were the economic conditions for a persuasive argument that women should be offered reliable and cost-effective contraception. Between 1870 and 1930 the number of employed American women increased by tenfold, bringing the total to over 10 million, or one fourth of the eligible female population. And increasingly higher percentages were older, married, and American born. As child labor laws prohibited the employment of young girls, and as immigration laws restricted the entry of foreigners, the numbers of single and foreign women in the work force diminished. By 1930, more than a quarter of the female work force were married, almost three fourths were native born, and studies showed that more than 90 percent of women workers contributed all or part of their incomes to the maintenance of families. No longer was it possible to sustain the traditional image of working women as immigrants gaining an economic foothold, as young girls biding time until they found husbands, or as spinsters who had never found them at all. And if married women were working in greater numbers than ever before, then rationalization and control of their fertility was paramount.

More important, perhaps, women's overall visibility as workers increased, even while the vast majority remained at home or were segregated in low-paying, entry-level jobs, such as personal and domestic services. As the nation's consumer and service economy developed, the numbers of women in clerical and service positions (store clerks, office workers, and telephone operators, for example) surpassed those in manufacturing. With more and more people living in cities, fewer women were left in inconspicuous, family-based agricultural pursuits. At the same time, though professional opportunities for women tended to be limited to teaching and nursing, the few intrepid pioneers who managed to enter the closed sanctums of business, law, medicine, and government achieved great notoriety. It was widely believed that their opportunities were increasing, even if aggregate statistics did not always bear out this impression.

Whatever the reality, the very perception of change itself provoked another round of vigorous public debate over the fertility of American women, and over the possibilities and practicalities of combining child rearing and career. In circles of progressive, educated women there was no issue more prominent. Even such an established feminist as Charlotte Perkins Gilman broadened her focus to embrace a concern about reconciling marriage and family with work. Margaret herself, though never shy on the subject, responded with special vehemence when queried by a reporter. Branding full-time domesticity "drab and monotonous," she claimed that work often disciplines a woman to appreciate her home more. Acknowledging that children need their mothers a great deal, she nonetheless argued that "young children are by nature selfish, and they will let you indulge them as much as you please." "It isn't good for them though," she concluded on a harsh, if personally revealing note. "As a matter of fact, they should be taught by example that a mother is not here merely to be their attendant, but that she is a superior human being, a personage as well. They have much more respect for her then."[9]

Margaret's message was intended to be prowoman, not antifamily, with emphasis on the new style of feminism she espoused, which accommodated and indeed encouraged sex and marriage. Once again, she advertised birth control as bridging the discontinuities of a feminist agenda that offered women a public role at the expense of their private lives. Only with universal availability of contraception could women hope to realize their full potential.

However halting and partial it may have been, the economic and political empowerment of married women during the 1920s forced yet another redefinition of their role within the home. Behavioral psychologists suddenly scorned Freud's developmental imperatives as overly sentimental and instead echoed John Watson's recommendation that women avoid their children's excessive reliance on mother love. At the same time, purveyors of the consumer frenzy driving the nation's economy forward reshaped the housewife into a domestic professional, freed by technology from the responsibility and drudgery that had bound her mother to the hearth. A burgeoning industry in advertising and public relations for electrical gadgets, packaged foods, storebought clothes, and other new commodities of the era encouraged women to be efficient managers of household goods and services. In high schools, colleges, and universities, courses in home economics were consciously designed to offer a reconstituted vision of marriage and family life, one that promoted time and labor-saving devices and emphasized the importance to women of the quality of their relationships in the family, not just of their material obligations and responsibilities as wives and mothers.

This vision of modern womanhood implicitly assumed the voluntary control of childbearing. It also consciously encouraged a more active sexual role for women on the practical grounds that the liberated homemaker and wife had time available for more romance in her life. Once considered scandalous, the ideal of mutuality in the sexual relations of husbands and wives found a large public audience in the 1920s. The most popular and enduring symbol of freedom for women of the decade was explicitly sexual. The youthful, eroticized flapper, her hemline dramatically and provocatively shortened, was emblazoned in national magazines and on billboards. Her figure lean and angular, her hair short and shingled like a man's, or marcelled in the new and somewhat softer style of middecade, she symbolized the assertion by women of social and sexual parity. Gone was the buxom, matronly woman common to advertisements in the past, whose very appearance assumed her primary maternal responsibility. In her place, a slender, stylish woman suddenly turned up, shopping in a department store, riding in an open roadster, or even dancing the night away at a speakeasy. This kind of woman used contraception within marriage and perhaps even outside it.[10]

With hindsight it becomes clear that not all of these developments were positive. Though present in the labor force in greater numbers than ever before, women in the 1920s did not necessarily consolidate and advance their economic power. And the decade's frenzied consumerism only escalated standards of domestic comportment, allowing housework along with affective relationships to continue to absorb female effort and time. What is more, the sexual revolution did not always leave women the equal partners of men, even as it fostered a new heterosexual intimacy. Yet as a gender consciousness and solidarity declined, the collective interests of women were left with no mobilizing agent or vehicle.

The popular journalist Dorothy Dunbar Bromley best expressed this shift in sentiment when she identified "new-style feminists" in 1928 as "intensely self-conscious" and professing "no loyalty to women *en masse*." Bored with the stridency of suffrage and the narrowly defined objectives of organized efforts on behalf of women's rights, a new generation of women who were coming of age took the struggles of their predecessors for granted. They listened to authorities like John Watson, who also claimed that militancy on women's issues betrayed poor social and psychological adjustment.

Indeed, the birth control movement provided one of the few women's causes that thrived in the 1920s, because it wed new personal and sexual interests to the larger set of public concerns that had motivated women in the past. Margaret Sanger wrote to much acclaim in *The Pivot of Civilization:*

> Women can attain freedom only by concrete, definite knowledge of themselves, a knowledge based on biology, physiology and psychology. . . . Birth control is no negative philosophy concerned solely with the number of children brought into this world. It is not merely a question of population. Primarily it is the instrument of liberation and human development.[11]

* * *

To many Americans, of course, this message was deeply disturbing. The advances of women and the new presumption that they might voluntarily control fertility became increasingly visible symbols of the rising stature of modern secular authority in matters of social and family life. *The Pivot of Civilization* also quoted Michael Higgins's old hero, the freethinking Victorian, Robert Ingersoll:

> Ignorance, poverty, and vice must stop populating the world. To accomplish this there is but one way. Science must make woman the owner, the mistress of herself. Science, the only possible savior of mankind, must put it in the power of woman to decide for herself whether she will or will not become a mother.

The specter of a pious Anne Higgins, marching compliantly to her early grave, was never far from the surface of Margaret's emotional life and professional motivation. By completing Ingersoll's mission, she would vindicate both her mother's death and her father's apostasy. As these private conflicts found constructive resolution, however, her public confrontations with the Catholic Church only grew more intense. She may no longer have had Anthony Comstock as a nemesis, and she might be trying hard to shed the taint of her prewar radicalism, but the Town Hall raid demonstrated that she now faced a still more contentious adversary. America's Catholic leaders were finally determined to discard their mantle of reticence. Birth control would become a vehicle for the church's institutional organization and political empowerment in this country.[12]

From prison in 1917, Margaret had written her sister Ethel and blamed the Catholic Diocese in Brooklyn for seeing that they were both punished. The letter quoted a local church newspaper with evident sarcasm. The judges, Margaret claimed, had been directed by the priests to give those "lovely intellectual women a serious dose of jail." This view would harden subsequently in response to more open and rigorous Catholic opposition. The dispute over birth control, in Margaret's mind, was first and foremost a battle for the allegiance of women. She came to believe that orthodox Catholic doctrine could only hope to survive on the blind faith of its parishioners—so many of them women in the home. The secular education and political enfranchisement of women, not to speak of their sexual emancipation, threatened to dilute the absolute authority over family life that the church tried to impose primarily through women.

During the war and immediately thereafter, intervention by politically powerful dioceses had forced the cancellation of public birth control activities on several occasions, or their removal to private homes or facilities. These local skirmishes then gave way to a national organizing strategy. American Catholics, seizing the offensive with respect to official church participation in the war effort, had established the National Catholic War Council at a convention of delegates from sixty-eight local dioceses in Washington in 1917. The agenda of the new organization was divided among teams of priests and laymen operating at the direction of an administrative committee of bishops, and the procedure worked so well that it was institutionalized after the war through the founding of the National Catholic Welfare Conference. This national body emerged over the combined protest of several bishops in this country, who resented the invasion of the autonomous jurisdiction they were accustomed to exercising in their own dioceses, and of some officials in Rome, who were wary of ceding authority to what they feared might be the precursor of a "national" church in the United States, where an apparent indulgence of modernist thinking in ecclesiastical theory and practice was already considered a problem. By the early 1920s, however, most of this internal dissent had been overcome with the assurance that the new body would assume a purely "advisory" role in matters of social and canonical dispute, and with the recognition of its immense public relations value. At the same time, local Catholic officials were empowered by the formation of a Catholic Charities appeal run by the bishops. In New York, the formidable Archbishop Hayes would raise nearly $1 million a year between 1920 and 1925, and spend at least some of this income to fight birth control in his own archdiocese.[13]

By 1920, the National Catholic Welfare Conference had also organized a social action department in Washington under the direction of an enterprising theologian by the name of Father John A. Ryan, whose mission was to articulate church doctrine on questions of social life and public policy in order to bring influence to bear, not only among Catholics, but outside the church as well. To this end, Ryan formulated an official Catholic position in opposition to women's suffrage, but he would become even more outspoken and better organized on the birth control issue.

Father Ryan had been building arguments against contraception for a long time. Echoing sentiments then being expressed in Europe, he had first warned against church complacency on the issue in the 1907 edition of the *Catholic Encyclopedia*. In that essay, Ryan identified Neo-Malthusianism as "intrinsically immoral" in its "perversion of natural faculties and functions," but he reserved his harshest words for the social and economic consequences of small families, claiming that they "foster a degree of egotism and enervating self-indulgence, which in turn diminishes the incentive to labor and reduces industrial production." The rising standard of living contemplated by Malthusians, Ryan wrote, leads not to "more genuine culture or lofty morals, but [to] more abundant physical enjoyments and a more refined materialism." Curiously enough, Ryan mentioned "natural faculties," but he cited no canonical precedent. His were essentially social, not moral, points of attack, no different from those of Teddy Roosevelt on the one hand or of orthodox Marxists on the other.

Ryan next wrote on the subject in 1916, in the *Ecclesiastical Review*, published by the Catholic University of America, where he encouraged more vocal opposition to birth control using the rationale that, only if reminded of the "mortal sin" of the practice, could good Catholics be expected to desist. He covered the same social arguments, again never explaining the precise doctrinal grounds of his opposition. It took three more years for the church to respond officially. In 1919, for the first time ever in this country, a joint pastoral letter was issued in the name of all American bishops expressly prohibiting artificial means of family limitation. Echoing Ryan, the bishops linked the practice to selfish individualism and demanded acceptance of the responsibility of bringing children into the world, "who may prove either a blessing or a curse to society at large." Children, the bishops reminded the faithful, are "the Lord's inheritance."

The following year, writing expressly in response to the endorsement of birth control by the New York State Federation of Women's Clubs, Ryan confronted the problem with intensified zeal. He identified three "evil results" of contraception: First, the "degradation of the marital relation itself since the husband and wife who indulge in this practice . . . cannot help coming to regard each other to a great extent as mutual instruments of sensual gratification, rather than cooperation with the Creator in bringing children into the world"; second, the weakening of "self-control and the capacity for self-denial" and the increasing of "love of ease and luxury," as evidenced by the fact that small families were most evident among the well-to-do; third, the inevitability of population decline. In his dire demographic prognosis, Ryan seized on eugenic arguments even while professing the church's love of all humanity.

Ryan's objective was to formulate a rational and defensible posture for the church, but he was not yet in a position to control the hysterical bombast from other official quarters. In 1922, the editors of the *Catholic Encyclopedia Supplement* baldly charged that women who use contraception accept "the conditions of a prostitute for those of married life." They linked the "unnatural and immoral principles" of the birth control movement to such "grave physical and moral disorders" as cancer, neurasthenia, sterility, infidelity, and divorce. Several years later, Archbishop Hayes, who was soon to be named a Cardinal, addressed the subject in self-conscious prose in his 1925 Catholic Charities appeal. He wrote:

> Latterly, into the public eye, has been thrust an open propaganda that shocks the moral sense of every true follower of Christ. Christian sentiment against it has found expression in the law of the land forbidding the dissemination of the knowledge of its practice. Yet, the downright perversion of human cooperation with the Creator in the propagation of the human family, is openly advocated and defended. It is not what the God of nature and grace, in His Divine wisdom, ordained marriage to be; but the lustful indulgence of man and woman. . . . Religion shudders at the wild orgy of atheism and immorality the situation forebodes.

A pamphlet issued by another official of the National Catholic Welfare Conference then condemned birth control because it "isolates sex passion from the normal controls and correctives and counterchecks placed upon it by nature and the God of nature and leaves it shorn and naked in all its degraded grossness and unloveliness. It reaps the pleasure of sex while evading the normally consequent sacrifices and responsibilities." The author cited authoritative testimony from such far-flung witnesses as Saint Augustine—whom he quoted as having said that contraception makes a "prostitute out of the wife and an adulterer out of the husband"—to Bernard Shaw, who called it "mutual masturbation." To this vitriol, *The Catholic Light*, a weekly published by the diocese of Scranton, Pennsylvania, added a scurrilous, ad hominem attack on Margaret and her "pals" who were allegedly "profiting" from birth control business.[14]

Margaret responded in kind. In a 1920 letter challenging a representative of the National Catholic Welfare Conference to debate, she accused the church of aligning itself "on the side of ignorance against knowledge, of darkness against light." Articles in the *Birth Control Review* took even cheaper shots. One piece berated "bachelor" priests for daring to pose as moral censors of marriage and also ridiculed the Church of Rome for associating Malthusian doctrine with a love of ease and luxury, "considering the state in which it is, itself, carried on." A direct reprint of a *New Republic* editorial of December 28, 1921, labeled the apparent influence of Archbishop Hayes over New York's police as "the last resort of authoritarianism" and "socially insane." In private, Margaret revealed an intensifying prejudice: "The R.C.'s are certainly taking their stand against this subject & me," she wrote Juliet Rublee. "Their attacks against 'the Sanger woman' are libels, but no time have me [sic] to bother about libels. Dearest I fear with you . . . but it may serve to awaken the Protestant element, in time to save the country later on."[15]

By decade's end, the Vatican would deliberately codify its own teachings on birth control, in the hope of elevating this level of discourse. Church officials would reassemble the intricate, scholarly edifice of Augustinian doctrine on natural law that had bolstered arguments against the practice many years earlier, but since then, scarcely been mentioned. But coming as it did, after fifteen years of more or less scurrilous propaganda on both sides of the issue, this recourse to natural law doctrine enjoyed only partial credibility. Margaret, for her part, could never accept Rome's intransigence on contraception as anything more than a last line of defense against the steady erosion of ecclesiastical authority in matters of family life and social behavior. Viewing birth control as a threat to the power of the church and its prelates, and not to their deepest moral principles, she let herself believe too quickly that Catholic opposition to contraception would in time be subject to compromise.[16]

In the early days before World War I, only such exceptionally outspoken religious figures as the Unitarian minister John Haynes Holmes of New York, or the Reform Jewish leader Rabbi Stephen

Wise, had dared to support birth control. But the situation was changing. In 1920, Margaret heard from the principal spokesman of the Anglican Church in London, the Very Reverend William R. Inge, Dean of St. Paul's. Inge had read *Woman and the New Race* and wrote Margaret how much he admired her courage and her conviction. He could not yet speak out in public, he explained, because of the regrettable use of contraception by some unmarried persons. Within a year, however, he went one step further and supported Neo-Malthusianism, expressing his concern about the social dangers of unchecked population growth. Though he stopped short of expressly endorsing contraception, this was a historic first step toward what would become an official reform of Anglican doctrine later in the decade. Through the 1920s, Margaret anticipated—incorrectly—that Inge's transformation was reason to assume the inevitability of doctrinal change elsewhere as well.[17]

Meanwhile, Margaret self-consciously sought the support of a growing community of secular thinkers who were suddenly enjoying new stature. Yet, many of these professionals, scientists, and academics had scarcely more inherent sympathy for her cause than the most determinedly conservative of clerics. They rejected contraception on the grounds that its use only discouraged the reproduction of people like themselves, who comprised the country's productive, educated, and upwardly mobile classes, while not reaching those individuals most in need. Like their progressive forebears, they were also visibly anxious about the broadening of public roles for women, and they almost always identified themselves as eugenicists.

"Such activity is distinctly antisocial; for it enables selfish people to escape their proper responsibilities, ultimately to their own detriment and certainly to the injury of the state," the prominent statistician and New York social welfare activist, Louis Dublin, told an audience of birth control sympathizers in 1925. Calling himself a progressive, Dublin insisted that economic intervention, and not birth control, would alone help the poor. "You do not solve the worker's problems by encouraging him to lose his greatest and noblest possession, his children," he added. This argument resonated with many Socialists and trade unionists in the audience, who at best saw birth control as a second or third line of defense in their struggle for the redistribution of economic opportunity, and who also shied away from it in fear of antagonizing Catholic workers they hoped to organize. Another speaker at the conference carried the point further by insisting that unfit children were being born to women who continued to work during their pregnancies.

Indeed, as overall birthrates continued to drop during the 1920s, qualitative theories of racial improvement again gained widespread public acceptance. As had happened briefly before World War I, eugenics became a popular craze in this country—promoted in newspapers and magazines as a kind of secular religion. A national advocacy organization, the American Eugenics Society, was founded in 1923 to foster broader public understanding of eugenic principles through such public relations gimmickry as sermon contests in churches and synagogues and "fitter family" contests at state fairs and other public gatherings. The great majority of American colleges and universities introduced formal courses in the subject, and sociologists who embraced it took on what one historian has called a "priestly role." Even a man as far to the left as Norman Thomas, then just beginning his long public career, had no qualms about adding his voice to the chorus of concern over the "alarming high birthrate of definitely inferior stock."[18]

Remarkably enough, this enthusiasm for eugenics endured, even as the putative science began to provide the intellectual rationale for socially conservative ends—for what became an unmitigated defense of property, privilege, and race baiting in its most conventional sense. By 1924, for example, an Immigration Act closed America's doors to new waves of foreigners from eastern and southern Europe and from Asia. The motivation behind the legislation was primarily economic. The country could no longer afford to assimilate hordes of unskilled workers, but the argument was framed in racial terms. In favoring white, northern Europeans, immigration restriction promoted a popular view that one nationality or stock can be distinguished from another on the basis of hereditary characteristics. Many supporters of eugenics, including Margaret, objected to this racial stereotyping, claiming that intelligence and other inherited traits vary by individual, not by group. But these distinctions grew more and more difficult to enforce.

What is more, nearly universal agreement was reached during the 1920s on the propriety of passing compulsory sterilization statutes to govern the behavior of individuals carrying deficiencies believed to be inherited, such as mental retardation, insanity, or uncontrollable epilepsy. This movement reached its zenith with the enactment of such laws in thirty states. Virginia's statute, authorizing the involuntary sterilization of inmates in state institutions, was, in fact, upheld by the United States Supreme Court in 1927, in the matter of *Buck v. Bell*. The majority opinion in this notorious case was written by

Justice Oliver Wendell Holmes, Jr., with Louis Brandeis and all but one other member of the court, voting in favor. (The lone dissent was from a Catholic, ostensibly opposed on moral grounds, though he presented no written comment.) Holmes and Brandeis had built their judicial reputations as liberals and proponents of free speech, but both were willing in this instance to sacrifice the rights of individuals who "sap the strength of the state," as Holmes put it. Arguing that collective social interests should take precedence in these circumstances, Holmes wrote without equivocation, "Three generations of imbeciles are enough."

By 1930, the state of California had sterilized 7,500 of its institutionalized dependents. Elsewhere enforcement was less zealous, if no less troubling, with 5,000 procedures accounted for throughout the rest of the country. The laws may also have acted, however, as an incentive for quiet coercion, and the extent to which individuals in populations at risk were pressured into agreeing to sterilization can never be fully determined.

Without any apparent concern for the potential of abuse, Margaret supported these initiatives and argued for the compatibility of this kind of eugenics and birth control. She deliberately courted the power of eugenically inclined academics and scientists to blunt the attacks of religious conservatives against her. Her principal intent remained, as it had been earlier, to redress economic and gender inequality and to promote healthier, happier families. Yet, there is no denying that she allowed herself to become caught up in the eugenic zeal of the day and occasionally used language open to far less laudable interpretations. At one point, for example, before an audience of eugenicists, she bemoaned the burden of the "unfit" on the productive members of the community and pledged to organize the "thinking population of this country" around the issue of birth control as a deterrent to poverty and human waste. She then committed birth control to the creation of "a race of thoroughbreds," having taken the phrase from an article in the popular *Literary Digest*. It had actually been written by a progressive physician, arguing for state endowment of maternal and infant care clinics, but it also carried other implications. A second lapse from her usual distinction between individual and racial definitions of eugenic fitness occurred in 1925 when, as a deliberate taunt to the Catholic Church, she suggested that the United States liberalize its immigration policies for Italian citizens, only if their government agreed to promote birth control.[19]

Yet even as Margaret strained to make an argument for contraception on biological grounds, the most prominent leaders of the eugenics movement—men such as Charles Davenport, head of the richly funded and highly profiled eugenic research laboratory at Cold Spring Harbor, New York—remained vocal opponents of birth control and actually feared that their own scientific credibility would be compromised by association with it. The California eugenicist and physician Paul Popenoe disparaged birth control in a private letter, referring to Margaret and her supporters as "a lot of sob sisters, grandstand players and anarchists." However extreme some of her pronouncements may seem by contemporary standards, Margaret continued to be identified popularly as a proponent of women and of a deep sympathy and compassion toward the overburdened poor. Only a handful of avowed eugenicists, such as the Johns Hopkins psychiatrist Adolf Meyer, the Harvard sociologist E. M. East, and the president of the University of Michigan, Clarence C. Little, were ever willing to associate with her publicly.

E. A. Ross of the University of Wisconsin, author of a popular diatribe against the unchecked reproduction of undesirables called *Standing Room Only*, admitted privately to Juliet Rublee in 1928 that some scientists were beginning to appreciate Margaret's work more and more, but he warned that posterity would judge her favorably only if she could demonstrate conclusively that providing clinical birth control services to women in need would save the world "from hordes of defectives." This was obviously not her intent, and Ross's begrudging acceptance of the birth control program proved a hollow victory.

By the end of the 1920s, the reputation of eugenics had finally begun to decline. Its primitive and largely specious underpinnings in genetic science were under attack, and the rise of Fascism in Europe was calling attention to its most perverse implications. In 1928, the American Birth Control League rejected a proposal to join forces with the American Eugenics Society. Still, however tenuous the association, Margaret's relationship with eugenicism has since provided ammunition for opponents to her left and to her right politically, who have argued that contraception is nothing more than an instrument of social control. Her intense desire to have the support of the major secular thinkers of her day may have cost her far more than it was worth.[20]

Margaret's growing prominence through the 1920s thus by no means conferred respectability in all quarters. The proverbial lists compiled each year of the nation's most admired women did not include her name beside those of social reformers or suffragists whose reputations were far less controversial—women such as Jane Addams, Alice Paul, or Carrie Chapman Catt. Only a more adventuresome opinion maker, such as the popular columnist and birth control sympathizer Heywood Broun, dared to identify her in his personal accountings of the most glamorous and important Americans of 1922. Three years later, Broun's wife, the journalist Ruth Hale, also featured her as a brave and defiant clarion of free speech and free thinking in one of the first profiles that ran in the new and fashionable *New Yorker* magazine. "She has carried her crusade for birth control through from the time when simply to mention it was to invite imprisonment . . . ," Hale wrote. "She is, by far, now and from the beginning the most effective friend that the cause of birth control has ever had. To see her, one is astounded at her youth, at her prettiness, her gentleness, her mild, soft voice."[21]

This flattering, if still somewhat flamboyant press, helped establish Margaret as a popular lecturer. Booked by agents in New York as "The International Champion of Birth Control"—or on another occasion as "the outstanding social warrior of the century"—she crisscrossed the country numerous times, addressing civic forums and women's groups and lending her support to the organization of local birth control federations. She also became a popular speaker on college campuses. In 1924, her appearance at Yale as the guest of the Divinity School was considered sufficiently newsworthy to merit coverage from *The New York Times*, yet the following year the administration at Tufts denied her the right to speak, forcing a liberal Unitarian minister in Somerville to provide his church as an alternative sponsor. Margaret cheerfully talked to a small group of adventuresome women who found their way there.

Whenever she went out on the circuit, Margaret addressed packed and enthusiastic audiences. Commercial lecturing on political and social topics was much in demand in America as an expanding economy provided the nation's growing middle class with leisure to explore new secular interests, but as yet without the competitive offerings of the talking film or the soon-to-be-universal medium of the radio. Margaret was a spirited advocate of her cause—an energetic and attractive figure who punctuated her remarks with moving human interest stories taken from the hundreds of letters she received from women every month. Her standard lecture in these days embraced a panoply of arguments for birth control—from the health, welfare, and personal rights of women and children, to the eugenic inheritance of the society, to global peace and prosperity. She typically spoke from notes, rather than a prepared text, in order to ease her nervousness in public and to allow her the flexibility to tailor her remarks to her audience. The few speeches where prepared texts or stenographic records survive have no ideological coherence but seem rather to wander among intellectual fads and fashions. In Hartford in 1923, for example, she belabored the problems posed by the feebleminded and the mentally unfit in the country, though at the same time she condemned the racial and class overtones of eugenicism. Overreaching in her effort to establish sound scientific credentials, she spewed forth a tedious litany of statistics about infant and maternal mortality, child labor and malnutrition, linking them all to overpopulation. Several months later, before a Chicago audience filled with professionals and volunteers from the fields of social work and public health, she identified birth control as an essential, preventive social service. An undated speech of the same period, by contrast, takes its theme from the country's overriding preoccupation with business. "A new generation of young American wives, a vast majority of whom have had business experience before marriage, is beginning to approach the central problem of life—that of motherhood—in a new manner," said Margaret. "In a word, these women are trying to put the business of bearing babies and rearing children on a basis of intelligent efficiency." In 1928, as part of a Pacific Forum, which included her old friend Will Durant who was touting the first volume of his best-selling history-of-civilization books, she offered her audiences a choice of topics bearing on birth control—one on world population trends, another on women's rights, and a third on domestic social welfare problems.[22]

No matter how much she had toned herself down, Margaret remained a target of repression. Her appearances in the heavily Catholic cities of Albany, Syracuse, and Boston were either canceled or interrupted in the several years following the Town Hall raid, and these incidents sustained her image as a daring and controversial figure, always slightly on the edge of respectability. Whenever she made a public appearance in New York City, police stenographers were assigned to cover her speech, no doubt with the intent of intimidating her. When a Bronx synagogue's board of trustees banned her from its premises, the rabbi resigned in public protest, and the congregation overruled the decision. In 1929, when civic authorities in Boston intervened and refused her the right to speak at Ford Hall, she dramatically stood silent, with a band of tape across her mouth, while the Harvard historian Arthur Schlesinger, Sr. rose beside her and read a brief prepared statement ending in the peroration: "As a pioneer fighting for a cause, I believe in free speech. As a propagandist, I see immense advantages in being gagged. It silences me, but it makes millions of others talk and think about the cause in which I live."

That same year, when film began to talk, and newsreels became a standard feature of the movie house, Margaret's appearance in a Fox Movietone reel aroused protest among some viewers, who thought birth control an inappropriate subject for audiences composed largely of young unmarried couples. Several of the newsreel companies capitulated to pressure brought by a Catholic voluntary association. Margaret was also kept off the airwaves until the mid-1930s, when a radio ban on discussion of the birth control controversy was lifted. Circulation-hungry newspapers, on the other hand, covered the subject with abandon, but still refused to endorse birth control outright in their editorial columns. One scion of the Gannett newspaper family admitted in a letter to Margaret that he personally supported birth control but just couldn't afford to agitate for it in his "semi-proletarian," large-circulation newspapers. He suggested the *New York Herald Tribune,* "a staunch organ of Protestant Republicanism" as a more likely ally.[23]

Despite this repression—in part, perhaps, because of it—Margaret remained a popular lecturer, even as the decade's prosperity waned. She wrote proudly to Havelock Ellis in April of 1930 that in the five prior weeks she had talked to nearly 20,000 people, as she moved east from Los Angeles, through Denver, Chicago, Madison, and Minneapolis to Oberlin, Ohio, and then back again through St. Louis and Chicago and on to Washington, D.C. On that trip, she earned a standard $250 fee per lecture appearance and spent her nights shuttling between cities on railroad sleeper cars. Subsequently she was paid as high as $500, a substantial fee for the period, which more than covered her own expenses. (By way of comparison, H. G. Wells, in 1937, also earned $500 per speech.) When Margaret's voice gave out, she replenished it with a special brand of cough drop made by an old German chemist, and she took pleasure in sharing her supply with other distinguished speakers of the day.[24]

She seemed remarkably pliant as a public figure in these years, willing to alter her image to suit the tastes—even perhaps some of the prejudices—of her audience. To a socially respectable volunteer in the New York office, in 1925, for example, she appeared "small, quiet, elegant in a stone beige coat trimmed with black persian lamb, carrying a large patent leather pocketbook . . . her titian hair was straight and swathed around her head. Wideset in a small heart-shaped face, her incredibly deep blue eyes [actually, they were hazel] met the gaze of acquaintances with the steadiest, most penetrating look one has ever seen. Her voice, calm and quiet answered questions without fuss or unnecessary elaboration. A smile of greeting to those who caught her eyes, then to her own office and desk."

This accommodating demeanor belied the far more complicated personality revealed in her journals and letters. A very different woman emerges from the private moments between the platform appearances and the organizational obligations, one who is often contemptuous of her own groveling for respectability and yearns instead for the more intense engagement of her youth. Yet without a well-defined political avenue of expression, the war in Margaret's nature between emotion and reason—between impetuosity and restraint—exhibited itself in a more subtle, and in the end a far more superficial, rebellion. She embraced wealth and privilege but continued her discreet support of radical friends and their causes. She maintained an appearance of social propriety through a second marriage, but secretly carried on passionate love affairs. Publicly, she identified herself with the increasingly rationalized world of science and medicine, but privately she maintained a fascination with the spiritual and the occult, frequently stopping between appointments to consult psychics, astrologers, and others who offered specious, but generally comforting, explanations of events and behavior she could not objectively explain.

Margaret absorbed these inherent contradictions in her life with the dry wit she took from the Irish circle of her childhood. She could be smug and self-righteous to a fault in public, but in private she was generally able to relax, to laugh at herself and at others, to appreciate human foibles and never tire of wondering at the ultimate folly of her predicament. As her days became more harried, she learned to rise early and savor her funniest observations in brief letters to scattered and often distant friends. She once wrote to Havelock Ellis from a train traveling somewhere in the Midwest, enclosing several newspaper clippings about a man with a fetish for pulling teeth. "The reporters have told me privately that they could not print all they knew about him," she confided. "But that was the way he gets his most intense sexual satisfaction. That the thought of pulling a *woman's* teeth gives him the only *erection* he ever gets, and the actual drawing out [of] the tooth brings on the ejaculation! It was a new one on me and I pass it along to you for your archives!"

It probably wasn't easy to reconcile the free spirit that traded off-color stories with reporters with the good manners and ladylike poise that made her the heroine of some opinion makers and society matrons. Yet she also accommodated to these contradictory elements of her nature. At one point, she consulted a psychic who offered an explanation of the still unresolved tensions between impulse and reason in her life through an analysis of her astrological signs. "You have originality, both in thought and action," she was told. "You have many of the masculine qualities of mind with a womanly heart that makes you self-reliant, gives executive ability, and the power to sacrifice yourself for others. . . . While you are practical, there is much of the dreamer inherent in your birth."[25]

CHAPTER ELEVEN

Organizing for Birth Control

If the dreamer in Margaret survived through the 1920s, it was hidden from all but an intimate few. What had been an outsider's begrudging accommodation to the role of elites in accomplishing change became an insider's willful determination to manipulate the system on her own terms.

In 1922, after considerable lobbying of dubious New York State officials, Margaret incorporated the American Birth Control League in accordance with the laws governing not-for-profit charitable institutions and set out an ambitious and far-reaching declaration of intentions that included public education, legislative reform, medical research in contraception, and the actual provision of services. The league was to be a national voluntary organization headquartered in New York. It would spawn affiliates at the state and local level throughout the country, while also acting as a vehicle for Margaret's leadership aspirations on an international scale.

To manage the new enterprise, she simply expanded the board of directors and staff that she already had in place to publish the *Birth Control Review*. She took charge with the assistance of her personally loyal, if not always professionally seasoned, entourage of women, some comfortably middle-class, and others who were very well-to-do, including Juliet Rublee as vice president of the board, Frances Ackerman, a long-standing Manhattan volunteer, as treasurer, and Anne Kennedy as a paid, full-time executive director. Margaret took no salary for herself, but lived off expense money, book and lecture fees, and eventually, most of all, the generosity of her wealthy second husband, Noah Slee.

Kennedy, a capable but somewhat eccentric and emotionally erratic woman, found her way into the birth control movement after a messy divorce. Margaret's sense of mission gave renewed meaning to her life, and her devotion in return was especially intense. In their first year, Kennedy and a handful of volunteers distributed an estimated 75,000 pamphlets, more than 300,000 letters, and twelve different books about birth control, including Margaret's own. Somewhere from 15,000 to 30,000 copies of the *Birth Control Review* were printed at the highest point of its circulation, with paid subscriptions augmented by newsstand distribution and by Kitty Marion's indefatigable street sales in New York. This outreach, in turn, produced 18,000 paid memberships and an additional 132,000 inquiries by letter and phone. The budget grew to more than $38,000, and a plan of expansion was adopted that nearly doubled that amount the following year. In 1925 alone, the league's Motherhood Department answered almost 30,000 letters from women who wrote for practical advice on contraception, infertility, and a whole host of sexual problems, referring them to sympathetic local doctors where possible, or just offering words of understanding, since the mailing of practical instruction remained illegal. In some instances, volunteers, including Margaret herself, also took letters home and answered them privately, removing the organization from legal liability.[1]

The mail was Margaret's link to popular American culture. Thousands of the letters she received were destroyed, but surviving examples bear witness to the often tragic circumstances of women from Maine to California who were unable to find reliable contraceptive guidance. They wrote of strict and falsely modest mothers who had told them nothing of sex or birth control, of callous physicians who claimed ignorance of reliable methods, of husbands who abandoned them when they chose continence over the risk of another pregnancy, of illegal abortionists who cost them their fertility. They wrote with a sisterly affection and intimacy made possible by distance and anonymity, often not even asking about contraception but instead confessing sexual anxieties or transgressions. A nineteen-year-old woman from Tarrant, Alabama, confided in 1924:

> Dear Friend. What I am going to tell you this afternoon has never been breathed to a single soul but the one who was the cause of it. . . . What I am fixing to tell you is a hidden chapter in my life, and the reason I choose you to "bare my heart to" was because you are far away and you do not know me and because I have to have some advice and I believe you will tell me what to do and tell me the right thing.

The overwrought letter went on to report a family history of poverty and parental abuse followed by a brief love affair with a young man named Tom whom the correspondent had met at work. He had made her pregnant, secured her an illegal abortion, and then abandoned her. The dilemma she posed for Margaret was this: should she tell a new boyfriend who wanted to marry her about this complicated—perhaps, some would say, sordid—past? Margaret wrote back immediately with enormous and respectful compassion:

> You must not think of yourself or your relations with Tom, whom you have loved, in the wrong light. If you loved him and he loved you, any relations between you were just as holy and as pure in the sight of God as if a marriage certificate had been given you. You must not look upon this relationship as if you were a bad girl.

Assuring the girl that no physical evidence of her prior relations was likely to be detected, she also encouraged her not to say anything if the knowledge would upset her new beau. "Keep your head high and your heart light," the letter cautioned.

The sheer volume of this confessional correspondence testified to Margaret's continued notoriety and the extent to which her personal magnetism helped sustain the birth control cause. Just how well-known she became is impossible to measure with precision, but the mail at least confirms that substantial numbers of poor women on farms and in small towns came to identify her with their concerns. "If I could only be one part as sporty as you have been, I'd be so happy," wrote the wife of a cotton-mill worker in Weaver, Alabama.[2]

In this respect, the birth control movement had a democratic impact, which its own paid constituency surely did not reflect. The typical league member was an upper-middle-class, thirty-five-year-old housewife still in her childbearing years—white, native-born,

Protestant, and identified as politically "independent"—though about one fourth reported foreign-born parents. And when willing to list party affiliation, just over half said they were Republicans, while 8 percent identified themselves as Socialists, reflecting the movement's, and Margaret's own, idiosyncratic histories. Nevertheless, the *typical* female member was also married to a college graduate who earned $3,000 per year, or well above the national average, and the vast majority of the men who belonged to the organization independent of their wives (about 17 percent of the total) were identified as professionals or academics.

At first, membership accounted for up to a third of the league's total budget, and an ambitious expansion was anticipated, but the various objectives of the organization quickly came into conflict. Along with advocacy, Margaret's goal was to mobilize local groups to provide clinical birth control services throughout the country. To this end, a field operation was immediately put into place to revive dormant interest in the nine states where it had existed prior to the end of World War I. As state and local leagues flourished, however, they drained energy and money from the parent organization. Over the years, various formulas would be adopted requiring them to share a portion of their membership receipts with New York, but the tension was never fully resolved. To offset its losses in 1925, the American Birth Control League tried assembling a national council of wealthy and professionally prominent individuals. Of some 250 members, almost half were listed in *Who's Who in America*, or had spouses with that distinction, but this did not automatically translate into funding, and the national operation's growth quickly leveled off and then declined, as did that of the *Birth Control Review*.[3]

Organized birth control, in fact, advanced only tentatively through the 1920s with the formation of state affiliates and local clinics as its major achievement. The most substantial impact by far was made in New York City, where Margaret concentrated her personal energies and resources on the Birth Control Clinical Research Bureau she founded in 1923, in an office next door to the league's. This pioneering medical facility later moved to independent space and became enormously successful, a story to which we shall return. Meanwhile, birth control organizations were, in fact, revived or begun anew outside New York through the efforts of women and social welfare activists.

In 1923 in Chicago, Rachelle Yarros, a physician and reformer who lived at Hull House and had long publicly advocated contraception, reactivated the Illinois Birth Control League, which had formed briefly after Margaret's speech at the Stockyards seven years earlier. Motivated by the extremely high incidence of illegal abortion she discovered among women in the city's Jewish immigrant neighborhoods, Dr. Yarros then opened a clinic modeled after the work of Marie Stopes in London. Her backers included a staid University of Chicago demographer by the name of James Field, and Harold and Anna Ickes, the prominent local attorney who would subsequently serve in the Roosevelt administration, and his first wife. At first they publicly disavowed Margaret, casting their lot instead with Mary Ware Dennett's organization, but after Margaret came to Chicago later that year, they changed their minds and sponsored a conference under the auspices of the American Birth Control League. This conclave was specifically targeted to social welfare groups concerned with "practical and feasible methods of decreasing dependency and delinquency." Its stated purpose was "to seek the reduction of the burden of charities and taxation resultant from the support of the dependent and the defective classes." Its clear intent was to distance Margaret from her former radical associations in order to make her more acceptable to new audiences like theirs.

The approach worked. Within a decade, five additional birth control facilities were operating in Chicago under Yarros's aegis, one of them at Hull House itself, and close to 22,000 indigent women had been served. All were affiliated with the American Birth Control League. The city's Jewish social service agency also opened a clinic, which gained national recognition with a program that sent visiting nurses into the homes of clients to instruct them in the use of diaphragms and other matters of sexual hygiene. By 1941, ten local facilities joined in a voluntary family planning confederation, for a brief time calling themselves Margaret Sanger Centers, to honor the woman who had in the interim gained international acclaim, and whose name was by then thought to have substantial publicity value with the larger public.[4]

Similarly, birth control agitation in Los Angeles, where a local league and the nation's third clinic were founded in 1925, traced its roots to Margaret's first appearance there before the war and to the subsequent organization of a local Committee of 100 in response to the national publicity generated by Ethel Byrne's hunger strike. With the war's interference, no further birth control activity occurred for nine years, until the Los Angeles Mothers' Clinic was formed with the cooperation of the city and county boards of health, the Bureau of Charities, several medical societies and philanthropic organizations. In the still progressive political atmosphere of the west, no effective political or religious opposition materialized, and the clinic's future was secured further by a substantial endowment from a local benefactress. Even so, it still only serviced about 1,500 clients a year.

No legacy survived of Margaret's prewar activity in San Francisco, where IWW activity and anarchist agitation had been particularly virulent, but a birth control league was founded there in 1924, in response to a visit by native daughter Anne Kennedy. Efforts to start a clinic failed until 1929, when several women doctors, working at the local Children's Hospital, encouraged a group of volunteer aides to join them in offering birth control services off the premises. Their first Maternal Health Center opened in a baby clinic sponsored by the local chapter of the American Association of University Women, which, regrettably, then reneged on its offer of space in the face of protest by Catholic members. The operation moved nearby, however, and a second one was also opened in an Oakland cottage belonging to the Children's Home Society.[5]

The pattern was similar elsewhere. Margaret had addressed a crowded audience of about 1,000 supporters in Detroit in 1916, but the only postwar emissary of her efforts there was a local dowager named Mrs. William McGraw, who used to return from vacations in New York carrying diaphragms from the birth control offices on lower Fifth Avenue, which she then distributed to needy women from her room in an elegant local residence hotel. In this manner, she evaded federal Comstock laws prohibiting shipment by mail. Mrs. McGraw was willing to finance a clinic but was unable to find any organizational support apart from a few members of the International Ladies Garment Workers Union. In 1926 several women active in Jewish philanthropy then raised $1,000 privately and prevailed on the local Jewish Welfare Board for an additional $3,000 to open the first birth control clinic between New York and Chicago. Several small clinics were also annexed to Detroit's two major maternity hospitals. A state group, calling itself the Michigan Maternal Health League in order to avoid some of the controversy associated with the name "birth control," organized in 1930 and expanded in response to heavy unemployment in the automobile and steel industries during the Depression. Still, inadequate funding, timidity in the face of opposition, and difficulty in getting supplies meant that fewer than 10,000 women were reached by Michigan's affiliated birth control agencies in their first decade of operation.

In nearby Cleveland, Margaret had been the guest of Eastern European Jewish radicals when she spoke before the war. Frederick Blossom then managed to mobilize an active local birth control constituency, including establishment reformers. This coalition fell apart, however, when anarchist Ben Reitman was arrested and jailed in Cleveland in 1916 for distributing birth control fliers, and when a visit the following year by the locally bred Socialist, Rose Pastor Stokes, again stirred controversy. The intense publicity left the progressive elite quite wary of the issue, and it was not until 1923 that several young women from the local Junior League again demonstrated interest, ostensibly propelled to action by the reported suicide of an indigent mother who drowned herself in Lake Erie, rather than face another pregnancy. The Junior Leaguers then formed a deliberately cautious Maternal Health League, and five years later, after a subsequent visit to Cleveland by Margaret, they also started a clinic. Operating with referrals from the Associated Charities of Cleveland, the facility served about 1,000 women per year.[6]

The Baltimore experience was unique. In 1927, the staid physicians of Johns Hopkins University, not yet convinced that Margaret Sanger was doing good work, agreed to sponsor a five-year experiment among their dispensary patients who exhibited clear medical indications for contraception. Their proposal was advertised to every physician, hospital, and social agency in the state of Maryland. But with a handful of women doctors working only part-time and devoting up to an hour for each patient visit, even this well-connected effort wound up handling little more than 1,000 cases in total.

Elsewhere, the American Birth Control League in New York sent its own organizers into the field. In 1925, Margaret hired James Cooper, M.D., a former instructor at Boston University's medical school, who had recently returned from medical missionary work in China. Cooper acted as her emissary to professional medical societies, which would never have deigned to listen to a lay woman propagandist. Until his resignation in 1929, he traveled to virtually every state in the nation and reached thousands of physicians through individual contacts and lectures, his reputation considerably enhanced by the publication of his *Technique of Contraception*, the first well-regarded technical text on the subject. In journeys of more than 40,000 miles, he also mobilized social workers, nurses, volunteers, and businessmen to support birth control affiliates. Another field secretary by the name of Henriette Hart explained in a memo summarizing her activities for 1927 that it had been necessary to hold a total of twenty-seven separate meetings in eleven different communities in order to get a state league going in New Jersey, which then raised several thousand dollars to open a single birth control clinic in downtown Newark.

By 1930, there were also small facilities advertising themselves as birth control clinics in Cincinnati, Atlanta, Denver, and San Antonio. A sociologist surveying the movement's progress identified thirty clinics nationwide, though her figure was deceptive, because it incorporated some negligible operations annexed to private practices or hospitals. Indeed, in 1930, Margaret's own Birth Control Clinical Research Bureau in New York alone serviced almost twice as many patients as all of the rest of the clinics in the country combined.[7]

The law prohibited contraception outright in Massachusetts and Connecticut, and for almost a decade Catholic threats there effectively quieted local activists. Then in 1928, Dr. Antoinette Konikow was arrested in Boston for distributing a handbill advertising a lecture on birth control and sex hygiene. The incident propelled the imperious Blanche Ames back into action to reform the state obscenity statute. Ames brought Margaret up to speak, but a birth control bill introduced in the state legislature never made it beyond committee, and several small clinics that opened around the state during the Depression were closed down by police raids in 1937—raids launched on the authority of the Commonwealth's original Comstock provisions of 1879. A case was brought on behalf of the clinic in Salem, but the statute was sustained in the lower courts and by the Massachusetts Supreme Court, which refused to make any exceptions to the ban on distributing contraception, even for licensed physicians. In neighboring Connecticut, clinics were opened in New Haven, Danbury, Greenwich, and Waterbury. The closing of the Waterbury facility in 1939 also provoked a legal challenge, but as in Massachusetts, state courts sustained the action, and all the clinics shut down after a final appeal was lost in 1940. Connecticut had no organized birth control services until 1961, when services were made available through Planned Parenthood in New Haven. The forced closing of this operation provided the test case that wound its way to the United States Supreme Court four years later and resulted in the historic ruling in *Griswold v. Connecticut*, when the Supreme Court finally accepted jurisdiction and declared contraception a constitutional right of married Americans.[8]

Yet even where birth control was legal, the cautious interpretation of provisions governing the transport of supplies and the eligibility of patients also acted as impediments to growth of the movement overall. Progress rested largely on the voluntary efforts of women whose financial and organizational resources never kept pace with their dedication to the cause, and whose sense of propriety in some cases actually compromised their effectiveness. Increasingly conservative by temperament, many of the new generation of activists outside New York shied away from publicity for fear of provoking controversy, and this made it especially hard for needy clients to find them. Many clinics, shunned by established social welfare networks that feared reprisals from Catholic voluntary agencies, were cut off from professional referrals. What is more, medical indications for birth control were often construed narrowly to conform to the letter of laws defining medical eligibility, while, at the same time, economic criteria for clinic service were also established, so as not to offend private physicians who were quick to voice their dismay about middle-class women receiving a subsidy. Finally, doubts were raised about the efficacy and cost of the recommended diaphragm procedure. All in all, there seem to have been almost as many constraints on expansion as there were incentives for growth.

Even so, numerous small clinics sprouted up, in response to increased attention and demand brought on by the Depression. By the mid-1930s birth control leagues existed in more than half the states, and there were at one point as many as 300 clinics. Still, it was unreasonable to expect that the essentially voluntary efforts of women could possibly result in comprehensive service delivery. Until the marketing of the pill and the provision of federal funding in the 1960s, the growth of birth control clinics stalled.

However halting, the slow progress of this clinic organization was still more substantial than the league's legislative accomplishments. Despite her bleak view of politicians, Margaret grew convinced that birth control would never win full acceptance as a social and medical practice while the onus of illegality still hung over it. In 1923 she persuaded Samuel Rosenman, then a well-connected young legislator from Manhattan, but soon to become senior speech writer and adviser to Franklin Roosevelt, to sponsor a new birth control bill in the New York State Assembly. The measure affirmatively licensed physicians to prescribe contraception for reasons of health, in accordance with the judicial ruling she had achieved earlier. The support of a mainstream Democrat was noteworthy, and the bill was also widely endorsed by grass-roots women's organizations, including, for the first time, the 10,000 member New York State League of Women Voters. Several leading Manhattan physicians also testified in its behalf, along with the same cast of liberal clergymen, university professors, and society women who had been to Albany to lobby for birth control in years past. To restore the effort's credibility as an issue for working people, Margaret also recruited Norman Thomas, then head of a Socialist Labor organization called the League for Industrial Democracy. Thomas gave a rousing speech to those who convened in the state capital to push the bill, but his appearance, however well-intended, did little to further its prospects.

When Margaret herself was scheduled to address this lobby, the mayor of the substantially Catholic town of Albany arbitrarily revoked the permit licensing the hotel meeting room where she was to speak. Her appearance was canceled and then moved to a private home. Once again, the intervention provoked a militant confrontation and created a rash of newspaper publicity, furthering the educational objectives of the movement but, at the same time, entrenching the opposition and effectively killing any hope of victory. In a sarcastic editorial in the *Birth Control Review,* Margaret then attacked the integrity of the elected officials who stood by in the face of this "despotism" and refused to grant her a respectful hearing. She suggested facetiously that "intelligence tests"—then still the rage of eugenicists and psychologists—be required for all legislators. The Rosenman bill never made it out of the Assembly Codes Committee, but the virtue of pursuing a strategy of legal reform at the state level was nonetheless affirmed, either because of Margaret's persuasiveness, or perhaps because the strategy replicated the prior efforts of suffragists, who had spent years in the states before focusing on Washington.

The weight of Margaret's argument for a doctor's preference also prevailed, even over Mary Ware Dennett's efforts in Washington. Dennett had strongly opposed Margaret's decision to pursue a legislative campaign in Albany. Earlier she had promised to support Margaret's efforts to establish clinics, if Margaret in turn stayed out of politics, a compromise Margaret saw no reason to make. In December of 1923, on her sixteenth request, Dennett finally enlisted Sen. Albert B. Cummins of Iowa, then president pro tempore of the Senate, to introduce her legislation, but this time she made a concession to Margaret by inserting a provision requiring five physicians to certify the reliability of any contraceptive product protected by law. Hearings were held by a joint subcommittee of the judiciary committees of the House and Senate, but the Cummins-Vaile bill (identified by the names of its Senate and House sponsors, the latter, Colorado Congressman William N. Vaile) then stalled and never got to the floor of either chamber. Support eroded for Dennett's goal of trying to repeal the federal Comstock statutes altogether, and within a year her Voluntary Parenthood League closed down, leaving Margaret's hegemony over the birth control movement uncontested. Dennett more or less retired to writing and subsequently attacked Margaret publicly in a book entitled *Birth Control Laws,* which made a final plea for the repeal of the federal Comstock statutes. "The poor sick woman has failed in her work and in order to explain her failure, she throws the blame on me and my work and early views, most of them very good but *radical,*" Margaret confided in a private letter. To Juliet, she described it as "devilish and cruel," but she refrained from public comment.[9]

However much she scorned Dennett in private, Margaret saw an opening for herself in this legislative setback on Capitol Hill. During the 1924 Presidential campaign, she quietly made an effort to put birth control on the national political agenda by enlisting Oswald Garrison Villard, the eminent publisher of *The Nation*, to talk to Progressive Presidential candidate Robert LaFollette about it. Predictably, however, LaFollette resisted embracing a contentious issue that would inevitably detract from the major domestic issues of his campaign. Delegates to the major party conventions were also lobbied on birth control that year, but to no avail.

After two years without any birth control activity in Washington, Margaret then decided to try to fill the vacuum by attempting some lobbying of her own devising. In 1926, she sent Anne Kennedy to Washington to test the waters for a "physicians' bill," but after surveying the scene, Kennedy left without even drafting legislation, convinced any effort would probably be futile, and that money was better expended elsewhere for the time being. Told by Senator Cummins that he had never been able to get his bill taken seriously—by others that it was "the laughing stock of the cloakroom"—Kennedy encouraged Margaret to invest in more public education.[10]

While in Washington, Kennedy also went to interview a National Catholic Welfare Conference public relations deputy by the name of Patrick J. Ward, whom she understood to be the official spokesman of the organization. Kennedy subsequently transcribed the interview, had Ward sign off on its contents, and then quoted him in an American Birth Control League circular saying that the NCWC was organizing a special committee to fight birth control openly and to legislate for Catholics and non-Catholics alike, according to the dictates of the church. When Kennedy made the contents of the interview public, however, Father John Burke, general secretary of the NCWC, first angrily denied that Ward had any authority to speak at all for the organization and then subsequently challenged the authenticity of Kennedy's account. Predictably annoyed, Margaret published a scathing attack in *The New Republic*.

She also intensified her public excoriation of the Catholic Church. In a particularly extreme example from 1928, the *Birth Control Review* carried an article by the journalist Floyd Dell called "The Anti-Birth Control Neurosis." A popularizer of Freudian theory, Dell boldly charged that Catholic clerics who opposed birth control were really just counteracting their own impotency anxiety. This kind of material was certainly not calculated to win support from Catholics—or from any politicians for that matter.

Having all but given up on partisan politics for the moment, Margaret attacked the Democrats for nominating New York's Catholic Governor, Al Smith, as their candidate for President and voted for Herbert Hoover, just to be safe. Nevertheless, she continued to file legislation in Albany to repeal the state's birth control laws, as she had been doing each year since 1923, only to have it repeatedly stalled in committee. By 1929, an opposition led by Catholic interests had rallied in force, and public lobbies for and against birth control met head to head in the Capitol chambers.[11]

The frustrations of continued setbacks and political defeats weighed heavily upon her, and Margaret blamed them for the periodic bouts of depression that began to plague her again in middecade. This recurrent malaise may also have been occasioned by the loss of her revered older sister, Mary, who died in 1926 from the complications of a ruptured appendix. Always the compliant domestic servant, Mary simply refused to tell anyone she wasn't feeling well before it was too late. In this respect and all others, the two sisters could not have been more different, or followed more divergent paths. They saw each other infrequently, if at all. Yet when Mary was operated on in 1925 in Buffalo, where for almost thirty years she had worked for the same family, Margaret at long last went up to visit. She returned soon thereafter for the funeral and noted in her journal that Mary had been "the stable sympathetic member of a large family. Her passing loosens up the foundations." With a small bequest from Mary, she built a rose arbor in her memory.

A still feisty Michael Higgins survived his oldest daughter, and Margaret also observed the irony of this situation, but within weeks of Mary's death, he suffered a severe stroke at the cottage in Truro, where he was living. He spent the following year as an invalid. When he then died at the ripe age of eighty-eight, most of his children did not even bother to attend the funeral. Margaret, however, did make the trip to Corning and took Grant along with her, who many years later recalled his horror that Michael had been buried apart from his wife at the cemetery's edge. Yet no observation of these events appears in Margaret's journals or correspondence, just as there is no record of any response by her father to her work. He would emerge as a far larger presence in her autobiographies than in these less self-conscious materials.[12]

Though scarcely mentioned, the deaths may nonetheless have been deeply felt. Margaret wrote frequently during this period to such intimate friends as Juliet and Hugh, confiding the wish that she might abandon America altogether for the more tolerant and happy atmosphere of Europe. Pampered and undisciplined, Juliet had long since tired of birth control and was preoccupied with archaeology and filmmaking, her two newest passions. En route to Italy in 1925, where she was about to descend to the ocean floor in a cylinder to look for ruins, she scribbled back to Margaret: "Darling—we must hurry—hurry—hurry—to pass B.C. on to others so that we can work for this other, super, bigger thing which will make men and women into Gods and Goddesses. B.C. was a necessary step, but useless unless we can also create finer human beings spiritually and mentally. . . . The desire and will to Freedom & free imagination & aspiration—Realization of all the Beauties & joys they have dreamed of, must be stirred and awakened in women just as you have succeeded in stirring & awakening them to a desire to control their own bodies."

Such romantic excess was characteristic of the letters the two women often exchanged. Juliet would tempt Margaret to slip away and indulge in the loftier personal and intellectual pursuits to which they had been introduced by the Wantley circle. This was no simple invitation to sexual promiscuity, but an honestly perceived commitment to the development of a higher and more spiritually attuned life—an idealized existence set apart from the turmoil of the real world. Invariably, Margaret would agree, promising to let go and allow others to carry on the more mundane matters of birth control, but then she would find an excuse to recant, usually arguing that she could find no one with comparable vision to succeed her.[13]

In fact, her international stature had grown substantially as a result of Dennett's decline and in the wake of the American Birth Control League's sponsorship in New York in 1925 of the Sixth International Neo-Malthusian Conference and Birth Control. Neo-

Malthusian sympathizers of various European nationalities had been meeting together since 1900, when a first conclave was held in Paris, which Emma Goldman attended. Delegates gathered again in Belgium in 1905, in the Netherlands in 1910, and in Germany a year later. Little came of these prewar sessions other than spirited debate about the relevance of Malthusian doctrine to Marxism. But the fifth session, in London in 1922, which Margaret attended, had attracted the attention of mainstream economists, demographers, social theorists and physicians, including such notable figures as John Maynard Keynes and H. G. Wells. As birthrates in the West declined, interest began to develop, albeit slowly, in the problems of unrestrained population growth in the developing nations.

The 1925 gathering in New York then drew more than 1,000 delegates, produced four volumes of papers, was covered extensively by the press and made a significant impression on professional, scholarly, and political audiences. Among the participants from Europe was Aletta Jacobs, M.D., and from the United States, the Freudian A. A. Brill, the Socialist Norman Thomas, and the flamboyant feminist and pacifist Rosika Schwimmer, who would be denied United States citizenship in 1929 in a historic Supreme Court case challenging her refusal to promise to bear arms in defense of her country. Also attending were numbers of professionals from medicine and the social sciences who were less controversial but perhaps more influential. Having hosted this event and been left with the responsibility of perpetuating international contacts and cooperation, Margaret was enjoying new prominence in what was becoming a movement of worldwide interest.[14]

The conference hardly provided an excuse to retreat from her public responsibilities as Juliet beckoned, but it did present an opportunity to indulge the fantasy of spending more time in Europe, where the demands of international leadership could more comfortably accommodate intellectual, aesthetic, and no doubt romantic opportunities, as well. With the business of clinic organization at home proceeding slowly, and with legislative reform in Albany and Washington stalled, Margaret decided to grant herself a sabbatical from her obligations in the United States and once again go abroad.

In June of 1926, she announced to the New York newspapers that she would be taking a leave of absence from the American league to study and prepare for another international conference scheduled the following year in Geneva, home of the League of Nations, whose delegates she sought to impress with the importance of population doctrine to world peace and prosperity. She did not resign from the organization, but instead named as acting president a formidable younger woman named Eleanor Dwight Jones, who had risen out of the ranks of birth control volunteers.

Mrs. F. Robertson Jones, as she liked to be known, was the wife of an establishment New York lawyer, and her many concessions to social convention may have deceived Margaret into believing that she had chosen a deferential stand-in. Instead, Jones emerged as a determined, independent presence, and with Margaret no longer around to interfere, she quickly instituted more professional standards of management for the organization. She regularized what had been fairly lax administrative practices, streamlined fund-raising, established formal accounting procedures, and instituted changes in governance, which diffused powers the president had previously exercised unilaterally.[15]

Margaret was not initially averse to these changes. She recognized the need to introduce formal procedures to an operation that had expanded substantially from its beginnings as a largely volunteer cause, whose leaders were emotionally driven. Indeed, she returned to the United States briefly in 1927 and agreed to a series of Jones's proposals, including her desire to remove Anne Kennedy, an original recruit and a close personal friend of Margaret's, from the organization altogether. Margaret apparently promised to find Anne a position in private business but then went back to Europe and did nothing about it. Later that year, Mrs. Jones then fired Kennedy outright, ostensibly because she had neglected to file daily expense sheets in connection with her field activities, though staff and board members who wrote confidentially to Margaret about the incident said that overall insubordination to Jones underlay the action. Recognizing the unhappy truth that the old-timers were accustomed to more or less making up rules as they went along and would probably never be able to accommodate to professional standards of accountability, Margaret brought Anne over to Europe temporarily to assist with the Geneva conference. She then sent her off to Cleveland, where she helped organize the clinic there, and then for an entire year drove herself by car through the midwestern states and as far away as Texas, in some cases literally knocking on the doors of strangers, to introduce herself and the birth control cause. Later, Margaret helped secure a permanent position for her with a company manufacturing diaphragms. Margaret complained that Jones had been clumsy in handling the departure but went along with it nonetheless. Indeed, of her own accord and in an identical spirit of committing herself to a higher level of professionalism, she also found a position outside the movement for Anna Lifschiz, her devoted secretary of more than thirteen years, who had been with her since the days of the Brownsville Clinic.[16]

Margaret may have been willing to sacrifice some of her most loyal associates, but she was not prepared to allow the league's new administrative regulations and procedures to interfere with her own work. In 1928, when she returned to New York permanently and resumed the presidency of the organization, she found herself in the untenable position of being a supplicant to a board of directors, whose views did not always reflect her own. Like most self-styled pioneers in social causes, she did not always move gracefully among a second generation of reformers who brought a corporate mentality to an endeavor in which they had far less of a personal stake. A deep emotional investment in her work and a temperamental disdain for the give-and-take of bureaucracy made her testy toward newcomers who thought they knew better than she did. On the other hand, she was happy to have them carry on independently when she wasn't prepared to pay attention, as this same group of women had done reasonably well during the eighteen months she spent in Europe.

On her return, minor disputes arose over the most trivial of expenditures, and in June of 1928, telling Juliet that she could not do her best work in an atmosphere that had sacrificed "spirit, love and trust" to "rules and regulations," Margaret submitted her resignation as president. She tried to name her own successor by engineering the election of Charlotte Delafield, a current vice president and director of the organization who had been loyal in the past, but when that maneuver failed, she acquiesced to the permanent election of Eleanor Jones. Her official letter of resignation acknowledged a growing interest in birth control research and clinical service, along with a recognition that the league had reached a new stage of "maturity and organization" and was moving forward in its educational and legislative objectives without her. She could afford to be gracious, because the league board had worked out an agreement allowing her to remain as a director and also retain her title as editor-in-chief of the *Birth Control Review*. She thought she could continue to exercise control where she wanted it, without being president.[17]

But within months, this carefully constructed détente proved unworkable. Margaret had initially incorporated and always administered the Birth Control Clinical Research Bureau as an autonomous legal and financial entity, wholly independent of the league, and she insisted it should remain so. Mrs. Jones argued instead that the parent organization had made important policy decisions with respect to the clinic and should continue in an advisory role. Cordial relations quickly deteriorated between the two women, and the resolution of legitimate differences became impossible. Margaret convinced herself that Jones was, on the one hand, a timid soul who only did what her lawyer-husband advised her to do, and on the other, a personally ambitious woman whose foremost interest was self-aggrandizement. In Margaret's view, Jones displayed an impertinent disregard for her own judgment and years of prior experience. The final break came when Jones, having lost the battle over the clinic, tried to reclaim control of the *Review* by appointing an editorial advisory board. Margaret then angrily resigned altogether, leaving the magazine behind, but taking the clinic with her.

"Politics, jealousies, selfishness, desire for glory and power kill the spirit always," she wrote to Hugh in a confession that may have described her own behavior as accurately as her adversary's. And yet she hardly seemed all that concerned over the entire matter, adding: "the movement grows and blossoms & I am getting happier everyday over it." She told the press that the controversy represented the maturing of the movement, which, like a growing cell, got to a certain point and then divided. "We are still the same body, however," she hastened to add.

Both women seem to have behaved badly, yet whatever character weaknesses they revealed, their personal dispute, much like those that had embroiled Margaret in the past, also reflected substantive differences in leadership style and in basic ideology. The schism was probably inevitable because Jones and the board members she controlled were intent on building an institution quietly and methodically by slowly compiling a record of endorsements, affiliations, and clinic openings. Margaret had little patience for this incremental approach and was, instead, eager to take risks and extend the organization beyond conventional and prudent tactics. Busy building institutions in the United States and in Europe, she had also been out of the press and the public eye for several years. As soon as she returned from Europe, she began to talk about throwing caution to the winds and mounting another major legislative campaign in Washington. She did not necessarily count on political victory but saw no other means except renewed lobbying to educate and arouse an increasingly apathetic public. She was willing to let Senators tell her what to do only for so long.[18]

Still defending her position to a wary ABCL leadership in 1932, she would admit that whether the Comstock laws actually still meant much or were enforced was not important to her. "There is no better way of educating public opinion than by changing the laws," she explained. "Such agitation arouses interest, awakens forces that have been sleeping or apathetic and creates a new attitude not only toward government, but toward our part in bringing about constructive changes in obsolete and vicious laws. In my estimation the agitation for legislation is the means, and precedes the knowledge and the awakening of interest in the establishment of clinics." Eleanor Jones, however, believed that lobbying would only divert energy and money from the practical, constructive work of bringing contraceptive services to the poor. As the Depression took hold, Jones also decided that propaganda was having a negative effect by encouraging a middle-class birthrate that was already too low. She could see no instrumental value in public relations arising from legal issues.[19]

While Margaret joined ranks with women of the establishment, she was also never completely comfortable with any but the most independent-minded—some might say the most eccentric—among them. She convinced herself that Jones, like Mary Ware Dennett before her, was simply not a compatible spirit, if for no other reason than that she looked down upon Margaret's social background and schooling. "I wonder if Mrs. J. thinks the N.R. asks 'uneducated' people to write for its columns," she wrote caustically to Juliet Rublee early in 1929, when *The New Republic* published a piece Margaret had prepared about her New York clinic. Her ego must still have been bruised a year later when Havelock Ellis responded to one of her letters in consolation: "The BC movement was magnificent in its day and it is splendid that you should be its St. Margaret," he responded, "but it is no longer a visionary movement, no longer an adventure, but, though always important, quite dull and commonplace and best left to dull and commonplace people."[20]

There was, indeed, a disturbing change of emphasis in the league under Jones's direction. For almost a decade, Margaret had pandered to a eugenically minded audience, but she was always careful to qualify her definition of hereditary fitness to exclude outright prejudice on the basis of race, ethnicity, or class. By contrast, Jones was unabashedly elitist and undemocratic. "Couples who cannot endow their children with health, vigor, and intelligence should have fewer children than those who can," she told the National Conference of Social Work in 1929. "In order that people of inferior stock shall have fewer children, all we need to do is to remove the obstacles put in the way of their getting birth control advice." The following year

Jones applied to the Rockefeller family-supported Bureau of Social Hygiene and to other foundations for funding to underwrite a "systematic campaign against the present dysgenic multiplication of the unfit." She explained her intentions this way: "The public is beginning to realize that scientific, constructive philanthropy does not merely care for the diseased, the poor, and the degenerate, but takes steps to prevent the birth of babies destined to be paupers, invalids, degenerates, or all three."

A tactful Lawrence Dunham, director of the Social Hygiene Bureau's staff, counseled his board that the application "assumed as facts statements which were in reality highly debatable opinions." Elsewhere he added: "The [birth control] movement has the support of many of the best and most intelligent people in the world and it also has the support of some persons whose mental balance is not the best. In between these two classes, we find the people who hold debatable opinions, the most capable group being the Eugenists [sic], some of whom make claims which many eminent scientists in the field of biology and other related sciences contend are utterly false, or at least unproven."

Dunham did not recommend support for the league's application. He instead took the advice of another member of his staff—to await the results of research on birth control being conducted under the auspices of Margaret Sanger's Birth Control Clinical Research Bureau. The American Birth Control League was given $10,000 to continue educational work among physicians, but its funding from the Rockefellers did not grow beyond that level so long as Eleanor Jones—"a martinet," as she was described in another Bureau of Social Hygiene memorandum—remained in charge.[21]

By contrast, Margaret's own reputation, however controversial she remained in many quarters, transcended the identity of the group she had founded. Freed of bureaucratic constraints and infighting, and fiercely determined to best her detractors, she moved forward on her own, expanding the Birth Control Clinical Research Bureau in New York, while also launching her proposed educational and lobbying campaign for birth control in Washington. Indeed, she fortuitously located the headquarters of this effort in the nation's capital just as that city found itself the center of the country's New Deal reform energies, and, in so doing, she valiantly attempted to ally the birth control cause with affirmative social welfare and planning initiatives in response to the economic crisis.

By leaving the league, Margaret deprived it of her firebrand temperament. She also took much of its fund-raising capability, as the Bureau of Social Hygiene records clearly confirm. Eroding the confidence of the Rockefellers was no small matter, but they did inevitably fund both the league and many of Margaret's new requests, as well, at least in small amounts. The far more significant loss proved to be a stately, monocled, self-made millionaire by the name of James Henry Noah Slee, who had become the birth control movement's principal benefactor by way of marrying Margaret Sanger. Having secured this one man's devotion and his checkbook, she was, for the time being at least, substantially able to pay her own way.

CHAPTER TWELVE

Happiness in Marriage

Born in Capetown, South Africa, in 1860 to a family of shopkeepers, Noah Slee, as he preferred to be called, migrated to America with his widowed mother at the age of twelve. At seventeen, he found a job in a company in Baltimore manufacturing machine lubricants. Subsequently, he patented his own formula for a blended, compound oil, which proved particularly successful at keeping bicycle chains in working order. When the country went crazy for bicycling in the 1890s, he promoted his 3-in-One Oil in a nationwide advertising campaign and cornered the emerging domestic market for such a product. Quick to see the benefits of mechanization, he then cut labor and production costs in his factories and substantially increased profits. The company he founded in 1894 with a $1,200 investment had capital assets listed at several million dollars thirty years later and annual international sales exceeding that amount. He reportedly sold it in 1929 for more than three times book value—nearly $7 million.

Slee had been married for more than thirty years to Mary Roosevelt West of New Windsor, New York, with whom he had two sons and a daughter. He was active in the socially impeccable Union League Club and in Episcopal Church affairs in New York City, where for years he scrupulously administered the Sunday school of St. George's Church on Stuyvesant Square. (Whenever Margaret told this story, she insisted that she had nearly fainted when she first heard it.) Beneath these appearances of respectability, however, lay a restless, unfulfilled man who had found no contentment in his relations with a wife he once described as so cold that each of his children had cost him dearly in gifts of diamonds and pearls. Margaret herself candidly portrayed Noah as a "babe in the woods—a deprived and hungry man with the passions of a youngster."

They met at a dinner party hosted by Juliet Rublee in 1921, where he had been coaxed by a friend under considerable duress. Expecting to face a coarse and militant feminist, he was instead beguiled by the evening's guest of honor. Within months, he left his wife at their estate in Dutchess County, New York, and placed his business in the hands of a grown son. He pursued Margaret tirelessly, standing by her side during the legal tribulations that followed her arrest at Town Hall in New York and thereafter for almost a year, as she lectured in a dozen American cities and then embarked from San Francisco for a round-the-world speaking tour.[1]

She was herself only recently divorced, having finally secured a legal separation from William Sanger in Barnstable, Massachusetts, in October of 1921, on grounds of desertion, since he still refused his consent. Following the death of Billy Williams and the marriage of Jonah Goldstein, she had been without a reliable companion in New York. Nonetheless, her calendar for 1920 and 1921 notes occasional evenings and holidays in the company of the still devoted Harold Hersey and others, including Sanger himself, with whom relations seem to have eased somewhat, once her independence from him was made official. Marriage made "not a whit of difference" to her, she confided in a letter to Hugh de Selincourt after the divorce was final. Earlier she had vowed that if she ever married again, it would be for money alone, and then, only so that she could come and live nearby him in England. She was "no fit person for love or home or children or friends or anything which needs attention or consideration," she admitted candidly in still a third letter, this one mentioning Noah Slee directly, though not by name. She referred to him only as "the millionaire."[2]

They could not have been a more improbable couple. She tended to be irreverent and fun-loving, he staid and sober. She was an atheist, he a pietist; she a Socialist, he a Republican; she a veteran of bohemia, he a pillar of the establishment. He remained wary of her zealous dedication to her work; she never stopped begrudging him his wealth and his leisure. Yet, though she bewildered and often exasperated him, he found her irresistible. She gave him satisfaction in love, and he, in turn, made her socially respectable, showered her with money, and instructed her in the habits of businesslike punctuality, reliability, and caution that made possible her transition from the birth control movement's wild-eyed and controversial pioneer to its preeminent, if still controversial, professional leader. He even persuaded her to bring men onto her staff, which she once acknowledged was a "big jump" for her.

The relationship was at once foolishly romantic and eminently practical. An early coworker recalled years later that Noah first secured Margaret's affections by providing her with an addressograph machine, an up-to-date filing system, and a new examination table for her office. The gifts were a ploy to encourage her to stay home and share breakfast with him in the morning, rather than go early to the office in order to answer the mail by hand.[3]

Slee's indispensability was never more apparent than when he accompanied Margaret to the Orient in February of 1922. Through the auspices of her friend, Agnes Smedley, she had been invited to lecture on population issues in Japan. The contact was made through Shidzue Ishimoto, a young Japanese woman of noble lineage, who first learned about birth control on a trip to New York. Margaret was to be part of a series sponsored by a liberal group that published *Kaizo Reconstruction*, a monthly review of politics, literature, and social theory. The group also extended invitations to such luminaries of the West as H. G. Wells, Bertrand Russell, and Albert Einstein.

Unwilling to endure a second, prolonged separation from her sons, she again took thirteen-year-old Grant out of school for a semester, and Noah came along ostensibly to provide companionship for the young boy aboard ship and during the month that she traversed the Japanese countryside, delivering lengthy lectures (painstakingly translated into the native tongue) before various groups of women and of medical professionals. Together, the Sanger party toured the temples, palaces, theaters, and gardens of conventional tourist interest, and Margaret also went off on her own to investigate working conditions for women and children in the cotton and silk factories, along with the relative living standards of geishas and lesser castes of Japanese prostitutes, whose independence from the repressive patriarchal norms of Japanese society she quite frankly admired.

She kept a journal and travelogue of her trip, but in 183 handwritten pages, Noah Slee's name only appears in passing—once as a facilitator of travel arrangements, and on another occasion when his "cross and disgruntled" behavior apparently spoiled her day. Allowing herself to become absorbed in material concerns was uncharacteristic of Margaret, and the absence of almost any reflection at all about her companion is striking, though she was, in fact, kept busy enough to be able to ignore him much of the time.

Her appearance in Japan sparked intense interest from the moment she arrived and was denied an entry visa, because Japanese representatives to the Washington Naval Conference, who were returning home on the same ship with her, ostensibly questioned whether their government ought to admit a woman whose right to free speech had been suppressed in her own country. Though the records are not clear, the American government may also have intervened, because the Federal Bureau of Investigation, still identifying Margaret as an individual with radical ties, feared her potential influence over the rise of Communist sentiment in Japan. Margaret succeeded in getting herself a visa by charming one influential vice-minister among the Japanese delegates aboard ship, but she was forced to agree in writing that she would not describe specific birth control techniques and would, instead, lecture only on the abstract social and economic implications of family limitation. So constrained, she found herself trailed everywhere by reporters and photographers. A nascent group of Japanese feminists was pursuing modernization for women by establishing their right at least to attend political meetings, and Margaret's lectures became a focus of their interest and public protest, as well. An article of Margaret's had already been published in Japanese, and her books were being translated and circulated among intellectuals. "It is very amazing the way interest in birth control has been aroused here through my coming," she wrote Juliet Rublee. "Every paper in the country carried headlines & front page stories & editorials on the subject for a full week."

From Japan, Margaret and her party traveled westward via Korea, mainland China, Hong Kong, Singapore, and Ceylon, across the Indian Ocean and through the Suez Canal to Egypt. In Peking they traversed the Great Wall for more than a mile, and she lectured at the National University. In Shanghai, she addressed a labor organization. "Six months here with you, Mrs. K, Anna, and Kitty, and we would revolutionize China," she again wrote enthusiastically to Juliet.

In Cairo, there was an enchanting, moonlight visit to see the Pyramids and the Sphinx. If Noah made any impression during these outings, however, once again she made no mention of him in her journal, though she did take the time to record Grant's enthusiastic responses. In Eygpt, Grant took ill with a fever, and nursing him back to health consumed all of his frantic mother's energies, but with his recovery, the idyllic journey continued to Alexandria and then, via the Adriatic Sea, to Venice, Milan, Paris, and finally London, where Margaret was scheduled to attend the Fifth International Neo-Malthusian Conference. She had collected fees for her lectures in Japan and China, but one can reasonably assume that her generous suitor picked up the tab for much of this exquisite return voyage.[4]

Margaret had been traveling for the better part of the year, but her supporters at home made certain that her fact-finding journey through the poverty-stricken Orient received sufficient press coverage to maintain and, indeed, enhance her domestic reputation and prestige. In London, she told a crowded public session at the conference that opinion makers and moral leaders of the struggling nations of the East were ready to acknowledge the value of birth control. Quite unlike the American birth control movement, where women predominated, British Malthusianism remained primarily the preserve of men, who emphasized the political, economic, and eugenic dimension of the subject over its humane, individual aspects. Margaret, as the only woman invited to chair a session of the 1922 conference in London, presented material on the Far East that proved to be of great interest to the men. But along with it she also painted a sentimental portrait of the downtrodden mothers of these nations, which won her the admiration of women delegates, who had been up in arms over the "male tone" of the assembly. Her celebrity was also enhanced by the publication of a revised British edition of *Woman and the New Race* under the more benign title of *The New Motherhood*.[5]

She shared a platform in London with H. G. Wells, and during her prolonged visit, they saw one another privately as well. She also found time for Hugh de Selincourt. Grant had gone back home to summer camp in the States, and she apparently kept Noah at bay. His whereabouts during at least part of her stay are unclear, but he did remain in Europe, and in August secured a French divorce from his American wife on the obviously specious grounds that she had refused to follow him to Paris. Then quite suddenly, on September 18, 1922, James Henry Noah Slee and Margaret Higgins Sanger were secretly wed by the registrar of marriages for the district of St. Giles, in Bloomsbury, London.

Earlier that year, before Margaret left New York, the same seer who analyzed the conflicting strains of her temperament had also predicted that she would soon find herself in a "fruitful and happy" second marriage. At the same time, the woman warned her against taking any precipitous action at all during the entire month of September. "You must be very careful," she said. "A flower may hide a snake." Margaret, however, needed no crystal ball to know that the marriage she was entering into was a risk. So uncertain were its prospects, in fact, that she at first chose not to make the news public beyond family and friends.

But eighteen months later *The New York Times*, the city's tabloids, and the national wire services got wind of the Cinderella story of how Sanger, "once a member of the advanced Greenwich Village set," had been wooed and wed by a millionaire. She told reporters that she hadn't bothered to make an announcement at first, because her private relations were not the public's business, yet she didn't seem in a hurry to own up to the decision. Even Bill Sanger was not informed until many months after the event, when he announced that he too would be remarried—to a woman by the name of Vedya Merz.

Margaret had, in fact, been counseled against the marriage by sources somewhat more reliable than the New York psychic. Harold Hersey wrote quite hysterically that for his "Margoldit" to marry "an old man" would most certainly destroy her. To Havelock Ellis, Margaret had described her suitor as "nice and kind and generous" but also inclined to disapprove and dislike everything she really stood for. Ellis took Slee's own best interests into consideration. "He seems a nice man," Ellis wrote back, "and deserves a more suitable wife."[6]

Yet, according to Margaret, Slee agreed in writing at their wedding that they would maintain separate residences with separate keys in New York, that she would keep her own name professionally, that, in all respects, she would maintain her freedom. And for the twenty-one years of the marriage, until his death in 1943, he held, however grudgingly, to this contract. Though they argued more or less constantly about her frequent absences from him and her fierce commitments to her work and to her friends, he always welcomed her home with warmth and affection. He called her "my adorable sweetheart" or "my precious love" or just "my darling Margy."

To what extent he was aware of her compromised affections—or of her intimacies with such men as Wells, de Selincourt, and Child—is not clear. She always wrote to him innocently of her European escapades, and even included him on several trips to London, so he could meet the Wantley circle. Though he remained distinctly an outsider to the group, he was welcomed on his visits with apparent good humor and was assigned his very own role to play. In the strange constellation of characters where Havelock Ellis was affectionately called "the King," and Hugh de Selincourt, "the poet," Noah became known simply as "the squire."

Whatever he may have suspected about the bonds that tied his wife to these people, he remained secure in the knowledge that no matter how frequent or long her trips to England, she would invariably return to him with her affections intact. Her emotional duplicity in this regard, however, seems undeniable, as is apparent from another letter she wrote to Hugh de Selincourt in 1924. As a wedding gift, Noah had built her a stately but gracious stone house several hours north of New York City in the town of Fishkill. Perched above a mirrorlike pond surrounded by willow trees, it was modeled after the romantic residence at Wantley and given the name "Willowlake." She wrote of her joy in living there:

> Spring—good health—new house—furnishing it—making roads, gardens, stone walls—a new Belgian police dog to be trained—moving trees—raising the lake three feet—building two bridges—learning to drive my new Franklin car—besides writing the new book which is nearly finished. I go to NY two days each week for BC.—If only I could fly by night to London to see you & Havelock & Harold—I'd be ready to say this is paradise.[7]

* * *

If by night Margaret had reservations about her second husband, however, she apparently kept them from him. His letters during the early years of their marriage convey the ardor of an adolescent boy discovering the warmth and pleasure of sexual intimacy for the first time. He had married for love and was totally captivated by the wife who, in his eyes, combined attractiveness, gaiety, and charm with intelligence and seriousness of purpose, as no other woman he had ever known. She would only have to appear on the path that led from her study to the main house at Willowlake, Olive Byrne Richard remembered, and her beaming husband would turn to his companions and remark worshipfully, "Isn't she the most beautiful creature in the world?"

The only problem was that, more often than not, Noah found himself alone with just pen and paper to appease the intensity of his newly aroused sexual appetite. In the early years of their marriage, Margaret traveled frequently throughout the United States and Europe. In both 1923 and 1924, she spent several months alone in London, where she achieved renewed celebrity when her *Family Lim-*

itation pamphlet was banned from circulation by a London court. (Contraception was legal in England, but the pamphlet was apparently censored because the sexual feelings of women were discussed not far from an illustration of proper diaphragm technique that showed a finger inserted into the vagina.)

During these separations Noah could only write her adoring letters, so filled with longing for her return and with protestations of his intense unhappiness that they began to get on her nerves. "He is such a dear lonely soul. I wonder how he goes on at all with so little within himself," she confided to Juliet Rublee in 1924, in a rather bleak assessment of the character of the man to whom she was lawfully joined. A year later she wrote again wondering why independent women like the two of them had attracted such "clinging husbands." And in still a third letter she also wrote of a dream in which a "white woman angel" was pointing her finger at Juliet and shouting "devastatingly cruel"—probably projecting as much misgiving about her own conduct as about her friend's.

The fact is that while Noah had been sexually awakened, he was not by inclination or experience a romantic sort. Nor was he a man of literary bent, as were many of Margaret's other suitors. In letters, expressions of sentiment were often sandwiched in among reports of mundane household matters and of the dental problems, intestinal complaints, and assorted other bodily ailments that increasingly plagued him as he grew older. He had an annoying habit of moving in his letters from the sublime to the absolutely ridiculous, without even the grace of a pause or a transition, and this often got in the way of the feelings he was trying to communicate. On one occasion, he told her that she was his "angel of love"—that he loved her "beyond life itself"—but then immediately reminded her to bring along an enema tube from home when she joined him for a vacation at the Homestead Resort in Hot Springs, Virginia. Requests of this nature were not likely to kindle great sparks of passion.[8]

However awkward, Noah's letters seem, nonetheless, heartfelt. Margaret's more fluid responses, by contrast, convey remarkably hollow sentiments, which often seem as though they were written more out of a sense of obligation than from genuine affection. Repeated assurances that she desired him, for example, quite clearly pandered to his insecurity in the relationship. This was particularly apparent when they spent their second wedding anniversary apart in 1924. She wrote from London that she missed him deeply and yearned for his embraces, even as she was carrying on again with

Wells and had begun a torrid new love affair with Harold Child. "England is nothing without my adorable lover husband. You are a magician to turn my life like this," she insisted. Yet, a journal entry only several weeks later mentions visits with Wells and describes Child as "so exquisite in his mind and response that it is beyond description to express the feeling he inspires." Child's steamy letters to her in New York when they parted also suggest that she had been lying outright. Several years later on another London trip, she almost got caught in her charade. In one letter, for example, it appears as though she first hurriedly scribbled: "Dearest Noah—Darling—It is really always lovely to be away from you even one day," but then discovered her unconscious error and corrected it, for her normally clear script is messy, and reads as though she scratched over the *v*, to make certain it read as an *n*, for the word "lonely."

Margaret's superior sexual sophistication and experience were part of her allure, and Noah may have been so blinded by his apparent victory in winning her away from other men more illustrious than he that he actually assumed they were all only part of her past. Indeed, she seemed to tantalize him with half-truths in this regard. She openly acknowleged that she partied with de Selincourt and took country jaunts with Child, as though this behavior were all very innocent. From London in 1927, for example, she wrote that she had run into Child, who was still lamenting that he had been spurned "for a millionaire." She described her "old beau" as a handsome and intelligent man who was "about to be knighted." "Someday you will meet him and be very flattered that I loved you *best. Perhaps*," she wrote, deliberately teasing and yet obscuring the intent of her qualification.[9]

By day, the marriage certainly flourished. There were, of course, the house in Fishkill and the adjoining apartments on New York's fashionable Gramercy Park, done up by an interior decorator from Wanamaker's. Thereafter the couple moved to a luxury building on lower Fifth Avenue, in the shadow of Mabel Dodge's historic salon. It was walking distance from the cold water flat on 14th Street where Margaret had lived before Noah paid the rent, but the two were worlds apart.

After years of warming herself by a coal stove, she could more than comfortably afford elegant clothes, fur coats, and winter holidays in posh, warm weather resorts. Even more cherished, however, was the money put at her disposal to educate her sons and to pamper other family members and old friends who had been generous to her when she was needy. Stuart, though never much of a student, graduated from the Roxbury School in Connecticut and secured admission to Yale after a year spent with tutors in Europe. Grant transferred from Peddie to the considerably more fashionable Westminster School, and from there went on to Princeton. Margaret was intent that her sons earn the academic credentials she lacked—that they never be made to suffer the slights she believed she had endured because she was not properly schooled. She even taught herself to enjoy Ivy League traditions. When she finally took the time to watch Stuart play in a Yale football game, she proudly carried a bunch of violets to represent the school colors and later entertained his girlfriends from Vassar at her house in nearby Fishkill.

The abrupt change in their economic and social circumstances and personal expectations, however, was not always easy for the Sanger boys to negotiate. Having next to no experience with money for nonessentials, they tended to squander whatever they were given and complained more or less constantly to their mother about never having enough. Stuart acted out some of his worst adolescent confusion and rage with a fair amount of drinking and carousing. He barely made it through Yale. Grant, on the other hand, managed external appearances quite well during these years. He worked hard, was determined to succeed, and always tried to be good-natured and ebullient. Yet he suffered bouts of introspection and brooding, which belied this superficial calm.

Margaret, in turn, tried to be patient and on occasion evidenced some degree of understanding of the toll her sons paid for having her as their mother: "We radical parents must stand by our children when they give out what we have fed them in the past," she once admitted in a letter to Havelock Ellis. "It's conflicting nevertheless to have the radical utterances consistent with the conservative education." Yet her boys' occasionally rebellious behavior was hardly a manifestation of radicalism but instead revealed their increasing deference to traditional values. In 1927, Grant, whose desire for order in his life was the more profound of the two, thought about signing up with the Reserve Officers Training Corps at Princeton. Margaret wrote him in protest, saying that the military was likely to crush out his "own incentive and ideas of freedom." Shortly thereafter he asked her advice about rejoining the Episcopal Church, where he long ago had been baptized as an infant. "I have outgrown the need of church by my interest in philosophy, psychology & humanity," she responded. "Very often I find the church narrows & limits the mental horizon of a person when in reality it should broaden & deepen . . . be sure you really want it." He ignored her warning and joined.[10]

The influence of Noah Slee, whom both boys affectionately called Pater, became increasingly evident. Despite his enormous wealth, Slee was a penurious man by temperament and habit, who complained frequently about the extravagances of the young. For all his carping, however, he seems, in fact, to have been exceedingly generous to his stepsons and to his many other new beneficiaries.

Margaret rarely saw or socialized with members of the extended Higgins family during these years, yet she remained bound to her brothers and sisters by an intense, irrevocable tie to their common past, and in her newly comfortable circumstances, she faithfully looked after their fortunes. Nan Higgins retired from her position as a private secretary in New York and was sent up to Truro to nurse the failing Michael Higgins in the last years of his life. Her devotions were then repaid with a holiday in Europe and supplementation of her modest retirement income, so she could spend winters comfortably in California. Richard Higgins received financing for a wholesale corset business in San Francisco from the famous sister in New York, who was promoting the biological emancipation of women, and Ethel, though far too proud to take money directly, permitted her daughter Olive to accept a loan to cover her tuition at Tufts—a loan that was then forgiven. Other nieces and nephews were sent to camp or to Europe or taken on shopping expeditions in New York with nothing asked in return. (Years later Margaret would be visibly shaken when one of her favorites, her brother Bob's daughter Virginia, returned from a holiday with her aunt in England, married a Catholic boyfriend, and had a parcel of children.)

Slee's largesse extended to Margaret's friends and coworkers as well. A stipend of $50 per month was made available for Agnes Smedley, when she needed a psychoanalyst in Berlin in 1924, and more money was sent for an abdominal operation four years later. Kitty Marion, whose employment was abruptly and unceremoniously terminated by the American Birth Control League in 1929, had only to ask for help, as did countless other wards. In the late 1920s, as the occasion of Havelock Ellis's seventieth birthday approached, Margaret entreated Noah to provide an annual income that would allow Françoise Cyon to work as "the King's" full-time companion and secretary. With this money Ellis was also able to purchase a house in the country. The $1,500 annual salary was reduced by a third during the Depression, when Noah suffered financial reverses, but Margaret did provide Ellis small sums of money until he died in 1939.

She grew accustomed to a life-style she could only have dreamed of without Slee, and yet the material enhancements he made possible always remained secondary to her work. Her remarriage and sudden wealth actually may have intensified her professional commitment, because she felt obliged to keep an upper hand with her husband by demonstrating that she could always manage to be economically independent, if necessary. She deliberately kept the income from her books, articles, and lecture fees in her own separate bank account, yet when she fell short of cash, showed no compunction about asking him for money—as had been the case in London in 1924, when he covered the fare for her first-class lodgings at the Stafford Hotel, where she held court for other admirers.[11]

Far more than these personal indulgences, however, it was Noah's extraordinary generosity to the birth control movement that solidified the bond between them. By 1925, he had already given nearly $50,000 to the American Birth Control League, which made him—by a factor of at least ten—its largest single source of support. At that point, Margaret began to barter herself for more money, promising her husband in a private letter that if he agreed to pay Dr. Cooper's salary for two years, and in so doing helped win medical endorsement for birth control, she would retire with him to "the Garden of Paradise." The commitment, no doubt, underscored her resolve the following year to take some time off in Europe, though predictably, perhaps, she would spend only a fraction of it with Noah.

Noah also made numerous in-kind contributions of time and management expertise on behalf of birth control. Though he needled Margaret incessantly about her devotion to the cause, and begrudged every hour she was away from him, he assumed an active role in the movement himself—one that became even more central to his life after he sold his business and had only economic investments to occupy his time. As assistant treasurer of the league (the official treasurer's title always remained with a woman, Frances Ackerman), and later at the Birth Control Clinical Research Bureau, he solicited contributions from wealthy friends and kept a watchful eye on operations, expenses, and accounting procedures.

He also put international business contacts and resources at Margaret's disposal when her New York clinic decided to dispense the rubber-spring diaphragm then manufactured in Holland and Germany but still unavailable in the United States. He had large quantities of the devices shipped to his factory in Montreal, and from there they were then smuggled into New York in 3-in-One Oil containers. When the clinic ran into a problem securing the spermacidal jelly used in conjunction with the diaphragm, he took the German formula and began to produce it clandestinely at his plant in Rahway, New Jersey. In 1925, he staked Margaret's former boyfriend, Herbert Simonds, in a business called the Holland-Rantos Company, which formally manufactured contraceptives and brought an end to the need for contraband supplies. Several years later a federal court decision allowed for the advertisement and shipment by mail of contraceptive devices to those states where they were lawful for the prevention of disease. A booming demand quickly developed among physicians and druggists, and established pharmaceutical companies began to compete in what became an extremely profitable trade. Noah was careful that Margaret's integrity as a reformer be uncompromised, and he never profited personally from this venture. It was, nonetheless, a virtuoso performance for a capitalist, if not exactly for a Sunday school rector.[12]

By most conventional standards, of course, Margaret's marriage to Noah Slee was a failure. She never seemed to care deeply for him or to find sustained happiness in his company. From the start they bickered a great deal when they were together, and she found constant excuses to be apart. At the same time, her appreciation for the considerable grace he brought to her life, not to speak of his boundless support of her work, was most certainly genuine. This was especially true after her success with the Sixth International Neo-Malthusian and Birth Control Conference in New York in 1925. In apparent gratitude for his making her personal triumph at that event possible, Margaret's attention to the relationship improved after the conference was over and only deteriorated again when she finally began to spend more time with her husband and confronted the dismal reality of his personal limitations.

It was with considerable excitement that they planned her sabbatical in Europe the following year to include several winter months together on the terribly fashionable southern coast of France. They rented a charming whitewashed villa, with a skylighted atrium and a roof of bright green tile, perched high above the Mediterranean in the village of Cap d'Ail. The American writer James Gould Cozzens, then just out of Harvard and chasing a Vassar girl who was also a friend of Grant Sanger's, spent some time as a guest there and later used the setting in his semiautobiographical novel, *Ask Me Tomorrow*, which had as its theme the subject of a young man's angst in coming to terms with youthful passion. Cozzens apparently made his hostess the model for one of the characters in the book—his American patron in Europe, a woman of about fifty whom he called Mrs. Cunningham and described as "rich, well-educated and domineering but kind"—just as Margaret might have appeared at this time: "The girl's face remained close behind the relaxed cheeks and the wholesome but aging skin. The shape was strangely unaffected; just as her wide, well-placed eyes and candid brow were not themselves affected by the glasses, horned-rimmed, she wore. Undoubtedly she had been beautiful."

Cozzens wrote palpably of the romance of the Côte d'Azur. A flight of stone steps led down to the Slee villa. The gentle fragrance of flowering vines and the softness of sea-washed sunlight enveloped it. If the location inspired reasonably good fiction, however, it does not seem to have had a comparably enriching effect on its erstwhile occupants. Despite her protestations to the contrary, Margaret's mind as ususal focused on her work and not on her husband that winter, and her emotions, once back in Europe, seem to have been engaged elsewhere.[13]

The family gathered for the Christmas and New Year holidays in 1926-27 at Cap d'Ail, and Margaret spent much of January there, but by the end of the month she was back in London alone, working out the details of the international population conference in Geneva later that year, at which she was planning to bring together a large roster of internationally renowned demographers, biologists, sociologists, and physicians. Noah accompanied Nan Higgins to Spain and then returned to the villa. Margaret wrote him from London:

> The movement now needs one dominating force to drive it to success—The interest is alive—the time is ripe, but I shall need to give time to it if it is to succeed. . . . Will you help me? Not by money darling one, but by seeing this thing eye to eye with me & giving me the time I need to work it up properly. I know how hard it is for you to let me be away from you & I shall try to arrange it so there will be few separations. . . . I can never believe that you have come into my life to hold me back, you who are so vigorous & glorious in your love & splendid in your ideals & generosity.

The following day, she sent repeated assurances: "Nothing gives me more power than to feel you love me and want me to succeed. No

1

Anne Purcell Higgins

2

Michael Higgins at work

Margaret Higgins (left) with sisters, Mary, Nan, and Ethel

4

Margaret Higgins at Claverack College with Corey Albertson

5

William Sanger

Stuart, Peggy, and Grant Sanger in Paris, 1913

6

7

Margaret Sanger (alias Bertha Watson), passport photo, 1914

8

Margaret in London, 1915

THE WOMAN REBEL

NO GODS NO MASTERS

VOL I. MARCH 1914 NO. 1.

THE AIM

This paper will not be the champion of any "ism."

All rebel women are invited to contribute to its columns.

The majority of papers usually adjust themselves to the ideas of their readers but the WOMAN REBEL will obstinately refuse to be adjusted.

The aim of this paper will be to stimulate working women to think for themselves and to build up a conscious fighting character.

An early feature will be a series of articles written by the editor for girls from fourteen to eighteen years of age. In this present chaos of sex atmosphere it is difficult for the girl of this uncertain age to know just what to do or really what constitutes clean living without prudishness. All this slushy talk about white slavery, the man painted and described as a hideous vulture pouncing down upon the young, pure and innocent girl, drugging her through the medium of grape juice and lemonade and then dragging her off to his foul den for other men equally as vicious to feed and fatten on her enforced slavery — surely this picture is enough to sicken and disgust every thinking woman and man, who has lived even a few years past the adoloscent age. Could any more repulsive and foul conception of sex be given to adolescent girls as a preparation for life than this picture that is being perpetuated by the stupidly ignorant in the name of "sex education"?

If it were possible to get the truth from girls who work in prostitution to-day, I believe most of them would tell you that the first sex experience was with a sweetheart or through the desire for a sweetheart or something impelling within themselves, the nature of which they knew not, neither could they control. Society does not forgive this act when it is based upon the natural impulses and feelings of a young girl. It prefers the other story of the grape juice procurer which makes it easy to shift the blame from its own shoulders, to cast the stone and to evade the unpleasant facts that it alone is responsible for. It sheds sympathetic tears over white slavery, holds the often mythical procurer up as a target, while in reality it is supported by the misery it engenders.

If, as reported, there are approximately 35,000 women working as prostitutes in New York City alone, is it not sane to conclude that some force, some living, powerful, social force is at play to compel these women to work at a trade which involves police persecution, social ostracism and the constant danger of exposure to venereal diseases. From my own knowledge of adolescent girls and from sincere expressions of women working as prostitutes inspired by mutual understanding and confidence I claim that the first sexual act of these so-called wayward girls is partly given, partly desired yet reluctantly so because of the fear of the consequences together with the dread of lost respect of the man. These fears interfere with mutuality of expression —the man becomes conscious of the responsibility of the act and often refuses to see her again, sometimes leaving the town and usually denouncing her as having been with "other fellows." His sole aim is to throw off responsibility. The same uncertainty in these emotions is experienced by girls in marriage in as great a proportion as in the unmarried. After the first experience the life of a girl varies. All these girls do not necessarily go into prostitution. They have had an experience which has not "ruined" them, but rather given them a larger vision of life, stronger feelings and a broader understanding of human nature. The adolescent girl does not understand herself. She is full of contradictions, whims, emotions. For her emotional nature longs for caresses, to touch, to kiss. She is often as well satisfied to hold hands or to go arm in arm with a girl as in the companionship of a boy.

It is these and kindred facts upon which the WOMAN REBEL will dwell from time to time and from which it is hoped the young girl will derive some knowledge of her nature, and conduct her life upon such knowledge.

It will also be the aim of the WOMAN REBEL to advocate the prevention of conception and to impart such knowledge in the columns of this paper.

Other subjects, including the slavery through motherhood; through things, the home, public opinion and so forth, will be dealt with.

It is also the aim of this paper to circulate among those women who work in prostitution; to voice their wrongs; to expose the police persecution which hovers over them and to give free expression to their thoughts, hopes and opinions.

And at all times the WOMAN REBEL will strenuously advocate economic emancipation.

THE NEW FEMINISTS

That apologetic tone of the new American feminists which plainly says "Really, Madam Public Opinion, we are all quite harmless and perfectly respectable" was the keynote of the first and second mass meetings held at Cooper Union on the 17th and 20th of February last.

The ideas advanced were very old and time-worn even to the ordinary church-going woman who reads the magazines and comes in contact with current thought. The "right to work," the "right to ignore fashions," the "right to keep her own name," the "right to organize," the "right of the mother to work"; all these so-called rights fail to arouse enthusiasm because to-day they are all recognized by society and there exist neither laws nor strong opposition to any of them.

It is evident they represent a middle class woman's movement; an echo, but a very weak echo, of the English constitutional suffragists. Consideration of the working woman's freedom was ignored. The problems which affect the

Cover page of the first issue of The Woman Rebel, *1914*

10

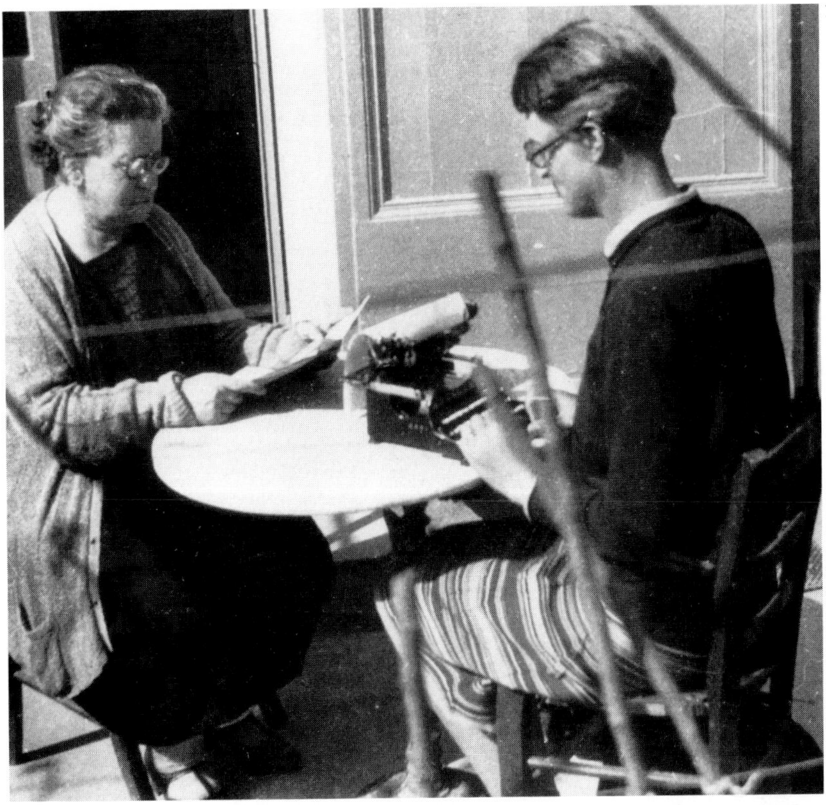

Emma Goldman dictating her memoirs

11

Anthony Comstock

MRS. SANGER TO BE TRIED

Back from Abroad to Face Indictments for Misuse of Mails.

Publicity photo, Margaret with Stuart and Grant, 1916

12

13

[ABOVE] *America's first birth control clinic, Brownsville, Brooklyn, New York, 1916*

[TOP RIGHT] *Mothers waiting in line*

[RIGHT] *Circular advertising the clinic*

14

MOTHERS!

Can you afford to have a large family?
Do you want any more children?
If not, why do you have them?

DO NOT KILL, DO NOT TAKE LIFE, BUT PREVENT

Safe, Harmless Information can be obtained of trained Nurses at

46 AMBOY STREET

NEAR PITKIN AVE. — BROOKLYN.

Tell Your Friends and Neighbors. All Mothers Welcome

A registration fee of 10 cents entitles any mother to this information.

מוטערס!

זיינט איהר פערטעגליך צו האבען א גרויסע פאמיליע?
ווילט איהר האבען נאך קינדער?
אויב נים, ווארום האט איהר זיי?

מערדערט נים, נעהמט נים קיין לעבען, נור פערהיט זיך.

זיכערע, אונשעדליכע אויסקינפטע קענט איהר בעקומען פון ערפארענע נורסעס אין

46 אמבאָי סטריט ניער פיטקין עוועניו **ברוקלין**

מאכט דאס בעקאנט צו אייערע פריינד און שכנות. יעדער מוטער איז ווילקאמען

פיר 10 סענט איינשרייבגעלד זיינט איהר בערעכטיגט צו דיזע אינפארמיישאן

MADRI!

Potete permettervi il lusso d'avere altri bambini?
Ne volete ancora?
Se non ne volete piu', perche' continuate a metterli al mondo?

NON UCCIDETE MA PREVENITE!

Informazioni sicure ed innocue saranno fornite da infermiere autorizzate a

46 AMBOY STREET Near Pitkin Ave. Brooklyn

a cominciare dal 12 Ottobre. Avvertite le vostre amiche e vicine.
Tutte le madri sono ben accette. La tassa d'iscrizione di 10 cents da diritto a qualunque madre di ricevere consigli ed informazioni gratis.

Margaret H. Sanger

15

Margaret outside the court-house, Brooklyn, 1917

[BELOW] *Margaret Sanger and Ethel Byrne in court, 1917*

WHILE
YOU WAIT.
WE DO
ALL KINDS OF
DYEING
WE
STERILIZE
173

Margaret leaving prison, Queens, New York, 1917 18

Portrait of Margaret Sanger, 1919 or 1920

Margaret in Egypt with Grant and Noah Slee, 1922

20

21

Havelock Ellis

22

Mary Ware Dennett, Margaret's rival for leadership of the early birth control movement

Volunteers selling The Birth Control Review, *Atlantic City, New Jersey, 1925*

Margaret with Dorothy Bocker, M.D., and Anne Kennedy, New York, 1924 24

Robert Latou Dickinson, M.D.

25

26 *Cover for the closing dinner of the Geneva Conference, 1927. Noah Slee is pictured on the far right. Margaret and all the other women were excluded.*

Margaret with Noah Slee in the Alps, 1927–28

27

28

Hugh de Selincourt with Grant Sanger at Stonehenge, England, 1929

29 *Hannah Stone and staff of the Birth Control Clinical Research Bureau being led into a police paddy wagon, April 15, 1929*

Margaret being censored in Boston, 1929

30

Portrait of Margaret Sanger, 1930s

32

Margaret with H. G. Wells and Katharine Houghton Hepburn, mother of the actress, New York, 1931

Margaret preparing to testify before the United States Senate Judiciary Subcommittee, with Senator Hatfield of West Virginia, 1932

33

34

Eleanor Roosevelt, silenced advocate of birth control

35

Margaret with Shidzue Ishimoto (now Shidzue Kato) of Japan, in New York, 1932

Margaret at the Tucson birth control clinic, 1936

[OPPOSITE LEFT] *Margaret with Gandhi in India, 1936*

[OPPOSITE RIGHT] *Margaret cooking curry, Tucson, 1941*

36

37

38

Margaret in a portrait by her friend Jay Sternberg, Tucson, 1952

Margaret with Abraham Stone, M.D., and others in India, 1952 40

Margaret with Grant and his six children, Michael, Peter, Stephen, Alexander, Morgan, and Anne, Mt. Kisco, New York, 1954

Margaret at the opening of a new Planned Parenthood facility in Tucson, 1953

43

Margaret with Nehru in India, 1959

Gregory Pincus, M.D., inventor of the birth control pill, with General William F. Draper, who first recommended to President Eisenhower that the United States make family planning aid available to foreign governments that request it, and Cass Canfield, Planned Parenthood Board Chairman, 1959–1962 44

45

46

Margaret in two caricatures by David Levine for Family Planning Perspectives, *1969 and 1978*

one in the world thrills me as you do or ever did, and as we go on together, it becomes lovelier." A third letter carried on in the same vein: "Blessed one I adore you more and more. You are my hearts desire. No one can take your place in the world." Beyond these remonstrances, however, and several coy expressions of her concern that Nan was the one secure in his arms, Margaret communicated little of substance to her husband.

Indeed, as a measure of her disingenuousness, one has only to compare these letters with those she was writing at the same time to Hugh de Selincourt, who had just dedicated his most recent book to her. She told Hugh on hearing the news: "You precious darling. You certainly have given me a surprise—a lift, a jolt and the greatest happiness. I reach up to kiss your dear face." Several days later, having read the book, she added that Hugh had a special talent for dealing with intimate and delicate subjects in an "entrancing way." Then she reminded him that Noah wanted to commission him to write up her life: "Won't you be shocked to know me really. How I smothered my little sister with a pillow whenever my mother left us alone! . . . how I stole money to buy flowers to put at the feet of the Virgin Mary! Oh-Oh—What fun we shall have—[But] You must promise not to publish it while I live—or at least while I am young enough to care." In the meantime, she asked him for biographical information in return, so she could line up a lecture series for him in America while they worked together on the book. "All that I know about you would not sound well from the wife of the Pres. of 3 in One," she teased. "No idea of your age, nothing about you but . . ." Several weeks later, when she was finally en route to rejoin Noah in France, she wrote again saying she would miss Hugh terribly at the villa. "I have no right to miss you, but I shall just the same."[14]

Margaret went to Cap d'Ail for several days and then returned to Paris via Geneva. The train trip through the lakes and mountains of Switzerland is one of the most majestically beautiful in the world, and there were plans for Noah to come along, but he apparently was wary of the strain of travel. She wrote to reprimand him gently for staying behind, telling him that a drunken man had tried to enter her compartment in the middle of the night. From February through April she moved back and forth between London and Paris, continuing the conference planning and also studying French. Noah and her sister took short excursions with Cap d'Ail as their base and then closed up the house. In early April, headquarters were opened in Geneva for the conference scheduled there in August. Noah joined her and remained in Geneva for the summer, but at the end of May,

Margaret was on her way back to the United States to deal with the tangled administrative affairs of the American Birth Control League, only to return in time for the actual proceedings to begin, during which her husband dutifully stood by her side at the social receptions.

Margaret had hired the British feminist Edith How-Martyn, an alumna of British suffrage battles, to help organize the Geneva Population Conference. As a young woman in London in 1907, How-Martyn relinquished a teaching post in mathematics to devote herself full-time to the suffrage cause. In 1915, she made the arrangements for the letter to Woodrow Wilson signed by prominent Britons in Margaret's behalf. Continuing to work as an organizer under the Pankhursts in the Women's Social and Political Union, she grew skeptical of the extremist politics of hunger strikers willing to compromise their health and spirits in merciless devotion to their cause and found herself sympathetic to the more moderate course of reform that Margaret was then charting for the birth control movement. Though she identified herself as a woman of "uncompromised feminist and democratic views," she was nonetheless willing to follow Margaret's lead in trying to encourage support from the professional mainstream, which, of course, meant reaching out to men. She managed the assignment with the clear understanding that the women would do all the work of the conference but give the men all the credit.

With How-Martyn's help, Margaret organized the entire event, paid her own expenses and funded the rest with grants from the Rockefeller-financed Bureau of Social Hygiene and from other smaller benefactors in New York and London, including Noah. Research papers were assembled that carefully documented the economic and social dimensions of population growth and change, while staying clear of propaganda and cant. Preliminary publicity was so extensive, however, that some number of the distinguished academicians who planned to attend became alarmed that they would be viewed as providing a platform for feminist birth control propaganda, with which they either disagreed outright or simply considered beneath their dignity. As a result, Margaret bought peace by agreeing that she would not participate in any of the formal meetings or discussions. With the single exception of a representative from Italy, who called her a tigress, most of the delegates took away a favorable personal impression and enhanced respect for her seriousness of purpose. In the end, she received a spontaneous standing ovation, which, in turn, inspired a round of "For she's a jolly good fellow" from the British delegation in attendance, and she felt especially good about her effort. How-Martyn, on the other hand, was more than relieved, as she put it with evident sarcasm in a private letter, to send "the distinguished scientists . . . back to their flies and mice." The men, in fact, did return to their laboratories, but only after organizing the International Union for the Scientific Investigation of Population, an association of demographers that for years had not one woman among its members.[15]

"I have had my hand kissed by every nation of Europe and Asia except Italy (whose ambitions are not ordinary)," Margaret wrote to Hugh, "and [I] have now decided never to live in USA longer than I can help it. . . . The squire, J.N. is well and talks of the 'poet' very often and misses it when you do not write to me !! Wonders why and so do I. When everyone knows I love you."[16]

No sooner were the sessions over than she summarily dismissed her husband once more on the grounds that the tribulations of the event, following on the heels of her difficult negotiations in New York, had left her in a state of exhaustion. She demanded time to edit the Geneva Conference proceedings for publication, while resting alone at a spa. The papers were mostly long and highly technical treatises on differential fertility by nation and region, and on patterns of migration, the consumption of natural resources, and mortality. It was not an easy job. "What a woman needs is to be alone, absolutely alone with God for a few days or weeks, until she has filled up the reservoir of her soul again with faith, hope & courage," she wrote Noah. "I have been impatient I know and really horrid at times. You have been tired & disappointed."

Noah went off to London, where he felt more comfortable than he had been in France, because he could at least speak the language. He occupied himself with visits to see Margaret's friends, but he was clearly miserable. The tensions in the marriage provoked Margaret to an uncharacteristic philosophical reflection about their differences. In her next letter, she told Noah bluntly that, despite their physical compatibility, they shared no common interests.

> My heart is troubled to have you lonely & apart from life's activities but I should wither up & die to be shut off from the intellectual currents of my contemporaries. All I want is a little more freedom. . . . I'm too grown up & too developed not to be free. My actions so far have been tempered with intelligence & I can't go back to chattel

> slavery. For that is what it really is dear when a woman is not made to feel that she can act without asking her husband's consent. Outside of financial affairs (which is & should be a joint affair between them) there should be utter liberty for both parties to enjoy tastes & friendships utterly free from the other. You will never see this I am certain, but until you can see it there will be no real happiness for the modern woman. If you could only be made to see what riches a woman can bring into your life, not only in outside forces, but in the joyousness of her own being, when she is fully conscious that freedom & love, faith & respect are the foundation of her marriage.[17]

The clinic's regimen of exercise, diet, and outdoor rest on a verandah, however, apparently restored Margaret's health and spirits. The couple reunited at the Ritz in Paris in October, completed final details of the publication of her conference report in London in November, and then visited Agnes Smedley in Berlin.

Smedley, the rebellious feminist and journalist, had become another of Margaret's emissaries abroad when she moved from New York to Germany in 1920, where she carried out intermittent birth control assignments. During World War I Smedley got herself into trouble in New York by supporting a community of insurgents, who were working for the seemingly just cause of home rule in the state of India. She came to the attention of American intelligence agents when several of her friends were accused of collaborating with Germany against the Allied war interests.

Berlin became a postwar haven for exiled Indian nationalists, and Smedley lived there for a time in a tempestuous common-law marriage with a Bengali freedom fighter by the name of Virendranath Chattopadhyaya, who was known for his extremism and his belief in the virtues of a socialist economy for a free India, and with whom she shared a growing intoxication with the Russian Soviet experiment. In 1928, she traveled to Moscow for the tenth anniversary of the Russian Revolution and wrote Margaret enthusiastically of the progress that had been achieved there.

> Lord when I see them working and building and starving, I could destroy the capitalist world for its blockade and its present policy of isolation. Americans come here and compare it with America. It is unfair. They ought to compare it with Czarist days. Now, instead of their miserable hovels, the workers here build huge apartment houses with community kitchens and kindergartens, with electric light and baths.

She was particularly optimistic about Russia's promise for women and provided a rhapsodic description of government-sponsored research on birth control, including pessaries, pastes, and an experimental "spermatoxin," which when injected into the blood of women, not only prevented impregnation, but allegedly also "restored vigor, sex energy and youthfulness."[18]

Smedley supported herself during these years by teaching English and selling sporadic pieces of journalism. She also leaned on friends at home in New York, especially Margaret and Noah, whose generosity she tried to repay by rounding up diaphragms from German suppliers and sending them under cover to New York. When they visited her in Berlin in 1927, Smedley arranged two lecture engagements for Margaret, the first before an association of German women doctors who were protesting a proposed law that would make criminal penalties for abortion more severe, the second before groups of Indian and Chinese students.

Basking in the success of Geneva, and still in a generous mood because of his then anticipated sale of 3-in-One Oil, Noah left Smedley with funds to establish a birth control clinic. Social welfare policies under the Weimar Republic were promoting secular, scientific attitudes toward marriage and family life. The German marriage bureaus that subsequently served as models for the Sanger Bureau's counseling services in New York were already open, and there were no formal laws against birth control. With the translation of her next book, *Happiness in Marriage*, into German, Margaret was determined to try to internationalize her reputation and influence. She encouraged Smedley and Josephine Bennett, a friend from the early days of birth control activity in New York who was living in Berlin, to find support for a clinic from local physicians.[19]

In July of 1928, the two women opened a small facility in Berlin with the help of a physician prominent in Germany's then reigning Social Democratic party. By this time, however, Smedley was working closely with German Communists, and the clinic also had a number of them on its board. To protect Margaret from the danger of red-baiting at home, to avoid provoking local opposition to the clinic as a conspiracy of foreigners, and quite possibly to avoid upsetting the politically conservative Slee, his seed money was never made public, and he was never asked to give any more.[20]

Margaret and Noah, meanwhile, had spent the winter months at fashionable St. Moritz in Switzerland, while Stuart and Grant went on a holiday cruise with college friends in the Caribbean. Margaret wrote them enthusiastically about her skating, alpine skiing, shopping, and other tourist conventions but admitted that "just now time hangs heavy on my hands. I am no good as a loafer." She might have developed doubts about the deprivations of Communism, but she found the amusements of the rich scarcely more tolerable.

When she returned permanently to New York in the spring of 1928, she wrote Juliet that she was trying to learn to relax with Noah at Willowlake by taking up swimming, tennis, and even some golf, though this new commitment to vigorous exercise seemed more a result of her concern that he had gained so much weight in Europe, than of anything else. Within the year, however, she was again fed up with him. "He will not let me out of his sight without a protest. I feel sorry for him & yet can I go on like this?" she asked Juliet, who had by then left her own husband in Washington and gone off to realize a long-held fantasy of making a movie in Mexico. "He's like a spoiled child," she added in another letter. "It simply breaks my heart to think of his loneliness. A few years ago I would not be moved by it, but now I am just sad at it all."

The truth was that Margaret had little capacity and no real desire to sustain a permanent intimacy with one man—and most assuredly not with Noah. He never satisfied her yearning for romantic love, and, indeed, the more time she actually spent with him, the poorer his prospects would become. Her emotions in this respect had come rather close to the surface in a letter written to Noah from the spa where she was working on the conference report after the event was over.

Without a trace of irony, she wrote that she had dreamed of a new packaging concept for 3-in-One Oil cans: "I saw it with a new cap [spout] which one could turn and let out a pouring stream—then turn half way around & it allowed only drops by drops," she explained. "Continue the turn & it checked the flow entirely. It was such a vivid dream & the picture of the handy can so real, I thought it like a good spirit trying to get to you." However valid an idea, her symbolic betrayal of a desire to influence Noah's output quite apart from his business enterprise seems apparent.[21]

Yet their shared public enterprise in behalf of the birth control cause continued to thrive. By supporting her work and immersing himself in its financial aspects so indefatigably, Noah won Margaret's enduring loyalty, and she apparently was warm and demonstrative toward him when she wanted to be. She once admitted, if rather too matter-of-factly, that "there is all the attraction between us that the world counts essential and necessary." Neither her commitment to her work, nor her apparent preference for men of more romantic excess—men who incidentally made no ongoing demands of her—ever seemed to compromise her ability to give him pleasure when they were intermittently together. Private letters testify to the fact that Noah remained sexually active into his old age. On one occasion, Margaret even wrote him that he was "a great lover, and there are few born or made," though she did so at a point in the marriage when they were spending so little time together that her candor seems highly questionable. Margaret stayed away for weeks, or often months, at a time and returned to find her husband "old and stooped and reluctant to action," as she put it in a confidential letter to Havelock Ellis: "But at sight of me and affection and harmony, he awakens—becomes active and happy—thinks clearly—his memory improves—dresses up—puts on gay neckties—sleeps and eats and walks at a different tempo. . . . He is just as alert at the sight of a lovely shape & just as urgent in his desires as he was when I first knew him at the age of 63."[22]

Margaret could scarcely claim absolute success in marriage, but she always thought of herself as an authority on the subject. Indeed, in 1926, when the market for domestic advice books was still strong, she published the third of the books comprising what she considered a kind of trilogy. As *Woman and the New Race* emphasized the relationship of birth control to women's rights and *Pivot of Civilization* its economic and social dimension, *Happiness in Marriage* stressed the central role it would play in family life. The book was intended to remove any remaining onus of immorality that still attached to the practice, and, perhaps not incidentally, it provided a product to compete with her competitor Marie Stopes's wildly successful advice manual, *Married Love,* when the ban on its publication in the United States was lifted.

Happiness in Marriage idealizes a conjugal relationship of shared companionship, obligation, and love. "Marriage no longer means the slavish subservience of the woman to the will of the man," Margaret insisted, carefully distinguishing the personal aspirations of her generation from what was universally perceived to have been the conventional arrangements of their parents. A "companionate marriage"—as it came to be known in the 1920s, and as she herself helped to define the arrangement—would follow a period of extended romantic courtship in which man and woman alike had ample opportunity to know, to seduce, and to freely choose one another. Once united, both parties to the relationship would respect each other's personal privacy and individual rights, even within the confines of small living quarters. To keep monotony and routine from threatening their happiness, they would freshen it each day with romantic gestures, no matter how stressed or tired they might be when they both returned home from their jobs. They would jointly establish a household budget, postpone childbearing until economically secure and comfortably situated, and share the chores and the responsibilities of child rearing. (The book skirts the issue of whether women with young children should work full-time.) They would practice birth control, so childbirth became "not a penalty or a punishment, but the road by which she [woman] travels onward toward completely rounded self-development."[23]

Margaret gave fair warning about common pitfalls in the marital relationship, offering descriptions of personal conflict quite obviously drawn from her own troubled experiences. "Petty quarrels, bickering and disagreements over details non-essential may become a habit," she wrote, undoubtedly thinking of Noah. "When they do, a separation, at least a spiritual separation, has already taken place. And a separation of the heart is more injurious to love than a physical separation. Petty quarrels inevitably lead to more serious ones." It was Bill Sanger, on the other hand, who probably inspired her recollection of "one charming young man with poetic and romantic longings, but absolutely irresponsible toward the prosaic matters as rent bills, grocery bills, gas bills and such unpleasant obligations. Constantly hoping to please his young wife, he spent money on orchids, violets, and trinkets of all kinds. These are gestures not to be condemned in themselves; yet in this particular case they did not make the wife happy . . . the children needed shoes. . . . The poetic husband sulked."[24]

She offered practical advice on how to overcome these problems, but the very title of her book betrayed a dangerous optimism and a flagrant dishonesty. Margaret remained an unrepentant romantic about love and sexuality, but she obviously joined the two to the institution of marriage solely for commercial purposes. This is nowhere more evident in the book than when she abandoned such routine subjects as housework and child care to talk directly about sex:

> As intelligent women seek to escape the trap of unwilling and enforced maternity, to change their position from that of docile, passive child bearers to comrades and partners of their husbands, they realize the need of a more abundant and deeper love life; As they attain equality in professional and social relations, they become conscious of the need for equality and fuller expression in the more sacred intimacies of the marriage relation. Husbands as well as wives today realize the importance of complete fulfillment of love through the expression of sex.

To this end, the entire second half of the book offers a frank and unabashed description of the human sexual and reproductive organs and also tackles the actual mechanics of lovemaking. Much of what Margaret had to say in the latter regard was premised on Havelock Ellis's assumptions about the periodicity of sexual desire in women, the presumably slower pace of their arousal, and the nature of their response patterns. She translated his guidelines into an elaborate seduction ritual culminating in coitus and mutual orgasmic satisfaction for both husband and wife. She wrote with a self-consciousness and uncharacteristic concern for delicacy:

> At this point, above all others, it is imperative that the husband shall not succumb to the temptation of merely satisfying his own bodily need. In the profoundest sense of the word, he must husband his resources and aim to bring to a climactic expression his wife's deepest love. Thus, while it is imperative that the woman should release her own deep impulses and give them full and unashamed expression, it is essential that the husband, with a deep effort of the subconscious will, attune his own desire to hers and aim to reach a climax simultaneously with that of his beloved.

But she then immediately added an important qualification: "In the ordinary normal woman this may be more retarded than the man might expect, gauging her nature by his own."[25]

In a subsequent passage, she repeated the admonition that women are "as a rule constitutionally unable to reach the climax of love at the same time as men," assuring her reader that this was no sign of frigidity. Her tortured prose undoubtedly reflected her concern about possible censorship and the fact that she was offering the first popular sex counseling, which proclaimed every women's right to an orgasm but, at the same time, also cautioned that many would not be able to achieve their desired response in a conventional marital posture. Despite her idealization of the relationship, she tried to keep expectations reasonable: "Each marriage is an individual problem, to be solved only by the participants. Happiness in marriage does not spring full grown from the bridal bed. To endure, it must be won gradually. Sex communion demands time and commitment."[26]

Such candid writing about sexuality, even if linked to wedded life, was not calculated to endear the book to moralists, and a lawyer for Margaret's publisher warned that it would probably be censored. His letter referenced the brief that had been submitted by prosecutors in Marie Stopes's censorship case. "Is there nothing else in the marriage state but degenerate thoughts of sexual passion and sexual indulgence?" the prosecuting attorney had asked the courts in seeking to ban Stopes's book. "If the marriage state has no higher aspiration than only the single gratification of sexual desire, then civilization has gone back to Pagan times, and the destiny of the human race and the expectations of the glorious future of our country have descended to the degenerate period of voluptuous Rome."

Jonah Goldstein, Margaret's longtime counsel, gave different advice. He submitted a long list of suggested deletions and changes, and then told her to go ahead and publish. No legal actions were, in fact, ever brought, and the view prevailed, as a reviewer for *The New York Times* put it, that "the terrible Margaret Sanger whom thousands of the pious have been taught to regard as the female Antichrist . . . is engaged in no more iniquitous enterprise than the effort to help people be happy." Indeed, Margaret's overriding desire not to be censored, and not to shock, may actually have made her seem a bit old-fashioned to those already inclined to support her by buying the book. This time, the liberal reading public in this country was ready for an even less inhibited sexual discourse than she was willing to risk.[27]

Much to her dismay, *Happiness in Marriage* never sold well and was quickly upstaged by the cookbook variety of sex manuals that have since become standard publishing fare. What is more, this sexually explicit literature then earned legal protection in 1930, ironically enough, when her old rival Mary Ware Dennett challenged the censorship of one of her own sex education pamphlets and won on appeal. In *United States v. Dennett,* the Second Circuit Court of Appeals in New York ruled that, in seeking to regulate obscenity, the Comstock laws should not interfere with serious, scientific sex instruction "unless the terms in which the information is conveyed are clearly indecent." The decision reconstrued *Swearingen v. United States*, a landmark case of 1895, where the Supreme Court had defined obscenity in printed matter as anything "calculated to corrupt and debauch the mind and morals of those into whose hands it might fall." The new rule of reasonable construction, as it was called, by insisting that the definition of obscenity inhere in the text itself whatever its intended motive, paved the way two years later for a lifting of the longtime ban in this country on Marie Stopes's *Married Love*, and for the publication of even more explicit manuals of scientific sex instruction. It would serve as precedent in the famous obscenity ruling on the importation of James Joyce's *Ulysses* in 1934, and also as the criterion for subsequent reinterpretations of the Comstock law with respect to contraceptive information and supplies.[28]

In the interim, in fact, an English translation was made available in this country of the work of the Dutch physician T. H. Van de Velde, whose graphic representation of the physiology and technique of lovemaking defied all prior standards of modesty. Van de Velde's *Ideal Marriage* was no less carried away in its enthusiasm for a higher level of sexual aspiration in marriage than Margaret's work. He was even more pietistic and far less cautious than she in promising a transcendent moment of sexual congress, which would transform marriage, as he put it, into a lifelong "honeymoon of rapture." He did, however, present a virtual encyclopedia of coital calisthenics and other erotic practices that had previously been labeled perverse but were legitimized as acceptable sexual practice with the help of his graphic and instructive discussion. The book became an immediate best-seller, eclipsing everything that had been written before it.[29]

Not one to take a flop lightly, Margaret read her rejection by the marketplace as a sure sign of her inadequacies as a writer. In 1927, she confided to Hugh that she would thereafter leave books to professional writers and never publish again. It was in this context that she and Noah came up with the idea that de Selincourt himself write her biography. She finished yet one more book called *Motherhood in Bondage*, a compilation of the most heartrending letters she had received over the years, which came out in 1928. But the tragic confusion about sexuality and reproduction communicated in her mail did not turn out to be popular reading material either, and so few copies sold that Noah graciously bought up all the remainders and gave them away.

None of Margaret's books, in fact, ever again attracted the big audience of her early work, but as with the debacle of the American Birth Control League, this setback did not deter her. Instead, she achieved renewed fame and public stature in the 1930s by committing herself to the very tactics of conventional political organization and lobbying she had previously slighted. Democratization of birth control during the Depression, however, presumed the legitimacy she also helped secure for it among the country's emerging medical and scientific elites. And this she accomplished by first making her birth control clinic in New York a priority.[30]

CHAPTER THIRTEEN

Doctors and Birth Control

Margaret had long hoped that the 1918 ruling of the New York State Court of Appeals in her Brownsville clinic conviction would embolden physicians in hospitals and public health stations to give out contraceptive advice to women with medical indications for its use. The following year, however, along with her friend and personal physician, Dr. Mary Halton, she had taken two sick women—one with tuberculosis, the other with syphilis—to virtually every hospital in Manhattan, and all had refused contraceptive service. She'd then sent out a questionnaire to fifty metropolitan area hospitals. Only a handful admitted to any policy at all on contraception, and of these, most said they did not give out information. Judicial clarification of New York's Comstock law regarding the rights of doctors to prescribe contraception for reasons of health had done little to help women who could not afford private health care. They continued to be denied access to medically sound advice.[1]

Physicians in private practice also betrayed a startling reticence and lack of information on the subject. Organized medicine remained notoriously sex shy, and a characteristic timidity was clear even among those doctors who made the effort to attend the American Birth Control League's inaugural conference in 1921. A session limited only to medical professionals began with a review of known commercial and folk methods for controlling conception, including the condom and suppositories made of occlusive jellies, such as vaseline and cocoa butter. The chairwoman, Lydia DeVilbiss, M.D., who had been trying to promote discussions of the subject at the New York Academy of Medicine since 1915, claimed that she had seen these suppositories work successfully when mixed with chemicals toxic to sperm, like quinine or zinc oxide, but this was as much as she could say for them.

The highly respected Baltimore psychiatrist, Adolf Meyer, whose early willingness to associate with Margaret was especially significant, then initiated a debate of the merits of the commonly employed practice of coitus interruptus, both in terms of its reliability and its potential side effects on hygiene and psychology. The self-consciousness of at least some of the participants was readily apparent. One speaker revealed, with some hesitation, what he claimed to have learned from his patients—that withdrawal worked best when combined with manual masturbation of the husband by his wife until orgasm was achieved. There was more candor, but still considerable confusion of fact, about whether or not the use of pessaries or diaphragms might impede female orgasm. Dr. Meyer nevertheless underscored the significance of the very fact that a group of doctors was openly discussing sexuality by urging them to take greater responsibility for sex counseling, "to individualize their outlook" and experiment with whatever contraceptive techniques seemed to work best for the maximum sexual gratification of their patients. He told them to be alert to the enormous changes taking place in sexual attitudes and behavior and deplored the continued refusal of the American Medical Association, the New York Academy, and other like-minded professional associations to endorse and give legitimacy to birth control.[2]

This professional discussion amply demonstrated that sexual prudery hindered medical acceptance of responsibility for contraception, but it also indicated scorn for unscientific, imperfect technology. Heavily invested in their campaign for professional stature during the 1920s, American physicians and the associations that represented them wanted little part of birth control practices long identified with the unorthodox approaches, and indeed in some instances the very medical and pharmaceutical quackery they were trying to conquer and overcome. Long after the passage of the first Food and Drug Act in 1906, progressive health reformers continued to bemoan the absence of strong regulations over the patent medicine industry. Medical literature frequently warned against commercial nostrums, along with cervical caps, pessaries, and other intervaginal apparatus sold in drugstores or by mail, which, if left in place for a long period of time or used in an unsanitary fashion, were thought to cause infections inducing sterility or perhaps even cervical cancer. At the same time, chemical douches, advertised for their alleged hygienic as well as contraceptive utility, remained suspect, because they tended to cause vaginal sensitivity or burns.

The best-selling douching agent in America at this time was the household cleaning product, Lysol, which was widely advertised as an antiseptic, disinfectant, and germicide, "invaluable for personal hygiene." The ads ran in the women's magazines along with notices for various "fountain syringes" or douche bags. Unlike bichloride, another popular douche, Lysol was not toxic in small doses, but women who mistakenly used it intensely put themselves at risk, especially if they were already pregnant, when the flooding of the vagina with chemical liquids under pressure could force air into the uterus, weakening blood vessels and causing spontaneous abortions and other vascular problems. When the Depression intensified many women's fears of getting pregnant, the Lysol ads became even more explicit, claiming the chemical's "penetrating power, reaching into every fold and crevice . . . soothing and healing enough . . . with no caustic alkali . . . to inflame tender feminine tissue. . . . It contributes to a woman's sense of fastidiousness, as well as to her freedom from fear."[3]

Many doctors also feared, or perhaps themselves shared, the public's still common confusion between contraception and abortion. Health professionals, especially in cities like New York, were increasingly concerned about their inability to reduce the country's appallingly high rates of maternal mortality, and they blamed the problem in part on the numbers of women dying from complications of illegal or self-induced abortion. In respectable circles, illegal abortion was universally condemned as primitive, dangerous, and disreputable, and this was clearly the reason why Margaret reversed the endorsement of the procedure she had made in her *Woman Rebel* days.

Even therapeutic and professionally supervised abortions, however, presented more difficult professional and ethical considerations than simple contraception. Complicating the matter even further, the line between the two was blurred by the sudden appearance on the medical market of a so-called wishbone or stem pessary, which was fitted through the cervix into the uterine canal and, much like the intrauterine devices marketed today, contravened pregnancy by preventing fertilization of the ovum. Medical literature of the period universally condemned these devices on the grounds that they acted as an abortifacient and were unsafe. And in an article in the *American Journal of Obstetrics and Gynecology* in 1924, Margaret was criticized for promoting the controversial procedure, which her friend and personal physician, Dr. Mary Halton, strongly endorsed. At the historic 1921 gathering of doctors, Halton had presented preliminary findings of a two-year test with more than 700 patients using an intrauterine coil made of silver or gold, which was then being more widely employed in Germany. She reported few harmful side effects in her sample. Chastened by the criticism, however, Margaret then took care to warn against coils in the chapter on contraception she included the following year in *Happiness in Marriage.* (Halton later began testing an IUD made of a ring of silk suture, but publication of her findings was still rejected by the *American Journal of Obstetrics and Gynecology* in 1947 as "too hot" an issue. It was not until the 1960s that the medical profession changed its mind about the procedure.)*

Explanations of recently developed sterilization procedures, still known to only a few practicing physicians, were also presented to the doctors attending this first conference in 1921, along with research findings demonstrating that neither surgical removal of a section of the female fallopian tube, nor male vasectomy, interfered with normal sexual functioning. Finally, Margaret, who was the only nonprofessional participating, reviewed the results of a five-year trial of the rubber-spring diaphragm by Dutch physicians, who reported a negligible failure rate when the method was employed in combination with individual examination and instruction. Indeed, until the marketing of oral anovulant birth control pills forty years later, the state of contraceptive technology did not advance measurably be-

* Mentioning Mary Halton's research raises the question of what form of contraception Margaret herself employed. Surprisingly, I have found virtually no mention in her voluminous personal papers, and therefore assume she used the diaphragm and jelly, the virtues of which she preached, or, perhaps, since Halton was her doctor, the I.U.D.

yond the collective knowledge gathered together for the first time at this very first discussion she sponsored.[4]

If reasonably sound knowledge was available, however, it enjoyed virtually no scientific credibility, and Margaret's suspect reputation with most doctors hardly helped the matter. In 1920, Robert Latou Dickinson, M.D., who had earlier decried the association of contraception with political radicals like Sanger, was elected president of the American Gynecological Society and began to stir up organized professional interest in birth control. In his inaugural address, he lamented the absence of authenticating clinical data on contraception and openly attacked his colleagues for shirking their responsibilities as specialists in gynecology and obstetrics by failing to study it. During his long experience in the private practice of obstetrics and gynecology in Brooklyn, Dickinson had come to the same conclusion Margaret reached in the course of her nursing among the poor. He believed that problems of sexual ignorance and maladjustment were widespread in American marriage, and he wanted an enlightened, scientific response to them, not what he characterized as the cant of propagandists. Determined to enlist the support of the right kind of people, he closed his private practice in Brooklyn and set up offices in the New York Academy of Medicine to conduct research. He asked the members of the gynecological society:

> What serious study has even been made bearing upon the harm or harmlessness of the variety of procedures or concerning the failure or effectiveness of each? Who has or can acquire any considerable body of evidence on these matters but ourselves? What, indeed, is normal sex life? What constitutes excess or what is the penalty for repression in the married? . . . It will take a few professional lifetimes of accredited histories to gather evidence to submit, but sometime a start must be made.[5]

However controversial this undertaking, Dickinson was himself a gentlemanly product of New York's social and professional establishment. He was, at least for the time being, willing to move ahead with caution and restraint. Margaret, of course, was not. Nor was she prepared to step aside for an individual, who by dint of gender, professional training, and social standing, quite clearly saw himself as her superior. In 1920, she had syndicated the chapter on birth control clinics that provided the peroration of *Woman and the New Race* in *American Medicine*, a popular health journal read by many doctors. And within a year she announced she would again open a clinic to treat patients presenting medical indications for contraception. This time she pledged to work within the framework of the law and also promised to collect case histories on which a scientific, clinical study of birth control could be based.

Margaret had arranged for the clinic to be administered by the same Lydia DeVilbiss who chaired the medical forum on contraception at the 1921 conference. But Dr. DeVilbiss, protective of her own professional credentials, refused to move forward as planned when New York State authorities arbitrarily denied the two women an operating license. In view of the venture's questionable legal status, the directors of the American Birth Control League also decided not to risk the new organization's tenuous stature, or their own personal liability, by linking themselves legally to it. The clinic finally opened in 1923 under a separate organizational umbrella—its medical delivery and research objectives carefully distinguished from the league's agenda of education and legislation. With contributions of $3,600 from Clinton Chance, a wealthy British manufacturer and Neo-Malthusian whom Margaret had met in London, and $2,500 from her longtime benefactor Dorothy Straight, she rented space across the hall from the league's office on lower Fifth Avenue and opened the Birth Control Clinical Research Bureau, so named in order to follow the spirit, if not the letter, of the law, which required any facility calling itself a "clinic" to have the state dispensary license she could not get. The operation was run essentially as the private practice of Dr. Dorothy Bocker, a graduate of Brooklyn's Long Island Medical College, who had been working in Georgia, running a division of the state's public health program. In order to land herself a guaranteed $6,000 salary back in New York, she dared to circumvent the law. Margaret warned Bocker that her medical license could be jeopardized as a result of her association with this undertaking, and in a letter explaining the terms of her job offer, she underscored that she did not anticipate "a peaceful, harmonious, uneventful year."[6]

In fact the only controversy that plagued the clinic in its first two years of operation was the quality of Dr. Bocker's research. With references from charitable and religious institutions, from some private doctors and nurses, and simply by word of mouth, the facility attracted a steady clientele of young women. They came predominantly from modest circumstances, two thirds having already attempted some form of contraception on their own, though without satisfactory results. Birth control had received extraordinary amounts of publicity and raised the level of demand among women in New York, but as so many of them lamented, their heightened expectations had not been easily met. Most claimed to have tried varieties of commercially available sponges, tampons, pastes, effervescent tablets, chemical douches, condoms, and pessaries. Many had resorted to abortion and, when examined, revealed a high incidence of pelvic disorder. One even claimed that she had gone in desperation for better advice to the keeper of a local brothel.

Bocker, however, was not an experienced researcher, and she ran into trouble when she employed thirteen different contraceptive regimens and failed to produce a statistically valid test with any one of them. Lacking sufficient funds to hire an assistant, she also neglected to follow up on those 20 percent of the women who did not return to the clinic for further instruction after their first visit. Assuming they were using the methods successfully, when, in fact, the opposite was more likely to have been true, she undermined her claim that she had achieved a failure rate of less than 10 percent.

When a report of her research was privately printed in New York by Noah Slee, it immediately came under the fire of Dickinson, writing in the *American Journal of Obstetrics and Gynecology*. Dickinson had, in fact, already sent undercover nurses to investigate the Sanger clinic and had learned to his surprise that Bocker, a graduate of his own alma mater in Brooklyn, had a good deal more professional standing than he had assumed. Whatever her qualifications, he was nonetheless obliged to challenge research he found far from unassailable. In his critique, however, he did take the trouble to distinguish "the present character" of Margaret Sanger's initiative from her prior undertaking in Brownsville. Less charitable was the judgment of the National Catholic Welfare Conference in Washington, which circulated a flier calling the Bocker report unscientific, unethical, and insensitive to the potential of contraception's harm to the "nervous system or morals" of its users.[7]

Dickinson had earlier prevailed on several of Margaret's own donors in the world of New York society, including Gertrude Pinchot, to fund an organization of eminent physicians to sponsor research. He named it the Committee on Maternal Health, and took office space for the group at the New York Academy of Medicine, though there was no formal affiliation between the two. A savvy operator in the politics of his profession, he also secured the qualified participation in this effort of George Kosmak, the prominent editor of *The American Journal of Obstetrics and Gynecology* who had once told his colleagues to counsel continence over contraception. Though a practicing Catholic and a vocal opponent of birth control, Kosmak joined up on the grounds that a responsible alternative was necessary to the work of the propagandistic and unprofessional Margaret Sanger.

To secure reliable data for his proposed study, Dickinson then enlisted the cooperation of the outpatient departments of seven leading Manhattan hospitals. He purchased the necessary supplies and also issued standard forms on which clinical case histories could be collected as data. He ran into a problem, however, when he was able to secure only condoms and spermicidal jellies for trial. He tried to import rubber diaphragms from Europe, but his shipment was intercepted by United States customs officials acting under the provisions of the Comstock laws. He was unable to find others until Margaret herself capitulated to him in 1925 and agreed to sell her contraband product at an extravagant 50 cents apiece.

Sensitive to a prevailing disdain and fear of social medicine among his colleagues, Dickinson agreed not to advertise the availability of his clinic services. He also established rigid procedures for the written referral of patients by reputable doctors in private practice, but then gave them no real incentive to get involved. His regulations were, in fact, so complicated that after eight months, only nine patients had made themselves available for research, and three of them were already pregnant. Even when the requirement of physician referral was later dropped—when hospitals were offered a small financial incentive to produce patients, and limited publicity was allowed—Dickinson could not seem to get his project off the ground. Five years' effort produced only 335 incomplete case histories, forcing him to admit the necessity of exactly the kind of propaganda he had criticized and to rely on the only available source of data he could find—Margaret Sanger's Birth Control Clinical Research Bureau.[8]

As it happened, Dickinson and Sanger in 1924 found themselves in competition for funding from the Bureau of Social Hygiene, the research institution established by John D. Rockefeller, Jr., which had for years been zealous in its investigations of commercialized vice and prostitution. The bureau was then run by Katherine Bement Davis, a patrician graduate of Vassar with a Ph.D. in sociology from the University of Chicago. Earlier she had distinguished herself as a progressive prison administrator in New York State and City, where she came under Margaret's venomous attack in 1917 as the individual responsible for the inferior conditions of the women's prisons in which she and her sister were incarcerated. Shortly thereafter, however, Davis had left city government for the safer harbor of foundation work, and under her tutelage the staid Bureau of Social Hygiene broadened its reach to embrace the larger study of normal human sexuality and social hygiene, not just problems of deviance.

Davis provided an avenue of reconciliation between the birth control propagandists she had reluctantly come to admire and her establishment friends in the medical profession. In 1924, she recommended that Rockefeller personally donate $10,000 toward Margaret's research, with the proviso that her data then be submitted to Dickinson's Committee on Maternal Health for professional analysis and review. At this juncture, Margaret also won the endorsement of the New York lawyer Raymond F. Fosdick, one of Rockefeller's most trusted counselors and a member of the Advisory Committee he established to supervise his personal charitable contributions. At Fosdick's urging, Rockefeller, using the Bureau of Social Hygiene as a conduit, anonymously donated $5,000 to Margaret. This private support was renewed each year thereafter at approximately the same levels, and in 1925 and 1926, the Bureau of Social Hygiene also made two additional anonymous contributions of $10,000 to facilitate the cooperation between Sanger and Dickinson that Davis desired. The following year, however, Margaret's bold request for increased funding of an expansion budget of $50,000 was turned down, with the Social Hygiene Bureau staff officially saying only that the cause remained too controversial for such substantial underwriting. In this period Rockefeller's policy limited his contributions to a fraction of any one institution's budget, and he was already funding her at a level comparable to all but the most exceptional of his beneficiaries. The millionaire industrialist whose assassination for crimes against working people she had once publicly advocated, thus became, after her own husband, her largest single source of support. He acted at the behest of Davis, another progressive do-gooder Margaret had once lambasted. Yet the only indication that either one of them may have held her accountable for her prior behavior was the demand that their contributions never be made public.[9]

With the Rockefeller money still at stake, Margaret sent her new medical emissary, Dr. James Cooper, to talk to Dickinson and inquire what she might do to win his approval. From Cooper, the word came back that to win his support she would have to jettison Dorothy Bocker. Though she had already signed off on Bocker's findings, she complied immediately, her discomfort apparent from the awkward manner in which she handled the firing, first saying she would help set Bocker up in a practice of her own, then agreeing to keep her on part-time, and only then severing the relationship completely. Bewildered but defiant, Bocker left in a huff taking all of the precious clinical files with her. Margaret then blamed the hapless woman for a "betrayal of trust" in leaving with the records, though as presiding physician of the clinic, they were technically hers to keep.[10]

The parting proved fortunate because in Bocker's place Margaret hired Dr. Hannah Meyer Stone, a thirty-two-year-old pediatrician affiliated with the Lying-In division of the distinguished New York Hospital and Medical College, from which she had graduated in 1920, after first earning a degree from the Brooklyn College of Pharmacy. Margaret also formed an advisory board for the bureau composed completely of men willing to support Stone's work. All of them were reasonably eminent professionals in either medicine or the social sciences, but because Dickinson had not as yet agreed to work with the clinic, most of them were not from New York City, and none were physicians with gynecological or obstetrical specialties. Finally, acceding to another Dickinson request, the clinic was physically separated from birth control propaganda activities and moved to freestanding space on West 15th Street.

Yet despite these accommodations and Stone's unassailable academic credentials, Dickinson's board at the Committee on Maternal Health still refused to cooperate. Since few prominent internships or residencies were then open to women doctors, and hardly any women taught on medical school faculties, Stone was without the kind of professional distinction that alone might have impressed them. She also happened to be Jewish and the daughter of immigrants, but even had she possessed more "acceptable" academic or social credentials, she probably would have remained suspect. "Men, in general, do not like to work under women, even when they do not have half as much sense; and doctors are particularly jealous cattle," E. M. East, the Harvard sociologist and Sanger clinic board member, reminded Margaret several years later as tortured negotiations with Dickinson continued. He doubted whether male doctors would ever volunteer for birth control service so long as Dr. Stone was in charge. Though she only worked for Sanger part-time, in fact, Stone was forced to give up her Lying-In privileges as a result of her birth control affiliation. Until 1932, she was also repeatedly denied membership in the New York Academy of Medicine, a situation that one admirer later described as a "kind of polite torture," which she accepted without "a trace of martyrdom."[11]

The equanimous Stone, nonetheless, went ahead and prescribed contraception to more than 1,600 women during her first year on the job. She kept extensive medical and sexual histories, along with socioeconomic data of interest to the Research Bureau's social scientists. Meticulous in her record keeping and determined not to repeat her predecessor's mistakes, she also dispensed a social worker to follow up on delinquent cases, a frustrating and enormously costly task in a city the size and complexity of New York, where residential and employment turnover made women difficult to locate—not to speak of the fact that some who came to the clinic undoubtedly gave false identities.*

So intense was the interest in this work that Margaret had to book a larger hall, and schedule a double session, when more than 1,000 physicians registered to hear Stone's preliminary report on her clinical experience at the well-publicized Sixth International Neo-Malthusian and Birth Control Conference in New York in 1925. This was so despite the fact that the Committee on Maternal Health officially vetoed the meetings, still refusing to have anything to do with the birth control propagandists. Dickinson, however, broke ranks and attended, ex officio, and, impressed by Stone's presentation, appealed two years later to the preeminent *Journal of the American Medical Association* to publish her research findings. When he was politely rejected there, he helped Stone find a place in a respectable professional publication called *Medical Journal and Record,* and, thereafter, worked with both Sanger and Stone in varying degrees of compatibility.[12]

At the behest of the Bureau of Social Hygiene, Dickinson had come up with a plan to create a Maternity Research Council composed of specialists in obstetrics and gynecology who would essentially take charge of the Sanger operation. The facility was still a shoestring operation when Margaret agreed to this proposal in exchange for the promise of professional endorsement and Dickinson's pledge to se-

* In January 1927, for example, fifty-four visits turned up only forty-six proper addresses, where only twenty-six patients were found to be at home, only fourteen of them reporting success with the diaphragm method. Of 167 mailed questionnaires, sixty-seven were returned, reporting a higher rate of fifty successes. Since these were women who did not return on their own for checkups, the rate of success was not all that bad, though certainly nowhere near what Bocker had claimed.

cure her a dispensary license from the New York State Board of Charities. The plan allowed her to back out if the license did not materialize, but, if all went well, she would cede her authority as head of the clinic to the physicians. Adolf Meyer, M.D., who had also become a member of the clinic's original advisory board, encouraged her cooperation with Dickinson at this time, as did the majority of his colleagues. One of them, though, C. C. Little, who was then president of the University of Michigan and a prominent eugenicist, objected on the grounds that it made no sense to reward the same medical men who had "made a mess" of the problem of contraception in the first place.[13]

As it turned out, Dickinson's colleagues also lacked enthusiasm for the proposal and only under duress agreed to appoint a three-member committee of the New York Academy of Medicine to investigate the clinic officially as a preliminary to formal affiliation. The vocal obstructionist, George Kosmak, was made a member of this group, and after a personal inspection of the facility, his vitriolic unofficial suggestion was that it ought to be closed down as "a violation of the law" and "a public menace." As an official matter, however, the investigating committee limited its objections to the fact that Hannah Stone was taking too liberal an attitude toward what constituted a medical indication for birth control under the law. She had added child spacing and other psychological factors to the long list of obvious physiological conditions that might make pregnancy hazardous. Any woman with a baby under the age of nine months, for example, was automatically given birth control. The doctors instead called for a more narrow interpretation of the law and also demanded that the *Birth Control Review* be removed from the reception area where it was prominently displayed, along with posters that explained the differences between contraception and abortion, so as to make clear that the clinic practiced medicine and not propaganda. A draft statement of principles also clarified that the committee wanted to help "legitimate" applicants for contraception "while not losing sight of encouragement to couples whose progeny promise to be of value to the community to bear as many children as they may."

Clinic policy at the time also permitted the "quiet" referral of patients presenting no health indications whatsoever to private physicians known to fit diaphragms under these conditions. This was particularly important because many newly married women sought service, and Stone very much wanted to accommodate them. The policy seemed suspect to the Committee on Maternal Health, however, not only because of its questionable legality, but also in light of its potential abuse by doctors given an incentive to work at the clinic in order to expand their own private practices. Indeed, one such physician actually quit in 1929 on the grounds that she wasn't receiving enough private business to make her time there worthwhile. At Margaret's direction, Stone thereafter took personal charge of all referrals for "no health reasons" as well as for any other recommended gynecological procedures, so as to enforce a uniform policy and avoid the appearance that staff physicians might benefit personally from their affiliation. At one point Margaret intervened personally and fired a doctor who had turned away a woman who deserved to be served at the clinic and not outside it.[14]

In the end, however, the issue of the license, and not the desire of Dickinson and his committee to regulate either the fertility of middle-class women or the ethics of women doctors, became the stumbling block to affiliation. After seven months of effort and two hearings on the matter, he came away empty-handed from the New York State Board of Charities, the professional panel authorized to grant medical licenses. Though no evidence survives to verify his claim, Dickinson charged that the board had added an unofficial fourth condition to the standard burdens of "proof of need, proof of character of the incorporators, and sufficiency of funds," required for a license. He accused it of demanding "a waiver of objection" to the license from the Catholic Church. He could get no further in Albany than Margaret had on her own.

Indeed, in what appears to have been a classic political shuffle, the three physicians who served as gubernatorial appointees to the panel simply announced that they found the granting of a license "inexpedient from the standpoint of public policy," while they quietly made it known through a representative of the Rockefellers that they would not interfere if Dickinson went ahead without a license, just as Margaret had been doing. New York's governor, Alfred E. Smith, was, of course, a Catholic with prospects as a Presidential candidate in the Democratic party. He was unwilling to risk the erosion of his political base of support by giving even a hint of legitimacy to Margaret Sanger. Though Dickinson was willing to proceed under these circumstances, his colleagues at the Committee on Maternal Health adamantly refused. Subsequent efforts on his part to interest New York Hospital in administering the clinic as an outpatient facility, covered under the umbrella of its own license, also came to naught. Fearful of giving up her independence to the lumbering bureaucracy of an elite hospital that at best would have had a marginal interest in providing women with access to quality birth control, Margaret ultimately refused to endorse this plan, and it was never pursued.[15]

For Margaret the clinic had by this time become nothing less than a crusade. What had once been only a lofty, rhetorical promise was transformed into a reality as more and more women crowded into the facility, fully two thirds of them on the recommendation of someone who had already been there before. By decade's end, the bureau was serving almost 5,000 new patients a year. Revisits for regular checkups and renewal of supplies brought the number of annual client contacts to well over 20,000—more than the aggregate of all the rest of the voluntary birth control clinics in the country combined. The facility was open five days a week and held evening sessions to accommodate working women. Several hundred private physicians were also receiving instruction each year in the proper fitting of diaphragms.

From the single nurse and social worker who had originally assisted Hannah Stone, the staff expanded to include twelve women doctors working part-time under her, assisted by a rotating battery of nurses, social workers, administrative personnel, volunteers, and field workers who indefatigably pursued delinquent cases either by letter or in person. To support this growth Sanger charged patients for consultation and supplies on a sliding scale, each according to her ability to pay, and made up the clinic's small deficit by dunning individual benefactors and by sponsoring any socially acceptable fund-raising gimmick she could come up with, including, on one occasion, the selling of chances on a string of cultured pearls.[16]

"Founded upon nothing more substantial than faith in its humble and despised beginnings," she wrote in an annual report for 1929, "it has grown steadily until it has become not only a clinic where individual women may receive expert medical advice for their most troubled and intimate problem, but a definite social force within the community." Elsewhere she again sounded the visionary themes of her early writings—the clinic would "lead woman out of darkness and despair into the light of sane living." It would place in her hand the "key of self-mastery and self-direction."[17]

Owing as much to these bold claims, perhaps, as to her considerable successes, Margaret once again found herself a target of the New

York City Police Department in 1929, whose impulsive intervention in the clinic's operation only served to help stimulate more business. On April 15, eight police officers entered the facility, drove out fifteen patients, arrested eight staff members, including the two physicians, and seized confidential medical records. The complainant was a married undercover policewoman named Anna McNamera, who several weeks earlier had been fitted with a diaphragm after her medical and social histories were taken, and she had received a thorough pelvic examination.

A young and still promising assistant district attorney by the name of Frank Hogan, soon to earn his reputation as one of the country's most respected municipal prosecutors, was put in charge of the case, but even he was no match for Margaret's longtime lawyer, Jonah Goldstein, who deftly turned the pretrial hearings into a referendum on the right of physicians to professional autonomy. The presidents of the New York Academy of Medicine and of the somewhat more professionally plebeian New York County Medical Society, along with Dickinson and a former commissioner of the New York City Department of Health, each testified that McNamera had exhibited reasonable medical indications for birth control under the provisions of the law. After two such hearings the charges were dropped, and the police commissioner issued a public apology. The administrator of the department's women's bureau, who had supervised the raid, was demoted from her position for exceeding the authority of the arrest warrant when she ordered the confiscation of confidential medical records, almost all of which were immediately returned.[18]

The outburst of publicity surrounding these events propelled a final round of discussions about affiliation with Dickinson and the Committee on Maternal Health. This time, however, all the doctors had to offer was a plan to supplant the existing nine-member advisory board of the clinic with local people of their own who would come around and make regular medical inspections. Dickinson was adamant about the need for trained obstetricians and gynecologists on the clinic's board and also proposed the continuation of efforts to have New York Hospital take it over altogether. An organizational plan was drafted that placed Margaret's Baltimore supporter Adolf Meyer, M.D., as president of an executive board, and left Sanger herself as vice-president. The prominent obstetrician J. Whitredge Williams and the gynecologist Frederick Holden, however, were also to join, along with Katherine Bement Davis of the Bureau of Social

Hygiene. Hannah Stone would remain as medical chief of staff but would be made to answer to an inspection and consultation committee of outside physicians.

Complicated negotiations went on for months, and the extensive talks produced reservations on the part of the clinic's existing Advisory Committee about the danger of compromising institutional autonomy. Stuart Mudd, M.D., an immunologist from Philadelphia who had long been a board member, may have done the most to provoke Margaret's concern when he encouraged her to cooperate with the Committee on Maternal Health, yet, at the same time, wrote of the "wonderful personal good will and humanitarian spirit you have introduced in the clinic, which could not be replaced by merely expert and scientific skill." She, in turn, complained to him that unless she swallowed "hook, line and sinker" every Dickinson proposal, she was accused of being "sassy"—"which makes me tired," she added frankly. The Advisory Board finally reached what was communicated as a unanimous conclusion that sharing authority for clinic policy would never work, and Margaret, basking in all the positive publicity she had just received, politely turned Dickinson down altogether, subjecting herself to his angry accusations that she was "playing fast and loose" with the prestige of the New York Academy of Medicine.[19]

If Dickinson went away mad, however, he did not stay that way for long. Margaret quickly announced her intention to solicit medical consultation independent of him. She approached officers of the Academy of Medicine directly and encouraged them to undertake another survey of the clinic's medical operations with the aim of adding several of its members to the existing clinic structure as consultants and visiting physicians. The investigation went forward, and this time the doctors claimed to be impressed by Dr. Stone's competence and sincerity. Margaret went out of her way to be charming personally, and even the dour and often abrasive George Kosmak found little to criticize. During his inspection, however, he apparently complained to the clinic's social worker, Mary Macaulay, that "husbands don't figure here at all," a comment which provoked some cynical comments about his condescending attitudes toward the autonomy of women in her private letter describing the visit. Kosmak also worried about the numbers of women who were receiving free services, a percentage that grew steadily as the onset of the Depression increased levels of unemployment and need, and provoked further anxiety among Academy members about the dangers of "socialized" medicine.

Nevertheless, the Academy published a favorable report on the clinic in its bulletin and actually issued its first official endorsement of the use of contraception for the prevention of disease—six years before the American Medical Association finally took a position in 1937. The Academy's director, Dr. Linsly R. Williams, then claimed, at least, that he made an effort to find recruits for a medical board but did not succeed, admitting to Margaret that a negative view of her work predominated among his members, who continued to believe that a birth control facility could never function in a scientific manner "as long as it is under private and independent control."[20]

Acting on his own and not in any official capacity, however, Dickinson did join the Birth Control Clinical Research Bureau's advisory board and added himself to the growing ranks of Margaret's fawning admirers. The two of them bickered over any number of policy issues and almost came to blows again three years later when Dickinson and his associate, Marie Kopp, published a historic report on the bureau's first 10,000 cases, which left Margaret's name—and Hannah Stone's as well—off the title page. The relationship of the two women to the Birth Control Clinical Research Bureau was mentioned only in passing in the text. Dickinson insisted that Margaret's reputation as a propagandist would compromise the scientific credibility of the document and accused her of a desire for "self-glorification," because she wanted the study to come out as a joint publication. Arguing that this had been the understanding when the research was first funded by the Bureau of Social Hygiene, she only relented after Ruth Topping of the Rockefeller staff said the arrangement had been left unclear. Dickinson's concession was to offer clinic board member Adolf Meyer, M.D., the opportunity to write a foreword to the study.

As further provocation, Margaret then went ahead and defiantly showed a prepublication draft to a reporter. Dickinson, in turn, called her "impetuous and indiscreet" but also tried to placate her with a patronizing request that she sit for a portrait to be hung in his offices at the academy. Within months, however, she was back in his good graces, and some years later, when she came under renewed fire from her adversaries in the American Birth Control League, he rose forcibly to her defense:

"Mrs. Sanger is the symbol, the international figure, possessed of ability to beget enthusiasm for this work beyond anyone else whatever. She has a way of delivering the goods. . . . She has ideas. She secures funds to set these ideas at work," he wrote. In a private letter, he also praised her for having remained steadfast through their many differences and confided: "Leadership sometimes means loneliness. Ideals so far in advance of public opinion as to be bitterly opposed, may breed sternness. For you to keep your kindliness and tenderness is one of the traits your friends most prize."

Until he died, Robert Dickinson kept a picture on his desk of Margaret Sanger, which was inscribed to him affectionately, and with self-evident humor, from "Saint Margaret."[21]

CHAPTER FOURTEEN

A Community of Women

Had Margaret capitulated to Robert Dickinson and relinquished complete authority for her clinic to the medical establishment, she undoubtedly would have achieved credibility in certain influential quarters. With the intervention of male physicians and hospital bureaucrats, however, she could not have maintained the clinic facility as the intimate sorority to which she remained fiercely committed—a community of women helping each other to achieve control over their personal lives. This alone, in her view, would empower them in a larger world governed by men. Her ambivalence toward male professionals, who exhibited an unmistakable gender and class bias in their dealings with her, and with clinic staff and patients as well, must be seen in the context of this consistent, if not always outspoken, motivation. Having ceded control of the American Birth Control League, she was also understandably more reluctant to give up the autonomy of her New York clinic in 1929 than she might previously have been, and she was a good deal more wary of the practicality of management by committee. She therefore consolidated her hold over the one institution that remained hers alone, rather than take a back seat, as Dickinson wanted, and as a team of management consultants she hired herself also advised that she do.[1]

Within a decade, in fact, the facility was renamed the Margaret Sanger Bureau in her honor. With these questions of governance resolved, she also turned her attention back to national and international organizing and began to spend less and less time in New York, keeping her hand in clinic policy and operations only by carefully selecting a staff and board of directors loyal to her vision and to her leadership, and always in touch with her by mail or by telephone. Yet surprisingly, she knew a great deal about what went on day to day, even when she was out of town. When a member of the clinic staff strayed from objectives she had carefully set, the behavior was immediately reported to her. On one occasion, a nurse's abrupt handling of a patient was called to her attention. "I am sure you know one of the dreams of my life has been to have our clinic different from every other so-called public clinic in the world," she immediately wrote in rebuke. The way to accomplish that goal is to "create an atmosphere of welcome, of kindness, of understanding, where women may come and tell us their troubles and be received with understanding and not with suspicion or *derision*," she added. The caring atmosphere of the clinic remained her paramount concern, and soon thereafter, when the nurse's behavior did not improve, Margaret summarily fired her.[2]

To preside over the facility in the manner she ordained, Margaret could not have chosen a physician of more steady but gentle temperament than Hannah Stone. Her face, serene and olive-skinned—her thick, dark hair wrapped in a neat and simple chignon at the nape of her neck—Stone was a madonna-like figure. She was legendary for her sensitivity to patients and her methodical attention to research. Calm, dignified, and intelligent, she was also a consummate professional—the perfect foil for her intensely driven boss, who nonetheless, by all accounts, revered her.

Stone is perhaps best captured in a transparently autobiographical scene from *The Group*, Mary McCarthy's comic and yet poignant novel about the rites of passage of American college women in the 1930s. Stone is seen through the eyes of Dottie Renfrew, an edgy Vassar College senior who has just lost her virginity to a man she hardly knows and, at his instruction, goes to get herself a diaphragm:

> The doctor's femininity was a reassuring part of her professional aspect, like her white coat. On her hand shone a broad gold wedding

> ring, which seemed to Dottie serene and ample, like the doctor herself. . . . Her skill astonished Dottie who sat with wondering eyes, anesthetized by the doctor's personality, while a series of questions, like a delicately maneuvering forceps, extracted information, that ought to have hurt but didn't.[3]

Stone's actual situation reflected the anomalous predicament of a generation of American women who came of age in the 1920s with serious professional aspirations but then confronted systematic opposition and institutionalized obstacles to their career advancement. She and hundreds of other similarly situated women doctors, denied hospital affiliation because of gender and class discrimination, found opportunity and challenge, as well as professional community, in birth control clinics throughout the country. Lena Levine, M.D., a gynecologist with additional training in psychiatry who also came to the Sanger clinic at this time, had been among only twenty-five women in her medical school class of 400 in New York and one of six who worked part-time at the clinic to get training in sexuality and birth control. Not a single male colleague ever showed.

Dr. Gerda Bruno had a similar experience. Fully a fourth of the medical school class at the University of Heidelberg in Germany, where she first trained in internal medicine, were women, but the young emigré physician found herself with no comparable network of gender support when she came to New York in 1934. She worked in hospital laboratories until she earned her American medical certification and then set up a private practice in a neighborhood of uprooted European Jews like herself. Married and soon pregnant with her first child, she started working part-time at the Sanger clinic despite the scorn of male associates, who joked about birth control and made no distinction between diaphragms and such traditional devices as condoms or nonmedical techniques like withdrawal. Her own mother could not understand her decision to affiliate with an institution whose reputation she thought scandalous. But Bruno believed in the diaphragm's clear scientific superiority over all other contraceptive options, simply because it gave women confident control over a responsibility she thought men would never take seriously enough.

To these younger women doctors, Margaret was an inspirational figure, if sometimes distant and imperious. "Fantastic, fantastic, charming, beautiful, petite and feminine . . . and she led such an interesting life," Bruno recalled years later, after her own retirement. Yet Cheri Appel, M.D., a strong-willed professional who had political ties on the left, felt quite differently. Appel traveled to the Soviet Union with Margaret in 1934. On this trip and in the clinic, in her view, Margaret was frosty and often appeared jealous of the professional credentials of the women doctors. Appel claims that the congenial atmosphere of the Sanger facility was due to the doctors themselves, who worked under the direction of the much nicer Hannah Stone.[4]

Clinic work demanded a high level of personal commitment from staff physicians, administrators, social workers, and nurses alike. A collective sense of mission linked these younger professionals to the older generation of volunteer activists. Mary Macaulay, who had been director of fieldwork for the Child Study Association of America, a prominent voluntary social welfare institution, came to the clinic as assistant director in 1929. Within a year she established a personal rapport with Sanger and become her resident eyes and ears in New York. Her letters, filled with detailed observations about the staff, the Dickinson controversy, and other official business, invariably ended with effusive, worshipful praise of Margaret herself: "Anyway be sure I love you and acclaim your truth and goodness, the precious dearness of your own life with its great meaning and purpose . . . ," went one typical example, written after Macaulay had left her position to pursue a love affair in England, the details of which she also confided.

Macaulay's shoes were then filled by Florence Rose, a former social worker no less devoted to the cause and to Margaret personally, whose typical, monthly summary of activities for February of 1936 exemplifies her characteristic zeal. In addition to working with patients, Rose held thirty-two interviews outside the clinic under the combined rubrics of fund-raising and field organization. She saw individuals ranging from a Methodist missionary group leader to the heads of the Brooklyn Association of Rabbis, the Jewish Board of Guardians, and the Federation of Jewish Women's Organizations of Greater New York. Other members of the medical and social work staff were also lecturing in the community at the time, with sixty-four total appearances listed for one calendar year. This level of commitment was best described by another zealous staff member, Cecil Damon, who wrote to Sanger of the need to "clean out those in the organization who consider the work a job."[5]

In its early years the clinic struggled with problems of organization and funding, and as might be expected in such fluid circumstances, it suffered a reasonable amount of staff turmoil and turnover. Like most social service and health institutions at the time, it paid low salaries that did not always keep pace with the high expectations made of employees. And although Hannah Stone may have acted as a force of moderation, Margaret herself remained a volatile and exacting personality who could easily drive a less zealous worker to despair with her endless demands that things happen better and faster.

Yet, archival material also reflects that Margaret went out of her way to praise and reward those who performed to her satisfaction. Marcella Sideri, for example, a young Italian nurse earning $135 per month, was arrested in the clinic raid of 1929. When she left to return to Italy with an unemployed husband two years later, Margaret sent her a personal check for $50 with a note about how much she would be missed. Lini Fuhr, a nurse who did follow-up work with delinquent patients, once wrote to Margaret: "Sometimes I feel I should not be paid for doing something which is not work to me, but living." Fuhr was a widow whose financial responsibility for a young daughter necessitated that she be more realistic about salary. She had been working for wages since the age of thirteen, when she started as a bobbin girl in the mills of Paterson, New Jersey. In 1937, she left her job and her daughter to volunteer in the Spanish Civil War but soon thereafter returned to work as a visiting nurse, while she also went to college for a degree in social work.[6]

Autonomy provided the Sanger Bureau with a great deal more administrative and ideological flexibility than it could possibly have had under corporate medical control. Despite dire warnings about the hazards of trying to sustain a "one woman movement," the facility continued to thrive even as the economic and social turbulence of the 1930s lowered expectations for its growth. It was, in fact, one of the only social welfare agencies in New York City that never incurred a deficit during the Depression. The budget, instead, steadily expanded, while other competitive organizations in the birth control field struggled to raise funds and barely survived, as was the fate of Dickinson's committee (renamed the National Committee on Maternal Health) and also of the American Birth Control League in the years Margaret did not head it.[7]

Once again, Noah Slee provided the financial foundation on which this success rested. In 1930, he purchased an elegant five-story town house at 17 West 16th Street in Manhattan for $80,000. The Birth Control Clinical Research Bureau moved its examination rooms to the parlors of this fine example of Greek Revival architecture, where it remained for forty-three years, rendering medical and counseling services to women in what had once been the handsome home of a prosperous nineteenth-century family. The distinguished building provided a warm and welcoming environment, not unlike a settlement house. Glowingly describing the charms of the new facility and its furnishings, Margaret boasted to Havelock Ellis, "We are grand as can be. Your picture hangs on our walls as always and graces and blesses our work." The facility was inaugurated, to considerable fanfare in the local papers, at a gala luncheon where the popular British scientist Julian Huxley was cheered for his proposition that only through the dissemination of birth control could man truly hope to control his destiny.[8]

When the Depression deepened in the winter of 1932, Noah suffered substantial financial reverses, but the clinic does not seem to have been affected. The records are sparse, because as treasurer of what was, after all, a private facility, Noah chose not to publish complete financial statements. Accounts that do remain, however, show no itemization of any payment of rent by the organization, which may mean that, despite the hard times, he personally carried the $33,000 mortgage on the building. This left only staff salaries, utilities, and the cost of supplies as major recurring expenses. During the worst years of the Depression, the operation continued to function on a substantially self-supporting basis, with occasional shortfalls of 10 percent of the budget at most—$5,000, for example, on $50,000 of reported expenses for 1931. At that point, several local social welfare agencies began to contribute a portion of the cost of supplies for women on relief, despite a disparaging view of welfare handouts typical even of reformers in this period, who felt that these materials would probably be used more carefully if clients themselves had to pay at least a small amount for them. The cost of supplies dropped, in any event, as a function of increased availability and the overall deflation. Staff salaries were also cut. Physicians' fees were apportioned on a sliding scale, and no one was turned away because of lack of funds.[9]

Margaret also stepped up her efforts to accommodate the new circumstances by replacing the volunteer women who had previously assisted her as fund-raisers with a weightier board of directors, which included the wives of some of New York's best known and wealthiest industrialists and financiers like J. P. Morgan, William K. Vanderbilt, Thomas Lamont, and Otto Kahn. Such prominent surnames—even if it was only the wives who participated—in turn made board service appealing to some prominent younger men in the legal and business community. The board seems to have exercised little, if any, influence on policy, but it did formally assume financial responsibility for all operating deficits.

Most significantly, perhaps, Margaret carefully cultivated Arthur Packard, who was by then the senior and most influential member of the Rockefeller charitable staff and could generally be relied on for small bequests whenever asked. Packard took Margaret's side in almost all of the disputes that arose among birth control factions in the 1930s, and when the Bureau of Social Hygiene formally disbanded, he continued to fund the clinic through other Rockefeller family charities. These anonymous donations constituted a substantial percentage of the clinic's small budget at the time, and were supplemented frequently with personal contributions from Abby Aldrich Rockefeller, which she would send in response to solicitations by mail.

Though critical to the clinic's survival, the annual Rockefeller gifts of $5,000 to $20,000 were, of course, negligible in comparison to the millions of dollars the family subsequently made available for family planning. The postwar population explosion would provide a more compelling rationale for the charity of a new generation than Margaret Sanger had given their parents, with her emphasis on the rights of women, the welfare of families, and even the growing public burden of the poor.

The obstacles Margaret faced, as a woman trying to raise money for what continued to be viewed as an institution dominated by women and of principal concern to women, cannot be overemphasized. Caroline Robinson, a Columbia University graduate student in sociology, betrayed an ivory-tower innocence when in 1930 she criticized birth control clinics for their inferior fund-raising efforts. Robinson may have been correct that the movement's brochures and other public relations efforts needed beefing up, but she was foolhardy at the same time to assume that birth controllers could easily "march with all the other health charities . . . depending calmly on the first-class arguments they are able to muster as well as on the first-class scientific men who have within the last three or four years become eager to lend their names to the movement." Male advisers undoubtedly opened some doors to the charitable and corporate world they themselves controlled, but so long as Margaret refused to concede her own authority and the paramount position of women in her organizations, her fund-raising abilities would inevitably be compromised. In this respect, the price of her autonomy was high.

Still, she was tireless as a fund-raiser, even as the economic crisis added to the burden of the undertaking. Refusing to be daunted by the much bemoaned declining fortunes of the rich, she wheedled money out of an extensive mailing list with one letter describing the tragedy of the harassed and anxious wife of a man who lost his job. Knowing of no reliable contraception, the woman ostensibly resorted to an illegal abortion, rather than raise another hungry child. This appeal, though genuinely humanitarian in tone, did cautiously play upon the anxieties of conservative, wealthy donors over the potential costs to them of supporting an increasingly dependent population. As the New Deal's welfare programs expanded, Margaret seemed to be tailoring special appeals to this group, even as Roosevelt sympathizers were being asked to give on the contrary rationale: that birth control constituted benevolent public policy and sound economic planning. She was never the least bit reluctant to target her pitch. At one point, five different texts were prepared, seeming to accommodate contradictory political viewpoints and rationales for supporting birth control. In the dry humor typical of her staff, one of these form letters was simply coded to "Dear Mrs. Generous."[10]

Clinic donors, whatever their politics, may also have been genuinely moved. The typical Clinical Research Bureau patient, as profiled in the monumental statistical study published by Dickinson and Kopp in 1934, was the thirty-year-old wife of a laborer in the manufacturing trades who earned from $1,000 to $3,000 a year, unless the Depression put him out of work and onto relief. (The study encompassed the years 1923 through 1931, and the economic breakdown corresponded fairly closely to figures for the city's general population, which was slightly above the national average.) She was native born, and Jewish or Protestant, though 26 percent of the clientele was Catholic, probably owing to the large numbers of Catholic women who were forced to enter the labor force in these years. A woman with only an elementary-school education, she had been married just over eight years and had been pregnant four times. One in five of her pregnancies had been aborted. The likelihood that she terminated her first pregnancy was only one in nine, but by the third, one in three, a figure which demonstrated the widespread motivation toward smaller families and a critical need for reliable contraception among married women, especially as the economic crisis worsened. Preclinical failure rates with prophylactics, jellies, suppositories, and other commercial contraceptives had ranged from 45 to 50 percent, suggesting that patients were fertile beyond average and less likely than average to be successful at contraception, whatever the method they employed. If they continued to use the clinic's diaphragm-and-jelly regimen properly, they could expect a failure rate of only about 7 percent.

The study thus proved the superiority of the diaphragm option over any other but also demonstrated that only 55 percent of the clinic patients, with whom contact was maintained, continued to use the diaphragm regularly after a year. Another 16.7 percent used it irregularly. A substantial number of the rejectors, however, did report a higher rate of success with the methods they had employed prior to visiting the clinic, demonstrating that some value attached to clinic visits, in any event.[11]

This problematic rate of acceptance substantially undermined claims of the efficacy of the method when properly used and, of course, became a source of considerable controversy. In an effort to better understand the rejection problem, Kopp, the statistician who actually conducted the research, analyzed her data in the context of social, economic, and personal factors, such as family income, education, age, and duration of marriage. The clinic had refused to adopt a policy against accepting well-to-do patients, despite the pressure brought by Dickinson and other physicians who feared competition with private practice. Margaret and Hannah Stone insisted on protecting "the personal preference" of any woman who favored the services and setting of the clinic over her own doctor. Approximately 20 percent of the patients were married to businessmen or professionals, and a small number were themselves so employed. Eleven percent were college educated, though these figures increased in subsequent years as more neighborhood facilities were founded to serve the poor, and the Sanger facility became instead a magnet for middle-class women citywide. Kopp demonstrated positive correlations between socioeconomic indicators and success with the diaphragm and thus underscored the limitations of the technique for young, newly married women—especially those of lower incomes and poorer education. Continuous and successful use of the diaphragm assumed a woman's understanding of basic elements of reproduction and sexual hygiene—her psychological willingness to anticipate and prepare herself prophylactically for sexual intercourse—and such elementary practical considerations as the proximity of a private toilet where she could insert it, remove it, and also keep it clean.[12]

Reservations about the clinic-diaphragm regimen were underscored as well by Margaret's failure to sustain a satellite clinic in Manhattan's substantially black neighborhood of Harlem. In 1930, she secured a $5,000 grant from Sears, Roebuck's merchandising magnate and philanthropist, Julius Rosenwald, and then raised equivalent matching funds to open the uptown facility. Her old friends at the Holland-Rantos Company contributed supplies, and most of the patients, 83 percent of whom were on public or private relief, were treated free of charge. At its peak of activity, the clinic was open four afternoons and one evening each week. It was endorsed by the powerful local black newspaper, the *Amsterdam News*, and by establishment political and religious leaders in Harlem, including the elder statesman W. E. B. DuBois, who condemned what he called "the fallacy of numbers" and deemed the "quality" of the black race more important to its survival. Margaret was invited to address Harlem's largest and most powerful congregation, the Abyssinian Baptist Church, and, after several years, her clinic moved into a larger welfare facility run by the Urban League. Yet, it never developed a steady following.

Part of the problem may have been the inevitable class and racial tensions between clinic personnel and clients. Part was the indisputable fact that many poor women, then as now, derive critical self-esteem and personal satisfaction from their childbearing. There were also important ideological differences in the black community itself. In the early 1920s, the integrationist philosophy of the NAACP had been sharply attacked by Harlem preacher and organizer Marcus Garvey, whose separatist doctrine rejected fertility control as genocidal. Garvey instead embraced traditional Biblical values and boldly encouraged black women to have babies. Though he was personally discredited by 1929, suspicion of contraception endured, especially in the churches.

Sensitive to this predicament, Margaret hired a black physician to improve patient rapport in the clinic and a black social worker to reach out to community social workers and preachers. Local doctors, who reasonably enough feared the competition of white women professionals and were reluctant to refer patients, were also invited in to observe the operation, but all to little avail. After four years fewer than 4,000 patients had been treated, and half of them were white. Margaret would turn the clinic over to the New York chapter of the American Birth Control League in 1936, which closed it a year later. But she refused to accept the verdict that failure was inevitable, because poor black women would not employ diaphragms regularly. To the contrary, she publicized statistics demonstrating that blacks and whites used the diaphragm with equivalent rates of success. Her data also revealed comparable patterns of intercourse in black and white marriages and undercut prevailing racist assumptions about black sexuality. The value of clinic services for blacks was further confirmed by the finding that the medical examination often had functioned as preventive health care. In a high percentage of patients, pelvic inflammatory disease and other conditions in need of treatment had been uncovered, some of them attributable to a high incidence of undetected venereal disease, which probably functioned as a natural check on fertility. Still convinced of the individual and social benefits of contraception, Margaret kept insisting that the problem was not in client motivation, but in the adequacy and accessibility of services. But once the Harlem clinic closed, the argument carried less weight.[13]

In view of research findings and the practical obstacles encountered by birth control advocates in places like Harlem, doubts about the large-scale utility of the clinic regimen continued to mount. Most damaging was a subsequent analysis of the patient load at the Sanger clinic by Regine Stix, a physician, and Frank Notestein, then a young Princeton University demographer who had sounded a major alarm about the nation's declining population in a 1930 study. The Stix–Notestein study was sponsored by the Milbank Memorial Fund, a prominent social science research institution of the era, then led by John A. Kingsbury, former commissioner of public charities in New York City and a personal champion of Margaret's. In 1928, the fund decided to devote its principal resources to the study of demography and sponsored the first comphrehensive study of differential fertility in America, according to social class. Though extremely cautious about guarding the scientific credibility and objectivity of research projects, it decided to cooperate with the Birth Control Clinical Research Bureau in order to study the effectiveness of contraceptive practice.

The work of Stix and Notestein was especially significant, because it unequivocally demonstrated the role of voluntary artificial contraception—as opposed to biological or other factors—in effecting fertility declines. Their more damaging findings had to do with the liabilities of the diaphragm, when its actual "use-effectiveness" was measured. They claimed that the condom offered greater contraceptive reliability, when the high failure rate of the diaphragm was taken into account, and though Margaret quickly took issue with their conclusions, her letter of protest to the Milbank directors was more inspired for its gift of rhetoric than for the weight of its argument: "I fully concur . . . that the *acceptability* of methods advised is a proper responsibility of the clinic—but I cannot agree that one can ascribe failure of a method to neglect to use it any more than one can say an automobile is not an effective means of transportation because one decided to walk instead of ride," she wrote. This disclaimer advanced, she then took pains to point out the many concessions the Clinical Research Bureau had made on its own accord as a result of the high diaphragm failure rate.[14]

While she continued to promote the diaphragm above all other choices, she also encouraged the research arm of her clinic to experiment with simpler contraceptive methods. "We have, alas, gotten into a rut and are working simply as a contraceptive clinic," she complained at one point to Hannah Stone and then personally instructed medical staff against bias *in favor* of the diaphragm, cautioning them not to give everything else a "black eye." But the files also bear testimony to the doctors' frequent rejoinder that the pressures of serving an expanding patient population with reliable goods continually pushed this research behind schedule. Margaret was especially concerned that evaluations be made of the effectiveness of the vast array of commercial contraceptive products that found their way onto the pharmaceutical market during the Depression as demand increased. Thus the clinic conducted laboratory tests on all kinds of commercial jellies, foams, powders, and other allegedly spermicidal compounds. At her direction, the quality of various condoms was also compared and the results offered to medical journals, though, at the same time, she remained sensitive to the linking of her name with commercial products.[15]

By 1936, the bureau had its own research publication called the *Journal of Contraception,* and later renamed *Human Fertility,* issued under the editorial direction of Hannah and Abraham Stone. But invariably research got short shrift, because of the clear emphasis on reliable service delivery. Robert Dickinson's National Committee on Maternal Health would prove a far more successful agent for pure research, on which it concentrated exclusively after 1935. His principal colleague and benefactor in this enterprise was Clarence Gamble, M.D, a self-styled do-gooder then teaching at the University of Pennsylvania Medical School, and an heir to the Ivory Soap fortune. Gamble had graduated from Harvard Medical School in 1920 but quickly grew bored with a career in applied medical research. Presented in his own marriage with the problem of finding an effective contraceptive, he became captivated by the broader pharmacological and sociological questions the subject presented and dedicated himself and a large part of his inheritance to the goal of discovering a simple and effective contraceptive product.

Gamble's first venture began in 1929 when he provided the seed money for a birth control clinic in his hometown of Cincinnati, Ohio, dedicated to the memory of his late mother and run by her distinguished friend, Elizabeth Campbell, M.D. He then mobilized the local charitable community in nearby Columbus to support another clinic, and as a Pennsylvania resident at the time, also became active in that state's new birth control league. Quickly despairing of the high costs of working through doctors and of the substantial diaphragm rejection rate, he then teamed up with Dickinson to try to establish laboratory standards for the effectiveness of the commercial contraceptives flooding the Depression market. Their research helped expose fraud in the industry and led to regulation by some states.

Relying on their data, *Fortune* magazine in 1937 would expose a $350 million-a-year industry in commercial contraception, where profits to manufacturers ran at the astonishing rate of 30 percent of retail sales. Condom sales represented little more than a tenth of this trade, with the balance comprising more than 600 known products marketed and widely advertised under the euphemism of "feminine hygiene." The diaphragm represented less than 1 percent of this huge market. Small businessmen could make enormous profits in birth control with very little capital investment, but unlike the Holland-Rantos operation Noah Slee had staked, many sold worthless products. *Fortune* called on the federal government to regulate the trade, but while the Federal Trade Commission did intervene on numerous specific occasions to stop individual companies from making insupportable statements about the contraceptive utility of their products, no systematic investigation was undertaken. This left only the voluntary birth control advocates to coordinate efforts on behalf of research and reform and created the paradoxical situation of making them advocate more and less birth control at the same time. Having made the nation conscious of birth control—having changed public attitudes and helped secure laws to protect its use—Margaret unwittingly left the market open to a commercial exploitation far more substantial than anything she could have contemplated.[16]

Yet Margaret's growing resolve in favor of research on simpler contraceptives did not diminish her enthusiasm for the kind of clinical facility she continued to operate in New York. To the contrary, she remained convinced that obstacles to success with the diaphragm and all other contraceptives could best be overcome if women were simply better educated and better served in matters of reproductive health and sexuality. To this end, she continued to promote voluntary birth control clinics with high standards, provoking the dismay and confusion of many social scientists and philanthropists, who dismissed them as costly and ineffective expressions of a kooky, sentimental feminism that was inconsistent with her larger and, in their view, more mature aspirations to affect economic and demographic trends on a broad scale. She, on the other hand, was never afraid to pursue different agendas at the same time. She could never fully explain her attachment to the New York clinic, moreover, because in several dimensions it operated perilously close to the edge of respectability and legality. Nowhere was this more evident than in the responsibility she assumed during the Depression for treating patients who became pregnant.

To safeguard her credibility with the public and with the medical profession, Margaret had carefully disassociated birth control from the even more controversial subject of abortion. She always emphasized the superior virtue of pregnancy prevention. A 1929 memorandum from Hannah Stone, for example, instructs physicians to refuse any new patient requesting a pregnancy examination. No risk was to be taken that an unknown woman who subsequently aborted her pregnancy and suffered complications would implicate the clinic. Registered clinic patients, however, were given the Aschheim pregnancy test and, if found to be pregnant, were referred to Hannah Stone for counseling.

Three years later, alarmed by a reported rise in the incidence of illegal abortion as a consequence of the deepening economic crisis, Margaret instructed Stone to permit staff physicians to administer pregnancy tests without qualification and to make direct referrals to hospitals when therapeutic abortion was indicated. She also created a fund to pay the laboratory costs of these procedures. Statistics prepared for her estimated an even higher incidence of abortion than the Dickinson-Kopp figures for her own clientele. A first study suggested that more than 1 million pregnancies had been aborted in the United States during 1930, representing an astonishing 40 percent of all conceptions, with 30 percent of the total having been performed criminally, and 3 percent, or more than 30,000, having resulted in fatalities. Subsequent estimates made on the basis of the Dickinson-Kopp data then pared these figures down to 700,000 abortions nationally, and 16,000 deaths, an admittedly conservative number. More refined data, published in 1935 on the basis of follow-up interviews in their own homes with Sanger clinic clients who came from the Bronx, showed an overall abortion rate of about 25 percent, with a sharp increase from 1929 to 1931, as the Depression set in, especially among young married women, acting out of economic considerations. (This final sample of living women obviously showed no fatalities.)

Whatever the exact dimensions of the problem, it was clear that therapeutic referrals could help save lives. Medical standards for determining when a pregnancy might endanger life were considerably more lenient at this time than they became after World War II, when pronatalist sentiments stirred public controversy over abortion and placed hospital policies under intensive scrutiny. The diagnosis of tuberculosis and many other diseases considered hazardous to pregnancy were routinely considered grounds for intervention. Therapeutic interventions, indeed, became so widespread during the Depression that they provoked a conservative reaction in the early 1940s, when legislation was introduced unsuccessfully by social conservatives in the New York State legislature to ban them altogether.

In 1932, Margaret also asked that a study be undertaken to determine how many women were becoming pregnant as a result of contraceptive failures and how many subsequently terminated their pregnancies through abortion. "It will always distress me to feel that women in this condition [more] desperately in need of sound advice than any other group have to be turned out without follow-up, check-up or any further notice," she wrote.

There were no secrets, yet nobody called special attention to what was going on. A private room at the clinic was set aside. A staff social worker volunteered to work over the lunch hour to accommodate the "overdues," as they were called, and in a year's time, Stone had gathered 430 case histories. Approximately half of the women surveyed turned out not to be pregnant and began to menstruate regularly once their anxieties were allayed. Of the 205 actual pregnancies, Stone could verify that only fourteen were carried to term. Seventy-five abortion referrals were made, several of them directly to hospitals, and the rest to physicians who presumably took charge of the necessary arrangements, though exactly how they did so is not clear. Stone claimed that "contact was lost" with the remaining 100 patients, a statistic which may have been legitimate or may have deliberately obscured known outcomes that were criminal.[17]

That at least one illegal abortion was arranged directly by a physician who worked on the clinic staff is documented in a random and unusually revealing letter to Sanger from 1932, which tells the story of an unmarried and unemployed Polish emigré, pregnant and allegedly deserted by her fiancé, who was referred to a "Dr. Seigal" for an abortion. The letter identifies three additional facts about the woman—that she was an "exceptional type of the class where you and I felt an exception could be made," that she had $100, and that she promised not to violate "the confidential nature of our assistance." The abortion went well, and the woman was also given job and personal counseling. Since clinic case records overall have been destroyed—and since abortion referrals of this sort were not characteristically documented in any event—the extent of this kind of situation, with its decidedly subjective criteria for referral, can never be determined with certainty. On at least three subsequent occasions, however, clinic personnel found it necessary to circulate a memorandum clarifying the official policy prohibiting physicians from referring patients for abortion, and it is hard to believe they would have brought the subject up if infractions were not, in fact, standard practice. One social worker, in making two abortion referrals to doctors employed at the clinic part-time, claimed that she thought she was acting in accord with Margaret's wishes.

Just how discreet the clinic doctors had to be is underscored by a memo from the lawyer Harriet Pilpel, who at this time was beginning her lifetime commitment to the cause of reproductive freedom as a young associate to Morris Ernst, who had replaced Jonah Goldstein as Margaret's counsel, when Goldstein became a judge. In 1942, Pilpel would advise birth control officials in New York not to risk taking a stand on the abortion question then being raised in Albany, since it had taken them so long to distinguish birth control from abortion in the public mind. Even in the 1960s, Mary Calderone, M.D., then medical director of the Planned Parenthood Federation of America, could still not get the organization to sponsor any kind of abortion counseling services officially, though doctors at the Sanger clinic, an affiliate of the parent organization, were still widely known as sources for therapeutic and illegal abortion referrals. No one talked about the situation, and no case records were ever kept, according to Charlotte Levine and Elizabeth Arnold, who administered the clinic at the time, but everyone knew what was happening and assumed that it had always been that way. Between 1967 and 1970, in the final years before New York's restrictive abortion law was repealed, the clinic would cooperate with the New York Clergy Consultation Service on Abortion, founded at the nearby Judson Memorial Baptist Church in Greenwich Village. This courageous voluntary effort would counsel nearly 30,000 women in just three years, many of whom were sent to the Sanger Bureau for examination and confirmation of their pregnancies before being referred to criminal abortionists, whose practices the concerned clergymen and their indefatigable staff then closely monitored. In Levine's view, this unofficial abortion referral policy exemplified a commitment to guaranteeing the right of women to autonomous control over their own bodies.

"We always thought of ourselves as feminists, protecting women's choices," she added, "even when that word was out of vogue."[18]

In many respects then, the Sanger clinic regimen was an exacting one, just as its critics charged. The costs and staff requirements of individualized services were high. Under Hannah Stone, initial examinations could run up to two hours. An extensive case history was taken from each patient, which included medical, sexual, and socioeconomic data. Painstaking instruction with the diaphragm followed. Stone or one of her subordinates employed a three-dimensional model of the female pelvis and explained the specific function and structure of each of the reproductive and sexual organs, often to women hearing this information for the first time. They then fit the diaphragm, removed it, and had the patient make the insertion herself. Return visits were scheduled within the week and at regular six month intervals thereafter. A conscious effort was made to establish an atmosphere where women could feel free of the inhibitions usually met with in standard gynecological practice.

Some patients welcomed this thorough indoctrination. One newlywed from Long Island, who came to the clinic four days after her marriage, exclaimed its success, saying she owed Stone "everything in the way of personal happiness." A few complained that the treatment was brusque and the instructions unclear—one client got pregnant because even after instruction, she used the diaphragm upside down. Still others were put off by the enforced intimacy and even found it condescending. The young, still unmarried protagonist of Mary McCarthy's novel, for example, is so uncomfortable with her sexuality—and finds the jelly-covered diaphragm so difficult to maneuver—that when she tries to insert it on her own, it shoots across the room, and she is horrified with embarrassment. She leaves Dr. Stone, walks to nearby Washington Square, and abandons the bulky package of contraceptive materials under a park bench.[19]

What complicated the clinic transaction was then not just the problem of technology. The intensive one-on-one client interviews uncovered the fact that concern over reliability and comfort with the diaphragm often masked a disturbing level of anxiety about sexuality itself. In this respect, the clinic became a social laboratory for testing the assumptions of prescriptive sex literature like Margaret's own

Happiness in Marriage. Only six out of ten women in the Dickinson and Kopp survey, for example, reported what was identified as a "normal" attitude toward sexual intercourse. The rest expressed opinions ranging from indifference to outright hostility—from toleration to loathing. In many cases concern about getting pregnant was itself the cause of the neurosis, and reliable contraception provided a solution. In others, however, the problems were deeper still, with many patients expressing frustration about the nature and adequacy of their sexual responses. Though eight of every ten women said they had experienced orgasm at least once in their lives, only half of those answering this question affirmatively claimed that climax was a usual occurrence, while the rest admitted the experience was seldom. Often the meaning of the term itself had to be explained before a response was possible. Few patients could locate the clitoris precisely or understood its function. The Sanger Bureau patients may have constituted a self-selected population, with a higher level of expectation about contraception and sexuality than the average woman who did not bother to pursue specialized services. The data, nonetheless, revealed a more serious level of disturbance than existing surveys by questionnaire typically uncovered.[20]

In the clinic's early years patients revealing sex problems were routinely referred to staff social workers for counseling. In 1931, convinced of the need for better trained advisers, Hannah Stone then inaugurated her own consultation service in conjunction with her husband, Abraham, a practicing urologist. The Stones worked initially under the auspices of the New York City Labor Temple and the Community Church, both nonsectarian institutions, but within a year they moved counseling into the bureau itself. Individualized services were provided free to established clinic patients, while outsiders paid a small fee. Sometimes husbands were invited in along with their wives. Premarital counseling, still a controversial moral issue, was also offered to newlyweds and included individualized sex education, along with actual medical intervention when surgical rupture of the bride's hymen was recommended. This procedure was intended to help alleviate anxiety and to facilitate diaphragm use by a virginal bride.[21]

Marriage counseling was still a new and innovative concept. It had originated in Germany where the Weimar Republic's pioneering social welfare system first funded marriage and sex advice bureaus in seven major municipalities. The Stones' practice in New York became the first freestanding American equivalent, though some established family welfare agencies were beginning to give their social workers special training in sexual counseling or hiring specialists in the field. The American Institute of Family Relations was also founded in Los Angeles in 1930 to promote education for marriage and parenthood, but its primary interests were eugenic not therapeutic, and it did not initially offer counseling services. Even as Fascism took hold abroad during the 1930s, and ideas about promoting human betterment lost an audience here, widespread consensus survived about the value of sex education and counseling in promoting human happiness. This was especially true for women, whose right of contentment as wives had only recently been proclaimed.[22]

It was this mission that inspired the Stones. Along with Havelock Ellis and Margaret herself, they blamed sexual dysfunction more on social repression than on individual psychological development. They believed that adult barriers to fulfillment generally derive from external taboos, which prevent adults from learning how to abandon themselves totally to sexual stimulation. Loosening standards of behavior had unleashed erotic expectations that were not always being met. Sex education and therapy were necessary to resolve these tensions.[23]

The Stones argued with good sense that the prescriptive sex literature of the 1920s had changed popular thinking about sex, fostering higher levels of sexual aspiration and intensifying anxiety about performance. The new sexual discourse licensed a freedom that many young Americans, by their own observation and according to interviews subsequently conducted by Alfred Kinsey, were claiming as their own. For some this freedom generated its own set of problems by establishing standards of behavior that were not necessarily easy to achieve. As a group, women seemed to have had the most difficulty and suffered the most severe letdown, because even as their capacity for sexual pleasure was affirmed, few could agree precisely on its components. Psychologists and sex counselors suddenly mobilized around the reported problem of female frigidity, but could not even offer a precise definition of the condition. Was the woman who experienced orgasm through clitoral stimulation, but not in conventional coitus, still to be considered frigid, for example? Orthodox psychoanalytic theory only exacerbated the confusion when Freud branded the clitoral orgasm as an immature, childlike response and demanded that adult women somehow learn to transfer their sexual sensitivity to the more womanly vagina.[24]

The Stones rejected the claim that female sexual response patterns are wholly subjective and instead tried to reduce their variable nature to physiological, rather than psychological, components. Their best-selling *A Marriage Manual,* first published in 1935, would repeat Margaret's earlier admonition that many women may only reach orgasm through direct manipulation of the clitoris. Far more clinical in orientation than she had been, they offered specific instruction on the importance of stimulation through sexual foreplay or digital manipulation during intercourse, devoting eight full pages to the subject. Male climax, by their observation, is rarely difficult to achieve, but as reported, erection in most men lasts only one to two minutes after penetration, thus not necessarily providing sufficient stimulation to evoke a female response.[25]

Yet, much like Sanger and Van de Velde before them, the Stones promoted the ideal of a synchronized mutual orgasm in coitus and sent a generation of young Americans searching for this often elusive ecstasy. The inherent contradiction between their clinical observations and the behavior they prescribed can only be explained by the title and format of their book, and by the precarious position they occupied as associates of a prominent woman, who was also pursuing a political agenda for birth control. *A Marriage Manual* was organized as a series of hypothetical counseling sessions between wholesome young couples and sober, scientifically trained doctors. The book was very deliberately confined to the subject of sex within marriage and not apart from it. It disparaged autonomous sexual experience through masturbation, condemned homosexuality, and argued emphatically for sexual fidelity in marriage. This intense moralism would only be dropped in editions published after the Kinsey reports of 1948 and 1952 had encouraged greater tolerance of deviance—and after Kinsey himself had registered his complaint: that too many women still reported failure to reach orgasm in conventional coital postures, and should be encouraged to achieve sexual pleasure by whatever direct stimulation is necessary.

The Stones' earlier writing, by contrast, reflected a widespread concern that external pressures brought on by the Depression and war were taking a severe toll on personal intimacy and on marriage as a social institution. Sexual expression is presented in the first editions of their book as a kind of palliative, a refuge from hard times, and they do seem overly optimistic in promising that every sexual relationship in every marriage can be made to work. The book also moves beyond the bedroom to touch upon such common domestic conflicts as work, money, household responsibility, and child rearing. Sex by the Stones' definition is intended to culminate a marital bond of "mutual love and affection, a community of interests, of tastes, of standards, an adequate economic arrangement and a satisfactory adjustment in many personal, family and social relationships." Far more than just an erotic experience, it is meant to be the foundation of a family life reorganized on democratic, rather than authoritarian, principles. The issue then is not technique alone, but the larger problem of mutuality for women in every aspect of marriage, including sex.*[26]

Quaint as all of this may now sound, *A Marriage Manual* endured several battles with censors over advertising and was rejected by the major book clubs because it was considered too explicit. It went on,

* How closely the Stones' prescriptive writing reflected actual counseling techniques at the Sanger Bureau is difficult to determine, since individual case records were destroyed. After Hannah's death, however, an experimental group counseling service was established in her memory by Abraham Stone and Lena Levine, his clinical colleague and coauthor after his wife's death, and transcripts of these sessions do survive.

A gynecologist who was also certified in psychiatry, Levine tended to be more sympathetic to Freudian paradigms and to do more impromptu "psychologizing" than Abraham Stone, who generally sat quietly through the transcribed sessions and let others do the talking. For example, she kept telling women who complained they were too tired for sex that fatigue was simply a rationalization for their lack of interest. So too, she tried to convince them of the possibility of "experiencing" their orgasm vaginally, even as she explained that the "two orgasms are essentially the same in terms of general bodily reactions." The distinction simply confused the issue for some of them—though several agreed in their own comments that orgasm with vaginal penetration was a "deeper" or "fuller" or "more meaningful" sensation.

The group experiment was intended to focus on cases of reported sexual maladjustment, not on more diverse marital incompatibilities, and in this respect, it had a more narrow orientation than individualized counseling services. Still, the complaints of some young mothers that they were not getting enough sleep may have been legitimate, and the reports of others that they simply could not reach a climax without direct and undiffused clitoral manipulation were undoubtedly valid as well. Stone apparently agreed and, contradicting Levine, told one woman who complained that her husband's climax invariably interrupted her own to learn to experience "external" orgasm.

The group sessions were held in the comfortable atmosphere of the clinic's library. They brought together a relatively homogeneous and upscale selection of clinic clients—newly married young women in their twenties, with a high school or partial college education, all of whom reported "maladjustments" ranging from a sense of total frigidity to concern simply over the vaginal orgasm dilemma. Husbands and wives met separately as groups, providing a rare and cathartic opportunity for open conversation and for reassurance that perceived inadequacies were not necessarily abnormal. Lena Levine achieved a remarkable degree of candor in her conversations with the women, several of whom shared long-buried revelations about masturbation, childhood sexual molestation, and adult infidelity, while others groped to describe their exact sensations and feelings in the experience of petting, intercourse, and climax. Even putative "perversions," such as oral and anal sex, were revealed, and then accorded legitimacy by the doctors, so long as they were incorporated as elements of a relationship ending in coitus, and not made exclusive preferences. Uninhibited and uncensored, the remarkably forthright conversations promoted a great deal of tolerance and understanding on the part of all who participated in them. For some they also had a direct behavioral impact. Stone and Levine's published evaluation of the project offered no specific results but did conclude that some women reported having achieved orgasm, "either clitoral or vaginal," after attending several sessions, while others at least reached a more acceptable level of satisfaction, even when what was labeled "a complete response" was not achieved. Still, for all the good they did, it is evident from the transcripts that the marriage counselors did not begin to resolve many of the problems they uncovered, and by raising expectations of compatibility, especially in terms of mutual orgasm, they may, in fact, have created additional ones.

nevertheless, to outsell the pathbreaking *Ideal Marriage,* a situation that pleased its publisher, Lincoln Schuster, who was both a personal friend of the Stones and an emerging rival of Van de Velde's publisher, Random House. Since the Stones also devoted an entire chapter to the subject of birth control, and listed Hannah as medical director of the Birth Control Clinical Research Bureau, their success may have enhanced Margaret's own reputation in some circles, while the controversy they inspired obviously extended to her as well. There is, however, no documentation of what she actually thought of their book.[27]

It would not be long, however, until the fundamental premise of *A Marriage Manual* found itself under attack. Soon, critics would argue that sex cannot be taught like any other subject—indeed, that too much obsession with sexual technique threatens to depersonalize human relationships and creates a "sex as work" ethic that robs human intimacy of the potential for individual expression and feeling. By the 1960s, one woman, quoted in a *Time* magazine feature on the subject, would capture the general complaint when she claimed that she could determine from the rhythms of her husband's lovemaking exactly when he was turning from one page of their marriage manual to another. Sobered by Kinsey's much talked about data on the variability of human sexual expression, a new generation came of age, rejecting the existing advice literature in favor of the dictum that the best sex is what comes naturally, and the most appropriate prescription for sexual behavior, none at all.

Even more salient from the standpoint of Margaret Sanger's legacy, however, was the argument that marriage counselors were overvaluing the sexual satisfaction of women at the expense of their autonomy and equality in the larger society—that they were undermining the very goals the pioneers in the field set out to promote. When a discontented writer, by the name of Betty Friedan, claimed in *The Feminine Mystique* of 1963 that the pursuit of greater sexual fulfillment was subverting women's aspirations for accomplishment as individuals outside the family, the liberation of one generation of women became another's tyranny.

Margaret would surely have been perplexed. She had long made it her business to try to win public approval with the tamest, most plausible, and least controversial arguments for birth control—the economic burdens, the negative health effects, and demographic consequences of large families—but, always, these arguments were meant to advance an underlying agenda.

What, after all, was the intent of her rhetoric and her jealously guarded clinical services, if not to end the enforced marriage and childbearing she once called an "an outrage upon the women"? Woman, as she said over and over again in her long career, was not meant to be a "brood animal for the masculine civilizations of the world."

To some who knew her well, this meaning was always obvious. "From time to time, in such remarks as these," a canny reporter for *The New Yorker* had pointed out in 1930, "Mrs. Sanger has let herself go and revealed a feminism so violent as to scare half her supporters out of their wits if they thought she meant it." Just how scared became clear that year when she left Hannah Stone in charge of the clinic in New York and traveled to Washington to fight for birth control in the halls of Congress.[28]

Grande Dame, Grandmere

CHAPTER FIFTEEN

Lobbying for Birth Control

There is no way of knowing for certain what prompted Margaret to undertake a new national campaign for repeal of the Comstock laws. Was it the continued frustration of working under a legal cloud? The timidity of demographers in Geneva, of physicians in New York, of volunteer women around the country? Was it an irrational thirst for power and celebrity or perhaps just a function of her own biological clock? She had, after all, celebrated her fiftieth birthday in September of 1929, observing the milestone in private, because she had long since stopped counting the years honestly, even to her own husband, children, and friends. Only Nan and Ethel Higgins might have set the record straight, but fame and fortune had by then shifted the balance of power among the sisters, and they knew better than to tell the truth. Yet the self is never wholly deceived. Margaret bounded across this most humbling of life's chronological divides with an unmistakable outburst of energy—perhaps a postmenopausal zest, as another remarkable woman of this era, the anthropologist Margaret Mead, might have characterized it.

First, she looked back. Venerated for her "magnetism," her "great personal courage" and "sincerity" in the same 1930 *New Yorker* profile that heralded her as a feminist, she was again courted by publishing houses. The scheme to make Hugh de Selincourt her biographer came crashing down along with the stock market's collapse, but she went ahead on the project anyway and in 1931 produced a workmanlike autobiography with the unacknowledged help of Robert Parker and Guy Moysten, another of the old Greenwich Village crowd of journalists.

At the urging of both Moysten and Havelock Ellis, she wrote in a genre of self-congratulation typical of the reflections of men in public life, but rather unusual for a woman, even one so flamboyant. She made no apologies and admitted no regrets for having chosen risk and exposure over the conventional, safer life she could have led. Destiny may have chosen her to vindicate poor Anne Higgins's predicament, but having been called to her work was not exactly an accident either. She made a secure claim for her talent, her indefatigable energy, her clairvoyance—for the place she thought she deserved among history's foremost rebels and pioneers. Working on the book was "like digging down into my subconscious and stirring its depths—not always a pleasant thing," she admitted to Hugh. So self-absorbed was the project that—to the dismay of many coworkers and friends who had loyally served the birth control cause along with her—she scarcely even mentioned their names. She also glossed over her youthful radicalism and willfully distorted information that might have embarrassed her, if only to make a better story and, at the same time, to serve her paramount goal: reform of the Comstock laws in Congress.[1]

Reviewers, nevertheless, tended to like the book and gave it considerable attention. It made the coveted front cover of the fall announcement issue of the *New York Herald Tribune*'s book section, illustrated by an attractive engraving of the author. "Margaret Sanger is one of our generation's world-changers," wrote social critic Mary Ross, "one of perhaps a half-dozen or so whose individual lives swerve or push the course of the world in a direction it might not know at that time except for them." The historian Mary Beard enthusiastically agreed in the *Saturday Review of Literature*, calling Margaret "a maker rather than a mirror of history." Her praises were sung in *The New York Times, The New Republic,* and in countless daily newspapers across the country, and Ellis branded the book simply "splendid."

Yet the condemnation of a single critic, writing in private, sent her into depths of despair for an entire week. She was devastated when Hugh, from his distant perch in England, attacked her as "egotistical" and unfair to public competitors like Marie Stopes and Mary Ware Dennett, a criticism which stung especially hard, because she thought she had succeeded in handling these women with forbearance. He reserved his harshest words, however, for her flagrantly dishonest portraits of the private aspects of her life. She had barely mentioned him at all, and to this, she offered only the reasonable response that however steadfast the personal commitments she maintained, she was hardly in a position to invite the public into her bedroom. Imploring him to understand the "staggering complexities" that faced a woman in her position, she hastened to assure: "There is no lie to any caress or kiss I have ever given—*Ever!*"[2]

Released in the depths of the Depression, *My Fight for Birth Control* never sold very well, although the favorable notices it received did confer a coveted degree of public respectability on the author. Several months after the book came out, Margaret held a dinner at the new Waldorf-Astoria Hotel in New York with 500 paying guests in attendance, the venerable educator John Dewey as chairman and H. G. Wells as honored guest. Still unchallenged in his preeminence as a writer, Wells actually loathed public speaking and only lectured for the money and the publicity. Appearing in Margaret's behalf was at least in part a gracious, personal gesture, and as they sat beside each other on the dais, he apparently whispered to her with the total absence of reserve that had long characterized their relationship. Amplifiers had been hidden in the table decorations to give resonance to his thin, reed-like voice when he got up to speak, and Margaret later reported to Havelock Ellis that she spent the entire dinner in a panic lest what Wells was saying in her ear be heard at the back of the room.

Introducing her honored guest and dear friend that night, she recalled that he had interceded with President Wilson on her behalf long ago in 1914. The "magic" of his name had saved her from jail, she insisted, taking considerable liberty with the facts, but then adding, with perhaps unintentional candor, that this was before he even knew of her "womanly charms." Wells's address was, in turn, courtly and respectful, and his salutation so eloquent that Margaret had him write it down on the occasion of a second dinner a month later, when she was finally honored for the first time by a prestigious, mainstream women's organization, the American Woman's Association, whose recognition of her inspired the epigraph of this book. Wells called her the "greatest woman in the world" and offered one of the prognostications for which he was famous. "The movement she started will grow to be, a hundred years from now, the most influential of all time in controlling man's destiny on earth," he said.[3]

These gala evenings certified Margaret's ability to attract money and attention even as the economic crisis worsened. The Wells event was a fund-raiser for the National Committee for Federal Legislation for Birth Control, the Congressional lobbying campaign she constructed out of her particular genius for public relations, her sheer tenacity, energy, and willfulness. The same development consultants from the John Price Jones Corporation who had told her to give up her New York clinic also predicted she could never raise money to change laws that were enforced only by exception and affected few potential donors personally. Others like Mary Ware Dennett and Rachelle Yarros of Chicago were willing to come aboard only if she agreed to abandon her medical exception strategy in favor of a bid for clean repeal of the Comstock laws.

Even the American Birth Control League wouldn't help and at the outset tried to make her life difficult by denying her access to mailing lists and other organizational tools she had helped develop. She went ahead without all of them, defiantly molding old arguments to new circumstances, disciplining her troops, vastly extending her organizational goals, and outperforming everyone else. Under pressure from many constituents, Eleanor Jones then relented and offered the board's tacit support, though never any active cooperation. Margaret, in turn, begrudgingly conceded the need for a unified front on the birth control issue, though she resented it and always believed that her own successes as a publicist were the engine of the league's limited organizational gains—that the women there needed her more than she needed them. The league operated at a deficit after 1932, quietly opening up clinics and taking credit for ones it actually had little to do with. Apart from a major rally at Carnegie Hall in New York in 1935, it would scarcely make a headline.[4]

Until 1931, Noah had kept the hope alive that he would succeed in a suit brought against the Internal Revenue Service, claiming the legitimacy of tax benefits for his contributions to the American Birth Control League. The league was officially chartered as a charitable and educational enterprise under New York law, but because it engaged in some political lobbying, the deductibility of contributions to it had been disallowed. Noah first initiated an action to overturn this ruling in 1926, when he tired of paying full taxes on the substantial income he had to draw out of 3-in-One Oil in order to pay his wife's bills. Represented by one of George Rublee's partners in the firm of Covington, Burling, & Rublee in Washington, his case wound its way over the course of four years through various administrative hearings and appeals and finally ended up in federal court in New York City. During these proceedings, investigators for the Internal Revenue Service not only confirmed the league's intermittent legislative activities, but also accused its officers of violating the federal Comstock law, because addresses of birth control clinics around the country were being mailed to any woman who requested them. For a time Margaret was concerned that legal charges would be brought over these infractions, and indeed the entire matter may well have added another element to her dispute with the league board. The Washington lawyers, in any event, advised her to maintain a low profile until all available legal recourse to her husband had been exhausted. They were particularly chagrined by the news in 1929 that she intended to organize an all-out legislative campaign in Washington, but she had given up on the case by then, convinced that no matter what the facts, the government would rule against Noah. Only when the lawyers lost a final appeal the following year, however, was she technically free to make as much trouble as she pleased, and by then, the outcome mattered less to her personally, since Noah's income was beginning to take a beating. His $40,000 settlement with the IRS appears to have been his last major outlay for birth control.[5]

These personal considerations aside, the early years of the Depression also provided a coherent public rationale for renewed organization for birth control reform, though surely no easy way to pay for it. With Herbert Hoover still in the White House, a path to national economic recovery was charted by way of lowered public expectations and reduced personal demand, and women were made targets of public consumer policy, because they usually controlled the vast bulk of family spending. What is more, the country's mood still tended toward cooperation and compliance. Volunteerism was still very much in vogue. There was not yet the despair of the later years of the crisis nor the zeal for wholesale reform that gave rise to the inventive, pump-priming expenditures and programs of the New Deal. Helping people to help themselves remained the only agreed upon agenda of reform, and in this context, stepping up the dissemination of reliable birth control to women had unassailable logic.

In 1930, the educator and Sanger clinic supporter Henry Pratt Fairchild went to see his friend, U.S. Secretary of the Interior Ray

Lyman Wilbur, about funding birth control through public health facilities under his aegis. He was rebuffed because of the notoriety that attached to the issue and to Margaret personally, but one man's reticence did not deter her. Like Fairchild, many religious leaders, social scientists, physicians, and opinion makers, who had remained shy of the issue earlier, were finally beginning to speak out more comfortably because of the economic crisis, and in light of Margaret's own clinical evidence testifying to the safety and reliability of certain methods. They might be counted on to add their stature to a lobbying effort.[6]

Margaret also gained a valuable ally when the Lambeth Conference of Bishops of the Anglican Church met in London in the summer of 1930 and, reversing its position of a decade earlier, officially sanctioned the use of artificial methods of conception control. Acting over the protest of a vocal minority of its own membership, the conference promulgated this historic edict with great care, emphasizing the delicacy of its situation by insisting that birth control never be used to violate the sanctity of marriage—that the spiritual obligations of family life never be made subordinate to either material or personal considerations. Emphasis was placed on the principle that the relations of husband and wife be disciplined and controlled and lived in the power of Christ, whose bond with the church is symbolized in the marital vow. The practice of contraception was condoned only by exception, "where there is a clearly-felt moral obligation to limit or avoid parenthood, and where there is a morally sound reason for avoiding complete abstinence." It was explicitly condemned when employed out of motives of "selfishness, luxury, or mere convenience." The qualified Lambeth ruling took great care not to endorse an unbridled liberalism, while still breaking the dam of official clerical opposition to the widespread practice of birth control. Yet whatever its reservations, the ruling was widely regarded as a major victory for reform.[7]

International debate of the issue in organized religious circles ensued. Universalists, Unitarians, and Reform Jews, representing the most advanced thinking in the United States, immediately followed suit with their own endorsements. Meanwhile, the Federal Council of the Churches of Christ in America, chaired by Reinhold Niebuhr and representing some 22 million Protestants ranging from Presbyterian elites to Baptist fundamentalists, took an intermediary step, first creating a Committee on Marriage and the Home to study the subject.

In what was, perhaps, the most stunning example of her transformation from Greenwich Village radical to uptown reformer, Margaret then arranged to raise funds for this committee anonymously. She worked quietly but determinedly through Worth M. Tippy, executive secretary of the organization and former dean of the Cathedral of St. John the Divine in New York. In large part through her unheralded efforts, dollars and arguments in support of birth control were marshaled, and a host of consultants was brought in, including psychologists and physicians from the New York Academy of Medicine. In April of 1931, the committee formally endorsed birth control on medical, economic, and social grounds, proclaiming the virtue of the practice as a safeguard to the health of women and children and as a deterrent to poverty and overpopulation. As to moral concerns, the committee's statement argued that the sexual union of man and woman in marriage is intended by God not only for the procreation of children but also as a "supreme expression of their affection and comradeship—a manifestation of divine concern for the happiness of those who have so wholly merged their lives." The inviolability of marriage was emphasized, but in framing these arguments around considerations of human contentment, the American document moved doctrinally far to the left of its British counterpart. So profound were the concessions to modernity that it even went on to acknowledge the possibility that extramarital sex relations might be encouraged as a consequence of greater knowledge of contraception. With this in mind, however, the committee endorsed sex education, rather than blind prohibition, as the more rational course toward the moral development of youth.[8]

"It's What I'd Have Written Myself," said Margaret in newspaper headlines about the report, though, of course, her role in bringing it about was never acknowledged. She congratulated the Federal Council on its intelligence and its scientific approach, yet when she mailed the statement to Havelock Ellis in London, he responded in mock horror at the thought that anything the two of them approved of could possibly be acceptable to officials of any church!

In fact, such advanced views did not prevail in America's largest Protestant hierarchy without considerable controversy. While the more liberal, elite constituents like the Congregationalists and Presbyterians went along with the statement, more conservative members of the organization, including some Methodists, protested, demanding additional study of the matter before the endorsement became official, an enterprise for which Margaret also raised funds. Disgruntled Presbyterians in the deep South briefly severed their affiliation with the parent body completely, resulting in a loss of revenue for which she also tried to compensate. Indeed, after two years of wrangling over the issue, no consensus was achieved, and the Federal Council actually never endorsed its own committee's report, though the document had by then received so much publicity that the absence of formal approval was barely noticed. The Federal Council enjoyed what was called a "cooperative" relationship with the Protestant Episcopal Church in America, and a "consultive" connection to the Lutherans, but the governing bodies of these denominations also did not immediately comply. A deeply divided Episcopal House of Bishops finally endorsed birth control in 1934, but only over the protests of many bishops who thought it indecent even to bring the subject before a house of God. Margaret's own lobbyists petitioned the Episcopalians with great determination, as they did nearly every convention of churchmen that met in the 1930s, but elsewhere they were not always so successful. The Missouri Synod, largest and most conservative of the Lutheran constituencies, for example, once accused the American Birth Control League of "spattering the country with its slime" and did not reverse its official opposition to contraception until the 1950s. Birth control remained a point of contention between left-wing and right-wing constituencies in the Protestant churches.[9]

Still, the support of liberal Protestants marked a critical turning point, the significance of which was underscored in the vituperative responses it occasioned. American Catholics called the Federal Council's report a "liquidation of historic Protestantism by its own trustees," an observation that simply replicated earlier pronouncements from the Vatican about the Lambeth Conference ruling.

In 1930, Pope Pius XI had issued the historic encyclical *Casti Conubii* (Of Chaste Marriage), which finally codified decades of ad hoc positions on birth control by Catholic officialdom in Europe and the United States. Referring specifically to his Anglican counterparts, the Pope wrote:

> Certain persons have openly withdrawn from the Christian doctrine as it has been transmitted from the beginning and always faithfully kept. . . . The Catholic Church, to whom God himself has committed the integrity and decency of morals, now standing in this ruin of morals, raises her voice aloud through our mouth, in sign of her divine mission, in order to keep the chastity of the nuptial bond free from this foul slip, and again promulgates: Any use whatever of marriage, in the exercise of which the act by human effort is deprived of its natural

power of procreating life, violates the law of God and nature, and those who do such a thing are stained by a grave and mortal flaw.

The Papal document went on to synthesize and distill a revisionist view of historical Christian doctrine on marriage, emphasizing the immutability of Augustine's ancient prohibitions against infidelity, divorce, contraception, and abortion, but affirming the value of conjugal love by proclaiming that the sex act in marriage bears "no taint of evil." While taking pains to dispute the darker Augustinian view of sex itself, the encyclical explicitly condemned "the false liberty and unnatural equality" of modern women and demanded recognition of the husband as head of household, so long as "the civil rights of women" were protected.

It could not have been more emphatic in its condemnation of any contraceptive practice at all. Yet, at the same time, it established a new precedent by proceeding to enumerate such "secondary ends" of marriage as "mutual aid, the cultivating of mutual love, and the quieting of concupiscence which husband and wife are not forbidden to consider so long as they are subordinated to the primary end and so long as the intrinsic nature of the act is preserved." To this end, the Pope explicitly approved the continued exercise of marital rights after menopause when "on account of natural reasons, either of time or of certain defects, new life cannot be brought forth."[10]

Casti Conubii was never intended to condone the affirmative, rhythmic use of the monthly sterile period for the purposes of contraception. As a result of its concessions to natural causes, however, it was widely subject to this reading, especially in the United States, where it made the front pages of newspapers and then continued to receive more attention than any papal edict ever had before. Ranking church officials here, especially the powerful Washington figure John Ryan, encouraged the most liberal interpretation possible to permit the deliberate use of the rhythm method by "any married person with a serious reason for avoiding offspring," even though this view remained highly controversial within the church.

The moral and physiological efficacy of using the sterile period as a deliberate way of avoiding pregnancy had, in fact, been debated intermittently and inconclusively among Catholic theologians since the 1870s, when Auguste Lecomte, a French churchman with some primitive training in biology, first recommended it. In the intervening years, scientific opinion on the precise boundaries of the fertile cycle had remained inconclusive, and so it mattered little that moral thinking was likewise.[11]

By 1929, however, what was considered a definitive medical finding—that ovulation occurs sixteen to twelve days before the onset of menstruation—was published by doctors working independently in both Germany and Japan, and their common conclusion inspired renewed consideration of the option. The concurrence of these scientific advances and the publication of *Casti Conubii* had a profound practical effect in the United States. Parish priests found in the doctrine of natural sterility a welcome answer to the most troubling problem of the confessional and began to counsel its use. Asked directly for further clarification on the matter, the Sacred Penitentiary in Rome in July of 1932 actually reissued the more strictly constructed papal prohibition against "Onanism" from 1880, but this response did little to end the confusion. Those Catholics who wouldn't condone rhythm outright used the 1932 communication as evidence that Rome was at least willing to countenance the sterile period in extreme circumstances, in preference to the even more detestable practice of withdrawal.

In 1932, Leo J. Latz, M.D., a Catholic physician on the staff of Loyola University Medical School in Chicago, wrote a book encouraging women to keep a calendar and confine their marital "cohabitations" to the twenty days per month at each end of the menstrual cycle when they are sterile by nature's intent. Simply titled *The Rhythm of Sterility and Fertility in Women* (or in later editions, just *The Rhythm*), the book was published through a private foundation organized with the support of prominent Catholics in Chicago and advertised in a circular headlined "The Big Problem of Married People Solved," which was distributed by mail order and through commercial bookstores. Within eighteen months, four editions of 60,000 copies of the book had been sold, along with an almost equal number of "record calendars." Even the American Medical Association gave its tacit approval, while still refusing to endorse the diaphragm or any other mechanical or chemical contraceptives. Almost overnight, the medical and moral efficacy of the procedure was widely established, though, within only a few years, studies would demonstrate that variability in menstrual cycles makes rhythm a risky method for most women.

The Latz book also constituted a wholesale reversal of Catholic moral and social doctrines enunciated in the 1920s, as the following excerpts suggest:

> ARE MARRIED PEOPLE OBLIGED TO BRING INTO THE WORLD ALL THE CHILDREN THEY CAN? Far from being of obligation, such a course may

> be utterly indefensible. . . . MAY THERE BE AN OBLIGATION IN CONSCIENCE FOR SOME MARRIED COUPLE TO TAKE ADVANTAGE OF THE RHYTHM OF STERILITY AND FERTILITY? Such a situation would exist where, on the one hand pregnancy is undesirable because of physiological, economic, or social reasons, and, on the other, continence would represent a serious danger for either one or both married persons. . . . WHAT GOOD IS EXPECTED TO FOLLOW FROM THE DISSEMINATION OF THIS KNOWLEDGE? First of all we have a right to expect that the married lives of many couples will be vastly enriched with the values, physical, psychic and moral, of married life, as it was intended by the Creator.[12]

Far from protesting, however, some church officials enthusiastically embraced the book. The Archdiocese of Chicago gave its official imprimatur, and a second work popularizing rhythm was published in New York, despite continued protests against the practice under any conditions by the archconservative Cardinal Hayes, who continued to stress the tragedy of the declining birthrate. In Washington, John Ryan did his part as well, even though the National Catholic Welfare Council and the National Conference of Catholic Charities never endorsed Latz's book as an approved statement of Catholic teaching. Indeed, many leading Catholic theologians Ryan had quoted in the past (especially the celebrated Arthur Versmeerch in Belgium) continued to inveigh against rhythm and warn against "the heresy of the empty cradle." The popular association of rhythm with Catholicism was so deeply rooted that it hardly mattered that the Pope never endorsed the practice until 1951, when Pius XII's *Moral Questions Affecting Married Life* appeared, again proclaiming childbearing as the primary obligation of married women, and reiterating the church's absolute condemnation of abortion, artificial contraception, and surgical sterilization. But it finally defended the moral use of the nonfertile periods when precaution against pregnancy was absolutely necessary on medical, eugenic, economic, or social grounds.[13]

Reduced to a dispute over natural versus artificial means, the Catholic argument against birth control lacked intellectual rigor, but it more than made up for this deficit with its practical utility. The rhythm method provided American Catholics a vehicle for joining the birth control debate on their own terms, a means to distinguish the behavior of the faithful from everyone else's. The church, in effect, had its own marriage manual, and for at least one generation, substantial numbers of Catholics—more than half, according to opinion polls—were willing to listen. By distributing daily menstrual calendars, the local dioceses maintained a measure of control over the personal behavior of their members. The situation among Catholics remained stable, until the pill was made available in the 1960s.

As these historic developments unfolded in religious circles, Margaret was quietly but effectively building a national political campaign for birth control by organizing the country from the bottom up, mobilizing volunteers and constituents by Congressional district and in turn by state and region. In 1929, she convened representatives from the Midwest in Columbus, Ohio, and the following year, she held a western conference in Los Angeles. By 1931, four regional directors, overseeing at least some presence in almost every state, were reporting to a national headquarters in Washington. Once again, the new recruits were predominantly Protestant and Jewish women, many of them also former suffragists, skilled in the art of political organization and lobbying. The Maryland state chairman, Mrs. Robert H. Walker, for example, came from one of the state's most prominent families but saw herself as a rebel because she had once gone to jail during a demonstration for the woman's vote in Washington. The head of the western region, Mrs. Verner Z. Reed of Denver, was also an advocate of women's rights and a major benefactor of Colorado hospitals, libraries, and universities. There were simpler folk, as well, like Viola Kaufman, a frugal retired schoolteacher and onetime suffrage volunteer in California, who was living in a boarding house paying $2.00 a week rent when she came to work for Margaret and then suddenly died, leaving to the cause an estate of Depression-devalued real estate holdings totaling $12,000.[14]

Major financial support also came from women, predominantly in New York and its environs, where Margaret's loyal lieutenant, Ida Timme, solicited contributions in increments of $1,000 and up. Timme fell short of her pre-Crash goals by about 50 percent, and managed to find only $25,000 in the first two years of trying, most of it from the same women who financed the New York clinic. The Rockefeller family's Bureau of Social Hygiene turned down an initial request for funds on the grounds that it did not support lobbying in general and didn't think it worthwhile in this instance. Donations of $4,000 and up, however, were secured from individuals like Mrs. Felix Warburg and Mrs. Felix Fuld, of the investment banking families, from Albert and Mary Lasker, the medical philanthropists, from Ethel Clyde, an eccentric, progressive Southerner, and from the Milbank Memorial Fund, which agreed to finance a campaign to have poor women seeking contraceptive advice write to their Congressmen.

Timme also solicited smaller sums, appealing in one mailing: "Do you, a woman, realize that true emancipation and acknowledgment of an equal status for women can never be realized until motherhood is by choice and not by chance? This is the first time in the world's history that an organized drive at race betterment, through conscientious intelligent, forward looking parenthood, is being launched and women must lead the way since women are the mothers of the race." Hundreds of gifts of $25 or less were received in response. When the Federal Committee finally closed its books in 1936, annual expenditures were more than $50,000, a respectable sum for the time, but never really enough. Even the Rockefellers' resistance had been worn down. Between 1934 and 1936, the family anonymously contributed $10,000, having adopted Margaret's theory that lobbying was justified from a public relations point of view, however slight the chances of actual legislative victory might be.[15]

Margaret was pivotal to every aspect of this operation, but nowhere was her influence more directly felt than in crafting its message. During the 1920s she had emphasized constituency development and institution building over public relations, with predictable results. As an index to popular thinking, for example, *The Reader's Guide to Periodical Literature* for 1925 through 1928, years she was also spending much of her time abroad, lists only thirty-one articles on birth control, the majority of them about the activities of Catholics and other opponents. Between 1929 and 1932, however, when she reassessed priorities and embarked on a deliberate strategy to combine propaganda and organization in order to educate public opinion, three times the amount of magazine coverage was produced, and a similar turnaround in daily reporting on birth control can be observed. Though she engaged in no antics so theatrical as the arrests and hunger strike of her days as a radical, she did go to great lengths to make headlines.

In March of 1931, for example, she produced front-page national coverage for hearings on a birth control bill in the United States Senate. Hoping to keep the story alive, she then traveled to Atlanta to debate Richard Russell, chief justice of the Georgia State Court and the father of seventeen children, one of whom had just been elected governor. The national wires also covered this event, declaring Margaret the winner. Back in the papers when her book came out in September, she again made the front pages later that month by tying birth control to the banking crisis and calling for a "two-year holiday" on babies for rich and poor alike. Captioned photos identifying Margaret as "attractive" and "fashionable" invariably accompanied these stories, and the overall tone and placement of the reporting about birth control improved.[16]

The movement's image was also immeasurably enhanced by the presence in Washington of Katharine Houghton Hepburn of Hartford, who joined the National Committee as legislative chairman. Long a loyal soldier for suffrage and birth control in Connecticut, Kit Hepburn was married to a physician active in social causes. Like Margaret, she was also a girl from the hills of Corning. Her grandfather, in fact, had been the founder of Corning Glass, but she was not herself a woman of substantial means, and stock market reverses left her unwilling even to cover her own expenses when she accepted Margaret's invitation to volunteer for the National Committee. That year, however, Hepburn's daughter and namesake was embarking on a stage career in New York and in Washington, and she'd soon made her historic film debut as the wholesome ingenue who fumbles her way to stardom in *Morning Glory*. When the young Katharine Hepburn won an Academy Award for this performance, the association of the name with birth control became far more valuable than anything money could buy.

Hollywood would reach the peak of its influence during the 1930s, with an average weekly audience of 85 million, but this extraordinary power was ordinarily directed toward preserving traditional values, not upsetting them. Katharine Hepburn was something of an exception. In *Christopher Strong*, a 1933 film made by Dorothy Arzner, the most successful and outspoken female director of the era, she starred as an aviator who kills herself after becoming pregnant by a married man. Even so, there was vehement protest from studio management when the redoubtable young Hepburn then told a reporter that she stood behind everything Margaret Sanger had to say. "I'd have spanked her if she hadn't," her perplexed but obviously pleased mother joked in a scribbled response to Margaret's enthusiastic note of thanks for the endorsement.[17]

Yet neither Hollywood glamour, nor the harsh reality of the Depression from which Hepburn's trademark films were intended to provide escape, was able to effect concrete political movement on the birth control question. An implacable Congress hardly budged even after a reasonably skillful assault by Margaret and her colleagues. The National Committee, with its disciplined, hierarchical organizational structure, had a substantial advantage as a lobbying institution over the loosely confederated American Birth Control League. When needed, thousands of supporters could be marshaled at short notice to make themselves heard. Within two years, a speakers bureau had lined up forty-one individuals for appearances before 858 civic and religious forums, social welfare associations, and women's groups in 319 cities and 26 states. Volunteer organizers spread an even wider net in the field, and, eventually, eight paid staff members were also sent out. In 1931, the organization claimed only 1,000 backers from Alabama to Wisconsin. By 1935, more than 50,000 individual endorsers had signed on, and more than 1,000 resolutions had been secured from groups representing a broad range of viewpoints. By the time the National Committee closed down in 1937, it would claim the direct endorsement of more than 12 million people across the country. In the single small town of Easton, Pennsylvania, for example, sponsors included a medical society, various women's clubs, the Social Service League, the Parent–Teachers Association, and the local chapter of the Socialist Party.[18]

The National Committee's phalanxes of volunteers, in turn, produced a steady barrage of mail. Margaret's combined staffs in New York and Washington were processing as much as 15,000 pieces of mail per month by 1932, while constituent letters and petitions also poured in steadily to key members of the Senate and House Judiciary Committees. "Let every mother in this land help me fight to change vicious laws which condemn us to conditions our Government would not impose upon a farmer's cattle," she entreated in the solicitation to poor women that was paid for by the Milbank Fund. And the responses she provoked provided the kind of material that would under less controversial circumstances propel almost any politician into action.

One bereft but still determined farm wife from Central City, Nebraska, who said she could not even afford her own stationery, scrawled a reply on the back of the form letter itself:

> My husband has been gone for more than 2 weeks looking for work, and I don't know where he is. I am almost barefoot and have only 2 badly worn dresses . . . and my 15 yr. old girl has been in the hosp. since Jan. . . . So, Mrs. Sanger, if my poor miserable letter that comes from bitterness and want can help other wives and mothers to have less babies and more common sense and comfort, then for God's sake use it.

A correspondent from Temperance, Michigan, only twenty-one years old but already with two young children, wrote:

> My husband has no job. He has been all over looking for work. He walked 28 miles the other day for the third time to the county seat to try and get a WPA job but he had no luck. We live in a small attic room that has two small windows. We've been happy in our love for each other in this little room . . . [but] I live in fear that I'll become pregnant again—more suffering and starving. Why must a woman suffer so much? I got some old newspapers from some people and I read about your campaign—about your signers for petitions concerning birth control. What is your plan? Can I help? Please let me know. Now I am going to bed and try to forget that I am hungry.[19]

Armed with the testimony of the needy and the endorsements of the powerful, Margaret mounted a diligent lobbying campaign each year from 1931 through 1936. She hired a tough professional lobbyist from the American Red Cross by the name of Hazel Moore, who was skilled in the internal dynamics of Congress. Deeply committed to the cause, Moore taught Sanger, Hepburn, and legions of volunteers how to pursue potential sponsors and supporters. They worked together with unflagging determination for six consecutive legislative sessions. Little time was wasted on formal organization, one volunteer later remembered, but everyone worked hard. "Margaret, were she not so gentle except when frustrated, was rather like a lion tamer. She kept us each on our boxes until she needed us—then we jumped and jumped fast."[20]

Moore was never afraid to let a recalcitrant legislator know just how many women could be lined up back home to oppose his re-election, if he voted the wrong way. Reporting to Margaret on a conversation with an objectionable Congressman, she observed:

> I told [him] if 2 million men had a toe ache within the last 60 years they would appropriate millions of dollars to care for them—pass all sorts of laws to remove all obstacles for the care of their toes etc—but because 2 million women had died from childbirth and God only knew how many from abortions since the fool law was enacted, they didn't have time to put a bill in a box and let us arrange for a hearing.[21]

Yet Congressional resistance to birth control proved subtle and complex. The hurdles were enormous. Despite the historic pronouncements of religious liberals, despite the indisputable economic need, the issue remained tainted for many politicians by its association with sex—a subject from which they generally shied away. It was perhaps especially so in this instance because Margaret Sanger, who had so much to say about it, was involved. Several distressed Congressmen indeed ejected her from their offices on claims of common decency. As the columnist Heywood Broun explained: "Birth control is in the eyes of politicians political dynamite. If they support it, they may lose some votes. If they oppose it, they may lose some votes. There is nothing a politician hates more than losing votes. He would much rather the subject never came up."[22]

It took almost the entire term in 1931 to identify a single sponsor for a birth control bill. Five male physicians and five women then serving in the Congress were targeted as possible supporters, but each was able to come up with an excuse for not getting involved. The next approach was to legislators who might feel insulated from potential voter reprisal by a combination of their seniority and the safety of their districts, but once again there were repeated rebuffs. Finally, a lame duck was identified. Sen. Frederick Huntington Gillett, a seventy-nine-year-old Massachusetts Republican, agreed to sponsor a bill. Gillett had served sixteen terms in the House, where he rose to the position of Speaker, but he was planning to retire after a single term in the Senate.[23]

The measure made it through a hearing of a subcommittee of the powerful Judiciary Committee, where Margaret testified in its behalf. She declared birth control a "Mothers' Bill of Rights," in an attempt to diminish anxiety about its sexual dimension, and emphasize its positive effects on the nation's high rates of maternal and infant mortality. J. Whitridge Williams, a supporter of the New York clinic and the prestigious chief obstetrician at Johns Hopkins University Hospital, then corroborated these arguments. Other speakers in support included academic and religious figures who also emphasized the individual and social benefits of the practice. Telegrams poured in from prominent opinion makers. Key members of the committee and of the Senate leadership were individually lobbied.

The *Congressional Digest* featured birth control reform as its lead story, and the potential of political reform seemed momentarily attainable, until the Catholic Church suddenly marshaled in force and sounded every possible alarm. Not just prudish politicians, but the substantially enhanced political sophistication and power of American Catholics stopped birth control reform in the 1930s. A determined minority was able to force its views on the entire country—not just in one city, state or region—and this was a development Margaret could not necessarily have foreseen.

A representative of the National Catholic Welfare Conference sounded uncannily like Anthony Comstock when he claimed Margaret's bill would open the "floodgates" to all kinds of pornographic and obscene literature. A second witness called the bill a subversive Soviet plot to undermine the morality of young Americans. Another deliberately confused contraception and abortion. At the NCWC's urging, the American Federation of Labor then also testified in opposition. Long petitions of protest were submitted to George Norris, the powerful chairman of the Judiciary Committee. And Margaret was again scapegoated with the charge that she was profiting from a commercial contraceptive venture somewhere in the Midwest, which was capitalizing on her name by calling itself the "Marguerite Sanger Company." In the Catholic journal *Commonweal,* she was then identified as the leader of a subversive "revolution."

When the Gillette bill died in committee, Margaret complained to Ida Timme in New York that the opposition was putting "terror and fear . . . in the minds of men." "We must work, not stop, raise our voices and make the men down here feel our votes are important too," she added. Timme copied the letter and sent it to key contributors.[24]

The following year, at the urging of ostensibly sophisticated lawyers at the firm of Covington, Burling & Rublee, a second bill was introduced by Sen. Henry Drury Hatfield. A powerless, freshman Republican from West Virginia, Hatfield was nonetheless a licensed physician and the former governor of his state, and it was hoped that he might diffuse the religious and moral opposition with medical arguments. In the House, a companion bill was filed by Franklin W. Hancock, a relatively progressive, second-term North Carolina Democrat, but, regrettably, he did little to help the cause when he acknowledged in public testimony that he had "reached no definite and determined view relative to its merits." With such politically ineffective allies, Margaret had no real hope of victory. What is more, it was a Presidential election year, and the thorny question of repeal of prohibition was also on the legislative agenda. One Senator told Margaret that prohibition posed a far greater national threat than the Comstock laws. "This was quite logical from his point of view," she then reported privately. "He never had to bear a child, and for him to do without a drink is a great hardship." In public, however, she maintained a less cynical posture, claiming that she was laying a base for reform in the future, at a more opportune moment.[25]

Sponsorship by a physician seemed especially meaningful to the lawyers advising Margaret, in view of a little-noticed ruling of 1930 in the United States Circuit Court in the Second Circuit in New York. The case, *Young's Rubber Corporation v. C. I. Lee & Co. Inc.*, involved two competing manufacturers of condoms in an accusation that one had pirated the trademark of the other, and it established the underlying legality of interstate commerce in contraceptives. Judge Thomas Swan ruled broadly that the transport of contraceptive articles was legitimate if they were to be used when "prescribed by a physician for the prevention of disease or for the prevention of conception, where that is not forbidden by local law." This doctrine of intent actually contradicted the ruling rendered only four months earlier by Swan's colleague, Augustus Hand, in the challenge to the Comstock definitions of obscenity in printed matter brought by Mary Ware Dennett over the confiscation of her sex education pamphlet. Yet even in retreating from Hand's "reasonable construction" principle, Swan offered another significant reinterpretation of the nineteenth-century statutes. Hand's liberal reading made possible a frank discussion of sexuality and contraception, and, since exemption provisions for physicians and druggists already existed in most states, Swan's decision opened the way for the vast expansion of the commercial contraceptive market that occurred during the Depression under the protection of intent to control venereal disease and promote feminine hygiene.

In 1931, the United States Post Office actually promulgated regulations for the implementation of the Swan ruling through case by case authorizations to manufacturers. And in 1933, in *Davis v. U.S.*, a federal judge in the Sixth Circuit in Washington again offered protection to a wholesale distributor of contraceptives, citing both Judges Swan and Hand. Margaret then briefly considered whether her legislative campaign ought to be abandoned altogether, since the Congressional action she sought would do little more than codify these judicial and administrative actions. She went ahead anyway, at the encouragement of her own lawyers, on the justification that laws are secure only when made by legislators, not by judges and postmasters, and in the conviction that the lobbying would have educational value, whatever its outcome.[26]

Her immediate strategy was to have Senator Hatfield lobby his colleagues on the hill about the critical need to clarify the rights of physicians and pharmacists under the new court and post office rulings. As governor of West Virginia, however, Hatfield had passed a coercive sterilization law, and he proved to be more interested in the eugenic implications of birth control than in its larger virtues. He turned out to be useful only as a participant in private negotiations that Margaret then initiated with the same representatives of the National Catholic Welfare Conference in Washington who had so strenuously objected to Senator Gillette's bill a year earlier.

As one doctor to another, Hatfield gained the confidence of a man by the name of Dr. Joseph J. Mundell of the Georgetown University Medical School, who regularly advised the NCWC on the medical aspects of legislation. In a private meeting with Mundell and Margaret, he then modified the language of the original Gillette bill and convinced Mundell that it would serve only the most narrow professional uses possible. Mundell, in turn, then assured John Ryan that clear, legal authorization of contraception would make doctors more comfortable about prescribing it to married women, but would also make possible more effective regulation of the vending machine and drugstore contraceptives available to the unmarried. Ryan was widely considered the official "censor" of all political positions taken by the Catholic hierarchy in this country, and his willingness to consider modifications in the language of the legislation was viewed as a major breakthrough.

This delicate bill-drafting session actually followed earlier, confidential meetings among NCWC staff, Mundell, Ryan, and Margaret's personal representative, a somewhat mysterious figure by the name of James Joseph Toy, who turned up in Washington in 1931 and volunteered his services to the National Committee. A former United States Army colonel, trained as an industrial engineer, Toy had lost some real estate investments in the early years of the Depression in California, and like many entrepreneurs in those circumstances, then tried his luck at the quick profits of commercial contraception, where he developed his knowledge and awareness of the birth control issue. Offering to help Margaret if she covered his expenses, he was first sent into the field as a representative to doctors. Once having proved himself, he was then employed as an emissary to John Ryan. A businessman, military man, and practicing Catholic, Toy seemed a valuable ally.[27]

Margaret could not have negotiated very well on her own. However hard she tried, she could never seem to contain her irreverence. In testimony on the Gillette bill in 1931, she identified Christ as a fine example of an only child, and in a special issue of *The Nation* devoted to the birth control controversy the following year, she made a mockery of the natural law doctrine in *Casti Connubii*. She wrote:

> The contention that it is sin to have dominion over nature is simple nonsense. The Pope frustrates nature by getting shaved and having his

> hair cut, as well, as by practicing continence. Whenever we catch a fish or shoot a wolf or a lamb, whenever we pull a weed or prune a fruit tree, we frustrate nature. Disease germs are perfectly natural little fellows which must be frustrated before we can get well. His attitude . . . is conditioned by disapproval of human enjoyment and an apparent relishing of the theory that suffering is good for our souls.[28]

John Ryan would probably never have consented to direct discussions with Margaret, and it appears he did not at first understand that Colonel Toy was her employee. By Toy's account, Ryan did not desist when told the facts, though he needed assurance that she was neither a fanatic nor a profit seeker, but rather an "idealist" whose goal was to bring contraception under stricter medical control. Ryan authorized Dr. Mundell as his agent to redraft the bill, and in light of the extreme delicacy of these maneuverings, he also recommended that Edward F. McGrady, the chief lobbyist for the American Federation of Labor and a prominent Catholic who would later become an assistant secretary of labor in the Roosevelt administration, be asked to quietly pass new voting instructions to Catholic members of the House and Senate. Toy quoted Ryan as saying:

> Of course you understand that the Catholic Church can take no conciliatory attitude publicly or officially towards birth control. It would be misunderstood. The press would play havoc with the situation. . . . Now remember that this must be held most confidentially. Any knowledge of my accepting your proposal becoming public would upset everything and create a continuation of controversy and animosity even greater than that which exists now.

Father Ryan had long espoused orthodox church doctrine on contraception, but on most other social matters he was a confirmed liberal. Educated in economics and sociology, he wrote extensively endorsing such then progressive ideas as minimum wage legislation, unemployment and health insurance, social security, public housing, and labor's right to organize. He would become a prominent political spokesman for Franklin Roosevelt. And, by 1937, Ryan would break publicly with his superiors in the church hierarchy when they refused to endorse the New Deal's historic child labor legislation on the grounds that it constituted undue governmental interference in family matters. Even on birth control, according to the Catholic historian John Noonan, though Ryan avoided any innovation beyond endorsing the rhythm method, "he did not like to be more rigorous than he felt constrained to be by authority."[29]

What happened following Ryan's meeting with Colonel Toy, and subsequent interviews with Mundell, McGrady, and Ralph E. Burton, a Catholic Congressman, is undocumented. It may have been that in this instance, as in the subsequent labor legislation dispute, superior authority did intervene, forcing Ryan to retreat from his earlier commitment. Certainly the hard line of Cardinal Hayes in New York would have carried greater weight than Ryan's views. And, of course, the interim developments with respect to the rhythm method may have been a consideration. Even though the conversation was taped and transcribed, it is also possible that Toy somehow misrepresented Ryan, or perhaps revealed the transcript to some unacceptable party, leaving no recourse but public denial. The sudden mobilization of Catholic constituencies in opposition to the bill may also have forced Ryan to rethink his position on the grounds that even the smallest appearance of defeat for the church could no longer be tolerated. While he was negotiating privately, such powerful groups as the National Council of Catholic Women and the Knights of Columbus either wrote or testified against the bill. One speaker, representing the International Federation of Catholic Alumni, baldly charged that birth control organizations were servicing and being financed by young, promiscuous people.

Whatever the reasons, on May 2, 1932, William Montavon of the NCWC's Legal Department wrote an emphatic denial of Colonel Toy's version of what had transpired. Dr. Mundell's efforts were repudiated, and the Hatfield bill, like its predecessor, was branded "immoral—destructive of fundamental relations of husband and wife and child, [and] consequently destructive of the family on the right order and dignity of which the whole welfare of human society rests." Ryan's own testimony marshaled his standard arguments against Malthusian doctrine, though they carried less weight in light of his endorsement of rhythm. He also emphatically rejected the suggestion that legislation would allow for more effective regulation of commercial contraceptives, the argument that had been discussed privately. The bill was narrowly defeated in committee after hearings in May, when the contemplated agent of compromise, Edward McGrady of the AF of L, refused to support any measure that the church officially denounced, though he did admit that this one was "not so sweeping or objectionable" as its predecessor. Morris Ernst was actually relieved. Though he recognized the public relations value of a detente with the Catholic Church and had encouraged Margaret in her lobbying efforts, he was concerned that the compromise bill would have been more restrictive than recent court decisions rendered the existing law.[30]

Far from any new gestures of reconciliation, the National Catholic Welfare Conference then dramatically intensified its opposition campaign. Mirroring Margaret's own public relations tactics, the organization distributed thousands of copies of a circular identifying birth control as a "national menace" through churches and other Catholic institutions. Catholic magazines editorialized against birth control, and the goal of overcoming the lobbying advantage of the birth control advocates by producing opposition mail in great quantities was handsomely achieved. Thousands of letters poured into Congress, and intimidation of birth control supporters also escalated at a local level. In New York City, for example, a well-known Catholic priest issued a press release demanding the removal of a local public school principal, who had allowed one of the doctors from the Clinical Research Bureau to give a presentation to a parents' association meeting, which included a detailed explanation of the diaphragm regimen. The release, accusing Margaret of "peddling immoral garbage," provoked a public protest from Worth Tippy on behalf of Protestants, but the intimidation worked against local Congressmen known to have been leaning toward supporting birth control. Emanuel Celler of Brooklyn, for example, later admitted to Margaret's lobbyists that he could not possibly be with them, because Catholics held the balance of power in his district and would surely defeat him. The window of opportunity for any political compromise with the Catholic Church had all but closed.[31]

CHAPTER SIXTEEN

Same Old Deal

Margaret retreated to Europe for much of the summer of 1932, where she renewed international contacts and then wandered around more or less aimlessly, finally settling down in a sanitarium in Switzerland for treatment of a lingering gallbladder ailment. She needed time to reassess her political strategy at home and to sort out personal concerns as well.

After Noah sold his company in 1929, he had put almost all of his money into the stock market and purchased his own seat on the New York Stock Exchange for more than half a million dollars, at the time one of the highest prices ever paid. His son, James, Jr., who had already left 3-in-One Oil for Wall Street, took charge of his portfolio, with some assistance from Stuart Sanger, who had also worked on the street for a brief time following his graduation from Yale. Many speculative investments were wiped out almost immediately in the great crash that year, but, fortunately, most of Noah's money had gone into industrials, railroads, utilities, and other blue-chip stocks that did not hit bottom until the Depression took firm hold during the winter of 1931-32. At that point Noah lost his seat on the exchange. During the bank holiday, the following year, when financial institutions were closed temporarily to avoid a run on deposits, he was devastated to find himself without even any cash. His banks were solvent, however, and he never liquidated what remained of his stock holdings, so that within a decade their value had been partially restored. But for the time being he had barely enough money to maintain his life-style and no longer considered himself a wealthy man. The losses seriously imperiled his sense of self-worth.

Like so many Americans of conservative inclination, Noah chose to view these reverses as evidence of personal failing and not of the more fundamental, structural weaknesses in the economy that underlay them. Unlike many of his contemporaries, however, he had children to blame for at least some of his troubles. Jim Slee and Walter Willis, a son-in-law, became scapegoats, first for having encouraged him to sell his company and then for his unfortunate timing in the stock market. He apparently never again spoke to them or his daughter Anne, or to a second son, Lincoln, with whom he had never been close.[1]

Margaret, by contrast, seems to have accepted Noah's losses with considerable equanimity. Money was the glue of their relationship, but it was not in the most basic sense the measure by which she judged an individual's worth, and his having less of it was hardly what diminished him most in her eyes. As to the impact on her own life and creature comforts, she wrote to Ellis of Noah's reverses, suggesting that her habits would need "drastic changing," but claiming, however disingenuously, that she was "not afraid of the simple life for really I never got very far away from it in my *very own way*." All the rich people she knew were learning to cut corners, and who knew better than she how to do so? She seemed far more concerned about what would become of Hugh and Janet de Selincourt, who had put their inheritance in the hands of stock speculators and lost everything. They were forced to rent out Sandpit, their only remaining asset, and with the loss of their home the personal freedom it symbolized seemed no longer possible to achieve. An entire way of life had been destroyed, and by comparison, her slightly diminished circumstances scarcely seemed significant.[2]

Although she could obviously no longer count on Noah's money, Margaret continued to engage him in her work by writing good-naturedly of the trials and tribulations of supporting herself on the road and raising funds for the movement in such difficult times. Describing her many ventures at economizing in Europe in 1932, she assured him that she was doing just fine with less—that she had been unnecessarily self-indulgent in the past, protestations of independence that may only have made him feel worse. When his spirits flagged, she simply insisted that he boost himself up and not be sorry for himself or lonely without her.

Being free of Noah's money actually gave her a new sense of liberation and rekindled her energy for work. Determined to support herself with substantial lecture and writing fees, she had new challenges to meet, and since Noah was no longer paying the bills, she also felt less of an obligation to be with him. He, in turn, made fewer demands on her time, perhaps not yet realizing exactly what this meant. They would, in fact, spend much of the remaining decade apart, their relationship sustained principally through frequent correspondence—Margaret's letters once again reflecting her capacity to idealize the marriage, so long as her husband remained a comfortable distance away. Their separations grew more and more prolonged as age, infirmity, and economic adversity intensified Noah's sanctimonious qualities and his many odd personal habits, creating a situation that would have tried the patience of just about any wife. Yet, the longer they were apart, the warmer, chattier, and more affectionate Margaret seemed to become. She would address him as "Dear Love," or "My Lovely Dearest One," or "Darling Noah," and often sign the letters with his name of endearment for her—"Lovingly," or "Devotedly, Margy."[3]

Noah spent winters with Margaret in Washington during the legislative seasons, but by and large he seemed absorbed in his own economic concerns and reconciled to his wife's absences. Evidently, he also occupied a good deal of his time alone, attending to the books of the clinic in New York and of the new federal lobbying organization. Piles of correspondence survive to testify to his obsessive concern for the administrative detail of her work. He drove Margaret's subordinates crazy with his frequent demands for accountings of travel expenses, postage, phone calls, office supplies, and the like—there was no item too petty for his personal scrutiny. "Watch the pennies," was his favorite dictum. As far as her personal needs went, however, he continued with considerable extravagance to send baskets of fruit or bottles of champagne to her departing ship cabins, and flowers to her faraway hotel rooms.[4]

Noah's estrangement from his own children seems to have intensified his emotional stake in Margaret and her sons. There was a warm family Christmas together at Willowlake in 1932, decorating a ten-foot outdoor pine by the side of the sleeping porch. By Margaret's enthusiastic description, its trim of silver and blue decorations became even more perfect when covered with silver frost. Devastated by the tide of events that left him unemployable, Stuart then left New York and traveled through the South and West for several years, with his mother and stepfather continuing to pay his bills. Grant, in the meanwhile, went on from Princeton to Cornell Medical School.[5]

Franklin Roosevelt's election in 1932 focused the nation's attention on reform and renewed Margaret's optimism about passing birth control legislation, at least for the moment. Before Roosevelt became governor of New York in 1928, his wife, Eleanor, had served on the board of the American Birth Control League. She'd also spoken in 1931 at the testimonial of the American Woman's Association that honored Margaret, but by that time her husband was a contender for the Democratic Party's nomination for President, and her vocal support of birth control received several unfavorable notices in the press. From then on, as she freely admitted, her position on the subject was something she simply never discussed, though she was continuously linked to the issue by reproving Catholic editorialists, nevertheless.[6]

Margaret faithfully voted for Norman Thomas once again in 1932, but she was inclined to support Roosevelt after he won in a landslide, and she confided to Ellis that both her sons had gone Democratic. Noah voted for Hoover, she admitted, but she had no use for the breed of rugged individualism Hoover represented and much preferred Roosevelt, whom she described as "an organizer . . . [he] will be more agreeable & will consult all kinds of people."

Her immediate intention was to lead a prestigious delegation to call on the new President when he took office in March of 1933, but it quickly became apparent that she would not be among those whose counsel was sought. An April letter from Roosevelt's appointments secretary politely regretted that "to accomplish his recovery objectives, the President is working under tremendous pressure, and we are, therefore, confining his appointments to matters having to do with the recovery program and legislative measures affecting it." One by one, members of the Roosevelt circle who had previously supported birth control formally severed their ties and refused to speak out on the issue. Harry Hopkins resigned from the board of trustees of the clinic in New York when he went to Washington to administer relief programs. Elinor Morgenthau, wife of the Secretary of the Treasury and a neighbor of the Slees in Fishkill, admitted that she had little patience with persons afraid to stand for their own convictions but then reminded Margaret of the violent letters she had received when her support was made public in the past and refused to allow the use of her name any longer, so as to avoid further controversy. Samuel Rosenman, Presidential adviser and speechwriter, who had sponsored Margaret's first birth control bill in the New York State Assembly, also refused to help. Only Anna Ickes, the imperious first wife of the Secretary of the Interior, continued to identify freely with the birth control lobby, refusing to be daunted by what certainly had the appearance of an unwritten administration policy. Her husband, however, whose agency then ran the government's public health programs, did not.[7]

Margaret's enthusiasm for Roosevelt quickly soured. "I'm getting sick of this stupid country," she would write Ellis by December of 1933. "Roosevelt 'experimenting' with peoples' existence, killing pigs, burning wheat, destroying provisions & the necessities of life, while welfare councils & Community Chests are driven crazy in an effort to feed starving millions." Her real concern, however, seemed less with the chaos of these initiatives than with the constituencies the President was courting. "He's losing the people's confidence," she continued. "Only the Irish Catholics & Southern Democrats are blind to the national disaster pending unless he stops experimenting and gets in gear." The apparent influence of urban Catholics in the emerging New Deal coalition aroused her to new heights of paranoia: "The class who have built up & supported the finest of arts & the cultural movements are impotent," she added with uncharacteristic bitterness. "Those who are grabbing it from them with the assistance of the govt. are concerned only with their cheap pleasures and will let culture, education rot or be taken over by the Hierarchy from Rome." Several weeks later she observed: "What depresses me more than the economic situation is the rise of the power of the Catholics in the Dem. party. Priests having tea at the WH."[8]

Margaret was understandably confused by the struggling Roosevelt administration's policies, and its attentiveness to individuals like the popular Catholic radio priest Father Charles Coughlin of Detroit, who was gaining a tremendous following by playing on popular fears and by invoking nostalgia for a simpler, more provincial era in the nation's past. (Coughlin had, in fact, been banned from CBS for addressing a host of sensitive subjects including birth control, but he then found an even larger audience through his own national hookup, and he was invited to the White House in the early days of the administration.) Yet whatever her private doubts, she carefully constructed a whole new set of public arguments for birth control tied to the enthusiasm for reform being generated by the New

Deal. She was determined to embrace some of Roosevelt's thinking, even if he would have no part of her.

As the New Dealers would themselves discover, the Depression was having a decidedly sobering effect on the social behavior of Americans. Even as the redoubtable Ethel Merman belted out the libertine anthem of Cole Porter's 1934 Broadway hit, "Anything Goes," the temper of the times turned increasingly conservative. Behavior once considered routine suddenly became a rare indulgence. Marriages were postponed. Birthrates plummeted. Women went to work, their opportunities expanded by public employment initiatives, but more than ever, they worked only to help families whose very survival and solidarity seemed in jeopardy. Their concerns as individuals were being set aside, and established arguments for birth control as a fundamental right of women lost salience as a public issue. Birth control needed a revised marketing strategy.

Always the pragmatist, Margaret responded to the Roosevelt administration's decision to try to enlist women in the recovery effort. No sooner had Mrs. Roosevelt and Secretary of Labor Frances Perkins launched a campaign called "It's Up to the Women," than Margaret repositioned her birth control campaign as an instrument to diminish human misery and reduce the staggering economic burden created by the Depression. This canny maneuver might have succeeded, but the Catholic lobby then acted quickly in response, leaving Roosevelt little choice but to capitulate to a key constituency. The new President and his principal domestic advisers knew better than to antagonize a unified church over legislation that was not yet viewed as a priority by all women or by many social theorists. The sometimes irascible Harry Hopkins, for example, had incurred his own share of ecclesiastical wrath in New York years earlier while working in the municipal government, where he investigated contract mismanagement in Catholic and Protestant welfare agencies. Having recently left his wife and three children in New York after a well-publicized love affair, Hopkins may also have felt personally vulnerable to religious attack. Nor can the President's own sensitivity on these grounds be discounted, given the problems in his own marriage that have since been amply documented.[9]

Finding herself spurned by the White House, Margaret took herself back to Capitol Hill. But Congress was consumed by the historic agenda of the first 100 days of the New Deal and never even got around to a hearing on birth control. The following year, with attention still focused on economic issues, public works and relief, she could inspire no better sponsor in the Senate than Daniel Hastings, a freshman Republican from Delaware, whose virulent opposition to the New Deal later cost him reelection. Walter Pierce, however, an enthusiastic, liberal Democrat from Oregon, who was insulated from local Catholic political pressure, was sponsor in the House, where the measure was finally scheduled for committee hearings in January of 1934.

In her 1934 testimony Margaret compiled evidence that birthrates in households on relief were close to 50 percent higher than those with at least one worker still employed. She pointed out that a quarter of a million children had already been born on public assistance, a figure clearly intended to shock federal legislators and administrators still struggling to comprehend the full cost of evolving social welfare policies. She argued that with so many married women entering the work force, reliable contraception was paramount. Always eager to incorporate the most current intellectual fads into her arguments, she called for a program of scientific "family planning," akin to what was being advanced in agriculture and industry. Her proposal was twofold: she asked the government to authorize birth control instruction for all families enrolled in relief and recovery programs and also demanded that a reasonable allowance for every child in need be provided. It was only sensible, she argued, that a society willing to subsidize children in need would help make contraception available at the same time.

In taking the position that birth control could help relieve the Depression, Margaret tackled the contrary opinion that the country's reduced rate of population growth was, in fact, at the root of its economic woes. By 1934, the fear of a declining United States birthrate, long advanced by economists like Louis Dublin, had been incorporated into an overriding economic explanation for the Depression. From an earlier emphasis on differential fertility rates, this school of thought turned its attention to a theory of "underconsumption," which viewed the country's economic collapse as the result of an insufficiency of purchasing power brought on, first, by the skewed income distributions of the boom years of the 1920s, and, second, by the static rate of national population growth. According to this argument, economic recovery depended on guaranteeing American workers a decent minimum wage along with other forms of income security, while also encouraging them to have more babies. By 1933, the overall national birthrate was below replacement level at 18.4 per thousand, and just about everyone was deferring marriage. All the more reason, perhaps, that conservative religious thinkers were reluctant to legalize contraception. By 1938, there would be only 1.5 million recorded marriages, as opposed to ten times that number a decade earlier, though by then the birthrate had begun to rise again to pre-Depression levels.

John Ryan forcefully advanced the Dublin position at the House hearings in 1934. "If we are not well on the way to recovery from this depression by the time any considerable number of children could be born, after the enactment of this bill, then we better get ready for something else in the social order, or a social revolution," he warned. Mrs. Sanger's idea of discouraging births among the unemployed is simply "fantastic," he concluded. Margaret had never once talked about coercive contraception, only of voluntary programs, but Ryan tried to scar her as an opponent of social justice, and this theme was echoed by the powerful Cardinal Hayes in New York.

Margaret, however, held the upper hand in this round. In reply, she submitted testimony from Wesley C. Mitchell, the economist who had headed the prestigious President's Research Committee on Social Trends under Herbert Hoover, along with Robert S. Lynd and other prominent social scientists. They minimized the significance of the decline in the overall birthrate, arguing instead for the importance of achieving a well-balanced population by class, region, and economic sector through the most democratic spread of contraceptive information possible and attacking restrictive legislation that interfered with the work of birth control clinics and propagandists.[10]

Still, linking birth control and relief was a risky business. It made sense on genuinely humanitarian grounds but also served to advance the interests of individuals and groups motivated by fear, prejudice, and unabashed elitism. Indeed, some of the more conservative eugenicists, who had long opposed birth control reform, finally changed their minds during the Depression on the practical grounds that it hardly made sense to argue for more children for the middle and upper classes at a time when most Americans could not afford to feed the ones they already had. In 1933, the American Eugenics Society formally endorsed contraception and joined Margaret's campaign, taking care, however, to define its objectives more carefully as the promotion of policies "to advance hereditary endowment without regard to class, race or creed." Nevertheless, a member of the organization, Guy Irving Burch, then volunteered his services in Washington, where he baldly wrote a letter on official birth control stationery admitting that he had worked for many years to prevent the American people from "being replaced by alien or negro stock, whether it be by immigration or by overly high birth rates among others in this country."

Burch was confiding his views privately, but similar sentiments were also being expressed by the American Birth Control League, with which Margaret was identified in the public mind, even though she had long severed her official ties. The same organization that had rejected a proposal to move closer to eugenicists in 1928 was now proclaiming: "The overproduction of the unfit is driving the American middle-class out of existence. Most serious of all, in the cradle of that second baby that many intelligent, middle-class parents hoped some day to have lies the dependent child of the prodigal proletarian. And usually not all that its foster-parents can do for him through welfare agencies and special classes, through camps and courts and clinics, can make him into a fine citizen." This was far afield from the argument Margaret made when she demanded that birth control be incorporated into national programs of social security and relief.[11]

Mounting ideological tensions within the birth control movement itself were apparent during a conference, Birth Control and National Recovery, that Margaret convened in Washington to coincide with the 1934 hearings. Nearly 1,000 people attended at her invitation, representing a broad spectrum of liberal and conservative viewpoints. The group as a whole made the plea that the country abandon its fascination with economic and population growth and called on President Roosevelt to legalize birth control and assume the obligation of providing it through public health and social welfare programs. Repeated attempts to set up appointments with the President, however, were once again rebuffed, even as Margaret pointed to studies showing that millions of American women were dying needlessly from the complications of self-induced and illegal abortions.

"What of the sex relationships between husband and wife in these normal self-respecting families, now on public relief," asked University of Pennsylvania Prof. James Bossard. "Shall they add further to their misery and their imposition upon the public treasury by having children at its expense, or shall they become the celibates of the New Deal?" The query was probably not ill-intended, but it provoked an unfortunate response. One openly racist Southern delegate raised his concern that prevailing differentials in fertility rates would one day produce an inferior "colored" nation, an accusation that prompted Dr. Ira S. Wile, Margaret's friend and supporter from New York, to point out quickly that the black birthrate, like the white, had already materially diminished. In another session, discussion about the growing burden of the poor on the more fortunate provoked a sharp warning from Rachelle Yarros of Chicago. "I hope this conference won't stress the privileged classes," she said to the amusement of the assembled crowd, "because we don't know who they are, and if we know now, we probably won't five years from now." Margaret's friend from London, Ettie Rout, soon made the same point in a sarcastic, private letter. "I'm glad they now believe in birth control," she wrote, referring to the eugenicists at the conference, but "eliminating them will improve the race!"

The conference closed with an inspirational dinner featuring the venerable feminist Charlotte Perkins Gilman, making a final public appearance before she died, along with the aviator Amelia Earhart, who had more recently established herself as a national figure of heroic proportion. Overall, it generated windfalls of positive publicity and well-informed lobbyists, who made calls to key committee members on Capitol Hill.[12]

In fact, opinion makers in both politics and the press appeared to understand the difference between the kind of birth selection some eugenicists supported and Margaret's advocacy of a more universal and democratic program of birth control. And regrettably enough, blatant expressions of bigotry and racism were tolerated far more in America sixty years ago than they are today. Indeed, there is no evidence that the birth control cause suffered politically because of the expressly classbound, or even racist, viewpoints of some of its advocates, despite the attack launched on these grounds by prominent Catholics.[13]

What is more, the church was itself vulnerable on the issue of prejudice, despite the undoubtedly genuine protestations of John Ryan. Far more influential than he was Father Coughlin, who returned to the birth control issue over and over again on his broadcasts in the early months of 1934. Coughlin was becoming increasingly strident and incoherent in these years and had already lost his credibility at the White House. He claimed that the proposed birth control law would make marriage "nothing more than a legalized bed of prostitution," and also kept calling for more babies and more mouths to feed, not fewer. He derided the airs of "the birth control ladies," but was himself openly biased. Although his most flagrant racism and anti-Semitism came later, he warned at this point that the dissemination of birth control information would make the United States lose its Anglo-Saxon and Celtic majority.[14]

Quietly, the Roosevelt administration joined forces with John Ryan and other Catholic officials in Washington to try to restrain Coughlin and blunt his influence. Margaret does not seem to have known of these efforts, but she too decided to take a conciliatory approach toward more moderate voices in the church. Rebuked by several of her own supporters for religious baiting in the past, she began to speak of the great significance of the new rhythm doctrine and encouraged all those who acknowledged the "principles and benefits to be derived from family limitation" to support her campaign in Washington. After all, as she put it, she was supporting a "permissive" not a "coercive" bill, which would simply legitimize a variety of contraceptive methods. What is more, Leo Latz's use of the public mails to advertise and distribute rhythm constituted no less a challenge to federal Comstock prohibitions than the activities of partisans of artificial methods. At one point she did investigate an idea advanced by the intrepid birth control pioneer, Blanche Ames of Boston, that the birth controllers sue Latz and the Chicago Archdiocese in order to establish a judicial test case on this question, which would have been guaranteed to make headlines. But her lawyers advised her that the post office could defend the validity of distinguishing between information on natural and artificial contraception, and she quickly dropped the matter.[15]

At the House hearings in 1934, she found herself in the curious predicament of praising the Catholics while watching them argue among themselves. She introduced Leo Latz's book on rhythm as evidence of ecclesiastical approval of the principle of birth control and reason for support of her bill, but Dr. Mundell of Georgetown then took exactly the opposite view, citing scientific confirmation of the natural sterile period as a reason that legalization of artificial birth control methods was no longer at all necessary. William Montavon of the NCWC, however, subsequently wrote to the committee contradicting both Margaret and Mundell, by claiming that the "official" Catholic position opposed all contraception and condoned the use of the sterile period only in the most extreme circumstances. Meanwhile, Protestant and Jewish clergymen testified that legal birth control would sanctify and secure marriage, the family, and the home. *Time* magazine's coverage made a mockery of the whole debate, and with all the confusion on who exactly stood for what, the committee reached no consensus.

"The word I got from the House is that it will be necessary for us to fight," Margaret confided to Blanche Ames when the hearings were over. "The Catholics are not only going to accept for themselves all the privileges and rights of the Mails and Common Carriers, but they are going to fight us to the death . . . we must be 'wiped out'."[16]

Thinking there was no more hope, Margaret could not have been more surprised herself when at the conclusion of its own hearings in March, the Senate Judiciary Committee, with only its three Catholic members voting in the negative, agreed to send Sen. Daniel Hasting's bill to the floor. Getting a birth control bill out of committee was a historic development. A victory in the Senate would have had no legal effect in itself, but might have increased the likelihood of a favorable outcome in the House the following year.

Like the original Comstock prohibition sixty years earlier, the reform measure was not calendared until the final day of the session on June 13, 1934, and when it came up for a vote, there were some 200 bills ahead of it. Hazel Moore expected that in the confusion of the day, opponents might simply overlook the measure. She positioned herself in the Senate gallery, tense but prepared for the extraordinary moment. At her insistence, the sponsor stood ready on the floor if, by chance, any objections were raised when the bill was called. His presence, however, turned out to be unnecessary. The birth control bill was read three times and then passed by voice vote, without debate.

Moore, not knowing whether she was "alive or dreaming," rushed into the Senate cloak room to confirm what had transpired, hardly able to believe it. In her brief absence from the gallery, however, the bill was then abruptly recalled by unanimous consent at the request of Sen. Pat McCarran of Nevada, soon to make himself known as a prominent Catholic anti-Communist, who had voted against it in committee.

As described in a later private account, an irate Moore then rushed back downstairs, grabbed the sergeant-at-arms of the Senate and confronted McCarran, yelling:

> "Sgt., arrest this man." "What are the charges?" said the Sgt. "Murder of thousands of women," said I. McCarran laughed and said "I had to object to that bill . . . because I do not believe in murder"—to which I answered "Are you accusing us who are backing this bill of being in favor of murder"—"That's what it is," said McCarran. I then said to the Sgt. "Arrest him for libel" and started on a tirade about an intelligent man making such a statement showing he didn't understand the bill (and probably a lot of other things)—by that time we reach the door of [the] Senate Judiciary Committee where McCarran was going. He laughed in his Irish manner and said something about being willing to be arrested with me—or some such rot—in order to wiggle out of a ticklish position.

Later in the day, demanding an explanation of why Senator Hastings had not objected to the recall, she was assured that tradition in the chamber demanded such courtesies—and that the measure would probably never have passed in the House, in any event.

"But why couldn't every man in favor have jumped to [his] feet and shouted 'No,' " she then asked, answering the question for herself with a personal observation that served as a fitting epitaph for the long and fruitless lobbying enterprise: "But men are men," she wrote, "and Senators are Cowards."[17]

Political defeat took its toll. The high personal price Margaret was paying had been particularly apparent during a recess in the first New Deal Congress, in March of 1933. Exhausted and exasperated by the continued failure of her efforts, she'd phoned Noah in Fishkill and suggested that he treat her to a week's holiday in Bermuda. His response, as she subsequently remembered it years later in an interview, was positively vitriolic: "She was wasting her life on a cause no one cared about, except a bunch of nuts," he screamed, while he remained alone in a big house with only servants as companions. "He might get sick, he might die in the night, who would care? She should take her vacation alone and not bother to come back!"

By this account of many years later, Margaret remained unfazed by this tirade, hung up the phone, booked a train reservation to New York, and then with a coworker set off surreptitiously for a week in Nassau in the Bahamas. She proudly paid for the trip out of her own money, and only when she was safely aboard ship wrote her husband to reveal her destination. Several contemporary letters also survive to verify the accuracy of what she remembered: "Be cheerful," she wrote Noah in a viciously patronizing tone. "Go to your club a few days a week. Go to visit your friends, take in the movies and a good play or two . . . be happy over what you have had and still have in the way of love."

Unbeknownst to her at the time, Noah had actually calmed himself and booked passage for the two of them to Bermuda. Expecting to find her at the boat despite his telephone outburst, he went down to New York the following morning and then sailed alone when she failed to turn up for the scheduled departure. A week later the two returned to Willowlake within several hours of each other, with Margaret determined to pack up and leave permanently in response to his recriminations. But Noah apparently salved his wounds, and they reunited over laughter, tears, and a fine bottle of French champagne.

"I opened the door to see the handsomest man I ever saw in a velvet smoking jacket, smoking a pipe by the blazing fire, the police dog at his feet," she recalled with no apparent awareness that the story was hardly flattering to either party. He looked up and said only, "Hello darling, did you have a good time?"[18]

Yet all was not forgiven, and, characteristically, more was at stake than Margaret willingly acknowledged, accounting, perhaps, for the unabashed insensitivity of her recollections. While the chronology of her private life is not precise for 1933, it is clear that sometime during the year—possibly before the reported contretemps with Noah—she had begun her first new love affair in many years, this one with a New York businessman by the name of Angus Sneed MacDonald. Trained as an architect at Columbia University, MacDonald owned a company that designed, manufactured, and erected iron book stack constructions for the New York Public Library, the Library of Congress, and other such major institutions. Like Noah, he was enterprising and successful, but he could not have been more different in personal temperament. Much closer to Margaret herself in this regard, he was incurably impulsive and romantic—and he loved to dance. Recently divorced and feeling lonely, he apparently walked into the offices of the Birth Control Clinical Research Bureau in New York to make a contribution and found himself seduced by more than just a worthy cause. He saw Margaret on and off through the summer of 1933, whenever she came down to the city on business from Willowlake.

"I long to talk and laugh and nestle close in your arms," she wrote him in August, but then she kept breaking appointments to meet, her unpredictability only intensifying his interest. "I'm no pal at all Angus dear," she warned him. "I'm a wild Irish Will of the Wisp and can't ever be counted on beyond your sight." However much she demurred, she was obviously happy to have found a suitable lover—one who also happened to reside on this continent, at long last—for she was again feeling lonely and misunderstood. The Wantley circle had provided a sustained illusion, but, in reality, only an intermittent emotional anchor to compensate for the detachment she felt from her marriage, and it was now lost forever. Hugh and Janet de Selincourt were completely broken in spirit by the collapse of their finances. Harold Child had finally gone off and remarried, and age and illness had taken its toll on him. H. G. Wells, who had never been more than a carefree diversion in any event, was also absorbed in a new relationship, though at least, he still traveled to the United States on occasion and always made it his business to see Margaret.

The accomplished and debonair MacDonald, on the other hand, would pursue her intensely for two years more with moonlit dances, amorous letters, flowers, and her favorite champagnes, often delivered anonymously to her home—making her feel young and heady with desire once again. She became flagrantly careless about the relationship, openly teasing Noah on one occasion, when he began to suspect that something was going on, chastising him in no uncertain terms when he dared to pry into her private papers, and then laughing with her lover about her incredibly callous behavior. She told MacDonald that she loved him best, but would never compromise her public stature by divorcing for a second time. "I still want to fly or climb difficult heights and be moving onward and upwards toward the unknown," she tried to explain. "[I'm] not a peaceful or restful person to know at all." In turn, he called her "the greatest woman that ever lived (and the most loveable) and the most impossible."[19]

In the fall of 1933, while the affair with MacDonald was still heated, Margaret took a three-week holiday in the Pocono mountains of Pennsylvania. She told her husband that she wanted to have time alone with Grant before he returned to medical school, so that she could get to know him better as an adult, but Juliet Rublee, who would have known of the dalliance, also came along for part of the time. On September 18, the anniversary of their marriage, Margaret wrote and told Noah she missed him, assuring him they would never again be apart on that day, a promise that turned out to be as hollow as it always had been in the past.

She spent much of 1934 without him, though in what was surely an effort at rapprochement, she did bring him to Washington for that year's round of lobbying for birth control reform. They found a lovely old house to rent with charming antique furnishings and a lovely yard, and they took it over Noah's objections about a faulty furnace and other impracticalities. No sooner did the Congressional session end in the spring, however, than she was off to London—then on to Truro for a brief summer holiday, while Noah for reasons unclear went to Woodstock, New York, and the house at Fishkill was rented to help pay the bills.

In July she and Grant left again for Europe, en route to Moscow, where they met up with H. G. Wells and his son, Kip. Noah met her in France on her return, but later that fall, she took Stuart out to Tucson, Arizona, to recuperate in the dry desert climate from an operation he had to correct a chronic sinus infection. Again Noah stayed behind. They reunited in Florida in December.

The following two years brought more of the same. Noah reconciled himself to being alone, while Margaret occupied herself with other interests and a renewed commitment to the birth control cause at home and abroad. They were together at length only for holidays. MacDonald finally gave up on her and married someone else, but he remained Margaret's close friend and occasional lover for years thereafter, and even as they grew older, she was able to rekindle his ardent passions whenever they met. Her capacity to disarm the men who loved her apparently did not diminish with age. Years later, his feelings scarcely moderated, he wrote: "Please understand that you are far and away the most important feature of my life. All else are details that must be made to fit in where they belong in proper order." And on another occasion: "Glorious Margaret, without your loving coming into my life it would have been drab and hardly worthwhile. You have the god-like power to touch a soul and make it bear better fruit than seemed possible!"[20]

Indeed, as she grew older and needier, Margaret refused all the more adamantly to compromise her personal freedoms or to put aside her public obligations in order to be with Noah or any other man. Yet far from thinking of herself as selfish in this regard, she accused her beleaguered husband of insensitivity to the stress and complications of her own predicament and said that if she was to be constantly misunderstood, she would have to keep far away from him even more. She would simply no longer tolerate his interference with anything she wanted to do.[21]

In all ways, then, Margaret seemed curiously emboldened by political defeat. The intransigence of Congress and the President infuriated but did not deter her. Instead, she vowed to maintain a presence in Washington, replicating the tactics of the suffragists, who had ultimately made themselves such a nuisance that Congress broke down and enfranchised women, in part just to be rid of them. To this end, she picked up a key endorsement in 1935 from the General Federation of Women's Clubs, whose New York membership had given birth control a critical boost in 1920. This time, however, the parent organization spoke for 2 million women nationwide.

Birth control also got the nod of the Young Women's Christian Association, sister organization to the very institution that had so many years earlier given Anthony Comstock his start. Even more important, perhaps, Margaret's legislative progress spawned a separate but complementary lobbying campaign by a committee of physicians funded by the Rockefeller family. This National Medical Committee proved no more successful than she on Capitol Hill, but it did succeed in convincing the still timid and noncommittal American Medical Association to sponsor a long overdue inquiry into the birth control issue. She was less successful herself with the American Nurses Association, which turned down a birth control endorsement at its annual convention. "Ah, self-control! Why don't you advocate that?" the association's prim president asked privately, when she reluctantly met with a birth control lobbyist.[22]

In February of 1935, Margaret also scored a crucial public relations victory by securing free radio time in New York to broadcast the closing program of a birth control fund-raising dinner. A major media breakthrough came again several months later when the Columbia Broadcasting System lifted its long-standing ban and gave her national air time for a talk on family planning. "The time has come for us to think of Family Security through Family Planning," she said, calling for support of legalized birth control on the simple grounds that it would secure the health of mothers, the earning power of fathers, and the well-being of children. The talk elicited hundreds of letters of appreciation and requests for information, none more eloquent than the brief note of a Brooklyn woman who paraphrased Roosevelt: "We need women like you to open the eyes of blind statesmen regarding the true position of long-suffering womanhood in our country," she wrote. "It's about time the 'forgotten woman' was remembered." Of course, there were dissenters, as well, including two men who equated Sanger's speech with the defense of "thievery, racketeering, murder or prostitution."[23]

Yet even as she spoke, birth control bills put before the 74th Congress were tabled in committee without so much as a hearing, while her lobbyists worked to stop a bill, introduced by Postmaster General James Farley, that was intended to protect consumers from fraud by cracking down on the transport of unregulated commercial contraceptives. As a prominent political operative among Catholics, Farley was a reasonable target of suspicion among birth control advocates, who feared that his efforts might also jeopardize the judicially guaranteed right of legitimate physicians and clinics to mail contraceptives.

Margaret again tried to reach the President personally, asking that he consider a new, measured approach to birth control, by creating a "population bureau" for the study of the effect of fertility patterns on "public health and social conservation." She received no recorded response but did not attack the Roosevelt administration publicly. Her restraint may have been influenced by Wells, who had spent a private evening in the White House in 1934 and come away especially impressed by the President's peculiar ability to at once maintain an open and flexible mind toward new ideas, while, at the same time, keeping "in constant touch with political realities and possibilities." Margaret and H. G. had been in Russia together immediately after that interview with Roosevelt, and Juliet Rublee, still a Washington insider, was also encouraging her to deal with the administration quietly and confidentially, at least until the election of 1936.[24]

Another important emissary for the birth control cause was Ruby Black, then a wire service reporter who had befriended Eleanor Roosevelt, when the two women traveled together in Puerto Rico in 1934. Black transmitted a personal letter from Margaret to the First Lady, emphasizing the anomaly of legal conditions that allowed the dissemination of information about the rhythm method but not about artificial contraceptives. Yet again, there was no official response.[25]

As the costs of conciliation mounted, Margaret could scarcely restrain herself. "Women's lives are being sacrificed by the thousands," she wrote, claiming no prejudice to Catholics, but then identifying their position on birth control as "barbaric and savage." This could not have made her relations with the White House any easier. The embattled President was privately polling the influence of Father Coughlin and Louisiana Senator Huey Long, to assess the threat they might pose to his reelection prospects the following year. Roosevelt was also contending with the dismay of church officials who were upset about a recommendation for public subsidy of contraception in Puerto Rico, where the administration had launched a major reconstruction program. Ernest Gruening, the young Department of Interior employee responsible for the controversial proposal (later a prominent Senator and family planning advocate from Alaska), was made to drop the idea when Cardinal Spellman of New York protested to Democratic National Committee Chairman Jim Farley. Gruening, however, did manage to help underwrite some programs indirectly, with private contributions from the philanthropist Clarence Gamble.[26]

Three years earlier, Harry Hopkins had expressly identified the murky legal situation surrounding birth control as an excuse for refusing to include it in public programs. Contraception was officially banned, yet a 1935 survey by the American Birth Control League discovered that the experience of the Sanger clinic in New York was not atypical. State and local officials occasionally circumvented policy guidelines and referred relief clients to clinics or private physicians. Asked by *Time* to comment on this practice, Hopkins admitted in 1935 that his agency would not interfere where birth control was legal under state or local laws. But in the entire country, only the state relief administrator of Michigan was willing to declare his support for birth control.

In several instances, however, relief agents quietly underwrote the cost of contraception. This was the case in localities without a powerful Catholic political presence, such as Los Angeles County, where the incorporation of birth control services into local public health clinics had been well-established prior to the infusion of federal relief dollars, and in the impoverished South, where rates of both birth and of infant death were alarmingly high. *Time,* for example, identified publicly run contraceptive programs in Lynchburg, Virginia, and Greene County, Missouri. In Miami, Dr. Lydia DeVilbiss, who years earlier had refused to start an unlicensed birth control clinic in New York, was able to hire Works Progress Administration employees as field workers for the maternal health clinics she had started. Yet the WPA would not pay for contraception directly and actually fired women workers on its rolls when they became pregnant. "Rather than lose their jobs, they are lacing themselves with corsets and bandages and are having their abortions in the WPA toilets," DeVilbiss reported to Margaret in 1936.[27]

These developments called for revised strategies. A dispirited Hazel Moore left the National Federation, but Margaret brought new blood into the organization. She hired the sister of pioneering Congresswoman Jeannette Rankin, Edna Rankin McKinnon, who, in turn, suggested new legislative initiatives intended to circumvent the bottleneck of the powerful judiciary committees in both houses of Congress. One of her ideas was to file legislation with the Post Office Committee, codifying existing administrative and judicial regulations regarding the transport of birth control material for medical purposes. Another was to amend the new Social Security Act to allow for the public provision of contraception, while a third contemplated adding a birth control rider to some omnibus appropriation bill, where it might be overlooked. None succeeded, however, and the situation deteriorated even further with the deaths of several key supporters in the House. Margaret orchestrated a new round of publicity with a "coming of age" dinner that honored the twenty-first anniversary of the birth control movement, but she then embarked on a long-delayed trip to India and the Far East, and in the increasingly contentious political environment of the waning days of Franklin Roosevelt's first term, birth control reform lost what little momentum it had briefly enjoyed.[28]

CHAPTER SEVENTEEN

Foreign Diplomacy

The Depression deterred, but did not defeat, Margaret's ambitions to promote herself abroad and build an international birth control organization. In 1930, she opened a Birth Control Information Centre in London with a $2,000 surplus resulting from Edith How-Martyn's rigorous management of the budget of the Geneva Population Conference. How-Martyn staffed the operation, and its letterhead identified "correspondents" for birth control in thirty-two countries, spanning the alphabet from Australia and Austria to Sweden, Syria, and the United States. Most of the members were physicians and social workers, many of them women, already at work in clinics or hoping to start such facilities, and Margaret's objective was to establish a network among them, comparable to what had been achieved for the men at Geneva.

When the economic decline dried up anticipated funding sources, she personally guaranteed a loan to cover the organizational costs of a second conference in Zurich in the summer of 1930. In fact, the event achieved her objective by bringing together the nucleus of women who would play key leadership roles in international population initiatives following World War II. It also provided an opportunity for Ernst Grafenberg, a German physician, to report on his clinical trials with an intrauterine contraceptive device made of silk gut and silver wire, similar to what Frances Halton had demonstrated in New York. Years later, when assembled from plastic components, the IUD would, of course, achieve medical credibility and revolutionize contraceptive technology.

Margaret then managed to scrounge together enough money to keep How-Martyn employed for another seven years as a link between her struggling birth control lobby in Washington and interested foreign parties. In 1934, How-Martyn scored a coveted success of her own in England, when Parliament passed a bill requiring the government to include contraception in its public health programs, which was, of course, a good deal more than the Americans had been able to accomplish. Yet she once described herself as no more than a "porter" on behalf of birth control during these years, with much of her time spent in India, where Margaret turned her own attention in 1935, when the complexities of politics in Washington wore her down.

How-Martyn spent most of 1934 in India, preparing the way for Margaret by establishing contacts among groups of women, physicians, and social scientists. She met with sympathetic personnel in the Raj bureaucracy and in the independence movement, as well. Plans were made for Margaret's itinerary and for the subsequent organization of demonstration clinics intended to provide practical instruction in contraceptive methods for local midwives.[1]

Birth control had first become a subject of public discussion in India in 1925 when Mahatma Gandhi condemned the separation of sex and procreation and called artificial methods of contraception undignified. He insisted that their use would undermine marriage by stimulating the sexual appetites of husband and wife and instead advocated the practice of continence as a means to limit fertility. Gandhi's ascetic doctrine had a distinct political motive. He exhorted his countrymen to conquer their carnal passions for food, drink, and sex so they would develop the personal discipline and moral character they would need to guarantee the larger success of political self-rule. When his views on sex and birth control were first made public, Margaret wrote in protest, and in a gracious letter of response, he professed to be open to more education on the subject.

Admiring his idealism, she then began planning a visit to India, but events at home intervened, and she never made the trip.[2]

Indians were accustomed to seeing graphic representations of divine sexual acts in their religious painting and sculpture, but physical sexuality had simply never been considered an appropriate matter of secular discourse, and Gandhi's pronouncements, though highly idiosyncratic, provided something of a breakthrough in social attitudes, even as they provoked bemused opposition from the country's professionals and intelligentsia. A small community of Neo-Malthusians and eugenicists was developing at the time in cities like New Delhi, Calcutta, and Bombay, where a physician by the name of A. P. Pillay also corresponded regularly with Margaret in New York and later began to publish an internationally respected journal, *Marriage Hygiene.* The local discussion at this juncture molded Western arguments about the social, economic, and health benefits of family planning, rather than outright continence, to Gandhi's larger political goals and led to the opening of a few small contraceptive clinics under medical auspices. Nevertheless, prudery generally prevailed among the associations of native elites and British missionaries who were best organized to advance health and welfare reforms on a wide scale.

In 1929, however, the All India Women's Conference, a prestigious voluntary association of Indians and British working to improve educational opportunities and claiming to represent some 10 million women, decided to add social issues to its reform agenda. Several years later, at the risk of alienating dissident members, the conference went on record in support of artificial contraception, making it the largest group in the world to have done so at the time. In 1935, it extended an invitation for Margaret to come to India and speak on birth control. Arrangements were made through Margaret Cousins, an Irish-born freethinker, feminist, and celebrated nationalist, who would soon go to jail to protest British restrictions on free speech. Cousins was a follower of Annie Besant, the Victorian reformer who had left England after her persecution for circulating birth control pamphlets in the 1880s, renouncing Western religion and culture for an Eastern regimen of material simplicity and spiritual containment. Until her death in 1933, Besant lived in Madras as the head of a colony of British expatriate Theosophists, whose metaphysical and psychic beliefs had also long drawn Margaret to the magic of India.[3]

Meanwhile, the plight of India's women had also been catapulted to the attention of their sisters in England and America as a result of the publication in 1927 of Katherine Mayo's controversial book, *Mother India.* In her scathing attack on the oppressive conditions of female life there, Mayo featured graphic descriptions of child marriage, sexual abuse, polygamy, bride burning, rampant venereal disease, primitive childbirth, and other pathologies. Excerpted in popular magazines, the book quickly became a best-seller and prompted extensive interpretation and analysis. Mayo, who had spent only several months in India, was criticized for condemning an entire culture on the basis of a narrow and uncharacteristic sample of female experience and for failing to mention the ongoing efforts of Indian women themselves to reform these anachronistic practices. Although she was dismissed by many as an apologist for British imperialism, the book shaped popular perceptions. Margaret, whose own views of India had largely been formed earlier by Agnes Smedley, shared Mayo's outrage over the indignities suffered by many of its women but advocated national sovereignty as their best hope for a better life. She did not see any reason why conflict over the dismantling of a colonial empire should stand in the way of common, humanitarian agreement on the need to disseminate birth control. She would try to rise above faction by pleading her cause without regard to competing political ideologies. But however well-intentioned, this goal was hardly practical, as the predicament in which her friend Agnes Smedley found herself, should have forewarned.[4]

Margaret had long been counting on Smedley to help accomplish her dream of undertaking a birth control campaign in the Far East. Soon after their visit together in Berlin in 1928 Smedley had published *Daughter of Earth,* the powerful autobiographical account of her childhood among the troubled mining families of Colorado, which established her international reputation as a writer. The following winter, carrying a three-year contract as a correspondent for the *Frankfurter Zeitung,* a left-leaning German newspaper, she'd made her way across Russia through Manchuria to Shanghai, then the economic, political, and cultural center of China and a cauldron of anticolonialist sentiment for the entire region. Tracked by British intelligence agents, she wrote to Margaret, asking for help in the event that she disappeared or was arrested.[5]

The two women had agreed privately that the one would organize birth control clinics in China in the other's behalf, and during her first year in Shanghai, Smedley wrote of her intention to do so in cooperation with a local employee of the YMCA. Margaret, in turn, sent $50 to get the project underway, but Smedley used the money instead to pay her way to Peking, ostensibly because a group of concerned Western reformers would be meeting with Chinese officials to plan a coherent birth control policy for the country. As it turned out, Smedley had no patience with the conference's hollow endorsement of birth control as "a vital contribution to maternal health" and quickly wrote Margaret of her increasing disenchantment. In her view, the local missionary movement was only interested in contraception as a means of approaching Chinese women with a Christian propaganda she could not abide. Nor could she countenance the strict social distinctions observed between Westerners and native Chinese. She refused to join British and American clubs that openly discriminated on the basis of race, and this made it all the more difficult for her to interact with potential Western allies.

What is more, as Smedley grew increasingly familiar with China, she uncovered living conditions so ghastly and a depth of poverty so overwhelming that she could no longer see the practical benefit of birth control to any but those among the ruling elites, who already had some access to it anyway. She pointed out to Margaret that the elementary hygiene necessary to practice contraception was simply not available to most Chinese, who lived without running water. "I am more and more convinced that no b.c. work is possible until there is a national revolution that will wipe out the whole capitalist class, the land-owner class, and the foreign imperialists," she wrote, endorsing an orthodox Marxist viewpoint.[6]

By 1932, Smedley was telling Margaret that their only hope was to get birth control into the few provinces already controlled by the peasant Communist governments. The logistics of so bold a strategy were then discussed, with Margaret, in response, describing the contraceptive properties of simple regimens that might be appropriate, such as using sponges soaked in quinine, then being tested at the Clinical Research Bureau in New York. Margaret's attention at this juncture was consumed by legislative developments in Washington, but she nonetheless continued to send small checks and supplies for the clinic in Shanghai that never materialized, all the while reiterating her confidence in Smedley, never challenging her political judgment or delving too deeply into her situation. It seems never to have occurred to her that birth control might be of little interest to the belligerent leadership of a fledgling Communist Party whose principle aim was to break the hold of the Western values over China that small families exemplified. Within a year, however, Smedley refused to accept any more assistance at all, and what had been a steady correspondence between the two women suddenly came to an end.[7]

Though personally loyal to Smedley, Margaret certainly harbored no ideological illusions of her own about Communism. Still curious about the Soviet experiment, she had eagerly made an on-site inspection of Russian health and welfare initiatives during her trip there in 1934 with Grant and H. G. Wells, but unlike her old friend, she did not discover a utopia for women. To the contrary, she had found the same disturbing incongruities that long bothered her about revolutionary movements at home. Russian women were accorded equal rights as a matter of law, and some maternal benefits were provided. Birth control was legal, and abortions were condoned as a necessary evil, but by Margaret's observation, the practical conditions of life for women did not match the stature they were granted in theory. She was especially disappointed by the poor quality of the medicine practiced in the clinics she visited—by the high numbers of abortions performed without any anesthesia and the primitive nature of what little contraceptive technology she was able to uncover.

Yet even as Margaret expressed her own disenchantment, she did not condemn old friends like Smedley, Ella Reeve Bloor, and Elizabeth Gurley Flynn, all of whom either joined the Communist Party or became high-profile sympathizers during the 1930s, and she never seemed to worry about being associated with them. So too, after Smedley went to Moscow in 1933–34, to write a book about the rural revolutionary movement emerging in China, she returned there via the United States where she visited with Margaret and rekindled their friendship.[8]

Perhaps naively, though possibly as part of a deliberate strategy, Margaret wrote in 1935 to the Chinese ambassador in Washington on behalf of Smedley, who was by then under attack in China and at home as a Soviet spy. She strongly defended her friend's sympathies for the cause of Chinese and Indian nationalism and flatly denied all Communist ties, maintaining instead that Smedley had gone to China to start birth control clinics at her request and with her financial support, a half-truth, but one that at least provided some evidence against the accusation that Smedley had enlisted as a Soviet agent from the start.* No matter how much Margaret tried to keep politics

* In fact, no formal tie between Smedley and the Comintern has ever been established, although strong circumstantial evidence links her to the Russians. During her years in Shanghai, she had a love affair with Richard Sorge, a German born in Russia, who was then ostensibly working as a correspondent for the German press, and who by some accounts sponsored her for party membership. Sorge later made his reputation as a master spy for the Soviets working in Japan, where he was arrested and executed during World War II. She also became involved in the defense of left-leaning Chinese intellec-

out of birth control, it always kept getting in the way, and India would be no exception.[9]

Bound for Bombay, Margaret departed New York via ship in October of 1935, laden with a large inventory of medical supplies and educational tools, including a demonstration film and fifty contraptions called gynaeplaques, which Hannah Stone used to instruct women at the clinic in New York. These life-sized, three-dimensional models of the female pelvis came apart to reveal the organs of the reproductive tract like pieces of a puzzle. They remained in use in India for years thereafter in the scattered villages Margaret visited, another anonymous gift of John D. Rockefeller, Jr., who at her personal request had donated the money to pay for them.

The main purpose of this trip, however, was to mobilize opinion, not to modify behavior, and the most important item in Margaret's cargo was the portable typewriter she carried everywhere, along with a carefully prepared press list and an ample stock of attractive photographs of herself for reproduction. Advised that it would be necessary to initiate and manage her own publicity, Margaret took along a young reporter from Pittsburgh by the name of Anna Jane Phillips, who, in turn, wrote daily releases for the local papers and wire services and kept a running diary of the trip that was reproduced in installments and sent home with great fanfare to American birth control supporters. Wherever Margaret went during her stay of several months, prominent coverage was generated in the local English language press and a steady stream of stories ran in American newspapers as well.[10]

This extraordinary propaganda machine first got underway during a stopover in London, where Margaret was toasted by H. G. Wells at yet another fund-raising dinner. Wells was most gracious on this occasion. "Alexander the Great changed a few boundaries and killed a certain number of men," he said, "but he made no lasting change in civilization. Both he and Napoleon were forced into fame by circumstances outside themselves and by currents of the time, but Margaret Sanger made currents and circumstances. When the history of our civilization is written, it will be a biological history, and Margaret Sanger will be its heroine."

While in London, Margaret also had the good fortune to meet with Indian nationalist leader Jawaharlal Nehru, who had recently

tuals being persecuted by the government and later helped open communication between Moscow and the Jiangxi Soviet outpost of the peasant Communists.

been released from a four-year prison sentence in connection with his agitation for home rule. Already considered the likely successor to Gandhi in the movement for independence, Nehru, by contrast to his mentor, possessed an aristocratic British education and a decidedly modern outlook. In town to select a school for his seventeen-year-old daughter and future successor as prime minister, Indira Gandhi, he enthusiastically endorsed the dissemination of birth control in India.[11]

India's population was growing at an astonishing rate of nearly 10 percent per decade, with 370 million people accounted for in the 1931 census. The adverse economic consequences of this demographic surge were severe. Ninety-five percent of the country's working population earned less than five cents a day, scarcely enough to provide one full meal, and the accelerating dislocation of peasants from traditional village culture was threatening to overwhelm the cities, where great Indian and British wealth and culture had been concentrated. Two hundred thousand people were sleeping on the streets of Calcutta alone. The chawls, or tenement houses of Bombay, teemed with impoverished, malnourished families, creating an unforgettable tableau that Anna Phillips vividly described in the newsletters Margaret sent home. At the same time, however, the country's rate of infant death remained tragically high, with one-half of all children dying before the age of five. Meaningful reductions in infant mortality awaited advances in medicine and antisepsis introduced after World War II and the war for independence.

Traveling from London aboard the *Viceroy of India* through the Suez Canal, Margaret arrived in December and was welcomed by local supporters who hung garlands of flowers around her neck. Crisscrossing the vast Indian subcontinent several times during her ten-week stay, she traveled a total of 10,000 miles by spending twenty-one nights on railroad trains. She held some forty formal meetings, spoke over the local radio, met with scores of influential individuals privately, and made a significant impact on the ongoing debate of the issue among the country's elites. Her appearance at the All India Women's Conference in Trivandrum in December sparked controversy when a local maharani capitulated to Catholic missionaries who ran the school system and objected to Margaret's appearance on the grounds that birth control would promote immorality and racial suicide. Proponents prevailed, however, and following her speech, a majority of delegates endorsed contraception on humanitarian and economic grounds and encouraged its initial distribution through existing public health channels in urban areas.[12]

The trip achieved its high point when Margaret met for an extended conversation with Gandhi at his simple ashram in the rural province of Wardha. Never one to miss the potential publicity value of such an encounter, she personally recorded the event in her diary and thus preserved it for interested partisans at home. An avid tourist, as well as a savvy publicist, she was careful to chronicle the experience with an eye to its most exotic details.

By her own telling, Margaret's party traveled in a horsecart from the train station and arrived in the early morning to be ushered immediately onto the verandah of the clean and peaceful guesthouse that formed part of the compound where the internationally acclaimed prophet of nonviolent resistance lived. With its white-plastered walls, bamboo roof, and rough-hewn stone flooring, the simple structure very much appealed to her. She was greeted by a gracious, smiling Gandhi—an unusual light emanating from his face like a mist, by her awed description—but since she had unwittingly come on his traditional day of silence, their conversation had to be postponed.

Margaret and her party spent the day inspecting the primitive industries connected with the colony. A satisfying dinner followed, consisting of the vegetable purees and soups, dry pancakes, rice, and fruits with which Gandhi was experimenting in his desire to eat only the most economical and wholesome foods. Evening prayers preceded a restful night of sleep on a porch open to the moon and stars, and the discussions began the following morning after a refreshing bath and a breakfast of sweetened porridge and milk.

With a personal rapport quickly established, Margaret solemnly inquired about the dignified leader's views on the social and economic degradation of women. By her account, he responded patiently, using his own marriage as a model and describing the depth of the personal struggle he had endured to overcome his own "animal passions," because of his determination to prove that pure love between men and women can and must transcend carnal lust. Led on by his astute interviewer's gentle insistence that men less extraordinary than he could hardly be expected to achieve a comparable degree of self-control, he enjoined women to resist their husbands, where necessary.

The discussion apparently went in circles from that point forward but continued throughout the afternoon, with Gandhi earnestly defending his dedication to the triumph of the spiritual bonds of marriage over its physical dimension. By the time she left, however, Margaret had secured two concessions from him, first that in the place of absolute celibacy, he might be willing to accept some reasonable regulation of the sex functions for the masses, so as not to "waste or exhaust their vital force through sexual intercourse," and second, that to this end, he might consider counseling the practice of sexual intercourse during the safe period of the menstrual cycle. Margaret shared this information in her private correspondence about the interview. Reeling from her most recent defeat at the hands of American Catholics, however, she could see little benefit from letting Gandhi give credibility to the rhythm method. Her public account of the interview in *Asia* magazine therefore neglected to mention these important distinctions altogether and dwelt instead on the superficial, if still intriguing, details of Gandhi's life-style.[13]

Margaret understood that from the standpoint of her American audience, the glamour of her personal association with the legendary Indian nationalist far outweighed any real philosophical differences between them. Wire service stories and photographs of their meeting ran in all the major newspapers at home. Meanwhile, in India, though she obviously had failed to convert Gandhi, she did leave a favorable impression among an urban bourgeoisie that would play an important role in the postIndependence political life of the nation. Before departing the country she added a prestigious national medical association to her list of endorsers. She also introduced foam powder as a potential product for mass distribution and established contacts between an American supplier and interested domestic manufacturers. On return trips in 1936 and 1937, Edith How-Martyn was able to observe with pride that twenty clinics had been established and that information on contraception could be obtained at some forty additional maternal welfare centers. Nevertheless, these institutions rarely succeeded in reaching beyond the middle classes. As in the United States, the limited, voluntary efforts of British and Indian elites failed to get through to the very poor and were soon halted, in any event, by political forces beyond their control.

Personally sympathetic to the home rule cause before she ever set foot in India, Margaret was nonetheless surprised and shocked by the depth of anti-British feeling she discovered there. So as not to provoke unnecessary antagonisms, she wound up having to downplay her British associations while in the country. At Margaret Cousins's advice, she maintained an itinerary totally separate from Edith How-Martyn's. The diary Margaret kept of her own travels records her deepening sensitivity to the increasingly desperate and autocratic manifestations of colonial rule she witnessed and to the growing local resistance.[14]

* * *

Margaret left India early in 1936, with the intention of continuing on to Malaysia, China, and Japan. In Hong Kong a recurrent bout of the gallbladder illness that had been plaguing her for years then forced her to cancel the remainder of her itinerary and return home for rest and recuperation. Within a year, however, she had rescheduled, and on this occasion, traveled with Florence Rose, her devoted secretary, Dorothy Brush, a favorite new supporter and friend, and Dorothy's son, Charles.

Ten years earlier, Brush had endured a great personal tragedy when her husband and a baby daughter died in quick succession, leaving her in her hometown of Cleveland, Ohio, with a substantial family fortune but nothing to do. She'd made her way to New York in search of an absorbing cause and wangled an assignment to interview Margaret Sanger for a woman's magazine. Typical of the free-spirited woman of means whom the birth control movement attracted, she started as a volunteer but wound up as a major benefactor. Beyond her own talents, she was also able to direct considerable amounts of money to Margaret's various enterprises through the Cleveland-based Brush Foundation, which under her influence developed its still flourishing interest in world population problems.[15]

Margaret had not been in Japan since her much publicized trip there in 1922, but a birth control platform had been advanced in the interim by her hostess on that first trip, the local feminist and birth control reformer Shidzue Ishimoto, who had become a significant propagandist and reformer in her own right. Ishimoto once compared the impact of Margaret's 1922 visit to Japan to the sensation Commodore Perry had created in the 1850s, claiming that she had appeared "like a comet" and left "a vivid and long-enduring impression."

In fact, the Sanger legacy in Japan owed its strength in part to the coincidence that her name, in transliteration, "Sangai-san," is understood to mean "destructive of production." For years a diaphragm-and-jelly kit was sold under that label in the nation's pharmacies, and other commercial abortifacients and suppositories also tried to capitalize on the identification. Beyond this happenstance, of course, deeper social and economic forces were at work in Japan, as they were in the West. The small country's burgeoning population, combined with an accelerating industrial revolution and an unusually high literacy rate, had greatly facilitated the dissemination of birth control in the wake of Margaret's first visit.

Through the 1920s, Ishimoto, in fact, pursued a Japanese organizational agenda almost identical to Margaret's in the United States. She tried to form a birth control coalition comprising different interest groups, reaching out to organized labor through a series of well-publicized lectures to miners and their wives in 1923, and later securing endorsements from physicians, Malthusian social reformers, and elite women anxious to establish some measure of autonomy and independence for themselves. With no legal restrictions or religious prohibitions standing in her way, she also set out to incorporate birth control into emerging public health programs.[16]

These efforts made her a favorite target of conservative social thinkers, who parodied her advanced social views in the popular press. This opposition gained strength after the Japanese invasion of Manchuria in 1931 and the rise to power of militarists who opposed the liberal social policies of the prior decade, which had tolerated contraception and declining birthrates. Ishimoto turned to the United States for moral and financial support. She made several trips here during these difficult years, raising money from a lecture tour arranged by Margaret's agents, and also serving her own apprenticeship at the Birth Control Clinical Research Bureau in New York. Her plan was to open a comparable facility in Tokyo under the medical direction of a Japanese physician, who had trained at the Sanger clinic in New York.

Her own personal circumstances also changed dramatically with the turn of events in Japan. The husband who had first encouraged her modern Western education suffered financial reverses, veered sharply to the right in his own politics, and went off to seek his own fortune and to promote his country's interests in Manchuria. Though divorce was not yet legally permissible, Ishimoto set up housekeeping on her own. Encouraged by another of her American friends, the historian Mary Beard, she then wrote the dramatic story of her transformation from feudal wife to modern feminist for publication in English. Margaret was prominently featured as an inspiration and muse in this book, which was called *Facing Two Ways* and enjoyed great critical acclaim in the United States, especially on the West Coast.[17]

Margaret arranged for an eccentric American birth control donor by the name of Ethel Clyde to fund Ishimoto's clinic and also sent supplies from the Clinical Research Bureau in New York. A Birth Control Consultation Centre quietly opened in Tokyo in 1934. By 1937 the facility had moved to a new location, and its dedication became the media highlight of Margaret's visit. With great fanfare, she called the clinic the first of its kind outside the West and placed Ishimoto's name in the company of such great women in history as Mary Wollstonecraft, Susan B. Anthony, Olive Schreiner, and Ellen Key. Ishimoto had by then come under intense political pressure, and she was grateful for Margaret's inspiring visit. Indeed, within weeks of these events, Japan's air force bombed Shanghai. All dissent from official government policy was suppressed, and domestic resources were diverted to the nation's military agenda.

"You left us a fresh strength to push back all the depressed feelings which are hanging around us," Ishimoto wrote Margaret in New York. "I am writing under dimmed lights—fear of war planes above us—with a heart full of love, admiration and gratitude." Four months later, on December 15, 1937, Ishimoto was arrested by Japanese authorities, charged with promoting "dangerous thoughts" and jailed for ten days. The clinic was closed, its records confiscated, and birth control activity suppressed in Japan until after World War II. On her release from what turned out to be only the first of several internments, she wrote again to Margaret with unusual grace and startling prescience:

> Some seeds must be planted during autumn and left underground covered with icy earth during severe winter, but spring will surely come back and the fresh leaves will grow during the warm sunshine. I believe that the new life is being prepared during the decaying process of [this] passing period in our history. I shall not [be] discouraged by this, but will look forward hand in hand with those who are internationally minded.[18]

* * *

By this time, Margaret was safely returned to the United States. She had planned a much longer trip that would have finally taken her to China and Malaysia, but once again personal circumstances intervened, when she fell and broke her arm. Very much in pain, she spent only eight days in Tokyo and then returned home, leaving her companions to seek further adventure without her. Florence Rose, in fact, was still in Shanghai when the bombing began.

Margaret responded to the news from Japan with a mixture of defiant anger and sad resignation. She renewed her membership in Jane Addams's International League for Peace and Freedom but privately acknowledged the inevitability of a war to stop the spread of Fascism in Asia and in Europe. The storm clouds blackening the two continents put a halt to her own international initiatives and to those of her emissaries abroad as well.

Agnes Smedley, in these years, was marching with the Red Armies across China, forging a friendship with Mao Zedong, and faithfully promoting the cause of a united Communist front for China through the articles and books she published in the West. She was never formally admitted to the Chinese Communist party and always claimed independent status as a freelance revolutionary. Indeed, highly considered British intelligence documents identify her as an anarchist and syndicalist, not as a Communist, but American intelligence thought otherwise.

Smedley kept in touch with Margaret, who collected a few thousand dollars from John D. Rockefeller, Jr., in 1937 and sent it to a Chinese doctor and an American missionary in Shanghai. They briefly opened a clinic and distributed sponges and foam powder. En route to the war front later that year, Smedley wrote to request that some of these supplies (along with a phonograph and records for her personal use) also be sent to her in the care of a friend at a YWCA in an outlying province. Margaret was also speaking on behalf of Chinese independence at the time under the auspices of Pearl Buck, who had become the Far East's most popular spokesperson in the West with the publication in 1931 of her best-selling and prize-winning book, *The Good Earth*. After Buck gave a highly publicized speech in Washington calling Margaret one of the most courageous women of the times, the two women quickly became intimate friends. Margaret in return lent support to East–West, the then mainstream China advocacy organization that would only come under anti-Communist fire years later during the McCarthy era.[19]

Agnes Smedley returned to the United States from China in 1939, her whereabouts tracked by FBI agents, who described her in confidential documents as having an extensive Communist background and many contacts with known party members at home, and who warned that she was always armed. Her last surviving correspondence with Margaret in 1941 would request support for birth control clinics in Hong Kong run by British relief organizations. If by this time Margaret harbored any suspicions of her old friend, she did not let on and immediately sent $500 for the use of a British friend of Smedley's, who was the head of a Hong Kong Eugenics League. Whether the two women ever met or spoke again, however, is not documented, though at the time of Smedley's death in England in 1950, of complications following surgery, the FBI was still linking them. Under interrogation by the House Committee on Un-American Activities the following year, a federal government employee, accused of Communist ties, testified that Smedley had given him a letter of introduction to Sanger, but he claimed never to have reached her.[20]

Terribly distressed over the deteriorating situation in Europe and in India, Edith How-Martyn retired with her husband to Australia. In the absence of adequate resources for foreign work, and unable to get to London herself, Margaret then resigned the presidency of the Birth Control International Information Centre, and it merged with Britain's National Birth Control Association (later renamed the Family Planning Association), a domestic advocacy and service organization, which served as an umbrella for local clinics, much as the American Birth Control League (and later the Planned Parenthood Federation) did in America.

Meanwhile, the civil war for independence in India put all other concerns there on hold. Many of the outspoken local reformers who had supported Sanger were jailed for their defiance of the Raj, and any hope of addressing the nation's pressing population problem awaited the partitioning of India and Pakistan in 1947 and the restoration of peace under the independent government of Prime Minister Nehru.[21]

In adversity, Margaret once again found renewed strength. The rise of Fascism, with its reactionary social goals and its sad consequences for her dearest friends, stirred her deepest passions, and the military campaigns advanced by men always rekindled her most strident feminism.

In impassioned remarks prepared for the Century of Progress exposition in Chicago in 1934 she had quoted from the American poet Walt Whitman:

Be not ashamed, Woman,
Your privilege encloses the rest,
and is the exit of the rest,
You are the gates of the body,
and you are the gates of the soul.

The achievements being celebrated as "progress," she pointed out, by and large reflected a "masculine psychology" or a "male supremacy." Men had spanned the oceans, conquered air, explored distant universes, harnessed energy, and controlled infection and disease here on earth. Yet these enormous scientific achievements were in danger of becoming little more than "instruments of destruction." Harkening back to the argument she had first made forcibly in the aftermath of World War I, she insisted that the most powerful nations of the world were again poised on the brink of war, because the control of population had never been made a priority. Indeed, the situation was getting worse. The world's population was increasing by an estimated 50,000 people a day. The expansionist aggressions of Germany and Japan were proving her point.

Echoing her earlier writings, she called on the women of the world to rise up and rebel, not through superficial remedies, but by concentrating all their energies on their reproductive rights. She again confidently predicted that "all the great grandiose schemes for world improvement" would fail until women empowered themselves by achieving control of their fertility.

"The solidarity of Woman is as noble as the brotherhood of man," she concluded. "Instead of a world created by irresponsible hordes in hatred and antagonism, *Free Woman* shall guide us into a future created by all-embracing love through the consciousness of birth control."

"Shall women of today be able to hold the freedom they have so far gained?" she again demanded in a 1937 speech. "Not unless they cease being incubators for war mad dictators."[22]

The stage was set for Margaret's postwar reemergence as a lonely voice for controlling the world's population by first recognizing and addressing the ever-precarious status of its women. But first there were matters at home to resolve.

CHAPTER EIGHTEEN

From Birth Control to Family Planning

During her long trip to India in 1936, Margaret had plenty of time to think over the question of whether a continued lobbying effort in Washington would be worth the effort. As a British colleague visiting the United States had put it the year before, perhaps she really was "needlessly knocking her head against a brick wall." Commercial contraception was overwhelming the government's meager regulatory and enforcement capacity, leaving little chance that licensed druggists and/or physicians would be harassed. Even the Sears, Roebuck catalog had begun to advertise "preventives." In 1935, the journal *American Medicine* had maintained that the mailing of contraceptive supplies and instruction was "as firmly established as the use of a gummed postage stamp," and while she was abroad, a much-anticipated report of the American Medical Association committee studying contraception found no actual evidence of interference with medical practice by existing state or federal laws. Margaret's rationale for lobbying as a tool to educate public opinion was also substantially undermined by the publication of polls showing that 70 percent of Americans, comprising at least a clear majority in every state, now supported the legalization of birth control. (Within two years a major poll commissioned by the *Ladies' Home Journal* would find 79 percent of its own readers in favor nationwide, a figure that included 51 percent of all Catholic women surveyed.) Economic issues were paramount: women wanted contraception, not because of abstract eugenic concerns or social considerations, but simply so they could space or limit the number of their children in accordance with family income. From an educational standpoint, her campaign had done its work, even if the Comstock laws technically remained valid.[1]

Still not ready to give up, Margaret at first dismissed the admonition of her British friend as hopelessly idiotic. "This sort of thing is so English," she told her aide, Hazel Moore. "They spend 3 weeks in USA and tell us how to run our government." But further controversy then erupted over the continued utility of her Washington enterprise when the American Birth Control League circulated a pamphlet claiming that the laws no longer served as any impediment whatsoever. Forced to respond, she asked her staff to find evidence to the contrary and came up with only a handful of cases, almost all of them involving overzealous customs officers who had stopped contraceptive literature and supplies at the borders on the authority of a 1930 amendment to the Tariff Act reiterating the original Comstock provisions. One such incident had involved Moore, who was detained while returning from England carrying birth control literature. There had been only one recent interstate incident, however, and it had never been litigated. Lawyers representing Margaret, the ABCL, and Robert Dickinson's National Committee on Maternal Health finally sat down with Morris Ernst and agreed that the courts had all but achieved the objectives of legislative reform.[2]

This was even becoming true in the remaining importation disputes. In 1932, a package of contraceptive supplies sent to Margaret by a Japanese physician, whom she had met at an international birth control conference, had been intercepted by United States customs. At the urging of Ernst, Margaret then requested that the materials be mailed again, but this time she had the shipment addressed to Dr. Hannah Stone, so as to stage a clear case on medical exemption. This would complete the recent judicial reconstruction of the Comstock prohibitions on obscene literature and interstate transport of contraception. The case, *United States v. One Package Containing 120, more or less, Rubber Pessaries to Prevent Conception*, was filed in the United States District Court for the Southern District in Manhattan on November 10, 1933, with Dr. Stone as claimant. Margaret found a donor to cover Ernst's fees.

The calendar moved slowly, but the trial finally got underway in 1935 and produced a ruling by Judge Grover Moscowitz that the tariff prohibitions could not be used to prevent the importation of contraceptives intended for legitimate medical use. The government appealed, and in the spring of 1936, with the backing of all factions of the birth control movement, Ernst defended the case before a three-judge panel in the Second Circuit Court of Appeals in New York, consisting of Judge Thomas Swan and the cousins, Augustus and Learned Hand. Swan and Augustus Hand had, of course, already delivered landmark readings of the Comstock provisions in the *Young's Rubber* and *Dennett* cases, and it came as little surprise when their ruling in this instance ordered the release of the confiscated package of pessaries. The sweeping nature of the decision, however, was unanticipated. Augustus Hand argued that although the importation statute alone was under consideration, all components of the Comstock law should be construed consistently. He advised that the language of the original law no longer be read literally—that the intent of the 1873 prohibitions had been to protect against materials thought problematic and dangerous fifty years earlier, but no longer so considered. Acknowledging an extensive body of medical and sociological evidence introduced by Ernst into the trial record as proof that contraception had become a safe and essential element of modern medical practice, Hand insisted that the law henceforth be interpreted to embrace "only such articles as Congress would have denounced as immoral if it had understood all the conditions under which they were to be used." He continued: "Its design, in our opinion, was not to prevent the importation, sale, or carriage by mail of things which might intelligently be employed by conscientious and competent physicians for the purpose of saving life or promoting the well-being of their patients." Hand admitted having relied on "common sense" to interpret Congressional intent in this manner.[3]

Margaret was out of the country when the decision was rendered, but on her return, she handily turned the victory into a public relations triumph. Claiming the "greatest legal VICTORY in the Birth Control Movement," she inveigled the press into celebrating with her. *Time* magazine branded the decision "another successful milestone" in her "tireless" campaign. The *Nation,* long an advocate on the left, applauded the emergence of the birth control movement into "the bright light of scientific acceptance and friendly publicity." *Life*, the newest addition to Henry Luce's burgeoning publishing empire, featured a four-page photo spread spanning her life in a series of flattering poses, along with shots of Noah, the two Sanger boys, and such prominent friends and supporters as Ellis, Wells, Pearl Buck, and Kit Hepburn, identified as the mother of the actress. In January of 1937, over the vocal protest of the city's Catholic community, Margaret received the annual award of honor given by the Town Hall Club, a New York civic association, and within months—on July 3, 1937, for publication on Independence Day—she announced the dissolution of the National Committee, "its work accomplished."[4]

Her news release acknowledged the Second Circuit's decision, and along with it, the historic endorsement of contraception by the American Medical Association at its annual meetings that year. A resolution to study contraception and to support state and federal legislative reform had first been introduced at the AMA convention of 1932, where it was voted down in executive session. It took until 1935 just to get an investigation of the matter underway and two years after that to complete the undertaking. In the interim, however, the powerful organization handed Margaret an official rebuke in the form of a resolution condemning the support of lay propagandists by medical doctors. The 1937 action finally granting a medical imprimatur to artificial contraception represented a dramatic policy reversal, one which also conceded Margaret's long-held view on what constituted the only acceptable standards for its use: "Voluntary family limitation is dependent largely on the judgment and wishes of individual patients," the report proclaimed. Although insisting that birth control remain under strict medical supervision, the AMA no longer regarded its proper use only in the event of pathological indications but as a responsible element of normal sexual hygiene in married life. To this end, it recommended that the subject be taught in medical schools, that scientific investigation of various commercial materials and methods be promoted, and finally that the legal rights of physicians in relation to the use of contraceptives be clarified. All in all, it was another page 1 story for birth control.[5]

The AMA may have been willing to yield at long last to the reality of established contraceptive use, but it was not prepared to accept any conclusive reading of the Second Circuit Court's ruling with respect to physicians' rights. Physicians were still not fully protected, the *Journal of the American Medical Association* cautioned, with a headline declaring "Contraceptive Advice, Devices and Preparations

Still Contraband." And, despite the conciliatory nature of its own committee report, the AMA once again accused Margaret directly of "misleading propaganda," jealously keeping its distance. To the AMA the court's ruling dealt narrowly with the issue of importation, not more broadly with "the right of a physician to advise the practice of contraception." What is more, the ruling technically applied only within New York, Connecticut, and Vermont, those states within the jurisdiction of the circuit court.

Morris Ernst, in a statement endorsed by an entire committee of birth control lawyers, replied to the contrary that the *One Package* decision explicitly stated the court's intent to move beyond the narrow issue of importation and provide a consistent reading of all parts of the Comstock law, in line with *Young's Rubber* and *Davis*. He insisted that the Second Circuit ruling did not "stand alone" but conformed to the Sixth Circuit's findings in *Davis* and represented "the last word on the subject." This was all but confirmed in his view by the fact that the United States solicitor general decided not to appeal the ruling to the Supreme Court. Ernst further argued that state courts could be expected to follow the lead of the federal judiciary. Forty of the then forty-eight states at this juncture either had no statutes prohibiting contraception or already exempted physicians and/or pharmacists. He told a conference of birth control advocates that "the law process is a simple one—it is a matter of educating judges to the mores of the day." Enthusiastic in his praise for Margaret's work in Washington, he added that "it is perfectly easy to win a case after Margaret Sanger has educated the judges, and she has educated any number of them. I have merely been a mouthpiece."[6]

In fact, as the legal setbacks to clinics in Massachusetts and Connecticut would soon demonstrate, subsequent judicial decisions at the state level did not turn out to be as salutary as Ernst predicted. The legal history of contraception during the following three decades would confirm the AMA's caution, along with the wisdom of Margaret's earlier observation that laws are best made by legislators, not judges. This was also the view expressed by Learned Hand in his separate, though concurring, decision in the *One Package* case. Though reluctant to dissent in this instance, Hand did declare his reservation about the underlying rationale of the majority's decision. He was unwilling to buy the view of his colleague and cousin, Augustus, that it had never been the intention of the original Comstock law to forbid contraceptives, whether or not they were prescribed by physicians and intended for lawful use. "Many people have changed their minds about such matters in sixty years," he wrote, "but the act forbids the same conduct now as then; a statute stands until public feeling gets enough momentum to change it, which may be long after a majority would repeal it, if a poll were taken." The courts in Massachusetts and Connecticut would soon echo these sentiments, and local prohibitions endured there until the *Griswold v. Connecticut* decision of 1965 established that the private use of contraceptives by married Americans is an inherent constitutional right.[7]

It would not be until 1970 that Congress finally rewrote the federal Comstock laws and formally removed the label of obscenity from contraception. Two years later, the Supreme Court, in *Eisenstadt v. Baird*, would extend the right of contraceptive practice to the unmarried.

Yet the full impact of the legal cloud that remained over birth control was felt less by the state courts than by the administrative agencies of the federal, state, and county governments, where contraception was incorporated into public health and social welfare programs only in the most haphazard fashion, and only in regions of the country where it would not stir controversy. In the final report of her National Committee, Margaret estimated that the country needed no fewer than 3,000 contraceptive clinics, approximately ten times the existing number of public and private facilities combined. She called on the federal government to provide them through existing public health channels.

"We urge caravans of education and help for mountain women, farm women, mothers on distant homesteads, mothers in all districts, city and country, who are now neglected," she wrote, and echoing her earliest and boldest pronouncements, she asked that "an army of equipped, sympathetic nurses take up this task." The statement revealed, if not explicitly, another reason for closing up the lobbying effort in Washington. She could no longer defend, even on pragmatic grounds, the pursuit of narrow legislation authorizing only doctors to prescribe contraceptives. Doctors were simply too expensive. Reversing her long-standing legislative position, she acknowledged that if the public was paying, the cheaper services of nurses and medical paraprofessionals should also be legalized.[8]

Earlier that year, in fact, when an official of the Farm Security Administration in charge of migratory labor camps in the South admitted to Hazel Moore that women were expressing interest in birth control, arrangements had quietly been made through the National Committee to equip FSA workers with privately funded supplies. Difficult to fund and to administer, the program there failed but did continue in California, where several nurses remained on duty through World War II.[9]

At the same time, Margaret sent Edna McKinnon from one government administrator to another to argue for an official change of policy on the basis of the *One Package* decision and the recent recognition of birth control by the American Medical Association. A representative of the American Birth Control League made the same rounds, but neither was successful. Without direct intervention from the White House, caution prevailed in federal agencies.

The policy constraint became most noticeable when maternal and child health services were first funded by the federal government under the Social Security Act. These funds, in turn, were administered by the Children's Bureau of the Department of Labor. For years the bureau's formidable director, Katherine Lenroot, a career civil servant, resolutely refused to be associated with the controversial birth control issue. Lenroot confessed outrage that people who were poor should not be allowed to have children—an idea she believed implicit in the suggestion that families on relief be given contraception. Margaret, in response to this allegation, pointedly distinguished the injunction to plan and space childbearing from absolute prohibition. Lenroot would not even consent to refer letters of inquiry about birth control to the American Birth Control League or any other voluntary agency, as was the policy of her colleague, Mary Anderson, director of the Woman's Bureau, and of several other federal administrators. Lenroot's position, however, was born less of concern for individual rights than of her commitment to the view that population decline was a principal element of the country's economic woes.

Beyond the nation's best interests, Lenroot also betrayed a transparent concern for protecting her own agency turf. These infant years of federal funding for health and social welfare, before the consolidation of services under one department, saw considerable jockeying among agencies for programs. Bureaucratic rivalry was particularly intense between the Children's Bureau and the U.S. Public Health Service at the Department of the Interior. The daughter of a Congressman and a savvy politician in her own right, Lenroot jealously courted the constituencies she needed to maintain her own power. In 1938, for example, she convened a National Conference on Better Care for Mothers and Babies and invited a representative of the

American Birth Control League. Margaret could not attend but Hannah Stone did and was ruled out of order when she tried to turn the group's discussion to birth control. Lenroot maintained that some of the groups represented would not have participated had they known that the birth control issue was to be considered, and she subsequently excluded any birth controllers from participating in the permanent committees that grew out of the conference.

These committees were established to help plan for Title V of the Social Security Act, which in 1938 provided some $5 million in new funds for maternal and child health services to be administered by the states. According to Martha May Eliot, M.D., who served as Lenroot's deputy at this time, the Children's Bureau encountered enormous resistance from Catholic lobbyists over Title V, because it decentralized a great deal of policy authority, the issue over which John Ryan broke with his superiors. Eliot, who drafted much of the measure herself, met with a delegation of bishops while the language of the bill was still being debated, ostensibly to work out a mechanism that would better protect the autonomy of Catholic agencies from the potential of arbitrary actions by state bureaucrats. A compromise was reached over general language, but the director of the Bureau of Catholic Charities then confronted Eliot directly with the question of whether the bureau would allow states to provide birth control through publicly funded facilities and programs. Much to his dissatisfaction she explained that this particular matter would be left to local discretion, but Lenroot herself then intervened, and no official statement of any willingness on the part of the Children's Bureau to let funds be used for such purposes was issued for the time being.[10]

Few states outside the South expressed interest in birth control in any event, and even there substantial resistance was encountered from private physicians, who objected on the grounds that birth control was just an example of socialized medicine in disguise. Eager for a statistically valid field investigation of a cheap contraceptive, Clarence Gamble in 1936 had sent a social worker to distribute a chemical jelly contributed by the Ortho pharmaceutical company among poor Appalachian women in Logan County, West Virginia. These women were enrolled in a public health project sponsored by the American Friends Service Committee, a Quaker philanthropy based in Philadelphia. The three-year study was also supported by Dickinson, the Milbank Memorial Fund, and the American Birth Control League. It recruited 1,345 women, out of a potential population three times that size, and achieved a 41 percent fertility decline among those who kept up with the method. But more than half of the participants expressed dissatisfaction and dropped out of the study, a rate worse than what had been achieved through the clinic-diaphragm regimen. This left only cost as a factor for recommending use of the jelly, and though it was cheaper, the expenditure required was still beyond the reach of existing public health budgets at the time. The Logan County study estimated that the cost of integrating contraception into existing public health programs would be from $2.00 to $3.00 a year, but the total yearly allowance per family on public health in Logan County was then only $1.25, a figure that incorporated just about all medical services available to the rural poor. Bringing contraception to the area would require a vastly expanded public commitment to health and social welfare, and since the effectiveness of mass marketing contraception could not really be proved, it was not even made a priority. Care of the malnourished and the sickly poor came first. Birthrates in the South for both whites and blacks were declining, but at a far less substantial rate than elsewhere in the country, and, of course, the region's levels of poverty, malnutrition, and disease remained disproportionately high.[11]

Nor could the problem of racism in the South be entirely overlooked. In 1937, the Sanger clinic in New York sent several field researchers to Miami to study Lydia DeVilbiss's use of a sponge and spermicidal foam powder that she was promoting as a resolution to the search for a cheap, effective, and democratic contraceptive. The problem they discovered was that DeVilbiss herself was hardly a democrat. Anxious about the high birthrates of the unemployed in Florida, she had earlier written Margaret proclaiming matter-of-factly, "It's either birth control and eugenic sterilization, or it is 'curtains.' " She then apparently calmed down somewhat as the overall demographic picture in Miami became clear, but she was unashamed of the number of women she sent from her clinic for sterilization at local hospitals on grounds of mental deficiency or psychiatric impairment under the state's eugenic law. She also admitted to Margaret that she routinely gave pregnant women capsules containing tiny portions of arsenic and other chemicals, which she encouraged them to take with quinine over a four day period, in order to produce an abortion.

Dubious about these procedures, Margaret privately undermined DeVilbiss's reputation in professional circles up North, but she continued to work with her and never challenged her publicly. She did, however, begin to recognize the severe limitations of "speakeasy" contraception—as she began to refer to the unregulated birth control clinics that sprouted up around the country during the Depression. In their place, she renewed her determination to legalize contraception and bring it under the closer scrutiny of public officials, who were at least legally accountable and responsible for the public's health and welfare. It was this motivation that sustained the last frustrating year of the National Committee's work, and with this intent, she also closed down the committee in 1937 and teamed up with Gamble and public health officials in the state of North Carolina to sponsor an official trial of DeVilbiss's foam powder there.[12]

Gamble agreed to pay Hazel Moore and Edna McKinnon of the National Committee to run a mass field distribution of sponges and foam. The two women worked with Dr. George M. Cooper, an enterprising official, though regrettably also a racist, in the State Board of Health, who incorporated the fieldwork directly into public programs. By 1940, three quarters of the county health stations in the state offered contraception, yet the programs were funded and administered so haphazardly that only a meager 4 percent of the eligible population was being served. Comparable demonstration projects were also tried with little success in five other Southern states, until a shortage of personnel during the war diminished interest altogether. Family planning programs in the South were not revitalized until new funding and new technology became available in the 1960s. Until then, when new appropriations were added under the Social Security Act for "special projects" in maternity and infancy, only thirteen states nationwide were providing any kind of publicly assisted birth control. And the Children's Bureau did not expressly commit funds until required to do so by the passage of the Child Health Act of 1967, which mandated that a fixed percentage of federal spending be allocated for family planning.[13]

In 1938, Margaret organized a Committee on Public Progress to keep constituent and journalistic pressure on federal agencies. At the same time, the American Birth Control League mounted a Citizen's Committee for Planned Parenthood. Both groups continued to lobby Congress for public funding of contraception through increases in the Social Security Act. Sen. Robert Wagner of New York, sponsor of the Title VI amendments of 1939, was apparently sympathetic to Margaret's view that birth control was essential to the kind of preventive public health initiatives he wished to promote. But, like others on the Hill, he was not prepared to stand up to Catholic opposition.

The patent absurdity of this situation became especially apparent when close to a million dollars in Social Security funds were channeled through the Public Health Service to fight syphilis. Millions more were explicitly authorized for this purpose through the National Venereal Disease Act of 1939, but all the money went into education and treatment, rather than outright prevention. Not a single dollar was allocated for condoms that contained the transmission of infection but were also self-evidently contraceptives. The U.S. Surgeon General, Dr. Thomas Parran, Jr., defended this policy on the grounds that the larger "scientific and social factors of birth control" were not sufficiently clarified to warrant government action. In response, Margaret circulated fact sheets demonstrating continued high rates of maternal death and disease in the country and emphasizing the spiraling incidence of abortion that was believed to account in large part for the persistence of the problem. She curtly reminded Dr. Parran that his responsibility was for public health and not for "conjectural considerations of population policy."[14]

Following her trip to Japan in the fall of 1937, Margaret finally took the time to recuperate from her broken arm and from long-postponed surgery to remove the gallbladder that had been causing her distress. Having completed Cornell Medical School, Grant was serving his residency in surgery at Columbia-Presbyterian Hospital, where he arranged for his mother to be treated. The routine procedure went smoothly, and the most memorable moment of her hospital stay occurred when H. G. Wells made a surprise visit to her bedside, causing quite a stir among those on the medical staff who knew of his personal notoriety.

On the doctor's strict orders, she then finally agreed to settle down for an extended period of postoperative rest and as a retreat chose the hauntingly beautiful, but still raw, desert landscape of Tucson, Arizona, which had captivated her several years earlier during a trip out west to visit Stuart. Noah was nearing the age of eighty, and she certainly owed him some sustained attention and time. They rented a charming adobe-style house in the foothills of the Catalina Mountains just north of the city limits.

Still little more than a trading outpost—though its first downtown skyscrapers were in construction—the town of Tucson was steadily gaining recognition for its restorative, healthful climate. The now fabled Arizona Inn had recently been opened by the elegant and cultured Isabella Ferguson Greenway, Eleanor Roosevelt's childhood friend, who was then also representing Arizona in Congress. Several other hotels and sanitaria were beginning to cater to a rather cosmopolitan population of winter visitors, and they could be counted on to provide welcome diversion. One of the most prominent was the cosmetics pioneer Elizabeth Arden, who befriended Margaret and supplied her with the latest in diets, vitamin creams, and other fads for the preservation of youth and beauty.

For more intellectual stimulation, the University of Arizona's community of scholars was nearby, and for occasional personal inspiration there was Juliet Rublee, who still spent her winters in Mexico. Margaret also used the publication of *Movers and Shakers*, Mabel Dodge Luhan's vivid memoir of New York's prewar bohemia, as an occasion to renew the acquaintance of her old friend. The eccentric Dodge had long since retreated from the frenzied East and married Tony Luhan, a Pueblo Indian from Taos, New Mexico, with whom she was exploring an alternative life-style ostensibly dedicated to the needs of the community over those of the individual. Guests were always welcome at their villa, and in the summer of 1937, the two women exchanged cordial letters and a first visit, which brought Margaret great pleasure and inspired the comment: "So few people mean anything to anyone in life that it's a joy to touch the fringe of the life of one like yourself who does."[15]

Always restless without some kind of project, Margaret also brought a team of best-selling authors along with her to Tucson and embarked for a second time on the tortuous enterprise of reexamining her life. *My Fight for Birth Control* was out of print, and the firm of W. W. Norton, Inc., had offered her a contract for a new autobiography, believing in its commercial potential in light of the tremendous publicity her Washington lobby and her trips abroad had received. Norton suggested as collaborators Rackholm Holt and Walter Heywood, two journalists who had just published a best-seller about the medical profession. The three closeted themselves in Tucson for days at a time, while Margaret spoke into a recording device. The final manuscript emerged out of a professional reworking of these conversations.

Margaret Sanger: An Autobiography has a narrative strength far superior to its predecessor—a slicker style and a more uplifting tone. This second venture in memoir writing is, in fact, far more typical of the way women have traditionally approached the genre—a good deal more modest and genteel than the first. Demure and lady-like, the book glosses over conflict and doesn't dare complain about the enormous obstacles Margaret was made to overcome in attempting to put her convictions into action. As such, it lacks essential credibility and, despite a bevy of favorable reviews, it also did not turn out to be the commercial triumph that had been expected. Margaret blamed a weak title and poor promotion by the publisher, but the truth is that in her own eagerness to be seen as an unqualified success, she had kept the best parts of herself hidden. The rough hide, the fragile core, the fiery temperament, the romantic yearning, the droll humor—all were lost, along with the complex dynamic of personal, political, and social conflict that had given her life its great resonance.[16]

Though she refused to hold herself accountable, the decision to be bland was clearly calculated. An unfettered woman might have sold more books, but Margaret had little to gain politically at this juncture by painting too complex a portrait of herself. She had spent too many years working to make herself mainstream, and even as she abdicated power, the fruits of these labors were being incorporated into the larger institutions she created.

"We have moved up into the social strata to get money to run the cause," she would admit sometime later to one of her most loyal supporters, Rabbi Sidney Goldstein of the Free Synagogue in New York, who was urging her to push for the incorporation of contraception into New York's public health services and was baffled by her diminished militance. "In this strata [sic] they do not like fighting crusading spirits, they want pleasant harmonious conciliatory efforts, to bring about results."[17]

Having passed on the official mantle of leadership, and with little immediate progress likely for birth control on either the domestic or international fronts, Margaret found herself out of the public eye for increasingly long stretches of time, filling her days as a private citizen in Tucson by enrolling in classes in drawing and painting and by planning extravagant parties, outings, and other entertainments. Under the right circumstances these frivolous activities might have provided a welcome sabbatical, but Noah's health and spirits were steadily deteriorating, and his condition put a decided damper on her opportunity for self-indulgence. She confided bitterly in her journal that, far from a sense of liberation, she felt herself bondaged to the care of an ailing and increasingly obdurate old man, whom she had come to abhor.

As is so often the case in old age, what had been the principal preoccupation of Noah's productive years became the virtual obsession of his decline. Money, no matter how small and insignificant the amount, remained his only interest, and he spent most of his time counting what he had left, and worrying about what he spent. Indeed, in his wife's less than charitable eyes, he became little more than a tyrant, intent on causing everyone around him only anguish and pain. After only a few months together out west, Margaret's diary began to refer to her husband vituperatively as "the sadist." One typical entry reads:

> January 30. 1938: evening spent mostly in reading financial bulletins from New York papers. Sadist sits in large, comfortable upholstered chair. Conversation must cease while he reads. Guests suggest a moonlight walk—he thunders out "Are you crazy—you'll get cold and then expect me to heat the house up."

Margaret apparently went out on her walk despite this protest, but by the next week, and the next, and for more than the year that followed, she could find little improvement in Noah's behavior. The complaints she recorded were always the same. He was forever scolding, grumbling, and nagging at her. He could only find fault in everything and everybody around him. He was, by her description, "sad and pitiful," his dinner table conversation, "trite and stupid."

Visitors were her only salvation. Grant and Stuart both came for vacations, as did Nan Higgins, and the charming, erudite cultural anthropologist, Bronislaw Malinowski, a friend of Havelock Ellis. Malinowski was also spending winters in Arizona and helped Margaret to manage as best she could by keeping herself intellectually current. With Noah in tow, Margaret also made a quick trip to London in the fall of 1938 to visit Ellis as he approached his eightieth birthday. There were, in addition, intermittent forays back East to keep pushing the Roosevelt administration on the birth control question, each of which became more and more critical to her sense of well-being and self-esteem. Occasionally she would give a lecture or accept an award from some local group as well. A tiny birth control clinic had been operating in Tucson since 1935, principally serving Mexican-American women, and sometimes she went over there to help out, but free of any real obligation, she had almost nothing to do.[18]

She wrote less and less in her journal, but the few sparse thoughts she did record reveal a deepening depression. She began to dream about dying, and at first the prospect frightened her. One evening during 1938, she reported having seen a man during her sleep who was walking with a lovely dog on a leash. A pack of wolves then came into view; the man let go of the dog into the pack; the dog fought until his fur and flesh were ripped apart and then lay down in front of Margaret, vomited, and died. When the wolves devoured his carcass, she woke up startled and recorded her dream without comment. The following year she had a similar dream of death, but on this occasion there was no recollection of fright on her part, or of any mediating symbols. Death had come to her directly in her dream and seemed welcome. She had felt her life going and seen a great figure with wings and light radiating over her head, and she awoke, by her own account, to a pleasant sensation.[19]

Of course, the troubles that disturbed Margaret's sleep were a good deal more complicated than Noah's provocations and other trivial discontents. She had been in the public eye for so many years—the focus of so much admiration, on the one hand, so much vilification, on the other—that her sudden isolation and anonymity became a kind of curse. However deep the sense of victimization she had often felt as a public figure (and more or less directly revealed in her dreams), it was also clear that she thrived on celebrity and felt herself lacking in vitality without it. It was, as she once said, "her intoxicant."

Far removed from the international stage on which she had long acted, she anxiously anticipated the arrival of mail each day from friends and colleagues around the world, and she rose early each morning to write some responses by hand from her big, old-fashioned, and comfortably pillow-laden white bed. In the still cool hours that followed, she might then sit with a secretary at a table on her terrace, dictating her more formal replies.

But her circle of correspondents was narrowing.

The most deeply felt loss came in July of 1939 with the death of Ellis, who for so long had been at the center of Margaret's cerebral world. He had seemed unusually frail during their visit the preceding fall, and sensing that the end was near, she spent the early months of the new year pulling together a "festschrift" in anticipation of his birthday. The contributions she gathered together instead served as inspiration for a memorial tribute.

In an international radio broadcast with the journalist Dorothy Gordon, Margaret praised Ellis as a physician, philosopher, and poet who would long be remembered for two qualities above all—his humanism and his feminism. As yet unaware of the degree to which Freud's expanding reputation would eclipse her friend, she predicted that future generations would honor him for dignifying sexuality and insisting on its importance to the "spiritual lives of men and women." To claim Ellis as a friend, she said, had been the greatest honor of her life. Indeed, so intense was her investment in the association by this time, that she embellished the truth, claiming he had guided her reading for one and a half years in the British Museum, when, of course, she had spent only about one and a half months, during which she was distracted by her other interests on the Continent. Several weeks later, however, in the privacy of her journal, she acknowledged that it was less the man himself she missed than the twenty-five-year habit of using him as a sounding board for her own observations and thoughts, often even her dreams. To Françoise Cyon she admitted that "it is as if a current of my very being has been cut off from its source."[20]

For this reason, Ellis's casually dismissive treatment of Margaret in the autobiography published the year following his death left her deeply shocked and saddened, even as she expressed an understanding of the complicated emotional context in which their friendship had first developed. Ellis had actually drafted the manuscript in 1918–1919, shortly after his wife Edith's premature death, and the book reads as nothing less than an elegy to their highly unconventional marriage. He had apparently never resolved a sense of responsibility for Edith's emotional turmoil and, perhaps for this reason, did not even mention Margaret by name in the book (only by the initial *M*), or acknowledge how intensely he had for a time pursued her. The two had, of course, remained devoted friends for the intervening twenty-one years and had visited and corresponded frequently. Margaret had gone to great lengths to build Ellis's audience and advance his reputation in the United States, and he had willingly accepted her money and other gifts. Yet the autobiography concludes that "beautiful as my new friend was to me and continues to be to this day, I have sometimes been tempted to wish that I had not met her," a passage that hurt deeply when she first read it in 1940, though she may have presumed the cause of her rebuke.

"Well I doubtless deserved it—no one gives us what we have not attracted to ourselves," she would admit some years later to Hugh. What she could never accept, however, was her longtime mentor's apparent remorse for a marriage that had been more compelling on a subjective or psychological plane than it had ever been in actuality, a relationship where passion had, quite literally, transcended the physical. In Margaret's view, the romantic intensity of the memoirs undermined the empirical, scientific basis of Ellis's sex research and theory, which for so long had provided a secure foundation, not only for his reputation, but for her own life and work. She saw the book as a repudiation of virtually everything he had advocated, and she, in turn, had advanced as practical marriage counseling. Worst of all, it was an implicit condemnation of her own personal behavior. She was bereft for weeks after it came out.[21]

But soon enough there was the welcome distraction of historic developments in the government's birth control policy. Escalating concern had finally propelled President Roosevelt to refer the matter to an Intergovernmental Committee to Coordinate Health and Welfare Policy, which included Surgeon General Parran and Katherine Lenroot. (An invitation was also extended for Margaret to visit privately with Eleanor Roosevelt at the White House, but the two women's schedules could not be coordinated at this time.) In January of 1939, the committee invited a delegation of birth control partisans, including Margaret, Robert L. Dickinson, Morris Ernst, and the demographer Frank Lorimer, to present testimony. Margaret's presentation pointed out that with 37 percent of the national income being spent on social welfare, it no longer made sense to prohibit funding of birth control. "It is not a panacea," she conceded, "but it will probably do more for the health and happiness of mothers and children then any other single instrument."[22]

As the committee was holding these hearings, lawyers at the Surgeon General's office also officially sanctioned the distribution of contraceptive supplies under the terms of the Venereal Disease Control Act, and assistants to Dr. Parran quietly began to issue approvals for some programs, but to no avail. Although the Public Health Service administered these programs, funding was still being channeled through Social Security dollars controlled by Lenroot, and she refused to have anything to do with the new policies, at least until the President personally intervened.

Birth control momentarily became a political issue in 1940, when Mrs. Roosevelt, for the first time since she had arrived in Washington, admitted to reporters that she favored "planned families" but would never impose her own views on others. Another invitation to the White House was extended to Margaret when she was to be in Washington in May, but a delayed flight prevented her from making the appointment. Promises were made instead to get together during the summer in Hyde Park. Following her husband's election to an unprecedented third term later that year, Eleanor Roosevelt finally felt free of political constraints altogether and called together birth control activists and government administrators at the White House. She acted at the behest of the philanthropists Albert and Mary

Lasker, friends and trusted confidants of the First Family, who had recently become the largest individual donors to birth control programs in the country. The Laskers were funding Margaret's birth control demonstration project among blacks in the South, and Mrs. Roosevelt was desperately concerned about helping this beleaguered population; it was, indeed because of this commitment that she finally got involved in birth control.[23]

Though self-consciously an experiment in social engineering, the Negro Project, as it was called, was expressly altruistic, and not racist, in intent. The project framers voiced concern that the country's largest minority population was being left out of locally administered public health efforts altogether and promoted as an alternative a "unique experiment in race-building and humanitarian service to a race subjected to discrimination, hardship, and segregation." The project proposal proclaimed, "Birth control, per se, cannot correct economic conditions that result in bad housing, overcrowding, poor hygiene, malnutrition and neglected sanitation, but can reduce the attendant loss of life, health and happiness that spring from these conditions."

Margaret was especially pleased to be involved in this effort to improve the quality of life and create opportunity for women and families often left out of existing social welfare initiatives because of race. The "Negro question," she predicted in a letter to Albert Lasker in 1942, would be "foremost on the country's domestic agenda" once the war was over. As in the past in Harlem, she was also sensitive to issues of racial self-determination and worked to involve black clergy, educators, and doctors in positions of leadership in the project, so as to temper racial divisions and any concern, as she wisely anticipated and candidly admitted in private, "that we want to exterminate the Negro population."

The advisory council for the project included W. E. B. DuBois, Mary McLeod Bethune, founder of the National Council of Negro Women and a Roosevelt appointee and friend of the First Lady, Adam Clayton Powell, Jr., pastor of the Abyssinian Baptist Church in Harlem, and other prominent leaders in the community. Still, there was simply no way to avoid the fact of endemic racism among many activists in the birth control movement, let alone among the white public health officials in the South on whom the success of any voluntary effort ultimately depended. The problems Margaret confronted in trying to bring contraceptive service to blacks only underscored the need for a public health initiative removed from the arbitrary and unaccountable control of local and privately subsidized leadership. Help from the President was crucial, though Margaret cynically reminded Mary Lasker in a private letter during the 1940 campaign that the Roosevelts had disappointed them many times before and suggested she also bring the subject before Republican Wendell Willkie. Margaret was especially incensed when the President, reaching for votes in the election of 1940, agreed to send an official United States emissary to the Vatican.[24]

Mrs. Lasker, however, did not share this suspicion. She was, indeed, no less enthusiastic about Franklin Roosevelt than she was about Margaret Sanger, whom to this day she unequivocally identifies as the most important woman of the century and the most important individual influence on her own life. And along with her well-connected husband, Albert, Mary Lasker was always eager to put political influence, as well as money, to work on birth control's behalf.

The White House meeting she helped convene on March 5, 1941, included representatives of the Public Health Service, the Children's Bureau, and the Department of Agriculture. Dr. Parran was unable to attend but sent his wife in his place as a conciliatory gesture. Margaret also sent a representative. The discussion was abstract and inconclusive but did secure a commitment from Mrs. Roosevelt to speak to the President about the matter, although as she later reminded Mrs. Lasker, "He knows that both Dr. Parran and Miss Lenroot are very anxious to have him take the rap on anything that is done about giving this information because they realize that there will be certain repercussions from the Catholic Church." This reservation aside, Mrs. Roosevelt, presumably with her husband's consent, then instructed Dr. Parran to establish a formal mechanism for reviewing state requests for information about "child-spacing" programs.

New procedures were announced the following October, but this action alone did not resolve the matter, and a second meeting on birth control took place at the White House on December 8, 1941, the day following the Japanese attack on Pearl Harbor, and just as war was being declared. Mrs. Roosevelt could not attend this time, nor could Margaret, but Edna McKinnon and Morris Ernst were there and made it clear that birth control activists would stand for no more obstructions. They wanted the cooperation of federal health agencies, especially among blacks in the South. Katherine Lenroot spoke up, insisting that "inclusion of birth control would jeopardize her other programs of maternal and child welfare," and citing the Congressional repudiation of Shephard-Towner in 1929 as a precedent. But the Washington D.C. obstetrician, Prentiss Wilson, who also attended, cautioned her to remember "at whose board we are sitting and under whose roof." He assumed Lenroot would cave in to White House pressure. "I consider this a most historic occasion and the most significant event in the history of the movement since the birth of Margaret Sanger," he added.[25]

Within two months, Dr. Parran issued a statement of his intent to approve state-initiated family planning programs, although he was careful to distinguish this gesture from active propaganda for birth control on the part of his own agency, and he insisted on a low-profile approach without publicity, until the extent of local interest could be measured. Lenroot first asked lawyers in her department for further clarification of her rights, and only after they expressed doubt that she could unilaterally oppose the White House, would she finally yield to its will and to pressure from public health officials, who were by then anticipating an increased need for reliable contraception from women working in vital war industries. In May of 1942, assured that Lenroot would not impound Social Security funds, the U.S. Public Health Service officially authorized a policy of "child spacing for women in war industries, under medical supervision." This small initiative opened the door to cooperation with the voluntary birth control movement and permitted a few public health programs initiated by the states to move ahead with official sanction.[26]

In the fall of 1941, Eleanor Roosevelt contributed $10.00 in response to a fund-raising solicitation signed by Margaret. She refused to accept a proposed award from birth controllers several months later, however, telling Mary Lasker, "There is no use antagonizing people at this time." The two friends corresponded frequently on the subject, and Mrs. Roosevelt extended a cautious salute to the birth controllers on their "extension of adequate maternal and child care health services" in 1943. But formal ties with the birth control movement were not established until after the President's death. Mrs. Roosevelt then lent her name as a sponsor of various international family planning initiatives, and Margaret, in turn, sent her a letter of appreciation in 1952: "It is amazing how many outstanding people in many walks of life who have the courage to stand by their ideas will hesitate, owing to the pressure of the Roman Catholic Church in this country, to give expression to their convictions and views on the question of population," she wrote. "But you have always been known for your courage—and especially for having the courage of your convictions and opinions—and for this, you have millions of friends throughout the world."

Still, all was not forgiven, and if Eleanor was excused, Margaret could not so easily overcome her resentment of the coalition Franklin Roosevelt built as a result of his capitulation to Catholic pressure. Continuing to cast her Presidential ballot for Norman Thomas, she would vote locally for Republicans after the war and forever disclaim Democrats who surrendered to Catholic influence.[27]

Contraceptive initiatives in U.S. Public Health programs never advanced very far, but the nation's armed forces did sell or freely distribute as many as 50 million condoms a month on military bases during World War II. Inaugurated as a security measure to contain the spread of venereal disease, this undertaking constituted the lone federal initiative for birth control of any real substance to emerge from a decade of political lobbying. Military largesse with respect to contraception, however, did not extend to women. Official regulations regarding sexual conduct by enlisted women were stringent. The navy delayed distribution of a film on sex hygiene made for women and canceled production of another one on birth control, a situation Margaret protested to no avail.[28]

The continued prospect of government support in this period, however, did serve as an important catalyst to internal organizational initiatives within the voluntary birth control movement. In 1939, citing the need for a unified force to petition the government and resist the Catholic Church, Margaret reunited with the American Birth Control League under the umbrella of a new entity called the Birth Control Federation of America. Her clinic in New York was struggling to continue to deliver services while vying with the American Birth Control League as chief lobbyist, cheerleader, fund-raiser, and sponsor for programs and clinics elsewhere in the country. It could barely meet its costs. Competition between the two organizations had been especially venomous since Margaret wooed Clarence Gamble away from several of his prior affiliations with the league and cajoled him to put her employees on his payroll as field workers in North Carolina. Likewise, the Rockefeller family and other common donors were fragmenting the impact of their contributions by splitting them between the two separate organizations.[29]

Reconciliation of the warring factions after a decade of suspicion and animosity was not easy. Margaret resented the unabashed bigotry of many of her adversaries at the American Birth Control League, believed emphatically that she had accomplished far more than they during the split, and knew for certain that she had raised more money. She demanded at least a token gesture of deference from women whom she referred to in private as "drawing room lizards." The reunion took more than a year of negotiation and required the intervention of an outside mediator from John Price Jones, Inc., in New York, the same management firm that earlier in the decade had so cavalierly dismissed her unique abilities and importance to the cause. This time the consultants acknowledged that the birth control cause could not possibly advance without her name, and she conceded a lack of interest in remaining in charge day to day. What is more, she could interest no woman among her own supporters in taking her place. Always one to hog the limelight, she had prepared no orderly succession. A committee comprising representatives of all interested parties—the league, the Clinical Research Bureau, and the National Committee on Maternal Health—named her as honorary chairman of the new organization and placed Richard N. Pierson, M.D., formerly head of the league, as active president of the new board of directors. D. Kenneth Rose of John Price Jones took over as national director.

"Our minds are miles apart in most things," Margaret admitted privately of these men, but "spirtually I have left the front and joined the ranks." Within months, however, she was busy drumming up more lobbying and fund-raising ideas and rebuking the new leadership for once again capitulating to alarm about the country's population decline by issuing a statement encouraging reproduction among the mentally and physically sound. "For us to start that kind of sentiment is just going to put the weapons in the hands of our opponents and soon the whole birth control movement will be sliding backward or into the Hitler and Mussolini phobia," she insisted. This was nothing more than "cheap twaddle."[30]

Nor did it escape Margaret's notice that the ascendence of men to positions of leadership in the movement reflected a deliberate change of strategy away from propaganda directed principally toward women. A new generation was determined to face the fact, as Rose himself put it, "that most pivotal groups upon which advancement of birth control is dependent are controlled by men, such as Federal and State legislatures, hospital boards, public health boards, etc." This was, of course, a polite way of saying what had been said before—that the voluntary birth control movement would only be taken seriously if men were put in charge. Rose and his new board also determined that after years of Depression-deferred marriage and overall fertility decline, the organization would benefit from a less belligerent image. "Birth Control," in his opinion, was simply too much of "a fighting word."

The new timidity was never more evident than in Holyoke, Massachusetts, in 1940, when Margaret was scheduled to speak at a Congregational church to inaugurate a citizens' initiative challenging the state's restrictive birth control law. The church closed its doors to her under pressure from businessmen on its board who were fearful of an economic boycott by local Catholics. Episcopalians, Methodists, the YMCA, and other civic organizations then followed suit, and municipal authorities refused to provide a public facility for a meeting. The situation looked hopeless until a young female organizer for the local Textile Workers' Union intervened. Margaret spoke in an old Socialist meeting hall, in front of a mammoth campaign poster for Franklin Roosevelt, a setting familiar enough to her, but hardly so to the largely elite membership of the state's birth control league. She then continued her tour without incident in eleven more cities.

Fifty thousand signatures were collected for the initiative petition, and a referendum was put on the ballot in 1942. Public opinion polls showed overwhelming support, even among Catholic voters, but the measure was defeated under a barrage of opposition orchestrated by the Archdiocese of Boston, which claimed the legislation would establish state control over childbirth and would legalize abortion. Margaret was incensed that birth control officials in New York did almost nothing to support the reform effort. Fearing further controversy, they also took no action when her autobiography was removed from the Boston Public Library under the alleged jurisdiction of the state obscenity laws.[31]

Indeed, in 1942, committing itself to child spacing rather than absolute limitation, the organization, through a membership referendum engineered by Rose, officially changed its name to the Planned Parenthood Federation of America. Margaret vigorously objected to this decision. While she had been among the first to market family planning as a tie-in to the New Deal, she was attached to the birth control nomenclature as a matter of sentiment and worried that the alternative concept, though perhaps friendlier, had none of the force or conviction that made the cause interesting and important, especially to women. The word "control," as she once defined it, meant "power to regulate," but just what did "planning" mean? "Family planning for what, for summer vacations?" her niece Olive liked to ask in jest. The change of name was symbolic to Margaret of a weak and spineless leadership, yet she was no longer in a position to enforce her will, though, as in the past, the new federation was largely dependent for its livelihood on donors she had recruited.[32]

In 1940, Albert and Mary Lasker had pledged $25,000 to the federation for four years, with the provision that their contribution be matched by two comparable gifts. Enchanted by Margaret personally, and convinced of the central importance of birth control to the country's economic and social vitality, the Laskers could not understand why the movement continued to beg for money. They encouraged a bolder fund-raising effort, but the only donations that came in of any substantial size were from Sanger admirers like Doris Duke Cromwell and assorted members of the Rosenwald and Rockefeller families. Mrs. Cromwell gave $15,000 with the express provision that it "be expended under the supervision and at the discretion of Mrs. Sanger," while Arthur Packard of the Rockefeller staff also defended Sanger against the innuendo of Rose and his staff. Some people find her "uncooperative and lacking the best judgment of any idea that is not her own," he wrote in a memorandum to his files, but "I have always found her judgment to have a rather good foundation in fact."[33]

Rose did streamline Planned Parenthood's tangled bureaucracy and vastly improved the relationship of the national office with its affiliates, but Margaret and Mary Lasker could never forgive him his cautious personality. They had little patience for what they viewed as a caretaker approach to the job and openly challenged his reluctance to establish a higher public profile—to exhibit "more of the crusading spirit, more fire, and more fight," as they put it to him directly in one of their last meetings. Rose, on the other hand, was maneuvering Planned Parenthood to serve as an unofficial agent of government in cooperation with public health programs and had recruited a public health service official to become medical director. To this end, he believed in the virtue of walking softly and provoking no further controversy, especially with the Catholic Church. Much to Margaret's chagrin, he had the board adopt a policy saying it would avoid religious controversy and emphasize only the health and social values of family planning. As Americans mobilized for war, he was also anxious that the organization not seem unpatriotic by encouraging a low birthrate. Whether a more militant approach would, in fact, have made greater inroads is impossible to determine. Certainly the coming of World War II gave new energy to the argument that American women ought to have more babies. Catholic journalists, in particular, stepped up their attack on "the woman's movement" and on the birth control movement for encouraging women to be "shirkers," and Margaret was identified personally as a "communist" and "anarchist."[34]

What is more, family planning advocates confronted an absence of resources for domestic initiatives of any kind that was even more devastating to their cause than the government's prior lack of will or fear of reprisal. Under Rose and his successors during the 1950s, Planned Parenthood foundered as it struggled to rid itself of a belligerent feminist reputation and to establish institutional credibility in a postwar era dominated by pronatalist sentiment, family values, and a tradition of urban social welfare voluntarism in which Catholic institutions steadily increased their influence. Having substantially raised its standards for affiliation, the federation actually ran fewer clinics in 1960 than it had twenty years earlier. It would rebound only as a result of technological advances in contraception, expanded public assistance, and a resurgent feminist movement.[35]

As the nation turned its attention away from domestic social issues during the war, Margaret retreated to Tucson where a voluminous correspondence kept her in touch with what was going on in birth control affairs, not just in New York, but around the world. With two sons serving in the military, she also had a high personal stake in the war's outcome. What is more, she was engaged intellectually and emotionally in foreign affairs as a result of her frequent trips to Europe and Asia. She spoke with the authority of an eyewitness to the pressure of internal population growth on the rise of expansionist, fascist militarism in Germany and Japan. In so doing, she anticipated the link between population and world peace that captured the attention of United States policymakers in the postwar era, and she prepared herself for it. Always one to be where the action is—never allowing herself to fret for long about an obstacle in her path—she turned her attentions abroad.

The new Birth Control Federation has "eliminated the kickers and consolidated the boosters," she had written in 1939 to her old friend George Plummer of the Rosicrucian Society, where she had long ago entrusted her spirit. "For myself I feel that twenty-five years is long enough to carry the baby, and so I want to give the younger generation the opportunity to push the cause over the top, and now within the next few years I hope to do a little research into my own individual life and to see which way this individual should go."[36]

If she had lost her appetite for people and politics at home, and they for her, still, the whole world beckoned.

CHAPTER NINETEEN

Intermezzo

From her safe harbor in Tucson, Margaret kept up a steady correspondence during the war with friends in London, whose plight she felt deeply. More than once, she remarked of her relief that Havelock Ellis had not lived to experience the terror of a second European conflict, but far from its corridors, she also seemed uncharacteristically disengaged. There were intermittent moments of commitment, to be sure: some help for George and Juliet Rublee, who were trying to evacuate Jewish friends from Germany; a contribution at the request of Lillian Hellman for the Abraham Lincoln Brigade in Spain; care packages of money, tea, cookies, canned goods, and other provisions for H. G., Hugh and Janet, the Drysdales, and Françoise, and still later, offers of peaceful shelter far away from the German bombings there.

She certainly kept herself current with foreign affairs. Entries in her journal between 1938 and 1941 remark on the historic occasions of Chamberlain's audience with Hitler, the signing of the Nazi–Soviet Pact, the formal declaration of hostilities by England and France, the controversy over Lend Lease and, of course, the fateful Japanese bombing of Pearl Harbor. Yet, so deep was her dread of the carnage of war, and so intense was her contempt for Winston Churchill—whom she held personally responsible for the worst manifestations of British arrogance in India—that she could only resign herself to the inevitability of American involvement on behalf of England and its Europeans allies. Though she grew increasingly alarmed by the Nazi threat, she would never bring herself to endorse American participation outright, as her more belligerent friends like H. G. and Juliet were pressing her to do.

"So it has come to pass as many Pro British Americans have wished & prayed it to be," she wrote in her journal, after the radio carried the fateful news of December 7, 1941. "Nation after nation will now join in this madness & God only can keep hearts true."[1]

For Margaret, World War II simply confirmed the failure of progressive reformers like herself who had tried for so long to stimulate interest in peaceful, scientific principles of planning for control of population, natural resources, and economic growth. She put most of the blame for this predicament on the shoulders of men but was willing to let women share some responsibility. Invited to join a 1940 Centennial Congress celebrating the political and social advancement of women, she responded contemptuously that it hardly seemed that emancipated women had gotten the world very far at all. She took the opportunity to chide the conference organizer, the now elderly Carrie Chapman Catt, for the continued unwillingness of the organized woman's movement in the United States to support birth control as a fundamental right, and she must therefore have been surprised and grateful several months later when Catt's colleague, Alice Paul, sent warm congratulations on the occasion of a celebration for birth control. Margaret in return agreed to lend her name to the advisory council of Paul's National Woman's Party, but when the group did nothing further to make its support official, she complained again to Nora Stanton Barney, the activist granddaughter of Elizabeth Cady Stanton, that organized women "really are so smugly satisfied with appearances and make no effort to achieve the reality" of equal rights with men.

On her own, Margaret spoke out against the increased hazards of sex discrimination during the war and for the need to protect the rights of women replacing male workers on the home front. During the summer of 1940 she visited Eleanor Roosevelt at Hyde Park to talk about a national health training program for women, an idea she had already proposed to various administration officials, encouraging them to train civilian women as nurse's aides, nutritionists, and in other skills that would benefit American citizens, help advance military preparedness, and not incidentally, promote the dissemination of contraception. In response, however, she received what appears to have been little more than a form letter from some minor government bureaucrat, who compounded the slight by misspelling her name. There was no federal money, and no broad institutional support, for the kind of expanded domestic health initiative she envisioned. All available health-care funds were being channeled to serve the troops abroad. Ironically, the greatest interest in her ideas came from the left, and after the *The Daily Worker* published an article she wrote on these subjects, she received a friendly middle-of-the-night phone call in Tucson from her old radical friend Marie Equi.[2]

The only real passion Margaret ever seemed to muster for the war effort derived from her hope that the Allies, if victorious, would punish the Roman Catholic Church for its apparent collusion with Mussolini and the Fascists. H. G. Wells shared her intensifying paranoia about the ties of the Vatican to the Axis powers and about the divided loyalties of American Catholics, who were in a position to influence the Roosevelt Administration's foreign policies. In 1943, Wells wrote *Crux Ansata*, a short polemic recapitulating an intellectual critique of Catholicism and its irrationalities that he had first published in his *Short History of the World*. He also then went on to pose the thorny question of why Rome was being spared Allied bombing raids that were pummelling other European cultural capitals. Published on both sides of the Atlantic, the book sparked a biting controversy and provided the basis of the last surviving correspondence between Margaret and H. G., who died in London in 1946, also just short of the age of eighty.[3]

With the passing of some of her dearest friends—with the world wholly absorbed by the war—Margaret made the personal decision to "stick out" her marriage, as she blithely characterized the nature of her intent in a journal entry for 1940. She also observed that Noah had mellowed a bit, once he got used to having her around more, and she was finding him less irritable than in the past. Confronted with a wartime rationing of gasoline, the couple had moved from the Tucson hills to a grand house closer to the center of town and just a few doors down from the Arizona Inn. Summers, of course, were spent back in Willowlake, but to escape the mounting tension of the news from Europe, Margaret and Noah took a Caribbean cruise together in August of that year, and a trip to Nassau with George and Juliet Rublee the following spring, where Margaret inaugurated a birth control program in the local hospital and had tea with the Duke and Duchess of Windsor.

This turned out to be their last holiday together, for Noah's health declined markedly through 1942. Normally stoic, he began to complain of feeling weak during the summer at Willowlake, where he suffered the first of several strokes. Barely strong enough to return to Arizona in the fall, he spent the entire winter in bed, content to gaze at the lovely mountains in the distance. By Margaret's telling, she "was close to him the whole year . . . the household revolved around his every wish, his food and his comforts," and they were alone together when he died peacefully in his sleep on June 21, 1943, just as he had hoped he would. In a conversation shortly before he died, he told her he could remember nothing about his life before she entered into it. "Only since I knew you have I lived," is what she remembered him saying, an idealized rendering of the marriage, to be sure, but a comforting one that may have been true enough for an old man.[4]

Noah's body was cremated, and Stuart and Grant flew out to pay their respects, but none of the Slee children or grandchildren ever turned up. Though Jim Slee was living not far away in California, Noah had made no attempt at a reconciliation with his eldest son, or with his only daughter, Elizabeth Willis, who acknowledged the occasion only by sending flowers. What remained of Noah's great fortune in real estate and stock must have been put in Margaret's name already, and this left her with more than a comfortable income on which to live, though she was never the enormously wealthy woman she would have been had the Depression not taken its toll. Noah had been paying their living expenses from an annuity that expired when he died, and less than $500 was left in his estate when it was probated. Loans still outstanding to his children were apparently forgiven, and Margaret instead made several subsequent attempts to restore a cordial relationship.[5]

Even at his death, Margaret had surprisingly little to say about her husband. She had mentioned him only once in her *Autobiography*, when she casually dismissed him as the "generous man" she married despite his "foibles." To Dorothy Brush, she acknowledged only that "22 years of *companionship* has made an impression & I shall find it difficult to go on the stage of life alone." Brush did better at capturing the essence of the relationship in the remarks she delivered at a memorial service at Willowlake in September, when Noah's ashes were buried.

"Margaret was quicksilver," she said. "You [Noah] never could quite catch her & she kept you always fascinated. . . . Without her, heaven won't be heaven for you, dear Noah."

With her husband finally gone, the "petty irritation & annoyances are wiped out," Margaret later disclosed in the privacy of her journal. "Death removes them all. It wipes out the memories of the unreal. Only the goodness, kindness & loving things remain in my thoughts of J Noah. I'm glad of that." It took several years alone, however, before she was willing to acknowledge him graciously in public, and before she ever once consented to identify herself as "Mrs. Margaret Sanger Slee." Yet quite unlike Havelock Ellis after his wife's death, she never made too much of these posthumous gestures to social convention. She never mistook sentimentality for love.[6]

With so little emotion invested in her marriage, Margaret had few problems adjusting to life on her own. There were hundreds of telegrams and letters of sympathy demanding response, and Noah had scarcely been laid to rest, when she was called back East after Nan Higgins suffered a heart attack and then died suddenly in January of 1944. In Margaret's lowest moments, she had always relied on her older sister's resourcefulness, and this death, much more than Noah's, came as a great shock to her. Nan was buried next to his gravesite in the plot at Willowlake, and Margaret wrote in her journal of the "big spot" left in her life. Feeling especially bereft in New York City, a place she could not visualize without the sister who had been there whenever she needed her, she quickly returned to Tucson, her despair intensified by the fact that relations with Ethel Higgins remained distant and tense. Nan had been living in an apartment Margaret kept above the clinic on West 16th Street. Ethel moved in when she died, but the two surviving women saw little of one another. For all practical purposes, Margaret was without sororal affection for the first time in her life.

What is more, she was frantic with concern for Grant and Stuart, both of whom shipped overseas as military doctors in the fall of 1943. Grant joined the navy, went off on an aircraft carrier to the South Pacific and then commanded a casualty control ship. Stuart—despite a medical history of sinus troubles and a complicating tubercular infection—finally made it into the army, and served with the American invasion forces on the beaches of Normandy, where he rose to the rank of major. "Thank God they are trained to save lives not shatter them," Margaret observed on first hearing of her sons' entering the service. But as the war dragged on, she found it more and more difficult to appease her persistent anxiety. "I've always said since Peggy's death that life could not hold me long if another of my children went before I do," she wrote in her journal. "It is lonely. Lots to do. East–West with Pearl Buck. My painting & B.C. All big interests, but one gets a loneliness nevertheless."[7]

Concern for the whereabouts and well-being of Stuart and Grant touched the wellsprings of her emotional life, and knowing that only one other human being in the world could possibly share her feelings, she reached out across the years to contact Bill Sanger, who was supporting his second wife and daughter by working as a humble architect on the staff of New York City's Department of Water Supply, Gas, and Electricity. The letter she wrote him on this occasion was destroyed, along with the rest of her correspondence, but, as always, she saved Bill's long, if halting, response, which overflowed with sentiments very close to those she was feeling.

"How strange it all seems," Bill wrote, "this meeting the final outcome of one's earlier view or ideal with the actual combat. This started out to be a war of invasion but it has reached the scope of world wide revolution." Pausing to reflect on the perversity of Fascism, with its intent to annihilate the innocents—pious Jews, on the one hand, and idealistic Marxists, on the other—the letter then went on: "Yes that mighty brow of old Karl would have been all wrinkled up if he had lived to witness the events of these times."

Bill reserved his most touching observations for personal matters—how he used to carry Stuart up Locust Hill in Hastings; how little Grant, all spruced up in a white corduroy suit, had once waddled into a neighbor's muddy lettuce patch; how Grant as a young man had come to see him from time to time, while Stuart resolutely stayed away. It was Margaret's apparent mention of Peggy, however, that aroused his deepest emotions.

"I have tried in the perspective of time to quiet the inward tears as the years rolled by; one had to steel oneself or go mad," he admitted. "I am told that time heals all wounds—yes some—but there [are] those that will linger to the last moment of living memory."

He went on with several disjointed references—from the furnishings for which Margaret and he had once shared great affection, to the eclipse of the art world in New York—and then closed his letter on a poignant note: "Grant & Stuart are in the service," he wrote, "and now in my little corner I feel I am part of the big surge to win this war."[8]

Coming of age had not been easy for Stuart Sanger, whose will was all but shattered by the early years of the Depression. Chastened by his hard luck on Wall Street, he finally straightened himself out professionally by following Grant to Cornell Medical School. Even as an intern at New York's Bellevue Hospital, however, he remained prone to intense emotional outbursts and occasional bouts with alcohol. Still living on money from his mother and stepfather as he neared the age of forty, he observed wryly that by the time he finished he would be able to claim old age insurance "so that the future does not seem entirely dark." The dependency nevertheless bred resentment and confusion, and on occasion he tried to explain himself to his mother, but she never seemed to have the time or inclination to listen.[9]

Like so many young men of this generation, the prospect of being drafted forced Stuart to make commitments and assume personal responsibilities he had long deferred. While training at the Leahy Clinic in 1941, he began dating Virginia Barbara Peabody, a young nurse from New Hampshire, twelve years his junior, who was also on the staff there. They were secretly married and in quick succession had two children: Margaret, born in November of 1941, six months after the wedding, and Barbara Nancy, born nineteen months later, only days after Noah's death—the first named for her illustrious grandmother, the second, for her mother and great-aunt, two quiet but stalwart women.

Relations between mother-in-law and daughter-in-law were strained from the outset. Margaret was never terribly good at disguising the fact that she found her daughter-in-law Barbara plain and uninspiring and resented what she considered as her slavish attention to family and household responsibilities. The two women could not have been more different in temperament and were never close. But a mutual respect developed between them, especially as the one grew older and increasingly dependent on the other for practical care.

The distance between them also never interfered with the warmth Margaret demonstrated toward her two spirited granddaughters, whose company in Tucson during and after the war provided her joyful companionship. Margaret lavished the time on these two little girls that she had long ago denied their father and frequently lamented that he was missing from their young childhood, as though she had never once been absent from his own. They called her Mimi (because when they were little she always said, "Come to me, Come to me") and quickly learned that, although she couldn't really be depended on to care for them in any responsible or sustained way, she possessed a very special gift. Whenever they were together, she made them feel as though they were the most important two people in the world. In their memory, she remains very much the "grande dame"—often distracted by worldly interests that seemed distant and unimportant to them, but able to charm and captivate as no one else could, whenever she took the time.[10]

By contrast to Stuart, Grant Sanger advanced with considerable ease during the difficult years of the Depression and as a consequence enjoyed more cordial relations with his mother. He shared her enthusiasm for birth control, her interest in politics and public policy, and her keen sense of humor. Once he earned his medical degree, however, they took opposing views on the wisdom of promoting public health programs that included contraception. Like most of his colleagues, Grant feared that government intervention would compromise his professional autonomy and income. In 1939, he wrote a friend at the AMA, suggesting that the organization write birth control into a pending public health bill as a sure way of seeing that it was defeated. "My sons, My sons!" Margaret exclaimed in a penciled comment on her copy of the correspondence.

Grant met his future wife, Margery Edwina Campbell, while they were both residents at Columbia Presbyterian. Tall, dark, and attractive, Edwina, as she was called, embodied all the qualities Margaret ostensibly admired and wished for in a daughter-in-law. The bright and determined daughter of a wealthy, established family, she'd graduated from Vassar in 1932, a year ahead of Mary McCarthy, with the intention of combining a family and a career. Grant seemed very much in love, and Margaret was pleased when they married after a brief courtship in 1939.

"You welcomed me very graciously into your family," Edwina wrote. "I have a feeling that we shall be good friends, and I hope that you will come to think of me as a daughter, and not as that anomalous creature—a daughter-in-law!" Thrilled with the furnishings Margaret provided as a wedding gift, she wrote again with enthusiastic thanks to "Mummy Sanger" about the charms of the new apartment she and Grant had found in Washington Heights and about their busy schedules at the hospital.

The future seemed unbounded in its promise for the young couple, until the war quickly altered their plans. Two sons, Michael and

Peter, were born before Grant went overseas, and Margaret visited them occasionally at the navy base in Coronado, California, which became their home during the war, doting over the boys, amazed by how much the one's plaintive sensitivity and the other's physical prowess resembled the same contrast between Grant and Stuart. These children called her Domah, the term of endearment that Grant and Peggy had long ago invented for Bill Sanger's mother.[11]

For the final two years of the war, Margaret remained in Tucson, her ear tuned to the radio. The harsh realities of combat hit her especially hard one day when she crossed paths at the local station with a trainload of young German prisoners en route to a detention facility in Mesa, Arizona. Mostly, she just waited quietly for letters from her sons, while admiring the hope and courage of their wives, especially at holidays. She learned to drive a car—though never with sufficient attention to who else was on the road, according to Stuart—and she could often be seen on errands around town, sporting a broad-brimmed straw hat to shield her delicate skin from the harsh sun, along with white cotton gloves to protect her hands. She lavished affection on a lovely, raven cocker spaniel called Beauty, and she attended an Episcopal Church regularly, for the first time in many years—amusing herself with a steady stream of friends, including the minister and his wife, who stopped by the house for drinks or dinner and kept her company on such momentous occasions as Roosevelt's 1944 election victory. Saddened by the President's sudden death the following April, and concerned for its potential effect on Allied morale, she was nonetheless annoyed by the three days of treacly tribute that played without interruption on the radio. She would not forgive Roosevelt his weaknesses, even in death.

A visit from Vijaya Lakshmi Pandit, Nehru's sister and later his official representative to the United Nations, provided temporary diversion in the several weeks following. The two women had met in India in 1936, when Madame Pandit started a birth control clinic in a provincial Indian hospital. In Tucson, Margaret gave a garden party in her honor and then prepared to leave for Willowlake. A long and languid summer followed before the dropping of the first atomic bombs in August, and Japan's subsequent surrender.

Grant returned to California on Thanksgiving Day, but he was off to New York almost immediately to begin the difficult job of reestablishing his medical career. Margaret would not let herself relax until Christmas Day, when Stuart had also returned, and both boys gathered together in Arizona with their new families for the happiest holiday she ever thought it possible to enjoy. To celebrate, she distributed several thousand dollars worth of shares from her portfolio of stocks, so they would have something from her with which to begin a new life.[12]

The pace of postwar adjustment was nevertheless rapid and confusing. Grant and Edwina found an apartment on New York's newly fashionable East End Avenue and tried to juggle jobs and family. A poignant letter to his mother describes the young soldier's conflicted emotions on trading the security of his uniform for the uncertainty of a civilian future. Two more sons, Stephen and Alexander, were born, but Grant was still eager for a daughter to fill the void left by Peggy's death. A fifth son, Morgan, came along first, and then with bittersweet success, their daughter, Anne, was born. Margaret "blushed," by her own account, whenever she had to acknowledge the size of Grant and Edwina's family, but she seemed willing to condone it on the grounds that they could at least support a large family. She even cashed in more of her stock and made them a loan to buy a house in Mt. Kisco, New York, that was large enough for everyone to fit. Assured that there would also be a room "for her old age," she chose to remain in Tucson and kept in touch through a ritual phone call every Sunday night. After selling Willowlake in 1946, she did spend some time each summer at Grant's house on Fishers Island in Long Island Sound, but generally showed up with the intention of staying a month and then found some reason to leave early, though never without first playing endless card games, where she endeared herself to the children by letting them cheat and pretending she didn't notice.

It was Stuart who remained in Tucson, built himself a successful practice in internal medicine, and wound up taking care of his mother. He and Barbara built a house on a piece of property just several blocks away from hers, which Noah had wisely purchased before his death. They saw each other every Sunday for lunch, and became devoted fans of the dishes prepared by Margaret's Mexican help. Sometimes Margaret did the cooking herself, experimenting with exotic cuisines like Indian curries, which the children did not always appreciate. But she redeemed herself afterward by having them stage an elaborate play of their own invention, complete with costumes and props gathered from her many travels all over the world. She was always the director, and children from all over the neighborhood participated, with their parents gathered in her living room to watch.[13]

Beyond family, Margaret was drawn during these years to a circle of artistically inclined refugees from the East, who like her had settled in Tucson because of its natural beauty and easy climate. Leighton and Catherine Rollins, two carefree retirees from Massachusetts, became favorite friends whose small theatrical ventures she helped finance in what would become a careless pattern of generosity to favorite companions and causes that Stuart and Barbara found especially unsettling. Through them and Dorothy McNamee, the owner of a local bookstore, she also met a young and commercially successful landscape painter by the name of Hobson Pittman. Though twenty-one years younger than she, Pittman was attracted by what he once called Margaret's "exuberant gaiety," and they began a casual love affair that lasted for six years and included many romantic weekends back East and trips to Europe. Pittman was witty, charming, and childishly devoted, and much to the chagrin of friends who were shocked by the disparity of age, Margaret kept up the relationship. Surviving letters profess a lighthearted love, but never anything too serious. There is one confession to Dorothy Brush that Hobson was fun to know, "but not for keeps." Another to Anne Kennedy, who'd remained a loyal correspondent since the early days at the American Birth Control League, confesses that, although some sort of "permanent companionship" might be possible, it was hardly worth the press it would invite. Brush, who had left her second husband, Alexander Dick, and was torturing herself over a married man, marveled at the ease with which Margaret began and ended affairs, and the freedom she extended to all of her lovers.

The two unattached women traveled extensively together during these years. They spent one long winter holiday together in Tucson, another in Haiti, and vacationed during the summer at Dorothy's ocean-front estate in Bridgehampton, New York, where they were sometimes joined by Juliet Rublee.

"They said that David & Jonathan had a love 'passing the love of women,' " Dorothy wrote Margaret after one such expedition. "Well I love you passing the love of men, I really do . . . no one has ever understood me as well as you do, or been as dear & patient & kind & considerate & thoughtful." Margaret's affections were no less genuine, but the friendship became even more valuable to her when Dorothy's easy access to money financed one last venture for birth control.[14]

* * *

Eager to be back in the public eye, Margaret had hosted a well-publicized cocktail reception for Eleanor Roosevelt when the former First Lady visited Tucson in March of 1946. Two months later, she was back in the papers again when she made a two-week cross-country tour of family planning clinics. Despite the favorable press, the trip left her despondent over the inadequacies of the diaphragm regimen. Millions of women were still in need of what she identified with great prescience, in a letter to Robert Dickinson, as a "birth control pill." Convinced that Planned Parenthood, more than ever before, was reaching only the middle classes, she rallied a group of supporters to petition the national organization's board to endow a fund that would be maintained for the sole purpose of research into simpler and cheaper methods.

Seasoned old-timers like Dickinson and Clarence Gamble shared her concern and echoed her cry, but they too had vastly reduced the scale of their own birth control activities during the war and enjoyed little credibility with the younger professionals at the organization's helm in New York, who were pressed for money just to maintain the status quo and, for the time being at least, advocated only token action on any new initiatives. Several years later, Planned Parenthood would enlist the National Research Council as a credible scientific sponsor of contraceptive research in the hope of raising funds from foundations unwilling to support mere activists, but the project would never get off the ground.[15]

Finding little reward in fighting the bureaucracy in New York, Margaret decided to take herself abroad, where opportunities for fresh approaches seemed more promising. She left for Europe in August of 1946, with Dorothy and Abraham Stone in tow, the occasion being a family planning conference convened in Stockholm by Elise Ottesen-Jensen, the Swedish pioneer in sex education and contraception, who had been in Zurich in 1930. The assembly called attention to the need for controlled population growth in light of the still precarious state of the postwar economy in Europe and formed a committee to work toward the establishment of a permanent international organization, whose leadership Margaret was not about to cede without a contest. Ottesen-Jensen, the seventeenth child of a Protestant minister, had a reputation as a formidable reformer in her own country, but she was no match for Margaret outside of it.

Stopping in London on her return, Margaret lined up a commitment from Britain's Family Planning Association to sponsor a follow-up meeting at Cheltenham, England. She pledged to cover

$5,000 in organizational costs from the proceeds of the anticipated sale of her large house in Tucson, and then back in New York, wangled a grant of similar dimension out of John D. Rockefeller III, whose philanthropic activities, like his father's, were still being guided by her old friend, Arthur Packard.

"It would be impossible to define Mrs. Sanger's work in this period," Dorothy Brush later remembered. "Almost single-handed, she created this conference, and those that followed, out of nothing but will power. She was unyielding, relentless, and egotistical in a way that was something to behold."[16]

No less important than the Rockefellers' money, Packard used the family's influence to help Margaret assemble a prestigious American delegation to Cheltenham in August of 1948, which included the influential and highly regarded demographers, Frank Lorimer and Pascal Whelpton, both of whom had long bemoaned the nation's declining birthrate and opposed organized birth control. Frank Notestein, the vocal critic of clinics and diaphragms, also lent his name, though in the end he did not attend.

The participation of these men signaled a dramatic shift of focus within their profession. Long preoccupied by the issue of stagnant fertility in the West, they were just turning their attention to a startling increase in population worldwide that had taken place as a result of dramatic wartime advances in the control of famine and epidemic disease. The populations of developing nations such as India were doubling in the space of years, as the conquest of death, especially among infants and children, outpaced the control of birth. A demographic transition that had transpired over the course of a century in the West was occurring in the East in the space of a few years and threatening prospects for economic growth and political stability among peoples newly unleashed from colonial rule and eager to improve their lives. The same demographers who had long argued that birthrates are largely determined by wholesale social and economic forces beyond the control of well-meaning reformers reluctantly began to heed Margaret's prophetic warnings that some kind of intervention was warranted—that even the slightest amelioration of the situation was better than none at all.

Any solutions, however, would have to accommodate a deep suspicion of Western motives, which endured in these countries as the legacy of centuries of colonial dominion. Postwar baby booms in America and Europe also made it especially difficult to counsel population control elsewhere. Margaret, to her credit, did not discriminate between East and West. She advised universal restraint in childbearing and indeed endured the ridicule of just about every newspaper in London, when, during a trip there in 1947, she admonished the British to limit their childbearing until postwar economic reconstruction was complete.

Beyond considerations of geography, race, and class, of course, there were even more intractable philosophical problems to confront. Preoccupied with the relationship of fertility to such abstract factors as migration, industrialization, urbanization, class, and race, most of the men who assumed positions of leadership in the postwar population control movement were not inclined to identify the poor, uneducated, and often unenfranchised peoples of the developing nations of the world as potential agents of change. They were even more baffled by Margaret's continued faith in the power of the contraceptive philosophy to take root among *women*, if only enough money and political support were put behind it. Convinced that few women outside the Western democracies would recognize the potential benefits of reproductive autonomy, they could scarcely conceal their contempt for propaganda that advocated birth control as a solution to the world's economic, social, and sexual ills. Arguing the relative merits of condoms, douches, and diaphragms, moreover, hardly seemed a terribly "manly" endeavor, as one participant in these debates put it. Indeed, the necessary association of contraception and sexuality became a distinct liability. Trapped in a largely self-defeating intellectual conundrum over what to do once reproduction rates were officially computed, even sympathetic advocates of population planning wasted precious years doing very little at all.

The program at Cheltenham's International Congress on Population and World Resources in Relation to the Family examined traditional Neo-Malthusian concerns about the relationship of birthrates and natural resources with an attempt at sensitivity to some of these thorny questions of sociology, religion, and politics. Papers were also presented that surveyed the latest medical research in contraceptive technology. For many of the men attending, however, the credibility of Margaret's program was compromised by the very fervor with which she approached her mission. Still, the conference drew 140 participants from seventeen countries, along with a representative from the newly formed United Nations.

The U.N. ought to have provided a continuing forum for discussion of population concerns, but family planning was quickly shelved from its technical assistance agenda by an unlikely alliance of Catholic and Communist nations opposed respectively on moral and ideological grounds. Committed to resisting American encroachment in the developing Third World, whatever its manifestation, the Communist bloc took the lofty position that family planning was a paltry substitute for full-scale economic justice.

This rapid politicization of the population issue left the field open to voluntary initiatives, and for the moment Margaret received the professional recognition she was long due. Though again she deliberately ceded the chair at Cheltenham to a prominent British physician, this time she did at least officially preside at a session on population trends, gave a conciliatory speech calling for "worldwide cooperation" and hosted a festive party, where the delegates mingled with her surviving British friends, among them Hugh de Selincourt, whom she hadn't seen in years. She was also treating her niece, Virginia Higgins—the one who later married and had so many children—to a first trip abroad, and when all the work of the conference was finally complete, they motored through Shakespeare country with Dorothy Brush and her young daughter, Sylvia, the child of Dorothy's failed second marriage to Alexander Dick.[17]

A decision was reached at Cheltenham to employ a permanent secretary in London who would maintain communications through an International Planned Parenthood Committee. Margaret leaned on Dorothy for another $5,000 from the Brush Foundation to cover the secretary's salary, and from far away in Tucson and New York then tried to press her own priorities on the work of that individual.

The range of viewpoints expressed at Cheltenham raised fundamental questions about what the proper emphasis of any permanent international organization in family planning should be. Inclinations divided, for example, over the relative importance of education and direct service. Was additional propaganda necessary before birth control could be successfully marketed in the developing nations of the world? Was research to find a simpler, cheaper contraceptive the most important priority? Did it make sense to export the traditional clinical approach pioneered in the West, with its female clientele and its emphasis on reproductive health and sexual education?

Frank Lorimer of Princeton, representing established demographic thinking, argued emphatically for rethinking the service delivery formula completely and for isolating contraception from what he perceived to be the complicating and variable factors of gender relations and sexual ethics that vary dramatically from one culture to another. He was firmly against the establishment of freestanding medical clinics, if not yet clear on what an appropriate alternative might be.

In this respect, he incurred the vocal opposition of formidable women in positions of leadership in countries like Holland and England, where voluntary initiatives had successfully paved the way for organized government support of contraception, and where clinics staffed largely by women provided exemplary health care services. Margaret, who had never been successful at making her New York clinic a model for publicly supported facilities, took the middle ground. Arguing that freestanding clinics would be too expensive, she advocated the immediate distribution of simple contraceptive regimens through existing public health channels, wherever they existed. Her thinking at this juncture may also have been governed by a second, strategic consideration. Frank Lorimer had considerable influence with the Rockefeller family, on whom she was counting for financial support.[18]

Without consulting Margaret, in fact, Lorimer in the spring of 1949 approached Arthur Packard of the family's charitable staff about financing the entire annual budget of an international population organization in order to influence its "sound directions." Projecting the costs at a negligible $25,000 a year, he presented a further caveat. He was uncertain of the wisdom of leaving Margaret Sanger in charge. The Planned Parenthood Federation of America had brought in a new president by the name of William Vogt, whose controversial book, *The Road to Survival*, identified the hazards of unrestrained population growth and claimed that if the United States had spent $2 billion developing a contraceptive, instead of the atom bomb, it would have done more for national security and also raised the world's standard of living. In light of all the attention the issue was receiving, the organization had reassessed its previous decision to concentrate resources at home. Lorimer thought it should take control of any international initiative.

Several months later, however, Margaret paid a visit of her own to Packard and expressed a predictably different view. She told him that the change of heart at Planned Parenthood had done little to renew her confidence in its leadership, and complained bitterly of Vogt's reasonable-enough request that the organization take 15 percent of all international revenues as the price of its supervision. She instead proposed a series of swift, and allegedly more cost-effective, actions she would herself oversee, including the convening of a second international conference in India, where the Nehru government, despite its Socialist leanings, had expressed interest in population programs and could probably be counted on for support. She also left Packard with a copy of a letter from Shidzue Kato (Ishimoto), who had achieved renewed prominence as one of the first women elected to the postwar parliament in Japan in 1946, and was already advancing population planning there.

Margaret had long been a favorite of Packard's. "Mrs. Sanger recognizes the crucial nature of population problems in the world today and is trying to carve out some kind of instrumentality that will get at things in a broader and more timely way than the rather grooved, rather beaten paths which characterize the present scene. This is characteristic of her pioneer spirit and social vision," he wrote in a file memorandum following her visit. Disturbed by her unusually frank and carping complaints about various professional colleagues and circumstances on this occasion, however, he also made a second observation: "Mrs. Sanger is perhaps losing her ability to enlist the cooperation, support and collaboration of key people at the policy level," he noted, all but auguring a future in which there would be less and less mainstream support for her endeavors.[19]

Several days before this meeting in New York, Margaret had attended commencement ceremonies at Smith College, where she received an honorary doctorate of laws. This was a milestone of great significance to her, and she wrote enthusiastically to Hugh with the news, coyly demanding that he pay her an appropriate respect now that she finally had a proper academic credential. Other colleges had declined to honor her in the past for fear of antagonizing constituents opposed to birth control, but Dorothy Brush, a Smith alumna, had intervened with the trustees there and then lined up distinguished friends all over the world to write on Margaret's behalf. Dorothy's deft pen was also evident in the official citation, which identified Margaret as "leader in the world-wide study of population problems and pioneer in the American Birth control movement; author, lecturer, and practical idealist; one who with deep sympathy for the oppressed and disinherited, yet with a dispassionate and scientific approach, has made a conspicuous contribution to human welfare through her integrity, courage and social vision."

Never one to shy away from accolades, Margaret may have been especially hungry for recognition at this time of profound personal transition in her life. She had finally sold the big Elm Street house in Tucson that she had shared with Noah and had also just given up their apartment in New York. Willowlake, of course, had long been passed on, and feeling very much uprooted, she saw Packard and left the city immediately to stay at Juliet and George Rublee's country house in the mountains of New Hampshire for several weeks, before returning to Tucson to pack up her belongings there and prepare to move.[20]

She was building herself a new and more manageable house on the empty lot she owned on Sierra Vista Drive next door to Stuart and Barbara. With characteristic zest, she had immersed herself wholly in the project, enrolling in a correspondence course in interior design and also traveling up to Scottsdale to consult with her reputable friend, Frank Lloyd Wright, before choosing a local architect. The innovative modern structure she planned could not have been more distinct from the Spanish style typical of residential construction in the Southwest at the time. Eccentric and yet pleasantly harmonious in form, the house is shaped like a fan, with a roof that slopes downward from expansive, interior windows and sliding doors that open to a rear terrace and yard. From almost any point inside, there is a tranquil vista of the mountains in the distance.

It was scheduled for completion in October of 1949, a gift Margaret may have intended to mark the milestone of her seventieth birthday, though, of course, she was admitting publicly to a more respectable age. Even for a woman of less vanity, turning seventy would have been an event of some consequence, but to make matters considerably worse, Margaret was suddenly confronted by unexpected illness. While overextending herself in the heat of the Tucson summer, she suffered a heart attack and found herself in a local hospital for two months, denied all contacts beyond the medical staff and her family.

The unexpected confrontation with death was a sobering experience, but she tried at first to take it in good humor: "There is no organ of the body that gives one pause like a heart attack. Just one little beat too few & out you go," she confided to Françoise Cyon in England, when she was finally feeling a little better. "But modern medical research has done miracles & I am no longer suspect to clotting and thrombosis & that's a relief."

From back in New York, however, Dorothy Brush offered a different prognosis. "You are 3/4 spirit & only 1/4 body, & keeping your spirits high will be the most important part of your cure," she wrote with exceptional clairvoyance. For even as Margaret slowly recuperated—even as she defiantly insisted on returning to work—she never fully recovered that indomitable spirit. During the remaining decade of her active, public life, she would essentially live on borrowed time, age and illness magnifying her eccentricities and compromising her effectiveness.[21]

CHAPTER TWENTY

Last Act

While convalescing in the fall of 1949, Margaret received a letter from a Pennsylvania journalist writing a feature story on how to handle life over sixty-five. She advised him to keep caring for a cause so much that you have little time to think of your own complaints. "All of life," she told him, "you must have a vital interest in something outside yourself."

Just as soon as the doctors would permit, she traveled to Chicago for a luncheon celebrating birth control pioneers; her speech was broadcast on national radio and received extensive newspaper attention, including an editorial in the *Washington Post* written by Agnes Meyer, the wife of the publisher and an old supporter and friend. Christmas was spent with Grant and his children, but easily exhausted, Margaret was home in Tucson by the new year. Comfortably settled in her new surroundings, she sent greetings to Hugh in London, reporting rhapsodically of the simple beauty of her sunshine-filled yard—with its lawn opening up to Stuart's pool next door—and the rose-copper hues shining off the distant mountains at sunset.

Yet this was a time of intense personal reckoning. Having brushed death so closely, she was gathering together the private correspondence and papers she would so carefully deposit in the archives at Smith College, and "veins of sadness," as she told Hugh, were opened by the exchange of old letters, filled with memories that "dim slowly."[1]

There were professional accounts to tally as well. For years she had remained nominally at the helm of the Margaret Sanger Research Bureau in New York, which continued to function as an independent not-for-profit facility, loosely affiliated with the Planned Parenthood Federation of America. Following the tragic and unexpected loss of Hannah Stone from a heart attack in 1941, Drs. Abraham Stone and Lena Levine had taken charge under the increasingly lax administration of a voluntary board of managers, which for a time included Grant Sanger, though his interest was always tepid. Margaret kept a distant watch over expenditures and policies through a regular correspondence with her personally loyal and devoted executive secretary, Mary Compton.

The clinic's volume of business remained steady during the war and immediately thereafter, but the nature of its clientele changed, with greater numbers of women, many of them unmarried, coming to have a diaphragm fitted and then never returning. It was difficult to predict income under such circumstances, and for several years, Margaret covered operating deficits and awarded bonuses to staff, by drawing on her own capital.

Without a substantial repeat clientele, the research objectives of the organization also suffered. It continued as a laboratory for testing new products—a plastic diaphragm to replace the latex variety, when rubber was scarce during the war, and simple remedies for mass marketing, such as tampons soaked in varieties of ordinary household spermacides. But technological advances of greater consequence would have required more substantial resources than Margaret could muster in these years. There was no progress, for example, on a biological solution to the problem of contraception—on a "spermatoxin," as she referred to it, using old-fashioned terminology. She corresponded extensively on the subject with clinic board member Stuart Mudd, M.D., of the University of Pennsylvania, whose own unavailing research in this field she did support with several grants. The single innovation of the clinic remained the diaphragm and jelly, and a landmark study of fertility in Indianapolis, Indiana, during the 1940s demonstrated that even it was beginning to lose the small market share it had enjoyed.

In fact, from a purely scientific standpoint, the Sanger clinic during these years made its greatest contributions to the treatment of problems of infertility, not to contraceptive research. Abraham Stone and Lena Levine were pioneers in sterility research and in artificial insemination, and with the postwar baby boom creating demand, they began to emphasize this speciality. At its peak, the service recorded nearly 7,000 patient visits per year, many of them referred by their own doctors after an article reporting substantial rates of success. From far away in Tucson, Margaret disputed the growing emphasis on fertility and marriage counseling at the expense of contraception and haggled over the myriad complications of maintaining the building on West 16th Street in which the clinic was housed. Though the records are unclear, there also appear to have been bureau accounts into which royalties from her books, articles, and lectures were paid, accounts on which, she, in turn, drew for some personal expenses. The determination of what was properly hers, and what was not, became an increasing problem, and she finally proposed that Dr. Stone and a group of friends purchase the outstanding mortgages of $23,350 on the handsome brownstone, thereby releasing her of all responsibilities and obligations. Working out the details of this arrangement took almost a year.[2]

During a summer vacation with Stuart's family in northern Arizona in the 1950s, Margaret then suffered a second heart attack and was returned to the hospital in Tucson. Following another prolonged convalescence, she emerged with a permanent, disabling case of angina, which caused episodic but extremely intense outbursts of chest pain brought on by the restricted flow of blood to her heart through clogged arteries. Corrective bypass surgery, which is commonplace today, was not yet standard medical practice, and she found herself uncharacteristically depressed, her anxiety about her health intensified by concern over the adequacy of her financial resources in the event of a protracted illness. The pyramiding expenses of doctors and nurses, along with other living costs and higher taxes, were taking a toll on her already diminished capital.

Loyal friends in New York tried to cheer her up by placing her name in circulation for the Nobel Peace Prize, an honor she had long sought and one not uncommonly connected with the intensity of the promotional effort launched in a nominee's behalf. In 1931, the reformer Jane Addams had received the award for her work with the International League for Peace and Freedom, and Margaret's efforts on behalf of birth control and world population seemed no less worthy of recognition. Periodic campaigns would be mounted for ten years but would never generate more than occasional letters of interest from various members of the prize committee.

As something of a consolation, Mary Lasker insisted in the fall of 1950 that Planned Parenthood present Margaret with the prize she and her husband had established to recognize pioneering work in family planning, much as the prestigous Lasker prize in medicine honored important research on disease. Margaret was far too weak to come East to accept the award, but Grant delivered her speech in her behalf.

It was not his mother's finest moment. Margaret's standard remarks in these years painted a sentimental, historical portrait of the birth control movement, emphasizing her own early heroism. But, on this occasion, she added a coarse note to her assessment of what had been accomplished by lampooning costly government welfare programs for their failure to weed out the "feebleminded and unfit," terms that were very much out of fashion following the tragic revelations of a decade of Nazi-inspired eugenic terror. Margaret proposed the idea that Planned Parenthood promote a program of "bonus" or "incentive" sterilization, calling on the federal government to guarantee a lifetime pension to any couple of "defective heredity" who would agree to the procedure. Pioneering research was just underway on the contraceptive effectiveness and safety of simple methods of tubal ligation, but sterilization still carried the stigma of coercion, and a new generation of leadership at Planned Parenthood wanted no association whatsoever with this dark legacy. Until the 1970s, Planned Parenthood would cautiously refrain from endorsing sterilization even under voluntary circumstances, and by then its use was already widespread among married American couples. Margaret's enthusiasm for the procedure, coupled with an uncharacteristic carping about the costs of social welfare, eroded her credibility with younger reformers. She sounded like the American Birth Control League ladies she had once deplored, and she never mentioned the idea again.

She was clearly losing patience altogether—for cautious bureaucrats unwilling to let her have her way, for individuals incapable of making responsible reproductive choices on their own. Her increasingly impulsive judgments may also have been the consequence of a tragic regimen of drugs and alcohol on which she began to rely more and more to diminish her pain and lift her spirits. To his subsequent regret, Stuart Sanger unwittingly prescribed a painkiller called Demerol for his mother, and she became dependent on it to the point of addiction. The drug was not always incapacitating or even apparent to most outsiders, but after a time, its ebbs and flows through her bloodstream would cause convulsions, sweating, and violent mood swings.[3]

Indeed, Margaret's disposition deteriorated not only under the influence of the drug but beneath the weight of news she was hearing from friends all over the world. Hugh de Selincourt died in London in 1951, followed by Bessie Drysdale and then Robert Dickinson in New York and Kit Hepburn in Hartford. Ethel Byrne suffered a heart attack at Truro, and Edith How-Martyn, a stroke in Australia. With her own husband dying in New Hampshire, Juliet Rublee, frantic as ever, warned Margaret that the secret of long life is in recognizing the importance of the magic word of "moderation" in all activities. "Happiness is the great thing. Enjoying things brings & keeps youth and beauty," she wrote. She encouraged Margaret to defy her illness through communication with "the cosmic forces," as the two women referred to them.

Margaret took the advice and enrolled in a Rosicrucian mail-order course in self-realization, complete with daily exercises intended to help her acquire "spiritual insight and first-hand spiritual experience." This regimen may well have sustained her by providing justification for her conviction that she would not yet die, as so many of her friends were doing, because she embodied the aspirations of all women on earth, and as their chosen agent of liberation, still had important work left to do in spreading the message and technology of contraception. Just as Anne Higgins had so long ago triumphed over adversity through the redeeming power of faith—just as she herself had once been rescued from the grief of Peggy's death with Rosicrucian homilies—so she now determined to try to make mind triumph over matter by reconsecrating her historic social mission and special destiny. A measure of her increasing self-absorption can be found in a letter she wrote to Ethel at this time requesting that her sister agree to a movie treatment being developed by a group of women in Hollywood. The proposed script would obliterate the dramatic role Ethel had played in the events surrounding the historic Brownsville Clinic trial and instead portray Margaret as the valiant hunger striker of 1916, an alteration allegedly necessary to give the plot dramatic unity. Ethel, bemused, ignored the request, and the movie project never got off the ground.

It was perhaps only the delusions of another old friend that helped lift Margaret, at least partially, out of her own. Since the death of

Havelock Ellis, Françoise Cyon had been living almost totally in the past. *Friendship's Odyssey*, an elegiac 1946 memoir of her life with Ellis, had totally repudiated the Wantley circle and especially condemned Hugh de Selincourt for his sexual excesses, causing him considerable anguish. The distant and complicated relationship was nonetheless still on her mind when Hugh died, and she wrote to Margaret of her hopes that he and Ellis might reconcile their differences "on the other side." Margaret had no patience whatsoever for this kind of remorse. As soon as she felt better during the summer of 1951, she decided to make a trip to London, where she occupied herself with meetings and paid a condolence call on Hugh's widow and daughter, but never even told Françoise she was in town.[4]

Little had become of the International Committee on Planned Parenthood during Margaret's long illness and absence. Scarcely any new funds had been raised or programs initiated, and Frank Lorimer, who might have lent the group credibility, had resigned. Yet, indigenous activities by family planning organizations in some twenty-five countries indicated the need of an independent coordinating body to serve as clearinghouse for information and education. The Indian government, in particular, was looking for family planning aid from abroad and under the auspices of the World Health Organization had hired Abraham Stone as a consultant to lay the groundwork for further technical assistance. To much fanfare, Stone designed a string of beads for Indian women, with colors denoting days of fertility and infertility between menstrual cycles. The simple device for observing the rhythm method was tested in clinics but met with little success. Stone meekly defended the expediency of his work to Margaret—predicting that only some simple biological method, preferably an oral one, would answer India's pressing needs—but she strongly repudiated his endorsement of the single contraceptive remedy approved by the Vatican. Absent a coherent family planning strategy, the Nehru goverment instead made economic development its priority, in the vain hope that modernization would somehow lower the birthrate.

Meanwhile in London, Margaret contributed her Lasker prize money to keep the international committee temporarily afloat and then secured another $10,000 from the Brush Foundation for a newsletter, which Dorothy Brush agreed to edit. Within two years, the publication would reach 13,000 government officials, civic leaders, and physicians in thirty countries around the world. Margaret also drummed up the money for another international conference in Bombay from G. J. Watumull, an Indian businessman in Los Angeles and Honolulu, who had created a foundation to reinvest in his native land some of the fortune he'd made in America.

That she was feeling much better for the moment is plainly evident from her report on a brief side trip to Paris for an interview with Eugene Cardinal Tisserant, a Frenchman, which was arranged by her old friend Angus MacDonald. By Margaret's telling, the allegedly progressive church official, though cordial, refused to concede that population growth was an international problem of any significance and insisted that all carnal relations between men and women should bear their accompanying burden of pain. In response, she took great pleasure in unleashing an unexpurgated version of her rather more dionysian sexual philosophy on him.[5]

Back in the United States, with at least a fraction of her old energy restored, Margaret drove her old friend Mary Beard up to Scottsdale for a weekend with Frank Lloyd Wright, and later reported bemusedly to their mutual friend, Dorothy Brush, that Beard, though dowdily dressed and far too talkative, was delighted by the visit. Margaret then spent the better part of a year preparing for the Indian conference. From sun-filled terraces in Tucson and by the sea in Santa Barbara, she corresponded with volunteers in London, New York, Washington, Los Angeles, Honolulu, Tokyo, and Bombay, all of whom had agreed to share responsibility for various aspects of the event. Out of the inevitable confusion and chaos, a program was finally agreed upon, lists of delegates and sponsors assembled, and small travel grants secured from foundations and individuals.

Scarcely a detail escaped Margaret's scrutiny. John D. Rockefeller, Jr., and his second wife, Martha, were vacationing at the Arizona Inn, so she invited them to tea and secured a token $7,500 contribution to pay the expenses of several American participants. She then reveled in securing an endorsement of the conference from Albert Einstein. "There is a school of thought, especially on the extreme Left, which holds that the fight against overpopulation can be waged successfully only by economic and technical help and not by a direct attempt to influence and educate people," wrote the gentle physicist whose theoretical insights had so dramatically changed the course of world affairs. "I am, however, fully convinced that this attitude is dangerously one-sided. It does completely neglect the fact that progress of hygiene and medicine has completely altered the earlier precarious equilibrium of the quantitative stability of the human race." Margaret gamely asked for permission to reproduce the quote in full. Yet, she was not just interested in assembling big names. She insisted on vetting the group. From a list of proposed delegates, she deleted the celebrated anthropologist Margaret Mead, claiming that in the early years, when Mead was climbing to fame, she had done nothing at all for birth control but "scoffed and giggled like an adolescent over the subject."[6]

Margaret's itinerary for October of 1952 routed her via ship from Los Angeles to Honolulu, where she arranged final details for the Bombay conference with G. J. Watumull and his American-born wife, Ellen. She then departed for an emotional return to Japan. Seven years earlier, following the war's end, she had written to Gen. Douglas MacArthur, commander of the Allied Occupation forces, in the hope of acquainting him with Shidzue Ishimoto and the history of birth control's suppression there. Her letter proposed that MacArthur establish a commission on the country's population pressures, but it received no response.

Ishimoto had spent much of the war in jail for espousing Socialist and pacifist doctrines in defiance of government policy. She'd finally divorced her husband and lost her one surviving son in battle, but her personal life was renewed when she met and married Kanju Kato, a fellow political detainee, who became a leader of Japan's postwar labor movement. In 1947, at the age of forty-eight, she gave birth to a daughter named Taki and wrote to Margaret that she hoped the baby would reincarnate the spirit of her own long-lost little Peggy.[7]

The Katos were also prominent in the Socialist majority that came to power in Japan in 1946 and worked closely with the American occupation forces on an anti-Communist agenda of social and economic reform. Among their many concerns was the need for a state-supported family planning policy. Postwar Japan, like the United States and Europe, experienced a tremendous baby boom when its soldiers returned home, while, at the same time, its women were granted many social and political benefits they had long been denied, including the right to vote, to hold public office, and to organize in labor unions, circumstances that facilitated the election of Mrs. Kato to parliament. Faced on the one hand with an expansion of opportunity, and on the other, with widespread unemployment and housing shortages that made large families a burden, Japanese women quickly sought to control their fertility. With a density of population more than ten times that of the United States, and with reliable contraception in short supply, rates of illegal abortion increased to alarming proportions, and Japan became the first country in the world to legalize abortion and sterilization, in an effort to promote greater safety in the use of these procedures.

The high incidence of abortion was so disturbing that Mrs. Kato encouraged Margaret to tour Japan in order to arouse interest in preventive birth control measures. General MacArthur, however, was particularly sensitive to the issue, for fear that any appearance of interest by the Americans in controlling Japanese fertility would be misunderstood. Arrangements were made for the publishers of Tokyo's largest newspapers to extend a formal invitation to Margaret, so there could be no doubt of her sponsorship, but on August 30, 1949, word was received from a ranking member of General MacArthur's staff that, despite this gesture, military clearance for Mrs. Sanger would be denied.

The incident provoked front-page newspaper coverage in both countries, and a column of protest from Eleanor Roosevelt. Long letters of dissent followed, but MacArthur held firm and was widely quoted as saying that birth control was a matter for the Japanese people to decide themselves. He later claimed in a letter to Charles Scribner, then chairman of the board of Planned Parenthood in America, that any interference by the Occupation might be viewed as "genocide," and rather contemptuously advised American birth control activists to concentrate their energies at home in Massachusetts, instead, where birth control activity was still illegal. Years later, however, Mrs. Kato took a less benign view of the general's motives, insisting that MacArthur overemphasized the issue of coercion in response to Catholic pressures and out of concern for his own Presidential ambitions in the United States.[8]

Prevented from traveling to Japan, Margaret defiantly raised funds in the United States to help her friend open several birth control clinics there. She also made arrangements for Clarence Gamble to oversee a field trial with simple contraceptives in a rural district. When American jurisdiction finally ended late in 1951, however, she was determined to make her long-anticipated trip and waited anxiously as her efforts to secure a visa were delayed while intelligence agents conducted an extensive security check, once again assembling the same old long list of her allegedly incriminating associations with Communist, Socialist, and civil libertarian causes. The file was sent off to U.S. Army and Navy officials in Japan, but there is no record of any follow-up.

Margaret's triumphant return featured a welcome in Yokohama from a group of fifty women in ceremonial kimonos bearing a wreath of golden chrysanthemums, which received widespread press coverage. The Sanger party then met with representatives from the government and the press, held round-table discussions for radio broadcast in Japanese and over the Voice of America, and visited birth control clinics established at a village school some miles outside the central city and at a welfare center in Yokohama. An automobile tour of several Tokyo slum districts drew hundreds of people out of their homes as sound trucks bellowed out the Sanger name, with its eponymous reference to "birth control" in Japanese. Notes in Margaret's handwriting for a speech from this trip make a strong plea for the benefits of birth control over abortion and also challenge the Japanese people, whom Margaret so greatly admired, to turn their backs on war. "You have a tremendous opportunity to apply your ancient wisdom, your strength of mind and body to the problems of 20th century Japan," she wrote, "and you may be a new force, guiding and strengthening the community of nations."[9]

Though comfortably housed at Frank Lloyd Wright's luxurious Imperial Hotel, which had only recently been vacated by the Occupation forces, Margaret was understandably exhausted by this schedule. From Japan, she then took what was still an adventurous and strenuous flight by passenger plane to Bombay. Just the last leg of the trip alone, from Ceylon to Bombay, took more than half a day of flying time. During stopovers in Hong Kong, Bangkok, Singapore, and on the tranquil island of Ceylon, she and a party that included Abraham Stone, Edna Rankin McKinnon, and her sister, the Congresswoman, conducted preliminary meetings with local officials interested in birth control.

The Family Planning Association of India, a voluntary association, officially hosted the Bombay conference under the able, if imperious, direction of Dhanvanthi Rama Rau, a past president of the All India Women's Association and wife of a local Brahman banker who had served as India's first ambassador to the United States. Prime Minister Nehru did not attend but did send his vice-president to deliver an inaugural address firmly establishing the government's endorsement of population control but offering no new financial support. Margaret and several other dignitaries dined at the Prime Minister's residence, and the conference delegation of some 500 individuals from more than a dozen countries was, in turn, entertained by the mayor of Bombay and other municipal officials. The government was already providing birth control services through some 106 clinics organized as part of a publicly funded maternal and infant care program, and Margaret was especially pleased to present a $2,500 check collected by friends in Tucson to fund one additional facility. She was also the conduit for small grants for clinic services from Clarence Gamble, the Watumulls, and her old friends at Ortho Pharmaceuticals, but this hardly made a dent in the need.

The historic significance of securing official government participation at Bombay cannot be underestimated, but absent comparable initiatives elsewhere, international family planning advocacy had no choice but to remain for the time being a voluntary enterprise. As a result, the International Planned Parenthood Federation was officially chartered at Bombay in order to unite the handful of autonomous family planning associations already at work in their respective countries. As a symbolic bridge between East and West, Lady Rama Rau and Margaret were together designated as honorary chairmen, and plans were laid for subsequent meetings in Sweden and Japan.[10]

At the urging of Iphigene Sulzburger, the formidable wife and mother of the publishers of *The New York Times* and a longtime admirer of Margaret's, the proceedings at Bombay received front-page coverage in America's newspaper of record, making it one of the first major stories to call attention to the world population problem. Margaret's efforts to stimulate further interest in her new organization, however, were soon complicated by the endeavors of John D. Rockefeller III, who had also just returned from a trip to Asia convinced that the world's future political and economic stability would depend on controlling its population—that population control would have to precede economic development and not the other way around. Wary of the controversy surrounding American birth control propagandists, however, he cautiously charted an independent course.

The Rockefeller Foundation, where his family had consolidated much, though by no means all, of its charitable giving, seemed the logical place to launch a population undertaking. The foundation was at this time concentrating its resources on international initiatives in public health and agricultural reform, and there was good reason to worry about the potentially extreme demographic consequences of such an agenda. J.D.R. III was the only one of the five Rockefeller brothers who served on the foundation board, but as a man of gentle and courteous demeanor, he refused to impose his priorities on officials there who were reluctant to compromise existing programs by spending money on new ones that few believed would work, in any event. They also feared that support for population control, even if handled with caution, would provoke opposition in countries with a strong Catholic influence where the foundation had already invested. The latter consideration raised an even more personal one. Nelson Rockefeller was sowing the seeds of a career in politics and needed to be protected from the potential sanction of Catholics at home.

Hoping to tred lightly, J.D.R. III asked the National Academy of Sciences, a research organization with which his family's charitable enterprises had long been associated, to sponsor a private meeting in Williamsburg, Virginia, where a group of distinguished individuals might quietly consider the international population issue. The list of invitees included demographers, such as Frank Notestein and Frederick Osborn, along with scholars in the related fields of public health, economics, anthropology, and sociology from the nation's most prestigious think-tanks and universities—men like Robert Merton, the Columbia sociologist, George Corner, the Johns Hopkins embryologist, and Thomas Parran, the former surgeon general. All were white and male, until someone added the names of two women to a second solicitation, a Dr. Dorothy Swaine Thomas of Philadelphia and Irene Tauber of Princeton's Office of Population Research.

The discussion at Williamsburg reflected the underlying suspicion of professional students of the subject about the merits of organized birth control intervention, though Kingsley Davis, then a young and relatively unknown sociologist doing work on India at Columbia, did stress the important contribution that educated elites had made in calling attention to the problem and in conducting basic research. No mention by name was made of Margaret Sanger, however, nor of her activities in America or abroad. William Vogt of Planned Parenthood, who had also been included at the last minute and was the only participant at Williamsburg with practical experience, argued that the incorporation of contraception into publicly assisted maternal health programs was at least worth a try, but even this modest proposal received no endorsement from the assembled group, most of whom believed that expenditures on Western-style family planning programs would be worthless.[11]

The Williamsburg conference nonetheless resolved to establish a permanent organization to address the population question "at a high level of professional competence and public esteem," and following a year's worth of continued discussion, the Population Council, Inc., was founded, with research and education as its stated purposes. The demographer and former U.S. Army official, Frederick Osborn, moved over from the United Nations to take charge under the direction of a board that included Rockefeller, Notestein, Parran, and other notables from government and academia who would give the population issue substantial credibility. Since this was to be a mobilization of professionals in fields where few women were represented, there were none on the board, nor on any of its advisory committees, though one, an assistant treasurer, did serve on the administrative staff. Nor was any sensitivity apparent at this juncture to the fact that no non-Westerners, and no people of color, were included in the decision making.

A few of the participants were privately skeptical. Marshall Balfour, formerly a regional director for the Rockefeller Foundation in the Far East, worried that the objectives of the new organization were too grandiose and—perhaps aware of the restraints on Rockefeller family giving—wondered where the money was going to come from. Bill Vogt also questioned the sole emphasis on scholarship, suggesting that "if we are to wait until all the data are in before taking action we shall find human beings piled up like cordwood."

In its first three years, however, the Population Council would authorize close to $400,000 in research grants in demography, and just under $100,000 in medical research, quickly establishing its institutional credibility and quietly laying the basis for subsequent technical assistance and medical research on a far grander scale. Every dollar of this initial support came from J.D.R. III personally, so his brothers could not be implicated, but the total substantially exceeded his entire family's aggregate contribution to birth control efforts during the prior three decades. Family gifts to the domestic and international Planned Parenthood organizations would continue, but only in insignificant amounts.

The first annual report of the Population Council did acknowledge a debt to prior initiatives in population research by the Milbank Memorial Fund, the Scripps Foundation, the National Committee on Maternal Health, and the United Nations, but again no reference of any kind was made to Margaret or to Planned Parenthood. The council would jealously guard its autonomy from "propagandists" on the grounds that only as an avowedly scientific organization, steering clear of controversy and dedicated to the narrow proposition that unchecked population remained an impediment to economic growth, could it hope to make itself eligible for major grants from controversy-shy institutions like the Rockefeller and Ford Foundations.[12]

When Margaret actually learned of Williamsburg—or what she may have thought about the news—is not clear. A passing reference to J.D.R. III in a 1953 letter to Clarence Gamble advises that trying to raise money for international work from him was a waste of time but blames the problem on unsupportive Planned Parenthood officials in New York—perhaps, sadly, proving the wisdom of Arthur Packard's observation that she had lost the capacity to work cooperatively or even to see things clearly. What is clear is that by refusing, for the time being, to fund the International Planned Parenthood Federation, the Rockefeller staff made its weak assessment of the organization's future into a self-fulfilling prophecy. In 1954 and again in the following year, Dana Creel, who succeeded the retired Arthur Packard as the family's principal philanthropic adviser, advised Mr. and Mrs. John D. Rockefeller, Jr., that Margaret's international work would probably never get off the ground and could not be recommended as a good charitable investment, while tactfully reminding them of their son's new competitive venture in the same field. Knowing of the long history of personal relations between Margaret and the senior Rockefellers, however, Creel, after checking with Population Council staff, did authorize a gift of $22,000 to help send delegates to an IPPF conference in Tokyo. It would do no harm, he explained, and would be "a nice thing to do for Mrs. Sanger."[13]

While all this was going on, Margaret was spending much of her time in Tucson, quite literally willing her body to repair itself through her daily courses of spiritual meditation and through intermittent indulgences in just about every health fad then known. She exercised to improve her circulation. She fasted on juice. She explored various diets, including yogurt, wheat germ, and honey, a concoction then just gaining notoriety as health food. She took at least thirty units a day of Vitamin E, and on learning that papayas are particularly rich in restorative substances, she had them shipped directly from Hawaii.

Still, there was plenty to make her heart ache. Her own situation distressed her no more than that of her adored son, Grant, who suddenly found himself overwhelmed by acute depression. Years of ignoring deeply buried anxieties and insecurities had finally caught up as Grant struggled to make a success of his medical practice and to support a large, demanding family. Angry and despairing of the future, he apparently confronted his mother with his problems during vacations they spent together in Tucson in March of 1953, and at Fishers Island in July. There is no record of what exactly transpired between them, but Edwina wrote following his return from Tucson to say that he looked better but "is not anymore cheerful about life in general & the income tax didn't help much."

Long accustomed to tolerating turmoil in Stuart's life, Margaret could simply not find room to accommodate it in her younger son. With characteristic optimism she tried to ensure Grant's happiness by relieving economic stress. She sent checks for the children and for household improvements and helped arrange for a trip of rest and relaxation in Europe, convincing herself that he suffered from no disease that some sightseeing in Spain or golf in Scotland could not cure. Tortured by far more elusive demons, however, Grant abandoned his private surgical practice in Westchester County in 1954 and took a less demanding post as a clinical professor at Columbia University's College of Physicians and Surgeons, where he remained until his retirement in 1976. Edwina inherited some family money, so the children were well provided for. The more significant loss was one of spirit, for like his father before him, Grant never completely recovered the resolve and enthusiasm of his youth.[14]

What his mother couldn't deny, however, she simply kept herself too busy to worry about. Sumiki Kato Ohmori, the stepdaughter of Shidzue Kato, lived with Margaret in Tucson during 1953 and recalls her as warm, genuine, and generous. The two women spent hours together reading *The New York Times* aloud for practice so that Sumiki could improve her English, and they also practiced cooking Western style. Margaret lavished a motherly affection on the young Japanese girl, held numerous parties and receptions in her honor, and paid all her living expenses.[15]

Margaret was also enjoying the flattering attentions of a new biographer. Lawrence Lader, a young Harvard graduate and contributer to *The New Yorker* and *Esquire*, spent parts of the winters of 1953 and 1954 with her in Tucson and Santa Barbara, and though he found her totally absorbed in her own mythology, he couldn't help being swept up by her powerful drive and feeling. She was still quite a handsome woman, by his recollection, very attentive to her hair and her skin, but her most memorable quality, by his telling, was her voice. With her eyes sparkling and her head half-cocked in a characteristic pose, she was able to captivate him for hours at a sitting with intricately woven and often very funny tales of her dramatic past. She also gave him access to many of her papers at the Library of Congress and at Smith.

Lader spent more than two years on his book project, interviewing just about everyone he could find, with the notable exceptions of William Sanger and Ethel Higgins, who both resolutely refused to talk. But having placed herself in the hands of an acolyte, Margaret then found it necessary to disavow the results. *The Margaret Sanger Story and The Fight for Birth Control,* as the book was ploddingly titled, is a reasonably well-researched and documented work, but Margaret had retained the right to edit the final manuscript, and it wound up recapitulating many illusions from her autobiographies and also creating some new ones. She quite clearly used Lader, for example, to correct the slight she had suffered in Havelock Ellis's memoir, and the book leaves the reader with the incorrect, but unmistakably deliberate, impression that Ellis had been the great love of her life, a situation that caused the hapless Françoise Cyon no end of consternation and all but brought an end to the long friendship between the two women. Deeply hurt, Françoise claimed that the book pictured Ellis as "a fool, a parasite and myself as having been handed over your leavings in his affection."

The essential problem with the Lader book, however, is less its factual inaccuracies than its sentimental excess. Dorothy Brush put it best when she accused Lader of enveloping Margaret in "clouds of gush," and Margaret herself disavowed the finished product, admitting candidly at one point that Lader hadn't balanced her finer qualities with her "pigheadedness and stubbornness," while complaining elsewhere that the manuscript was a portrait of "Joan of Arc and Florence Nightingale." Yet never once did she acknowledge her own contribution to these distortions.[16]

Margaret was also preoccupied during these years by a dramatic breakthrough in the field of contraceptive research, for which she was indirectly responsible. Though little progress had been made toward the development of a biological contraceptive, the possibility of immunizing the female body to fertilization with antigens derived from plants remained under investigation. With developments in the fields of endocrinology and steroid chemistry, the pursuit of an artificial agent to inhibit female fertility suddenly began to look more and more promising.

During the 1920s the innovative, Rockefeller-supported Bureau of Social Hygiene had funded a Committee for Research in Problems of Sex, under the sponsorship of the National Research Council. Among its accomplishments was the discovery and isolation of estrogen, the principal hormone secreted within the female ovaries, which is responsible for changes in the uterine lining that permit adaptations necessary for reproduction. Subsequently, scientists at the University of Rochester also identified progesterone, the hormone secreted by the ruptured egg sack of the ovary and later by the placenta, which allows the uterus to accept and maintain the fertilized ovum. The therapeutic applications of hormone extracts to stimulate conception in cases of natural sterility were quickly recognized, but the costs of producing the substances from animals proved prohibitive. By 1943, however, an American chemist working in Mexico, and building upon his earlier research with steroid substances derived from plants, had successfully synthesized progesterone, using the roots of a wild Mexican yam. By this time a Columbia University researcher had also discovered that beyond its applications in sterility cases, the therapeutic administration of steroids can inhibit ovulation by, in effect, tricking the body into a state of pseudo-pregnancy. With this determination, the various scientific principles necessary for the manufacture of synthetic hormonal contraceptives existed. But still missing were the motivation and the money necessary to assemble them in a manner that would safely work for women.[17]

The two came together in 1953 at the Worcester Foundation for Experimental Biology, a nonprofit, tax-exempt corporation in Shrewsbury, Massachusetts, founded by Gregory Goodwin Pincus and Hudson Hoagland. These two intrepid survivors of academic politics and tenure rejection at Harvard had first found their way to nearby Clark University and then, with the backing of a prestigious board of directors, struck out on their own as scientific entrepreneurs. The early success of their enterprise rested on their expertise in steroid research, which was thriving as a result of grants from the federal government, assorted voluntary agencies, and the drug industry. Great interest in steroids had been generated, however, not for the purposes of contraceptive research, but for the alleviation of diseases such as rheumatoid arthritis, which is caused by a malfunction of the adrenal glands.

The Worcester Foundation had lost out in a fierce competition to synthesize cortisone cost-effectively on behalf of its principal benefactor, G. D. Searle & Company, a drug manufacturer in Illinois, which then refused Dr. Pincus's proposal for the development of a hormonal contraceptive. In the interim, however, he had identified two highly motivated women who were prepared to help him in this new venture.

At the urging of Abraham Stone, Margaret first met Gregory Pincus in 1951 and soon thereafter introduced him to Katherine McCormick, an old friend and occasional birth control contributor, whose husband had just died and left a substantial inheritance from the International Harvester Company. The McCormicks had been married since 1904, shortly after Katherine graduated as one of the first two women to receive a degree in science from the Massachusetts Institute of Technology. After showing great promise in the management of his family's business, however, young Stanley McCormick suffered a mental breakdown from which he never recovered, and his wife was forced to find a new focus for her life through her philanthropy. She first heard Margaret speak in Boston in 1917 and then helped her smuggle diaphragms into the United States. In 1927, she also entertained the delegates to the World Population Conference at her lavish château in Geneva.

Trained in biology, McCormick developed a special interest in contraceptive technology and research, but during the many years she corresponded with Margaret about developments in this field, she was also spending a great deal of time and money searching for a cure to her husband's schizophrenia. This inevitably led her to endocrinologists at Harvard who were investigating the possibility that some kind of malfunction of the adrenal cortex might cause the disease by producing a hormonal deficiency, which undermines the body's ability to deal with stress. Quite by coincidence, these Harvard scientists became collaborators of Hudson Hoagland's own clinical research with mentally ill patients at the Worcester State Hospital, though they were never able to develop an effective therapy.[18]

With her husband's death, Katherine McCormick inherited more than $15 million and in the fall of 1950 asked Margaret for advice about how to put it to good use. Margaret immediately suggested that she fund a crash program of $100,000 per year to be distributed to several university laboratories. This was to be handled by a new Committee on Human Reproduction that Planned Parenthood was trying to organize under the auspices of the National Research Council, the same group that subsequently helped get the Population Council started. Complications involving the disposition of her husband's estate delayed her acting on this recommendation, and the council proposal died for lack of funding. But McCormick did send $5,000 for Margaret's international efforts and offered her seaside estate in Santa Barbara as a retreat from which to organize the Bombay conference.

McCormick also made a few small contributions of several thousand dollars to a research fund established by Planned Parenthood in memory of Robert Dickinson. The money was, in turn, contributed to the Worcester Foundation for preliminary investigations in hormonal contraception being conducted by Dr. Pincus and his collaborator, M. C. Chang, an investigator of mammalian reproduction who has since gained international renown. This investment paid off handsomely when early results demonstrated conclusively that injections of progesterone suppressed ovulation in rabbits and that oral administration of the hormone had a 90 percent rate of effectiveness.

"These data demonstrate definitely the contraceptive ovulation-inhibiting activity of an oral progestin, and suggest that with proper dosage and regimen of administration control of ovulation may be effective," Gregory Pincus wrote in a progress report to Planned Parenthood in 1952. The findings did not generate much enthusiasm from William Vogt, however, who never even bothered to communicate them to Katherine McCormick, even though she was financing the work and was clearly in a position to fund an expanded clinical research agenda, if necessary. Privy by then to the Population Council's decision to pursue an exclusive research agenda in demography and biomedicine, Vogt had all but decided to leave research to them and concentrate Planned Parenthood's meager resources on education and clinic organization.[19]

Totally bewildered by Vogt's indifference, Margaret and Katherine McCormick took the situation into their own hands and traveled to Shrewsbury in June of 1953 for a historic meeting with Dr. Pincus, where McCormick immediately promised $10,000, a commitment that would grow exponentially within a year. Vogt, who had never even bothered to visit the Worcester facility, insisted that they were wasting their money and particularly disparaged a $50,000 commitment toward the construction of an expanded animal testing facility. Seriously misjudging McCormick's single-mindedness when she subsequently came to see him in New York, he asked her for money to expand his administrative offices without ever fully explaining his revised priorities. The entire situation, as she described it to Margaret, was "vague and puzzling—really mystifying."

McCormick returned to her home in Boston and made the Worcester Foundation the focus of her life until she died at the age of ninety-two in 1967, while awaiting the dedication of a women's dormitory she had also contributed to MIT. By that time, she'd given Pincus and his colleagues more than $2 million and left them another $1 million in her will. Until the marketing of the first anovulant birth control pill, she would channel a token amount of that money through Planned Parenthood as a tribute to Margaret, who reluctantly conceded that the organization's name might lend credibility to the project despite her utter contempt for its leadership.[20]

With Mrs. McCormick's support, Dr. Pincus set Dr. Chang to work with his newly housed rabbits and rats, testing hundreds of different steroid compounds prepared by chemists in the laboratories of G. D. Searle, which became the only participant in the project to benefit financially when it patented the formula that proved most effective as Enovid, its first oral contraceptive. At the same time, Pincus moved quickly to initiate human testing under the auspices of John Rock, M.D., a senior Harvard professor in gynecology and obstetrics, with whom he was already collaborating on sterility research. At Pincus's suggestion, Rock tried out a twenty-day cycle of progesterone, interrupted to allow for menstruation, on a small group of highly motivated, middle-class women in his sterility practice at the Lying-In Hospital in Brookline. It quickly became clear that the regimen inhibited ovulation while in regular use, and when terminated, actually increased the likelihood of conception, providing a potential benefit in cases of sterility. Dosages were gradually lowered to decrease such side effects as nausea and tenderness of the breast, and a fortuitous accident then all but eliminated a third problem of breakthrough bleeding. Laboratory contamination of a batch of the substance with a small amount of estrogen suggested the advisability of combining the two hormones, and the essential compound that Searle would eventually market, and others would copy, was considered ready for mass testing.

McCormick would involve herself in virtually every stage of Dr. Rock's clinical investigations, defending him all the while to Margaret, who at first objected to his participation in the effort, because, despite his demonstrated interest in contraception, Rock was a practicing Catholic. Dr. Rock, however, attempted to reconcile his scientific and religious beliefs by arguing that a pill created from synthetic hormones inhibiting ovulation would provide no less "natural" than periodic continence, and while the Vatican would never accept this rationale, he became an important salesman for the pill and even earned Margaret's confidence. "Being a good R.C. and as handsome as a god," she would later admit to Martha Rockefeller, "he can just about get away with anything."

Margaret's concern about Rock also reflected her sentimental investment in the reputation of the Margaret Sanger Clinic as a first-class research facility. She insisted that clinical testing be conducted there as well and even cajoled McCormick into paying for it. Outside of a few women in the clinic's sterility service, however, Abraham

Stone was never able to come up with substantial numbers willing to cooperate, although his 1956 report on a negligible sample of thirteen did confirm Rock's optimistic conclusions.

Finding women with the motivation, time, and tenacity to participate in the testing of an oral contraceptive was not easy. The procedure involved frequent temperature and urine analysis, vaginal smears, and of course the risks and side effects of taking an experimental medication. Pincus and Rock also used a small group of mental patients in Worcester, a standard practice of this era before the research exposés of the following decade, but McCormick's impatience for a foolproof survey was already apparent in 1955 when she demanded of Margaret: "How can we get a 'cage' of ovulating females to experiment with?" [21]

So confident were the two women of the pill's revolutionary consequences that they seemed positively immune to any objection to it whatsoever and interpreted reasonable concerns about the liabilities of experimenting with so potent a drug as just one more round in the arsenal of opposition that birth control advocates had confronted for years. Had she been younger, McCormick acknowledged at one point, she would have happily participated in the research herself.

When official announcement of the historic scientific breakthrough came in a 1956 article in the magazine *Science*, Margaret dashed off a note to McCormick with the fervor of a schoolgirl. She wrote:

> Dear Kay, You must, indeed, feel a certain pride in your judgment. Gregory Pincus had been working for at least ten years on the progesterone of reproductive process in animals. He had practically no money for this work. . . . Then you came along with your fine interest and enthusiasm—with your faith and wonderful directives—[and] things began to happen.

"Nothing matters to me now that we have oral contraception," McCormick responded enthusiastically several months later. "Pincus' genius brought us the oral contraceptive we have been seeking and now we must implement it. We must keep on testing indefinitely—that goes without saying."[22]

The very prospect of scientific progress had revived Margaret and rekindled her enthusiasm for missionary work on behalf of the birth control movement. From her meeting with Dr. Pincus in Shrewsbury in June of 1953, she went to visit Juliet at Cornish, then on to Smith

College, Fishers Island, and the Connecticut home of her old friends Betty and Herbert Simonds, who had sold their company that manufactured diaphragms and jellies to Ortho Pharmaceuticals. In August, she then sailed for an IPPF conference in Stockholm, traveling with Harriet Pilpel, Planned Parenthood's longtime lawyer, as her companion.

Years later Pilpel could still recall the fanfare that attended Margaret's arrival in Sweden. She was welcomed with bouquets of flowers and christened an "international citizen" of the world. At a closing dinner she delivered an anecdotal speech on the history of the birth control movement, which is preserved on tape in the Smith archives. Her tenuous and frail voice is nonetheless absorbing. A seasoned orator, she had learned to speak in public with a good sense of timing and the ability to balance anecdote and humor with more profound and inspirational observations about the enterprise in which her audience was engaged.

"Build thou beyond thyself, but first be sure that thou thyself be strong in body and mind," she quoted from an Indian proverb and then continued in a similar inspirational vein:

> I believed it was my duty to place motherhood on a higher level than enslavement and accident. For these beliefs I was denounced, arrested, I was in and out of police courts and higher courts, indictments hung over my life for several years. But nothing could alter my beliefs. Because I saw these as truths, I stubbornly stuck to my convictions.

Portions of the speech were subsequently broadcast as a "This I Believe" segment on CBS radio to an audience estimated at 39 million Americans, and the script was also selected by Voice of America for distribution overseas. Margaret was especially pleased by the attention, because interest generated by the publication of the Kinsey Report earlier that year had been making her feel unappreciated and forgotten.[23]

Unhappy just playing muse to the struggling new international organization, Margaret then insisted on more active involvement. She returned from Tucson to New York in December to participate in the drafting of an organizational plan dividing IPPF's seventeen member-nations into three regions worldwide, one in the West to raise consciousness and money, and two in the East, where the needs were great and the money would be spent. The plan contemplated a $250,000 annual budget and, for the first time in her long history as an advocate and organizer, it also provided that her own personal expenses be covered. Hugh Moore, the entrepreneurial founder of the Dixie Cup Corporation and a recent convert to the world population cause, also assigned Tom Greissemer, a capable young executive in his employ, to work full-time out of the Sanger Clinic in New York. Almost all the money the two men raised, however, was consumed by administrative overhead, and, for the time being, the only significant developments abroad would require indigenous foreign support.

By 1954, a group of private Japanese citizens was ready to advance family planning there under the leadership of Shidzue Kato. In April, IPPF sent Margaret to participate in the first national meeting of the newly chartered Japan Federation of Family Planning. The group was then invited to affiliate formally with the international federation—over the strident objections of such members as Dhanvanthi Rama Rau, who was never bashful about expressing her contempt for the people who recently had so aggressively pursued a position of dominance in Asia.

Margaret, with her deep admiration of Japanese culture, refused to blame the sins of its military on its civilians. The highlight of her third visit to the country was an address to the Committee of Public Welfare in the House of Councillors of the Diet, arranged by Mrs. Kato, who had moved over to this senior parliamentary chamber in 1950 and would serve there for another twenty years. It was the first time a foreigner had ever been invited to address the national legislature. But Margaret's testimony regrettably betrayed her deteriorated health. Overwhelmed by the emotion of the occasion and by the fatigue of travel, she rambled on when given the opportunity to speak and seemed to stimulate interest in what she was saying only with a passing reference to the historic, scientific research going on in Shrewsbury and Boston, a subject she was not at liberty to discuss further. During her trip to Tokyo, however, she also helped organize the family planning conference scheduled there for the following year, the historic significance of which would derive from the fact that Gregory Pincus used the occasion to report for the first time on his preliminary findings. Margaret valiantly attended the event over the protestations of a family growing increasingly concerned about her health, and she was officially presented to Emperor Hirohito.

Heads of state were, indeed, beginning to take notice of the population issue, especially following meetings held in Rome in the fall of 1954 by the United Nations in conjunction with the Union for the Scientific Study of Population, the group that had been founded years earlier at the Geneva Conference. Data were presented at this time showing an alarming worldwide birthrate of 40,000 babies per day, but a coalition of Catholics and Communists blocked all recommendations for action. An International Planned Parenthood Federation application for membership as a consultive organization to the United Nations Economic and Social Council was then voted down in 1955, with the United States abstaining. Constrained by a handful of its members, the United Nations would refuse to endorse affirmative family planning policies or support any programs until the late 1960s.[24]

Without the support of governments or of broad-based international institutions, IPPF could only struggle to stay alive, yet sadly enough, Margaret herself came to be viewed as part of its problem. So long as she chose to remain active, no one in the organization was willing to challenge her openly, but almost everyone indulged her schemes and paid her bills while complaining bitterly to each other in private that she was too erratic and no longer had the capacity to make things happen. Even Dorothy Brush lost patience and accused Margaret in a moment of pique of becoming uncharacteristically self-absorbed—"bitchy, ruthless and cruel"—as the conversation was later reported. Margaret responded by becoming only more convinced that she was being pushed out. "The big heads that grow bigger & bigger with the growth of the movement just sicken me!" she later complained to Dorothy, confirming her observations.

Increasingly frail during these years, Margaret would recuperate from her intermittent bouts of angina long enough to scurry across the country looking for money, but even then she could only manage to come up with a handful of $5,000 checks from longtime supporters like Doris Duke, Mary Lasker, Martha Rockefeller, Amy Dupont, and Mary Scaife of the Mellon family in Pittsburgh, who conveniently spent part of her winters in Tucson at the Arizona Inn. Until Margaret officially retired in 1959, IPPF's annual budget never exceeded $35,000, nowhere near the millions needed for a serious undertaking, and, of course, nowhere near the money available to the Population Council.

A successor generation filled with talent and good intentions was eager to take charge—such women as Elise Ottesen-Jensen of Sweden, Dhanvanthi Rama Rau of India, Dr. Helena Wright, a prominent sexologist in England, and Eleanor Pillsbury and Frances Ferguson of Planned Parenthood in the United States. These women, however, were all divided in their loyalties between international work and competing domestic obligations. Even as they disparaged Margaret, they acknowledged the difficulty of identifying substantial resources for foreign work, and the indignity of having to grovel before a handful of interested and wealthy men for what little money they could raise. Yet she, in turn, always found a reason to criticize them, and grew especially harsh in her condemnation of family advocates who were supporting marriage counseling, sex education, and infertility programs contributing to baby booms in the West, while trying to advocate population decline elsewhere. Once it became clear to her that activities she had long tolerated as enhancements to her central program might actually be subverting it, she refused to have anything to do with them whatsoever.[25]

The struggling IPPF found itself at the mercy of entrepreneurs like Clarence Gamble, who was willing to underwrite its initiatives abroad, but only under the condition that he be given a measure of control. Long grateful for what little credibility he had provided her among fellow physicians and philanthropists, Margaret for a time staunchly defended the eccentric Gamble among a widening circle of skeptics. In 1955 she sent him off to Ceylon with IPPF's imprimatur, but he immediately set off a fracas there by treating local women with unabashed insensitivity and arrogance, allegedly addressing them with terms of derision like "coolie" and "native." His obdurate defense of the contraceptive utility and cost-effectiveness of a simple rag soaked in salt water was viewed under these circumstances as the symbol of an elitist contempt for the poor women of the developing world. Although she continued to defend his good intentions and his personal generosity, Margaret had no choice but to repudiate him, while taking pains not to alienate him altogether from the organization. The situation underscored the complexity of reconciling the diverse constituencies supporting birth control.[26]

Her newest and most sympathetic benefactor, Hugh Moore, then stirred up even more trouble the following year with a pamphlet called *The Population Bomb*, distributed as a fund-raising vehicle on behalf of a group of men in business and the professions to some 10,000 notables identified in *Who's Who in America*. Claiming concern over the spread of Communism in underdeveloped countries, the document encouraged support for population control with the rationale that a hungry world "may quite likely succumb to the blandishments of Moscow" and with a specific disclaimer of any interest in the "sociological or humanitarian aspects of birth control." The original language was so insensitive that the new president of Planned Parenthood of America, Loraine Campbell of Massachusetts, wrote along with other irate recipients to demand that it be changed.

Moore's Cold War zealotry did succeed in generating popular interest in the subject, but at the same time it shocked and offended the more seasoned activists, who despaired that incendiary American rhetoric would stir up Communist and Roman Catholic propaganda and threaten the little progress that had been made in building indigenous constituencies for family planning abroad. A prolonged fracas over the pamphlet helped scuttle Margaret's own plans for a population conference in Washington in 1957, which she reluctantly canceled on the advice of Frederick Osborn of the Population Council. Pointing to developments in India, Japan, Egypt, and even mainland China, where Socialist and Communist governments were already supporting birth control clinics, Osborn convinced her that Washington was no place to meet, because the United States, as he put it, was becoming "backward" on population issues compared to other countries in the world.[27]

As these developments unfolded, Margaret found herself in and out of the hospital once again. She suffered two more acute heart attacks in 1956, and under these circumstances, what may have been nothing more than the inevitable fits and starts of institution-building left her simply weary and confused. She took everything personally and was especially distressed, as she put it, by having to listen to the opinions of "young men too lazy to read history . . . who sound as though the BC movement began with their arrival as paid and hired hands." She summoned what little sense of humor she could muster, however, and admitted in another letter to Dorothy that "all this is enough to *give* you a heart attack, but I am getting better."

During the early winter months of 1957, she then took herself off to Hawaii to recuperate as the house guest of Ellen and Goma Watumull in Honolulu. Meanwhile, far away in New York and London, IPPF officials concentrated their attentions on the slow and largely unheralded work of developing solid regional structures for family planning in central Africa, the Soviet Union, Australia, Asia, and the Carribbean. A conference was held in the Virgin Islands in 1958 with support from Laurance Rockefeller, who had demonstrated a strong interest in the controlled development and conservation of the islands there. These were not initiatives in which she had any significant role to play, and although she retained her title as president, she became little more than a figurehead.

Back in Tucson, she continued to wrangle small contributions out of old friends like Mary Lasker, who sent her money with few questions asked, allowing her to hire a pandering young secretary by the name of Jonathan Schultz, who at her direction then drafted a series of memoranda that offered elementary suggestions about policies and operations to IPPF members all over the world. Margaret disputed the wisdom of decentralizing IPPF along regional lines, since neighboring countries like India and Pakistan or Japan and China were often at odds. She disparaged marriage counseling and infertility services and designated as the movement's primary goal the integration of contraception into public health programs. These controversial proposals were handed down in an imperious tone, with only the most elementary analysis of Margaret's thinking. Few paid them any heed, though several did try to respond out of respect and courtesy. C. P. Blacker, Margaret Pyke, and others at the headquarters in London found the situation "impossible . . . and tragic," and it only grew more and more troubling through the following year as Margaret's health deteriorated further, and her memory began to fade. Dorothy Brush sadly reported the precipitous deterioration and its unfortunate consequences to Margaret Grierson, the librarian at Smith College, who was assembling the Sanger archive. Brush attributed the extreme insecurity and vanity to Margaret's age, illness, and loss of physical appeal. "The collection ought to have letters which show the unfortunate change in character of old age," she added wistfully. "But I hate to spoil the otherwise remarkable picture of the most selfless woman I ever knew."[28]

As it turned out, however, there was no need of betrayal on Dorothy's part. Hungry for recognition of just about any kind, Margaret did all the damage she could possibly do to herself when she went on national television in September of 1957 as the guest of Mike Wallace, who was just beginning his long career as a combative investigative journalist. The format was a half-hour interview show on ABC offering, as Wallace promised in the promo, "an unrehearsed, uncensored . . . free discussion of an adult topic . . . that we feel merits public examination."

Wallace certainly got what he was looking for. Intent on uncovering the titillating story of how the old—and shockingly wizened—woman who sat across from him had become involved in a life of controversy, he spent far more time trying to expose Margaret's psyche than ferret out her thoughts. It was not recent developments in birth control that interested him, but, rather, his guest's attitudes toward divorce, infidelity, promiscuity, and God, and he put her through a cross-examination for which she was wholly unprepared.

What prompted the inquiry was Wallace's reading of Lawrence

Lader's biography, from which he baldly quoted material out of context. The interview began with nothing less than the accusation that Margaret had abandoned her husband and children when she was a young woman, because the birth control movement gave her "joy and interest and freedom." "Now, what was this joy, this freedom, that you craved?" Wallace demanded to know. She responded meekly that simple humanitarian motives had been enough to justify her calling—that she hated to see women suffer or children starve—but he then countered with statistics suggesting that the world's agricultural resources were plentiful, and she didn't seem to know what to say.

Following a commercial interruption, the discussion turned to religion and went further downhill. Margaret challenged Catholic attitudes toward love, marriage, and contraception, and questioned why celibate clergy were empowered to instruct married people on how to live their lives, allowing her host to respond with a defense of the integrity of natural law doctrine, as though he actually believed in it.

Is birth control a "devastating social force, which tends to weaken the moral fibre of the community," he inquired abruptly, quoting a recent article in a popular magazine? Did Margaret really just advocate it as a way "for single women to avoid bearing illegitimate children"? What, exactly, were her religious beliefs? Did she believe in a God "who rewards or punishes people after death"? Did she believe in sin?

She tried to punch back by responding that the greatest sin she believed in was the sin of bringing children into the world who would never have a chance. "But sin in the ordinary sense that we regard it," Wallace insisted. Is infidelity a sin? And what about murder? And what about America's high divorce rate?

"May I—may I ask you this," he admonished haltingly, perhaps betraying an uncharacteristic reluctance to say what was clearly on his mind: "Could it be that women in the United States have become too independent—that they have followed the lead of women like Margaret Sanger by neglecting family life for a career?"

The interview was nothing less than a knockout. Margaret's teenaged granddaughters were watching with their parents in Tucson and remember being floored, hoping that she would fight back—astonished that a woman who had once been so powerful now seemed so submissive and overwhelmed. Bill Sanger, watching in New York with his daughter Joan, began to cry. Writing in *The New York Times* the next morning, the television critic Jack Gould attacked

Wallace for his determination to explore Margaret's personal life rather than the significant aspects of her career—for trying to trap her in inconsistencies, at the cost of the more important story.

But Gould may have missed the point. Wallace got exactly the interview he intended. For more than forty years, Margaret had been trying to posture birth control as a scientific and social issue, but she could never escape its moral dimension, because the truth was that her own life engaged it. For all her efforts to conceal herself—for all the compromises she had made in order to get ahead—she could never wholly escape her own past.

With the same unforgiving clarity that the television camera gave to his guest's wrinkled old face, Wallace explained just why Margaret Sanger's life really did make a compelling story, but not necessarily one that a new generation of professional leadership in the family planning field wanted told.[29]

CHAPTER TWENTY-ONE

Woman of the Century

Had Mike Wallace actually been interested in reporting on developments in family planning, there was quite a bit to say. In the waning years of the 1950s, basic assumptions that had long constrained movement activists were finally being altered in a manner that would allow for dramatic gains during the following two decades.

The big news, of course, was scientific. Planned Parenthood's own clinical experience had long demonstrated the limitations of the diaphragm and jelly and provided the most convincing rationale of all for better technology, if birth control was to be truly democratized. It was hardly surprising, therefore, when the preliminary findings on the pill published by Gregory Pincus and John Rock in 1956 led immediately to expanded field trials. Within a year, the Population Council had agreed to joint meetings with the International Planned Parenthood Federation to discuss technology and was directly supporting field research on a small sample of pill takers in Los Angeles. And a larger experiment was begun in Puerto Rico, under the direction of a local public health physician by the name of Edris

Rice-Wray, whom Pincus had met while giving a lecture in San Juan.

As a legacy of Ernest Gruening's and Clarence Gamble's quiet cooperation during the Depression, the Puerto Rican legislature had legalized birth control in 1937, over the strident objections of the Catholic Church. Sixty-three family planning clinics remained in operation on the island, one of them in a housing project for indigent families where Dr. Rice-Wray worked. A tradition of sexual modesty and the absence of reliable methods prevented the island's women from practicing conventional contraception effectively, however, and sterilization had instead become their contraceptive of choice. Promoted by private physicians eager for the business and inadvertently by Catholic pastoral letters condemning it, sterilization was not just reliable but had the distinct advantage of requiring only a one-time absolution in the confessional. In a pattern that the United States mainland would begin to replicate in the 1970s, one third of all women ages twenty to forty-nine were having the operation. Yet the Puerto Rican birthrate still remained twice as high as the United States national average.

Under these circumstances Dr. Rice-Wray had no trouble finding recruits for her pill research and no compunction about recommending that they take a risk on experimental medication. In one year she collected data for several hundred patients, aggregating forty-seven years of pill-taking, without a single pregnancy. Problems with side effects such as nausea, fluid retention, and dizziness caused a quarter of the original sample to drop out, but eager substitutes were found, and experiments with placebos then demonstrated that at least some of these reactions were psychological, while the administration of the actual medication in lower dosages resolved even more problems, with still no effect on contraceptive reliability.

Anxious officials in the local public health ministry, nevertheless, put a stop to the research when they learned of it, and Dr. Rice-Wray left the country for a position in Mexico. A second field trial was then arranged privately in the village of Humacao as the result of a proposal by Clarence Gamble to Dr. Adaline Pendleton Satterthwaite, a Quaker medical missionary there. Having spent years delivering babies and then sterilizing desperately poor women, she too had no trouble defending her work on humanitarian grounds and wound up providing a fourth of the case histories on which Gregory Pincus would base his successful argument for the safety and effectiveness of Enovid before the United States Food and Drug Administration three years later.[1]

Physicians and policymakers in the continental United States were, at first, considerably more cautious. During the summer of 1957, Planned Parenthood officials in New York issued a tentative statement of support for the Pincus–Rock studies in Brookline, but admonished enthusiasts who were already proclaiming the dawn of a new era that it was still much too soon to regard the medication as safe. Dr. Carl Hartman, then chairman of the organization's medical committee, expressed many reservations about the possible consequences of altering the body's natural hormonal chemistry and predicted a fifteen-to-twenty-year period before the drug's safety could be assured. (This prompted Margaret to pencil in the comment on her copy of the statement that he was simply "jealous.") In fact, Planned Parenthood would take close to two years after FDA approval before authorizing the pill's use by its affiliates, during which time Searle and Ortho Pharmaceuticals, its first major competitor, substantially reduced the drug's progestin and estrogen content, further diminishing reported side effects and enhancing safety.

Private physicians who had never liked the diaphragm, because prescribing it was neither medically challenging nor terribly remunerative, turned out to be a good deal more enthusiastic about the pill, and within five years it became the most popular contraceptive in America, used by 29 percent of married, non-Catholic women under the age of forty-five and by more than half of all women with a college education. It would soon revolutionize contraceptive practice among Catholics as well. Close to 50 million women around the world would be taking oral contraceptives by the 1970s, a population more than adequate to establish their reliability and safety for women of normal health—outside a small and readily identifiable group of high-risk users. Sixty million use it today. Periodic alarms about the relationship of the pill to embolisms, cancers, and other serious complications have been sounded, but never substantiated in large enough numbers to dissuade use. From a medical standpoint, the potent drug, whose actual physiological effects to this day remain poorly understood, has proved remarkably benign, even as women have continued to question the wisdom of taking it over long periods of time.[2]

The demographic consequences of oral contraception have also been substantial, though never enough so to satisfy population planners. The pill's early and rapid success did demonstrate the motivation of large numbers of women, across a broad spectrum of classes, creeds, and cultures, and helped undermine prevailing assumptions about who would use contraception and who would not. But because it remained a relatively costly medication, requiring prescription by a doctor and individual daily administration, it never lived up to the hopes of its early patrons. International population professionals have continued to look for an inexpensive technology that does not depend on the regular cooperation of the people using it—something on the order of the inoculations against epidemic disease that have more successfully revolutionized maternal and child health around the world.

These inherent liabilities were, in fact, recognized from the start. In 1957, while field trials on the pill were still underway, officials at the Population Council continued to despair over the prospects for ever bringing about meaningful change through voluntary family planning initiatives. A long-term experiment with conventional barrier and chemical methods of contraception in Khanna, a rural district of India, was resulting in poor compliance and negligible changes in fertility. And even in the United States, where knowledge of contraception was nearly universal, and its use controversial only among a few groups, national fertility surveys were still uncovering substantial numbers of unwanted births. Accidental, unplanned pregnancies in and out of marriage remained a problem of statistical significance, especially among the poor, who appeared to have more difficulty anticipating the need for contraception, and less access to pharmacies or health care services that could provide it.

In 1958, the Population Council decided to invest in the development of a contraceptive device that could be left in place for a long period of time. Alan F. Guttmacher, M.D., then chief of obstetrics at Mt. Sinai Hospital in New York, and a member of the council's medical advisory board, recommended the support of preliminary research by Lazar Margulies, a German-trained physician on his staff, who was experimenting with a variation on the Grafenberg ring that Margaret had promoted years earlier and then been pressured to reject. The new intrauterine device substituted a pliant plastic material for the metal components that had always been difficult to insert and more likely to cause uterine punctures and infection. The once controversy-shy organization then contracted with Christopher Tietze, M.D., another German émigré who had become the protégé of Robert Dickinson and had continued working on his own with a shoestring budget at the National Committee on Maternal Health following Dickinson's death. During the early 1960s several million dollars would be channeled through Tietze for the refinement, testing, and evaluation of various intrauterine devices. And the organization would reserve to itself the international marketing rights for a loop-shaped apparatus developed by the Buffalo physician Jack

Lippes, that gained the highest rate of acceptance and caused the fewest side effects. By 1967, when the success of the pill had legitimized active intervention in family planning on a broad international scale, the Population Council would incorporate this research and technical assistance capacity as its own Bio-Medical division, where further testing and refinement of various IUDs, injectable contraceptives, and other experimental medications have continued.

IUDs were widely distributed in the 1970s and 1980s, but their use has declined subtantially in recent years as a result of concerns about safety. IUDs have been associated with an increased risk of pelvic inflammatory disease, which, if left untreated, can cause sterility. The fear of malpractice liability has left many physicians in the United States unwilling to insert the devices, and they are also less frequently recommended anymore for use in countries where adequate follow-up medical care is not available to women. More successful in recent years has been the Population Council's investment in research on subdermal contraceptive implants that slowly release an ovulation inhibiting synthetic hormone containing progestin, and can remain in place for up to five years. Close to a million women in the rest of the world are currently using this procedure, and it has recently been approved for use in the United States by the Food and Drug Administration.

In the United States and many other countries, however, barrier contraceptives are still widely employed, sterilization remains a preferred option of married women who have completed their desired childbearing, and legal abortion is a widely utilized backup. This is likely to remain the case, so long as all artificial methods pose the risk of any side effects or more serious complications. As a result, the primary objectives of family planning policymakers today must be to promote additional research to ensure that existing services are tailored to the individual needs of women in disparate cultures and circumstances.[3]

Political barriers to change were also eroding in the late 1950s. As Margaret had long complained, Planned Parenthood, after rejecting her own flamboyant, confrontational tactics, never formulated a coherent strategy for combating, or even neutralizing, the power of Catholic opposition to family planning and instead more or less accommodated to its marginal political and legal stature in this country. Something of a turning point, however, came in 1955 when Agnes Meyer of Washington admonished new recruits to the organization to be less cowardly and encouraged them to articulate a positive vision in opposition to Catholic absolutism, thus demonstrating that they could no longer be intimidated.

The ideal circumstances for putting this advice into practice developed several years later, when a doctor in a municipal hospital in Brooklyn found that he could not get permission from New York City's health commissioner to fit a diabetic patient with a diaphragm. Hospital administrators and city officials sensitive to New York's large and powerful Catholic constituency had never challenged the unwritten but widely acknowledged policy that kept contraceptives out of publicly assisted health clinics, despite the legal protection state law provided birth control when prescribed for medical reasons. Indigent women could only find medical birth control through a handful of Planned Parenthood facilities and clinics in voluntary hospitals or settlement houses.

Working behind the scenes, Planned Parenthood staff in New York, under the direction of Frederick Jaffe, then a young and savvy public relations specialist, assembled a broad coalition of support from non-Catholic medical, social, and religious institutions. They also brought the situation to the attention of the local press, where it received extensive coverage, especially from Joseph Kahn, a crusading investigative reporter for the *New York Post*, who helped frame the issue as a matter of freedom of information, medical discretion, and religious tyranny. After months of concerted lobbying, the policy was overturned with the quiet acquiescence of Democratic Mayor Robert Wagner, Jr., though he remained neutral in public. Contraceptive services were subsequently incorporated into postpartum clinics in the city's three largest municipal hospitals, though only physicians, of course, not social workers or other nonmedical personnel, could legally give information.

The New York City confrontation raised popular awareness of the substantial political constraints on birth control in this country. Editorial opinion was nearly unanimous in its approval of government's taking a more assertive role and gave Planned Parenthood professionals the courage to assist similar confrontations elsewhere. The victory also exposed emerging divisions of opinion within the Catholic Church itself. "It should be clear," suggested an article in *Commonweal*, by then considerably more liberal editorially than it had been in the past, "that there are many sound and compelling reasons why Catholics should not generally strive for legislation and directives which clash with the beliefs of a large portion of society . . . they almost inevitably strengthen in the minds of non-Catholics the already present worries about Catholic power." Two years later a Planned Parenthood poll of lay Catholics would establish that more than half believed public officials should respect freedom of religious belief in all medical institutions. An editorial in *The Pilot*, the publication of the Boston Archdiocese, then acknowledged that although Catholic principles remain constant, "the social, political, economic, legal and cultural context in which these principles are applied is itself in flux and they must be applied differently." No longer would the church be able to present itself as a monolith, absolutely resistant to change.[4]

Margaret was in Tucson during the many months of the New York City encounter, preoccupied by the prosaic task of keeping herself alive. Her only participation was a telephone interview in which she called the city policy "disgraceful." She was no longer well enough to remain more than intermittently active. An increasingly constricted flow of blood to her weakened heart muscle was causing more frequent paroxysms of chest pain, and when stricken she required oxygen and extended rest. A New York specialist advised surgery, but her own doctors thought that an open-heart procedure was too risky for a patient of her condition and age.

She was absorbed as well in something of a personal obsession that she blew way out of proportion—the question of who would replace her as president of the International Planned Parenthood Federation. The obvious candidates were Lady Rama Rau of India, who had for a time already shared the title with Margaret, and Elise Ottesen-Jensen of Sweden, who had brought considerable distinction upon herself as the conduit through which her government became the first Western nation to assist family planning programs in the developing world through a joint program with the government of Ceylon. With the United States and the United Nations still uninvolved, the agenda for a well-run and ambitious voluntary organization was pressing. The job would demand strong administrative skills and special sensitivity to the nuances of international diplomacy. On both grounds each candidate had liabilities acknowledged by many of Margaret's correspondents, yet her own reservations were scarcely rational. No one seemed to please her, and other women were especially threatening. Mrs. Rama Rau was too nationally minded, Mrs. Ottesen-Jensen, too temperamental. Fearful of finally having to yield her own authority completely, she promoted the candidacy of her longtime loyal lieutenant, Dr. Abraham Stone, but he died unexpectedly of a heart attack in 1959, and with international attention focused on India's population explosion, first Rama Rau and later Ottesen-Jensen got the job.[5]

Margaret also insisted on attending the Sixth International Conference on Planned Parenthood in New Delhi in February of 1959, though her doctors and her family strongly advised her not to go. Grace Sternberg, a friend and Planned Parenthood volunteer from Tucson, agreed to act as travel companion and watched over an extremely frail patient who resolutely made her way from Los Angeles to Honolulu, Tokyo, Hong Kong, and Bangkok, complaining at each stop that she could not tolerate the fact that everyone thought she was dying, even as she wearily retreated from each festivity tendered in her honor.

Ample reward for her determination and stamina came when Prime Minister Nehru warmly welcomed Margaret to the meetings in New Delhi on February 14, 1959, and then cautiously ushered her on his arm to the podium as the 750 delegates who had assembled from twenty-eight nations put aside their differences to cheer the moving sight. Nehru pledged $10 million in public health funds for family planning, earning Margaret's praise as the world's greatest living statesman, along with a trenchant warning that he be careful to send doctors into the villages who were sympathetic to the "shy, simple woman who comes to them, asking for information as to how to space her pregnancies and how to take care of the children that she has already borne." It was a final opportunity to reiterate her view that how an individual woman perceives her own self-interest may be as important to her decisions about fertility as larger economic and social conditions. Stories and photographs ran in major newspapers and news magazines throughout the world, and Margaret was given the honor of being named president emeritus of IPPF.

The following day Gregory Pincus dedicated his historic report on field trials with oral contraception to Margaret as "the product of her pioneering resoluteness," but by then she was too weak to leave her hotel room and celebrated quietly with old friends over a favorite meal of champagne and chicken sandwiches. They presented her with a two-volume testimonial, entitled "Our M.S.," filled with the often poignant, personal reminiscences that have appeared throughout this book, and dedicated to the woman who "blazed a trail through the Jungle of Man's prejudice and Ignorance and Stupidity." The surprisingly strident tone of the collection was established by Blanche Ames of Boston, the first of more than a hundred contributors listed alphabetically, who observed acidly that monuments had been erected to the deeds of men since the time of the pyramids, but rarely was the work of a woman ever honored.[6]

Yet even as Margaret's contemporaries tried to establish her place among history's foremost emancipators of women a newly empowered generation of activists was questioning the fundamental wisdom of her approach to family planning for the very reason that it enlisted women as clients and talked in terms of their self-interest. Dudley Kirk, a demographer on the Population Council staff, reminded his audience at New Delhi that "male" methods of contraception, such as the condom and coitus interruptus (as though neither required female participation) had actually been responsible for the great demographic revolutions of the West, and he advocated a policy for India that placed priority on these simple techniques rather than on expensive medical ones requiring individualized instruction. A proponent of sending convoys of helicopters laden with condoms into rural villages, Kirk was glad to observe the evolution of Planned Parenthood away from "emphasis on family limitation as primarily an interest and responsibility of women," he said, "toward emphasis on the value and indeed the necessity of joint responsibility in family planning."

Indeed the view that a "feminist bias" was subverting family planning programs in the developing world, where a medical-clinical approach to the problem was believed to be simply too expensive and likely to fail, would continue to inform the thinking of demographers and policy makers, even as new contraceptive methods for women revolutionized the field. In 1961, Katherine McCormick sadly admitted to Margaret in the last surviving letters between them that no one any longer believed that the pill was the answer to overpopulation. Her letter also said that Gregory Pincus was experimenting with injectable contraceptives but correctly predicted that effective inoculations would take years to develop. Meanwhile, programs offering economic incentives for male sterilization would probably be necessary in places like India, where the Nehru government was already supporting policies that have since engendered widespread controversy and been widely repudiated.

Since 1965, however, the rate of population growth has unexpectedly slowed in almost all countries in the world outside Africa, even as absolute numbers continue to grow precipitously everywhere but in a handful of developed nations. Most baffling, however, have been the extreme cultural variations in reproductive behavior and in the success of organized family planning initiatives. Efforts to understand these patterns, and to analyze alternative strategies for intervention, are finally reawakening interest in the relationship between fertility and the status of women. Contemporary population policymakers are more inclined to concede Margaret's insistent view that women are inherently better motivated to limit their fertility and should be identified as primary agents of change. Programs seem to work best, moreover, when contraception is offered as part of a larger package of maternal and infant health care reforms delivered under paramedical auspices, just as she always intended. Prodded by contemporary feminists in the field, population planners are finally investing in the overall health and welfare of women, because it has been demonstrated that to do so reduces birthrates most effectively.[7]

Margaret returned from New Delhi in a wheelchair, a rather pathetic sight in Grace Sternberg's memory, except that she good-naturedly wore a straw hat purchased in Honolulu, which was adorned by a chicken whose wings flapped up and down when she pressed air through a bulb. Within months, however, she was feeling strong enough to fly back to Tokyo to meet with the Prime Minister and receive a key to the city from its governor. Accompanied by her teenaged granddaughters and several of their friends, she basked in an official recognition and esteem that had long been denied her at home. But the trip was a struggle, and she confided to Mary Lasker, who graciously underwrote its costs, that "I pray I will be well enough to do all that is expected of me."

The young girls, meanwhile, were entertained in memorable Japanese style by Sumiko Ohmori, who had married since her visit to Tucson and was anxious to return Margaret's gracious hospitality. Young Margaret and Nancy Sanger were astonished to find that, in Japan, not only family planning activists, but even taxi drivers had heard of their grandmother.

This would turn out to be Margaret's last trip abroad, and just how much it meant to her is apparent not only in her enthusiastic reports to Mrs. Lasker, but in a touching notation in the deteriorated handwriting of Margaret's old age, which remains on a scrap of paper included in the archive at Smith College. It records the wish that she be buried next to Noah in the family plot on the grounds of Willowlake, but only after her heart had been removed for entombment in Japan, the one government in the world that ever granted her a public honor.[8]

Though birth control remained a politically sensitive issue at home, Margaret came back to a country suddenly paying attention. In response to pressure from Democrats on the powerful Senate Foreign Relations Committee, Pres. Dwight David Eisenhower had appointed a special committee to assess his administration's policies on foreign military and economic aid. The ten-member panel of men who had all served previously in high-ranking government positions was chaired by Gen. William H. Draper, an investment banker and former army commander who had supervised postwar economic recovery programs in Europe. Prompted by a telegram from the ever-resolute population watchdog Hugh Moore—and given explicit authorization to do so from Eisenhower himself—Draper placed world population growth on the committee's agenda. There was considerable rumbling from his staff about potentially explosive political consequences and particular resistance from one especially anxious Catholic member of the panel. But while Margaret herself was still out of the country, Draper decided to recommend that the United States government should, on request, assist foreign governments receiving our economic aid in formulating plans to deal with population growth and with maternal and child welfare problems.

The report's release in July of 1959 received extensive press coverage and an immediate, but reasonably restrained, response from the National Catholic Welfare Conference branding its birth control recommendations "not only immoral [but] also a counsel of defeatism and despair." Popular interest in the issue built steadily in the months following, however, especially after CBS News in November ran a prime-time documentary on conditions of rural poverty and population growth in India, which would air twice and be seen by an estimated audience of more than 18 million Americans.

At meetings in Washington later that month, the American Catholic hierarchy then released a considerably more vituperative statement, attacking public discussion of the "population explosion" as nothing more than a "smoke screen behind which a moral evil will be foisted on the public" and denouncing efforts to build support for the use of public funds for artificial contraception. The church instead urged greater efforts to feed and uplift "backward peoples around the world," and in pledging to work actively against population control programs, provoked the immediate condemnation of numbers of Protestant officials, one of whom, James Pike, the Episcopal bishop of San Francisco and a long-time Planned Parenthood supporter, also demanded to know if the church's policy was binding on Catholic candidates for political office.

The question had special resonance, of course, because the first Catholic candidate since the defeat of Al Smith in 1928 was seeking the presidency. Sen. John F. Kennedy of Massachusetts immediately told James Reston of *The New York Times* in a telephone interview that it was absolutely not in America's interest to promote birth control overseas—that it would be a "mean paternalism . . . a great psychological mistake for us to appear to advocate limitation of the black or brown or yellow peoples whose population is increasing no faster than in the United States." But Kennedy was equally insistent, on this and subsequent occasions, as the issue dogged him through the campaign the following year, that he would act only on the basis of what he considered to be in the public interest, without regard to his private religious views or the public position of his church. Making birth control a condition of foreign aid was never the real issue. When later pressed about what he would do if foreign governments like India affirmatively requested American assistance, or if Congress took the initiative, he retreated somewhat from his initial formulation but insisted that the likelihood of any President ever having to sign a bill authorizing expenditures on birth control was "very remote indeed" and repeated that, whatever he did, his actions would be based solely on his assessment of the national interest. Even Eleanor Roosevelt was willing to endorse this position.

Kennedy could afford to beg the more pointed question of cooperative assistance programs, because President Eisenhower, fearing the potential divisiveness of the matter on the upcoming campaign, then repudiated the Draper Commission recommendations, much to the surprise and dismay of its members. After the Kennedy story broke, the President responded with unusual brusqueness to a reporter's inquiry by saying he could not imagine a less "proper political or governmental activity or function or responsibility" than for the United States to promote family planning abroad. He advised instead that concerned foreign governments seek assistance from private groups.[9]

From Tucson, Margaret announced immediately that she was prepared to debate Eisenhower in order to "straighten him out" on the question of family planning, and her statement made headlines as far away as Tokyo. She then wrote a letter to *The New York Times* insisting on the importance of population control to future world peace and protesting the position of the Catholic Church. Prominently displayed in the Sunday edition, it provoked an immediate exchange between Senator Kennedy and reporters on that morning's edition of "Meet the Press" in which he again protested his independence.

Shortly after the program aired, the telephone rang at Margaret's house, and her old friend, Norman Thomas, was on the line. Margaret almost always stayed clear of partisan politics and quietly cast her Presidential ballot for Thomas, but the lively, perennial candidate of the Socialist Party urged her to become more actively involved on this occasion by pointing out to the press that Kennedy's longtime acquiescence to church interference during successive referenda on the question of reforming punitive birth control laws in Massachusetts surely belied his claims of autonomy. She rose to the challenge and immediately wrote Kennedy a letter along the lines Thomas suggested, but when she never received any response, she seems to have dropped the matter. Nor did Thomas pursue it, his restrained, gentlemanly demeanor in campaigns being legendary.[10]

Had Margaret been twenty years younger, or perhaps just a bit healthier, she might have been less reticent. She did create international headlines once again after Kennedy's nomination, when she baldly announced that she would leave the country if he were elected, but the empty threat of an old woman in the middle of a hot summer hardly stirred up much of a fracas. Just two weeks before the November vote, however, three Catholic bishops in Puerto Rico issued a pastoral letter instructing their parishioners to oppose the island's popular incumbent governor, Munoz Marin, because he had endorsed public schools and birth control, and Washington's political reporters went crazy over the story. Catholic spokesmen in Washington quickly repudiated the statement, and Kennedy himself condemned the church-state interference, but according to the memoir by his aide, Theodore Sorensen, he knew he had been hurt. "If enough voters realize that Puerto Rico is American soil," Kennedy is reported to have said, "this election is lost."

It was, indeed, won with just over 100,000 votes out of more than 68 million cast, and various pollsters estimated that from 1 to 2 million voters deserted Kennedy in the last two weeks of the election when the Puerto Rican story broke. For the second time in her life, Margaret voted for a Republican Presidential candidate and announced publicly that religion was the reason. She then added that mutual friends were assuring her that the new President had an open mind and promised to give him a year before making good on her threat to find another place to live.[11]

The election controversy generated a windfall of publicity for birth control advocates. More Americans than ever before became aware of the world population problem. *Reader's Digest*, with some 15 million subscribers, featured a flattering biographical portrait of Margaret. NBC News tried to match the ratings of the CBS show on India with an investigative piece of its own on Hong Kong. *Newsweek* prepared a special report on the "crisis," and Vance Packard wrote a best-seller on the subject. Planned Parenthood presented a statement of conviction about overpopulation to the United Nations, signed by 200 internationally prominent individuals, including thirty-eight Nobel laureates. Even the once publicity shy Population Council contracted with a public affairs agency and issued a pamphlet called *This Crowded World*.

According to population policy analyst Phyllis Tilson Piotrow, the election of a Catholic President, publicly committed to analyzing the matter in terms of objective national interest—rather than as a religious or moral dilemma—put great pressure on all parties to work toward reconciliation. Perhaps, as President Eisenhower is reported to have said privately, a Catholic in the White House might be able to accomplish what a Protestant could not.[12]

For the time being, however, the matter remained in private hands. Incensed by Eisenhower's public disavowal of the Draper Panel, Hugh Moore called a group of prominent citizens together in Princeton, New Jersey, in March of 1960 to consider what could be done voluntarily to address the population issue. Margaret promised to be there—"if humanly possible, if I have to crawl," as she put it. Though quite nervous about her health, she did make the trip and brought along $25,000 from Martha Rockefeller toward the $100,000 that Moore put together to launch a World Population Emergency Campaign, which would run for two years and generate a membership of 10,000 individuals and more than a million dollars in funding for the International Planned Parenthood Federation.

So long as Moore could attract powerful men to the cause, like General Draper and Lammot duPont Copeland, of the industrial family, Margaret was willing to forgive the Dixie Cup king his rhetorical excesses, not to mention the fact that he was already on his fourth wife, whom she not so incidentally described as "beautiful and young," in a gossipy letter to Mrs. Rockefeller. Moore, in turn, recognized the mass marketing potential of Margaret's name, and asked her to sign a direct mail fund-raising appeal and a full-page advertisement in *The New York Times*, after agreeing to her demand that the population crisis be postured as a humanitarian concern, with all references to the threat of Communism excised from the text. Responses came back with small contributions and tender greetings from women who had followed Margaret's career throughout the years—one who first heard her speak in 1916 and then organized clinics in California, another who said that reading *Woman and the New Race* had changed her life. An ever vigilant Federal Bureau of Investigation also noticed the salutation and, seeing Margaret's name, transmitted a copy of the letter to the agencies in its regular security network. Only one apparently bothered to respond. A baffled William Josephson, then the young and earnest general counsel at the Peace Corps, took the time to note that he didn't think the matter warranted any further investigation.[13]

Had Margaret known about this internal communication, the interest J. Edgar Hoover and his agents demonstrated in her might have meant a great deal, or, at least, given her a good laugh. Alone much of the time in Tucson, she was drinking more and taking stronger doses of Demerol to ease her pain. In March of 1961, a fund-raising consultant hired by the World Population Emergency Campaign orchestrated a tribute in New York to honor her forty-fifth anniversary as a birth control advocate. The tragic deterioration in her physical and emotional condition is evident in the handwritten note she sent in response to his invitation, admitting that she was not "so rugged" as in the past but nevertheless hoped she could "pep up" and come to New York for the celebration. With the help of a secretary, she then wrote a more cogent reply admitting no less poignantly: "I cannot tell you how my heart goes out to you for all you are doing. As a matter of fact, you are the only one in recent years who has any knowledge of the history of the Movement or that Margaret Sanger had anything to do with it. It is to laugh, but that is the way it is."

The notable British scientist Sir Julian Huxley chaired the event, which included a dinner and a symposium of eminent scholars, physicians, and policymakers speaking about world population. Agnes Meyer, who had died in the interim, gave the initial gift that made it all possible, and Katherine McCormick provided the basis of a $100,000 endowment for IPPF to be maintained in Margaret's name. An eloquent testimonial was prepared, including greetings from friends in thirty-five countries and a charming printed program with old photographs of Margaret. *The New York Times* made her its "Woman in the News," while to everyone's surprise, an article in the Catholic journal, *America*, for the first time acknowledged the existence of an international population problem but rejected the position of those who would "Sangerize" the world, contending that so long as Communist countries were encouraging growth, so should nations in the free world.

Stuart Sanger accompanied his mother to New York, and he assisted her to the podium to deliver a brief message of thanks. Emotionally overwhelmed and exhausted by the experience, however, she then nodded off to sleep at the dais and was returned immediately to her hotel room. It was her last appearance in public.

Back in Tucson a new doctor slowly weaned Margaret of her addiction to painkillers and limited her to one drink a day. By the testimony of friends, she was serene and at peace with herself as she had not been in years, but even as she grew stronger and more coherent, she could no longer live alone or manage her own affairs. Barbara Sanger dutifully came in every day to check up on her, but the Sanger girls were grown and had left Tucson, and Stuart seemed utterly incapable of dealing with the dependency of the figure whose difficult but forceful presence had dominated his life for so long. Neither he nor Grant ever told their mother of William Sanger's death at the age of eighty-seven from a heart attack on July 25, 1961. And Bill, in turn, never saw the poignant letter Margaret had written forty-two years earlier to be given to him after her own death. She had looked at it herself on several occasions, but never made any practical arrangements to ensure its delivery.

Olive Byrne Richard had retired to Tucson and stopped by regularly to assist Margaret with correspondence and other domestic chores. She remembers her sitting for hours in the corner of the large living room she had furnished in a minimalist Oriental style. All of a sudden, Margaret began to fill every available surface with old photographs of family and friends that seemed strangely out of place in these spare surroundings. Yet they provided the only company she could find.[14]

In the fall of 1961, Ellen Watumull asked friends and former colleagues to join her in a friendly conspiracy. Margaret was feeling much better than in the past, but there are times when she feels completely forgotten, Watumull confided. Would they write occasionally with news of what was happening in their part of the world? Would they bring some problem to Margaret's attention, ask her advice, needle her a bit about some controversy? Would they send her a book review, a news clipping, or just a postcard?

A typical response came from John D. Rockefeller III, who had just received the Lasker Award for family planning and had also spoken in Rome before a United Nations assembly. "In these two public appearances I realized that what I was doing was following in your footsteps—in a small way helping to carry forward the tremendously important work for which you were so largely responsible," he wrote. And then, lest the letter sound too programmed, perhaps, he added a personal note. "I remember so well how much my mother and father used to enjoy their visits with you in Arizona. They spoke of you often. My personal regret is that our paths have not crossed more often."

Within two weeks, Rockefeller received two responses to his greetings. The first carried on obsequiously about the "splendid heritage" of the Rockefeller family. The second, asking for money to fund the deficit of the Margaret Sanger Research Bureau in New York, demonstrated that Margaret might be down but could not yet be counted out. Rockefeller instructed his staff to investigate why Planned Parenthood in New York was not taking responsibility for the clinic, which seemed to him only proper, but on the grounds that he did not support freestanding medical institutions, he never made a contribution and never wrote again.[15]

In his remarks at the Sanger anniversary symposium, Marriner Eccles, a former New Dealer and chairman of the Federal Reserve, had predicted that the rate of world population growth might prove more explosive than the atomic or hydrogen bomb. The alarmist rhetoric occasioned an editorial in *The New York Times*, which called on the Kennedy administration to accept the recommendations of the Draper Report and assist friendly nations in population planning at their request. Key appointees at the State Department did not disagree with this proposal in principle but determined, after extensive internal debate, that active intervention by the United States was simply not "feasible" because of religious and social obstacles at home. A compromise strategy recommended that the federal government quietly support more extensive demographic and medical research through the National Institutes of Health, but a report proposing a preliminary agenda for work by the agency was then quashed in 1962 by politically timid advisers to the President. All this in spite of an increasing recognition that the Kennedy Administration's desire to leave a strong and innovative foreign aid program as its legacy was being compromised by the magnitude of a staggering world population problem. Further capitulation to fears of inciting the Catholic Church was also evident that year at the United Nations, where the United States at first supported, but then, by abstaining on a necessary second vote, helped to defeat, a resolution introduced by the government of Sweden permitting technical assistance in population planning to nations requesting it.[16]

As the Kennedy administration waffled, however, an extraordinary mobilization of private resources for addressing the population issue took place. The budget of the Population Council expanded fivefold, while the Ford and Rockefeller Foundations got ready to make a major commitment of their own resources to programs in the population field. Following its dramatic successes in fund-raising and public relations, the World Population Emergency Campaign merged with the Planned Parenthood Federation of America on the grounds that a single organization marketing family planning at home and abroad would be more effective. Cass Canfield, the highly considered and well-connected head of the publishing firm of Harper & Row, who was already serving as chairman of Planned Parenthood's board, took charge of the combined organization. The venerable Alan Guttmacher of Mt. Sinai Hospital in New York then retired from medical practice and replaced William Vogt as a full-time president and chief executive officer.

Within a year, Planned Parenthood clinics in the United States would be serving nearly 200,000 patients, a gain of more than 30 percent. With the introduction of the pill, caseloads expanded so fast that some facilities had to impose limitations on service because of lack of funds. About 20 percent of this clientele was on public assistance, and the need for expanded distribution of services to indigent women through tax-supported hospitals and welfare agencies quickly became apparent. In many areas of the country, however, there were no public institutions in place providing the sustained preventive health care that medical contraception required, so Planned Parenthood had no choice but to expand its services to fill in the gaps, a situation that continues today. To this end, the politically skillful and diplomatic Guttmacher announced his determination to eliminate the movement's elitist reputation by broadening the base of its constituency to include better representation from organized labor, ethnic groups, and racial minorities.[17]

Meanwhile, from a political standpoint, the publication in 1963 of John Rock's book, *The Time Has Come, A Catholic Doctor's Proposals to End the Battle Over Birth Control*, was also especially important. Though the church hierarchy did not accept Dr. Rock's inventive defense of the pill as a natural contraceptive, a deliberate effort was made at conciliation in public comments on the book by Richard Cardinal Cushing of Boston, who also met privately with Alan Guttmacher. Even more important, in Rome, Pope Paul VI appointed a commission of clerical and lay Catholics to review the subject. Its ostensible aim was to reconcile Catholic theology with the most current scientific expertise in family planning. Three years later,

American newspapers would report rumors that the commission was struggling with a recommendation to leave the matter of choosing a specific birth control technique to individual Catholic conscience. These stories could never be confirmed, however, and the Vatican made no official announcement until the publication in 1968 of the papal encyclical *Humanae Vitae*, which suddenly reconfirmed the immutability of natural law doctrine. Because the commission had never been able to reach a consensus, the Pope simply reiterated the doctrine that "every marriage act must remain open to the transmission of life." Only natural laws and rhythms of fecundity might constrain fertility. Man does "not have unlimited dominion over his body in general . . . or over his creative faculties." The statement also expressed concern that artificial birth control was making men especially vulnerable to "infidelity and the general lowering of morality" and to the use of women as a "mere instrument of selfish enjoyment."

From a theological standpoint nothing had changed, but as a practical matter, no significant efforts would be made to enforce this reiteration of Catholic orthodoxy about contraception on secular social policy in America or elsewhere in the world. The situation politically would revert to quiet acquiescence, just as in the nineteenth century, the church-state battleground shifting, instead, to the debate over legalizing abortion.[18]

Undoubtedly aware of the internal debate going on within the church, President Kennedy, in his last statements on population, hinted at the potential for a change of his administration's policy when he finally acknowledged the seriousness of population growth and a willingness to have the United States make better "information" about it available to the world. In July of 1963, the Senate Foreign Relations Committee chairman, William Fulbright of Arkansas, insulated from Catholic intimidation by his largely Protestant constituency, seized the initiative from the executive branch and added an amendment to the foreign aid bill specifically authorizing programs in population research and technical assistance. Within months, Adlai Stevenson, who was serving as ambassador to the United Nations, went before a Planned Parenthood audience to talk about the issue, and Dwight David Eisenhower publicly disavowed the position he had taken as President that family planning was not the government's business. Together with his predecessor Harry Truman, he then accepted the honorary chairmanship of a Planned Parenthood fund-raising campaign.

On Dec. 16, 1963, only weeks after the Kennedy assassination,

Pres. Lyndon Johnson signed the historic Fulbright bill into law. It was less than four years following Kennedy's prediction that the possibility of a President's ever having to authorize funds for family planning was remote.[19]

Just several weeks earlier, the journalist Lloyd Shearer of *Parade* magazine had interviewed Margaret in her room at the House by the Side of the Road, a convalescent home in Tucson, where she had been living for the past year. He found her bedridden, but still spirited and "irrepressibly pedagogic," as he put it. She talked mostly about the past:

> Fifty years ago I realized what was coming—the population explosion we hear so much about today, women having more and more babies until there's neither food nor room for them on earth. And I tried to do something about it. Now I have thousands of people all over the world aware of that problem and its only possible solutions—family limitation and planned parenthood. But 50 years ago, what opposition I had: the law, the police, the government, even my own father! He was the most broad-minded Irishman I ever knew—Michael Higgins was his name. But he kept saying, "Margaret! Get out of it. Get out of it. The kind of nursing you're doing, the kind of project you're involved in—that's no life for a girl!"

By Shearer's account, Margaret was happy to observe the change in the tide of international opinion about population and deeply satisfied that the American government had finally authorized the funding of family planning assistance abroad. He praised her for "having fearlessly faced imprisonment, condemnation and ostracism" and concluded: "To many persons, both her name and her views are still objectionable. But in the eyes of many she has lived to become a respected prophet in her own time."[20]

Stuart Sanger sat in on the interview with his mother. It was one of her better days. She had been confined to a wheelchair or to bed since her return from Christmas dinner the previous year. That had been an especially festive occasion, because young Margaret Sanger, who married her second cousin, Olive Byrne Richard's son, Dom Marston, had just given birth to her first child, a little girl. Born on November 5, 1962, the baby was named Margaret but called Peggy after the child who would have been her great-aunt.

The matriarch of the family spent most of the day quietly reposing in bed, but when her great granddaughter was brought to her, she suddenly became animated and kept repeating: "Peggy's come back. Peggy's come back." She then ran her hands over the infant's head to discern her personality from its shape and contour, as Michael Higgins's phrenology books had instructed her to do so long ago. Observing this compelling but strange behavior, Margaret Marston despaired that her grandmother was growing more and more disoriented and confused. She did not then understand that her new baby had been born nearly forty-seven years to the day of little Peggy Sanger's death. She did not then know that her grandmother had stood by her own daughter's deathbed all those many years earlier actually believing she saw the light of Peggy's tiny soul ascending to the heavens, nor that she had kept up imaginary conversations with the dead child for years, fully anticipating that one day they would be reunited.

This extraordinary reunion with little Peggy Marston and her family turned out to be Margaret's last journey outside the nursing home. As they were driving back that day, Margaret Marston also remembers that her grandmother became quite agitated and began to cry, protesting that she wanted to go back to her own bed in her own home. It was an especially difficult moment. Stuart stopped the car and after a silence that seemed interminable told his mother firmly that she simply could not go home again, because her bed there was no longer made. The elementary reasoning quieted her down, but Stuart was distraught for days thereafter. It was the only time his daughter ever remembers seeing him express any visible emotion.[21]

For the remainder of her life, Margaret was most often too tired to read or talk and had only infrequent visitors. She was only coherent some of the time, and was able to remember the distant past far more clearly than anything recent. Old colleagues from the birth control movement and several friends from Tucson were deeply distressed that she had been placed in an institution by her family, and bending to criticism of the particular facility, Stuart had her transferred to a different one nearby called the Valley House and Convalescent Center. He then retired and moved with his wife to Mexico. Occasionally someone would come by to see Margaret, bearing a plate of her favorite chicken sandwiches, a birthday cake, or some other treat, but she had little appetite and seemed almost to waste away. Unable to sit up on her own any longer, she nonetheless had the presence to request that a nurse bring her a paper cup and straw so she could drink the champagne that Grant and Edwina brought when they came out to visit for Christmas in 1964. Young Anne Sanger admired one of the paintings she had done that hung on the wall of her little room, and she gave it to her as a gift with this message: "H. G. Wells says I was the greatest woman who ever lived." Yet when all six of Margaret's New York grandchildren lined up against the wall of her room so she could see them together, she couldn't keep track of their names.[22]

Several months later the Planned Parenthood Center of Tucson sponsored a testimonial dinner in Margaret's honor and hailed her as "the woman of the century." She was unable to be there, of course, but 1,000 guests attended, including the Duke and Duchess of Windsor, the former New Dealer and American ambassador to England, Lewis Douglas, who lived in Tucson, and the wife of the Arizona Senator and Republican Presidential candidate, Barry Goldwater. They heard Dr. John Rock praise Margaret's remarkable ability to combine "practical action with idealism," while Mrs. B. K. Nehru, wife of the Indian ambassador to the United States, declared that she had "single-handedly carried the torch of responsible motherhood" to the women of India and all over a crowded world. The celebration received extensive news and editorial coverage in local papers, where embittered organizers called attention to the fact that neither Planned Parenthood–World Population in America nor the International Planned Parenthood Federation had sent an official representative. Nonetheless, there was some good news. Margaret's old friend Grace Sternberg had been campaigning for years to have her awarded an honorary doctorate from the University of Arizona and finally succeeded over the protest of several Catholics on the board of trustees. Announcement was made of the degree to be granted at commencement ceremonies in May.[23]

In conjunction with the dinner, Ambassador Douglas and other leading Democrats in Arizona, including the United States Secretary of the Interior, Stewart Udall, also attempted to have President Johnson award Margaret Sanger a Presidential Medal of Freedom. Since the honor was intended to be nonpartisan, they lined up Republican support for the nomination from the conservative Goldwaters and the more liberal New York Senator, Jacob Javits. The publisher of Tucson's newspaper and many other prominent Arizonans wrote to the White House and to the members of the Distinguished Civilian Service Awards Board of the United States Civil Service Commission, which handled the awards process. Pointing out that Margaret was terribly old and ill, they argued that she deserved to be honored before she died for the freedoms she had struggled for so long to win for the world's women and families.[24]

As a political issue, family planning had been put on hold because of the Kennedy assassination, the initiation of the Johnson administration, and the contentious election campaign of 1964. The White House was embroiled in historic civil rights legislation, and in the dramatic escalation of American military involvement in Vietnam, yet federal agencies were quietly beginning to address the matter. On the international front, the Agency for International Development assigned Dr. Leona Baumgartner, a former New York City health commissioner with a long-standing interest in birth control, to meet with government personnel and outside policy experts in anticipation of putting together practical programs, and at the State Department population officers were being assigned through the Alliance for Progress initiative to desks in every major country in Latin America. Secretary of State Dean Rusk and McGeorge Bundy, then chief White House foreign policy adviser, had also met with population activists, following the election. They rejected a proposal for the creation of a special commission but did see that a pledge was incorporated into President Johnson's State of the Union Message in 1965 to "seek new ways to use our knowledge to help deal with the explosion in world population and the growing scarcity in world resources." Four more specific references to the international population problem were made by the President that year, representing what the activists understood to be a "calculated escalation" to test public opinion and encourage government officials to act.

Meanwhile, on the domestic front there was even more demonstrable progress. During 1965, a dozen pilot projects were jointly developed by the new Office of Economic Opportunity and various Planned Parenthood affiliates around the country to bring contraceptive services to married indigent women as part of the Johnson administration's emerging War on Poverty. Only one major condition for this initiative was set by OEO administrator Sargent Shriver, the brother-in-law of the late President: that there be absolutely no publicity.

For the time being at least, President Johnson also insisted on keeping a cautious distance in public from family planning activists. White House staff firmly rejected all requests for formal meetings. They did not want the administration's policies to provoke resistance from Catholics and, in fact, maintained informal procedures for keeping in touch with key church officials about what was going on. Johnson himself wrote to Lew Douglas, who was a longtime personal friend, saying that he was "not unaware of the innovations and trail blazing" of Margaret Sanger but was constrained by the recommendations of the panel he had appointed to review award nominations. He clearly intended to do nothing.

No record of the panel's deliberations can be found, but subsequent correspondence with Johnson refers to "certain difficulties" that arose in connection with the 1965 Presidential Medal of Freedom, and given the President's acknowledged sensitivity to thinking within the Catholic Church, it is not hard to contemplate what those difficulties might have been. It was one thing to inaugurate pilot family planning programs, quite another to honor the country's best-known antagonist of Catholics.

In fact, the Johnson administration would move ahead on family planning with circumspection. Following Margaret's death, the President did agree to accept an award from Planned Parenthood for his international achievements which was given in her name, but he did not show up in person for the presentation ceremony. He was increasingly preoccupied by Vietnam and by the violence spreading through the country's urban ghettos, where black militants were becoming increasingly vocal. Johnson would not dramatically expand family planning assistance abroad or at home until legislated to do so by Congress in 1967. At that time, the historic Title X Amendment to the Foreign Assistance Act authorized $35 million for family planning assistance to foreign governments, United Nations agencies, and private nonprofit organizations (including the International Planned Parenthood Federation), while amendments to the Social Security Act designated that no less than 6 percent of funds for Maternal and Child Health Services be spent on domestic family planning programs. These were not Presidential initiatives, however, but rather the work of a bipartisan coalition in the Senate, including Democratic Senators Fulbright and Gruening, who chaired extensive hearings, along with Joseph S. Clark of Pennsylvania, Joseph D. Tydings of Maryland, Alan Cranston of California, and the maverick Republican, Robert Packwood of Oregon. In the House, critical leadership was provided by two liberal Democrats, Morris Udall of Arizona and James Scheuer of New York, and by two Republicans, Robert Taft of Ohio, and a newcomer from Texas. His name was George H. Bush, and he would remain a staunch advocate of reproductive freedom for women until political considerations during the 1980 Presidential elections accounted for one of the most dramatic and cynical public policy reversals in modern American politics.[25]

* * *

Margaret did not live long enough to witness these developments. Happily, she did die with the comfort of knowing that the United States Supreme Court had made its historic decision in *Griswold v. Connecticut*. Though increasingly senile and frail, she also appeared to understand when told that the government of Japan in 1965 had granted her one of its highest honors, the Third Order of the Sacred Crown. She never learned, however, of a letter of August 11, 1966, sent by Lady Bird Johnson at the urging of mutual friends, wishing her good health and happiness on behalf of the President, though this informal communication was as close to official recognition as she ever received from her own country.[26]

She died of arteriosclerosis on September 6, 1966, just a few days short of her eighty-eighth birthday. *The New York Times* ran a front-page obituary, and Edwina Sanger, traveling with her younger children in Greece, learned of the death from a cover photograph and story in *The Times* of London. On the floor of the United States Senate, Ernest Gruening mourned the passing of "a great woman, a courageous and indomitable person who lived to see one of the remarkable revolutions of modern times—a revolution which her torch kindled—the breakthrough which enables us to discuss birth control and the population explosion and to seek acceptable solutions."[27]

A private funeral service was held two days later at St. Phillips-in-the-Hills, the Episcopal Church Margaret had occasionally attended in Tucson. Grant flew out with his oldest son, Michael, and Stuart came up alone from Mexico, but aside from a few local friends, no one else could make it. The Rev. George Ferguson delivered a eulogy that did not ignore Margaret's achievements on behalf of humanity but remembered her more for the marvelous sense of fun she brought to Tucson during the many years they knew each other, with her lively interests, festive parties, and essential joy in living.

On September 21, 1966, the autumnal equinox, the extended Sanger family, along with numerous colleagues from the birth control movement, gathered for a memorial service at St. George's Church on Stuyvesant Square in New York, where Noah Slee had long worshipped. Included among the famous and powerful was Mrs. Rose Halpern, then a spry little lady of eighty, who had been one of Margaret's first patients in Brownsville and a member of the welcoming party that greeted her when she left jail.

The city's heaviest rainfall in sixty-three years produced gale-force winds and tortuous traffic congestion that day, and many of the mourners arrived late for the service in the large and beautiful church. A choir of twenty members robed in scarlet flanked an altar adorned with the flowers Margaret had most loved. Morris Ernst eulogized her in a light vein, enumerating her courageous accomplishments but emphasizing her wit and charm, and Hobson Pittman offered an even more personal remembrance. The new rector at St. George's had never met Margaret, but her long-devoted secretary, Florence Rose, sent along copies of past tributes, so he had good material with which to work. The weather provided him his best line. It was, he said, "a stormy day to end a stormy life."[28]

But the last word must be Margaret's own.

In one of their final conversations, Margaret Marston asked her grandmother what she wanted said after she died. And Margaret said she hoped she would be remembered for helping women, because women are the strength of the future. They take care of culture and tradition and preserve what is good.

That, she hoped, would be her remembrance.[29]

Notes

1: GHOSTS

1. The chapter title is taken from *Ghosts* (1881) by Henrik Ibsen in *Four Great Plays* (New York: 1959), Introduction by John Gassner, which observes: "It is not just the things we inherit from our parents. It is the ideas that live on in us as ghosts which define our path of duty."

The Sanger memory is from Margaret Sanger, *My Fight for Birth Control* (New York: 1931), p. 13. The incident is paired with a recollection of running away from the house and inadvertently getting lost, a commonly understood sign of separation stress. Both are dropped from Margaret Sanger, *An Autobiography* (New York: 1938), a journalistically polished and considerably more upbeat account of her life, produced with the help of a team of best-selling authors.

2. The Higgins family Bible was deposited in the Margaret Sanger papers of the Sophia Smith Collection at Smith College, hereinafter MS-SS. For the census data, see the Planned Parenthood of the Southern Tier Newsletter, special Margaret Sanger issue, Jan. 1973, MS-SS.

3. The material in quotation on the perfectly formed new babies is in *My Fight,* p. 12, and *Autobiography,* p. 14. A Higgins family tree is in MS-SS, but does not seem totally correct as a result of confusion caused by changes of names. The siblings, in order, were Mary, 1870, Joseph, 1872, Anna (Nan), 1874, John, 1875, Thomas, 1877, Margaret, 1879, Ethel, 1883, Clio (changed name to Lawrence), 1886, George McGlynn, 1887, Richard, 1889, Arlington (changed named to Robert), 1892. Also see Richard Higgins to M.S., Sept. 11, 1936, Margaret Sanger papers in the Library of Congress, hereinafter MS-LC; and Robert Higgins to M.S., n.d. (1938), MS-SS, enclosing newspaper clipping of his election to the College Football Hall of Fame with a note that reads "by the grace of God I had four wonderful sisters."

A particular Yeats line that comes to mind is: "Not Beauty to make a stranger's eye distraught/ Or hers before a looking glass, for such,/ Being made beautiful overmuch/ Consider beauty a sufficient end/ Lose natural kindness and maybe/ The heart-revealing intimacy/ That chooses right, and never find a friend." From "A Prayer for My Daughter," in William Butler Yeats, *Selected Poetry* (London: 1974).

4. *Autobiography,* p. 12. Higgins's 1846 birth date is on the Steuben County Census records for 1880 and 1900. His Volunteer Enlistment record, dated Dec. 1863, New York City has the 1843 date, suggesting that he was lying in order to qualify. His military record is chronicled in the Abstracts of Civil War Muster Rolls, New York State Archives, Albany, New York (which includes a Medical File Card) and in the Records of the 12th Regiment of New York Cavalry at the National Archives, Washington, D.C. I am indebted to Alex Sanger, Margaret's grandson, for providing me with copies of these documents, which he has collected for a family genealogy. Margaret's handwritten notes on a letter about

her father's pension application from her uncle, Sen. William Purcell, to his sister, Anne Higgins, May 23, 1910, tell the mule story, MS-LC. Also see Harold Hersey, "Margaret Sanger: The Biography of the Birth Control Pioneer" New York (1938). Hersey's completed manuscript was printed but never published when his publisher went bankrupt during the Depression. It was discovered in the New York Public Library by Alex Sanger in 1969 and can be found there and in MS-SS, and MS-LC. Hersey was a journalist who met and fell in love with Sanger in 1919 and contributed to her first periodical publication *The Birth Control Review*. He wrote this biography long after their love affair had ended, and she adamantly refused his request for permission to publish the book because she did not want it to compete with her own and because Hersey's numerous interviews with people who knew her as a child challenged her own sanitized account of her family. The book is an important source of information from the only contemporary of Sanger's who wrote about her. Correspondence from Harold Hersey to M.S., 1920 and 1938, is in MS-SS. James Reed, *The Birth Control Movement and American Society: From Private Vice to Public Virtue* (Princeton: 1984), fn. p. 395, discusses Hersey.

5. Again, my thanks to Alex Sanger for the genealogical record on Anne Higgins (sometimes called Annie), and for extracts from the 1870 census for Hunterdon County, N.J. (M-583, Roll 870, Raritan Township, Flemington), which identifies Joseph Purcell's family and real estate holdings. Also see Hersey, pp. 10, 27–28, 32. The Higgins family Bible in MS-SS, chronicles the family's early travels by listing the birthplaces of the older children. The question of where Sanger was born is discussed in Ronni MacLaren and Elissa Mautner, "Corning's Margaret Higgins Sanger," *Andaste Inquirer* 7:1 (May 1978), pp. 9–18 (a publication of the Painted Post Historical Society of Corning, New York, to which I am grateful for a copy). MacLaren and Mautner were students in a 1977 Smith College seminar on Sanger, and some of the research materials for their article remain in MS-SS. Sanger's *Autobiography* says she was born in a house in the woods, beyond the city limits, where her father had gone because of her mother's poor health. Finally, for context on nineteenth century Irish family life, see Hasia Diner, *Erin's Daughters in America: Irish Immigrant Women in the 19th Century* (Baltimore: 1983), passim.

6. Hersey, "Margaret Sanger," pp. 12–13. The extent of Higgins's drinking is disputed. Grant Sanger, who spent time with him as a boy on Cape Cod during the 1920s, says he was an "alcoholic" for many years, but Olive Richard, who lived with him as a child in Corning, vehemently denies this, saying that though he carried a whiskey flask, and liked an occasional nip, he actually drank in moderation.

See author's interview with Grant Sanger, M.D., Aug. 1976, for the Schlesinger-Rockefeller Oral History Project, Schlesinger Library, Radcliffe College, p. 3. Olive Richard's comments are from an interview with the author on Mar. 28, 1985, in Indian Shores, Fla. On modernization see Richard D. Brown, *Modernization: The Transformation of American Life, 1600–1865* (New York: 1976). And on the disruption of the American artisan system, Sean Wilentz, *Chants Democratic: New York City and the Rise of the American Working Class, 1788–1850* (New York: 1984), esp. pp. 4–5.

7. Hersey, "Margaret Sanger," pp. 14, 39. Recollection of the glassworkers' strike is from Nelson L. Somers, *Corning Memories*, Collection of the Painted

Post Historical Society, Corning, New York. On glassblowing at Corning, also see *Fortune,* 1:1 (Jan. 1930) with photographs by Margaret Bourke-White and text by Dwight Macdonald.

8. On the church and organized labor, see John Tracy Ellis, *American Catholicism* (Chicago: 1969), pp. 106–108. *My Fight,* p. 7, *Autobiography.* p. 21, and Hersey, "Margaret Sanger," pp. 22–24 discuss the Ingersoll incident, which may be part truth, part fabrication. Orvin Larson, *American Infidel: Robert G. Ingersoll* (New York, 1962), has Ingersoll stopping in Corning, the best documentation of Sanger's story that exists. For an early example of how Sanger wove the Ingersoll story into a moral lesson about the courage to speak one's convictions, see Ruth Hale, "The Child Who Was Mother to a Woman," *The New Yorker* 1:8 (Apr. 11, 1925), pp. 11–12, an extremely flattering profile written in the magazine's first year of publication. For Ingersoll on birth control, see the reprint of an address he delivered at the Hollis Theatre in Boston on June 2, 1899, published as "Robert Ingersoll on Birth Control," *The Birth Control Review* 3:10 (Oct. 1919), p. 1.

9. *Autobiography,* p. 23. Henry George's *Progress and Poverty* was first published in 1879, the year of Margaret's birth, and sold 5 million copies in its first twenty-five years in print. For Sanger on Ingersoll's influence, also see the correspondence between Sanger and Lawrence Lader in MS-SS. Sanger cooperated with Lader on a biography, Lawrence Lader, *The Margaret Sanger Story* (New York: 1955).

10. *My Fight,* p. 21, *Autobiography,* p. 33, Hersey, "Margaret Sanger," p. 33. Olive Richard told the story about the milk in her interview with the author. Also see Catherine Shafter to Ronni MacLaren and Elissa Mautner, Apr. 28, 1977, MS-SS.

11. *My Fight,* pp. 19–2l, *Autobiography,* pp. 30–31. On the intense separation of gender spheres common to Irish families, see Diner, *Erin's Daughters,* p. 16. On the significance of the Victorian daughter's special sense of having been "chosen" by her father and given a taste of a man's life, see Judith Thurman's distinguished biography, *Isak Dinesen: The Life of a Storyteller* (New York: 1982), p. 26. On changing attitudes toward the idea of infant damnation in the nineteenth century, see Barbara Welter, "The Feminization of American Religion: 1800–1860," in *Clio's Consciousness Raised,* edited by Mary S. Hartman and Lois W. Banner (New York: 1974), p. 140.

12. *My Fight,* pp. 11–12. Sigmund Freud, *The Interpretation of Dreams* (New York: 1965), p. 235.

13. Michael Higgins to Mary Higgins, July 31, 1902, in MS-LC tells of his lady chasing. Further commentary on how the women of the Irish immigrant community typically deemphasized romance and sexuality are in Diner, *Erin's Daughters,* pp. 16–17, 22–23, which contains a favorite folk proverb of the community of Margaret's childhood: "The three things that leave the shortest traces are a bird on a branch, a ship on the sea, and a man on a woman." For a feminist theory of how women negotiate oedipal attachments, see Nancy Chodorow, *The Reproduction of Mothering: Psychoanalysis and the Sociology of Gender* (Berkeley: 1978), p. 140. As a physical legacy of the childhood bout with typhoid, Sanger suffered from lifelong gallbladder colic, and had gallbladder surgery in 1938, according to Dr. Grant Sanger in his interview with the author for the Schlesinger Library, p. 50.

My interpretation of Sanger's relationship to her father disputes David Kennedy, *Birth Control in America: The Career of Margaret Sanger* (New Haven: 1970), p. 3, which reaches the peremptory conclusion from this incident that Sanger associated her father with an "aggressive, threatening, masculine sexual instinct . . . that continued to color her attitudes toward men and sex." Since Kennedy did not explore the archival materials on Sanger's personal life, he could not have known much about her sexuality or her feelings about men. His rush to judgment may nonetheless explain his skepticism about her. The mistaken view of Sanger as completely antimale is deep-rooted. See also Christopher Lasch, *The New Radicalism in America: The Intellectual as a Social Type* (New York: 1965), p. 62, and William O'Neill, *Everyone Was Brave* (New York: 1969).

14. Rev. Robert F. McNamara to Ronni MacLaren and Elissa Mautner, "Easter Sunday, 1977," enclosing notes he had compiled for a history of the parish in Corning, which was published privately in the 1940s as *A Century of Grace*, in MS-SS. The birth date on the baptismal certificate was listed as Sept. 14, 1880, and the middle name as "Elizabeth," the first disparity suggesting how early Margaret may have begun to lie about her age, the second, that she may have taken the middle name of a sponsor outside her immediate family. Hersey, p. 21, confirms the incident and says he interviewed people who remembered it. Margaret wrote herself about the significance of religious feeling in the lives of adolescents in the newspaper column that launched her career: "What Every Boy and Girl Should Know," *The Call*, Sunday Supplement, Collections of the Tamiment Library, New York University, hereinafter, Tamiment–NYU. On the rigid sex segregation of the Irish immigrant church, see Diner, *Erin's Daughters*, pp. 22–23. Reflections on adolescent religion and identity formation are in Erik Erickson, *Identity, Youth and Crisis* (New York: 1968), esp. p. 27, and Chodorow, *Reproduction*, pp. 79, 137–38.

15. *My Fight*, p. 22, *Autobiography*, p. 34, Hersey, "Margaret Sanger," pp. 56–57.

16. Printed brochures describing Claverack are in MS-SS. Also see correspondence with Sanger's school friend, Amelia Stuart Mitchell, in MS-SS and *My Fight*, p. 22.

17. Claverack photos are in MS-SS. Also *My Fight*, pp. 23–28, *Autobiography*, pp. 35–36, and Hersey (interview with Amelia Stuart Mitchell), p. 62. M.S. to Mabel Pyott, Amelia Stuart's daughter, after Amelia died in 1955, describes Margaret's affection for her mother, in MS-SS. There are abundant letters in the Sanger files from old friends at Claverack, especially when the photograph of Margaret and Corey Albertson was published in *Life* in 1937. See, for example, M.S. to Gola Beagle, July 23, 1937, MS-LC. On female adolescent sexuality in the nineteenth century, also see Nancy Sahli, "Smashing: Women's Relationships Before the Fall," paper delivered at the Third Berkshire Conference on the History of Women, Bryn Mawr, Pa., June 11, 1976, and Carroll Smith-Rosenberg, "The Female World of Love and Ritual: Relations Between Women in Nineteenth-Century America," in *Disorderly Conduct: Visions of Gender in Victorian America* (New York: 1985), pp. 53–76. Margaret's theatrical aspirations are described in *Autobiography*, pp. 13, 32, 38, and in *My Fight*, p. 24, and are confirmed in Mary Higgins's diary, Mar. 2, 1898, MS-SS. On the role that clothes and material aspirations played in the fantasy

life of Irish servant girls, see Christine Stansell, *City of Women: Sex and Class in New York, 1789–1860* (New York: 1986), p. 157.

18. Mary Sanger diary, Aug. 25, 1897, MS-SS. For the experience of Irish domestics in acquiring modern bourgeois tastes, see Diner, *Erin's Daughters,* p. 84, and on the rise of the Victorian bourgeoisie, Robert Wiebe, *The Search for Order 1877–1920* (New York: 1967). Stansell, *City of Women,* pp. 155–68, and 219–20, takes a bleak view of the relations between homemaker and servant in New York City, yet agrees that bourgeois values ultimately triumphed, reshaping the aspirations of servants and destroying their cultural autonomy.

19. *My Fight,* p. 21. *Autobiography,* p. 28. Sanger's lifelong preoccupation with wealth and status is evident in her private correspondence with her longtime friend, Juliet Barrett Rublee, recently discovered in the attic of Rublee's former summer house in Cornish, New Hampshire, and now housed in the Dartmouth College Library, hereinafter, MS-DC. Also see Grant Sanger interview, Aug. 1976. Stuart Sanger also talked about his mother's conflicts over money in an interview with the author on March 17, 1986, in Tucson, Ariz. On status incongruity, see Richard Sennett and Jonathan Cobb, *The Hidden Injuries of Class* (New York: 1972), pp. 21–31.

20. *Autobiography,* p. 16. *My Fight,* p. 11. Diner, *Erin's Daughters,* pp. 22–23, suggests that the Higgins marital intimacy was indeed unusual for the Irish community. See Chodorow, *Reproduction,* p. 197, on how women take refuge in romance as a reasonable response to actual economic and social subordination and dependence.

21. The Higgins family photographs are in MS–SS. Sanger's descriptions of her mother are in *Autobiography,* p. 11 and *My Fight,* p. 4. On the influence of Anne Higgins and the contempt of the Higgins children for their father, see Grant Sanger interview, pp. 1–5.

22. On FitzGerald see "Edward FitzGerald, 1809–1883, Poet and Translator," in Leslie Stephen and Sidney Lee, *Dictionary of National Biography* (New York, 1908), pp. 111–13; Alfred Terhume, *The Life of Edward FitzGerald, Translator of The Rubaiyat of Omar Khayyam* (London: 1947), and Grant Sanger interview, p. 1.

23. *Autobiography,* p. 16, *My Fight,* p. 5. Author's interview with Margaret Sanger Marston, Arlington, Va., Feb. 1986.

24. *My Fight,* p. 12. On the Victorian culture of TB, see Susan Sontag, *Illness as Metaphor* (New York: 1979), p. 14. For an understanding of the etiology of TB, I am grateful to Paul Brandt-Rauf, M.D., of the Columbia University College of Physicians and Surgeons, who lectured on the subject at the Center for the Study of Society and Medicine on July 26, 1984.

Anne Higgins's suffering was only alleviated by popular notions that identified victims of TB as particularly edified and gave rise to such enduring heroines as Mimi in Puccini's *La Boheme,* who, in a febrile blush, meets her death in a Parisian garret—beautifully and peacefully and without apparent remorse. This cultural stereotype may also have reinforced the refined aura Anne and her daughters so deliberately cultivated.

25. My analysis of nineteenth-century contraception and American social behavior is based on a wide reading in the rich secondary source material now available. Among the best general treatments are the following: Smith-Rosenberg, *Disorderly Conduct,* esp. pp. 79–89 and 167–81; Carl Degler, *At*

Odds: Women and the Family in America from the Revolution to the Present (New York: 1980), pp. 3–85; John D'Emilio and Estelle B. Freedman, *Intimate Matters: A History of Sexuality in America* (New York: 1988); Peter Gay, *The Bourgeois Experience, Victoria to Freud,* Vol. 1: *Education of the Senses* (New York: 1984); Christopher Lasch, *Haven in a Heartless World: The Family Besieged* (New York: 1977), pp. 3–22; Wiebe, *Search for Order*; Kennedy, *Birth Control,* pp. 36–71, and Reed, *Birth Control Movement,* pp. 19–33. For case studies on the communities of upstate New York earlier in the century, but providing important context for the Higgins family, see Paul E. Johnson, *A Shopkeeper's Millennium: Society and Revivals in Rochester, New York, 1815–1837* (New York: 1978), and Mary P. Ryan, *Cradle of the Middle Class: The Family in Oneida County, New York, 1790–1865* (Cambridge, Eng., and New York: 1981), esp. pp. 145–242.

Stuart M. Blumin, "The Hypothesis of Middle Class Formation in Nineteenth-Century America: A Critique and Some Proposals," *American Historical Review* 90 (Apr. 1985), pp. 299-337, challenges the theory that a middle-class cohered on distinct economic grounds in the nineteenth century but nonetheless agrees that personal and social values converged in such a way as to define a perceptible middle-class experience, against which the Higgins family history can be judged.

On demographic trends and contraceptive use, specifically, see Reed, *Birth Control Movement,* pp. 3–18, 39–41 and 44–45. Especially important is his use of data compiled by Maris A. Vinovskis, "Demographic Changes in America from the Revolution to the Civil War: An Analysis of the Socio-Economic Determinants of Fertility Differentials and Trends in Massachusetts from 1765 to 1860," doctoral dissertation, Harvard University, 1975, p. 12, and his citation of Charles Goodyear, *The Applications and Uses of Vulcanized Gum Elastic* (Connecticut: 1853). Also see the demographers Ainsley J. Coale and Melvin Zelnick, *New Estimates of Fertility and Population in the United States* (Princeton: 1963), pp. 36, 40; Linda Gordon, *Woman's Body, Woman's Right: A Social History of Birth Control in America* (New York: 1976), esp. pp. 64–70; Degler, *At Odds,* pp. 210–26, D'Emilio and Freedman, *Intimate Matters,* pp. 57–66; Daniel Scott Smith, "Family Limitation, Sexual Control and Domestic Feminism in Victorian America," *Feminist Studies* 1:3 (Winter–Spring 1973), and Janet F. Brodie, "Family Limitation in American Culture: 1830–1900," doctoral dissertation, University of Chicago, 1982, esp. pp. 396–428. On the development of Christian sexual doctrine, see John T. Noonan, Jr. *Contraception: A History of Its Treatment by the Catholic Theologians and Canonists,* 2d ed. (Cambridge, Mass: 1986), pp. 31–55. The story of Onan is from Genesis 38: 8–10, quoted and analyzed in Noonan, *Contraception,* pp. 10 and 33–35, and in Gordon, *Woman's Body,* pp. 5–7. On the distinction between Hebrew and early Christian interpretations, also see Alvah Sulloway, *Birth Control and Catholic Doctrine* (New York: 1959), Chap. 3. For a brilliant interpretation of Augustinian doctrine and its historical significance, see Elaine Pagels, *Adam, Eve and the Serpent* (New York: 1988) and W. H. C. Frend, "The Triumph of Sin," a review of Pagels in *The New York Review of Books,* June 30, 1988, pp. 27–30. Clinical studies of birth control practice from the 1930s confirm the endurance of withdrawal as a contraceptive practice. See Degler, *At Odds,* p. 212. On specific nineteenth century contraceptives, see One *Hundred Years of*

Birth Control: An Outline of Its History, pamphlet distributed at the First American Birth Control Conference, Nov. 1921, copy in MS-SS; Brodie, "Family Limitation in America," pp. 56–57, 101–102, 145, 158, 161, 167, 179–206, 375–78; Noonan, *Contraception,* pp. 392–94; Norman E. Himes, *Medical History of Contraception* (Baltimore: 1936), pp. 212–18; Gordon, *Woman's Body,* pp. 42–44, 64–66, 78–79, 86–87, 166–70; Reed, *Birth Control Movement,* pp. 10–13; Degler, *At Odds,* pp. 213–17. Folk remedies are the focus of Brodie, "Family Limitation in America," pp. 61, 112–21, 136–38, 143, 360–67, 462–64.

26. Brodie, "Family Limitation in America," pp. 469–74; Degler, *At Odds,* pp. 262–64.

27. An excellent comparison of the moral absolutism of Catholics and the relativism of Protestants is in Kennedy, *Birth Control,* pp. 143–44. On the nineteenth century struggle of "control v. conscience," also see Gay, *Bourgeois Experience,* p. 263; on Roman Catholic stipulations, Sulloway, *Catholic Doctrine,* pp. 44–45, 198–99 and Noonan, *Contraception,* pp. 395–406. Noonan also covers the French experience on pp. 387–90. On the politics of American Catholicism, see Ellis, *American Catholicism,* p. 83.

28. *Autobiography,* p. 21, is less than candid about the Catholicism in her background. The Bible is in MS-SS. On the burials see Rev. Robert McNamara to Ronni MacLaren and Elissa Mautner, "Easter, 1977," MS-SS, and Grant Sanger's interview with the author. On women and religion in the late nineteenth century and the rebellion of their daughters against piety, see Lasch's essay on Jane Addams in *New Radicalism,* p. 3, and Kathryn Kish Sklar, *Catherine Beecher: A Study in American Domesticity* (New Haven: 1973).

29. Michael Higgins's pension records are in the files of the Department of the Interior, Bureau of Pensions, at the National Archives, Washington, D.C. He made his first application in 1896, alleging poor vision preventing his working, and he was awarded $6.00 a month. His condition was in no way the result of "excesses or vicious habits," according to an affidavit filed for an increase (to $12 monthly) by a Corning physician in 1907. The intervention of his distinguished brother-in-law raised the award to $30 in 1911. See especially "Commissioner of the Bureau of Pensions (signature unclear) to Hon. W. G. Purcell," Dec. 13, 1910, and "Special Act of the Senate and House of Representatives of the United States of America in Congress assembled," Feb. 25, 1911, both in the National Archives. Also see Sen. William Purcell to Anne Higgins with Margaret's handwritten notations, May 23, 1910, MS-LC; and William Purcell to M.S., Sept. 25, 1926 and Oct. 25, 1928 with Margaret's scrawled note "and a good roman c too" in MS-SS. On William Purcell's service in Congress, see *Congressional Directory: 91st Congressional Session,* p. 92, and Purcell family genealogy, p. 4.

30. *Autobiography,* p. 16, photos in *My Fight,* Hersey, "Margaret Sanger," p. 28, quoting a man named Charles Dolan.

31. Though I have tried to excise psychological jargon from the narrative as much as possible, these views have been informed by readings in object-relations theory, which provides an account of personality development that forges an intermediary path between the instinctual determinism of Freud and the environmental determinism of the cultural school of psychoanalysis represented by Karen Horney, Melanie Klein, and others. Object-relations theory maintains

that social relations from birth determine the course of the child's psychological growth, that personalities form and flourish, not in any single relationship, but through a dynamic series of connections with significant and beloved individuals. The achievement of an independent sense of self depends on the quality of the mother's primary nurture, which, in turn, affects secondary attachments with father and siblings, friends and colleagues, husband and children—pretty much common sense. Object-relations theory, and more particularly what is known today as "self-psychology," place as much emphasis on the subjective reality of the analysand as revealed in conscious or "screen" memories—the very memories that biographers have at their disposal—as they do on the buried revelations of the unconscious that Freud spent so much time trying to uncover. The clinical particulars here are less important, however, than the validity for a biographer of an overall approach to personality that uses the psychoanalytic vocabulary to understand human development without succumbing to any didactic fixations. This is what I have tried to do throughout this book.

See especially, Heinz Kohut, M.D., *How Does Analysis Cure?* (Chicago: 1984), which was edited after his death by Arnold Goldberg and Paul Stepansky and is more accessible to the lay reader than earlier writings, esp. pp. 54–56. For another variant of this approach and its relevance to the study of a gifted individual, see Alice Miller, *The Drama of the Gifted Child,* originally published as *Prisoners of Childhood* (New York: 1981), esp. pp. 9–21. Also see Margaret Mahler, "Thoughts about Development and Individuation," in *The Psychological Study of the Child* (New York: 1963), pp. 307–22. My thanks especially to Peter and Cathy Buirski for acquainting me with the work of Kohut.

The specific memories I cite are from *Autobiography,* pp. 25–26, and *My Fight,* p. 18. Mention of Margaret's jealousy of Ethel is also in Jacqueline Van Voris's interview with Olive Byrne Richard, p. 6. "Their mother used to arrange Ethel, my mother's, hair in long curls, and Margaret said she hated Ethel because of the long curls and also because their mother spent so much time with her."

Chodorow, *Reproduction,* p. 96, talks about the precarious situation of girls who do not form secure maternal attachments, and Phyllis Rose, *Woman of Letters: A Life of Virginia Woolf* (New York: 1978), pp. 109–25, traces the pathways among emotion, creativity, and political commitment in her subject's life with admirable ingenuity and control. Reading Rose's book frankly forced me to consider my own work in a whole new light, one that I hope is respectful of Rose's insights without being unduly derivative. Also see Phyllis Rose, "Fact and Fiction in Biography," *Writing of Women: Essays in a Renaissance* (Middletown, Conn.: 1985), pp. 64–85. Final thanks to my friend and neighbor, Francis Beaudry, M.D., for his many insights about the application of psychoanalytic theory to the study of creativity.

32. Hersey, "Margaret Sanger," p. 114, Grant Sanger interview, p. 11. On teaching as a career for the Irish, in particular, see Diner, *Erin's Daughters,* p. 96. Margaret may have rejoined her mother's family in New Jersey, though Hersey says that Anne Higgins herself never saw her parents after she moved away.

33. Again, thanks to Alex Sanger for a copy of Anne Higgins's death certificate. Also see Mary Higgins's diary, Mar. 31 and Apr. 1, 1899, and MacLaren and Mautner materials, both in MS-SS.

34. Margaret Sanger, *Woman and the New Race* (New York: 1920), *Autobiography*, pp. 41–42. Kohut, *How Does Analysis*, p. 156. Here again, I am indebted to Phyllis Rose, since parallels to the life of Virginia Woolf suggest themselves. In *To the Lighthouse,* Woolf creates enduring testimony to her dependent embrace of her mother in the exquisitely drawn portrait of the saintly and selfless Mrs. Ramsey, an idealized mother who derives her only satisfaction from assuring the comfort of family and friends. The invention of a perfectly realized maternal presence helped resolve Woolf's unspent grief for the mother she herself lost at the age of thirteen and helped set her free of an emotionally controlling past. See Rose, *Woman of Letters,* pp. 110, 170, Bell, p. 18, and, of course, Virginia Woolf, *To the Lighthouse* (New York: Harcourt, Brace & World, 1927).

2: LOVE AND WORK

1. *Autobiography,* pp. 42–45, *My Fight,* pp. 29–30. The Higgins family Bible, MS-SS, has Margaret's handwritten notes describing what became of her brothers and sisters. Additional information is in Harold Hersey, "Margaret Sanger: The Biography of the Birth Control Pioneer," New York (1938), pp. 28–30, and in a genealogy Margaret compiled in 1930, given to me by Alex Sanger.

Ronni MacLaren and Elissa Mautner in "Corning's Margaret Higgins Sanger," made a search of the local police docket between 1895 and 1905 and turned up the Richard Higgins incident, along with two earlier arrests of Joseph Higgins for petty burglary and fast driving.

Hasia Diner, *Erin's Daughters in America: Irish Immigrant Women in the 19th Century,* (Baltimore: 1983), p. 19, suggests that Irish mothers typically overdominated, pampered, and protected their sons, but sent the daughters out to work earlier, which gave them greater autonomy and motivation. Surely, the Higgins sisters dominated the family.

2. Regina Morantz-Sanchez, *Sympathy and Science: Women in American Medicine* (New York: 1985); Paul Starr, *The Social Transformation of American Medicine* (New York: 1987), pp. 79–180; George J. Annas, Sylvia A. Law, Rand E. Rosenblatt, and Kenneth R. Wing, *American Health Law* (Boston: 1990), pp. 701–703.

3. Morantz-Sanchez, *Sympathy and Science;* Lavinia Dock and Isabell Stewart, *A Short History of Nursing* (New York: 1931), p. 145., Mary Adelaide Nutting, *A Sound Economic Basis for Schools of Nursing* (New York: 1926), pp. 155–63. Barbara Melosh, *The Physician's Hand: Work, Culture and Conflict in American Nursing* (Philadelphia: 1982).

4. Annas, et al., *Health Law,* pp. 703–705. On the requirements of a nursing degree, see James Reed, "Margaret Sanger" in *Notable American Women, A Biographical Dictionary,* edited by Barbara Sicherman and Carol Hurd Green (Cambridge: 1980), p. 623. Also see N. Tomes, "The Silent Battle: Nurse Registration in New York State, 1903–1920," in *Nursing History: New Prospectives, New Possibilities,* edited by B. Conliffe Lagemann (New York: 1983) p. 107. My thanks to Sylvia Law for this reference. Finally, see M.S. to Mary Higgins, June 20 and July 15, 1902, in MS-SS. M.S., *Autobiography,* pp. 46–53, has Sanger's description of the backbreaking conditions, and Hersey, "Margaret

Sanger," pp. 74–75 and 77–79, corroborates her recollections by quoting from the hospital's turn-of-the-century annual reports.

5. M.S. to Mary Higgins, June 1901, and "My Dear Maggr," n.d. (1901), where she talks about treating the case of intestinal cancer, both in MS-LC; M.S. to Agnes Smedley, July 7, 1924, on the consequences of having been ill for so long, in MS-LC. Also see the Olive Byrne Richard interview with Jacqueline Van Voris, and James Reed, *The Birth Control Movement and American Society: From Private Vice to Public Virtue* (Princeton: 1984), p. 121. Grant Sanger, M.D., in his Schlesinger Library interview of 1976 offered this diagnosis of his mother's tuberculosis.

6. M.S. to Mary Higgins, Dec. 29, 1901, in MS-LC. Photos in MS-SS. Olive Byrne Richard interview with Jacqueline Van Voris, p. 25.

7. M.S. to Mary Higgins, May 12, 1902, says she's to graduate in June and then has a month to make up from her operation. Also see, M.S. to Mary Higgins, June 20 and July 15, 1902, MS-SS. Grant Sanger interview, p. 11. *My Fight*, p. 35, and *Autobiography*, p. 30, which distorts the narrative to cover up the fact that she married before she completed her degree. On the tension between personal and professional fulfillment for women of this era, see especially, Barbara Sicherman, *Alice Hamilton: A Life in Letters* (Cambridge, 1984), introduction.

8. M.S. to Mary Higgins, May 12, 1902, and n.d. (Aug. 1902), and William Sanger to Mary Higgins, Aug. 18, 1902, MS-LC.

9. M.S. to Nan Higgins, n.d. (Aug. 1902), and to Mary Higgins, "Sunday 12n," n.d. (Aug. 1902), and William Sanger to Mary Higgins, Aug. 18, 1902, MS-LC.

10. William Sanger to Mary Higgins, July 27, 1902, and Aug. 18, 1902, MS-LC. Whether she actually quit before finishing the makeup credits for the two-year degree, or did not continue the third year for registration, is unclear, though the latter seems more likely, since she did subsequently work as a practical nurse.

11. W.S. to M.S., "Dearest," Wed., May 1, n.d. (1901), MS-LC (in unidentified correspondence).

12. W.S. to M.S., Dec. 8, 1914, MS-SS. For confirmation of his virginity at marriage and his wife's pre-marital relations, see W.S. to M.S., Jan. 1915, MS-SS. Karen Horney theorized extensively on why women tend to marry their fathers. On conflict and desire in marriage, also see Phyllis Rose, *Parallel Lives: Five Victorian Marriages* (New York: 1984), p. 7.

13. M.S. to Mary Higgins, July 15, 1902, MS-SS.

14. The Sanger version of her first husband's genealogy is in *Autobiography* p. 56, and M.S. to Trena Senger, Sept. 11, 1939, MS-SS. It is wholly disputed by Ely Sanger's immigration papers, Port of New York, Oct. 3, 1878; his naturalization records, Superior Court of the City of New York, Feb. 6, 1891, and the death certificates for Ely Sanger and Henrietta Wolfberg Sanger, dated respectively Feb. 1, 1903, and Sept. 24, 1913, all cited in a Sanger family genealogy given to me by Alex Sanger. On William Sanger also see Ralph Waldo Fawcett, *The Trial of William Sanger* (New York: 1915) in MS-SS.

15. Bill Sanger conspired in the subterfuge. His daughter Joan (now Joan Sanger Hoppe of Great Barrington, Mass.) was also never told of her Jewish grandparents, never met her Jewish aunt, and said in a 1985 letter to the author

that religion was simply never discussed in the family, because her father was a confirmed atheist. Bill may also have tried to protect himself from the rampant anti-Semitism in the New York architectural profession. The quote is from M.S. to Virginia Gildersleeve of Barnard College, May 10, 1944, MS-SS. Joan was admitted. Olive Byrne Richard, in her interview with me, remembered visiting the Sangers in New York when relatives in traditional religious garb came to visit.

For an example of Margaret's concern about an anti-Semitic comment made by Havelock Ellis, see M.S. to Hugh de Selincourt, Jan. 16, 1927, MS-LC, and on the need to bring Mrs. Henry Morgenthau and New York's Jewish elite into the birth control cause, M.S. to Juliet Rublee, n.d. (1928) in MS-DC. Also, Sanger Journal entry, Sept 14, 1938, MS-SS, on reference to the Rublee's efforts in London to help get Jews out of Germany and Austria because of Hitler's "sadistic outbursts."

Once again, there is a parallel here with Virginia Woolf, who also married a Jew. See Rose, *Woman of Letters,* p. 89, which makes the point about the attraction of social disadvantage. The unfortunate self-consciousness and self-loathing of several American Jews of Sanger's acquaintance who became public figures is chronicled in Ronald Steel, *Walter Lippmann and the American Century* (New York: 1980) and in Vicki Goldberg, *Margaret Bourke-White* (New York: 1986).

16. *Autobiography,* p. 60. *My Fight,* p. 36. Byron Caples, M.D. to M.S., Feb. 6, 1930, MS-SS. The TB was apparently a problem even before the pregnancy, and Bill spoke of sending Margaret to Saranac in his letter to Mary of Aug. 18, 1902, MS-LC. The Trudeau Sanitarium at Saranac Lake, N.Y., destroyed its individual patient records from this era in the 1950s and cannot confirm that Margaret Sanger was a patient.

17. Sanger's illness is described in *Autobiography,* pp. 49, 53, in M.S. to Mary Higgins, June 1901, MS-LC, M.S. to Ethel Remington Hepburn, Apr. 11, 1938, MS-LC, and M.S. to Philip Bourke, editor of the *Fluoroscope,* a magazine about TB, June 5, 1935, the latter cited in Reed, *Birth Control Movement,* p. 396. Also see Hersey, "Margaret Sanger," pp. 71, 75. For a popular account of Saranac that does not document Sanger's stay but offers some perspective on her experience, see Robert Taylor, *Saranac: America's Magic Mountain* (Boston: 1986). Also, Susan Sontag, *Illness as Metaphor* (New York: 1979) on TB and sexuality, pp. 12–13.

18. W.S. to M.S., Feb. 15, 1914, Grant Sanger, Schlesinger interview, p. 12, and author's interview with Olive Byrne Richard.

19. *Autobiography,* p. 61, *My Fight,* p. 40. Olive Byrne Richard interview with Jacqueline Van Voris.

20. M.S. to Lawrence Lader, Oct. 27, 1953, MS-SS; *My Fight,* pp. 43–44, *Autobiography,* pp. 62, 66.

21. Ibid.; W.S. to Grant Sanger, October 21, 1952, MS-SS, Hastings clipping from Feb. 20, 1908, in MS-LC, Scrapbooks; M.S. to Juliet Rublee, "Wednesday" (Bronxville), n.d. (about 1919) MS-DC. Joy G. Dryfoos, "Margaret Sanger's Suburban Interlude," *The Westchester Historian,* 63:3, Summer 1987, pp. 73–78. My thanks to Charlotte Fahn, the current occupant of the house, for a copy of this article.

22. *Autobiography,* pp. 66-67; W.S. to Grant Sanger, Oct. 21, 1952, MS-SS.

3: SEEDS OF REBELLION

1. The standard references on this cultural transition are Henry F. May, *The End of American Innocence: A Study of the First Years of Our Own Time* (New York: 1959), which cites the Brooks quote; see esp. pp. 21, 23, 30, 39; and Morton White, *Social Thought in America: The Revolt Against Formalism* 2d ed. (Boston: 1957). For Lippmann quotes, see *Walter Lippmann: Early Writings,* edited by Arthur Schlesinger, Jr. (New York: 1970), introduction, and Ronald Steel, *Walter Lippmann and the American Century* (New York: 1980) p. 45; and for Floyd Dell, see *Love in Greenwich Village* (New York: 1923), p. 27. Also see Leslie Fishbein, *Rebels in Bohemia: The Radicals of the Masses, 1911–1917* (Chapel Hill: 1982); Irving Howe, *Socialism in America* (New York: 1985) and Robert A. Rosenstone, *Romantic Revolutionary: A Biography of John Reed* (New York: 1975).

2. *Autobiography,* pp. 69–70; Hersey, "Margaret Sanger," pp. 86–92; letter from William Sanger, n.d. (1911), in Socialist Party Local New York Letter Books, 1907–1914, Tamiment Library, New York University, hereinafter SPNY,Tamiment-NYU. Election results are in *Report of the Board of Election of the City of New York for the Year Ending December 31, 1911* (New York: 1912), cited in Alexander Campbell Sanger, "Margaret Sanger, The Early Years, 1910–1917," senior thesis, Princeton University, 1969, p. 31, in MS-SS. Just under 10,000 total votes were cast in the district.

3. *Autobiography,* pp. 69–72.

4. For Socialist Party electoral results, see Howe, *Socialism in America,* and on women and socialism, *The Papers of Eugene Victor Debs,* microfilm edition, in Tamiment, NYU, p. 11; E.V. Debs, *Woman: Comrade and Equal,* undated pamphlet issued by the National Office of the Socialist Party, Chicago, in MS-SS; "Women and Socialism," an editorial in *The Masses* 1:2 (Dec. 1911), p. 4, and Mari Jo Buhle, *Women and American Socialism, 1870–1920* (Urbana, Ill. 1983), Chaps. 4–7 and especially pp. 147–56. An advertisment for "Margaret Sanger, Women's Organizer" is in *The Call,* Nov. 20, 1911, and for Sanger on suffrage, see her article in *The Call,* Dec. 24, 1911, both in Tamiment-NYU. Finally, see Alex Sanger, "Early Years," p. 35.

5. Elizabeth Griffith, *In Her Own Right: The Life of Elizabeth Cady Stanton* (New York: 1984).

6. For this dimension of suffrage, see especially Aileen Kraditor, *The Ideas of the Woman Suffrage Movement 1890–1920* (New York: 1965), esp., pp. 53–55, and Ellen Dubois, *Feminism and Suffrage: The Emergence of an Independent Women's Movement in America, 1848–1869* (Ithaca, N.Y.: 1978), passim. Also, William H. Chafe, *The American Woman: Her Changing Social, Economic and Political Role, 1920–1970* (New York: 1972), pp. 10–13. After Stanton's death at the age of eighty-seven in 1902, she was all but obliterated from the official memory of the suffragists. Matriarchal honors were instead bestowed on Susan B. Anthony.

7. The Roosevelt remark is quoted in David Kennedy, *Birth Control in America: The Career of Margaret Sanger* (New Haven 1970), p. 42. Also see "Race Suicide and Racial Stamina," *The Literary Digest* 47:676 (Oct. 18, 1913). Roosevelt's views are also summarized in his article "Race Decadence"

in *Outlook,* Apr. 8, 1911, p. 765, and in James Reed, *The Birth Control Movement and American Society: From Private Vice to Public Virtue* (Princeton: 1984), pp. 201–203 and Linda Gordon, *Woman's Body, Woman's Right: A Social History of Birth Control in America* (New York: 1976), pp. 135–58.

8. Charlotte Perkins Gilman, *Women and Economics* (New York: 1966), originally published in 1898, esp. p. 33, and Carl Degler's thoughtful introduction. Also see Charlotte Perkins Gilman, *The Man-Made World* (New York: 1911).

9. Jacqueline Van Voris interview with Olive Byrne Richard, pp. 2–3, 18–19 (quote from p. 9), and author's interview of Mar. 28, 1985.

10. Reed, *Birth Control Movement,* p. 83. My thanks for the Visiting Nurses information to Karen Buhler-Wilkerson and Ellen Baer of the University of Pennsylvania Center for the Study of the History of Nursing. Also see Karen Buhler-Wilkerson, "Public Health Nursing: In Sickness or in Health?" *American Journal of Public Health* 75:10 (Oct. 1985), pp. 1155–61.

11. *Autobiography,* pp. 89–92. *My Fight,* pp. 46–55.

12. Reed, *Birth Control Movement,* pp. 3–33; Gordon, *Woman's Body,* pp. 3–71. On the great upsurge in abortion between 1840 and 1880, also see James C. Mohr, *Abortion in America: The Origins and Evolution of National Policy, 1800–1900* (New York: 1978), pp. 46–85, and on the crusade to end it, pp. 147–245. A popular account of abortion in the Jewish ghetto is in Kate Simon, *Bronx Primitive* (New York: 1982), pp. 68–69. Also see Richard and Dorothy Wirtz, *Lying In: A History of Childbirth in America* (New York: 1978), pp. 155–61; Carl Degler, *at Odds: Women and the Family in America from the Revolution to the Present* (New York: 1980), pp. 196–97, 228–29, 279–97; Carroll Smith-Rosenberg, "The Female World of Love and Ritual: Relations Between Women in Nineteenth Century America," in her *Disorderly Conduct: Visions of Gender in Victorian America* (New York: 1985), pp. 217–44; Paul Starr, *The Social Transformation of American Medicine* (New York: 1987), pp. 79–144; and Brodie, "Family Limitation in American Culture: 1830–1900," doctoral dissertation, University of Chicago, 1982, pp. 469–74. On the late nineteenth century fertility decline among native-born and immigrant, see Degler, *At Odds,* pp. 219–22, citing, among others, Tamara Hareven and Maris A. Vinovskis, "Marital Fertility, Ethnicity and Occupation in Urban Families: An Analysis of South Boston and the South End in 1880," *Journal of Social History* 8 (Spring 1975); Norman E. Himes, *Medical History of Contraception* (Baltimore: 1936), pp. 333–52; John D'Emilio and Estelle B. Freedman, *Intimate Matters: A History of Sexuality in America* (New York: 1988), pp. 59–64; and Gordon, *Woman's Body,* p. 66. The data on New York is from Morris H. Kahn, M.D., "A Municipal Birth Control Clinic," reprint from *The New York Medical Journal* (Apr. 28, 1917), MS-SS.

13. Margaret Sanger, "To Mothers Our Duty," *The Call,* Mar. 26, 1911, and "Impressions of the East Side," *The Call,* Sept. 3, 1911, both at Tamiment-NYU. For the maternal mortality statistics see Louis I. Dublin and Lee K. Frankel, "Visiting Nursing and Life Insurance: Statistical Summary of Eight Years," *Quarterly of the American Statistical Publication Association* (June 1918), in the collections of the New York Academy of Medicine, hereinafter NYAM. On the role of the Visiting Nurses, see Louis I. Dublin, *A Family of 30*

Million: The Story of the Metropolitan Life Insurance Company (New York: 1943), also at NYAM; and Diane Hamilton, "Faith and Finance," *Image: Journal of Nursing Scholarship* 20:3 (Fall 1988), pp. 124–27. Comparative national data is in Louis I. Dublin, "The Problem of Maternity: A Survey and Forecast," *American Journal of Public Health* 29:11 (Nov. 1939) pp. 1207–208; and Robert Woodbury, *Maternal Mortality: U.S Department of Labor, Children's Bureau Publication 158* (Washington, D.C.: 1926), pp. 1–30. Finally, see Ellen A. Kennan, "Maternity: A Hazardous Occupation," *The Birth Control Review* 3:7 (July 1919) pp. 10–11.

14. *Autobiography*, p. 111. "What Every Girl Should Know," ran weekly in *The Call,* Sunday Supplement, Women's Page, Nov. 17, Nov. 24, Dec. 1, Dec. 8, Dec. 15, Dec. 22, and Dec. 29, 1912; Jan. 12, Jan. 19, Jan. 26, and Feb. 2, 1913. The article for Feb. 9 was censored but ran on Mar. 2, 1913. Also see letters and editorial comment for Dec. 29, 1912, Jan. 5, Jan. 12, Jan. 19, Jan. 26, Feb. 2, Feb. 9, Feb. 19, Feb. 11, Feb. 11, Feb. 14, Feb. 16, Mar. 2, Mar. 16, and June 5, 1913, all at Tamiment, NYU. The articles were subsequently collected, edited, and bound in paper under the title *What Every Girl Should Know* (New York: 1920), but much of the original political rhetoric is deleted; copy in MS-SS.

15. Mary Alden Hopkins, "Birth Control and Public Morals," *Harper's Weekly,* 60:3048 (May 22, 1915), pp. 489–90. Heywood Broun and Margaret Leech, *Anthony Comstock: Roundsman of the Lord* (New York: 1927), p. 15. This journalistic account is still the best biography of Comstock. For a psychoanalytic interpretation of Comstock and his hold on conservative public opinion, see Robert W. Haney, *Comstockery in America: Patterns of Censorship and Control* (Boston: 1960), pp. 172–77.

16. Anthony Comstock, *Traps for the Young* (New York: 1884), p. 9, also cited in C. Thomas Dienes, *Law, Politics and Birth Control* (Urbana Ill.: 1972), p. 33.

17. On late Victorian social purity reform, see especially William Leach, *True Love and Perfect Union: The Feminist Reform of Sex and Society* (New York: 1980), esp. pp. 85–96.

18. Dienes, *Law, Politics,* pp. 35–39; Alvah W. Sulloway, *Birth Control and Catholic Doctrine* (New York: 1959), pp. 3–7.

19. Section 211 of the Federal Criminal Code is cited in full in Mary Ware Dennett, *Birth Control Laws: Shall We Keep Them, Change Them, or Abolish Them?* (New York: 1926), pp. 9–10; Sections 1142 and 1145 of the New York State Penal Code are summarized on pp. 10–11. For the chronology of events, also see Dienes, *Law, Politics,* pp. 20–48; Dennett, *Birth Control Laws,* pp. 19–45; John T. Noonan, Jr., *Contraception: A History of Its Treatment by the Catholic Theologians and Canonists,* 2d ed. (Cambridge, Mass.: 1986), p. 412; Sulloway, *Catholic Doctrine,* p. 23 and notes on pp. 181–87; and Harriet F. Pilpel and Theodore S. Zavin, "Birth Control," *Marriage and Family Living,* 14:2 (1952). Finally see, James F. Morton, "The Origin and Working of the Comstock Laws," *Birth Control Review* 3:5 (May 1919), pp. 5–7; and Reed, *Birth Control Movement,* pp. 34–45.

20. Mohr, *Abortion in America,* pp. 196–99, Broun and Leech, *Anthony Comstock,* pp. 121–22, Hopkins, "Public Morals." Also see, "A Physician,"

Madame Restell: An Account of Her Life and Horrible Practices Together with Prostitution in New York: Its Extent, Causes and Effects Upon Society (New York: 1847). A copy of this paperbound book is in the rare books collection of the New York Public Library.

21. Brodie, "Family Limitation in America," pp. 280, 288, 306, 316, 323, 325, 330, 342–44, 354.

22. For contrasting interpretations of the Mosher survey, see Degler, *At Odds,* pp. 262–64, and Peter Gay, *The Bourgeois Experience, Victoria to Freud,* Vol. 1: *Education of the Sexes* (New York: 1984), pp. 135–44, both of whom use the data as evidence of sexual enthusiasm, v. Rosalind Rosenberg, *Beyond Separate Spheres: Intellectual Roots of Modern Feminism* (New Haven: 1982), pp. 180–87, and Carroll Smith-Rosenberg, "A Richer and Gentler Sex," paper delivered at the Berkshire Conference on the History of Women in America, Bryn Mawr, Pa., June 1976, both of whom take a more cautious view. On Kinsey, see Alfred Kinsey, et al., *Sexual Behavior in the Human Female* (Philadelphia: 1953), pp. 267–69 and 330–32. Ira L. Reiss, *Premarital Sexual Standards in America* (Urbana, Ill.: 1953), pp. 126–45, Reed, *Birth Control Movement,* pp. 54–63; and Gordon, *Woman's Body,* pp. 192–94. Daniel Scott Smith speculates that a loosening of standards may have occurred even earlier in lower middle-class culture where individuals, and especially women, were less vulnerable to rigid sanctions. See Smith, "The Dating of the American Sexual Revolution: Evidence and Interpretation," in *The American Family in Social and Economic Perspective,* edited by Michael Gordon (New York: 1973). Robert Latou Dickinson, M.D. and Lura Beam, *The Single Woman: A Medical Study in Sex Education* (Baltimore: 1934), an analysis of clinical records from a private practice in Brooklyn, New York, uncovered an 8 percent incidence of premarital intercourse in the 1890s, but 18 percent by 1918; pp. 62–64, 430, also cited in Rosenberg, *Beyond Separate Spheres,* p. 202. On the antiprostitution hysteria, see "Sex O'Clock in America," *Current Opinion* (Aug. 1913), pp. 113–14. For a statistical breakdown of periodical coverage of the 1910–1914 hysteria over prostitution and sex morals, see President's Commission on Social Trends: *Recent Social Trends in the United States* (New York: 1933), pp. 414 and 422. The principal secondary source on the campaigns against prostitution is David Pivar, *Purity Crusade* (New York: 1973). Allan M. Brandt, *No Magic Bullet: A Social History of Venereal Disease in the United States Since 1880* (New York: 1985), pp. 7–51, analyzes the progressive response to venereal disease. Also see Smith-Rosenberg, "Richer and Gentler," pp. 176–77; Reed, *Birth Control Movement,* pp. 57–58, and Kennedy, *Birth Control,* pp. 66–68.

23. Broun and Leech, *Anthony Comstock,* pp. 17–18, 229–30, 249, 257–58; Gertrude Marvin, "Anthony and the Devil: An Interview," *The Masses* 5:5 (Feb. 1914), p. 16. The cartoon was also from *The Masses,* Sept. 1915, cited in Broun and Leech, p. 11. For Emma Goldman on Comstock's influence, see "Victims of Morality," *Mother Earth,* 8: 1 (Mar. 1913), pp. 19–21.

24. For a variation on this analysis, see Max Eastman, "Revolutionary Birth Control: A Reply to Some Correspondence," *The Masses* 6: 10 (July 1915), p. 15, which refers to opponents of birth control as those who see any reference to sexuality as "a libidinous violation of something sacred."

4: THE PERSONAL IS POLITICAL

1. Memos on Women's Committee Activities from Mar. 11 to May 25, 1912, in SPNY, Tamiment-NYU. The Ashley dispute is No. 77. Sanger on Ashley is in *Autobiography*, p. 71.

2. Mari Jo Buhle, *Women and American Socialism, 1870–1920* (Urbana, Ill.: 1983), p. 171. Nancy Shrom Dye, *As Equals and As Sisters: Feminism, the Labor Movement, and the Women's Trade Union League of New York* (Columbia, Mo.: 1980).

3. Margaret Sanger, "The Women of the Laundry Workers' Strike," *The Call,* Jan. 14, 1912, Tamiment-NYU, and *Autobiography,* pp. 79–80. U.S. Congress. House. Rules Committee., *Hearing on the Strike at Lawrence, Mass.,* H.R. 671, 62d Cong., 2d sess., Washington, D.C., 1912, pp. 226–33. "Mrs. Taft Hears Strike Children Tell Woes to House Rules Committee," The *New York Herald,* Mar. 6, 1912, clipping with a photograph of Sanger, along with a clipping from The *New York World,* Mar. 3, 1912, in MS-LC. "Mrs. Taft Listens to Strike Charges," *The New York Times,* Mar. 6, 1912, 6:2–3. Also see Raimond Fazio, an IWW official in Chicago, to Julius Gerber, a Socialist Party organizer in NYC, Jan. 31, 1912, SPNY-Tamiment, NYU. Sanger wrote on Lawrence for *The Call,* Feb. 15, 1912, 6:3, and Feb. 18, 1912, 15:6, Tamiment-NYU.

A warm personal recollection of Sanger leading the children into New York City comes from Rada Bercovici, daughter of the radical writer, Konrad Bercovici, whose family took in several of the evacuees, author's interview, Mar. 24, 1986.

On Sanger at Lawrence, also see Carlo Tresca, "Autobiography," unpublished manuscript in the Carlo Tresca Papers, Manuscript Division, New York Public Library, hereinafter CT-NYPL, pp. 124–41, and Elizabeth Gurley Flynn, *The Rebel Girl* (New York: 1973), p. 142. On Lawrence in general: Melvyn Dubofsky, *We Shall Be All: A History of the Industrial Workers of the World* (Chicago: 1969), p. 248, and on the role of women at Lawrence: Meredith Tax, *The Rising of the Women: Feminist Solidarity and Class Conflict, 1810–1917* (New York: 1980), pp. 260–70. Additional clippings on Sanger's arrest in Hazelton are in MS-LC, Scrapbook 2. Also see M.S., "With the Girls in Hazelton Jail," *The Call,* Apr. 20, 1913, 15:6–7, Tamiment-NYU.

4. Also see Hersey's interview with Flynn, "Margaret Sanger," p. 108.

5. Flynn, *Rebel Girl,* pp. 152–53; Tresca, "Autobiography," pp. 208–14, 218. Socialist Party resignations are in SPNY, Letterbooks at Tamiment, although Sanger's is not among them, so we have to take her word. Also see Camp manuscript; *The Papers of Eugene Debs,* microfilm ed., introduction, p. 24, Tamiment-NYU; Dubofsky, *We Shall Be All,* p. 257, and Henry F. May, *The End of American Innocence: A Study of the First Years of Our Own Time* (New York: 1959), pp. 219–21, 228.

6. Flynn, "The Truth About the Paterson Strike," typed copy of a speech in Tamiment-NYU, quoted in Dubofsky, *We Shall Be All,* p. 272.; *idem,* pp. 266–79, and Robert Rosenstone, *Romantic Revolutionary: A Biography of John Reed* (New York: 1975), p. 123.

7. Accounts of Sanger in Paterson are in William Haywood, *Bill Haywood's Book* (New York, 1929), pp. 260–62; in *The Call,* Apr. 30, 1913, and *The New*

York Times, Apr. 30 and May 1, 1913, cited in Anne Huber Tripp, *The I.W.W. and the Paterson Silk Strike of 1913* (Urbana, Ill., 1987), p. 51. On the pageant, see *The Call,* June 26, 1913 (cited in Tripp, p. 145); *Autobiography,* p. 85; Flynn, "The Truth About Paterson"; Mabel Dodge Luhan, *Movers and Shakers* (Albuquerque, N. M.: 1985), originally published in 1936, pp. 188–89, 194–95, 203–207; Rosenstone, *Romantic Revolutionary,* p. 127; Dubofsky, *We Shall Be All,* pp. 281–83, and the Camp manuscript, Chap. 3. Interpretations of the strike are in David Montgomery, *Worker's Control in America* (Cambridge: 1979), pp. 91–92.

8. *Autobiography,* esp. p. 110. Hersey, "Margaret Sanger," pp. 89–90, David Kennedy, *Birth Control in America: The Career of Margaret Sanger* (New Haven: 1970), pp. 9–15. The Eastman quote is in *Enjoyment of Living* (New York: 1948).

9. For his sense of defeat, see W.S. to M.S., letters from Paris, 1914, passim, MS-SS. On the generational conflict between individual and social renewal, see Leslie Fishbein, *Rebels in Bohemia: The Radicals of the Masses, 1911–1917,* (Chapel Hill: 1982), Chap. 1, and May, *End of Innocence,* pp. 195–219 and 283.

10. W.S. to M.S., Sept. 3, 1913, MS-SS; M.S. "What Every Girl Should Know," *The Call,* Feb. 6, 1913, Tamiment-NYU, also cited in James Reed, *The Birth Control Movement and American Society: From Private View to Public Virtue* (Princeton: 1984), p. 76; Hersey, "Margaret Sanger," p. 110, quoting an interview with M.S. Boyd re: Paterson, also cited in Reed, *idem,* p. 78.

11. *Autobiography* p. 85.

12. On Flynn's social reticence, see Camp manuscript, Chap. 2. On Goldman, see Candace Falk, *Love, Anarchy and Emma Goldman* (New York, 1985); Alice Wexler, *Emma Goldman: An Intimate Life* (New York, 1985) and Richard Drinnon, *Rebel in Paradise: A Biography of Emma Goldman* (Chicago, 1961).

13. Once again, I am indebted to the rich secondary material from this period in American history and women's studies: Carl Degler, *At Odds: Women and the Family in America from the Revolution to the Present* (New York: 1980), esp. pp. 5–9, and 101–10; John D'Emilio and Estelle B. Freedman, *Intimate Matters: A History of Sexuality in America* (New York: 1988), pp. 4–17, 27–30, 40–58. Linda Kerber, *Women of the Republic: Intellect and Ideology in Revolutionary America* (Chapel Hill: 1980), pp. 51–55, 99–111; Mary Beth Norton, *Liberty's Daughters: The Revolutionary Experience of American Women 1750–1800* (New York: 1980), pp. 188–90, 195–210, 230–32; Nancy F. Cott, *The Bonds of Womanhood: Woman's Sphere in New England, 1780–1835* (New Haven: 1977), pp. 126–59. On illegitimacy in particular, see Ellen K. Rothman, *Hands and Hearts: A History of Courtship in America* (New York: 1984), p. 141. And finally, Sylvia A. Law's reconsideration of women and the Constitution: "The Founders on Families," *University of Florida Law Review* 39:3 (Summer 1987), pp. 583–612. Also see Paul E. Johnson, *A Shopkeeper's Daughter: Society and Revivals in Rochester, New York, 1815–1837* (New York: 1978), pp. 136–41; Mary P. Ryan, *Cradle of the Middle Class: The Family in Oneida County New York, 1790–1865* (Cambridge, Eng., and New York: 1981), pp. 145–85; Carroll Smith-Rosenberg, "The Female World of Love and Ritual: Relations Between Women in

Nineteenth-Century America," in her *Disorderly Conduct: Visions of Gender in Victorian America* (New York: 1985), pp. 79–89, 129–33, 137–43; and Peter Gay, *The Bourgeois Experience, Victoria to Freud,* Vol. 1: *Education of the Senses* (New York: 1984), esp. 19 and pp. 47–49.

Recent studies of Freud argue the influence on psychoanalytic theory of the distinctive social anomie of the secular Jewish community of nineteenth-century Vienna, alienated on the one hand from orthodox religious and cultural values and on the other from the Christian society around it. An analogous situation may have presented itself in the intensely fragmented culture of nineteenth-century America, accounting perhaps for the unusually receptive audience that psychoanalytic theory and practice subsequently received in this country.

On culture and personality, see especially Christopher Lasch, *Haven in a Heartless World: The Family Besieged* (New York: 1977), pp. 63–75, and for the definitive work on Freud in America and the legacy of popular Victorian culture, Nathan G. Hale, Jr., *Freud and the Americans: The Beginnings of Psychoanalysis in the United States, 1876–1914* (New York: 1971), pp. 24–46. On liberal Protestantism see Ann Douglas, *The Feminization of American Culture* (New York: 1977), pp. 17–142. The best analysis of nineteenth-century domestic advice literature remains Kathryn Sklar's biography of Catherine Beecher, popular writer on domestic economy, daughter of the revivalist preacher Lyman Beecher and sister of abolitionist Harriet Beecher Stowe. See Kathryn Kish Sklar, *Catherine Beecher: A Study in American Domesticity* (New Haven: 1973), esp. pp. 134–42, 153–93.

14. Smith-Rosenberg, "Female World," pp. 115, 129–64, 173; Linda Gordon, *Woman's Body, Woman's Right: A Social History of Birth Control in America* (New York: 1976), pp. 17–21, 23–95, 108–109, 123; N. Hale, *Freud and the Americans,* Sklar, *Catherine Beecher*, pp. 116–27: Cott, *Bonds of Womanhood,* pp. 197–206: Ryan, *Cradle,* esp. 191–210, Degler, *At Odds,* esp. pp. 26–51, 279–98; Sheila M. Rothman, *Woman's Proper Place: A History of Changing Ideals and Practices, 1870 to the Present* (New York: 1978), pp. 67, 82–83; and Rosenberg, *Beyond Separate Spheres: Intellectual Roots of Modern Feminism* (New Haven: 1982), introduction.

15. Peter Gay, *Bourgeois Experience,* pp. 168–69, 230–32; D'Emilio and Freedman, *Intimate Matters,* p. 45; Smith-Rosenberg, "Female World," pp. 182–96; 217–44; Degler, *At Odds,* pp. 249–78 (takes the most skeptical view of the significance of repressive ideology and of the conspiratorial theories linking it to status anxiety on the part of doctors). Also see Nancy F. Cott, "Passionless: An Interpretation of Victorian Sexual Ideology, 1790–1850," in *A Heritage of Her Own: Toward a New Social History of American Women,* edited by Nancy F. Cott and Elizabeth H. Pleck (New York: 1979), pp. 162–79 and especially p. 168; Judith Walzer Leavitt, *Brought to Bed: A History of Childbirth in America 1750–1950* (New York: 1986), pp. 32–55; Ann Douglas Wood "The Fashionable Diseases: Women's Complaints and Their Treatment in Nineteenth-Century America," Regina Morantz, "The Lady and Her Physician," in *Clio's Consciousness Raised: New Perspectives on the History of Women,* edited by Mary Hartman and Lois W. Banner (New York: 1974), pp. 1–22, and 38-53. The most extreme of the misogynist interpretations of female sexuality were in the writings of Drs. William Acton and William A. Alcott, see Gay, *Bourgeois Experience,* and Rosenberg, *Beyond Separate Spheres.* Contrar-

ily, examples abound of physicians who stressed the value of sexual pleasure for women such as Dr. Edward B. Foote, the advocate of contraception, and Elizabeth Blackwell, the first woman physician in the United States, see Degler, *At Odds.* Nonetheless, sexual control for both sexes was widely endorsed. Finally, for a modern-day, Freudian analysis of these gender arrangements, see Dorothy Dinnerstein, *The Mermaid and the Minotaur: Sexual Arrangements and Human Social Malaise* (New York: 1976).

16. Smith-Rosenberg, "Female World," pp. 167–81, 197–216. A compelling case study of how gender tensions undermined one brilliant but sensitive Victorian daughter and led to a lifetime of neurasthenic conditions is in Jean Strouse, *Alice James: A Biography* (Boston: 1980), pp. 97–143. Feminist Charlotte Perkins Gilman powerfully recorded her own breakdown in *The Yellow Wallpaper* (New York: 1973).

17. The Goldman quote is from "Rebel Thoughts," in Margaret Sanger, *The Woman Rebel* 1: 4 (June 1914). Also see Emma Goldman, "The Tragedy of Woman's Emancipation," *Anarchism and Other Essays* (New York: 1910), p. 237; and Emma Goldman, "Anarchism" in *Mother Earth* 9: 7 (Sept. 1914), p. 212.

18. Goldman, *Anarchism,* p. 237, also cited in Falk, *Love, Anarchy,* p. 193, and Wexler, *Emma Goldman,* p. 153.

19. Wexler, *Emma Goldman,* p. 166; Gordon, *Woman's Body,* pp. 213–21; Reed, *Birth Control Movement,* pp. 46–53. The Reitman verse is in Reitman to Norman Himes, Feb. 13, 1938, in the Norman Himes Papers, Countway Library, Harvard University, cited in Reed, *idem,* p. 53.

20. Goldman's reference to Sanger is in *Living My Life* (New York, 1931). Also see Falk, *Love, Anarchy,* pp. 212 and 379. Sanger denies their association in M.S. to Ethel Clyde June 12, 1935, MS-LC. The quote is from M.S. to James Pond, Feb. 23, 1934, in MS-LC.

21. William Sanger to Emma Goldman, Mar. 17, 1916, in MS-LC. For the nature of Goldman's lecture material before 1915, see "Review of New York Activities 1913–1914," *Mother Earth* 9:2 (Apr. 1914), p. 54. For escalation of her rhetoric and activities after 1915, see Emma Goldman, "The Social Aspects of Birth Control," *Mother Earth,* 11:2 (1916), pp. 468–75. A copy of the pamphlet entitled *Why and How the Poor Should Not Have Many Children,* is in the Ben Reitman Papers at the University of Illinois, Chicago Circle, also cited in Reed, *Birth Control Movement,* p. 393, f.n. 17.

5: BOHEMIA AND BEYOND

1. William Sanger to M.S., Dec. 8, 1914, and Jan 5. 1914, which says how he hates "wage slavery," MS-SS.

2. Mabel Dodge Luhan, *Movers and Shakers* (New Mexico: 1985), pp. 25–38, 90.

3. On the Dodge artists see Patricia R. Everett, *Mabel Dodge: The Salon Years, 1912–1917* (New York: 1985), the catalog of a show at the Barbara Mathes Gallery. On art as liberation, see Leslie Fishbein, *Rebels in Bohemia: The Radicals of the Masses, 1911–1917* (Chapel Hill: 1982), p. 30. For an assessment of Bill Sanger's painting, I have relied on the discussions in his letters to Margaret from Paris, especially W.S. to M.S., Jan. 14 and Jan. 20, 1914,

MS-SS, on my own observations of his work in the possession of his children and grandchildren, and on the comments of Joan Sanger Hoppe in a letter to me of Mar. 21, 1985. Also see Caren Sands and Donna McWhalen, "William Sanger," a paper prepared for the Smith College seminar on Margaret Sanger, May 13, 1977, MS-SS.

4. W.S. to M.S., Mar. 25, 1914, MS-SS, and also his letter of Feb. 25, 1914, which says: "So 'Art' is in the Parlor with its present Rendezvous at Madame Dodge. If art doesn't get out 'quick like' it will share the same fate with all the Revolutions that have swept over the movement in New York."

Also see Luhan, *Movers and Shakers,* pp. 84, 88–91, Fishbein, *Rebels in Bohemia,* pp. 37–38, 85–86, Henry May, *The End of American Innocence: A Study of the First Years of Our Own Time* (New York: 1959), pp. 233–36, and Ronald Steel, *Walter Lippmann and the American Century* (New York: 1980), pp. 50–53.

5. The "overbearing" quote is from W.S. to M.S. Mar. 25, 1914, MS-SS. The Hutchins Hapgood quote is in *A Victorian in the Modern World* (New York: 1939) p. 170. Also see *Autobiography,* 93–94.

Sanger critics have argued that she artificially inflated her own place in history by undervaluing the quality of information available in this country before her efforts, but the undeniable fact is that her initial endorsement and support of the rubber-spring diaphragm and later, of the oral contraceptive pill, would permanently alter medical opinion about birth control and dramatically change the preferred contraceptive choices of American women. She never claimed to have accomplished anything more.

David Kennedy, *Birth Control in America: The Career of Margaret Sanger* (New Haven: 1970), p. 19, indicts her for saying in her autobiography that she found information no more reliable than that exchanged by "back-fence gossips in any small town." Kennedy points out that the U.S. Surgeon General's index listed two pages of books and articles on "prevention of conception," discussing such methods as condoms, vaginal douching, suppositories, tampons, and pessaries. But this was precisely her point. She never claimed, as he says, that before her work doctors knew little about contraception, only that they changed their advice after her work—which, as we shall see, was substantially true. For statistical information on the shift to diaphragm use between 1910 and 1930, see the data on contraceptive practices of white, married women collected by the Kinsey Institute for Sex Research, and in Paul Gebhard et al., *Pregnancy, Birth and Abortion* (New York: 1958), Table 46, p.131, cited in James Reed, *The Birth Control Movement and American Society: From Private Vice to Public Virtue* (Princeton: 1984), pp. 123–25. Reed persuasively refutes Kennedy on this point. This material is discussed further in Chaps. 14 and 15.

6. W.S. to M.S., Feb. 5, 1914 and Mar. 25, 1914, MS-SS. Grant Sanger, Schlesinger Library interview, p. 15, and interview with the author, Dec. 18, 1987.

7. W.S. to M.S., Sept. 3, 1913, MS-SS. Henrietta Sanger's death certificate is on file with the New York City Department of Health, Bureau of Records. Again, my thanks to Alex Sanger for a copy.

8. *Autobiography,* p. 105, Grant Sanger, Schlesinger interview, pp. 15–16.

9. W.S. to M.S. Dec. 28, 1913. As Bill became more and more desperate, his

prose and his handwriting began to run away from him. I am especially grateful to James Reed, who helped me decipher many of his letters.

10. The quotes are, in order, from W.S. to M.S., Jan. 11, Jan. 5, n.d. (Spring 1914), and Mar. 12, 1914, all in MS-SS. Also see, W.S. to M.S. Mar. 3, 1914. Mention of his receiving £50 from her is in the Feb. 5 letter. An accounting of his receipt of a total of $160 is in his letter of Mar. 19, 1914. Mention of the end of the Hastings mortgage payments is in May 25, 1914.

11. See W.S. to M.S., Mar. 19, 1914. Quotations are in order from W.S. to M.S., Mar. 12, June 1, and Apr. 2, 1914, all in MS-SS. Further impressions are also drawn from letters of Jan. 21 and 28, Feb. 14, Mar. 25, Apr. 2, June 1, 1914, and n.d. (June 1914), MS-SS. The divorce statistics are from President's Commission on Social Trends: *Recent Social Trends in the United States* (New York: 1933), p. 692.

12. Luhan, *Movers and Shakers,* pp. 69–71. On the disillusion of the Greenwich Village crowd with sexual liberation, see Fishbein, *Rebels in Bohemia.*

13. The undated poem is in the Walter Roberts correspondence, MS-SS. The fact that she liked the poem is mentioned in his letter to her of May 13, 1914, MS-SS.

14. Otto Bobsein to M.S., Oct. 25, 1953, M.S. to O.B., Oct. 27, 1953, in MS-SS; Roma Brashear (a librarian) to Florence Rose (secretary to M.S.) Dec. 24, 1934, MS-LC; *Autobiography,* pp. 107–108.

15. *Autobiography,* pp. 107–109. By emphasizing that the feminists turned her down, Sanger gave the conservatives in the established birth control movement an excuse for her early radicalism—that, in effect, she had nowhere else to go—hardly the only rationale of her alliance. Kennedy, *Birth Control* and Linda Gordon, *Woman's Body, Woman's Right: A Social History of Birth Control in America* (New York: 1976), however, tend to read her literally and continually question her bona fides as a "radical." Both argue, from different perspectives, that Sanger saw birth control as a single issue early on and isolated herself from radical labor politics, but the facts substantially dispute this interpretation. Sanger's vision of a feminist alliance for social change, moreover, had considerable effect among women radicals of the day. Her break with the left, as we shall see, came much later. See Kennedy, *idem,* p. 22; Gordon, *idem,* pp. 221–22. On heterodoxy, see Judith Schwarz, *Radical Feminists of Heterodoxy, Greenwich Village, 1912–1940* (Lebanon, N.H.: 1982), and Nancy Cott, *The Grounding of Modern Feminism* (New Haven: 1987), p. 40. On women as a "united front," Meredith Tax, *The Rising of the Women: Feminist Solidarity and Class Conflict, 1810–1917* (New York: 1980).

16. *The Woman Rebel,* 1:1, (Mar. 1914), pp. 1, 3, 8; 1:2 (Apr. 1914), pp. 10, 12; 1:3, (May 1914), pp. 20, 22, 28: 1:4 (June, 1914), pp. 25, 31, reprinted in Alex Baskin, ed., *Woman Rebel* (Stonybrook, N.Y.: 1976). Unidentified clippings of Sanger newspaper interviews are in MS-LC scrapbooks.

17. Max Eastman in *The Masses,* 5:8 (May 1914), p. 5. Emma Goldman to M.S., Apr. 9, 1914, and June 23, 1914, MS-LC.

18. G. F. Murphy, asst. postmaster, to M.S., Apr. 2, Apr. 7, and Aug. 27, 1914; A. Snowden Marshall, U.S. attorney, to M.S., Oct. 7, 1914; Otto Bobsein to Postmaster E. M. Morgan, Esq., Apr. 4, 1914, and Morgan to Bobsein, Apr. 7, 1914, all in MS-LC.

19. Tresca, "Autobiography," unpublished manuscript in the Carlo Tresca papers, CT-NYPL, pp. 279–80; Elizabeth Gurley Flynn, *The Rebel Girl* (New York: 1973), p. 182; Camp manuscript, Chap. 3.

20. On Tannenbaum, see Luhan, *Movers and Shakers,* pp. 265–277; Tresca, "Autobiography," p. 264, and *The New York Times* for 1914, Mar. 3, 1:3; Mar. 4 (editorial) 10:3; Mar. 5 (lead story) 1:8 and 8:2; Mar. 6, 1:1; Mar. 12, 1:3; Mar. 17, 9:3; Mar. 24, 2:6; Mar. 25, 6:4; and Mar. 26, 5:3. Also see *The Woman Rebel,* 1:6 (Aug. 1914), pp. 45, 46, 48.

21. The Modern School archives are housed in the manuscript division of the library of Rutgers University and include the following on this period: "The Prospectus of the Francisco Ferrer Association," 5:11 (Jan. 1911), pp. 348–59; Carl Zigrosser, "Memoir of The Ferrer Center"; Bayard Boyeson, "The Modern School," *Everyman* 10:10 (Dec. 1914), pp. 11–12; Harry Kelly, "The Ferrer Modern School, 1920"; and the Modern School of Stelton, *Twenty-Fifth Anniversary Bulletin, May 17, 1940,* which includes an article by James Dick, "Some Memories and Passing Thoughts." *The Modern School Monthly Magazine*, Vols. 1–8 (1912–1922), is in the New York Public Library. Also see Paul Avrich, *The Modern School Movement: Anarchism and Education in the United States* (Princeton: 1980), especially pp. 9–15, 47, 80. I am indebted to Professor Avrich for his help with these references. Finally, see Will and Ariel Durant, *A Dual Autobiography* (New York: 1977), p. 41.

22. Tresca, "Autobiography," pp. 292–323. Avrich, *Modern School Movement,* pp. 183–326. "The Realization of a Dream," *The Modern School Magazine* 2:6 (June 1915).

23. Herbert A. Thorpe, "A Defense of Assassination," *The Woman Rebel* 1:5 (July 1914), pp. 33–34. M.S. to Helena Huntington Smith, July 1930, MS-LC.

24. Margaret Sanger, *Family Limitation,* copies of various editions (most of the earlier ones undated) in MS-LC and MS-SS. Also see Joan Jensen, "The Evolution of Margaret Sanger's Family Limitation Pamphlet," *Signs* 6 (Spring 1981) pp. 548–67.

25. "Woman Rebel Editor on Trial," *The Call* Oct. 20, 1914, 4:4, Tamiment-NYU. "Margaret Sanger," *The Masses,* Nov. 1914, 6:2 p. 20. *Autobiography,* pp. 117–18; Kennedy, *Birth Control,* p. 25.

26. *My Fight,* p. 6., Sanger Journal, Nov. 3–6, 1914, MS-SS.

6: A EUROPEAN EDUCATION

1. Passport and photograph are in MS-SS. Also see *Autobiography,* p. 121.

2. Journal entry, Nov. 3, 1915, MS-SS; "Opinions of American Women in Europe," unpublished manuscript, MS-LC. This manuscript offers an interesting contrast to the portraits in Henry James's turn-of-the-century novels and stories about self-indulgent daughters of the American aristocracy, who meet with tragic consequence when they seek romance and adventure on the Continent.

3. W.S. to M.S., Dec. 25, 1914, Dec. 27, 1914, Jan. 10, 1915, which says that "the letter excommunicating me from your life was cold and calculating," all in MS-SS.

4. W.S. to M.S., Dec. 1914, May 21, and Sept. 21, 1915, in MS-SS speak of

Peggy and the "steampipes," as he referred to the brace on her leg; Stuart Sanger to M.S., Apr. 29, 1915, and to W.S., May 6, 1915, and Grant Sanger to M.S. n.d. (1915) and July 31, 1915, all in MS-SS. Olive Byrne's interview with Jacqueline Van Voris, pp. 4–5, recalls visiting her mother when she was living with Bill Sanger and his children. M.S. to Nan Higgins, Feb. 22, 1915, and n.d. ("Barcelona, Spain, 1915") in MS-LC convey her concern about Peggy and her wish that Bill do nothing about "her little foot" until she returns. Sanger Journal entries for Nov. 25 and Dec. 17, 1914, MS-SS, contain the material in quotation. For biographical information on Helen Marot, see Nancy Shrom Dye, *As Equals and as Sisters: Feminism, the Labor Movement, and the Women's Trade Union League of New York* (Columbia, Mo.: 1980); and also Sol Cohen "Helen Marot," in *Notable American Women, 1607–1950: A Biographical Dictionary,* edited by Edward T. James and Janet Wilson James (Cambridge, Mass.: 1971). On Caroline Pratt, see her autobiography, *I Learn from Children: An Adventure in Progressive Education* (New York: 1948), especially the reference on p. 203 to her intolerance for parents "slow to mark distress signals, to see children in trouble and offer help."

5. Journal, Nov. 13, Nov. 18 and Dec. 16, 1914, MS-SS. The Dec. 16 entry has the quote. Also see M.S. "Notes on Nietzsche" (1915), MS-LC, in which she extracts the following teachings: "sincerity and heroism plus delicacy of sentiment and refinement"—"understand the aristocracy and acquire subtle methods of thinking."

6. Journal, Nov. 25, 1914, MS-SS; James Dick, *Some Memories and Passing Thoughts,* bulletin published by the Ferrer Association, refers to Portet as Ferrer's successor. Dick was a young British sympathizer who came to teach at the school in Stelton.

7. Journal, n.d. (sometime after a previous entry on Nov. 15, 1914); additional references to Portet in London and Paris on Dec. 24, Feb. 1, 1915, Feb. 2, May 1915, etc. Biographical data is from Margaret Sanger, "Notes on Portet and Ferrer," MS-LC. Also see William Archer, *The Life, Trial and Death of Francisco Ferrer* (London: 1911), a compilation of articles first published in *McClure's Magazine,* Nov. and Dec. 1910; Dick, *Some Memories,* p. 31; and Paul Avrich, *The Modern School Movement: Anarchism and Education in the United States* (Princeton: 1980), p. 27.

8. Journal, Apr. 12, 20, and May 4, 1915, MS-LC.

9. W.S. to M.S., Jan. 21, 1915, MS-SS, in typescript to ensure that she would read and understand all of it, since his handwriting was often illegible. Also see, "Sanger Held for Trial as Comstock Testifies," *The Call,* Feb. 3, 1915, 3:5; "Is the Truth Obscene?" *The Masses,* 6:6 (Mar. 1915), pp. 5–6; and "Anthony Comstock's Latest Victim," *The Modern School Magazine* 7: 2–3 (Feb. and Mar. 1915).

10. Margaret wrote of her financial woes and of her annoyance in M.S. to Nan Higgins, n.d. (Barcelona, Spain), MS-LC, and in M.S. to W.S., May 31, 1915, MS-SS, one of the few of her letters to him that survives. He also used the term "excommunicating me from your life" in W.S. to M.S., Jan. 5, 1915, a very bitter letter, considerably different in tone from those that followed his arrest, esp. W.S. to M.S., Jan. 17 and Jan. 21, 1915.

11. Margaret Sanger, "Modern Schools in Spain," *Modern School Magazine,* 8: 1&2 (May–July 1915). The Portet reference is from M.S. to Nan

Higgins, n.d. ("Barcelona, Spain"), MS-LC.

Her letter to Nan from Amsterdam on Feb. 22, 1915, MS-LC, refers to "so many tongues and gossips ready to put a knife in your back" and claims that she was planning to return to Canada and claim her children. A vitriolic letter from M.S. to W.S., May 31, 1915, attacks him for turning people against her, especially Helen Marot and Caroline Pratt, who were caring for the children and whom she refers to as "splendid women."

She wrote of Portet to Leonard Abbott in M.S. to L.A., May 1915, MS-LC (this letter is filed in unidentified cc). The recollection of Portet is from a telephone interview on Oct. 3, 1985, with Nelle Dick, then age ninty-three, living in Miami, Fla. Nelle Dick was married to James Dick and also taught at Stelton. My thanks again to Paul Avrich for putting me in touch with her.

12. The four cablegrams from Portet in Barcelona to Margaret in New York, dated Nov. 14, Nov. 21, Dec. 8, 1915, and Jan. 3, 1916, in MS-SS, convey his hope that she would get her case dismissed and prepare to return to him. They are variously signed "lovingly" or "ever yours." A letter from "L. Portet to Mrs. Margaret H. Sanger," dated Feb. 10, 1916, on "Casa Editorial" letterhead formally offers her a job and must have been intended for customs purposes. The Sanger references to Portet are in yearbook entries for Feb. 13 and Feb. 15, 1919, MS-LC, and letters to Juliet Rublee from London, June 7, and Aug. 25 (1920), in MS-DC. M.S. to Hugh de Selincourt (a subsequent lover), "Chamonix," July 14 (1928 or earlier), refers to her association of Portet and Paris, MS-LC. Noah Slee (Sanger's second husband) to M.S., Feb. 7, 1927, MS-SS, tells her he had been in Barcelona and recalled the "vivid details" of "your affair," which she had apparently shared with him. Also see *Autobiography*, pp. 153–68.

13. See Annie Besant, *The Law of Population* (London: 1884), and George Drysdale, *The Elements of Social Science: An Exposition of Cause and Only Cure for the Three Primary Social Evils: Poverty, Prostitution and Celibacy* (London: 1886), both in MS-SS. Also see Peter Fryer, *The Birth Controllers* (New York: 1966), esp. pp. 43–192, Rosanna Ledbetter, *A History of the Malthusian League, 1877–1927* (Columbus, Ohio: 1976), Linda Gordon, *Woman's Body, Woman's Right: A Social History of Birth Control in America* (New York: 1976), pp. 73–81, and James Reed, *The Birth Control Movement and American Society: From Private Vice to Public Virtue* (Princeton: 1984), pp. 89–90.

14. Edward Carpenter, *Love's Coming of Age: A Series of Papers on the Relations of the Sexes* (Kansas: 1927), esp. pp. 28–51, and C. V. Drysdale, *The Small Family System, Is It Injurious or Immoral?* (New York: 1914). On Neo-Malthusianism and labor, see Ledbetter, *Malthusian League,* pp. 87–115, and Sheila Rowbotham, *Hidden from History: Rediscovering Women in History from the 17th Century to the Present* (London: 1976), pp. 70–76.

Both Besant and Carpenter were Fabian Socialists. Even in the 1920s, the Labour Party, then in power, refused to endorse contraception, despite efforts to place it on the party platform by Mrs. Bertrand Russell and other prominent members.

15. Sanger Journal, Dec. 22, Dec. 28, 1914, MS-LC; Havelock Ellis, *My Life* (New York: 1940), p. 520. The first evidence of Sanger lying about her age as an adult is on the Bertha Watson passport in MS-LC.

A more skeptical view of Karezza is in H.E. to M.S., Jan. 1921, MS-LC, in which he cautions that her apparent enthusiasm may be a bit excessive—"while there is much good and beautiful" about it when it can be achieved, there is "no need to belittle other things." On Stockham and her mentor, John Humphrey Noyes of the Oneida Colony, see Janet Brodie, "Family Limitation in American Culture: 1830–1900," doctoral dissertation, University of Chicago, 1982, pp. 69–71.

16. Ellis, *My Life,* esp. pp. 59, 84–86, 162–63, 169–71. Also see Phyllis Grosskurth, *Havelock Ellis: A Biography* (New York: 1980), Chap. 1; and Arthur Calder-Marshall, *A Life of Havelock Ellis* (New York: 1956).

17. The ten volumes were condensed for a Modern Library edition in the 1930s which contains the essentials and is a good deal more readable than the originals. See Havelock Ellis, *Studies in the Psychology of Sex:* Vols. 1 and 2 (New York: 1936), esp. Part II, "The Sexual Impulse in Women." The best analysis of Ellis's contributions to the history of sexual ideology is in Paul Robinson, *The Modernization of Sex* (New York: 1976), pp. 1–41. A brief but elegant portrait of Ellis appears in François Lafitte, "Havelock Ellis," *Alta: University of Birmingham Review* 5 (Spring, 1968). Professor Lafitte, the son of Françoise Lafitte Cyon, the companion of Ellis's mature years, shared this article and his personal recollections of Ellis and Sanger in an interview of Jan. 29, 1987, at his home in Birmingham, Eng., for which I am very grateful. Sanger's comments are in *Autobiography,* p. 94.

18. Ellis's quotes on Freud are from Joseph Wortis, M.D., *Fragments of an Analysis with Freud* (New York: 1954). Wortis was a follower of Ellis who became interested in psychoanalysis and was analyzed by Freud in Vienna during the 1930s. See esp. pp. 11–16, 30, 45, 63, 168, 175, 199.

Wortis's own critique of Freud in his "Retrospect and Conclusions," pp. 185–203, reflects much of Ellis's thinking and quotes letters from Ellis warning him against psychoanalysis. Ellis and Wortis foreshadowed the criticism of Freud explored by the ego psychologists in their emphasis on complex family and social relationships and situations over sexual absolutism, although they were not willing to accept even the basic analytic assumptions that shape this revisionism. I am grateful to James Reed for this citation. See Reed, *Birth Control Movement,* p. 91, and p. 398, f.n.

I am also grateful to Joseph Wortis, who reminisced about Ellis with me on Mar. 13, 1987, at his home in Brooklyn, New York, after I had written a first draft of this chapter. Also see Joseph Wortis, M.D., "Havelock Ellis," *Recent Advances in Biological Psychiatry* (New York: 1960). The relationship of Ellis and Freud is also explored in Grosskurth, *Havelock Ellis,* pp. 232–35, 291–93, 387–93. Dr. Wortis, I should add, takes great exception to the Grosskurth biography, which, he claims, is biased toward Freud and provides a mistaken evaluation of Ellis's personality and intellect, unfairly reducing his stature to that of "some kind of kook."

19. For these viewpoints also see Havelock Ellis, *The Task of Social Hygiene* (Boston: 1914); reprinted with an introduction by Sheila M. Rothman, (New York: 1978), pp. 49–133, and *Essays in Wartime: Further Studies in the Task of Social Hygiene* (Boston and New York: 1917), esp. p. 186 on marriage.

20. Ellis, *Studies,* especially in Vol 1., Part II: "Analysis of the Sexual Impulse" and "Love and Pain," and Part IV, "Sexual Inversion," passim. The references to fetishism and the material in direct quotation about erotic sym-

bolism are also from *Studies,* Vol. 2 of this edition, p. 113, also quoted in Reed, *Birth Control Movement,* p. 91, and Grosskurth, *Havelock Ellis,* p. 228. Ellis's views on the uniqueness of human sexuality informed the final volume of his studies, originally published in 1910 as *Sex in Relation to Society.*

Also see, Havelock Ellis, "The Love Rights of Women," *The Birth Control Review* 2:5 (June 1918), pp. 5–6, and Robinson, *Modernization,* pp. 6–27. Criticism of Ellis's views on female homosexuality and his heterosexual imperative are in Carroll Smith-Rosenberg, "The New Woman as Androgyne: Social Disorder and Gender Crisis, 1870–1936," in her *Disorderly Conduct: Visions of Gender in Victorian America* (New York: 1985), pp. 275–81. Finally, see Grosskurth, *Havelock Ellis,* pp. 216–235 passim, though her analysis of Ellis's sexual theories is, in my view, the weakest part of the biography. Sanger's comment on Ellis's explicitness is from *Autobiography,* p. 94. Her comments on lesbianism are in *Woman and the New Race* (New York: 1920), pp. 18–19.

21. Ellis, *Studies,* Vol. 1, Part II, "The Sexual Impulse in Women," passim. Havelock Ellis, *Man and Woman: A Study of Human Secondary Sexual Characteristics* (New York: 1904), esp. pp. 1–20, and p. 362. Similar views about female sexuality were also advanced at this time in England by Edward Carpenter and by the German sexologist, Dr. Iwan Bloch. See Peter Gay, *The Bourgeois Experience, Victoria to Freud,* Vol. 1: *Education of the Sexes* (New York: 1984), p. 133. Also, see Ellis, *Task of Social Hygiene,* pp. 113–33, and *Essays in Wartime,* p. 233; Grosskurth, *Havelock Ellis,* pp. 225 and 229–31, and Robinson, *Modernization.*

I have taken the polarity of "guilt v. responsibility" in Ellis's writings about sex from Professor Lafitte's article "Havelock Ellis." On romanticism and materialism in sexuality, also see Herbert W. Richardson, *Nun, Witch, Playmate: The Americanization of Sex* (New York: 1971), esp. p. 12. A measured criticism of Ellis's sexual ideology is in Sheila Rowbotham and Jeffrey Weeks, *Socialism and the New Life: The Personal and Sexual Politics of Edward Carpenter and Havelock Ellis* (London: 1977), p. 23, and of Sanger's, in Linda Gordon and Ellen Dubois, "Seeking Ecstasy on the Battlefield: Dangers and Pleasure in Nineteenth Century Feminist and Sexual Thought," *Feminist Studies* 9:1 (Spring 1983), p.18.

22. Ellis, *My Life,* 388–447, Robinson, *Modernization,* pp. 3, 29–33, 191–95.

23. Ellis, *My Life,* pp. 223–34, 244–68, 348, 388–89, 447. On Edith's lesbianism, see M. S. to Vincent Brome, Jan. 6, 1954, MS-SS; and Françoise Lafitte Cyon to M.S., Dec. 1, 1955, uncollected letters now in MS-SS; Calder-Marshall, *Life of Havelock Ellis,* p. 143, and Mrs. Havelock Ellis, *Steve's Woman* (New York: 1909), published in England as *Kit's Woman.* Grosskurth says that Ellis identified Schreiner as the only "true woman of genius" he ever knew, which, in this respect, certainly delimits the nature of his attraction to Margaret Sanger.

24. Françoise Delisle, ("Delisle" was an anagram of the French "de Ellis"), *Friendship's Odyssey* (London: 1946), pp. 278–79. Calder-Marshall, *Life of Havelock Ellis,* pp. 249–55 accepts Cyon's impression of a gradually transformed relationship; Grosskurth, *Havelock Ellis,* pp. 285–87 has doubts, pointing out that Cyon never explicitly states that there was conventional consummation of their relationship.

25. H.E. to M.S., Dec. 30, 1914, Jan. 5, Jan. 6, Jan. 22, Feb. 2, Feb 27, and "Friday afternoon" (n.d.) 1915, all in MS-LC. For an interpretation of the Reading Room of the British Museum as symbolic of liberation to women of the era, see Clive Bell, *Virginia Woolf: A Biography,* p. 145.

26. H.E. to M.S., Jan. 13, Jan. 15, Feb. 10, 11, 12, 15, 18, Mar. 29, Apr. 1, 3, 8, 9, 21, 22, 28, 1915, MS-LC. Ellis himself loved Spain and had written quite passionately about the countryside and the people in Havelock Ellis, *The Soul of Spain* (London: 1908).

27. I emphasize this point because the impression of a complete compatibility is so firm in Reed, *Birth Control Movement,* p. 94, and in the Ellis biographies, especially Grosskurth, *Havelock Ellis,* 242–53, 255–56. Grosskurth also says that Ellis did not know about Portet, though she does not document this assertion, and his letters quite clearly suggest otherwise. See H.E. to M.S., Mar. 15, Apr. 22, May 27, June 1, 3, and 17, 1915, in MS-LC. Ellis's letter to his wife is quoted in *My Life,* p. 550. The relationship with "Mneme" is chronicled in Grosskurth, *idem,* pp. 161–62, 257.

28. Ellis, *My Life,* pp. 337–43, 513–19, Calder-Marshall, *Life of Havelock Ellis,* pp. 198–201, and Grosskurth, *Havelock Ellis,* 247–53. H.E. to M.S., Mar. 13, 1915, MS-LC, quotes Edith's letter about her, which is reprinted in *My Life,* p. 437, with the "fanatical and unbalanced" part left out. Also see H.E. to M.S., Mar. 15, 1915. Margaret's comments on Edith are in the Brome letter cited above.

29. H.E. to M.S., June 1, 3, July 8, 14, 15, 22, Aug. 25, 29, Sept. 1, 6, 1915, in MS-LC, Calder-Marshall, *Life of Havelock Ellis,* p. 205. In her autobiography, Margaret wrote that there had been discussion of Edith's bringing her daughter, Peggy, to Europe, but Grosskurth finds no evidence to support this claim, see Grosskurth, *Havelock Ellis,* pp. 251–52. Edith's letter is quoted in Ellis, *My Life.*

30. M.S. to Vincent Brome, Jan. 6, 1954, MS-SS. A letter to Calder-Marshall from the same period is completely evasive on these issues and calls his questions "impertinent," also in MS-SS.

31. I am struck by the similarity of Sanger's situation and Margaret Mead's, as described by her daughter, Mary Catherine Bateson, in her enchanting memoir, *With a Daughter's Eye: A Memoir of Margaret Mead and Gregory Bateson* (New York: 1984), p. 127. Bateson says Mead "moved generously through a diversity of relationships," that while she might have wished for more order in her personal affairs—and wanted the intimacy of having shared many experiences with only one significant companion—she accepted this fragmentation as the price of her professional autonomy.

32. See especially Margaret Sanger, "Havelock Ellis," an editorial clipped from the *Birth Control Review,* Jan. 21, 1929, MS-LC, and M.S. and Dorothy Gordon, "Let's Talk It Over," transcript of a radio interview, July 17, 1939, on the occasion of Ellis's death, further discussed in Chapter 18. Also see Havelock Ellis, *Little Essays of Love and Virtue* (New York: 1922) and *The Dance of Life* (Cambridge: 1923), both offering light, philosophic reflections on love and life that convinced Sanger of Ellis's essential humanism, and the importance of sexual expression to sane living. Sanger reviewed *Little Essays* in *Birth Control Review* 7:4 (Apr. 1923), p. 95.

When Ellis's writings were condensed and republished in the United States in

1933, she wrote in M.S. to H.E., n.d. (1933), MS-SS: "& now you have combined some of the essentials from your 'studies' with the findings of modern reports & one feels a great satisfaction in the result. I am deep in it now & as always when reading your books I melt in reverence & admiration for your great spirit & wisdom."

33. On Ellis's politics see Grosskurth, *Havelock Ellis,* pp. 259–60, which quotes his own description of his interest in "socialization" from *The Labour Manual of 1895.* Also, Ellis, *Man and Woman,* pp. 1–20, 122–23, and *Task of Social Hygiene,* esp. the introduction, pp. 1–48, "The Significance of a Falling Birth Rate," pp. 181–92, "Eugenics and Love," pp. 195–97, "Individualism and Socialism," pp. 381–405. On eugenics in the United States see, Donald K. Pickens, *Eugenics and the Progressives* (Nashville, Tenn.: 1968), esp. pp. 3, 12, 18, 28–29; John Higham, *Strangers in the Land: Patterns of American Nativism, 1860–1925* (New York: 1974), pp. 149–50, 158–162; and the more recent study by Daniel J. Kevles, *In the Name of Eugenics: Genetics and the Uses of Human Heredity* (New York: 1985), first excerpted in a four-part series in *The New Yorker* (October 7–29, 1984). Many of these observations come from Part II of that series. Another example of a progressive argument for the compatibility of eugenics and social reform is in Scott Nearing, *The Super Race: An American Problem* (New York: 1912), esp. pp. 15–24, 26–27, 41–42. The Kropotkin quote is from his lecture to the Eugenics Congress in London in 1905.

34. Ellis, *Task of Social Hygiene* (material in quotation, on p. 12). Also see Ellis, *Essays in Wartime,* esp. pp. 92–115; Ellis, *Little Essays,* passim; Sanger's review of it in the *Birth Control Review,* 7:4, (Apr. 1923), and Ellis, "The World's Racial Problem," a review in *Birth Control Review* 4:10 (Oct. 1920), p. 16., of a book by eugenicist Lothrop Stoddard, *The Rising Tide of Color Against White World Supremacy,* in which Ellis is skeptical, but not wholly dismissive.

My impressions of Ellis's increasing "bewilderment" about eugenicism are drawn from his later writings and also from the interviews with François Lafitte and Joseph Wortis, previously cited. Though Ellis shared many of the prejudices of his upper-class English milieu and privately may have made snide remarks, he exhibited no overt anti-Semitism and worked diligently to help Jewish refugees relocate out of Germany in the late 1930s.

35. For Ellis's views, see his *Man and Woman,* esp. the introduction and pp. 447–51, and "The New Aspect of the Woman's Movement," in *Task of Social Hygiene,* pp. 67–112. Material in quotation is on p. 81. Sheila Rothman's introduction to the edition of the work previously cited presents a derogatory interpretation of Ellis's thinking about women, with which I respectfully disagree. Also see Rowbotham and Weeks, *Socialism and the New Life,* pp. 146–48 and 170–172.

On Ellis and Goldman see E.G. to H.E., Dec. 27, 1924, and May 30, 1928, in the Emma Goldman Papers, Tamiment, NYU. Ellis returned the tribute and contributed in 1928 to a fund being raised to enable Goldman to write her memoirs.

On his relationships with Schreiner and Key, see Olive Schreiner, *Woman and Labor* (New York: 1911), esp. pp. 20–21, 46–51; Ellen Key, *The Century of the Child* (New York: 1909), p. 85; Ellen Key, *Love and Marriage* (New York:

1911), esp. pp. 229–33; and for the material in quotation, Ellis's introduction, pp. vii-xiii, Ellen Key, *The Renaissance of Motherhood* (New York and London: 1914), esp. p. 88. For Ellis, Schreiner, and Key's influence on emerging feminists, see Nancy Cott, *The Grounding of Modern Feminism* (New Haven: 1987), pp. 41–46.

For modern-day thinking on these same issues, see Carol Gilligan, *In a Different Voice: Psychological Theory and Women's Development* (Cambridge, Mass., and London: 1982), pp. 68–70, and Sylvia Ann Hewlett, *A Lesser Life: The Myth of Women's Liberation in America* (New York: 1985) passim. Sylvia A. Law, "Rethinking Sex and the Constitution," *University of Pennsylvania Law Review* 132:5 (June 1984), pp. 955–1039, offers a provocative, revisionist legal argument on women's rights to constitutional protection of their biological role as child bearers.

36. Margaret Sanger, "Comstockery in America," speech at Fabian Hall, July 5, 1915, MS-LC. Also see the form letter of invitation to hear the speech, July, 1915, MS-LC, and M.S. to "Comrades and Friends," Aug. 1, 1915, MS-LC.

37. Leonard Abbott to M. S., May 1915, June 1, and Aug. 15, 1915, MS-LC; E. G. Flynn to M.S., Aug. 1915, MS-LC; Caroline Nelson in San Francisco to M.S., June 12, 1915; Charles Schultz of the Oakland IWW to M.S., Nov. 7, 1915; Mrs. F. E. Daniel, publisher of *The Texas Medical Journal,* to M.S., Aug. 19, 1915, MS-LC; Harry Breckinridge, "The Persecution of Margaret Sanger," *Mother Earth* 9: 9 (Nov. 1914), pp. 296–97; M.S., "A Letter from Margaret Sanger," *Mother Earth* 10:2 (Apr. 1915), pp. 76–78.

38. "Statement of William Sanger," Sept. 10, 1915, Court of Special Sessions, New York, MS-SS; James Waldo Fawcett, *The Trial of William Sanger* (New York: 1917) in MS-SS; "The Conviction of William Sanger," *Mother Earth* 10:8 (Oct. 1915), pp. 268–71; "Criminals All," *The Masses,* Sept. 17, 1915, an article enclosed in the William Sanger correspondence, MS-SS; "Sanger Trial in Comstock Case Ends in Uproar," unidentified New York newspaper clipping, scrapbook, MS-LC. Also see, "William Sanger on Trial," *The Call,* Sept. 10, 1915, 6:1–2; "The Case of Sanger," editorial, Sept. 11, 1915, 6:1–2; "What They Say About the Sanger Case," Sept. 11, 1915, 1:6 and "William Sanger Sentenced to Thirty Days in Jail," Sept. 11, 1915, 1:7.

39. On her defensiveness about her absence from the children, see M.S. to W.S, May 31, 1915, MS-SS; also *My Fight,* pp. 117–18, 126, and *Autobiography,* p. 175.

7: THE FRENZY OF RENOWN

1. *Autobiography,* p. 180. For a statistical breakdown of birth control coverage in popular magazines listed in the *Readers' Guide to Periodical Literature* and in select newspapers and books, see Hornell Hart, "Changing Social Attitudes and Interests," in President's Research Committee on Social Trends, *Recent Social Trends in the United States* Vol. 1 (New York: 1933), pp. 382–83, 414–16, 422–23. Also see James A. Field, "Publicity by Prosecution," *The Survey,* Feb. 19, 1916, p. 599, in MS-LC. For parallels between Sanger and Besant, see "Three Rebel Women," *Birth Control Review* 13:4 (Apr. 1929), p. 106.

2. See, for example, Max Eastman, "Is the Truth Obscene?" *The Masses* 4:6 (Mar. 1915) and successive articles in the May, June, July, Sept. and Nov. issues. I took this particular quote from *The New Republic* because it was widely circulated through a condensation of the articles that appeared later in "The Battle over Birth Control," *Current Opinion* 59: 339–41, (Nov. 1915). For the original, see "The Age of Birth Control," *The New Republic* 2: 113 (Feb. 28, 1915), "The Control of Births," *The New Republic,* 2:114 (Mar. 6, 1915), and subsequent articles and correspondence on the subject in the issues of Mar. 13, Mar. 20, and July 3, 1915.

3. Mary Alden Hopkins, "The Control of Births," *Harper's Weekly,* 60:3042 (Apr. 10, 1915), pp. 342–43, and subsequent articles in the series, especially, "Dead Babies," Apr. 17, 1915, pp. 369–70, "Spacing Out Babies," Apr. 24, 1915, pp. 401–402, and "The Falling Birth Rate," June 12, 1915, pp. 567–68. *The New York Times Index* for 1914 and 1915 lists relevant articles under "family," "birth control," and "Sanger." The first entry is on William Sanger's arrest and the decision of the Free Speech League to help defend him, Feb. 6, 1915, 12:5; followed by articles on July 19, 16:7, July 25, II:14:7, Sept. 5, II:8:5, Sept. 11, 7:2, and Sept. 12, II:15:1. Also, see John Reed to M. S., Jan. 12, 1916, MS-LC. A tabulation of birth control coverage in *The Times* and *The Reader's Guide* between 1866 and 1926 was made by Francis McLennon Vreeland, "The Process of Reform with Especial Reference to Reform Groups in the Field of Population," doctoral dissertation, University of Michigan, 1929, pp. 296–312, and Tables 85 and 87.

4. On feminism and the declining birth rate, see "Birth Control Calendar," clippings from *The New York Times* for 1915, including "Women and the Fading Maternal Instinct," Sept. 5, 1915, MS-LC. On the formation of the NBCL, see "Birth Control," *The Masses* 6:8 (May 1915), p. 20. On the original NBCL membership, see Vreeland,"Process of Reform," p. 690. On Mary Ware Dennett, see biographical entry in *Notable American Women, 1607–1950: A Biographical Dictionary*, edited by Edward T. James and Janet Wilson James, (Cambridge, Mass: 1971) pp. 463–65. The Parsons incident is recounted in Elsie Clews Parsons, "Wives and Birth Control," *The New Republic* 6 (Mar. 18, 1916) pp. 187–88; in Rose Pastor Stokes to Elsie Clews Parsons, n.d. (1915–16), RPS, Tamiment-NYU; and in Sanger, *Autobiography,* p. 189, where she "doctored" the incident by saying that twenty-five women were asked to "plead guilty" with her in court, and only one agreed. The second Parsons quote is from Elsie Clews Parsons, *Social Freedom* (New York: 1915), cited in David Kennedy, *Birth Control in America: The Career of Margaret Sanger* (New Haven: 1970), p. 60. Finally, see Carrie Catt to M.S., Nov. 24, 1920, MS-SS.

5. On the suffrage victory see Eleanor Flexner, *Century of Struggle: The Woman's Rights Movement in the United States* (New York: 1973), originally published in 1959, pp. 262–75. For a discussion of the ideological distinctions between older suffragists and women activists and the younger generation of "feminists" who added sex to their rights agenda, see Nancy Cott, *The Grounding of Modern Feminism* (New Haven: 1987), Chap. 5. The rash of birth control publicity from 1915 to 1918 is analyzed in Vreeland, "Process of Reform," and in Hornell Hart, President's Commission on Social Trends: *Recent Social Trends in the United States* (New York: 1933), pp. 414–16, which makes the point that birth control did not again receive comparable attention until the

1930s, when, as we shall see, Margaret Sanger abandoned an interim strategy of quieter organization and lobbying and intensely pursued national publicity for a second time.

6. Anita C. Block, "The Sanger Case," *The Call,* Sept. 19, 1915, Sunday Supplement, p. 13:2–3. A critical reply to the editorial was written by Jessie Ashley. See "Differs on the Sanger Case," *The Call,* Sunday *Magazine,* Sept. 26, 1915, p. 13: 1–2. The quote is from William Sanger to M.S., Sept. 27, 1915, MS-SS. Also see W.S. to Mabel Dodge, Feb. 28, 1915, and Leonard Abbott to Mabel Dodge, Feb. 3, 1915, in the Mabel Dodge Luhan papers, Beinecke Rare Book and Manuscript Library, Yale University, and W.S. to M.S., Sept. 21, 1915, MS-SS. (The second benefactress was Grace [Mrs. John Sargeant] Crane.) Stuart Sanger discussed his aunt's role in his placement at the Winnwood School on Long Island in his interview with the author, Mar. 1986.

7. Wm. Sanger to Mabel Dodge, Sept. 27, 1915; W.S. to M.S., Feb. 14, 1914; Mar. 25, 1914; Jan. 10, 1915, with threat of suicidal impulses; Sept. 3, 1915, enclosing the poem; Sept. 14, 1915, on her birthday; Oct. 6, 1915, all in MS-SS. M.S. to W.S., Oct. 13, 1915; Mar. 21, 1917 (wishing to give back his name) and Mar. 24, 1917, also all in MS-SS.

8. Author's interviews with Olive Byrne Richard, Mar. 1985, and Stuart Sanger, Mar. 1986.

9. Dreams of Peggy in Journal, May 1, 1926, MS-LC, and memory of the cremation in 1936 India Diary, MS-LC; M.S. to Juliet Rublee, Nov. 3, n.d. (1923), MS-DC; and M.S. to H.E., May 30, 1929. *Autobiography,* p. 182. Additional dreams of babies are in Sanger Journal entries for Oct. 6, 1924, Feb. 14, 1936 and May 28, 1951, in MS-SS.

Margaret often wrote about her dreams to Havelock Ellis, whose own interpretations of dream content disputed the dominant psychoanalytic theory of sleep as the province of highly charged sexual symbols. Ellis insisted instead that dreams represent no more than a random sorting out of the significant events of one's conscious life, possibly affected by such physiological factors during sleep as body temperature or position.

Freud on dreams of babies is in Sigmund Freud, *A General Introduction to Psychoanalysis,* translated by Joan Riviere (New York: 1960), p. 143, where he interprets unconscious images of babies as representations of the genitalia. Ego-pyschologists would more likely read a generalized anxiety pattern stemming from early childhood into these dreams. Of course their meaning could only be determined in relation to direct conscious associations, but the sustained pattern is nevertheless compelling.

The depth of Margaret's grief for Peggy is also evident in contemporaneous letters of condolence. See, for example, Jessie Ashley to M.S., Nov. 8, 1915; Stella Brown to M.S., Dec. 5, 1915, and April 6, 1916; and Emma Goldman to M.S., Dec. 7, 1915, which entreats her to stop blaming herself, all in MS-LC. M.S. to Grant Sanger, May 31, 1942, in MS-SS, reminds him that it is Peggy's birthday, and that "the bond of mother and child never dies." Olive Byrne Richard, Margaret Sanger Marston, and Nancy Sanger Ivins also spoke of the special bond among Peggy, Grant and Margaret in their oral reminiscences with Jacqueline Van Voris, for the Sophia Smith Collection, Smith College, Nov. 25, 1977.

M.S. to Lawrence Lader, Dec. 3, 1953, answers his question about her use of the word "guilt" in a letter about Peggy to Emma Goldman by saying "guilt" was a "hackneyed word" and that she preferred the term "regret," because it did not imply wrongdoing on her part. "As to leaving the children I knew it was a necessary sacrifice to leave them to prepare my defense in order to leave them a clear record of their mother's work," she continued. Her behavior at the time of the tragedy, however, suggests the appropriateness of the term "guilt," even by her later definition.

10. These "psychic experiences," and Margaret's conflicted responses of both comfort and disbelief are reported in notes on a conversation with Dorothy Brush, dated Aug. 17, 1937, MS-SS. Margaret also told Brush that several years following the death, she attended a meeting led by a Parsee Indian, where she met a small woman psychic who claimed to have communicated with Peggy. The woman described the child accurately and then, to Margaret's astonishment, said Peggy was with "Domah," the name which the Sanger children used for Bill Sanger's mother. Letters Margaret kept from the Parsee woman are also in MS-SS, but there is no confirmation of the psychic experience.

11. Margaret discusses the meaning of mysticism and of Rosicrucianism, specifically, in a letter to Lawrence Lader, Mar. 2, 1954, MS-SS, and in handwritten notes on correspondence with the Rosicrucians, in MS-LC. She liked them, as well, because of their interest in the enhanced spiritual powers of women and their sympathy for political feminism. See George Plummer to M.S., Apr. 13 and Apr. 19, 1944, and Apr. 14, 1944, MS-SS; and R. Swinburne Clymer, M.D., *The Rosicrucians: Their Teaching, Their Manifestos* (Quakertown, Pa.: 1941). A 1974 undergraduate thesis by Barbara Livingston of Wesleyan University, entitled "Dreams and Inspirations: A Footnote to a Biography of Margaret Sanger," provides an interesting summary of this fascination with the mystical and the occult, MS-SS. On "talking" to the dead, see M.S. Journal, July 28, 1919, MS-SS, and M.S. to Juliet Rublee, n.d (1923 or 24), MS-DC.

12. Sanger's resentment of the Ferrerists over Peggy's illness is from my phone conversation with Nelle Dick; that she nevertheless courted them after the death is evident from Margaret Sanger, "To My Friends and Comrades," in *Revolt* 1 (Jan.–Mar. 1916), a short-lived anarchist journal edited by Hippolyte Havel, available at the New York Public Library.

13. A sampling of Sanger's letters to and from her sons is in MS-SS. For the Grant Sanger quotes, see G.S. to M.S., Feb. 20, Mar. 6, and Nov. 17, 1918. These impressions and the Stuart Sanger memory are also taken from my personal interviews with Grant Sanger, Stuart Sanger, Alexander Sanger, and Margaret Sanger Marston. Again, my thanks to Alex for piecing together old family films.

14. Edith How-Martyn to M.S., Mar. 26, 1916, MS-SS.

15. *Autobiography,* pp. 183, 186; Morris Kahn to "To Whom It May Concern," Dec. 30, 1915, MS-LC, contains Sanger's margin notes on refusing to use it. Criticism of her trial strategy is in Max Eastman to M.S., Jan. 11, 1916, and Samuel Guggenheimer to M.S., Dec. 6, 1915, in MS-LC; support is in Bolton Hall to Leonard Abbott, Dec. 13, 1915; Leonard Abbott to M.S., "Saturday," n.d. (1915), and Emma Goldman to M.S., Dec. 7, 1915, all in MS-LC. Also see M.S. to "To My Friends and Comrades, Jan. 5, 1916, MS-LC, and M.S., "To My Friends," *Mother Earth* 10:12 (Feb. 1916), p. 405.

16. *Autobiography,* p. 186. M.S., "To My Friends," Jan. 26, 1916, soliciting

letters to President Wilson and Judge Clayton of the Federal District Court, is in the Rose Pastor Stokes Papers, Department of Manuscript and Archives, Yale University Library, hereinafter RPS-Yale. A similar appeal on National Birth Control League letterhead, dated Feb. 7, 1916 is in RPS, Tamiment-NYU. Petitions to Judge Clayton and to the President from all over the country are in MS-LC. M.S. to Marie Stopes, n.d. (1915), "Torrington Square," in the Marie Stopes Papers, in the Manuscript Division of the British Museum in London (hereinafter Stopes-BM), discusses a draft of the Wilson letter. Also see Marie Stopes to M.S., n.d. (1915), enclosing a personal letter she sent to Wilson and a copy of the official letter from "H. G. Wells, Marie Stopes et al. to the President of the United States," Sept. 1915, both in MS-LC. For the effect of all the publicity, see "Mrs. Sanger's Federal Trial Scrapbook," MS-LC; James Waldo Fawcett, "The Sanger Case," *The Call,* Jan. 13, 1916, 6:3; and subsequent articles on the trial in *The Call,* Jan. 18, 19, 21. *The New York Times* also covered the story. See, for example,"Mrs. Sanger Draws Crowd," Jan 19, 1916, 22:4. For general support mail, see Edric B. Smith to M.S., Jan. 29, 1916; Georgia Kalsch to "Dear Comrades," Jan. 18, 1916, and B. Greenberg to M.S. Feb. 19, 1916, all in MS-LC.

17. Margaret Sanger, Hotel Brevoort Speech, Jan. 17, 1916, MS-LC. Mrs. Sanger's Federal Trial Scrapbook, MS-LC. Correspondence regarding the dinner and a list of prospective attendees are in RPS, Tamiment-NYU.

Sanger was considerably less than forthright in her *Autobiography,* p. 189, about the support she had received from the National Birth Control League, an omission that reflected the long and intense rivalry she was to engage in with Mary Ware Dennett. Other discrepancies in her account of these events—such as that Walter Lippmann had been present, when, in fact, it was his colleague, Herbert Croly—seem the result of honest confusion after more than twenty years, but with respect to anyone who ever crossed her, such as Dennett or Emma Goldman, she clearly altered the facts.

18. Clippings from Mrs. Sanger's Federal Trial Scrapbook, MS-LC, include "U.S. Drops Birth Control Suit Against Woman Rebel," *The Call,* Feb. 21, 1916, 3:3, and "Drops Mrs. Sanger's Case, Federal Actions Followed by Plans for a Celebration," *The New York Times,* Feb. 19, 1916, 12:2.

19. "Mrs. Sanger Glad: Thanks Authorities for Aiding Birth Control Cause by Publicity," clipping from *New York Herald* Feb. 21, 1916, in scrapbook, MS-LC. Margaret Sanger, "Original Speech Given in 1916," with handwritten notation that she delivered it 119 times, in MS-LC. Margaret Sanger, "Chicago Address to Women," n.d. (1916), and "Itinerary for Feb. 6–17, 1916 for M. Sanger, Son, and Secretary," MS-SS. Details of the stockyard speech in Chicago are in Bernice J. Guthmann, *The Planned Parenthood Movement in Illinois, 1923–1965,* a 1965 pamphlet, published by the Planned Parenthood Association, Chicago Area, and collected by the author in a 1976 research trip there. The Baldwin recollection is from Harlan B. Phillips, Interview with Roger Baldwin, Columbia University Oral History Project, 1953–54. Vol. 1., pp. 48–49. (Baldwin misidentifies the year as 1912.) Also see William M. Morehouse, "The Speaking of Margaret Sanger in the Birth Control Movement from 1916 to 1937," doctoral dissertation, Purdue University, 1968, pp. 56, 74–75, 89–91, a copy of which is in MS-SS.

20. Alexander Berkman to M.S., Dec. 9, 1915, MS-SS, is terribly affection-

ate and also offers condolences on Peggy's death, saying, "I would hold you in my arms again." Also see "Edward" to M.S. n.d. (1914) MS-LC. Berkman either wrote about birth control without a byline or using the pseudonym of "Reb Raney." See "Not Guilty," *The Blast* 1:1 (Jan. 9, 1916); "The Meaning of Margaret Sanger's Stand," *The Blast* 1:6 (Feb. 19, 1916); and the cover cartoon showing a physician handing birth control information to a well-dressed woman and turning away a poor woman and her children, with the caption "The Boss's wife can buy information to limit her family. The Boss can buy your children to supply his factories with cheap labor." *The Blast* 1:5 (Feb. 12, 1916). *The Blast* is available as a Greenwood Reprint (Fairfield, Conn.: 1968). A clipping of the Anita Block editorial comment in *The Call* is in the Rose Pastor Stokes Papers, Tamiment-NYU. Also see Marie Equi to M.S., October 20, 1916, MS-LC.

Years later, on depositing this letter in her papers at Smith College, Margaret penciled in the following description of Marie: "a rebellious soul, generous kind, brave, but so radical in her thinking that she was almost an outcast. Upon arrival she captured every well known woman who comes to Portland. Her reputation is Lesbian but to me she was like a crushed falcon which had braved the storm and winds of time and needed tenderness and love. I liked Marie always."

21. Goldman in the wings is from *New York Herald,* Feb. 21, 1916, clippings, MS-LC; "Respectable" quote is from "Observations and Comments," *Mother Earth,* 10:5 (July 1915) and Reitman remarks from "The 1915–16 Tour," *Mother Earth* 11:8 (Oct. 1916); persecution of Goldman (with recognition that she was being singled out especially harshly) is in "Emma Goldman's Defense," *The Masses* 8:8 (June 1916) and "Birth Control," *The Masses* 8:9 (July 1916). Also see Emma Goldman, "My Arrest and Preliminary Hearing" in *Mother Earth* 11:1 (Mar. 1916) and *Mother Earth* 11:2 (Apr., 1916) and 11:3 (May 1916), essentially entire issues devoted to the birth control controversy that never once mention Sanger. Subsequent issues of *Mother Earth* contain only a scattered article or two on birth control. Sanger telegram in "Carnegie Hall Meeting endorsed by M. Sanger in Telegram," *The New York Times*, Mar. 2, 1916, 20:4, and statement for the later Emma Goldman rally, n.d. (1916), MS-LC; clippings on Rose Stokes at Carnegie Hall, RPS, Tamiment-NYU.

22. Conversation on pacificism is from Harold Hersey, "Margaret Sanger: The Biography of the Birth Control Pioneer," New York (1938), p. 223, also cited in James Reed, *The Birth Control Movement and American Society: From Private Vice to Public Virtue* (Princeton: 1984), p. 96.

23. *Autobiography,* p. 204. For "pink tea" reference, see "Copy of part of Mrs. Dennett's statement," Nov. 18, 1921, MS-LC, in which she says Margaret repeatedly spoke of organization and legislation as "bourgeois, pink-tea and lady-like."

24. See especially Mary Ware Dennett to Marie Stopes, Oct. 31, 1921, Stopes-BM. Christopher Lasch's profile of Dennett in James, *Notable American Women,* says that her divorce was over the fact that she had become a suffragist.

25. "Birth-Control," *The Masses* 8:9 (July 1916), p. 21. A copy of the bill introduced by Abraham I. Shiplacoff, Socialist, is in MS-LC. Also see Shiplacoff to Frederick Blossom, Feb. 20 and Feb. 27, 1917, and M.S. to Ship-

lacoff, Mar. 2, 1917, on her decision to endorse Assemblyman Greenberg's version of the bill. Also see Mary Ware Dennett, "Beating Around the Bush With State Legislation," *Birth Control Laws: Shall We Keep Them, Change Them or Abolish Them?* (New York: 1926), pp. 72–93; and Reed, *Birth Control Movement,* pp. 97–105. The best documentary record of the Sanger-Dennett controversy as it developed is in Dennett's letters to Marie Stopes, Stopes-BM. See especially, Stopes to Dennett, Jan. 5, 1920, and Dennett to Stopes, Jan. 27, 1920, June 14, 1921, Sept. 2, 1921, and Dec. 30, 1921. Also see the Marie Stopes papers, Wellcome Institute for the History of Medicine, London, hereinafter Stopes-Wellcome: Stopes to Dennett, Nov. 19, 1921, and July 31, 1931.

26. Margaret Sanger, *Birth Control Review* (Jan., 1919) p. 2. and *Birth Control: The Proceedings of the First American Birth Control Conference* (New York: 1922), pp. 91–92, both cited in Reed, *Birth Control Movement,* pp. 102–103.

27. Dennett, *Birth Control Laws.* Reed, *Birth Control Movement.*

28. *Autobiography,* pp. 143–48. The autobiography, as in so many other respects, takes some liberty with the facts here, embellishing the dimension of her Dutch investigation, turning what had been only days into months. Also see Johannes Rutgers to M.S., Nov. 15, 1916, May 16, 1917, Oct. 10, 1920, MS-LC. Leonard Abbott to M.S., Feb. 11, 1916, MS-LC, and Henriette Hendrixholtz, "Aletta Jacobs," *Birth Control Review* 12:5 (May 1928), p. 139.

29. Margaret Sanger, "Chicago Address," MS-SS; *Autobiography,* p. 190.

30. Paul Starr, *The Social Transformation of American Medicine,* (New York: 1987), pp. 180–97 (clinic data on pp. 191–92).

31. S. Adolphus Knopf, M.D., "Birth Control: Its Medical, Social, Economic and Moral Aspects," *The Survey* 37:11 (Nov. 18, 1916), pp. 161–64, reprint of an address delivered at the 44th Annual Meeting of the American Public Health Association, Cincinnati, Ohio, Oct. 27, 1916. C. V. Drysdale, *The Small Family System: Is It Injurious or Immoral?* (New York: 1914), pp. 59–62, applauds the Dutch example. Also see "Judge's Views Delight Birth Control Advocates," *The New York Times Magazine* 5:8:1 (Oct. 22, 1916), and "Abraham Jacobi Favors Regulation in Address to Free Synagogue," *The New York Times,* Nov. 29, 1915, 18:4, and "Dr. Jacobi Presides Over Meeting and Urges Physician Advisors as in Europe," *NYT* May 27, 1915. Finally, see Kennedy, *Birth Control,* pp. 173–74.

32. The actions of the committee were reported in *Pediatrics* 29 (1917), pp. 17–23, cited in Kennedy, *Birth Control,* p. 174. Dickinson's remarks are in *Surgery, Gynecology and Obstetrics* 23 (1916), pp. 185–90, cited in Reed, *Birth Control Movement,* pp. 167–68. Also see Starr, *Social Transformation,* pp. 140–44, 215–32, 252–57, 260–66.

33. Robert Dickinson to M.S., Nov. 7, 1945, MS-SS, recalls his rebuke. M.S., *Autobiography,* pp. 210-15, claims that four other doctors did offer her support, on the condition that she find a doctor to staff the clinic, but the only confirmation is in William J. Robinson to M.S., July 1916, MS-LC, from which this material is taken. Also see "Mrs. Sanger Plans Clinic," *The New York Times,* July 22, 1916, 4:3, and "For Birth Control Clinic," *NYT,* Sept. 12, 1916, 11:4.

8: THE COMPANY SHE KEPT

1. A photo marked "46 Amboy St., Brownsville, Brooklyn," is in MS-SS. A copy of the circular is reprinted in M.S., *My Fight for Birth Control,* p. 155.

2. I have taken my narrative of the clinic's operation and the events surrounding Margaret's arrest from contemporary newspaper accounts and from the transcript, *The People of the State of New York, Plaintiff Against Margaret H. Sanger, Defendant,* Court of Special Sessions of the City of New York, Part Two. Brooklyn, N.Y., January 29 and Feb. 2, 1917, copy in the National Archives, Record Group 267, Box 7093, File 26412, hereinafter, NA-SC (for Supreme Court). These records were kept as a result of Goldstein's subsequent appeal to the Unites States Supreme Court. Many thanks to David Garrow for helping me to uncover this document. Transcripts of state court proceedings were not generally kept at this time, but in this instance apparently enough interest was anticipated, so that one was kept. Briefs from the first appeal in the Supreme Court of New York, Appellate Division, 2d Dept. (179 App. Div. 1939 [1917]), are in MS-SS. Also see People of N.Y. v. Margaret H. Sanger, Defendant-Appellant New York Court of Appeals, 222 NY 192 (1918). Finally, see C. Thomas Dienes, *Law, Politics and Birth Control* (Chicago: 1972), pp. 85–87.

Sanger gives her own version in *Autobiography,* pp. 210–37, and I have tried to correct significant discrepancies. Mary Halton, M.D., a tuberculosis specialist at Grosvenor Hospital on Manhattan's Lower East Side, was a supporter of Sanger through the National Birth Control League. She had once been reprimanded (Sanger says she was asked to resign) from the staff for prescribing birth control to a patient. She may have been a candidate to work in the clinic, but there is no confirmation of that fact. Also see Elizabeth Stuyvesant, "The Brownsville Birth Control Clinic," *Birth Control Review* 1:2, Feb. 1917, pp. 6–8. The article featured illustrations by William Sanger.

Excellent use of some of these sources was made by Marybeth Albanese Petschek in "The Brownsville Clinic Trial: 1916–1919," a paper prepared for Prof. Stephen Isaacs's master's seminar at the Columbia University School of Public Health, Dec. 1981. Although our accounts and our interpretations vary, I am grateful to Ms. Petschek for sharing her paper and some of these citations with me.

3. *Autobiography,* p. 112. "Sanger et al. arrested at Clinic in Brownsville," *The New York Times,* Oct. 28, 1916, 8:4.

The single column story also mentioned Emma Goldman's arrest for literature circulation at a Union Square rally. Two days later (Oct. 30, 9:2) the paper gave comparable coverage to an announcement by faculty at Fordham University that they would fight the birth control movement, and the following day (Oct. 31, 9:5), to Jessie Ashley's having been found guilty and fined for distributing birth control literature.

4. "Mrs. Sanger fights as Police Seize Her in Raid on Clinic," *Brooklyn Daily Eagle,* Jan. 26, 1916, 1:3, cited in Petschek, "Brownsville Clinic," p. 17; "Mrs. Sanger, Mrs. Byrne and Miss F. Mindell in Court and Held for Trial," *The New York Times,* Nov. 7, 1916, 8:4; "Mrs. Sanger Released on Bail to Await Trial; Reopens Clinic in Brownsville Under Observation of Police," *NYT,* Nov. 14, 1916, 4:2; "Mrs. Sanger Rearrested at Her Clinic on

Charge of Maintaining a Public Nuisance," *NYT,* Nov. 16, 1916, 17:1; "Seize Mrs. Sanger in Raid on Clinic for Birth Control," *New York World,* Nov. 27, 1916, 7:1.

5. *The New York Times,* Nov. 27, 1916, 13:6; Nov. 28, 24:2; Dec. 5, 11:1; Dec. 12, 15:1; Dec. 13, 11:3; Dec. 23, 5:3. Jonah J. Goldstein, "The Birth Control Clinic Cases," *Birth Control Review* 1:1, Jan. 1917, p. 8, and Jonah Goldstein, Brief for the Defendant Appellant in People v. Sanger, Supreme Court Appellate Division, p. 3, MS-SS. Also see "Jonah J. Goldstein," *The National Cyclopedia of American Biography,* p. 256.

6. *The New York Times,* Jan. 5, 1917, 4:2; Jan. 9, 11:1–2; Jan. 23, 20:3; Jan 24, 20:2. Goldstein, "Birth Control Case"; Goldstein, *People of the State of New York ex rel. Margaret H. Sanger, Ethel Byrne and Fannie Mindell. Appellants' Brief in Support of Motion for Stay of Proceedings* (New York: 1917), pp. 11–56. Copy in the New York Public Library. *People of the State of New York v. Margaret H. Sanger,* transcript, passim, NA-SC. Jonah J. Goldstein, *People of N.Y. v. Margaret H. Sanger, Defendent-Appellant* (New York: 1917). This was Goldstein's brief, published by the Hecla Press, obviously because of all the publicity and interest. The major precedent for ruling on other than legal precedent was the decision won by Louis Brandeis, then still a young lawyer from Boston, in Muller v. Oregon, 208 U.S. 412 (1908). Goldstein also cited several additional such rulings in the courts of New York State. My thanks to Sylvia Law for helping to clarify some of this legal strategy for me.

7. *The New York Times,* Jan. 25, 1917, 20:2; Jan. 26, 1:2, Jan. 27, 1:4, Jan. 28, 1:3, Jan. 29, 1:4, Jan. 30, 4:2. David Kennedy, *Birth Control in America: The Career of Margaret Sanger* (New Haven: 1970), p. 87, says that the corrections commissioner was the same Katherine Bement Davis whom Margaret excoriated in *The Woman Rebel* for her treatment of Becky Edelsohn's hunger strike, but who would later became an ally. Actually Davis was still a prison official but no longer commissioner. The commissioner responsible was a man by the name of Burdette S. Lewis. Though Margaret would thereafter cite the precedent of British suffragists, Becky Edelsohn's example in 1914 was better known to her. See Margaret Sanger, "The History of the Hunger Strike," *The Woman Rebel* 1:6 (Aug. 1914), p. 47, and "The Old and the New," a comparison of Davis and Edelsohn, on p. 48.

8. Minutes of what appears to be the first meeting of the Committee of 100 are in RPS-Yale. A Planned Parenthood Federation of America reprint of the original manifesto written by Rublee is in MS-SS.

9. *The New York Times,* Jan. 9, 1917, 4:2, also cited in Lawrence Lader, *The Margaret Sanger Story* (New York: 1955), p. 124.

10. "Mrs. Byrne Pardoned," *The New York Times,* Feb. 2, 1917, 11:5; Feb. 3, 8:2–3; Lader, *Sanger Story,* p. 125–26.

11. Ethel Byrne to M.S., n.d. (Feb. 1917), MS-SS; M.S. to Byrne, Feb. 14, 1917, MS-LC. The sisters had to communicate by letter, because Margaret by then was in jail. Quotes are from author's interview with Olive Byrne Richard, Mar. 28, 1985, and Richard interview with Jacqueline Van Voris, Nov. 25, 1977, p. 2. Also see p. 5. For the public tribute to Ethel, see Margaret Sanger, *Woman and the New Race* (New York: 1920), p. 217.

12. *The New York Times,* Feb. 3, 1917, 8:2, *The Call,* Feb. 3, 1917, 2–3;

and especially, the *New York Herald* account cited in Lader, *Sanger Story,* p. 127.

13. Margaret Sanger, "A Victory, a New Year and a New Day," *Birth Control Review* 3:2 (Feb., 1919), p. 3.

14. *The New York Times,* Nov. 14, 1916: 4:2, Nov. 16, 1916: 17:1. *People of N.Y. v. Margaret H. Sanger,* NA-SS, pp. 22–73.

15. *People of N.Y. v. Margaret H. Sanger,* NA-SC; *The New York Times,* Feb. 3, 1917, 8:2; *The Call,* Feb. 3, 1917, 1:2–3, Lader, *Sanger Story,* p. 131.

16. Excerpt from prison letter of Feb. 9, 1917, in *Birth Control Review* 1:2 (Feb. 1917), p. 3. Sanger Diary entry from prison, Feb. 8, 1917, MS-LC, tells of supper of bread, molasses, and tea; oatmeal and salt for breakfast; and dinner of stew. Also see M.S. to Ethel Byrne, Feb. 21, 1917; MS-LC; *The New York Times,* Feb. 6, 1917, 20:5, and Feb. 9, 1917, 13:5. Letters on prison reform include the following: Mrs. Powell, President of the Woman's Prison Assn., to M.S., Mar. 8, 1917, and Virginia Young to M.S., May 13, 1918, MS-LC. When Margaret on leaving prison made public statements condemning corrections official Katherine Bement Davis, she received letters from women prisoners. See Golden Rule League, Blackwell's Island, to M.S., Mar. 9, 1917, and Branch Pen, Harts Island, to M.S."on behalf of hundreds serving indefinite sentences" n.d. (1917). In M.S. to Winthrop Cane, Mar. 17, 1942, she says that "the only great cause after birth control is won will be the investigation of the treatment of prisoners. If I can't do it now, I'll book it for the next trip." He'd apparently written her, having just read the prison reminiscences in her *Autobiography.*

17. *Autobiography* p. 243. Anonymous letters of support from the women inmates to Sanger are in MS-LC. Theodore Debs to "My Dear Comrade Sanger," Feb. 25, 1917, MS-LC. Also see Eugene V. Debs to M.S., Feb. 14, 1917, MS-LC.

18. *The New York Times,* Mar. 6, 1917, 11:4; Mar. 7, 1917, 20:5–6 and *New York Herald,* Mar. 7, 1917, emphasizing the fingerprinting squabble, clipping in MS-LC. A Sanger Diary entry for Feb. 8, 1917, records her first refusal to be fingerprinted, and a later undated entry says the warden was being very decent about it, but still kept asking, MS-LC. Harold Hersey, "Margaret Sanger: The Biography of the Birth Control Pioneer," New York (1938), p. 243, identifies the welcoming committee, which also included a Columbia professor named Robert Lesher, whose presence is not explained. The Halpern story is from the author's interview with Paula Gould, Halpern's sixth and youngest child, on July 26, 1976, in New York City.

19. *Autobiography,* pp. 249–50.

20. Decision in *People of N. Y. v. Margaret H. Sanger,* New York Court of Appeals, 222 NY 192 (1918), reprinted in *Birth Control Review* 4:6, (June 1920), p. 1. The Supreme Court actions are chronicled in NA-SC, which includes Goldstein's petition of Jan. 20, 1918; the docket of April 3, 1918; notification of the matter's being carried over to October, 1918; scheduling of an oral argument for May 2, 1919 and an April 30, 1919 telegram from Goldstein requesting a postponement; Goldstein's brief submitted on Aug. 29, 1919; and finally, notification of the dismissal, dated Nov. 17, 1919. Also see "Dismisses Birth Control Case," *New York Times,* Nov. 18, 1919, 17:3. My thanks to Kevin Hahm for retrieving the file. Ethel Byrne to M.S., n.d. (Feb.

1917), MS-SS. M.S. to Jonah Goldstein, judge of Court of General Sessions, n.d. (1931), MS-LC.

In a letter to the author on April 30, 1990, Prof. Sylvia Law underscored the significance of Goldstein's ingenuity, or perhaps his simple good fortune, in getting an appellate ruling on behalf of physicians when his client had no real standing to raise the question. Perhaps this is why the Supreme Court would not hear the matter. For more on the importance of the decision to the future course of the movement, see, especially, Chapter 13.

21. David M. Kennedy, *Over Here: The First World War and American Society* (New York: 1980), pp. 26–27; Melvyn Dubofsky, *We Shall Be All: A History of the Industrial Workers of the World* (Chicago: 1969), pp. 389–425. Robert A. Rosenstone, *Romantic Revolutionary: A Biography of John Reed* (New York: 1975), pp. 320–37, discusses the impact of repression on the intellectuals and on John Reed, in particular. Randolph Boehm, ed., *U.S. Military Intelligence Surveillance of Radicals in the United States 1917–41,* (Frederick, Md: University Publications of America, 1984), Reel 6, documents surveillance of Goldman, Berkman and other IWW activists, Ferrer Center anarchists, and Socialists in New York City in 1917 and 1918 (including the arrest of Tresca and Flynn). The microfilm is available in New York at Tamiment-NYU.

22. Joan Jensen, "The Evolution of Margaret Sanger's *Family Limitation* Pamphlet," 1914–1921, *Signs* 6 (Spring 1981), pp. 548–67, analyzes the editing from this standpoint. Also see James W. Walker to M.S., Apr. 5, 1917, MS-LC, which regrets her excluding references to the "ennobling effects of sex gratification on women." M.S. to "Friend" (on "163 Lexington Ave." letterhead n.d., 1917–18), MS-SS, is an example of the covering letter Margaret sent out with pamphlets, acknowledging she was technically violating the Comstock Law, making a feminist argument for doing so, and requesting contributions. The clipping cited is from the *Herald,* Rochester, N.Y. n.d. (1917), in Scrapbooks, MS-LC.

According to Peter Engelman of the Margaret Sanger Papers Project, the Lusk Committee did nothing more than collect several of Margaret's pamphlets and notices of her speeches, which are in the committee's records in the New York State Archives in Albany, N.Y. But federal agents later became more diligent. See, U.S. Department of Justice, Federal Bureau of Investigation, file on Margaret Sanger, supplied on May 13, 1985, in response to the author's request under the Freedom of Information Act. Included are the following documents of interest: A memorandum titled "In Re: Margaret Sanger: Alleged Violation Section 211," dated Jan. 19, 1920, New York City, but of unclear departmental origin; File "Re: Oswald Garrison Villard Radical Activities," identifying Margaret as an associate, June 9, 1922; Edward Brennan to director, Bureau of Investigation, General Intelligence Division, Department of Justice, "In Re: The League for Amnesty of Political Prisoners," Jan. 27, 1922; report of Special Agent Walter Foster on Sanger's speech in Philadelphia on Jan. 30, 1922; and, finally, Part 5, Vol. 3 of the Fish Committee Report of Hearings before a Special Committee of the House of Representatives to investigate Communist Activities in the United States in 1939, which links Margaret to the American Civil Liberties Union.

23. M.S. to Theodore Debs, Feb. 20, 1918, Mar. 4, 1918, Aug. 21, 1918,

and M.S. to Eugene V. Debs (in the federal penitentiary in Atlanta), Oct. 17, 1921, all in the Debs Papers, Tamiment-NYU. On the exception she made in 1928 to her usual vote for Norman Thomas, see M.S., Journal, Willowlake, Oct. 1, 1928, MS-SS, and H.E. to M.S., Oct. 26, 1928. In 1932, she told Ellis that she again voted for Thomas, though her sons voted for Roosevelt, M.S. to H.E., Nov. 29, 1932, MS-LC. See Chap. 16. On her opposition to John F. Kennedy in the 1960 election, see the correspondence with Norman Thomas, MS-SS. See Chap. 20.

24. The article from *The Call,* Feb. 29, 1919, is cited in Janice R. and Stephen R. MacKinnon, *Agnes Smedley: The Life and Times of an American Radical* (Berkeley: 1988), p. 66. Also see, Bill Haywood to M.S., n.d. (1919), MS-SS, and M.S. to Rose Pastor Stokes, Feb. 5, 1925, and Stokes to M.S., March 12, 1925, RPS, Tamiment-NYU.

25. Haven Emerson, M.D., commissioner of health, to George H. Bell, New York City Department of Licenses, May 11, 1917, copy in MS-LC. *The New York Times,* Mar. 28, 1917, 11:2; May 7, 1917, 18:4; June 7, 1917, 10:7; and July 14, 1917, 7:3. Also see clipping from the *New York World,* May 7, 1917, Scrapbooks, MS-LC. All copies of the film were destroyed, but several still transparencies remain in MS-SS, and several were reproduced as still photographs for an advertisement in *Birth Control Review* 1:3 (Apr.–May 1917), p. 11. On the National Birth Control League's support for the film, see Mary Ware Dennett memo on wartime activities of the NBCL in RPS-Yale. Also, Sanger, *Autobiography,* p. 252.

26. Theodore Roosevelt, "Birth Control from the Positive Side," *Metropolitan Magazine,* 46:5 (Oct. 1917), p. 5. Margaret Sanger, "Birth Control: Margaret Sanger's Reply to Theodore Roosevelt," *Metropolitan Magazine* 47:1 (Dec. 1917), p. 66.

27. The figure of twenty leagues is taken from pp. 16–17 of a pamphlet called *The Birth Control Movement* published by the National Birth Control League in 1917, in MS-SS. On the general tone of the *Review,* see Frederick Blossom to "Dear Comrades," n.d. (1917), MS-LC: and "To the Men and Women of the United States," *Birth Control Review* 1:2 (Feb. 1917), introduction. Pacifist sentiment is in M.S., "Woman and War," *BCR* 1:3 (Apr. 1917), p. 5; *BCR* 1:4 (June 1917), cover; and *BCR* 1:6 (Nov. 1918), p. 4.

28. M.S. to Frederick Blossom, July 2, Oct. 15, Oct. 22, 1917, MS-LC; Blossom to M.S., Oct. 11, Oct. 18, and Nov. 13, 1917, Jan. 16, 1918, MS-LC. A copy of Sanger's sworn statement to the district attorney "State of New York, City of New York, Margaret H. Sanger, being duly sworn," is included with these materials. Also see Blossom to "My dear Judge," May 18, 1918; Jonah Goldstein to "Birth Control League of New York," June 7, 1918; M.S. to Jonah Goldstein, June 5, 1918; Cerise Carmen Jack to M.S., June 7, 1918, all in MS-LC. Sanger's subsequent accounts are in Margaret Sanger, "A Statement of Facts—An Obligation Fulfilled," *Birth Control Review* 2:6 (June 1918), pp. 3–4, and in M.S. to Juliet Rublee, Aug. 10, n.d. (1918), MS-DC; in M.S. to Elizabeth Gurley Flynn, Nov. 3, 1922, MS-LC; and in William Williams to M.S., "Saturday," n.d. (1917), MS-SS. Finally, see Francis Vreeland, "The Process of Reform with Reference to Reform Groups in the Field of Population," doctoral dissertation, University of Michigan, 1929, p. 90.

29. "M.W. Dennett Reports on Eastern States Birth Control Conference,"

Birth Control Review 2:5 (June 1918), p. 17. Mary Ware Dennett statement, Nov. 18, 1921, MS-LC. On tensions between the NBCL and the NYBCL, see Marion Rawson to "Mrs. Max Heidelberg," Jan. 24, 1917, and Frederick Blossom to "Mrs. Carey," Jan. 17, 1917, both in RPS-Yale. On NBCL support of Sanger after her split with Blossom, see Virginia Heidelberg to Rose Pastor Stokes, Mar. 1, 1918, and an enclosure reporting wartime progress, RPS-Yale. Finally see, "The Fight from Coast to Coast," *BCR*, 2:3, (Mar. 1918), pp. 5–6.

30. Gertrude Pinchot to M.S., April 16, 1917, MS-LC; M.S. to Mrs. Willard Straight, June 13, 1917, MS-LC; M.S. to Juliet Rublee, Feb 21, n.d. (1918) and August 10, n.d. (1918), both in MS-DC. On financial conditions when Blossom left, see "statement of loans to and notes for *The Review,*" and M.S. to Postmaster, New York City, both in MS-LC.

31. See the Sanger–Rublee correspondence in MS-SS and MS-DC, passim; the Schlesinger Library Grant Sanger interview, pp. 6–8; and "George Rublee," in *Who's Who in America,* 1930–31. A personal perspective on Rublee is in Frances Hand Ferguson's June 3, 1974 interview with James Reed in the Schlesinger Library Oral History Collection. Ferguson, the daughter of Learned Hand, became president of the Planned Parenthood Federation of America in the 1950s. Her mother had been a close friend and Cornish, New Hampshire neighbor of Rublee.

32. M.S. to Juliet Rublee, Feb. 21, n.d. (1918), Aug. 10, n.d. (1918), and n.d. (1918–1920), all in MS-DC. M.S. to Rose Pastor Stokes, Dec. 4, 1917, RPS-Yale, also makes clear that she was fitting pessaries.

33. A miscellaneous file of early *Birth Control Review* documents is in MS-SS, Box 132, including handwritten statements of credits and disbursements for May of either 1918 or 1919 that list the directors on the letterhead. Minutes of the directors' meeting for Feb. 14, 1919, talk of including labor. Stock certificates in Margaret's name, dated Apr. and Nov. 1918, and for Jan. 15, 1922 (she owned only a handful of shares), are in MS-LC. On Florence Guertin Tuttle, see her unpublished "Autobiography" and a typewritten biographical statement in the Florence Guertin Tuttle papers, Sophia Smith Collection, Smith College, Northampton, Mass.

34. Compare, for example, Walter Roberts, "Birth Control and the Revolution," *Birth Control Review* 1:3 (Mar.–Apr., 1917) p. 7, to three articles in *BCR* 3:10 (Oct. 1919), on tuberculosis, infant mortality, and the defective child. An account of the Agnes Smedley arrest is in MacKinnon, *Agnes Smedley,* pp. 48–49, which cites articles in *The Call* and *The New York Times* for the assertion that Smedley's indictment actually included charges against local ordinances prohibiting the dissemination of birth control information. Ruth Price, however, who is also working on a book about Smedley, says that she has found no such charges in the court records. The resolution quoted is in *BCR* documents at MS-SS, Box 132. Endorsers included Mrs. Frank Cothren, who followed Rublee as president, Francis Ackermann, the treasurer, Mary Ware Dennett, Ethel Byrne, Jessie Ashley, and Juliet Rublee.

35. Margaret Sanger, "Large Families and the Steel Strike," *Birth Control Review* 4:1 (Jan. 1920), p. 11; editorial, "A Birth Strike to Avert World Famine," p. 1; and "The Call to Women," *BCR* 4:2 (Feb. 1920), pp. 3–4. Mary Ware Dennett to the board of directors of the New York Woman's Publishing Company, Jan. 20, 1920, MS-LC. Mary Ware Dennett to Marie Stopes, Jan. 27,

1920, Stopes-BM. Also see minutes of the board of directors of the N.Y. Women's Publishing Committee, MS-SS.

36. The material in quotation is from Kitty Marion, "Hail and Farewell," *The Birth Control Review,* 14:2 (Mar. 1930), p. 92; Agnes Smedley to M.S., Nov. 1, 1918; and Agnes Smedley,"Cell-Mate, No. 4," n.d. (1918), both in MS-LC. Also see Margaret Sanger, "Trapped," *BCR* 2:9 (Oct. 1918), p. 3; Kitty Marion, "Scattered Memories," *BCR* 5:9 (Sept. 1921), p. 11; "Kitty Marion," *BCR,* 12:1 (Jan. 1928), p. 30. On police interference see Jonah Goldstein to Frederick Blossom, Apr. 18, 1917; F.B. to Police Commissioner Arthur Woods, Apr. 25, 1917, and Woods to F.B., June 19, 1917; unsigned vendor to Jonah Goldstein, Oct. 2, 1919; R. E. Enright, police commissioner of the City of New York to M.S., July 15, 1919; and Enright to Jonah Goldstein, Oct. 21, 1919, all in MS-LC.

37. Blanche Ames, "Margaret Sanger's Influence," remarks prepared for a celebration of Margaret's seventy-fifth (actually her seventy-ninth) birthday in 1958, p. 7, in the Blanche Ames papers at the Sophia Smith Collection, Smith College, hereinafter BA-SS.

Daughter of a Union Army general, Adelbert Ames, and wife of Oakes Ames, a Harvard University botanist, Mrs. Ames had a distinguished career as a botanical illustrator and birth control activist. She had four children, including Amyas Ames and Pauline Ames Plimpton, mother of the irreverent writer, George Plimpton, who was shipped down as a child to his grandmother's Florida retirement estate when his mother despaired of ever disciplining him herself. See biographical data and miscellaneous family correspondence in BA-SS.

38. On the Allison case, see "V.K. Allison . . . Jailed for Three Years," *The Masses,* 8:2 (Sept. 1916), p. 15., and F. C. Cowan, "Memorandum Concerning the Case of Commonwealth v. Allison 227 Mass. 57 (May 24, 1917)," dated Mar. 14, 1950, in the Planned Parenthood of Massachusetts Papers, Sophia Smith Collection, Smith College, hereinafter, PPLM-SS. On reaction to Ames, see clipping from the *Boston Post,* Nov. 26, 1916, BA-SS. On Massachusetts, Pennsylvania, Illinois, and progress of other local efforts, see "The Fight from Coast to Coast," *Birth Control Review* 2:3 (Mar., 1918), pp. 6–11. Also, Bernice J. Guthmann, *The Planned Parenthood Movement in Illinois, 1923–1965,* a pamphlet prepared in 1965 for the Planned Parenthood Association, Chicago area, a copy of which was given to the author during a trip there in 1976.

39. Margaret Sanger, Diaries and Yearbook, 1919, MS-LC. See especially entries for Feb. 12, Feb. 17, Feb. 18, Feb. 19. On her illness in 1918, see M.S. to Juliet Rublee, n.d. (Aug. 1918), MS-DC, and H.E. to M.S., July 1, 1918, Aug. 12, 1918.

40. Sanger Diaries, 1919, MS-LC, Feb. 13, 15, 17, 23, 24; Mar. 1, 4, 9, 16; Apr. 7, 11, 15, 22, 23. Quotation in letter to William Sanger is from M.S. to W.S., Mar. 24, 1917, MS-SS.

41. See Walter Roberts to M.S., Jan. 11, "1915" (actually 1916, he was so overcome with emotion, he apparently forgot the new year), and Feb. 11, 1916, MS-SS, and M.S. to Walter Roberts, Sept. 24, 1919, when fearing that she might die from scheduled TB surgery, she returned his intimate letters and expressed her appreciation of what she placidly described as their "lovely friendship." She must have reclaimed them at some point, however, for the entire correspon-

dence survives in MS-SS. Also see Roberts to M.S., Apr. 5, 1929, and Mar. 30, 1935, MS-LC.

42. The William Williams correspondence is even more substantial than the Roberts, also all in MS-SS. See especially, M.S. to W.W., Oct. 16, 1920, when he was dying in the hospital, and also Dr. Mary Halton to M.S., n.d. (Oct. 1920), describing Williams's last hours and how beautifully he spoke of her, and enclosing a last letter to her. The correspondence includes a clipping of *The Call* obituary of Oct. 24, 1920, along with John Reed's. Also see Margaret's 1919 diary references to Williams.

43. Williams diary entrance is from May 1, 1919, along with the "chemistry of love" speculation. Jonah Goldstein diary references are on Feb. 6, 8, 15, 17, Mar. 8, and May 9, from which the quotation about him is taken. She also comments here on the "Jewish reactions" that "enslave" him, meaning, it appears, that she found Goldstein too controlled and moralistic, but also suggesting further evidence of a reluctance on her part to marry another Jew. Stuart Sanger recalled that Goldstein bought him his first pair of real "men's pants" at a tailor on the Lower East Side. On Herbert Simonds, see his printed "Recollections," pp. 44 and 79, in MS-SS. Also, see Harold Hersey to M.S., Aug. 6, 1940, and her explanation of their relationship, dated June 13, 1947, for inclusion with the letters at Smith, both in MS-SS. Finally, see M.S. to Juliet Rublee, Aug. 27, 1921, MS-DC.

44. The Ellis quote is from H.E. to M.S., May 19, 1918; the apology to Bill in M.S. to William Sanger, Dec. 1, 1919, MS-SS. On her operation, see Ethel Higgins to Mary Higgins, n.d. (1920), MS-SS, and Margaret Sanger to Mary Higgins, n.d. (1920), MS-SS. The diary quotation is from June 10, 1919, MS-LC.

9: NEW WOMAN, NEW WORLD

1. Margaret Sanger, appointment calendar, May 9, 1920, through May 2, 1921, MS-LC. M.S. to Juliet Rublee, May 18, May 27, June 7, July 7, 1920, MS-DC. Lawrence Lader, *The Margaret Sanger Story* (New York: 1955), p. 157, reconstructs the story of Glasgow Green from an interview with Sanger in 1953. Sanger's *Autobiography* says Alice Vickery made the arrangements with the Cooperative Guild, p. 273. Also see the announcement of Sanger's lecture at Caxton Hall, Westminster, sponsored by the Malthusians, in MS-LC, and Margaret Sanger, "London Birth Control Meetings," *Birth Control Review* 4:9 (Sept. 20, 1920), pp. 5–7.

2. On Sanger's role in publishing *Married Love* in the United States, see M.S. to Marie Stopes, July 6, 1915, Oct. 1, 1917, Nov. 9, 1917, Dec. 20, 1917, and July 22, n.d. (1916) in Stopes-Wellcome. Also, Marie Stopes to M.S., Mar. 30, 1916, included with the Rublee correspondence, MS-DC; and William Robinson to M.S., Oct. 3, 1917, MS-LC. The quotation from *Married Love* is taken from the fine biography of Stopes, Ruth Hall, *Passionate Crusader: The Life of Marie Stopes* (New York: 1977), as is the assessment of her personality. The playground chant serves as the epigraph of this book. For the deterioration of relations between the two women, see M.S. to Marie Stopes, three notes marked "52 Rotherwick Rd. Garden Suburbs," n.d. (1920) at Wellcome: Marie Stopes

to M.S., May 26, 1920; M.S. to Stopes, May 16, 1920, July 1, 1920; M.S. to Stopes, Apr. 11, May 7, Oct. 28, Oct. 29, 1921, also in Stopes-BM; H.E. to Stopes, Sept. 15, n.d. (1921); May 21, 1922; Jan. 15, 1923, Stopes-BM. M.S. to Marie Stopes, Oct. 29, 1921, in Stopes-BM, has the Mary Ware Dennett incident. In the same collection, also see Stopes's correspondence with Dennett, 1921–31, passim. Finally, see *Autobiography,* p. 296.

3. M.S., appointment calendar, May–August 1920, passim, MS-LC. H.E. to M.S., Aug. 13, n.d. (1920), Aug. 17, Aug. 19, 1920, "8 Cliff Terrace, Plymouth," n.d. (1920), and "Wednesday," n.d. (1920), MS-LC. *Autobiography,* p. 277.

4. The first quote is in M.S. to F. Cyon, n.d. (from the Stafford Hotel, London) which was among the correspondence given to the author by François Lafitte, Cyon's son by her first marriage—now deposited in MS-SS. Another of these letters, dated only "Saturday," has the housecleaning reference. Also see M.S. to F.C., May 5, 1929, Jan. 8, 1930, Dec. 9, 1931, Jan. 11, 1931, Nov. 10, n.d. (1936), Aug. 31, n.d. (1930s), in which she encourages Cyon to keep up her fortitude and courage in the face of Ellis's declining health and also sends money to make their lives easier, MS-SS.

5. The Sanger–de Selincourt correspondence is in MS-LC. See especially de Selincourt to M.S., "17th August, Wantley," n.d. (1920), where he speaks of "a lovely foundation on which to build our mutual love of Havelock." Ellis's "sexual athlete" reference is in *My Life.* Also see H.E. to M.S., Nov. 2, 1920, MS-LC, and M.S. to Françoise Cyon, Aug. 31, 1931, MS-SS.

6. Hugh de Selincourt to M.S., June 2, 1920; and M.S. to H. de S., "Saturday" n.d. (1922), MS-LC. My impressions of the Wantley circle are drawn from the large number of references to what went on there in Sanger's correspondence with Juliet Rublee, Hugh and Janet de Selincourt, Havelock Ellis, Françoise Cyon, and Harold Child. See especially Harold Child to M.S., Oct. 24, 1924, included in the Sanger–Rublee letters, MS-DC. On Ellis's only visit, see M.S. to Hugh de Selincourt, Oct. 28, 1927, MS-LC. The final quote is from M.S. to Françoise Cyon, Oct. 1, 1946, now at MS-SS. On the reputation and lure of the Byron-Shelley circle in Edwardian England, see the biographical sketch in George Edward Woodberry, ed., *The Complete Poetical Works of Percy Bysshe Shelley,* Cambridge, Ed. (New York: 1901), pp.xv–xviii.

7. M.S., appointment calendar, Sept. 1920, MS-LC. The quoted material in order of presentation is from M.S. to H.de S., n.d. (1920 or 21); M.S. "Introducing Hugh de Selincourt," *One Little Boy* (New York: 1924), MS-LC; M.S. to H.de S., Aug. 12, n.d. (1930), MS-LC; H.de S. to M.S., "Wantley," n.d. (1920); "Nov. 20," n.d. (1921); Aug. 5, 1921; Jan. 20, 1923, and Feb. 14, 1927, all in MS-LC; H.E. to M.S., Sept. 13, 1921, and Jan. 18, 1921, MS-LC: M.S. to H.de S., "Aug. 1, Zermatt, Switzerland," n.d. (1928); Jan. 7, 1927; "Feb. 18 en route to Bermuda," n.d.; "Hey there Poet," n.d. (1931 or '32, after her first biography was published); and Oct. 5, 1932 ("Willowlake"). The letter telling him to meet Rublee is M.S. to H.de S., "Saturday," from the Hotel Russell in London, n.d. (1921). The final Rublee references are in letters dated Sept. 20, 1932, and "October Willowlake," n.d. (1932), all in MS-LC. For the attempted lecture tour, see M.S. to James Pond, Oct. 1, 1930, MS-LC.

I emphasize the lighthearted nature of the Sanger–de Selincourt relationship, in part, because Madeline Gray, in her often inaccurate portrait in *Margaret Sanger: A Biography of the Champion of Birth Control* (New York: 1978), makes a great deal more of it. See esp., pp. 131–36, 141–42 and 219. In the absence of other biographical work on Sanger, however, more substantial books, such as Phyllis Grosskurth, *Havelock Ellis: A Biography* (New York: 1980), p. 307, make reference to Gray.

8. The Sanger quote is from M.S. to Juliet Rublee, "Stafford Hotel," n.d. (probably 1925), MS-DC. The Child quote is from a collection of essays first published as *Love and Unlove* in 1921 and referenced posthumously in the introduction to Harold Child, *Essays and Reflections* (Cambridge and New York: 1938), p. vii.

9. The quote is from the introduction to W. Warren Wager, ed., *H. G. Wells: Journalism and Prophecy 1893–1946* (Boston: 1964), p. xvi, as is some of the biographical data. I have also made use of the two principal biographies of Wells: Norman and Jeanne Mackenzie, *H. G. Wells, A Biography* (New York: 1973), especially pp. 299–351, and the recently published, David C. Smith, *H. G. Wells, Desperately Mortal, A Biography* (New Haven: 1986), esp. pp. 361–427, both of which document the relationship with Sanger. On Wells and Rebecca West also see Gordon N. Ray, *H. G. Wells and Rebecca West* (New Haven: 1974), though much of the view of their relationship it presents is disputed by the highly controversial portrait of Wells in Anthony West, *H. G. Wells: Aspects of a Life* (New York: 1984), an affectionate and eloquent memoir written by the son born of Wells's liaison with West. The late Anthony West spoke to me by telephone about his father's deep and sustained affection for Margaret Sanger on Oct. 10, 1986.

10. H. G. Wells, *Ann Veronica* (London: 1909). Also see H. G. Wells, "War and the Status of Women," and "Socialism and the New World Order," in Wager, *Journalism and Prophecy,* pp. 103–109 and pp. 392–403, and H. G. Wells, *Socialism and the Family* (London: 1908), pp. 29–31, 35–37. On Wells's influence on his generation in America, see Henry F. May, *The End of American Innocence: A Study of the First Years of Our Own Time,* (New York: 1959), esp. p. 238.

11. H. G. Wells, *The Secret Places of the Heart* (London, New York, Toronto, and Melbourne: 1922). The material in quotation is from p. 183, other references from pp. 144, 162–63, 167, 169–71, and 178, respectively.

12. *Ibid.* The material quoted is from pp. 189, 214, and 276, respectively. Anthony West discusses the novel and its meaning in *Aspects of a Life,* pp. 87–88. In a conclusion that suggests he didn't quite know how to resolve the story, Wells kills off Sir Richmond in an accident and then brings his permanent lover, Martin Leeds (Rebecca West), back on stage to mourn for him. Wells's own autobiography admits that the novel was written to provoke Rebecca. See Smith, *Desperately Mortal,* p. 382.

13. Author's telephone conversation with Anthony West, Oct. 10, 1986. Smith, *Desperately Mortal,* pp. 270–71, 403–405. M.S. to Juliet Rublee, Aug. 27, 1921, says, "H.G. wired me to come for a weekend," MS-DC. The direct Wells quotes are, in order, from H.G.W. to M.S., Sept. 14, 1921, in unidentified cc., MS-LC, and from H.G.W. to M.S., Dec. 7, 1921, and Oct. 8, 1924, in MS-SS. Also see the more chatty later correspondence, esp. H.G.W. to M.S., Jan. 3, 1943, on how amusing he found her letters. The "way out" message is

undated, presumably from the early 1920s, in MS-LC. The Mackenzies, *H. G. Wells, A Biography,* disparage his love life on p. 345. Sanger's description of him is in *Autobiography,* pp. 268–69.

14. The Wells quote about Sanger is from his introduction to Margaret Sanger, *The Pivot of Civilization* (New York: 1922), p. xvi. Lenin's characterization of Wells is in Smith, *Desperately Mortal,* p. 271.

15. Margaret Sanger, *Woman and the New Race* (New York: 1920), p. 94. The Macmillan Co. to M.S., Jan. 9, 1920, MS-LC, and author's conversations with Grant Sanger.

16. Ellis to Sanger, "Saturday AM," n.d. (1915), MS-LC; *Woman and the New Race,* pp. 9–29, 167–85.

17. *Woman and the New Race,* quote is on p. 7; pp. 138–50 comprise a chapter called "Will Labor Benefit?"

18. *Woman and the New Race,* pp. 167–85 and introduction, passim. The Library of Congress papers contain publishing data in a file of *Woman and the New Race* correspondence. Also, for examples of the misleading advertising, see Francis McLennon Vreeland, "The Process of Reform with Especial Reference to Reform Groups in the Field of Population," doctoral dissertation, University of Michigan, 1929, p. 100. Finally, H.E. to M.S., Aug. 19, Sept. 21, and Nov. 16, 1919, all in MS-LC.

19. The Wells quote is from Sanger, *Pivot of Civilization,* p. xvi. My discussion of the text thus far essentially summarizes the arguments in the book on pp. 1, 9–13, 23–26, and 148–49. (The "too flattering a doctrine" quote is on p. 9, "entering wedge," on p. 24.)

20. *Ibid.,* "cradle-competition" on p. 25; "self-directed . . ." on pp. 22–23; also see pp. 170–71, 180–81, 186–189. Sanger took the passage about eugenics almost directly from a statement she had delivered in October of 1921 to the Second International Congress of Eugenics in New York. See Margaret Sanger, "The Eugenic Value of Birth Control Propaganda," *Birth Control Review* 5:10 (Oct. 1921), p. 5. Also see H.E. to M.S., Nov. 18, 1930, where he worries over a Eugenics Society scheme for legalizing sterilization, which he called "ridiculous and harmful and quite contrary to all my ideas." Important new insights into the popularity of eugenicism are in Carl N. Degler, *In Search of Human Nature: The Decline and Revival of Darwinism in American Social Thought* (New York: 1990); my thanks to Meris Powell for my copy of this book. For doctrinaire criticism of Sanger's eugenic sympathies, see Donald K. Pickens, *Eugenics and the Progressives* (Tennessee; 1968), pp. 75–76; David Kennedy, *Birth Control in America: The Career of Margaret Sanger* (New Haven: 1970), p. 115, and Linda Gordon, *Woman's Body, Woman's Right: A Social History of Birth Control in America* (New York: 1976), esp. p. 332, which quotes Sanger extensively out of context. A corrective is offered in Charles Valenza, "Was Margaret Sanger a Racist?" *Family Planning Perspectives* 17:1 (Jan.–Feb. 1985) pp. 44–46. However, Valenza, a public relations officer for Planned Parenthood of New York City, although he clarifies Sanger's ideas, is too quick to excuse her for the company she kept.

21. Sanger, *The Pivot of Civilization,* p. 13, pp. 210–11.

22. The Wells quote is from *ibid.* introduction, p. ix. Also see Ellis to Sanger, "New Year's Eve," n.d. (apparently 1922—when he would have been reading a draft), MS-LC. On Robert Allerton Parker, see Dorothy Brush to Margaret

Grierson (the former chief archivist at Smith College), Dec. 12, 1959, DB-SS, and Olive Byrne Richard's interview with Jacqueline Van Voris, MS-SS. For reviews, see Leta S. Hollingworth, "For and Against Birth Control," undated clipping from *The New Republic,* in MS-LC, and E. M. East, "Margaret Sanger's Pivot of Civilization," *Birth Control Review,* 6:12 (Dec. 1922), p. 253. Hollingworth reviewed *Pivot of Civilization* along with a book titled *Birth Control* by Halliday G. Sutherland, M.D. (New York: 1922). The "yesterday's criminal" quote is from "Birth Control as a Conquering Movement," *Current Opinion* 72 (Feb. 1922), p. 212. Book sales data is from a report prepared by Anne Kennedy, executive director of the American Birth Control League, Oct. 5, 1926, Planned Parenthood Federation of America Papers, Sophia Smith Collection, Smith College, hereinafter PPFA-SS.

23. M.S. to Juliet Rublee, n.d. (on *Birth Control Review* letterhead, 1920 or 1921, in New York), MS-DC; M.S. to H.E., Jan. 1, 1921, MS-LC; M.S. to Juliet Rublee, n.d. ("Juliet Dearest," 1921 in New York); Aug. 25, 1921 (from Lucerne); and Aug. 27, 1921 (from Amsterdam), all in MS-DC.

10: THE CONDITIONS OF REFORM

1. Margaret Sanger to "Dear Friend," Sept. 28, 1921; M.S. to Dr. E. W. Ritter, Scripps Institute of Biological Research, La Jolla, Cal., Aug. 12, 1921; *The First American Birth Control Conference: Why?* promotional pamphlet, n.d., all in MS-SS.

2. Mary Ware Dennett, "The Voluntary Parenthood League," statement presented for the American Birth Control League Conference, Nov. 11–13, 1921, in MS-LC; Dennett, *Birth Control Laws: Shall We Keep Them, Change Them, or Abolish Them?* (New York: 1926), p. 100 and p. 180; and "Outline of Birth Control Legislation," draft prepared for the *Congressional Digest,* Mar., 1931, MS-LC. Also, "Woman's Federation Endorses Birth Control," *Birth Control Review* 4:11 (Nov. 1920), p. 5, and the clipping of an article on the General Federation of Women's Clubs resolution that appeared in *The Call,* Oct. 15, 1920, MS-LC. Arthur Gleason, "Birth Control," *Survey* 47:22 (Oct. 1921), pp. 113–14, summarizes developments. Also see *Autobiography,* p. 415.

3. Clippings on the welcoming luncheon from *New York Herald* and *The Call,* Dec. 9, 1920, in MS-LC. Responses to Rublee's appeals of 1920 and 1921 are also in MS-LC. See, for example, Mrs. Robert Perkins Bass to J.R., Oct. 12, 1920; Herbert Croly to J.R., Sept. 12, 1921; Lillian Wald to J.R., Sept. 13, 1921; Florence Lamont to J.R. (n.d.), where she says that she was glad to give her name, but her husband, Thomas Lamont, was not. Rublee was also turned down by such physicians she contacted as the then prominent New York gynecologist Howard Kelly. On legislative work, "Outline of Legislative Work at Albany," *Birth Control Review,* 5:5 (May 1921) p. 11. Reference to Rublee's earlier visit to Belle Moskowitz is in M.S. (from London) to J.R., June 7, 1920, in MS-DC.

A breakdown of the responses to the 1921 mailing and questionnaire is in MS-LC. It shows that condom and pessary use were split about evenly among 900 of the women, while the remainder indicated preference for suppositories or sponges. The high incidence of pessary use may have reflected the influence of Margaret's own propaganda on women who supported her. I found no breakdown of how much money the mailing raised. Margaret referred to the survey in her Town Hall speech at the First American Birth Control Conference in 1921. See the stenographic record of the speech, Proceedings of the First American Birth Control Conference, pp. 21–22, MS-SS, and *Autobiography,* pp. 292–94.

4. Charles Valenza, "Was Margaret Sanger a Racist?" *Family Planning Perspectives* 17:1 (Jan.–Feb. 1985), pp. 44–46. Transcript of First American Birth Control Conference, Opening Session, Nov. 11, 1921, pp. 1–7, 36–42, 75–76, MS-SS. Sanger quotes are on p. 4 and p. 7. In all other respects, the views of the two women were actually quite close: see Antoinette F. Konikow, M.D., *Voluntary Motherhood* (Boston: privately printed, 1923) and *Physician's Manual of Birth Control* (London: 1931). Finally, see *The New York Times,* Nov. 10, 1921, 12:2, and Nov. 12, 1921, 18:1.

5. "Birth Control Raid Made by Police on Archbishop's Order," *The New York Times,* Nov. 14, 1921, 1:4. Coverage continued throughout the week: Nov. 15, 1:3; Nov. 16, 17:1–2; Nov. 17, 5:3; Nov. 18, 18:2–3; Nov. 19, 1:4; Nov. 21, 1:4. Nov. 22, 16:2; Nov. 23, 9:1–2; Nov. 25, 7:1. The Hayes statement was printed in full in the *Times,* Nov. 21, 1921, 6:2–3. Another spate of coverage followed the inquiry proceedings in January. See *NYT,* Jan. 18, 1922, 36:3; Jan. 22, 5:2; Jan. 24, 1:5; Jan. 25, 14:5 (editorial); Jan. 25, 1922, 36:3. Also see "Brief Submitted in Behalf of Paul D. Cravath and Others," *Birth Control Review* 6:4 (Apr. 22, 1922), p. 54–55; and "The Press Protests," *Birth Control Review* 5:12 (Dec. 1921), pp. 16–17.

6. *The New York Times,* Nov. 19, 1921, 1:4; Lawrence Lader, *The Margaret Sanger Story* (New York: 1955), p. 180, also quotes from the Hearst's, *New York American.* Transcripts of Cox's speech and of Sanger's are in the stenographic record of the conference, MS-SS, with quotations respectively on pp. 10, 21–22.

An actress by the name of Mary Shaw also spoke, and Juliet Rublee made the evening's pitch for money, asking for support of a proposed birth control clinic under medical auspices.

Also see, Morehouse, "The Speaking of Margaret Sanger in the Birth Control Movement from 1916 to 1937," Doctoral Dissertation, Purdue University, 1968, pp. 120–28, MS-SS, and Anne Kennedy to Harold Hersey, Feb. 19, 1937, in MS-LC. Finally, compare the text to "Notes for Town Hall Speech, 1921," MS-LC, to see how Sanger capitalized on the alleged church intervention.

7. "Topics of the Times: Resistance Was Not the Remedy," *The New York Times,* Nov. 15, 1921, actually criticized the birth controllers for acting like "anarchists" by resisting the police. A day later, however, the paper recanted with "Topics of the Times: No Basis Found for Action," Nov. 16, 1921, 18:4–5. Also see "Birth Control and Free Speech," *Outlook* 129:30 (Nov. 1921), p. 507. Editorial comment is summarized in "The Press Protests," *Birth Control Review* 5:12 (Dec. 1921), pp. 16–17. The hearings and the Rublee incident are reported in "Digs into Leader's Birth Control Past," *NYT,* Nov. 23, 1921, 9:1–2; "Arrest Mrs. Rublee for Views on Birth," Dec. 3, 1921, 9:1–2 and continued coverage on Dec. 4, 20:1–2; Dec. 8, 16:2; Dec. 10, 15:6; Dec. 18, 16:1. Also see "Mrs. Rublee's Arrest: A Record and a Protest," *Birth Control Review* 6:1 (Jan. 1922), pp. 5–7, and M.S. to H. de S., "March, Syracuse N.Y."

n.d. (1924), MS-LC, where she says that the best way to fight the Catholics is in "old Yankee fashion."

8. "The Case of Birth Control: The National Woman's Party," *Birth Control Review* 7:6 (June 1923), pp. 141–42. Another example of Sanger's frustration with the failure of feminist leaders to support birth control is in M.S. to Kitty Marion, Jan. 4, 1935, MS-LC. Nancy F. Cott, *The Grounding of Modern Feminism* (New Haven: 1987), pp. 53–114, offers a thoughtful analysis of feminist politics in the 1920s. The best prior interpretation of Sanger's contribution to these debates is in Sheila Rothman, *Woman's Proper Place: A History of Changing Ideals and Practices, 1870 to the Present* (New York: 1978), pp. 188–209, with mention of Sheppard-Towner specifically on p. 136. Sanger discusses her reservations about this reform in *Pivot of Civilization* (New York: 1922), p. 116.

The term "social feminism" was first used by the historian William O'Neill in 1969 to group together women who put their concerns as labor organizers, social activists, and reformers ahead of their direct concern for women's rights. On the limitations of this categorization, see Nancy Cott, "What's in a Name? The Limits of Social Feminism; or Expanding the Vocabulary of Women's History," *The Journal of American History* 76:3 (Dec. 1989), pp. 809–29.

9. The employment statistics are from a two-part article by Chase Woodhouse, "The Status of Women," *American Journal of Sociology* 35:6 (May 1930), pp. 1091–95, and 36:6 (May 1931), pp. 1011–16. Also see S. P. Breckinridge, "The Activities of Women Outside the Home," President's Commission on Social Trends: *Recent Social Trends in the United States* (New York: 1933), pp. 709–43. The best analysis of this data is in Alice Kessler-Harris, *Out to Work: A History of Wage Earning Women in the United States* (New York: 1982), pp. 217–49.

For evidence of the intense concern these trends aroused, also see Suzanne LaFollette, *Concerning Women* (New York: 1926), Virginia MacMakin Collier, *Marriage and Careers, A Study of One Hundred Women Who Are Wives, Mothers, Homemakers and Professional Workers* (New York: 1926), esp. tables on pp. 27–29, 56–58; Nancy E. Scott, "The Effects of the Higher Education of Women Upon the Home," *Journal of American Sociology* 32:2 (Sept. 1926), p. 257; Viva Boothe, "Gainfully Employed Women in the Family," *Annals of the American Academy of Political and Social Science* 160 (Mar. 1932), pp. 75–78; Ethel W. Cartland, "Substitutes for Motherhood," *Outlook* 134 (June 20, 1923), pp. 229–30; "Is The Younger Generation in Peril?" *The Literary Digest* 69:7 (May 11, 1921). The latter article appeared under the magazine's "Topics of the Day" and dealt essentially with the danger of shorter skirts, dance, makeup, etc., to young women. The Sanger quotations are from Hannah Stein, "Does Marriage Interfere With a Career? Interview Margaret Sanger," the *Syracuse Herald,* April 5, 1926, clipping in MS-LC.

William O'Neill in *Everyone Was Brave* (Chicago: 1969) took the view that this kind of emphasis on personal liberation for women detracted from political and economic concerns raised in earlier struggles for suffrage and labor reform and inadvertently produced "the feminine mystique," which Betty Friedan and other pioneering women's rights advocates bemoaned in the 1960s. In this respect, O'Neill positioned Margaret Sanger as a reactionary figure in the long history of the women's rights struggle, influencing the subsequent work of David Kennedy, who failed to appreciate fully the burden of social and sexual repression on women of Sanger's generation. More recent historical writing explains why this arbitrary and one-dimensional view of feminism's decline in the 1920s is unwarranted. See especially Cott, *Grounding,* pp. 179–239.

10. John B. Watson, *The Psychological Care of Infant and Child* (New York: 1928). Cott, *Grounding,* pp. 145–74; Rothman, *Proper Place,* pp. 178–88.

A dynamic interpretation of images of liberation for women in the 1920s was presented at the Seventh Berkshire Conference on the History of Women held at Wellesley College, June 19–21, 1987. I have adapted some of this material from a session titled "The New Woman Revised: Images in 1920s and 1930s Art and Theatre," which included a paper by the art historian, Ellen Todd, "New Types and Old Traditions: Images of Women and Consumer Culture, 1920–40." Perhaps the most cogent analysis of what happened to women and marriage in the 1920s is in Margaret Mead, *Male and Female: A Study of the Sexes in a Changing World* (New York: 1949), esp. pp. 292–98, 304–29.

11. Dorothy Dunbar Bromley, "Feminist-New Style 1927," *Harper's Monthly* 155 (1927), p. 556. John B. Watson, "The Weakness of Women," *The Nation* 25 (July 6, 1927), pp. 9–10. Sanger, *Pivot of Civilization,* pp. 238–39.

12. Sanger, *Pivot of Civilization,* p. 220.

13. The quote from Sanger is in M.S. to Ethel Byrne, Mar. 1917, MS-LC. On the formation of the NCWC, see John A. Ryan, "The National Catholic Welfare Conference," unpublished manuscript for an autobiography, pp. 144–150, in the John A. Ryan Papers, Catholic University of America, hereinafter, JR-CU; John Tracy Ellis, *American Catholicism* (Chicago: 1969), pp. 140–44, and Esther McCarthy, "Catholic Women and War: The National Council of Catholic Women," paper delivered at the Berkshire Conference of American Women Historians, Bryn Mawr, Pa., June 9–11, 1976. Ellis, p. 118, identifies Rome's distrust of American church liberalism as evidenced by a papal communication (*Testem Benevolentiae*) of 1899. Also see Patrick Cardinal Hayes, "Cardinal's Pastoral, Catholic Charities Appeal, April 26 to May 3, 1925," copy in MS-SS.

14. On the contraceptive canon and Ryan's role in reformulating church policy in this country, see John T. Noonan, Jr., *Contraception: A History of its Treatment by the Catholic Theologians and Canonists,* 2d ed. (Cambridge, Mass.: 1986), pp. 414–24, and Alvah W. Sulloway, *Birth Control and Catholic Doctrine* (New York: 1959), pp. 37–43. The quotes, in order, are taken from Sulloway, *idem,* p. 38 and p. 199, citing *The Catholic Encyclopedia,* 12 (1907), p. 279; Noonan, *idem,* pp. 423–24, citing Rev. John A. Ryan, D.D., "Family Limitation," *Ecclesiastical Review* 54 (1916), pp. 684–96; and the Pastoral Letter of the Archbishops and Bishops of the United States, Sept. 26, 1919, in Guilday, ed., *The National Pastorals,* pp. 312–13; Rev. John A. Ryan, D.D., "The Attitude of the Church Toward Birth Control," *Catholic Charities Review* 4:10 (Dec. 1920), pp. 299–301, copy in MS-SS; Sulloway, *idem,* p. 41, citing *The Catholic Encyclopedia Supplement* (1922); and Hayes, "Cardinal's Pastoral," April, May, 1925, MS-SS; John M. Cooper, Ph. D., associate professor of sociology at Catholic University of America, *Birth Control* (Washington: n.d. [1920s]), pp. 17, 21, MS-SS; and finally, Rev. Thomas J. Cawley, *Those Dangerous Babies!* (reprint from *The Catholic Light,* weekly newspaper of the

Diocese of Scranton) n.d. (1920s), pp. 16–18, MS-SS. The NCWC began circulating anti–birth control propaganda. See Memorandum from "Father Burke, Father McGowan," Aug. 6, 1925, National Catholic Welfare Conference Papers, Catholic University of America, hereinafter NCWC-CU.

15. M.S. to Michael Slattery, executive secretary, NCWC, Dec. 31, 1920, MS-LC; Genevieve Grandcourt (probably a penname), "Bachelors Oppose Birth Control," *Birth Control Review* 5:2 (Feb. 1921), p. 13; "The Sin of Birth Control," reprint of an article from *The New Republic,* Dec. 28, 1921, in *BCR* 6:2 (Feb. 1922), p. 17; M.S. to Juliet Rublee, n.d., MS-DC.

16. For a contrary interpretation of the Catholic controversy, which essentially blames Sanger for having failed to understand the legitimacy of the church's immutable moral position, see David Kennedy, *Birth Control in America: The Career of Margaret Sanger* (New Haven: 1970), pp. 147–53. Kennedy, however, neither acknowledges the low end of the debate on both sides through the 1920s, nor concedes that the American church was late in articulating and publicly advancing its natural law arguments as moral doctrine. Sanger met the attacks of the Catholic Church on its own muddy terrain. Still, she never gave up. In 1929, she even sent John Ryan a complimentary copy of one of her books. See M.S. to Father John A. Ryan. Feb. 6, 1929, and J.R. to M.S., Feb. 9, 1929, in which he promises to send comments. JR-CU.

17. Wm. Inge to M.S., Oct. 27, 1920, MS-LC. Reference to Inge's public remarks on population is from the pamphlet titled *The First American Birth Control Conference: Why?,* MS-SS. Also see Margaret Sanger, "The War Against Birth Control," *American Mercury* (June 1924), clipping in MS-LC; and Francis McLennon Vreeland, "The Process of Reform with Especial Reference to Reform Groups in the Field of Population" doctoral dissertation, University of Michigan, 1929, pp. 285–86.

18. The first quote is from Louis I. Dublin, "The Excesses of Birth Control," address delivered before the Sixth International Neo-Malthusian and Birth Control Conference, New York, Mar. 26, 1925, copy in MS-SS. The speech was covered in "Population Rise No Menace," *The New York Times,* Mar. 27, 1925, 8:1–2. The second reference is to a "Dr. Schlapp" who spoke several days later. See "Finds Excitement Injures the Race," *NYT,* Mar. 29, 1925, Sec.1, 6:1–5. Dublin was chief statistician for the Metropolitan Life Insurance Company. The speech was revised for publication as "The Fallacious Propaganda for Birth Control," *Atlantic Monthly,* Feb. 1926, reprint also in MS-SS. For a critique of Dublin, see Norman Himes, *Medical History of Contraception* (Baltimore: 1936), pp. 398–405. For support of Dublin's viewpoint from organized labor, also see J. B. S. Hardman, an official of the Amalgamated Clothing Workers of America, "Organized Labor and Birth Control," *Birth Control Review* 13:9 (Sept. 1929), pp. 245–51. The Norman Thomas quote is from the same *Birth Control Review* forum, "A Socialist's Viewpoint," p. 255.

19. On the continuing popularity of eugenics, see Daniel J. Kevles, *In the Name of Eugenics: Genetics and the Uses of Human Heredity* (New York: 1985), and John Higham, *Strangers in the Land, Patterns of American Nativism, 1860–1925* (New York: 1974), p. 149. In the years immediately before World War I, popular magazines carried more articles on eugenics than on the major progressive issues of slum and tenement reform; Higham, *idem,* pp. 264–65, on the "tribal twenties"; and Donald K. Pickens, *Eugenics and the*

Progressives (Nashville, Tenn.: 1968), pp. 89–93, 131–37. Carl N. Degler, *In Search of Human Nature: The Decline and Revival of Darwinisim in American Social Thought* (New York: 1991), underscores the point that many eugenicists objected when their principles about individual inheritance were applied collectively, with race as a basis. The phrase, "to create a race of thoroughbreds," appears on the pamphlet advertising the First American Birth Control Conference, MS-SS. For its derivation, see Dr. Edward J. Kempf, "Rearing Human Thoroughbreds," *Literary Digest* 69:24 (May 14, 1921), and also, Charles Valenza, "Was Margaret Sanger a Racist?" *Family Planning Perspectives* 17:1 (Jan.–Feb. 1985), p. 44–46. The Italian reference is from M.S., "The Incident at Williamstown," *Birth Control Review* 9:9 (Sept. 1925), pp. 246–47.

20. Kevles, *Name of Eugenics*. For Davenport's opposition and the Popenoe quotation, see Pickens, *Eugenics and the Progressives,* p. 91. For a description of Sanger's "compassion for the poor," see Caroline Hadley Robinson, *Seventy Birth Control Clinics: A Survey and Analysis Including the General Effects of Control on Size and Quality of Population* (Philadelphia: 1930), p. 39. The E. E. Ross quote is from Juliet Rublee to M.S., Aug. 1, 1928, MS–SS. The rejected proposal to invite eugenicists to contribute to the *Birth Control Review* is in "A Question of Policy," *Birth Control Review* 12:6 (June 1928), p. 188, and editorial, *BCR* 12:12, (Dec. 1928), p. 306.

21. *Birth Control Review* 6:18 (Aug. 1922), p. 161, mentions articles in *The Nation* and other newspapers and periodicals that ignored Sanger. By contrast see Heywood Broun, "It Seems to Me," clipping from *The World,* Feb. 1922, in MS-LC, and Ruth Hale, "The Child Who Was Mother to a Woman," *The New Yorker* 1:8 (Apr. 11, 1925), pp. 11–12. Some years later the Brouns divorced, and Heywood converted to Catholicism, much to Margaret's shock and disbelief.

22. See yearbooks (especially for 1925) and the brochures for Sanger's "First American Lecture Tour" in 1923–24 and for James B. Pond, "Margaret Sanger: The International Champion of Birth Control," in MS-LC and MS-SS. Also, see Morehouse, "The Speaking of Margaret Sanger in the Birth Control Movement from 1916 to 1937," doctoral dissertation, Purdue University, 1968, pp. 132–44. The Yale reference is from "Mrs. Sanger Talks at Yale," *The New York Times,* Dec. 5, 1924, 21:7, and Olive Byrne Richard told the story about Tufts in her interview with the author. Examples from specific speeches are taken in order from "Address of Margaret Sanger, President, American Birth Control League, Inc.," Parson's Theatre, Hartford, Conn., Sunday afternoon, Feb. 11, 1923, MS-SS; "The Chicago Birth Control Conference," *Birth Control Review* 7:12 (Dec. 1923), pp. 316–17; "This Business of Bearing Babies," n.d. (1920s), MS-SS. Also see, "Speech at the Auditorium Theatre, Oakland, California," Dec. 19, 1928, MS-LC. A Sanger diary entry for Dec. 19, 1928, describes the Oakland audience as large (over 1,000) and friendly, but not excited. On her speaking style and use of notes, see M.S. to Juliet Rublee, Jan. 7, 1929, MS-SS.

23. For a complete record of the confrontations with Catholics between 1922 and 1925, see Vreeland, "Process of Reform," pp. 139–40, 285–87. Examples of police surveillance are in *The New York Times,* Oct. 21, 1922, 36:3, and Dec. 7, 1924, 21:7. The synagogue controversy is in *NYT,* Apr. 22, 1923, 5:7 and April 23, 1923, 15:2. The Ford Hall remarks, dated April 16, 1929, are in MS-SS. On the newsreel controversies, see "Editorial Paragraphs,"

The Nation 128 (May 1929), pp. 574–75; Woman's Club of Upper Montclair, N. J., to M.S., Mar. 14, 1929; and M.S. to Mrs. A. J. Lins, Mar. 20. 1929, MS-LC. The final quote is from Lewis Gannett to M.S., May 20, 1929, MS-LC.

24. Olive Byrne Richards interview with the author, Mar. 1985. M.S. to Havelock Ellis, Mar. 23, 1930, Apr. 3, 1930, MS-SS. Random notations on her lecture fees, and her need to speak in order to earn money, are in correspondence with her agent James Pond in MS-LC; the $500 fee for an appearance in Washington, D.C., on May 12, 1931, is mentioned in Pond to M.S., Apr. 22, 1931, MS-LC. Wells's fees are in David Smith, *H. G. Wells, Desperately Mortal, A Biography* (New Haven: 1986), p. 336. On the cough drops, see M.S. to Samuel Seabury, Mar. 31, 1933, MS-LC.

25. The first quotation is from "Reminiscences of Elizabeth Grew Bacon," in "Our M.S.," 1958, MS-SS; the second, from M.S. to H.E., Mar. 23, 1930, MS-SS. On hero worship of Sanger, see Vreeland, "Process of Reform," p. 147. The Sanger horoscope and psychic reading for 1922 is titled "Margaret Higgins 2–4–8, 1–5–7," signed by Elizabeth Aldrich, MS-SS.

11: ORGANIZING FOR BIRTH CONTROL

1. The incorporation controversy is in "Birth Control Wins Charter Fight," *The New York Times,* Apr. 14, 1922, 36:2, and Apr. 23, 1922, Pt.1, 2:3. On Anne Kennedy, see M.S. to Juliet Rublee, "Juliet darling, Your special letter with enclosure came yesterday . . . ," n.d. (1924) MS-DC, and *Autobiography,* p. 261. On the organization of the ABCL, see "Report of the American Birth Control League Activities," 1922, and "Minutes of the American Birth Control League for 1922," in PPFA-SS. The goals were announced in an editorial in the *Birth Control Review* 5:11 (Nov. 1921), pp. 4–5. Also see Francis McLennon Vreeland, "The Process of Reform with Especial Reference to Reform Groups in the Field of Population," doctoral dissertation, University of Michigan, 1929, p. 135. The league actually claimed distribution of 600,000 pamphlets in 1923, but I use Vreeland's estimate, pp. 146, 240, and he maintains that these early figures may have been inflated, accounting for some falloff when he himself kept more accurate records while working in the ABCL offices in 1926–27, as part of the research for his study. On the Motherhood Department, see Bertha Potter Smith's report for Jan. 12, 1926, PPFA-SS, and Helena Huntington Smith, "Profiles, They Were Eleven," *The New Yorker*, 1930, clipping in MS-SS.

2. For published examples of the early correspondence, see "The Doctor Only Laughed," *Birth Control Review* 7:6 (June 1923); "Prevention or Abortion—Which?" *BCR* 7:7 (July 1923); "Is Continence the Solution?" *BCR* 7:9 (Sept. 1923). The quotes are from Bobby Walls to M.S., Mar. 2, 1924, a twenty-four-page handwritten letter; M.S. to Bobby Walls, Mar. 7, 1924; and Mrs. M. M. Gardner to M.S., June 21, 1935, all in MS-LC. As we shall see, Margaret collected and published less controversial letters in *Motherhood in Bondage* (New York: 1928).

3. This statistical profile of the membership is taken from Vreeland, "Process of Reform," pp. 153, 164–67, 171, 192, 208, 210–11, of contributors, p. 252, of the budget, p. 327, and of the National Council, pp. 428–29. On *Birth Control Review* distribution, also see M.S. to Francis Fitzgerald, Aug. 11, 1924, MS-LC. (Fitzgerald was the librarian at Creighton University, a Jesuit school,

and although a free subscription had been donated to the library by an alumnus, he refused to accept it.) ABCL memos dated Jan. 13, 1927, and Jan. 20, 1932, in PPFA-SS discuss a reduction of affiliate contributions from 25 percent to 10 percent of annual membership receipts.

4. M.S., form letter, July 15, 1923, asking support for the Chicago conference. Also see, Clara L. Rowe (the conference organizer) to Prof. Michael Frederick Guyer, July 6, 1923, both in the American Birth Control League Papers, 1923–28, Houghton Library, Harvard University, hereinafter, ABCL-Houghton. On the high incidence of abortion among Jewish immigrant women in Chicago, see Harry L. Lurie, "The Sex Hygiene of Family Life," *Jewish Social Service Quarterly* (Dec. 1926), cited in Caroline Hadley Robinson, *Seventy Birth Control Clinics: A Survey and Analysis Including the General Effects of Control on Size and Quality of Population* (Philadelphia: 1930), p. 66. Also see Bernice Guthmann, *The Planned Parenthood Movement in Illinois, 1923–1965,* a 1965 pamphlet published by the PPFA, Chicago Area, pp. 3–6; Rachelle Yarros, M.D., "Illinois Looks Ahead," *Birth Control Review* 2:4 (Jan. 1935), p. 2; and Vreeland, "Process of Reform," p. 367. On Yarros, see Christopher Lasch, "Rachelle Slobodinsky Yarros," in *Notable American Women, 1607–1950: A Biographical Dictionary* (Cambridge, Mass.: 1971), edited by Edward and Janet James, pp. 693–94.

5. On the organization of the L.A. clinic, see Vreeland, "Process of Reform," pp. 365–68, and on the endowment of $180,000, see Robinson, *Seventy Clinics,* p. 33. Patient data is in Robinson and in *The Los Angeles Mothers' Clinic Association Annual Report,* 1930, copy in MS–LC. On San Francisco, see *Alameda County Birth Control League and Mothers' Health Clinic,* 1929 pamphlet in MS-SS; and Planned Parenthood League of Alameda County and Planned Parenthood Association of San Francisco, *Joint Annual Report, 1969,* pp. 5–7, a pamphlet also collected by the author.

6. On Detroit, see Eloise K. Sulzberger, "Instant Birth Control," and Betsy Graves Reyneau, "Nobody Came," in "Our M.S.," Sanger Seventy-Fifth Birthday Reminiscences, pp. 264–67 and 230–32, MS-SS; Anne Kennedy to Mrs. Willard Pope, Jan. 5, 1944, MS-SS; and "Birth Control League of Michigan," *Birth Control Review* 16:1 (Jan. 1932), p. 23. On Cleveland, see Vreeland, "Process of Reform," pp. 401–409; *The Maternal Health Association of Cleveland,* 1937 pamphlet summarizing the history of their clinic program in MS-SS; Dorothy Brush, "Impressions of Margaret Sanger," in "Our M.S.," MS-SS; and finally, Nancy Peacock, "Everything You Wanted to Know About Noblesse Oblige But Were Afraid to Ask," *Cleveland* (May 1988). My thanks to my mother, Celia Chesler of Cleveland, for this last citation.

7. On Baltimore, see "The Baltimore Birth Control Clinic," *Birth Control Review* 13:5 (May 1929), p. 137, and Bessie L. Moses, M.D., *Contraception as a Therapeutic Measure* (Baltimore: 1936), esp. introduction and pp. 3–7, 14, summary. Moses' primary purpose was to test and compare the efficacy of the diaphragm against Sanger's New York statistics, which are discussed in Chapter 13. On Cooper, see M.S. to J. Noah. H. Slee, Feb. 22, 1925, with a handwritten notation by Sanger's secretary, Florence Rose, that Cooper spoke to 248 groups in practically every state, and M.S. to James Cooper, Feb. 5, 1925, both in MS-LC. Schedules and reports for Cooper's tours are in ABCL-Houghton, along with some early correspondence, including J.C. to M.S., Sept. 14, 1923, and J.C.

to Clara L. Rowe, July 19, 1923. Miscellaneous reports from Cooper in the field including "Report on St. Louis, Mo. October, 15, 16, 17, 1925"; and "Report on North Jersey Medical Society (colored), Tioga County Medical Meeting and Indianapolis, Indiana," October 1925, are in MS-LC. Monthly reports from 1926–28 are in James Cooper, M.D., "Clinical Report File," uncataloged papers, Margaret Sanger Center, N.Y.C.; and a summary of 1928 activities is in MS-LC. Also see James F. Cooper, M.D., *Motherhood and Birth Control,* and *Some Reasons for the Popularity of the Birth Control Movement,* pamphlets in BA-SS. Biographical material in S. Adolphus Knopf, M.D., "In Memoriam: James F. Cooper," reprint from *The Medical Journal and Record,* May 20, 1931, in MS-SS and clipping from a *New York Herald Tribune* obituary, Mar. 28, 1931, in MS-LC. On New Jersey, see "Report of ABCL Executive Secretary Penelope B. Huse," Mar. 8, 1927; and Henriette Hart, "Report of the New Jersey Field Work," Apr. 12–May 8, 1927, both in PPFA-SS. Also see "News Notes," *BCR* 12:1 (Jan. 1928), p. 25. Aggregate data for 1930 is in Robinson, *Seventy Clinics,* passim. Robinson's outlook about the future of the clinic movement was optimistic, and her statistics were inflated by the inclusion of case data from facilities in Europe, as well as the United States. When one actually looks beyond the Sanger clinic in New York, however, her conclusion seems unfounded. For more on the Sanger clinic, see Chaps. 13 and 14.

8. On Massachusetts, see Lucile Lord-Heinstein, M.D., "An Account of the Salem Raid and Trial," July 28, 1937, PPLM-MS; "Massachusetts Clinic Case," an account of the Massachusetts Supreme Court ruling of May 26, 1938, n.d. (1938), MS-SS; and Ruth Smith, ed., *PPLM Reports* 24 (Spring 1974), copy in PPLM-SS. My thanks to David Garrow for summarizing the situation in Connecticut.

9. On the Albany lobbying effort, see "Despotic Government at Albany," *Birth Control Review* 7:2 (Feb. 23, 1923), p. 47; "To All Our Friends," *BCR* 7:3 (Mar. 23, 1923) p. 71; "Intelligence Tests for Legislators," and "The Hearing at Albany," *BCR* 7:5 (May 1925) pp. 107–108 and 111–12. Also see "Albany Mayor Fails to Halt Birth Control Meeting," *The New York Times,* Feb. 21, 1923, and assorted clippings from local Albany papers in MS-LC. The denouement of Dennett's efforts is chronicled in the Stopes correspondence, MS-BM. The Sanger quotations are in M.S. to J.N.H.S., Mar. 2, 1927, MS-SS, and M.S. to J.R., n.d. (from Geneva), MS-DC. Also see U.S. Congress. Joint Subcommittees of the Committees on the Judiciary. *Joint Hearings on the Cummins-Vaile Bill.* 68th Cong., 1st sess., Apr. 8 and May 9, 1924.

10. Anne Kennedy, report on "Federal Work," n.d. (1926), and Anne Kennedy to the Board of Directors and National Council of the ABCL, "Facts You Should Know," Jan. 19, 1926, both in MS-LC. The quotations are from Anne Kennedy, "Short Synopsis of Interviews with Senators," a sixty-page document. She quoted Vaile and George W. Norris, among many others, see esp. pp. 1 and 4.

11. On the 1924 campaign, see Oswald G. Villard to M.S., Sept. 3, 1924, MS-LC and "Summary of Events for 1924," PPFA-SS. The 1926 events are in Anne Kennedy, "Report of an Interview with Father Ward of the National Catholic Welfare Conference, Washington D.C., Also Father Ryan of the Publicity Department," n.d. (1926); Mrs. Anne Kennedy, "Report of an Interview with Mr. P. J. Ward of the NCWC, Washington, D.C.," Mar. 2, 1926, copies

in MS-SS and MS-LC; Patrick J. Ward to Clarence C. Little, president of the University of Michigan, Mar. 18, 1926; Rev. John J. Burke, general secretary of the NCWC, to M.S., Apr. 21, 1926; M.S. to John J. Burke, May 13, 1926, and June 24; Burke to M.S., June 12 and July 28; Patrick J. Ward to the editor, *The New Republic,* Oct. 29, 1928, all in MS-LC. From 1928, see Floyd S. Dell, "The Anti-Birth Control Neurosis," *Birth Control Review* 12:9 (Sept. 1928), pp. 252–54, and "Mrs. Sanger Calls Catholics Bigots . . . Attacks Smith Candidacy," *The New York Times,* Apr. 25, 1928, 14:2–3; and on the Hoover vote, M.S. to Juliet Rublee, n.d. (Nov. 1928), MS-DC. Finally, on New York lobbying efforts: "Legislators Wake to a Vital Problem," *BCR* 9:5 (May 1925), pp. 143–55. A copy of Assembly Bill 684, dated Feb. 1, 1927, is in MS-LC. A summary of the progress made on a subsequent bill introduced in 1929 is in "Doctors and Birth Control," American Birth Control League, Report of the executive secretary for 1929, PPFA-SS.

12. Grant Sanger, Schlesinger Library interview, p. 54; interview with the author, Dec. 18, 1987. Olive Byrne Richard, Jacqueline Van Voris interview, Smith College, p. 17. Margaret Sanger Marston, Jacqueline Van Voris interview, Smith College, p. 44.

13. Sanger Journal, Mar. 7, 1925, Jan. 11, 1926, MS-SS. M.S. to "Juliet Dearest," n.d. (possibly as early as 1921) and M.S. to J.R., "Aug. 20," n.d. (sometime in the 1920s) on Mount Royal Hotel letterhead, MS-DC. The quote is from J.R. to M.S., Sept. 11, 1925, MS-SS, also see letters dated Sept. 11, Oct. 7, and Oct. 12, 1925.

14. Margaret Sanger, ed. *The Sixth International Neo-Malthusian and Birth Control Conference,* 4 vols. (New York, 1925–26), copy in MS-SS. The conference was held at the McAlpin Hotel, March 25–31, 1925. Also see, news releases and other materials from the event in ABCL-Houghton. *The New York Times* coverage began with "Birth Control Conference; Noted Advocates from Abroad to Attend Sessions Opening Tomorrow," Mar. 25, 1925, 12:2, and continued for a week. See *NYT,* Mar. 27, 1925, 8:1–2; Mar. 28, 9:1; Mar. 29, Sec. 1, 9:1, Mar. 30, 10:3; Mar. 31, 7:1; Apr. 1, 15:1; Apr. 2, 17:2. Also, "Neo-Malthusians," *The Nation* 120:15 (Apr. 15, 1925), p. 401; John Langdon-Davies, "Race-Suicide No Murder," *The New Republic* 42: 541 (Apr. 15, 1925), pp. 209-11. On the participation of Rosika Schwimmer, see R.S. to M.S., Mar. 17 and Dec. 4, 1924, Jan. 30, 1925, and M.S. to R.S., Mar. 26 and Dec. 9, 1924, Jan. 17 and Apr. 6, 1925, all in the Schwimmer-Lloyd (Lola Maverick Lloyd) Collection, New York Public Library.

15. "Margaret Sanger Begins to Study Birth Control; Leaving League She Created 'to Catch Up With Subject,' " *New York World,* June 6, 1926, clipping in MS-LC. *Autobiography,* p. 393, and David Kennedy, *Birth Control in America: The Career of Margaret Sanger,* (New Haven: 1970), p. 103.

16. Sanger's positive assessment of Anne Kennedy and the league's progress is in Journal, "Notes during the Geneva Conference, 1928," MS-SS. The events surrounding the Kennedy firing are chronicled in the following correspondence: Eleanor Jones to M.S., "Friday, July 8," n.d. (1927); M.S. to E. J., Dec. 20, 1927; M.S. to A.K., Dec. 22, 1927, and A.K. to M.S., Jan. 10, 1928, and "Geneva, Sat. the 5th," (n.d.) (1927 or 1928); P. B. Huse to M.S., Nov. 3, 1927; Annie G. Porritt to M.S., Dec. 29, 1927; Frances Ackerman, Nov. 3–13, 1927, and Dec. 3, 1927; and Charlotte Delafield to M.S., Nov. 29, 1927, all in

MS-LC. On Lifschiz, see Anna Lifschiz to Margaret Sanger, Aug. 15, 1930, MS-SS. Without apparent rancor, Lifschiz went to the western office of Holland-Rantos, manufacturer of diaphragms, in Los Angeles, saying to M.S., "There are no words to express how I cherish my contact with you."

17. M.S. to Juliet Rublee, May 17, 1928, MS-DC. M.S. to "The Board of Directors," the American Birth Control League, Inc. June 8, 1928, MS-SS. Charlotte Delafield to M.S., Apr. 16, 1928, indicates her refusal to serve as a replacement President.

18. "Minutes of Special Meeting, Sept. 20, 1928," MS-LC, discuss the dispute over the autonomy of the clinic. MS. to Juliet Rublee, Sept. 14 and Sept. 23, 1928, and "Juliet dear" on 39 Fifth Ave. letterhead (n.d.), reveal her view of the dispute as it was developing, all in MS-DC. M.S. to "the Secretary of the A.B.C.L., Inc. January 31, 1929," communicates her formal resignation as editor and director, and M.S. to Mrs. F. Robertson Jones, Feb. 11, 1929, and Eleanor Dwight Jones to J.N.H.S., testily explain the differences between the two women, all in the ABCL papers, MS-SS. The direct quotes are respectively from M.S. to H.de S., Feb. 19, 1929, MS-LC; and from a story in the *Brooklyn Eagle,* Dec. 28, 1930, clipping in MS-LC. Also see, "Mrs. Sanger Quits Birth Control Post," *The New York Times,* Sept. 12, 1928, 11:1–3 and "Mrs. F. Robertson Jones Becomes Head of Birth Control League," *NYT,* Sept. 13, 29:8. Kennedy, *Birth Control,* pp. 103–104, attributes the break to Sanger's emotionalism and her "autocratic and often chaotic leadership," without giving her any benefit of doubt and without fully examining the particulars of the controversy that led up to it.

19. M.S. to Dr. Alice Boughton, executive director, ABCL, in 1932 ABCL correspondence, MS-LC. Also M.S. to Annie G. Porritt, secretary of the ABCL board, Jan. 20, 1930, MS-LC.

20. M.S. to Juliet Rublee in Mexico, "Willowlake, Friday 26, Darling Juliet," n.d. (1929) MS-DC, and H.E. to M.S., Nov. 3, 1930, MS-LC. For the article, see Margaret Sanger, "The Birth Control Raid," *The New Republic* (May 1, 1929), pp. 305–306, clipping in MS-LC.

21. The first quotes are from Eleanor Dwight Jones, "Birth Control: First Aid in Social Work," speech reprinted in *Birth Control Review* 13:8 (Aug. 1929), p. 218. The next two are from Eleanor Dwight (Mrs. F. Robertson) Jones to Lawrence B. Dunham, Nov. 3, 1930, Bureau of Social Hygiene Papers, Rockefeller Archive, Record Group 2, Pocantico Hills, New York, hereinafter Rocky, followed by the appropriate record group number. My thanks to Joan Dunlop for helping to facilitate my use of the Rockefeller archives by putting me in touch with Peter Johnson, the Rockefeller family archivist whose preliminary search helped me locate these papers, which, to my knowledge, have not been previously examined. For the Bureau of Social Hygiene Response, see memorandum: "To Mr. Dunham from Dr. Sellin," Nov. 17, 1930; and Lawrence Dunham to Thomas M. Debevoise, Mar. 5, 1931, and R. (Ruth) Topping to Mr. Dunham, "ABCL-Comments on Report of Activities for 1931," Jan. 5, 1932, and RT (Ruth Topping), "File Memorandum re: ABCL," Dec. 2, 1932, in which she quotes Robert Dickinson, M.D., calling Jones a "martinet," all in Rocky-RG2. When the Bureau of Social Hygiene closed down, Topping ironically took a job with the league, but by that time, it was supporting Sanger.

12: HAPPINESS IN MARRIAGE

1. The biographical information on Slee is from a Planned Parenthood Federation of America press release issued at his death on June 22, 1943, copy in MS-SS; and from his obituary in the *New York Herald Tribune*, June 23, 1943, a clipping of which is in the Abraham Stone papers, Countway Library of Medicine, Harvard University, hereinafter AS-Countway. There is no indication that Slee's first wife was related to the Roosevelt presidents. Also see a deposition for a suit against 3-in-One-Oil in MS-LC. The dollar figure on the 3-in-One sale is from Juliet Rublee to MS., Sept. 28, 1929, MS-SS. Olive Byrne Richard, in her interview with the author, also recalled this figure, and told the story of Margaret having said she nearly fainted.

2. The Sanger divorce decree, dated Oct. 4, 1921, Barnstable, Mass., is in MS-SS. Also see Herman Harding, counselor and attorney-at-law, to M.S., Apr. 16, 1920. Carl Degler, *At Odds: Women and the Family in America From the Revolution to the Present* (New York: 1980), p.169, says that desertion and failure of support were typical grounds for divorce. On time spent with Hersey and Sanger, see Sanger Journal entries for Oct. 1920, MS-SS, and also William Sanger to M.S., Jan. 5, 1922, MS-SS, where he tells her that he is "thrilled" by a recent letter that must have expressed some sense of sustained affection or caring for him, because he said that it had lifted "the pall over my being—your indifference." Also see M.S. to H.de S., Nov. 15, 1921, "Aug. 6, Sunday am," n.d. (1921) and "Hotel Russell," n.d. (1921), all in MS-LC.

3. On Slee's influence see M.S. to Lawrence Lader, Mar. 29, 1954, MS-SS. M.S. to Juliet Rublee, on "One Hundred-Four Fifth Avenue, New York" letterhead, with "Juliet dearest" as a salutation, n.d. (1923 or '24), tells of bringing a man on staff. The final recollection is from Elizabeth Grew Bacon, "M.S. A Memory Picture," in "Our M.S.," MS-SS.

4. My impressions of the Sanger-Slee marriage are drawn from their extensive correspondence, which she saved and left to Smith College, to be opened to researchers ten years after her death. Specific letters are cited throughout the text that follows. Also see M.S. to Lawrence Lader, Mar. 29, 1954, MS-SS; Dorothy Brush, "I Just Love Margaret," in "Our M.S," MS-SS. A Japan journal is also in MS-SS. See especially entries for Mar. 9, 10, 13, 16, 18, 19, 21, 29; Apr. 4, 11, 21–22, May 31, June 10, and June 30, 1922. Additional information on the trip is from the Sanger FBI file. See "Weekly Intelligence Report, Seattle, Washington District, Feb. 20, 1922"; Report on "Japanese Situation—San Francisco District" to Mr. J. Edgar Hoover, Feb. 18, 1922; and General Intelligence Division, Special Reports of Radical Activities, periods ending Feb. 25, Aug. 19, and Oct. 14, 1922. Sanger's affidavit allowing her entry into Japan, along with a letter from Baroness Ishimoto to Anne Kennedy, Mar. 9, 1922, and other correspondence is in MS-LC. Letters quoted are M.S. to Juliet Rublee, "The Grand Hotel, Yokohama," n.d. (1922), and Apr. 16, 1922, from "Grand Hotel de Pekin." Finally, see *Autobiography*, pp. 315–55, which never even mentions Slee's presence on the round-the-world trip.

5. *Report of the Fifth International Neo-Malthusian and Birth Control Conference,* Kingsway Hall, London, July 11–14, 1922 (London: 1922), copy in MS-SS. See especially, Sanger's introductory address to the session, "Individual and Family Aspects of Birth Control," pp. 24–31, and Annie G. Porritt, man-

aging editor of the *Birth Control Review,* "Publicity in the Birth Control Movement," pp. 302–306. American press coverage of the trip included the following: "Birth Control in Japan," *The New York Times,* June 5, 1921, Sec. 6, 10:1–3, announcing her intention to go; "Mrs. Sanger Shocks Her; Chinese Girl Interpreter Breaks Off Birth Control Lecture," *NYT,* June 22, 1922, 3:2; and "Mrs. Sanger Tells of Trip; Says Japanese and Chinese Hailed Birth Control," *NYT,* Oct. 11, 1922, 19:4. Also see coverage of the conference in *BCR* 6:9 (Sept. 1922), especially, "British and American Birth Control Movements," p. 172, and "Margaret Sanger's Impressions," pp. 175–76; and Francis McLennon Vreeland, "The Process of Reform with Especial Reference to Reform Groups in the Field of Population," doctoral dissertation, University of Michigan, 1929, p. 138. Margaret Sanger, *The New Motherhood* with introductions by Harold Cox and Havelock Ellis, came out in London in 1922.

6. The divorce decree and marriage certificate are in MS–SS, as is a copy of William Sanger's certificate of marriage to Vedya Merz on July 6, 1924. The seer's pronouncements, under "Margaret Higgins, 2–4–8, 1–5–7," are in MS-SS. Clippings on the announcement of the marriage in Feb. 1924 are in MS-LC scrapbooks. See for example "Mrs. Sanger Reported Wed," *The New York Times,* Feb 18, 1924, 4:4; "Meet the Wife," and "Millionaire Won Mrs. Sanger with Hunt over Globe," *New York Daily News,* Feb. 18, 1924. Also see Harold Hersey to M.S., "July 19th" n.d. (1921 or 22), MS-SS. H.E. to M.S., Jan. 15, 1922, MS-LC. William Sanger learned of the marriage from Michael Higgins in 1923 and was exceedingly distressed by the news. See William Sanger to M.S., Feb. 27, 1923, MS-SS.

7. M.S. to H.de S., July 17, 1924, MS-LC. Also see *Autobiography,* pp. 356–57. The marriage "contract" is alleged in Lawrence Lader, *The Margaret Sanger Story,* (New York: 1955).

8. Richard quote from her interview with the author, Mar. 1985. Sanger quotes in M.S. to Juliet Rublee, n.d. (1924), on "Canadian Pacific Hotels" letterhead, M.S. to J.R., Aug. 6, 1925, and M.S. to J.R., n.d. (sometime in the 1920s), all in MS-DC. The Sanger–Slee correspondence is in MS-SS. See, for example, J.N.H.S. to M.S., telegram, Apr. 5, 1923; May 20, 1923; Oct. 7, 1923; Oct. 30, 1923; Nov. 12, 1923; Oct. 9, 1924; Apr. 1, 1927; and for the material in quotation, Apr. 23, 1925, from The Homestead, Hot Springs, Ga. The *Family Limitation* controversy is chronicled in Charles V. Drysdale to M.S., Feb. 25, 1923, MS-SS, and *Birth Control Review* 7:4, (Apr. 1923), pp. 84–85. It became another opportunity for competition between Sanger and Marie Stopes, who resented the fuss made over it and claimed that the obscenity ruling posed no larger threat to the legality of birth control in England.

9. Examples of correspondence from Sanger to Slee are the following: M.S. to J.N.H.S., Feb. 29, 1924; Sept. 18, 1924 (from London where she is spending their wedding anniversary alone); Oct. 19, 1924, from Wells's home in Easton Glebe; Oct. 23, 1924, from London's Stafford Hotel. The material in direct quotation is from M.S. to J.N.H.S, Nov. 7, 1924, and Dec. 5, 1926, and Mar. 2, 1927, all from the Stafford Hotel in London. Some of these letters, including M.S. to J.H.N.S., Dec. 5, 1926, are reprinted in Elizabeth S. Duvall, ed., *Hear Me for My Cause, Selected Letters of Margaret Sanger, 1926–1927,* a pamphlet published by Smith College. Duvall takes them at face value. Also see Journal, Oct. 6, 1924, and, passim, correspondence of Harold Child to M.S., 1924 and

1925, MS-SS. An intimate account of the Sanger-Slee marriage is in Joan Dash, *A Life of One's Own: Three Gifted Women and the Men They Married* (New York: 1973), pp. 69–113. Dash apparently failed to read Sanger's correspondence with other lovers during this period, however, so she also missed the critical element of the story.

10. M.S. to J.H.N.S., Apr. 17, 1925 (complains that Stuart was feeling uncomfortable about Slee's preoccupation with money); Ethel Byrne to M.S., Apr., 1925, talks about Stuart's problems with money, as does M.S. to J.H.N.S, Apr. 17, 1925, both in MS-SS. For more concern about Stuart's and Grant's spending, see M.S. to Grant Sanger, Apr. 18, 1928; "Aug. 2," n.d. (probably 1931); undated (also probably 1931). On the boys' concerns in general, see, for example, Grant Sanger to M.S., "Dear Mother," on "Westminster" letterhead, n.d., and Nov. 3, 1924, both in MS-SS; Sanger Diary entries for May 23 and Nov. 14, 1925; and the horoscopes for Grant, MS-SS. The final quotes are respectively from M.S. to H.E., Dec. 3, 1933; and M.S. to G.S., Oct. 23, 1927 and Apr. 18, 1928, all MS-SS.

11. Margaret's generosity to the Higgins siblings is detailed in the Higgins family correspondence, MS-SS. See especially the letters from Bob about his daughter and her marriage. On Nan's retirement income, see M.S. to J.N.H.S., Dec. 4, 1928, MS-SS. On the corset business financing, see Richard Higgins to M.S., Sept. 11, 1936, in MS-LC. Olive Richard spoke of the college loan in her interview with Jacqueline Van Voris, pp. 10–11. Agnes Smedley to M.S., May 9, 1924 asks for money, and M.S. to A.S., June 4, 1924 pledges $50 a month. Jo Bennett to M.S., Mar. 2, 1928, thanks her for sending a check to Smedley, MS-LC; Kitty Marion to M.S., Feb. 2, 1930, and Feb. 16, 1930, thanks her effusively for her check—the latter is addressed "My Darling Beloved Lady and Pal," MS-LC. H.E. to M.S., Aug. 1, 1930, describes the new comforts of his household and his gratitude for "this new life"; M.S. to H.E., Aug. 29, 1931, says the salary would have to be diminished, as does M.S. to Joseph Wortis, Sept. 21, 1934. H.E. to M.S., Mar. 13, 1932, says not to let the payments become a burden, all in MS-LC. M.S. to Françoise Cyon, "April third," n.d. (1938) talks of another check for Ellis to buy a comfortable bed for the country house they had rented with money she collected from American friends, and Cyon to M.S., Oct. 9, 1957, bickers over Lawrence Lader's portrayal of Sanger as Ellis's benefactress, both in MS-SS. MS. to J.N.H.S., Nov. 7, 1924, coyly requests extra hotel money, MS-SS.

12. A full and precise accounting of Slee's early contributions to the movement is in M.S. to "Dear Frances," (undoubtedly, Frances Ackerman), Aug. 1, 1928, MS-LC. The letter is included with the correspondence and papers that relate to Slee's appeal, carried on between 1926 and 1930, of an Internal Revenue Service disallowance of the deductions he took for his contributions on the grounds that the American Birth Control League was a valid educational and charitable institution, and not a political lobbying group. Further discussion of this case and its implications is in Chap. 15. The appeal was brought by Covington, Burling, & Rublee in Washington D.C. The letters between the firm, Slee, and Sanger date from June 25, 1927, through Mar. 24, 1930, MS-LC. Other examples of Slee's fund-raising efforts are in J.N.H.S. to Frances Ackerman, Dec. 19, 1922; J.N.H.S. to Thomas L. Lamont, Dec. 19, 1922; J.N.H.S. to Clarence V. Evans, Feb. 29, 1924, MS-LC; and John A. Kingsbury (of the

Milbank Memorial Fund) to J.N.H.S., Mar. 17, 1926, all in MS-LC. The Cooper request is in M.S. to J.H.N.S., Feb. 22, 1925, MS-LC. The smuggling is documented in J.N.H.S. to Murray Agency, Montreal, Oct. 16, 1924; J.N.H.S. to Messrs. Hechtel & LeNoir, Berlin, Germany, Oct. 16, 1924; and "Mr. O'Rourke" to J.N.H.S., Apr. 10, 1928, all in MS-LC. M.S. to Hannah Stone, June 11, 1926, MS-SS, says not to order supplies without consulting Slee first about problems with deterioration of rubber.

A statement dated Nov. 25, 1925, on 3-in-One Oil letterhead signed by Slee chronicles the smuggling and jelly manufacturing story. It is included in MS-LC with a note from Sanger's secretary Florence Rose, dated Sept. 1943, saying Mrs. Sanger was "much entertained at the recollection of this period of Mr. Slee's activity . . . [that] it always brought a chuckle." On the founding of Holland-Rantos, see the recollections of Herbert Simonds in MS-SS. A brochure from the early 1930s advertising Holland-Rantos products says they were used by 105 clinics, 121 hospitals, and 52,000 physicians, in National Archives-Margaret Sanger bill files. Finally, on the commercialization of contraception after 1930, see Chaps. 14 and 15, and David Kennedy, *Birth Control in America: The Career of Margaret Sanger* (New Haven: 1970), p. 212.

13. On her appreciation of Noah after the conference, see M.S., Journal, Mar. 22, 1925, MS-SS. Also see James Gould Cozzens, *Ask Me Tomorrow* (New York: 1940). Cozzens later won the Pulitzer Prize for his 1957 novel *By Love Possessed.* On his writing, and on the quasi-autobiographical nature of *Ask Me Tomorrow,* see Granville Hicks, *James Gould Cozzens* (Minneapolis: 1966). Grant Sanger remembered the Cozzens link.

14. M.S. to J.N.H.S., Feb. 1, Feb. 2, and Feb. 6, 1927, MS-SS. M.S. to H.de S., Jan. 10, Jan. 13, Jan. 22, Feb. 9, 1927, MS-LC. Some of the Sanger-Slee letters from this period are reprinted in Duvall, *Hear Me,* MS-SS.

15. M.S. to J.H.N.S., Feb. 22, 1927, and letters, passim from Feb. through Mar., MS-SS.

16. The initial quotes are respectively from E.H-M. to M.S., Mar. 15, 1929 and "Margaret darling, Have been awake since 1.30 A.M.," n.d. (1928), MS-SS. Also see E.H-M. to M.S., July 19 and July 27, 1915, June 15, 1916, Dec. 22, 1925, Sept. 28, 1926, Sept. 26, 1927, Oct. 31, 1928, MS-SS. E. H-M to Marie Stopes, Feb. 18, 1916, and Louise Thompson to M.S., Mar. 31, 1938, all in MS-SS, and the clipping of a 1934 interview in the *New York World Telegram,* "Repeal of 'Silly Comstockery . . . Should Be U.S. Women's Next Objective,' Says Pioneer," MS-LC. Sir Bernard Mallett's tribute to Margaret is in Margaret Sanger, ed., *Proceedings of the World Population Conference* (London: 1927), p. 356. Homage to Margaret for her role at Geneva was formally offered by Frank Lorimar, "The Role of the International Union for the Scientific Study of Population," in Clyde V. Kiser, ed., *Forty Years of Research in Human Fertility: Retrospect and Prospect* (New York: 1971), pp. 86–87. Also, see James Reed, *The Birth Control Movement and American Society: From Private Vice to Public Virtue* (Princeton: 1984), p. 337. On the events at Geneva, also see assorted printed documents from the World Population Conference in MS-SS, and "Miscellaneous Notes and Comments" in "Journal, 1927," and "Geneva Diary, 1925–27," both in MS-SS; as well as observations in the correspondence between Edith How-Martyn, who helped organize the conference, and M.S. 1925–29, passim, MS-SS. For the Italians, see Grant Sanger, Schlesinger Library

interview, p. 36; and Abraham Stone, M.D., "Speaking of the Conference," *Birth Control Review* 12:2, (Feb. 1928), pp. 48–49. The final quote is from M.S. to H.de S., May 22, 1927, MS-LC.

17. M.S. to J.H.N.S., Sept. 21 and Sept. 27, 1927, MS-SS. Also see M.S., ed., *Proceedings.*

18. Agnes Smedley to M.S., Nov. 19, 1928. Also see A.S. to M.S., Jan. 30, 1928, both in MS-LC. Janice and Stephen MacKinnon, *Agnes Smedley: The Life and Times of an American Radical* (Berkeley: 1988), pp. 51–133, provides a detailed account of her life in these years, which makes use of the Sanger correspondence.

19. A.S. to M.S., 1924–6, in MS-LC, especially May 9, 1924, Feb. 12, 1925, Nov. 5, 1925, Jan. 13, n.d. (1926). The file also contains copies of American Express foreign money orders Margaret sent to Smedley in denominations of $50. Also see MacKinnon and MacKinnon, *Agnes Smedley,* pp. 98, 113–14, 127–130.

20. A.S. to M.S., Apr. 23, 1928, July 1928; M.S. to Edith How-Martyn, Apr. 11, 1929, all in MS-LC; MacKinnon and MacKinnon, *Agnes Smedley,* pp. 128–31.

21. On the Swiss holiday see M.S. to Grant Sanger, Dec. 28, 1927, MS–SS and J.N.H.S. to H.de S., Jan. 16, 1928, MS-LC. For the material quoted directly, see M.S. to Juliet Rublee, June 24, July 10 (1928), July 13 (1928), Aug. 15 (1928), Oct. 21, 1929. MS-DC; and finally M.S. to J.N.H.S, Sept. 18, 1927, MS-SS.

22. M.S. to J.N.H.S., Sept. 27, 1927, and n.d. (from her trip out west in the fall of 1934); M.S. to H. E., June 20, 1939, marked "confidential," June 20, 1939, all in MS-SS.

23. Margaret Sanger, *Happiness in Marriage* (Elmsford, N.Y.: 1969), reprinted from the original 1926 edition, pp. 177–86, 191–203, 221–31, quotations on pp. 197 and 199.

24. *Ibid.,* Quotations from pp. 181 and 229 respectively.

25. *Ibid.,* pp. 5–6, 105–62, final quote on p. 139.

26. *Ibid.,* p. 170, p. 121. My reading of the text here disputes Linda Gordon's interpretation in *Woman's Body, Woman's Right: A Social History of Birth Control in America* (New York: 1976), p. 373.

Gordon says Sanger wrote nothing at all on the technique of physical love and confined herself to romantic philosophy, which is simply not true. It is true that Sanger obviously felt constrained writing about physiology, because she was a laywoman, eager for popular acceptance of her cause, and more importantly, perhaps, because she wrote under the threat of censorship. Both Sanger and Marie Stopes should be credited as transitional figures in the movement toward sexual candor, characteristic of the marriage manuals of the 1930s and of our own time. Gordon also attacks Sanger for promoting mutual orgasm in coitus, and implies that she did not distinguish between clitoral and vaginal responses, which is also incorrect, though Gordon is right that she did establish mutuality of response as an ideal.

27. A copy of the letter from the lawyer (name unclear) to Charles Herold of Brentano's, with the Stopes quote enclosed, Jan. 29, 1926, is in MS-LC, as is Jonah Goldstein to Anna Lifshitz, Margaret's secretary, Feb. 15, 1926. Also see "Some Notes on How to be Happy if Married," unsigned review in *The New*

York Times, July 4, 1926, clipping along with other notices in MS-LC. The book was also reviewed in the *New York Herald Tribune, Saturday Review of Literature, Booklist, Survey* and many local newspapers.

Margaret was also taken aback by the criticism of her friend, Agnes Smedley, who wrote from Europe that the parts on romantic courtship seemed terribly strange. On the other hand, she said that she found the sections of practical sex instruction "very, very excellent," and promised to review the book favorably in an Indian publication for which she wrote frequently. See Agnes Smedley to M.S., Jan. 3, n.d. (1927), MS-LC. On sales, see Lowell Brentano to M.S., June 9, 1930.

28. United States v. Dennett, 39 F. 564 2d (1930) and U.S. v. One Obscene Book Entitled "Married Love," 48 F. 2d (1931). On these cases, and their reinterpretation of Swearingen v. United States, also see Kennedy, *Birth Control*, pp. 243–44. Margaret's book was reissued by Blue Ribbon Books in 1930, which guaranteed her a royalty of 10 cents each on 15,000 copies, and when the censorship laws were eased, she tried to restore some of the originally expurgated material, but what became of this effort is not clear. See Lowell Brentano to M.S., June 9, 1930, and M.S. to Eugene Reynal, both in MS-LC. On the contraceptive rulings, see Chap. 16.

29. T. H. Van de Velde, M.D., *Ideal Marriage: Its Physiology and Technique* (New York: 1930), passim. The translation was by Stella Browne, the British radical feminist, who had by then accused Sanger of embracing a bourgeois agenda, so its success must have infuriated Margaret all the more. Between 1940 and 1962, Van de Velde was continuously reprinted, sometimes twice a year. See esp. pp. 105, 148–49, 164–65, 168–69, 178–83, 188–89. On the history of marriage manuals, see Michael Gordon, "From an Unfortunate Necessity to a Cult of Mutual Orgasm: Sex in American Marital Education Literature, 1830–1940," in *Studies in the Sociology of Sex*, edited by James M. Henslin (New York: 1971), and Edward Brecher, *The Sex Researchers* (New York: 1969), which compares Van de Velde's prescriptive writing to behavioral changes charted by Kinsey.

30. M.S. to H.de S., (no date, 1927), MS-SS. Margaret Sanger, *Motherhood in Bondage* (New York: 1928). The files on this book in MS-LC contain numerous letters she wrote giving it away, as well as records on her royalties, dated Apr. 19, 1920, reflecting the poor sales. Anna Lifshitz to Noah Slee, Nov. 12, 1929, details the cost of remainders. For her initial optimism about the book, see M.S. to Françoise Lafitte Cyon, Aug. 16, 1928, MS-SS. For glowing reviews of the book, see Freda Kirchway in *The Nation* 127 (Dec. 12, 1928), and Katherine B. Davis to M.S., Jan. 23, 1929, MS-LC, which suggests she send it to President Hoover. It was also reviewed favorably in just about every major progressive publication of the day.

13: DOCTORS AND BIRTH CONTROL

1. *Autobiography*, pp. 290–297. M.S., "Clinics the Solution," *Birth Control Review* 4:7 (July 1920), pp. 6–7. M.S. to Samuel Untermyer, Dec. 31, 1920, asks his advice on whether the law must be changed before a dispensary license can be granted. There is no surviving response. Responses to Sanger's hospital questionnaire are detailed in a Jan. 1, 1923 memo marked "Birth Control

Clinical Research Department, Private, Confidential to Council Members only," MS-LC.

2. Transcript of the Evening Medical Session, First American Birth Control Conference, 1921, MS-SS, pp. 7–35, Meyer quote, pp. 32–33. For historical context, suggesting just how forthright and unusual this discussion was for its time, see Sophie D. Aberle and George W. Corner, *Twenty-Five Years of Sex Research: History of the National Research Council Committee for Research in Problems of Sex, 1922–47* (Philadelphia: 1953). The book speaks of the courage it took to sponsor sex research in 1921 and credits the birth control and feminist movements for helping to advance interest in and tolerance of the study of the physiology of sex. See especially p. 3. Also see Regina Markell Morantz, "The Scientist as Sex Crusader: Alfred C. Kinsey and American Culture," *American Quarterly* 29:5 (Winter 1977).

3. Janet F. Brodie, "Family Limitation in American Culture," doctoral dissertation, University of Chicago, 1982, p. 182. On the patent medicine trade, also see, for example, George Creel, "Poisoners of Public Health," *Harper's Weekly* 60:3028 (Jan. 2, 1915), pp. 4–6, and "Suffering Women," *Harper's Weekly* 60:3029 (Jan. 9, 1915), pp. 28–30. For examples of Lysol ads, see the *Ladies Home Journal,* 32:3 (Mar. 1915), p. 58; *LHJ* 36:7 (July 1919), p. 73; *LHJ* 42:9 (Sept. 1925), p. 136; and for the "Wearever Fountain Syringe," *LHJ* 32:2 (Feb. 1915), p. 31. The final quotes are from an ad in *McCall's* (July 1933), p. 85, cited in Norman Himes, *Medical History of Contraception* (Baltimore: 1936), p. 329. Ellen Chesler, Interview with Sarah Marcus, M.D., Schlesinger-Rockefeller Oral History Project, Schlesinger Library, Cambridge, Mass., p. 17; Dr. Marcus talks about the popularity of Lysol. Several physicians in the early 1920s complained that the *Birth Control Review,* in order to make money, also carried advertisements for some of these questionable products. See, ABCL Minutes for 1922, PPFA-SS. A discussion of the hazards of douching is also in *Moneysworth: The Consumer Newsletter* 5:5 (Dec. 9, 1974).

4. Transcript of the Evening Medical Session, First ABCL Conference, MS-SS. (The sterilization material is separate from the main body of the transcript, see esp. pp. 4–5.) On IUDs and abortion, see R. S. Siddal, M.D., "The Intrauterine Contraceptive Pessary—Inefficient and Dangerous," *American Journal of Obstetrics and Gynecology,* July 8, 1924, pp. 76–79; Maraget Sanger, *Happiness in Marriage* (Elmsford, N.Y.: 1969), pp. 210, 214, and also, David Kennedy, *Birth Control in America: The Career of Margaret Sanger* (New Haven: 1970), pp. 184–85 and Janet F. Brodie, "Family Limitation," p. 182. On Mary Halton and IUDs, also see James Reed, The *Birth Control Movement and American Society: From Private Vice to Public Virtue* (Princeton: 1984), p. 275.

5. Robert Latou Dickinson, M.D., "A Program for American Gynecology," Presidential Address to the American Gynecological Society, reprint from *The American Journal of Obstetrics and Gynecology* 1:1 (Oct., 1920). Also see Dickinson, "The Business of Preventive Gynecology," reprint from *The Long Island Medical Journal,* Jan. 1908, and "Office Gynecology," reprint from *Practical Lectures Delivered under Auspices of Medical Society of the County of Kings* (New York: 1925). The reprints are in the library of the New York Academy of Medicine. Dickinson analyzed his own case records in R. L. Dickinson and Lura Beam, *A Thousand Marriages: A Medical Study of Sex Adjust-*

ment (Baltimore: 1953). The papers of Robert Latou Dickinson are in the Countway Library of Medicine, Harvard University, hereinafter, RLD-CL. My thanks to James Reed for sharing his research on Dickinson with me. The best biographical information on Dickinson and the best analysis of his relationship with Sanger is in Reed, *Birth Control Movement,* pp. 143–80. Reed convincingly disputes David Kennedy's view that Sanger's erratic personality was to blame for the problems she encountered from the establishment medical community in New York, an interpretation which misrepresents the class and gender bias she endured and thus misreads her reluctance to compromise the autonomy of her clinic by acquiescing to medical authority. See Kennedy, *Birth Control,* pp. 172–217.

6. M.S. to Dorothy Bocker, Oct. 17, 1922; J.N.H.S. to Bocker, Jan. 1, 1923; Bocker's résumé, dated 1922; budget for Clinical Research Fund, Jan. 1 to Dec. 31, 1923, shows contributions from Chance and Straight, along with smaller donations that brought the total to almost $8,000; all in MS-LC. Also see Clinton and Janet Chance to M.S., Nov. 3, 1922, telegram, MS-SS. A memo dated Jan. 27, 1932, explains the choice of the Research Bureau name to circumvent the problem of a dispensary license, MS-SS. Also see Reed, *Birth Control Movement,* p. 113.

7. Dorothy Bocker, M.D., *Birth Control Methods* (New York: 1924), copy in MS-SS. Slee paid to print the report privately. Also see Bocker, "Summary of 2000 Cases Treated from Jan. 1, 1923, to 1924," MS-LC; Robert L. Dickinson, "Contraception: A Medical Review of the Situation," First Report of the Committee on Maternal Health of New York, *American Journal of Obstetrics and Gynecology* 8:5 (Nov. 1924), pp. 583–88; *The Question of Birth Control, Authoritative Medical Report on Birth Control Methods,* one in a series of fliers published by the National Catholic Welfare Conference, 1925, copy in MS-LC. In a response Margaret graciously thanked Dickinson for his interest but called his findings "tainted with bias." See *Birth Control Review* 9:1, (Jan. 1925), pp. 20–21. Also see Reed, *Birth Control Movement,* p. 115 and pp. 168–69.

8. Minutes of the Committee on Maternal Health for Dec. 7, 1923, Dec. 11, 1924, Dec. 10, 1925, Jan. 12, Mar. 9, and Mar. 12, 1926, and Oct. 11, 1927, cited in Reed, *Birth Control Movement,* pp. 172–75. R.L.D. to M.S., Nov. 6, 1929, and M.S. to R.L.D., Nov. 26, 1929, MS-SS. Beyond the rubber spring diaphragm, Sanger had also amassed a collection of other vaginal contraceptives made in Germany, which Dickinson coveted. She lent them to him when they became allies in 1929, and he published the first comparative study to appear in an American medical journal. For Kosmak's early views, see George W. Kosmak, M.D., "Birth Control: What Shall Be the Attitude of the Medical Profession Toward the Present-Day Propaganda?" *Medical Record* 91:17 (Feb. 1917), pp. 268–73.

9. Biographical material on Davis is from *Notable American Women, 1607–1950: A Biographical Dictionary,* edited by Edward T. James and Janet Wilson James (Cambridge, Mass.: 1971), pp. 439–41. On the early research work of the Bureau of Social Hygiene, also see Havelock Ellis, "The Sex Life of Married Women," *Birth Control Review* 7:10 (Oct. 1923), pp. 266–69. A detailed account of the Rockefeller contributions to birth control exists in the John D. Rockefeller, Jr. papers, Rocky RG 2 and 3.

The Rockefeller staff prepared extensive memos on the internal workings of the birth control movement in the 1920s and 1930s, including what appear to be quite accurate assessments of various institutional and personality conflicts. Sanger emerged as a favorite of the staff and of John D. Rockefeller, Jr., and his two wives, Abby Aldrich and Martha Beard Rockefeller.

See, for example, Katherine Bement Davis's memo for the Rockefeller staff on Sanger's request for funding, June 10, 1924; John D. Rockefeller, Jr., to Davis, June 17, 1924; Raymond Fosdick to John D. Rockefeller, Jr., June 13, 1924, and Rockefeller to Fosdick, June 17, 1924; Fosdick to R.L.D., July 17, 1924; memo on the American Birth Control League, Inc., Apr. 16, 1925; M.S. to K.B. Davis, "The Homestead, Hot Springs, Virginia," n.d. (1925); M.S. to Davis, Sept. 24, 1925, enclosing a request for up to $50,000 to fund an expansion budget, which was turned down. Also see Sanger to Davis, Oct. 11, 1926, and memos on the ABCL annual requests for funding prepared for the advisory group, dated 12/3/25, 12/9/26, n.d.(1927), and 12/13/28. Annual reports of the advisory committee show total levels of funding during these years in the $700,000 range, all of it in contributions of $10,000 or less. A memo dated Feb. 27, 1926, sets forth the principles of the advisory committee with the proviso that contributions to current expenditures not exceed 5 to 10 percent of the total budget. All in Rocky-RG2.

10. M.S. to Dorothy Bocker, Nov. 18, 1924; memo from Bocker to M.S., Nov. 24, 1924; M.S.to Bocker, n.d. (Dec. 1924); M.S. to George Kirchway, Esq., about Bocker, all in MS-LC. Journal entry for Jan. 1, 1925, MS-SS, refers to her shock over the "betrayal of trust."

11. Autobiographical material on Hannah Stone is in AS-Countway. The East quote is from E. M. East to M.S. Feb. 1, 1929, MS-LC (copy also in PPLM-SS). Also see M.S. to East, Jan. 29, 1929, PPLM-SS. Hannah Stone to M.S., Mar. 27, 1932, recounts the ordeal of her membership hearing before the Academy of Medicine, MS-LC. The quotes on her "torture" are from the lawyer Morris Ernst, written for a memorial at her death, Oct. 28, 1941, MS-LC.

12. Hannah M. Stone, "Report of the Clinical Research Department of the American Birth Control League for the Year of 1925," MS-SS. In 1976, I also found scattered reports of Stone's follow-up work in uncataloged historical materials at the Margaret Sanger Center of Planned Parenthood of New York City. Linda Gordon, *Woman's Body, Woman's Right: A Social History of Birth Control in America* (New York: 1976), pp. 312–13, criticizes the failure to do more casework through home visits without fully considering the commitment of resources such visits required.

On the medical session at the 1925 conference, see R. L. Dickinson, "The Birth Control Movement," *Medical Journal and Record* 125: 10 (May 18, 1927), and Hannah M. Stone, "Therapeutic Contraception," *Medical Journal and Record* 126:6 (Mar. 21, 1928), pp. 8–17. Newspaper coverage highlighted the fact that Margaret was not permitted to attend, because she was not a physician. See "Doctors in Shut Meetings," *The New York Times,* Mar. 30, 1925, 10:2.

13. Committee on Maternal Health Memorandum, Mar. 12, 1925; CMH memorandum, "Proposed Standards for Medical Direction of Clinical Research Connected with the American Birth Control League," Apr. 17, 1925; "Report of Conference of the Maternal Health Committee and the Clinic Committee of the American Birth Control League," Nov. 29, 1925, all in MS-LC. M.S. to

Adolf Meyer, May 28, 1925; C. C. Little to M.S., Oct. 26, 1925, and R.L. D. to M.S., Dec. 17, 1925, all in MS-LC. Also see Reed, *Birth Control Movement*, pp. 177–79.

14. CMH, Apr. 17, 1925, memorandum, MS-LC; "Report of the Sub-Committee to the Public Health Committee on the Medical Work and Clinic of the American Birth Control League," RLD-CL; and Kosmak to Dickinson, Feb. 16, 1925, both cited in Reed, *Birth Control Movement*, p. 177. A list of the official health indications for contraception is in "Report of Birth Control Clinical Research Bureau, January 1st 1929 to November 28th 1929," MS-SS. Early clinic policy on child spacing and on referring women exhibiting "no health reasons" or NHRs, as they were called, is in James Cooper to Hannah Stone, Aug. 28, 1928, and in an internal memorandum dated "4/16/28," which apparently came from Stone herself, though it is not signed, both in the uncataloged papers at the Margaret Sanger Center in New York. "Minutes of the Staff Meeting of the Clinical Research Bureau, Apr. 29, 1929," MS-LC, revisits the issue and says "it is up to the doctor to prove that she gave information in good faith."

Ella M. Hediger, M.D., to M.S., Apr. 22, 1928, MS-LC, complains that she had opened an office on West 9th Street to be convenient to the clinic but was not getting enough private patient referrals. Whatever the official policy, referrals continued to be made. A memorandum "To Staff Physicians," dated Oct. 3, 1932, and signed by Hannah Stone with an "O.K. M.S." at the bottom, reiterates the official prohibition on private referrals as a result of "recent infractions." A second memo from Stone, dated Nov. 12, 1940, and titled "Policy Regarding Referral of Patients," specifies that women should be referred back to their own private physician or to a local hospital clinic, or if neither exist, they were to be given the names of three doctors in their own neighborhoods. Both memos are in AS-Countway. Finally, see M.S. to Hannah Stone, June 26, 1929, MS-LC.

The willingness to treat patients exhibiting no health reasons became even greater during the Depression, when the clinic physicians were anxious to provide contraception on economic grounds. See Sigrid A. Brestwell (head nurse) to M.S., Nov. 10, 1932, MS-LC. By 1939, an official view was adopted that any married woman who wanted contraception should be given it, and to that end, "marital adjustment" was added to the list of health indications, and birth control was legitimized for its psychological benefit. See memorandum, "DOCTORS MEETING," May 31, 1939, uncataloged papers at the Margaret Sanger Center in New York City.

To understand just how threatened George Kosmak was by the specter of "socialized" medical services for women and children, one should know as well that his testimony at Congressional hearings in 1929 on the Sheppard-Towner Act helped defeat this pioneering legislation. See Sheila Rothman, *Woman's Proper Place: A History of Changing Ideals and Practices, 1890 to the Present* (New York: 1978), p. 151.

15. Dickinson's comments are in "England and Birth Control," notes made in 1926, RLD-CL, cited in Reed, *Birth Control Movement*, p. 177. Also see CMH minutes for Jan. 21, 1926 and Dec. 10, 1926, cited in Reed, *idem.* A transcript of the hearing before the Board of Charities on Jan. 15, 1926, is in MS-LC. Members of the panel were Lee K. Frankel, M.D., Wm. R. Stewart, M.D., and Richard J. Kevin, M.D. Their private comments to Michael M.

Davis, of the Rockefeller-funded Committee on Dispensary Development, which had endorsed the Dickinson-Sanger merger plan, are documented in the CMH minutes for Jan. 17, 1927, cited in Reed, *idem,* pp. 178–79.

16. "Annual Report: Birth Control Clinical Research Bureau," Dec. 1, 1929–Nov. 1, 1930, MS-SS. Also see, Marie E. Kopp, Ph.D., *Birth Control in Practice: Analysis of 10,000 Cases and Stories of The Birth Control Clinical Research Bureau* (New York: 1934). Various directories of staff nurses and doctors, all of them women and many of them also affiliates of local hospitals, are in MS-SS. A memo from Sanger to Hazel Zbrowskie, the administrator of the clinic, dated Feb. 2, 1935, directs her to advertise the availability of evening hours for working women, MS-LC. On Sanger's scrambling for funds, see M.S. to Edwin Embree of the Julius Rosenwald Fund and Embree to M.S., May 9, 1929, MS-LC. The clinic's $30,000 budget in 1928 was largely self-financing, with contributions of more than $500 to make up the small deficit coming from Mrs. Otto Kahn, Mrs. Thomas Cochran, Mrs. Henry Phipps, and an R. J. Caldwell. Rosenwald then personally pledged $1,000. The sale of the cultured pearls, the scheduling of an afternoon tea and other fund-raising initiatives are discussed in BCCRB Report of Board of Manager Meetings, Sept. 19, 1929, Dec. 2, 1929, June 11, 1930, MS-LC.

17. "Report of Birth Control Clinical Research Bureau, January 1, 1929 to November 28, 1929," MS-SS. Finally, see M.S., "Education and the Birth Control Clinic," unpublished manuscript, 1930, MS-LC.

18. "Raid Sanger Clinic on Birth Control—Dismissal Predicted," *The New York Times,* Apr. 16, 1929, 31:3. "Doctors Aroused Over Raid," *NYT,* Apr. 19, 1929, 27:2; "500 in Court to Aid 5 Seized at Clinic," *NYT,* Apr. 20, 1929, 21:6. Stories ran in the paper for more than a week, and regularly thereafter through the resolution of the trial and the demotion of Sullivan: "Doctors are Freed in B.C. Raid," *NYT,* May 15, 1929, 20:4–5. Also see "The Raid," *Birth Control Review* 13:5 (May 1929), p. 139. "The Raid," *BCR* 13:6 (June, 1929), p. 154, and editorial on p. 148 of the same issue; Margaret Sanger, "The Birth Control Raid," *The New Republic,* May 1, 1929, clipping in MS-LC. Finally see J. J. Goldstein to M.S. June 3, 1929, and M.S. to J. J. Goldstein, June 6, 1929, MS-LC; M.S. to Havelock Ellis, May 29, 1929, MS-LC; and M.S. to Juliet Rublee "Friday 26" (1929), MS-DC.

19. "Maternity Research Council Memorandum on Plan as made originally with Mrs. Sanger . . ." dated "9–17–29," MS-LC. Minutes of BCCRB Advisory Committee, Nov. 20, 1929, MS-LC. M.S. to R.L.D., Nov. 26, 1929, MS-LC. The extensive debate over the matter is chronicled in the following letters: Louise Bryant to M.S., Feb. 25, 1929; E. M. East to M.S., Mar. 29, 1929; John Favill to M.S., Mar. 14, 1929; Adolf Meyer to M.S., Mar. 14, 1929; M.S. to John B. Solley, Jr., M.D., Mar. 15, 1929; Ira. S. Wile to M.S., Mar. 15, 1929; Benjamin Tilton, M.D., to M.S., Mar. 27, 1929; Louise Bryant to M.S., July 17, 1929; M.S. to Adolf Meyer, Dec. 14, 1929; M.S. to Stuart Mudd, Dec. 31, 1929; Morris Waldman to M.S., Dec. 12, 1929, and M.S. to Waldman, Dec. 31, 1929, all in MS-LC. The Mudd quote is from Stuart Mudd, M.D., to M.S., June 30, 1929, MS-LC; the Sanger quote, from M.S. to Stuart Mudd, Oct. 17, 1929, MS-SS; and the Dickinson quote, from R.L.D. to "My Dear Doctor," Dec. 4, 1929, MS-LC. Also see R.L.D. to M.S., Dec. 4, 1929, and M.S. to R.L.D., Dec. 9, 1929, MS-LC.

20. John A. Hartwell, M.D., president of the New York Academy of Medicine to M.S., Dec. 20, 1929, and Sanger to Hartwell, Dec. 31, 1929, MS-SS; Hannah M. Stone to M.S., Jan. 12, 1930, MS-SS; Mary Macaulay to M.S., Jan. 31, 1930, MS-LC. "Excerpt from letter written to Mrs. Margaret Sanger by Linsly H. Williams, M.D.," Dec. 31, 1931, MS-SS. Linsly R. Williams, M.D., to M.S., May 23, 1932, MS-LC. The best summary of these events is in Ruth Topping, "File Memorandum: Action of New York Academy of Medicine in Relation to Birth Control," May 5, 1931, Bureau of Social Hygiene papers, Rocky-RG2. Also see Hannah M. Stone, M.D., "The NYAM and Birth Control," *Birth Control Review* 16:6 (June 1932), pp. 188–89.

21. On the initial dispute over the study, see "Marie Kopp Study: Summary of Controversy Over Funding and Attribution," n.d., MS-SS. Also, Ruth Topping "File Memorandum: BCCRB Report—Providing Mrs. Sanger with a Copy," Feb. 18, 1931, BSH, Rocky-RG2; M.S. to R.L.D., Oct. 5, 1933, and M.S. to H.E., July 15, 1933, MS-SS. Finally, see Marie E. Kopp, *Birth Control in Practice: An Analysis of 10,000 Cases of the Birth Control Clinical Research Bureau* (New York: 1934), foreword and pp. 1–47.

Another perspective on the Sanger–Dickinson relationship is in M.S. to Dr. Wells P. Eagleton, Nov. 29, 1932, MS-LC, previously cited. Sanger was apparently sufficiently accommodating to Dickinson that she asked him to speak in her stead before physicians who protested her presence at medical meetings. "You have done exactly the best and biggest thing—to fight on issues and principles and *not* on personalities," she wrote when her invitation was withdrawn. For Dickinson's change of heart on Sanger, see R.L.D. to M.S., Dec. 14, 1933, MS-LC; R.L.D., "Concerning Teamwork for Birth Control," memorandum to the directors of the American Birth Control League, Mar. 23, 1937, copies in MS-SS, and in the Norman Himes papers of the Countway Library of Medicine, Harvard, also cited in Reed, *Birth Control Movement,* p. 180. The final quote is from R.L.D. to M.S., May 20, 1942, MS-SS. Also see Dorothy Dickinson Barbour to M.S., n.d. (1950s, after her father's death), MS-SS.

14: A COMMUNITY OF WOMEN

1. Admonition to Sanger about the dangers of her leadership hold are in John Price Jones Corporation, "A Survey and Plan of Fund-Raising for the Birth Control Clinical Research Bureau and the National Committee on Federal Legislation for Birth Control," copies in MS-SS and MS-LC. See especially pp. 108–23. The report cost $3,500, which was paid by Noah Slee. Sanger's acid response to paying that amount, only to be told to step down, is in a note attached to her personal secretary's letter paying the bill. See Florence Rose to J.P.J. Company, Sept. 29, 1930, MS-LC.

2. M.S. to Francis Warren, Jan. 13, 1932, and M.S. to Marjorie Prevost, Mar. 28, 1932, both in MS-LC.

3. Sanger's own description of Stone is preserved in a handwritten eleven page Journal entry for July 14, 1941, the day following Stone's funeral, MS-SS, from which the quote is taken, and in a public statement that was included in "Hannah M. Stone—In Memoriam," *The Journal of Fertility* 6:4 (Aug. 1941), pp. 109–110, copy in MS-SS. An editorial from *The Nation,* July 26, 1941, also cited in this memorial volume, p. 112, provides additional perspective. Miscel-

laneous Sanger–Stone correspondence from the 1920s and 30s is in MS-SS. Only one letter suggests even a hint of any acrimony. On Apr. 1, 1930, Sanger complained to Stone that a recent publication of hers mistakenly listed the BCCRB as a division of the American Birth Control League and left off Sanger's name altogether. "I know you don't mean it," she wrote, "but it seems to me that it is time for us who are working together to come out and stick together and make no bones of where we stand." The mistake was never repeated. The Mary McCarthy quote is from *The Group* (New York: 1954).

4. Lena Levine's recollections are from her remarks in *Proceedings of the Birth Control and National Recovery Conference* (Washington, D.C. 1934):, p. 361, MS-SS. The Bruno recollections are from Regina Markell Morantz, "Interview with Gerda Bruno, M.D.," Lawrence, Kansas, 1976. Morantz shared the taped interview along with additional recollections of Bruno's that were not on the tape in a private letter to the author in 1976. Bruno, who fled the rise of anti-Semitism in Germany, did not deny that eugenic considerations underlay some of the support for the early birth control movement, but she insisted that Margaret Sanger was "different" and that overall, "humanitarian motives" predominated and masked any less benign impulses. A clinic "Doctor's List" for Sept. 1935 identifies fifteen employees including Stone and Levine. "Memo: to Mrs. Sanger from M.W.," Mar. 15, 1933, describes a visit to the clinic by Sophie Aberle, M.D., of Yale Medical School, who came in search of instruction for her students.

5. The Appel recollections are from my own interview with Cheri Appel, M.D., on Feb. 1, 1989, in Manhattan, the transcript of which is now at Smith. A Hunter College graduate, Appel was one of five women in her class at New York University Medical School in 1927. She went to work at the Women's Infirmary in Manhattan and then interned in gynecology at Morrisania Hospital in the Bronx. She was married to Benjamin Segal, M.D. Hazel Zaborowski, executive secretary of the clinic, to Dr. Cheri Appel, Feb. 21, 1936, arranges for her to return to work one day a week, after she has been absent having a baby of her own. Also see Macaulay's résumé, letters of recommendation, and her correspondence with Sanger, 1929–1931, all in MS-LC. The quotation is from an undated letter from England, apparently in 1931. Florence Rose, "Summary of Activities, Feb. 24, 1936," is in MS-SS. Additional Rose papers and correspondence are also collected under her own name at the Sophia Smith Collection, Smith College, hereinafter FR-SS. Finally, see "Lectures Arranged from N.Y. Office," Dec. 1, 1934, to Dec. 1, 1935, MS-SS and Cecil Damon to M.S., Aug. 3, 1936, MS-SS.

6. The Sanger correspondence with Marcella Sideri, 1928–1932, is in MS-LC, see especially Sanger to Sideri, May 26, 1931. Lini Fuhr to M.S., Jan. 12, 1936, MS-LC, is in a file that also contains an article on her return from Spain from *The Daily Worker,* May 20, 1937, and subsequent correspondence containing biographical information.

I have offered examples of satisfactory staff relations, in part to dispute the view of Sanger as an uncompromising elitist offered by Linda Gordon in *Woman's Body, Woman's Right: A Social History of Birth Control in America* (New York: 1976). Gordon is correct that Sanger favored vibrant, intelligent, and personally loyal staff, that she demanded a high level of dedication from them, and that she often drove them beyond reasonable endurance, but these are characteristic traits of impassioned reformers, and hardly seem deserving of unqualified condemnation. Gordon's further demand that the clinic ought to have been unionized is well-motivated but unrealistic. Certainly comparable health care and social work facilities had not begun to unionize either. See Gordon, *idem,* p. 329. In 1939, Sanger did agree to meet with a former employee of the American Birth Control League who was interested in organizing clinic labor. "I have always believed it wise to listen to complaints & I have never avoided expressing my own opinion re: unionization of labor & where such should apply," she wrote in M.S. to D. K. Rose, Mar. 25, 1939, MS-SS, making it clear that the clinic was not one of those places.

7. On BCCRB finances, John Price Jones Corporation, "Survey and Plan," copies in MS-SS and MS-LC. On the financial and organizational struggles of the ABCL and the NCMH (the Committee on Maternal Health went "National" in title after 1930), see Helen Payne to Miss Topping, Nov. 12, 1932, Bureau of Social Hygiene Memo, Rocky-RG2; annual memorandums on the ABCL funding requests for 1934, 1935, 1936, and 1937 in Rocky-RG2; Arthur Packard (head of the Rockefeller charitable staff), memos "To Files—NCMH (Conversation with Dr. Louise Bryant)," dated May 8, 1934 and July 9, 1934; and Raymond Fosdick to J. D. Rockefeller, Jr., Feb. 5, 1934, all in Rockefeller Archives, RG2. Also see NCMH, *A Statement of Its Programs and Needs, November, 1940,* pamphlet in the archives of the New York Academy of Medicine, and, finally, James Reed, *The Birth Control Movement and American Society: From Private Vice to Public Virtue* (Princeton: 1984), pp. 181–93.

8. Cost of house and discussion of the finances is in Minutes of the Board of Managers, BCCRB, Sept. 19, 1929, Dec. 2, 1929, June 11, 1930, June 12, 1930; and in J.N.H.S. to Mrs. Felix Fuld, Feb. 18, 1937, all in MS-LC. There is a discrepancy in the figures with the Slee letter citing $75,000 as the original purchase price, but I assumed the earlier figure to be more accurate. Description of the architecture is from Alexandra Howard, "Sanger House Faces Landmark Designation," *Our Town,* a local neighborhood paper, Sept. 24, 1976. Quotation is from M.S. to H.E., May 28, 1930, MS-SS. The Huxley speech was covered in stories in *The New York Times* and *New York Herald Tribune,* Oct. 29, 1930, clippings in MS-LC. Additional information comes from Charlotte Levine's interview, with the author, Nov. 18, 1987, Brooklyn, N.Y.

9. BCCRB Minutes of the Board of Managers, *idem,* 1930, 1931, MS-LC. BCCRB, Memo on Unemployment, Feb. 26, 1932, MS-LC. M.S. to H.E., Aug. 29, 1931. Ruth Topping to Mr. Dunham, Application from BCCRB, Feb 3, 1931, BSH, Rocky-RGII. M.S. to Dr. Abraham Stone, Mar. 30, 1950, mentions Noah's reticence about making the clinic's complete financial statements public. Certainly, its financial accounting was a good deal looser than would be required today. "Is Preventive Work the Next Step?" story in *Birth Control Review* 16:2 (Feb. 1932), pp. 42–43.

10. On fund-raising, compare the 1931 listing of the board of managers of the BCCRB with a memo titled "Status of Tentative Directorate," Jan. 11, 1932, and minutes of the original meeting of the new board of trustees, Dec. 21, 1931, all in MS-LC. Also see M.S. to Mrs. William K. Vanderbilt, Jan. 7, 1932, and M.S. to Charles Scribner, Feb. 22, 1932, MS-LC, in which she says that she will not cede authority to a board unless it is legally bound to assume financial and administrative responsibility for the clinic. Robert Dickinson to Dr. Linsly

Williams, Mar. 8, 1932, MS-LC, claims that the legal obligation was secured, and says that, while Sanger would remain on the board, she desired to withdraw from active participation. Dickinson was writing to secure Williams's help in recruiting a medical board for the clinic and may have wanted to understate Sanger's role. She does not seem to have become any less active in day-to-day operations until several years later. Finally, see Ruth Topping, BCCRB file memo, June 28, 1932, and "BCCRB-Reorganization Meeting, March 5, 1932"; Mr. Packard to files (on conversation with Raymond B. Fosdick about the BCCRB); Arthur Packard to Miss Anna Kelly (secretary to Mrs. John D. Rockefeller, Jr.) Dec. 6, 1932, and Nov. 14, 1932; John D. Rockefeller III to "Dear Father," Mar. 17, 1934; "Statement of Appropriations in the Field of Social Hygiene and Sex Research, 1929–1933"; and Mr. Packard to J.D.R. III, Dec. 19, 1936, all in Rocky-RG2. For a personal side to Arthur Packard's friendship with Sanger, also see Sanger's letter introducing him to Havelock Ellis, July 7, 1937, MS-SS. Also revealing are Anna Kelly to M.S., May 24, 1929, and M.S. to Mrs. J.D.R. Jr., Sept. 29, 1930, Nov. 19, 1931, Jan. 12, 1932, Oct. 21, 1933, and Jan. 3, 1935, all in MS-LC. The letter of 1933 has the abortion pitch.

Caroline Hadley Robinson, *Seventy Birth Control Clinics: A Survey and Analysis Including the General Effects of Control on Size and Quality of Population* (Baltimore: 1930), pp. 116–17, has the fund-raising reference. Gordon, *Woman's Body,* p. 313, wears the same blinders when she accepts Robinson's criticism of Sanger's fund-raising without qualification. Robinson (and Gordon) are correct, however, that the clinic was not receiving as many large foundation grants as it should have, although there were exceptions they may not have known about, such as the anonymous Rockefeller and Bureau of Social Hygiene support.

Finally, see M.S. to George A. Hastings, Feb. 22, 1938, and M.S., to "Dear Mrs. Generous," n.d. (1937), both in MS-SS.

11. Dickinson and Kopp, *Birth Control in Practice,* pp. 48–52, 56–57, 61, 109–23, 130. On the relationship of this data to New York City norms, see Norman Himes, *Medical History of Contraception* (Baltimore: 1936), p. 367. Median family income for the country overall had come back to $1,160 by 1935–36, but $2,500 still placed a family in the top tenth percentile. See Susan Ware, *Holding Their Own: American Women in the 1930s* (Boston: 1982), p. 2.

12. Dickinson and Kopp, *Birth Control in Practice,* pp. 58, 61. Also see Florence Rose memo, n.d., and Florence Rose to M.S., June 29, 1936, and "How to Establish a Birth Control Clinic," BCCRB, 1938, all in MS-SS.

13. Records of the Harlem clinic are divided between MS-SS and MS-LC. At Smith, see Harlem Clinic Annual Reports, Feb. 1931, Nov. 1932, and Nov. 1934; minutes of organizing meetings, May 20, 1931, June 17, 1931, Mar. 23, 1932, Oct. 25, 1932, and listing of advisory committee formed of local black leaders and physicians. At the Library of Congress: "Totals for Harlem Branch, Feb. 1–Nov. 1, 1930; M.S. to W.E.B. DuBois, Nov. 11, 1930 and Dec. 8, 1930; Dubois to M.S., Nov. 17, 1930; Dr. M. O. Bousfield (a black physician who inspected the facility) to Michael Davis (medical director of the Rosenwald Fund), Apr. 9, 1932; Dr. Lucien M. Brown, "Keeping Fit," clipping from the *Amsterdam News,* n.d. (1932), in which a black doctor argues the vital importance of birth control to achieving a "higher standard of physical fitness, mental

capacity, and financial stability"; and W. E. B. DuBois in *Negroes and Birth Control,* a pamphlet published by the Birth Control Federation of America (New York: 1939), MS-SS.

For the contrasting views of Marcus Garvey, I am indebted to Rebecca McKay, a student in my senior research seminar at Barnard College, 1988–89. Also see minutes of the Harlem Clinic Advisory Board for Oct. 18 and 25, 1932; press release on Sanger speech at Abyssinian Baptist Church, Dec. 7, 1932; Marie Levinson Warner (medical director of the clinic) to M.S., July 11, 1933; Florence Rose to "M.P." (Marie Pichel Levinson Warner), Jan. 31, 1936. The statistics are from Marie Warner, M.D., "Birth Control and the Negro," a four-year summary and progress report, paper delivered at a symposium, Birth Control and Depression Problems in Harlem in 1935, copy in MS–SS. On black fertility in Harlem also see Clyde V. Kiser, "Harlem Negroes," *Milbank Memorial Fund Quarterly* 13:3 (July 1935), pp. 273–85.

Bessie L. Moses, M.D., *Contraception as a Therapeutic Measure* (Baltimore: 1936), pp. 72, 82–83, also analyzed statistics on birth control practice by race. Twenty percent of the Baltimore clientele was black. Less than half of the total succeeded with the diaphragm regimen—a success rate even worse than in New York—yet Moses still maintained the virtue of her clinic experiment. She insisted that most of her patients were able to learn the diaphragm method, that only factors of "emotion"—a term that encompassed the patient's overall attitude toward sex—compromised their effectiveness. She saw no distinctions on the basis of race, intelligence, or income. She claimed, as well, that a marked "physical" and "emotional" improvement could be seen in all women who participated in the research for as long as one year, whether or not they managed the diaphragm, and thus endorsed clinical contraception in all circumstances, insisting that it be made a standard practice of preventive social medicine.

Recent analyses of black fertility patterns have confirmed Margaret's views, finding comparable numbers of desired children among black and white women, but demonstrating that fertility outcomes only remain greater for black women because so many first become pregnant as teenagers. See, for example, Harriet B. Presser, "The Timing of the First Birth: Female Roles and Black Fertility," *Milbank Memorial Fund Quarterly* 49: 3 (July 1971), pp. 329–61.

14. Regine K. Stix, M.D., and Frank W. Notestein, "Effectiveness of Contraceptive Practice in a Selected Group of New York Women," *Milbank Memorial Fund Quarterly* 12:1 (Jan. 1934), pp. 57–68, and Stix-Notestein follow-up study in *MMFQ* 13:2 (Apr. 1935), pp. 162–78. Stix and Notestein published the same findings and other research in book form in 1940. See Regine K. Stix, M.D. and Frank W. Notestein, *Controlled Fertility* (Baltimore: 1940). For the quoted material on her concerns about the book, see M.S. to Frank G. Boudreau, M.D., executive director of the Milbank Memorial Fund, June 25, 1940, uncataloged papers of the Margaret Sanger Center, New York City. Also see Reed, *Birth Control Movement,* pp. 204–10. At the height of his career in the 1950s, Notestein would serve as president of the Rockefeller-funded Population Council. See Chaps. 19 and 20.

15. Quote is from M.S. to Hannah Stone, Jan. 13, 1932, MS-SS. On BCCRB research and testing of simple methods and commercial contraceptive products, see, for example: "Statement to Commercial Concerns Who Offer New Con-

traceptive Devices or Materials for Trial and Error," signed by Margaret Sanger, director, and Hannah Stone, M.D., n.d. AS-Countway; M.S. to Hannah Stone, Feb. 2, 1932, MS-SS; Helen Holt, "Confidential Report to Members of BCCRB Advisory Council, Plan and Scope of Research, June, 1933," and Helen Holt, "The Spermicidal Powers of Commercial Contraceptives," Dec. 30, 1933; "Contraception and Birth Control," clipping of an editorial reporting on BCCRB tests of commercial products in *Journal of the American Medical Association,* Sept. 8, 1934, all in uncataloged papers, Margaret Sanger Center, NYC. Examples of her concern over specific products are in M.S. to Mrs. Post, manager, Peck & Sterba Company, n.d., and in various letters to and from Herbert Simonds, the owner, and a Mr. Hicks, the general manager, of Holland-Rantos Co., Inc., on the occasion of its twentieth anniversary in 1944, all in MS-SS. Also see M.S. to Mr. Ralph Hull, Sept. 24, 1931, regarding a vaginal irrigator he invented, MS-LC; M.S. to Ira S. Wile, M.D., July 6, 1933, and L. J. Cole, Ph.D. to M.S., Oct. 21, 1933, comment on Holt's research plan, both in MS-SS. Finally, see selected minutes of medical staff meetings, for example, Mar. 27, 1934, and Oct. 29, 1941, and memo from Hazel Zabrowski to M.S., "Drugstore Contraception," May 10, 1935, all in MS-SS. Again, Gordon in *Woman's Body,* pp. 308–10, leaves the impression that the clinic only recommended the diaphragm, which is not true, as these materials, along with the Dickinson–Kopp study and the Stix–Notestein data, make clear.

16. For additional information on Gamble and his career, see Reed, *Birth Control Movement,* pp. 225–46. A clipping of a reprint of the Editors of *Fortune* magazine, *The Accident of Birth,* 1938 pamphlet, is in MS-SS. T. Lane Moore, U.S. General Services Administration, National Archives and Records Service, to the author, Sept. 24, 1975, describes the results of a search of the indexes of the *Federal Trade Commission Decisions, Finds, Orders and Stipulations* for the 1930s. Also see Elizabeth Garrett, "Birth Control's Business Baby," *The New Republic* 77 (Jan. 17, 1934), pp. 269–72. Commercial exploitation did not end with the Depression. See Grace Naismith, "The Racket in Contraceptives," *American Mercury* 71:319 (July 1950), pp. 3–13; and Christopher Tietze, M.D., *The Condom as Contraceptive,* 1963 publication of the National Committee on Maternal Health, copy in the library of the New York Academy of Medicine. Locally, the Sanger clinic also had to be wary of disreputable practitioners who tried to capitalize on its reputation and name. See, for example, Josephine Franklin to Planned Parenthood Federation of America, Oct. 2, 1945, regarding a facility on East 12th St. listing its name as the Birth Control Association, AS-Countway.

17. Memoranda, n.d., "Registered Clinic Patients" and "Non-Registered Clinic Patients," Margaret Sanger Center, NYC. BCCRB Memorandum, "Medical Policy, April 29, 1929," MS-LC; State by State Statistics on Abortion and Maternal Mortality in 1930, prepared for the National Committee on Federal Legislation for Birth Control, MS-LC; 1933 data gathered by Fred J. Taussig, M.D., in Helena Huntington Smith, "Wasting Women's Lives," *The New Republic,* Mar. 28, 1934, reprint in MS-SS; Regine K. Stix, M.D., "A Study of Pregnancy Wastage," *Milbank Memorial Fund Quarterly* 13:4 (Oct. 1935) pp. 347–65; Memo re: "Policy Regarding Aschheim Test," Oct. 18, 1932, signed "M.S.," AS-Countway; M.S. to Hannah Stone, Jan. 30, 1933; "Special Consultation Bureau, Monthly Reports, April 1, to May 4, 1933, and January, 1934," MS-LC.

Hannah Stone, "The O. D. Clinic: An Analysis of 450 'Overdue' Cases," unpublished manuscript, n.d., Margaret Sanger Center, NYC; minutes of medical staff meeting for Nov. 1, 1938, re: A–Z tests, MS-SS. Cheri Appel, M.D., in her interview, Feb. 1, 1989, says she knew nothing of this abortion study but confirmed that many women who came to the clinic had been aborted or were pregnant, and that some things that went on at the clinic were "sub-rosa."

18. The letter from Marjorie Prevost to M.S., Feb. 10, 1932, is in MS-SS. Dr. Appel (whose husband may have been the "Dr. Seigel" referred to) did not remember the incident. Memo, "Policy Concerning Over-Due Patients," signed by Hannah Stone, one with n.d. and one dated Nov. 12, 1940, are both in AS-Countway.

Mary Compton to M.S., Apr. 14, 1942, reports the story of the social worker, who also said that one of the doctors actually gave a woman $20 to pay the fee of an illegal abortionist. Also see Compton to M.S., Dec. 8, 1942, both in MS-SS. The case history is also cited in Gordon, *Woman's Body,* p. 382, which claims without substantiating evidence that this was an exception, and that the clinic turned away most abortion requests. Gordon did not consult the Countway archive or the uncataloged Sanger Center papers in New York, so she was not aware of Stone's data, which demonstrates that almost half the requests for abortion in the period studied were, in fact, accommodated directly, all of them presumably through licit professional channels. On the basis of the one letter, Gordon also says that the BCCRB practiced a double standard of abortion referral—one for the worthy middle-class and another for the poor. She makes this claim because Prevost was explicitly elitist in characterizing the client as someone trustworthy on the basis of her appearance. Gordon is correct that Sanger and many clinic personnel had social biases, but any class distinctions in their abortion referrals were probably less a function of overt discrimination than of the obvious need for caution in getting involved in something so controversial. That middle-class women could afford to pay the price of arrangements made privately with sympathetic physicians may also have been a factor. What happened to those who could not pay anything at all is less clear. Charlotte Levine admits that, at least when she arrived at the clinic in 1959, the doctors quietly provided the names of cheaper, illegal abortionists as well. Levine's testimony is taken from her interview with the author, Idem. Elizabeth Arnold, R.N., in her interview with James Reed for the Schlesinger Library Oral History Project, Nov. 13, 1974, p. 57, said she saw thousands of pregnant women during her seventeen years on the clinic staff and "hustled" them to psychiatrists or to known abortionists.

The Sanger clinic relationship with the New York Clergy Consultation Service on Abortion was explained by Arlene Carmen in a Jan. 1976 interview with the author conducted for the Oral History Project on Women in Population, the Schlesinger Library, Radcliffe College, pp. 27–29. Carmen ran the service on behalf of Judson pastor, the Rev. Howard Moody, who founded it.

On the Planned Parenthood Federation of America's abortion policies, see Harriet Pilpel to D. Kenneth Rose, Apr. 3, 1942, and Mary Calderone, M.D., to Alan Guttmacher, M.D. (then the organization's president), Dec. 8, 1960, both in the Mary Calderone Papers, Schlesinger Library. I am grateful to Harriet Pilpel for a personal interview at her New York office in February of 1986, in which she recalled having first heard of Margaret Sanger as a girl, when birth control first stirred controversy in the North Bronx community in which she grew up.

19. Marie Kopp, *Birth Control in Practice: Analysis of 10,000 Cases and Stories of the Birth Control Clinical Research Bureau* (New York: 1934), p. 40, 145–47, 172. Also see Hannah Stone, "The Vaginal Occlusive Pessary," *Practice of Contraception: The Proceedings of the Seventh International Birth Control Conference* (Baltimore: 1930); and Hannah Stone, "The Birth Control Clinic, Some Problems in Procedure," an apparently unpublished manuscript in MS-LC, which discusses the relative merits of questioning women about their sex lives. For a brief time, the sex questions were dropped because they embarrassed many patients, but they were quickly restored in the belief that effectiveness with contraception was impossible for those with major sexual anxieties.

The quote from Helen S. Isaacson is in a condolence letter to Abraham Stone, Aug. 1941, AS-Countway. The McCarthy incident is from *The Group*. Other examples of unhappy client mail include Helene Simon to M.S., Mar. 28; Anna E. Nash to M.S., May 2, 1929; Mrs. Harry H. Revelle (the upside-down user) to M.S., Sept 28, 1931, and M.S. to Revelle, Oct. 12, 1931, all in MS-LC. These complainants received cordial responses.

20. Kopp, *Birth Control in Practice*, pp. 101–103. For comparable data on sexual behavior drawn from questionnaires, see R. L. Dickinson and Lura Beam, *A Thousand Marriages, A Medical Study of Sex Adjustment* (Baltimore: 1953), pp. 438–42. Also see Hannah M. Stone, M.D., and Henriette Hart, "Contraception and Mental Hygiene," *Mental Hygiene*, 17:3 (July 1933), pp. 417–23.

Lewis Terman in *Psychological Factors in Marital Happiness* (New York: 1938) downgrades the emphasis of sexologists on sex factors in marital happiness, yet, at the same time, confirms the Stones' findings about frequent inability to reach orgasm among women. Terman's point is that he found just as many happy couples among the sexually maladjusted as there were unhappy ones among the sexually compatible.

21. Abraham Stone, "Presidential Address to the American Association of Marriage Counselors, May 26, 1950," copy in AS-Countway. On the controversy over premarital instruction, see R. L. Dickinson, "Premarital Examinations as Routine Preventive Gynecology," *American Journal of Obstetrics and Gynecology* 8:5 (Nov. 1928), p. 631. On the issue of whether rupturing the hymen should be "comme il faut" for doctors with patient authorization, see Marjorie Prevost to M.S., Nov. 23, 1931, MS-LC.

22. Ralph P. Bridgeman, "Guidance for Marriage and Family Life," *Annals of the American Academy of Political and Social Science* 160 (Mar. 1932), pp. 144–62. Abraham Stone, M.D., "Presidential Address to the American Association of Marriage Counselors, 1950," p. 1; "The First Ten Years of The American Institute of Family Relations, A report from the Board of Trustees;" "Margaret Sanger Research Bureau Marriage Consultation Service," typescript, n.d., all in AS-Countway.

Blank examples of the marriage consultation service case record, also in the Stone papers at Countway, show that, although a history of hereditary diseases was taken for each patient, the emphasis was on medical, sexual, and social factors that affected the individual directly, the latter including economic status, housing conditions, etc.

23. For a succinct summary of their views, see Hannah Meyer Stone, M.D.,

and Abraham Stone, M.D., *A Marriage Manual: A Practical Guide Book to Sex and Marriage* (New York: 1935), esp. pp. 18–27, and Hannah Stone, "Marital Maladjustments," *The Cyclopedia of Medicine, Surgery and Specialties* (Philadelphia: 1940), pp. 820–29, copy in MS-SS.

24. Hannah Stone, M.D., "Marriage Counseling: Marital Problems and Adjustments As They Arise in Birth Control Clinics," remarks at the Conference on Birth Control and National Recovery, Washington, D.C., Jan. 17, 1934, copy in MS-SS. Freud's commentary is in "Three Essays on Sexuality," in Sigmund Freud, *Collected Papers* (London: 1940), pp. 219–35.

25. Stone and Stone, *Marriage Manual,* esp. pp. 203–33, "The Art of Love." Also see Hannah Stone, M.D., and Abraham Stone, M.D., "Sexual Disharmonies," unpublished manuscript in AS-Countway, esp. proposed chapters "Frigidity in Modern Woman," "Female Orgasm," and "Premature Ejaculation." This highly technical manuscript on female orgasm, evidently intended for a professional audience, was never completed for publication.

26. Stone and Stone, *Marriage Manual,* Chaps. 1, 2, 3, 5, and 7, and quotation on p. 206. Also see Abraham Stone, M.D., "The Case Against Marital Infidelity," *The Reader's Digest* (May 1954), copy in AS-Countway. Alfred C. Kinsey et al., *Sexual Behavior in the Human Female* (Philadelphia: 1953); and Regina Markell Morantz, "The Scientist as Sex Crusader: Alfred C. Kinsey and American Culture," *American Quarterly* 29:5 (Winter 1977), p. 573. On sexual counseling technique, see "Margaret Sanger Research Bureau, Marriage Counseling, Group Sessions," Transcripts for Oct. 1946 through Jan. 1947, in MS-SS. Also, Abraham Stone, M.D., and Lena Levine, M.D., "Group Therapy in Sexual Maladjustment," *American Journal of Psychiatry* 107:3 (Sept. 1950), copy in MS:SS.

I have cited these transcripts at length because they form the basis of Linda Gordon's indictment of the Sanger Bureau's marriage counseling on the grounds that it tended to victimize unhappy women, and thus exemplified the abandonment of Sanger's commitment to female autonomy and the transition of birth control from a female to a family-centered institution. Although I share some of Gordon's criticisms of the actual sex counseling, I have attempted to offer a more complex and, I believe, more accurate reading of what actually transpired in these sessions. The question of how representative these group sessions really were must also be raised. Finally, it may be worth pointing out that, although the counseling was done under Sanger's official auspices and she obviously bore responsibility, it appears that she only knew of the group experiment after the fact. See "Memo to Mrs. Sanger from Dr. Stone via Compton re: marriage counselling service," May 10, 1947, MS:SS. There is no response from Sanger in the files.

27. Profit and sales data and information on legal entanglements are referenced in correspondence between Lincoln Schuster and Abraham Stone, in AS-Countway. See, for example, L.S. to A.S., Sept. 30, 1941, Jan. 19, 1942, Sept. 20, 1944. The book was declared unmailable by the post office in 1941.

28. On the popular critique of marriage and sexual advice literature, see Jean L. Block, "Are Those Marriage Manuals Any Good," *Cosmopolitan* (Oct. 1948), pp. 42–43, 136–40; "Love & Marriage: By the Book," *Time* (June 28, 1963); "Sex Manuals: How Not To," *Newsweek,* Oct. 18, 1965, pp. 100–01, clippings in a file on marriage manuals, Kinsey-Bloomington. Ironically, the

Newsweek piece quoted Dr. Mary Calderone, then medical director of the Planned Parenthood Federation of America. Also see Betty Friedan, *The Feminine Mystique* (New York: 1963). The final quote is from Helena Huntington Smith, "They Were Eleven," profile of Sanger in *The New Yorker* 6:20 (July 5, 1930), pp. 23–24.

15: LOBBYING FOR BIRTH CONTROL

1. Helena Huntington Smith, "They Were Eleven," profile in *The New Yorker* 6:20 (July 5, 1930); *My Fight.* On beginning to write the book, also see M.S., Journal, July 23, 1930, MS-SS, and Guy Moysten to M.S., Jan. 31, 1930. Sanger had apparently written asking for advisory and editorial help on a "history" of birth control. Instead Moysten urged a "personal chronicle"—all she had done in a purely "objective way" with "no compulsion to weigh facts." Ellis made the same observation in H.E. to M.S., Nov. 18, 1930. Finally, see M.S. to H. de S., Aug. 4, 1930, MS-LC. My observations on the autobiography are informed by the insightful views of Carolyn Heilbrun, *Writing Women's Lives* (New York: 1988).

2. Review clippings are in MS-LC. See especially, Mary Ross's review in the *New York Herald Tribune*, "Books," Sept. 27, 1931; Mary Beard in the *Saturday Review of Literature,* Nov. 2, 1931, and assorted clippings from *The New Republic,* Nov. 11, 1931; the *New York Post,* the *Philadelphia Inquirer,* the *New Haven Journal-Courier,* and *The New York Times,* Sept. 28, 1931, 26:1. Ellis's views are in H.E. to M.S., Aug. 25, 1931, and Oct. 13, 1931, MS-LC. For Sanger's distress about de Selincourt, see M.S. to H.E., Nov. 28, 1931, MS-SS, H.E. to M.S., Dec. 14, 1931, and M.S. to H. de S. Oct. 30, 1931, MS-LC.

3. Sanger's 1931 dinner speech is in MS-SS. Wells's transcribed quotation was used as a salutation for a dinner honoring Margaret on the occasion of her receiving the medal of the American Woman's Association. Also see, H. G. Wells, Apr. 11, 1932, MS-LC. Sanger's private description of the dinner is in M.S. to H.E., Nov. 28, 1931, MS-SS. Also see Ruth Topping, "Social Notes on H. G. Wells Birth Control Dinner," Bureau of Social Hygiene Papers, Rocky-RG2; and "Wells Dinner in New York," *The New York Times,* Oct. 18, 1931, clipping in MS-LC. *NYT* also covered the AWA dinner and Wells's tribute, Apr. 21, 1932, 23:3, and ran an editorial in praise of Sanger, headlining her as a "Gentle Crusader," Apr. 10, 1932, Sec. 9, 2:8. Linda Gordon, *Woman's Body, Woman's Right: A Social History of Birth Control in America* (New York: 1976), p. 328, uses the dinner as an example of Sanger's wholesale conversion to snobbish pretense.

4. M. W. Dennett to M.S., Feb. 15, 1930, and M.S. to M.W.D., Mar. 4, 1930, MS-SS; National Committee for Federal Legislation for Birth Control, hereinafter NCFLBC, "Transcript of Middle Western States Conference on B.C.," Columbus, Ohio, Nov. 12, 1929, discussion with Yarros on p. 14, MS-SS; John Price Jones Corporation, "A Survey and Plan of Fund-Raising, for the Birth Control Clinical Research Bureau and the National Committee on Federal Legislation for Birth Control," copies in MS-SS and MS-LC. On the ABCL's refusal to support Sanger or give her access to its membership files, at a board meeting of Dec. 12, 1929, see resignation resolution of the New Jersey

Birth Control League, Jan. 1, 1930; and M.S. to Annie G. Porritt (ABCL secretary), Jan. 20, 1930, MS-LC.

On the continuing ill-will, see M.S. to Annie G. Porritt, Jan. 2, 1930, MS-LC; M.S. to Mrs. F. Robertson Jones, Dec. 8, 1930, and Eleanor Dwight Jones to Mrs. Edward A. Norman, Jan. 2, 1931, both in MS-SS and both examples of the manner in which the two women continued to undercut each other's priorities and solicit support for their respective organizations, at the other's expense. On the identity confusion caused by the existence of competing birth control entities, see, for example, Howard Knight to M.S., Mar. 13, 1931, MS-LC, when the league and Margaret competed over who would have a booth at the National Conference of Social Work. The league's formal endorsement of Sanger's bill is in Mrs. F. Robertson Jones to M.S., telegram, n.d. (1930) in NA-MS, Sen. 71, A-E 1, Washington, D.C. However, "Aims of the American Birth Control League," a statement dated Sept. 13, 1933, PPFA-SS, is one of many documents that never even mentions birth control legislational, although it does commit the organization to advocating "the enactment of laws for the sterilization of certain classes of persons with incurable hereditary defects." The situation improved when Ruth Topping became executive director of the league in 1933. See, for example, Mrs. Louise deB. Moore, chairman of the executive committee, to Mrs. Edward Cornish, Mar. 6, 1935, MS-SS, which urges support of Sanger's bills. Margaret was not invited to the league's Carnegie Hall rally in 1935, which did make front-page news. See, "A Night That Will Make History," *Birth Control Review* 3:4 (new series) (Dec. 1935), copy in MS-SS.

Once again, I have gone over this controversy in some depth to explain its substantive, as well as personal, dimension, since the narrative of these events in David Kennedy's *Birth Control in America: The Career of Margaret Sanger* (New Haven: 1970), makes it seem that Sanger's intemperate ego was the critical issue in the dispute, which is unfair.

5. On the Slee tax appeal, see M.S. to Messrs. Covington, Burling & Rublee, Aug. 1, 1926; Newell Ellison to M.S., June 25, 1927; J.N.H.S. to Messrs. Covington, Burling & Rublee, May 22, 1928; Ellison to J.N.H.S., enclosing a new petition on the 1926 case, July 3, 1928; M.S. to Messrs. Covington, Burling & Rublee, Aug. 1, 1928, and their response of Aug. 2; Ellison to J.N.H.S., Oct. 9 and Oct. 18, 1928; Penelope Huse to M.S., Oct. 24, and Nov. 30, 1928; Ellison to J.N.H.S., Mar. 6, 1929; Ellison to M.S., Mar. 24, 1930; Ellison to Walter I. Willis (Slee's son-in-law and a vice president at 3-in-One Oil), Jan. 15, 1930, and Willis's response, Mar. 19, 1930, all in MS-LC. The size of Noah's settlement is mentioned in M.S. to Juliet Rublee, Oct. 1 (1930), MS-DC. The matter got press attention in "Birth Control," *Time* 13:11, Mar. 13, 1929, pp. 36, 38. The ABCL tried again unsuccessfully to gain not-for-profit status in 1937 by distinguishing itself from Sanger's group. See memo dated Oct. 15, 1937, MS-SS. Ironically, Margaret was finally able to establish the tax exempt status of her own New York clinic the following year. See John R. Kirk, deputy commissioner, U.S. Treasury Department, to "Birth Control Clinical Research Bureau, c/o Greenbaum, Wolff and Ernst," Oct. 24, 1938, MS-LC.

6. On women in the early years of the Depression, see Susan Ware, *Holding Their Own: American Women in the 1930s* (Boston: 1982), esp. the introduc-

tion, pp. xii–xiii, and pp. 1–5. Also see "Report of Interview with Secretary of the Interior, Ray Lyman Wilbur," May 5, 1930, MS-SS.

7. The qualifications were meant as a salvo to social conservatives and as a rebuke to the more socially minded among the bishops, such as Margaret's correspondent of years back, Dean William Inge, whose vocal support of Malthusian arguments appeared to his colleagues to elevate considerations of individual and social need over fundamental moral laws governing family life. The Lambeth Conference resolutions are cited in John T. Noonan, Jr., *Contraception: A History of Its Treatment by the Catholic Theologians and Canonists,* 2d ed. (Cambridge, Mass: 1986), p. 409. The resolutions and subsequent events in England received front page newspaper coverage in America. See, for example, coverage of an address on birth control by the Archbishop of Canterbury, in *The New York Times,* Nov. 16, 1930, clipping in MS-LC.

8. The textual quotations are from the "Report of the Federal Council of the Churches of Christ in America," which appeared as "Birth Control: Protestant View," *Current History* (Apr. 1931), and was then reprinted as a flier distributed by Sanger's committee, copy in MS-SS. Also see "Memorandum on the revised Social Ideals of the Churches and the Action on Birth Control by the Quadrennial Meeting of the Federal Council of Churches at Indianapolis, Dec. 8, 1932," MS-SS, and Committee on Marriage and the Home, Federal Council of the Churches of Christ in America, *Moral Aspects of Birth Control: Some Recent Pronouncements of Religious Bodies,* 1938 pamphlet, copy in MS-SS. As an example of endorsement, see "Resolution Passed by the General Council of the Congregational and Christian Churches in Seattle, Washington, at Its Meeting June 25 to July 3, 1931," MS-SS. Conservative Jews joined their Reform brethren in 1934; see "Statement of United Synagogue of America," Feb. 27, 1934, MS-SS. The matter got front page coverage. See "Council of Churches Hold Birth Control Morally Justified," *The New York Times,* Mar. 26, 1931, 56:5–6, and later "Hails Church Move for Birth Control," *NYT,* Apr. 15, 1931, 56:2. On Sanger's role, see Worth M. Tippy to M.S., June 24, 1931; M.S. to Tippy, June 30, 1931; Tippy to M.S., July 1, 1931; M.S. to Frances Ackerman, July 1, 1931; M.S. to George Blumenthal, Oct. 29, 1931; M.S. to Tippy, Nov. 5, 1931; Amelia Wyckoff (for Tippy) to M.S., Nov. 30, 1931; Tippy to M.S., Feb. 27 and Nov. 22, 1933; L. Foster Wood to M.S., June 7, 1934, and Jan. 10, 1935; M.S. to Wood, Jan. 21 and Feb. 16, 1935, June 15, 1937, Jan. 5, 1939, Feb. 4, 1940, all in MS-LC.

9. The Sanger quote is from stories in the *New York World-Telegram* and the *New York Herald Tribune,* Mar. 21, 1931, clippings in MS-LC. Ellis's remark is in H.E. to M.S., Apr. 9, 1931, MS-LC. On the Episcopalians, see M.S. to Bishops of Episcopal Church, Dec. 3, 1934, MS-SS; Hazel Moore to M.S., "Year of the Bishops, 1934 Episcopalian Convention," MS-LC; and "Church to Retain Canon on Divorce—Birth Control Also Before Bishops," *The New York Times,* Oct. 16, 1934, 28:2. On the Lutherans, see Alan Graebner, "Birth Control and the Lutherans: The Missouri Synod as a Case Study," *Journal of Social History* 2:4 (Summer 1969), pp. 309–32.

Kennedy's interpretation of these events differs substantially from my own. He does not give Sanger as much credit as she deserves for influencing the report of the Committee on Marriage and the Home, and, in turn, asserts that her treatment from Protestants was little better than from Catholics, which is true only of conservative denominations, a critical distinction. He then emphasizes the controversial nature of the committee's document to the point of losing sight of its enormous public impact as a statement of liberal thinking. See Kennedy, *Birth Control,* pp. 154–71.

10. *Commonweal,* Apr. 1, 1931, p. 589. Pius XI, *Casti Conubii: On Christian Marriage* (Washington, D.C.: 1931); and Arthur Versmeersch, "Annotationes" (on the encyclical *Casti Conubii*), cited in Noonan, *Contraception,* pp. 426–27. Also see Kennedy, *Birth Control,* pp. 150–51, and Lucy Freibert, "American Catholics and the Rhythm Method from the 1930s to the 1960s," paper delivered at the Berkshire Conference on the History of Women in America, Bryn Mawr College, June 1976, pp. 6–9. Dorothy Dunbar Bromley discusses the significance of the encyclical in *Catholics and Birth Control: Contemporary Views on Doctrine* (New York: 1965), p. 1.

11. Noonan, *Contraception,* pp. 120 and 438–44. The Ryan quote is from John A. Ryan, "The Moral Aspects of Periodical Continence," *Ecclesiastical Review* 89 (1933), p. 29, also cited in Noonan, *idem,* p. 443. For an opposing view on the legitimacy of rhythm, see William F. Montavon to Hatton Sumners, chairman, Committee on the Judiciary, U.S. House of Representatives, Jan. 23, 1934, MS-LC. On the impact of the encyclical, see "Pius XI Condemns Trial Marriage, Divorce and Birth Control," a front page story in *The New York Times,* Jan. 31, 1931, along with clippings from other papers in MS-LC. Also see Ernest R. Groves, "The Family," *American Journal of Sociology* 36:6 (May 1931), p. 997.

12. Noonan, *Contraception,* p. 443. Leo J. Latz, M.D., *The Rhythm of Sterility and Fertility in Women* (Chicago: 1932), quotations consecutively from pp. 119, 128, and 131. Also see, *The Big Problem of MARRIED PEOPLE Solved,* circular advertisement for Latz, *The Rhythm,* copy in MS-SS.

Hannah Stone conducted preliminary research at the clinic in 1936 and could identify only one women in 150 who experienced a regular menstrual cycle over the course of a seven month investigation. Her preliminary data on rhythm is in "Safe Period Calendars (Preliminary Report)." By the 1950s, however, the clinic took a more favorable view and actually set up a Rhythm Service. See, "Description of Special Service Established at Bureau, April, 1959." Both documents were in MS-NYC uncataloged papers, now in MS-SS. Finally, see Freibert, "Rhythm Method," and, on the AMA and rhythm, Kennedy, *Birth Control,* pp. 210–11.

13. For the Hayes view see Canon Valere Coucke and James J. Walsh, *The Sterile Period in Family Life* (New York: 1933); and Noonan, *Contraception,* pp. 443–44. Pope Pius XII, *Moral Questions Affecting Married Life: The Apostolate of the Midwife* (New York: 1951), esp. pp.13–15. For John Ryan's views on rhythm, see his lecture notes, "Rhythm of Fertile and Infertile Periods," pp. 13–23, in JR-CU.

14. Transcript of Organization Meeting, NCFLBC, Columbus, Ohio, Nov. 12, 1929; "Proceedings, Western States Conference on Birth Control and Population Problems," Los Angeles, Feb. 20–23, 1930, both in MS-SS; "Report on Maryland," Feb. (probably 1930), MS-LC; Katharine Hepburn to M.S., Apr. 3, 1930, MS-LC. Memo, "Federal Contributions: 1929–31" and *Autobiography,* p. 429, tell the Viola Kaufman story, MS-SS, as does M.S. to Juliet Rublee, Jan. 9, 1932, MS-DC. "Outline of Birth Control Legislation" prepared for Congress

in 1931, MS-LC, identifies state-by-state organizational progress to that point. Other NCFLBC organizational documents, identifying state-by-state progress are in MS-LC and MS-SS. Ida Timme to Mrs. Willard V. King, Convent, N.J., Feb. 24, 1930, is an example of organizational outreach. Also see *Autobiography,* pp. 415–30.

15. Mrs. Walter Timme to Mrs. William K. Vanderbilt, Oct. 24, 1929, and accompanying mailing list for $1,000 letter; Felix Warburg to Mrs. Walter Timme, Feb. 11, 1930, all in MS-LC. "Birth Control Unit Plans $100,000 Fund," *The New York Times,* Jan. 11, 1930, 9:4. Ruth Topping, file memorandum, "Interview with Mrs. Sanger," Apr. 16, 1931, and R. Topping to Mr. Dunham, "Application from Committee on Federal Legislation, Mrs. Sanger, Chairman," Oct. 2, 1931, Rocky-BSH papers; funding memoranda on National Committee on Federal Legislation for Birth Control, Dec. 26, 1934, Nov. 1, 1936, Dec. 11, 1936 and NCFLBC Treasurer's Reports, Nov. 1, 1935, and Oct. 31, 1936, all in Rocky-RG2. John D. Rockefeller, III also gave $500 personally in response to an appeal by mail, but would not allow his or his wife's names to be used. See J.D.R. III to Arthur Packard, Aug. 16, 1934; J.D.R. III to J.N.H.S., Dec. 10, 1935, and Blanchette Rockefeller to Mrs. Harriman, Feb. 6, 1935, MS-LC. Another example of where Sanger was turned down for money to lobby but funded for the clinic is in M.S. to Julius Rosenwald, Apr. 6, 1931, M.S. to Ed Embree, president of the Rosenwald Fund to M.S., April 18, 1931, and M.S. to Julius Levin of the fund, June 29, 1932, all in MS-LC. The quotes are from Mrs. Walter Timme to "My dear Mrs.," general letter, n.d., MS-LC. Timme replaced Frances Ackerman, Sanger's original treasurer at the American Birth Control League, who died in 1934. In the fall of 1933, Margaret engaged Tamblyn & Brown, a professional fund-raising firm, to help, and expanded her goals. See John Brown to M.S., Oct. 7, 1933, MS-LC. Finally, see *Autobiography*, p. 429.

16. *The Readers' Guide to Periodical Literature* 1925–28, pp. 236–37; 1929–32, pp. 240–41; 1933–35, pp. 217–18. Also see Gloria Moore and Ronald Moore, *Margaret Sanger and the Birth Control Movement: A Bibliography, 1911–1984* (Metuchen N.J./London: 1986), pp. 63–92. Assorted clippings on birth control activity and Senate hearings in February and March of 1931 include the *New York Herald Tribune,* May 24, 1931, the *Brooklyn Eagle,* May 1, 1931, *The New York Times* and *New York World-Telegram,* May 18, 1931, all in MS-LC.

17. Katharine Houghton Hepburn to M.S., Mar. 1, 1929; M.S. to Mrs. Thomas Hepburn, Nov. 6, 1929, Dec. 11, 1933, Jan. 26, 1934; M.S. to the young Katharine Hepburn, Jan. 25, 1934, and Hepburn to M.S., Jan. 25, 1934, all in MS-LC. Also see, "Katharine Hepburn," *Current Biography* (New York: 1969), pp. 209–11 and Christopher Anderson, *Young Kate* (New York: 1988). On the influence of the movies, see Ware, *Holding Their Own*.

18. NCFLBC, "Endorsing Committee of 1,000," Summary Report, Nov. 1, 1933 to June 1, 1934; Annual Report for Nov. 1, 1934–Oct. 1, 1935, both in M.S. to Arthur Packard, Oct. 12, 1935, Rocky-RG2. Resolutions from Easton, Pa., and elsewhere, all in MS-LC. Sanger's *Autobiography* claims that, when the committee folded in 1937, organizations representing 12 million people had endorsed it, see p. 430. Eighteen drawers of file cards record the range and breadth of individual and institutional endorsements nationally, MS-LC. So

strong was the emphasis on field organization that the Washington headquarters closed for the half of the year that Congress was out of session, both to save money and to augment the field operation. See, M.S. to Hazel Moore, telegram, June 8, 1933, MS-LC.

This analysis disputes Linda Gordon's claim that Sanger ignored mass organization in favor of the mobilization of elites. The two were not mutually exclusive. See Gordon, *Woman's Body,* p. 328.

19. M.S. to "Dear Friend of Our Cause," Apr. 29, 1932; unknown (signature unclear) to "Margaret Sanger, Dear Friend," May 9, 1932; and Mrs. Geraldine Kish to M.S., Apr. 22, 1936, all in MS-SS. For an assessment of Sanger's mail, see Application to the Elmhurst Foundation, n.d. (probably 1933), MS-SS.

20. Dorothy Brush, manuscript for "Impressions of Margaret Sanger," in "Our M.S," 1957, p. 3, Dorothy Brush Papers, Sophia Smith Collection, hereinafter DB-SS.

21. Moore résumé and Hazel Moore to "Dear Girls," n.d. "The Day After the Day" (1932); M.S. to "To Whom it May Concern," May 13, 1939, an enthusiastic letter of reference for Moore, remarks on her "courage, sincerity, integrity of purpose and boundless perseverance," all in MS-LC.

22. Recollection of these early incidents is in NCFLBC, Annual Report, Nov. 1, 1934–Oct. 1, 1935, p. 8, copy in Rocky-RG2. Quotation is from Heywood Broun, *New York Herald Tribune,* Oct. 15, 1930, clipping in MS-LC.

23. Mrs. Donald McGraw to Katharine Hepburn, Feb. 28, 1930; Katharine Hepburn, "Outline of Report of Legislative Chairman," New York, Apr. 24, 1930.

24. U.S. Congress. Senate. Subcommittee of the Committee on the Judiciary, *Birth Control, Hearings on S. 4582,* 71st Cong., 3d sess., Feb. 13–14, 1931, esp. pp. 2–7 and 76–83; "The Mother's Bill of Rights." U.S. Congress. Senate. Subcommittee of the Committee on the Judiciary. 71st Cong., 3d sess., Feb. 13, 1931, statement by Margaret Sanger, NCFLBC reprint; clippings from *Congressional Digest,* 10:4 Apr. 1931, pp. 97–116; lists of speakers and endorsements of the Gillett Bill, including medical societies, women's clubs, junior leagues, social and child welfare associations, settlement houses, religious associations, and the American Civil Liberties Union; lobbying memos and logs from Feb. to Dec. 1931, all in MS-LC. The NCWC testimony in opposition, dated Feb. 13, 1931, and a statement by William Green, president of the AFL, Feb. 17, 1931, are in MS-LC. A copy of the bill and evidence of the testimony and mail in opposition is also in MS-NA. See especially M.S. to Frederick Gillett, regarding a Dr. Henry Cattell's statement about "Sanger Pro-Tex Tubes," Feb. 20, 1931, and Mrs. Randolph Frothingham to Hon. George W. Norris, Feb. 26, 1931. The first quotes are from "Bill to Legalize the Importation and Dissemination of Contraceptive Literature and Devices," *Commonweal* 13, Mar. 4, 1931, p. 479, and Michael Williams, "The Religion of Death," *Commonweal* 15 (Dec. 30, 1931), pp. 234–36. The last quotes are from M.S. to Ida Timme, Dec. 10, 1931, MS-LC. Finally, see M.S. to the Hon. George W. Norris, Nov. 17, 1942, MS-LC, a letter filled with praise for all the help he had given her, written on the occasion of his defeat.

25. U.S. Congress. House. Committee on Ways and Means, *Birth Control: Extracts from Hearings on H.R. 11082.* 72d Cong., 1st sess. Also quoted in

Kennedy, *Birth Control,* p. 234. U.S. Congress. Senate. Subcommittee of the Committee on the Judiciary. *Birth Control, Hearings on S. 4436,* 72d Cong., lst sess., May 12, 19, 20, 1932, M.S. to Kate Hepburn, Jan. 12, 1932, and M.S. to Ida Timme, Dec. 10, 1931, MS-LC. Also see coverage in *The New York Times,* May 13, 1932, 40:5–6, and May 20, 1932, 11:2, and Robert S. Allen, "Congress and Birth Control," *The Nation* 134:3476, Jan. 27, 1932, p. 104.

26. For the significance of these rulings and an argument for achieving social change through the courts and not the legislature, see Morris L. Ernst to M.S., Dec. 9, 1931, and Jan. 28, 1932, along with Morris L. Ernst, "How We Nullify," *The Nation* (Jan. 27, 1932), both in Ernst files in MS-LC; and also Kennedy, *Birth Control,* pp. 246–48. On the legal status in the states: "Proceedings of the American Conference on Birth Control and National Recovery, Jan. 15–17, 1934, Washington, D.C.," p. 49, MS-SS. On Sanger's strategy: M.S. to Kate Hepburn, Jan. 12, 1932, and Col. J. J. Toy to M.S., Dec. 10, and Dec. 12, 1931, all in MS-LC. M.S. to Mrs. Jessie Ames Marshall, June 1, 1934, rearticulates her position on the educational value of fighting.

27. A résumé is in James Joseph Toy to Adelaide Pearson (secretary of the NCFLBC), Dec. 18, 1931. Toy offered to help with the promise that he would first sell off his entire interest in an Ohio company manufacturing spermicidal jellies, but there at first remained concern that he was using his position in the field to advance his own products. He apparently then earned Margaret's trust, however, and she agreed to pay him $200 a month for three months. See telegram from Sanger to Toy, dated Nov. 17, 1931. Also see J. J. Toy to M.S., Sept. 21, 1931, Oct. 26, 1931; Dec. 11, 1931, Jan. 6, 1931 (actually 1932), Jan. 21, 1932; M.S. to J. J. Toy, Oct. 20, 1931, Oct. 29, 1931 (telegram), Dec. 16, 1931, Jan. 13, 1932, Feb. 22, 1932, Oct. 7 and 20, 1932, and Jan. 19, 1932, all in MS-LC.

Toy's transcriptions of his interviews with William F. Montavon, legal representative of the NCWC, and Edward F. McGrady, lobbyist for the AFL, on April 13, 1932; and with John A. Ryan and Dr. J. J. Mundell, on Apr. 15, 1932, all in MS-LC, chronicle the allegedly confidential discussions that led to the legislative redraft.

28. *Hearings on S. 4582,* 1931. Margaret Sanger, "The Pope's Position on Birth Control," *The Nation* 134:3473 (Jan. 27, 1932), p. 103.

29. Transcript of Toy interview with John A. Ryan and J. J. Mundell, Apr. 15, 1932, MS-LC; Noonan, *Contraception,* pp. 422–23. On Ryan's differences with the hierarchy, also see Leo H. Lehmann, *The Catholic Church in Politics,* reprint by Birthright Inc. of articles that appeared in *The New Republic,* Nov. 16 and Dec. 21, 1938; and Francis Lyons Broderick, *Right Reverend New Dealer, John A. Ryan* (New York: 1963). On his relations with Roosevelt, see Franklin Roosevelt to Very Rev. John A. Ryan, Sept. 1, 1932; Ryan to Raymond Moley, Nov. 29, 1932; Ryan to FDR, April 19, 1933; Louis Howe to Ryan, April 7, 1933; FDR to Ryan, Sept. 24, 1935 and especially, FDR to Ryan, Jan. 7, 1937, inviting him to give the benediction at his inaugural. All in JR-CU.

30. W. F. Montavon to J. J. Toy, May 2, 1932, MS-LC; "Copy of Statement of Edward F. McGrady Before a Subcommittee of the Judiciary Committee of the United States Senate," May 12 and 20, 1932, MS-SS. Mrs. F. Robertson Jones to Mrs. Thomas A. McGoldrick (quoting the testimony), Oct. 27, 1932, MS-LC. Morris L. Ernst to Florence Rose, May 2, 1932, and M.L.E. to M.S.,

May 9, 1932, MS-LC. I uncovered no documentation of these meetings in the Ryan papers at Catholic University. The archive does contain Ryan's testimony. See "Economic and Social Objections to Birth Control," Statement by Dr. John A. Ryan, May 19, 1932, JR-CU. Ryan was also an active member of the American Civil Liberties Union, and a friend of Roger Baldwin. He opened his testimony on the defensive, insisting that the bill extended beyond reasonable limits on freedom of speech.

Readers of my presentation of these events, who are familiar with David Kennedy's discussion of the same material in *Birth Control,* his biography of Sanger, will once again find considerable discrepancy of fact and interpretation. Kennedy refuses to concede that Sanger made any effort at all toward compromise. On page 268, for example, he cites a 1932 letter from Morris Ernst urging conciliation without ever mentioning that she did indeed follow Ernst's advice. Earlier, on pp. 236–37, in his otherwise detailed text, he relegates his account of the private meetings with Father Ryan and his emissaries to a footnote, but nonetheless attacks Sanger alone for torpedoing what he characterizes unfathomably as this Catholic gesture toward compromise. Offering no information on the resolution of the meetings, however, he cannot explain why she alone was at fault. He simply condemns her failure to comprehend the moral principles at stake and neglects to mention the dramatic change in Catholic doctrine on natural methods of contraception underway at this juncture. By not considering this development, he fails to acknowledge its inevitable impact on the larger public policy controversy. What's most curious about this oversight is that earlier in his text, on p. 210, he does credit the significance of rhythm as a medical development in the 1930s.

31. NCWC, "The Question of Birth Control: A National Menace," n.d. (1933). A copy of this circular accompanies an affidavit from a stenographer at the Clinical Research Bureau in New York who said that, on Feb. 2, 1933, she had been given the circular by a man named T. J. Hillis, who identified himself as a former socialist, and said his son-in-law was studying at Fordham University. He had been told, he said, that 30,000 letters would be written by Catholics to every member of the Judiciary Committee to protest birth control and showed her a copy of a solicitation for such protests, dated Jan. 30, 1933; all in MS-SS. For an example of the opposition mail, see Margaret McGuire, president, San Francisco County Council of Catholic Women, to Hon. Henry F. Ashurst, chairman, Judiciary Committee, U.S. Senate, Mar. 2, 1934, *SEN A-E 1,* NA-MS. Also see "The Birth Control Racket," *Commonweal* 16:6, (June 8, 1932), pp. 141–42, and "Editorial Comment," *Catholic World* 135 (July 1932), pp. 480–87. On the New York incident, see Rev. Worth M. Tippy, press release dated Mar. 26, (1933), MS-LC. Also see Margaret Benson (executive director of the American Birth Control League) to Dr. George J. Ryan (president of the Board of Education) Mar. 19, 1935, in which Benson condemns Dr. Marie Warner of the clinic for exhibiting bad taste by going beyond a general discussion and actually demonstrating how the diaphragm works with the help of a diagram. The letter was reprinted in local newspapers and elicited a vituperative response from Margaret, who accused Benson of "disloyalty to the cause" and of washing her "soiled linen in public." See M.S. to Benson, Mar. 29, 1935, both in MS-SS. Finally, the Celler conversation is reported in "Notes to Margaret Sanger from Guy Irving Burch," Jan. 20, 1935, MS-LC.

16: SAME OLD DEAL

1. Stuart Sanger to J.H.N.S., Nov. 14, 1929, and Oct. 5, 1931, describe the stock purchases and advise him not to sell his seat on the exchange. On the purchase and loss of the seat, also see M.S. to H.E., Feb. 23, 1932, and for more on the bottoming out of their finances, M.S. to H.E., Mar. 12, 1933, MS-SS. The developing acrimony between Noah and his son is chronicled in their correspondence during the winter of 1931–32, all in MS-SS. Relations had, in fact, been strained between them since 1924, when Jim Slee left 3-in-One Oil and went on his own to Wall Street because his father refused to grant him a salary increase. An affidavit dated May 26, 1938, signed by Noah Slee and witnessed by Grant Sanger, makes reference to an agreement of July 24, 1929, just before the crash, in which Noah had lent his son $438,000 for investment purposes, in MS-SS. Lincoln Slee was described by Stuart Sanger as a "drifter," whom Slee never had much to do with, author's interview, Mar. 19, 1986. Grant Sanger had similar memories in an interview of Dec. 18, 1987.

2. M.S. to H.E., n.d. (1930), M.S. to J.N.H.S., from London, n.d. (sometime in the summer of 1930).

3. On her capacity to make him feel involved in her life through her well-narrated letters, see M.S. to J.N.H.S. Jan. 1931, from Pittsburgh; Apr. 10, 1932, from New York City; and miscellaneous letters postmarked Marienbad, Villa Serena, Italy, Paris, etc., Aug. 8, 14, 20, 22, 29, Sept. 3, Sept. 20, 1932, MS-SS.

4. On a typical marital evening in Feb. 1932, see M.S. to H.E., Jan. 31, 1932, MS-SS. Slee's penurious supervision of the accounts is exemplified in correspondence with Adelaide Pearson in Washington in 1930 and '32 and with Stella Hanau, in 1935 and '36, (especially an unsigned memo, probably from Pearson, dated June 8, 1932), all in MS-LC. Also see Florence Rose to J.N.H.S., Apr. 23, 1931. For one among many of Margaret's thank-yous for his gifts, see M.S. to J.N.H.S., June 28, 1934, MS-SS.

5. M.S. to Françoise Cyon, Dec. 28, 1932, MS-SS.

6. Minutes of 1928 ABCL Annual Meeting record Eleanor Roosevelt as an active member, PPFA-SS; newspaper clippings on Eleanor and birth control include a Heywood Broun column in the *World-Telegram,* Feb. 1, 1933; "Mrs. FDR Assailed by Priest on Birth Control," *Chicago Tribune,* Aug. 16, 1932; "Roosevelt v. Roosevelt," *San Francisco News,* Nov. 27, 1931; and editorial in *New World,* which appears to be a Catholic publication in Chicago, Dec. 4, 1931, all in MS-LC. Mrs. Roosevelt's refusal to discuss B.C. in an interview is reported in Hazel Moore to M.S., n.d. (1935 from Atlantic City), MS-LC. Finally, see "Worse than any "Ism," *Catholic World* 149 (Aug. 1939), pp. 513–16.

7. M.S. to H.E., Nov. 29, 1932, MS-SS; M.S. to Mrs. Thomas Hepburn, Jan. 6, 1933, MS-LC; Marvin McIntyre to M.S., Apr. 20, 1933, Presidential Papers, Franklin Delano Roosevelt Library, Hyde Park, N.Y., hereinafter "FDR Papers." The McIntyre letter bears a buck slip with the designation, "for President's approval." H.L. Hopkins to M.S., Aug. 1, 1933, MS-LC. Hopkins still wouldn't lend his name in 1942: M.S. to Harry Hopkins, Apr. 9, 1942, MS-SS. Elinor Morgenthau to M.S., Nov. 4, 1933, MS-SS. Even after Roosevelt won a third term in 1940, Samuel Rosenman still claimed it would be "out of place"

for him to attend, or even send greetings to, a birth control dinner, though he did request an autographed copy of Margaret's latest book. See M. S. to Samuel Rosenman, Oct. 3, 1941; Rosenman to M.S., Oct. 8, 1941; Rosenman to Florence Rose, Oct. 16, 1941; and Rose to Mrs. Albert Lasker, Oct. 22, 1941, which includes the citation Sanger put in his copy of her book: "To Samuel Rosenman whose courage and vision helped us to fight the fight. My life-long gratitude." Mrs. Ickes' support is noted in "Birth Control's It," *Time,* Feb. 18, 1935, clipping in MS-LC.

8. M.S. to H.E., Dec. 3 and Dec. 30, 1933, MS-SS.

9. Alan Brinkley, *Voices of Protest: Huey Long, Father Coughlin and The Great Depression* (New York: 1983), pp. 100–101. Robert E. Sherwood, *Roosevelt and Hopkins: An Intimate History (New York 1948),* p. 25, p. 37. Joseph P. Lash, *Eleanor and Franklin* (New York: 1970). (Lucy Mercer Rutherford, with whom Roosevelt had had an earlier affair, renewed her acquaintance with him while he was President and was present at his death.) Also see David J. O'Brien, *American Catholics and Social Reform: The New Deal Years* (New York: 1968). One hundred thousand women were employed by the Civilian Works Administration by the end of 1933.

10. Hearings on H.R. 5978, pp. 61–66, 151–52; David Kennedy, *Birth Control in America: The Career of Margaret Sanger* (New Haven: 1970), pp. 238–39. "The Federal Hearing," *Birth Control Review* 1:6, Mar. 1934, p. 2. Cardinal Hayes is discussed in Worth M. Tippy to Stella Hanau, Dec. 10, 1935, MS-LC. Also see "The Gods of the Machine," *Commonweal* 23:9 (Dec. 27, 1935), pp. 225–26, in which Hayes attacks birth control as a Malthusian tool of "mechanized, materialistic industry": and John A. Ryan, "Fallacious Arguments of the Birth Controllers," *Catholic Action,* 16:4 (Apr. 1934), pp. 9–11, 23. Warren S. Thompson and Pascal K. Whelpton, "The Population of the Nation," in *Recent Social Trends,* Vol. 1, makes the argument against restrictive birth control legislation. On women in the 1930s, and particularly during the critical year 1933–34, see William H. Chafe, *The American Woman: Her Changing Social, Economic, and Political Role, 1920–1970* (New York: 1972), pp. 43–65; Susan Ware, *Holding Their Own: American Women in the 1930s* (Boston: 1982), pp. 16, 66–67, 104–105, which has marriage and birth data, and also Susan Ware, *Beyond Suffrage: Women in the New Deal* (Cambridge, Mass.: 1981), pp. 43–67. Linda Gordon, *Woman's Body, Woman's Right: A Social History of Birth Control in America* (New York: 1976), p. 310, condemns Sanger for abandoning feminist arguments at this time but fails to consider the context in which she had to operate.

11. The Guy Burch quote is from G.I.B. to Dr. Arthur J. Barton, Chairman of the Southern Baptist Convention, Jan. 23, 1934, MS-SS. The ABCL quote is from Margaret Lee Woodbury, "A Plea for the Middle Class," *Birth Control Review* 1:9 (June 1934), p. 5.

The first idea for a proposed merger of the American Eugenics Society and the American Birth Control League is discussed in a memorandum dated Mar. 2, 1933, which cautions that the foundations of eugenic thinking are weak because the mechanisms involved in the transmission of heredity are insufficiently understood, PPFA-SS. On the ultimate capitulation of eugenicists to the birth control argument, see *Practical Eugenics: Aims and Methods of The American Eugenics Society,* a 1938 pamphlet, copy in PPFA-SS, esp. p. 12; and minutes of the Conference on Eugenics and Birth Control of the American Eugenics Society, Jan. 28, 1938, PPFA-SS. Also see Arthur Packard to files, "American Eugenics Society," Feb. 3, 1938, in Rocky- RG 2. Several prominent eugenicists nonetheless continued to inveigh against birth control propaganda, saying that it did more harm than good. Henry Fairfield Osborn began to espouse what he called "birth selection" over indiscriminate control. See H. F. Osborn, "Birth Selection vs. Birth Control," *Forum,* 88:2 (Aug. 1932), pp. 79–83, a report on his address to the Third International Congress of Eugenics in New York.

Gordon, *Woman's Body,* pp. 303–313, once again distorts Sanger's eugenicism at this juncture, as does a present-day reading of it from the point of view of the New Right: George Grant, *The Legacy of Planned Parenthood* (Brentwood, Tenn.: 1988), esp. pp. 87–101. My thanks to Molly Ivins for this reference.

12. "Proceedings of the American Conference on Birth Control and National Recovery," Jan 15–17, 1934, Washington, D.C. See especially, "Opening Remarks" by Prof. Henry Pratt Fairchild, p. 9; responses from Sanger and Rachelle Yarros, pp. 40–45; remarks by Rabbi Sidney Goldstein of New York, pp. 76–79; remarks by Lydia Allen DeVilbiss, M.D., p. 286; and closing speeches by Sanger, Charlotte Perkins Gilman, and Prof. William McDougall of Duke University, pp. 446–74. Also see press release, Dec. 31, 1933, and "Resolution to the President of the United States," Jan. 17, 1934, in MS-SS; and "Summary of the American Conference on Birth Control and National Recovery," MS-LC. The Bossard quote is from "The New Public Relief and Birth Control," *Birth Control Review* 1:8 (May 1934), p. 1, an excerpt of his conference speech. Roosevelt's responses are in M.S. to Marvin McIntyre, Jan. 8, 1934; M.M. to M.S., Jan. 13, 1934, and Jan. 18, 1934; and M.S. to M.M. April 19, 1934, all in FDR papers. Press coverage included the following: "Will Link Recovery with Birth Control: 500 Leaders in Medicine, Education and Religion Will Confer at Capitol, Jan. 15–17," *The New York Times,* Jan. 7, 1934, 21:4; "See Birth Control as Recovery Need," *NYT,* Jan. 16, 1934, 6:6; "Ask Roosevelt Aid for Birth Control," *NYT,* Jan. 18, 1934, 28:5; "Birth Control: Capital Has Bill to Repeal Comstock Law," *News-Week* 3:27, Jan. 1934, pp. 28–29. The final quote is from Ettie Rout to Hazel Moore, Jan. 27, 1934, MS-SS. Also see, Mary S. Lovell, *The Sound of Wings: The Life of Amelia Earhart* (New York: 1989).

13. Gordon, *Woman's Body,* p. 315, acknowledges the validity of Sanger's disappointment with the New Deal, but claims without evidence that the overall impact of her lobbying effort was to aid the right-wing opposition to Roosevelt. On the other hand, Gordon admits that most birth controllers identified themselves as New Dealers, and that public opinion still largely identified Sanger as a rebellious figure, not as a conservative. Gordon simply does not account for the incongruity in her analysis.

14. A summary of Coughlin's statements in Jan. 1934 is in MS-LC. Also see Mrs. Leo Schmitt to M.S., Mar. 25, 1934, MS-SS, which tells the sad story of not being able to feed her five starving children, debunks Coughlin's arguments and simply says: "Tell him for me, he is all wet!" By contrast, a single letter in opposition to Sanger survives in the Roosevelt Presidential papers, charging that "it is nearly only the ignorant & the colored women who does (sic) not follow this wicked advice." See Lydia Paquette (of Alabama) to FDR, Sept. 13, 1936,

FDR papers. M.S. to Westbrook Pegler of *World Telegram,* Feb. 14, 1940, congratulates him for claiming that the government and press had been treating Coughlin too gently for too long and for encouraging a full investigation of his relationship to a group believed to be a Nazi front organization in the United States, MS-LC. Also see, Brinkley, *Voices of Protest,* pp. 119–26.

15. For the change of public posture, compare "Mrs. Sanger Assails Birth Control Ideas," *The New York Times,* Feb. 7, 1933, 3:3, to Margaret Sanger, "Catholics and Birth Control," *The New Republic,* 79:10 (June 13, 1934), p. 129. Also see Anne Wheaton to M.S., Apr. 17, 1932, MS-LC; M.S. to Mrs. Oakes Ames, Feb. 14, 1934; Leo J. Latz, M.D., to Mrs. Oakes Ames, Feb. 24, 1934; Karl A. Crowley, solicitor, U.S. Post Office Department, to Mrs. Blanche Ames, May 2, 1934; Frederick A. Ballard to Mrs. Oakes Ames, all in BA:SS. And finally, Morris Ernst to Florence Rose (secretary to Sanger), Oct. 3, 1935, which recounts his inquiries in late 1933 on this matter, MS-LC. The direct Sanger quotes are from *Excerpts From the Rhythm of Sterility and Fertility in Women,* pamphlet issued by the NCFLBC, n.d., MS-SS. On Roosevelt and Coughlin, see Brinkley, *Voices of Protest,* pp. 131–32. On Ryan's efforts to blunt Coughlin's influence see Francis Broderick, *Right Reverend,* pp. 213–214. Roosevelt received an honorary degree from Catholic University in 1933.

16. U.S. Congress. House. Committee on the Judiciary. *Birth Control Hearings on H.R. 5978.* 73d Cong., 2d sess., 1934, pp.6–9, 230–39. Wm. F. Montavon to Hon. Hatton W. Sumners, chairman, Committee on the Judiciary, U.S. House of Representatives, Jan. 23, 1934, and M.S. to Hatton Sumners, Mar. 6, 1934, MS-LC. M.S. to I. Van Meter of *Time,* Feb. 12, 1934, MS-LC. "The Federal Hearing," *Birth Control Review* 1:6 (Mar. 1934), p. 2. The final quote is from M.S. to Mrs. Oakes Ames, Feb. 6, 1934, BA-SS.

17. U.S. Congress. Senate. Committee on the Judiciary. *Birth Control Hearings on S.R. 1842.* 73d Cong., 2d sess., Mar., 1, 20, 27, 1934, especially pp. 149–75. Hazel Moore, Memorandum, "June 13th—year of the Devil and Roman Catholic—1934," copies in MS-SS and MS-LC. Also see John O'Donnell and Doris Fleeson, "T'was Legal, for 5 Minutes to Talk of Birth Control," *The New York Daily News,* June 15, 1934, clipping in MS-LC.

18. On the Nassau incident, see M.S. to J.N.H.S., Mar. 21, 1933, from aboard ship to Nassau, and "Saturday Evening 2/33," from Nassau (actually Mar. 1933), both in MS-SS. Her recollection of the incident is from M.S. to Lawrence Lader, Mar. 29, 1954, MS-SS.

19. Biographical information is from a clipping of the MacDonald obituary in the *Orange County Review,* Orange County, Florida, Feb. 23, 1961, (where he moved with his second wife), MS-SS. Also see notes on a conversation about MacDonald with John Muller of Bridgehampton, N.Y., May 10, 1963, MS-SS. Quotes from M.S. to A.M., Aug. 23 and Sept. 4, 1933, and from A.M. to M.S., Sept. 29, 1933, all in MS-SS. M.S. to A.M., Feb. 2, 1934, talks of deceiving Noah and guests about flowers that arrived at her house and Nov. 26, 1937, speaks of champagne; M.S. to J.N.H.S., May 24, 1934, mentions the private papers, also all in MS-SS.

20. A.M. to M.S., Sept. 12, 1949, Aug. 19, 1951, MS-SS.

21. See especially M.S. to J.N.H.S., Sept. 18, 1933, May 24, 1934, June 28, 1934, n.d. (Fall 1934, headed "R.F.D.Box 276"), May 6, 1935, "Christmas 1935" and Feb. 1, 1936, all in MS-SS, though there are many other communi-

cations in the Sanger-Slee file for these years, which also support the generalizations made here. M.S. to Havelock Ellis, Oct. 23, 1933, MS-SS, has the particulars on the house in Washington and M.S. to H.E., July 3, 1934, and Dec. 7, 1934, help establish the chronology for that year.

22. The suffrage analogy is mentioned in Elizabeth M. Lappin to Arthur Packard, June 18, 1934, Rocky-RG2. On the endorsements, see "YWCA Endorses Birth Control Legislation," in *Birth Control Review* 1:9 (June 1934) and Dorothy Dunbar Bromley, "Clubwomen, Doctors Back Birth Control," the *New York Mirror,* June 13, 1935, clipping in MS-SS. The educational reach of the clubwomen is evident in "Social, Economic and Health Aspects of Birth Control: An Outline Designed for Group Study," a document prepared to guide women's club discussions of birth control and distributed nationally in 1937 and 1938. It included a prepared speech for use by program chairwomen, praising the birth control advocates, copy in MS-SS. Also see memo, "The National Committee on Federal and State Contraceptive Legislation," Dec. 26, 1934, and Prentiss Willson, M.D. to Arthur W. Packard, Nov. 2, 1934, both in Rocky-RG2. The final quote is from Susan B. Francis, R.N., president of the American Nurses Association, conveyed in a memo from Florence Rose to M.S. "Re: National Convention of American Nurses Association, Los Angeles, June 21, 1936," MS-SS.

23. Copies of "Family Planning, A Radio Talk By Margaret Sanger," Apr. 11, 1935, are in MS-LC and MS-SS. Correspondence includes the material quoted from Edna M. Graff to M.S., Apr. 11, 1935, MS-SS, and from James J. Mohen and Frank J. Seuferling, Astoria, N.Y., Apr. 15, 1935, MS-LC.

24. H. G. Wells, "Franklin Delano Roosevelt," in W. Warren Wager, ed., *H.G. Wells: Journalism and Prophecy 1893–1946* (Boston: 1964), pp. 348–49; Juliet Rublee to M.S., May 30, 1936, MS-SS. M.S. to F.D.R, Mar. 1, 1935, FDR papers.

25. Hazel Moore to Mrs. Franklin Delano Roosevelt, Nov. 9, 1934; Hazel Moore to Malvina Schneider, secretary to Mrs. Roosevelt, Nov. 15, 1934; Ruby A. Black to Mrs. Roosevelt, Apr. 16, 1935, enclosing M.S. to Mrs. F.D.R., Apr. 9, 1935, all in the Eleanor Roosevelt papers, Franklin Delano Roosevelt Library, Hyde Park, N.Y., hereinafter "ER papers."

26. Margaret's frustration is in M.S. to C. D. Brown, Jr., Aug. 5, 1935, MS-LC. The Puerto Rican situation is chronicled in the following: Henry Wallace to A.J.S. Weaver, July 14, 1934, FDR papers, Hyde Park, directly instructs that no references to contraception in Puerto Rico be made from official sources. The President wrote personally in response to a telegram about the Puerto Rican situation from Father John Burke of the National Catholic Welfare Conference, promising that Harry Hopkins would look into the matter: John J. Burke to FDR, April 1, 1935, and FDR to J.B., April 23, 1935, FDR papers, Hyde Park. Also see Phyllis Tilson Piotrow, *World Population Crisis: The United States Response* (New York: 1973), p. 31; and James Reed, *The Birth Control Movement and American Society: From Private Vice to Public Virture* (Princeton: 1984), pp. 259–60.

27. Hazel Moore, Memorandum, "Interview with Harry Hopkins, June 6, 1934," and "Survey of Policies of F.E.R.A. Administrators," Feb. 25, 1935, both in MS-LC; "Relief and Babies," *Time,* Apr. 8, 1935, clipping in MS-LC. Nadina Kavinoky, M.D., "List of Public Clinics in Los Angeles," Sept. 1937,

MS-LC. The quotation is from Lydia DeVilbiss, M.D. to M.S., Sept. 30, 1936. Also see DeVilbiss to M.S., Jan. 2, 1935, and DeVilbiss to Stella Hanau, Jan. 2, 1935, all in MS-SS. The Puerto Rico incident is recounted in an unpublished manuscript of Ernest Gruening, cited in Piotrow, *World Population Crisis*, p. 31. Also see James Reed, *The Birth Control Movement and American Society: From Private Vice to Public Virtue* (Princeton: 1984), pp. 259–66.

28. NCFLBC, Annual Report, Nov. 1, 1934–Oct. 1, 1935, pp. 6–8, copy in Rocky-RG2; Hazel Moore, memo to M.S., Jan. 8, 1935, "Year of Our Lord and Miracles," MS-LC; M.S. to Hazel Moore, Oct. 18, 1935, and H.M to M.S. "Spit 12–no year," n.d. (1936), both in MS-LC. (There did not seem to be any hard feelings. Sanger offered Moore a field position in the South. At first she declined and went back to work for the Red Cross, but then shortly thereafter returned to birth control work.) Also see "Birth Control Bill Shelved in House: Mrs. Sanger Declares Fight Will Go On," *The New York Times*, Feb. 6, 1935, 15:3–4) and "Undiscouraged," *NYT*, Feb. 10, 1935, sec. 4, 2:5. U.S. Congress. House. Committee on the Post Office. *Offenses Against the Postal Services: Hearings on H.R. 154 . . . H.R. 5370*, 74th Cong., 1st sess. Mar. 8, Apr. 4, Apr. 10, 1935. Sanger testimony is on pp. 45–49, 95–101. Finally see Edna R. McKinnon, "Outline of Campaign for Passage of a Birth Control Bill," memorandum, Dec. 8, 1936, esp. p. 4, MS-LC. Morris Ernst objected to this Post Office bill, again thinking it more restrictive than existing conditions guaranteed by the courts. See Morris L. Ernst to Stella Hanau, Feb. 17, 1936, MS-LC. The two supporters who died were House Speaker Thomas Rainey and Percy L. Gassaway of Oklahoma, who had agreed to sponsor a new bill. See M.S. to Hazel Moore, Sept. 15, 1936, MS-LC, on Gassaway, a "cowboy" Congressman from Oklahoma, whose first wife had died in childbirth. Gassaway's second wife asked Sanger for information about the best "preventives" to give to her newly married daughter, and Sanger carefully responded by asking for the name of the daughter's physician, since she could only legally mail the appropriate medical texts to him. Press on the 21st anniversary dinner includes "Will Honor Mrs. Sanger," *NYT* Feb. 10, 1935, sec. 2, 4:6; and "New Drive Mapped for Birth Control," *NYT* Feb. 13, 1935, 8:4.

17: FOREIGN DIPLOMACY

1. Periodic reports on the Birth Control International Centre are in MS-LC, along with copies of some of How-Martyn's correspondence, fund-raising invitations, circulars, etc. On the Geneva Conference budget and expenditures, see M.S. to "Catherine" [sic] B. Davis, Jan. 4, 1928, Clinton Chance to Katherine Bement Davis, Jan. 25, 1928, and Davis to Chance, Mar. 25, 1928, all in Rocky-BSH. "Preliminary Programme of the Seventh International Birth Control Conference," Sept. 1–5, 1930, in Zurich, including a roster of attendees, is in MS-SS. On the finances see M.S. to Juliet Rublee, June 9, 1930, MS-DC, and M.S. to Abe Stone, May 19, 1931, MS-LC. Dr. Ernest Grafenberg, "An Intrauterine Contraceptive Method," is in Margaret Sanger and Hannah M. Stone, M.D., ed. *The Practice of Contraception: An International Symposium and Survey. Proceedings of the 7th International Birth Control Conference.* (Zurich: 1930), p. 275. On the legacy of Zurich, also see Berryl Suitters, *Be Brave and*

Angry: Chronicles of the International Planned Parenthood Federation (London: 1973), p. 4. The "porter" quote is from Barbara N. Ramusack, "Embattled Advocates: The Debate Over Birth Control in India, 1920-40," *Journal of Women's History* 1:2 (Fall 1989). Also see: memo, "Edith How-Martyn's Visit to India, 1934-35; E. H-M. to M.S., Jan. 23, 1935, Apr. 1, 1935, Sept. 17, 1935, MS-LC; and Birth Control International Information Centre, News Letter, No. 3, Feb. 1935, International Planned Parenthood Federation Papers, University of Cardiff, Cardiff, Wales, hereafter "IPPF-Cardiff." My thanks to Esther Katz of the Margaret Sanger Papers Project, who xeroxed the IPPF collection and brought copies to New York.

2. M. K. Gandhi to M.S., July 8, 1925; M.S. to Dr. Malinibai Sukthanker, July 16, 1924: N.S. Phadke to M.S., June 3, 1926, all in MS-LC. Also see B. Ramusack, "Embattled Advocates," pp. 34–64. My thanks to Dr. Ramusack for sharing her work with me when it was still in draft.

3. M.S. to Capt. A. P. Pillay, Dec. 20, 1929; M.S. Krishnamurthi Ayyar to M.S., Oct. 5, 1929; Dr. S. L. Kalra to "Dear Sirs, American Birth Control League," Aug. 3, 1930; Margaret E. Cousins to M.S., Mar. 14, 1932; M.S. to Rukmini Arundale, Mar. 23, 1933; memo on "Indian Contacts on file in Washington Office, Sept. 7, 1935," all in MS-LC. (There are two full boxes of Indian correspondence from 1922 to 1935, perhaps 1,000 letters in all.) Also see Margaret Cousins, "Annie Besant: Super-Woman," an article from *The Theosophist,* Jan. 1934, included in an undated letter from Cousins to Sanger, MS-LC; and Ramusack, "Embattled Advocates," pp. 39–45.

4. Katherine Mayo, *Mother India: Slaves of the Gods* (New York: 1929). Also see Barbara N. Ramusack, "Catalysts or Helpers? British Feminist, Indian Women's Rights and Indian Independence," in *The Extended Family: Women and Political Participation in India and Pakistan,* edited by Gail Minault (Columbia, Mo.: 1981), pp. 124–30; and Barbara N. Ramusack, "Sister India or Mother India? Margaret Noble and Katherine Mayo as Interpreters of the Gender Roses of Indian Women," paper presented at the Seventh Berkshire Conference on the History of Women, Wellesley College, June 20, 1987. On Smedley's views, see Janice R. and Stephen R. MacKinnon, *Agnes Smedley: The Life and Times of an American Radical* (Berkeley: 1988), p. 127. A recent perspective on Mayo's influence is in Elisabeth Bumiller, *May You Be the Mother of a Hundred Sons: A Journey Among the Women of India* (New York: 1990), pp. 21–22.

5. A.S. to M.S., Oct. 30, 1928, MS-LC; MacKinnon and MacKinnon, *Agnes Smedley,* pp. 132-33.

6. A.S. to M.S., Nov. 21, 1929. Also see letters for June 13, Oct. 12, and Dec. 6, 1929, all in MS-LC; MacKinnon and MacKinnon, *Agnes Smedley,* pp. 134-46.

7. A.S. to M.S., Jan. 3, May 2, 1932; M.S. to A.S., Jan. 29, 1931, Jan. 26, 1932, all in MS-LC.

8. M.S. Journal, "Russia 1934," MS-SS, pp. 3–15. At Smith also see Grant Sanger's handwritten journal of the trip, especially the "July 22, Moscow," entry which reports on the sorry state of the abortion clinics, and also on a meeting with an expatriate American anarchist, identified as "Dr. Kavinoky's father, an old friend of MS." Sanger reported on the trip in one of the only articles she contributed during these years to the *Birth Control Review.* Mar-

garet Sanger,"Birth Control in Soviet Russia," *BCR* 2:9 (June 1935), p. 3. Sanger sent greetings for publication on the occasion of Bloor's birthday in 1942. See FBI file clipping, July 7, 1942.

9. M.S. to His Excellency, the Honorable Sao-Ke Alfred Sze, Feb. 16, 1935, MS-LC.

10. E.H-M. to M.S., Aug. 23, 1935; M.S. to Marian Paschal, an assistant to Doris Duke, who helped fund the trip, Aug. 13, 1935; according to "News from Margaret Sanger," Mar. 1936, MS-LC, additional funds were provided by Juliet Rublee and by a Mrs. Elmhurst and a Mrs. Robert P. Bass. Press release, "Leader of International Birth Control Movement to Vist India," Nov. 20, 1935; Florence Rose to Anne Kennedy at Holland-Rantos Company, Oct. 14, 1935, all in MS-LC. For the Rockefeller contributions, see M.S. to Arthur Packard, Oct. 23, 1935, and A.P. to M.S., Sept. 15, 1936, Rocky-RG2. Examples of the press coverage include Julian Huxley, "Birth Control's Greatest Propagandist," *Times* Nov. 11, 1935, and "Birth Control Has Vital Contribution to Make," *The Bombay Chronicle,* Nov. 23, 1935, clippings in MS-LC. A staff memo summarizing American press coverage of Sanger's return from India in May 1936 said 377 papers in 43 states carried stories, MS-LC.

Much of my information about the India trip comes from an interview with the late Anna Jane Phillips Shuman in Pittsburgh, Pa., in 1976. My thanks to Elaine Light for arranging it.

11. "News from Margaret Sanger," Letter No. 1, London, Eng., Nov. 1935; itinerary for Sanger and Phillips, Oct. 16, 1935, both in MS-LC. The Wells quote was reprinted in *Round the World for Birth Control,* a pamphlet issued by the Birth Control Information Center in London, n.d. (1937), copy in MS-SS. M. J. Akbar, *Nehru: The Making of India* (New York: 1989) is a good recent biography.

12. "News from Margaret Sanger," Letter No. 2, Dec. 9, 1935, and Letter No. 4, Mar. 1936; India scrapbook; Mrs. S. O. Mukerjee, secretary of All India Women's Conference, to M.S., Nov. 26, 1935, and M.S. to Mukerjee, Nov. 20, 1935; memo, "Resolutions passed by All-India Women's Conference and Women's Indian Association," 1935; M.S. to "Greetings Everybody, Jan. 2, 1936," all in MS-LC. The Sanger Journal in MS-SS also contains extensive lists of contacts in India and handwritten notes and observations about the country. Finally, see M.S. to H. E., Feb. 2, 1936, MS-SS.

13. M. K. Gandhi to M.S., handwritten invitation, Nov. 12, 1935, and M.S. to M.K.G., Nov. 27, 1935, MS-LC; M.S. Diary, Wardha, Dec. 2, 1935, MS-SS; "Gandhi and Mrs. Sanger Debate Birth Control," *Asia* 26: 11 (Nov. 1936), pp. 698-702, copy in MS-LC; M.S. to Dr. Maurice Newfield, Dec. 4, 1935, MS-LC. Also see B. Ramusack, "Embattled Advocates," pp. 50-52

14. Sanger Journal, "Notes on India," pp. 22, 27, MS-SS; M.S. "India Diary," 272 pages, MS-LC; M.S. to Margaret Cousins, July 16, 1935, and M.C. to M.S., Aug. 27, 1935; M.C. to M.S., May 15, 1936; Dr. K. Choudhury to M.S., Dec. 12, 1935; Florence Rose to Mohamaya Debi, Dec. 16, 1935; Florence Rose to M. O. Varghese, Dec. 18, 1935; Philip Stoughton (manufacturer of foam powder) to Dr. Pillay, Jan. 6, 1936; Dr. G. S. Melkote, Indian Medical Assocation, to M.S., Jan. 7, 1936; M.S. to Dr. Pillay, June 9, 1936; M.S. departure letter for publication in Indian newspapers, Feb. 1, 1936; clippings on Gandhi interview from *The New York Times,* Dec. 29, 1935, the *Washington*

Post, Jan. 2, 1936, and many other papers; all in MS-LC. Also see the Sanger-How-Martyn correspondence, 1937–39, in MS-SS, and B. Ramusack, "Embattled Advocates," pp. 57–59.

15. Anna Jane Phillips to Adelaide Pearson, Mar. 8, Mar. 27, 1936, MS-LC; M.S. to Juliet Rublee, Apr. 1, 1936, MS-DC; Dorothy Brush reminiscences, in "Our M.S.," MS-SS. Charles Brush shared his recollection of the trip with the author in an interview in New York on Oct. 16, 1985. My thanks to him and his wife, Ellen.

16. Shidzue Ishimoto, *Facing Two Ways: The Story of My Life* with Introduction and Afterword by Barbara Molony (New York: 1925, reprint ed. Stanford, Cal.: 1984), esp. p. 229; Shidzue Kato, *A Fight for Women's Happiness: Pioneering the Family Planning Movement in Japan* (Tokyo: 1984), pp. 50–74, esp. p. 52. (Ishimoto was divorced and remarried during World War II and took the name of her second husband.) Also see Malia Sedgewick Johnson, "Margaret Sanger and the Birth Control Movement in Japan, 1921–1955," doctoral dissertation, University of Hawaii, 1987, pp. 74–78. My special thanks to Taki Katoh, daughter of Shidzue Kato, for sending me materials and talking to me in New York in June, 1988, when her mother was ill and could not be interviewed as planned in Tokyo. Olive Richard, in her interview with Jacqueline Van Voris, recalled that the "Margaret Sanger" contraceptive kits were still being sold when she visited Tokyo in 1959, p. 13.

The history of Ishimoto's experience in Japan is chronicled in her correspondence with Sanger, which is preserved in MS-LC. See, for example, S.I. to M.S., Apr. 5, 1923, Apr. 7, 1924, Oct. 12, 1929, June 5, 1931. There are scattered additional letters from this period in MS-SS.

17. Ishimoto, *Facing Two Ways,* pp. 237–310; Kato, *Women's Happiness,* pp. 65–74; Johnson, "Birth Control Movement in Japan," pp. 78–85. S.I. to M.S., Aug. 8, 1930, Mar. 8, 1931, Nov. 20, 1931; M.S. invitation for tea at Willowlake in honor of Ishimoto, Nov. 28, 1932; correspondence with William B. Feakins, Margaret's lecture agent, in regard to booking Ishimoto as a lecturer, Apr. 11, 1932; S.I. to M.S., April 12, 1934; M.S. to S.I., with congratulations and enclosing copies of book reviews, Sept. 12, 1935; correspondence of Gladys Smith and Ishimoto, relating to Ishimoto book tour arranged by Margaret's staff, 1937; all in MS-LC.

18. The quotes respectively are from "Remarks of Margaret Sanger," Tokyo clinic, 1937; S.I. to M.S., Sept. 18, 1937, both in MS-LC; and S.I. to M.S., Jan. 11, 1938, MS-SS. Also see M.S. to S.I., Mar. 22, 1937, re: the Clyde contribution; S.I. to Florence Rose, Aug. 16, 1937, re: the danger of talking about birth control; Arata Ishimoto to M.S., Jan. 2, 1938, about his mother's arrest; M.S. to S.I., Jan. 2, 1938, enclosing American newspaper clippings about the arrest; and S.I. to Florence Rose, Feb. 23, 1938, and July 5, 1938, being forced to cease all birth control activity. The Sanger Journals at MS-SS contain long handwritten notes on Japan in 1937, see esp. pp. 14–17.

19. A.S. to Florence Rose, Sept. 19, 1937, MS-LC. M.S. to Arthur Packard, July 4 and July 16, 1937, and A.P. to M.S., July 9, 1937, Rocky-RG 2, documents the expenditure in China. Sanger FBI file: memorandum, Jan. 27, 1937, along with miscellaneous correspondence with Juliet Rublee from this period in MS-SS reveals Margaret's conflicting views about peace and war. The Buck speech is in the Sanger correspondence with Pearl Buck in MS-SS.

Margaret subsequently got Florence Rose a job with East–West. See also, P.B. to M.S., Sept. 24, 1944, in which she says that Sanger's coming to her was "a miracle," and Dec. 28, 1950, in which she talks about closing down East–West. Pearl Buck, *To My Daughters with Love* (New York: 1967) is a book about female sexuality and gender relations that incorporates all of Margaret's philosophies.

20. A.S. to M.S., June 10, 1941, MS-LC, has Sanger's handwritten note that she sent $500 to Mrs. Selwyn-Clarke of the Hong Kong Eugenics League. Also see Sanger FBI file: Agents' reports on Smedley dated Apr. 24, 1945, Jan. 28, 1946, Apr. 28 and May 25, 1950; security check memorandum on Margaret Sanger Slee, Feb. 12, 1952, with quotation from an ad Margaret signed in *The Daily Worker,* Aug. 20, 1947, opposing measures to repress the rights of members of the American Communist Party; and memo about Oliver Edmund Chubb, containing his testimony at the U.S. House of Representatives, Committee on Un-American Activities, Aug. 20, 1951.

21. M.S. to Mrs. M. A. Pyke, secretary, National Birth Control Association, June 3, 1938, IPPF-Cardiff; M.S. to E.H-M., Feb. 1, 1938, and E. H-M. to M.S., Sept. 6, 1939, June 20, 1940, Sept. 6, 1940, MS-SS.

22. The initial quotes are from M.S., "Woman of the Future," an undated 15-page manuscript prepared for the Century of Progress Exhibition, MS-SS. The speech also condemned domestic policies that kept contraception illegal, despite a spiraling rate of illegal abortion. For an earlier exposition of these themes, also see Margaret Sanger, *The Pivot of Civilization* (New York: 1922), and Dorothy Dunbar Bromley, "This Question of Birth Control," *Harper's Monthly* 160 (Dec. 1929), pp. 34–35.

18: FROM BIRTH CONTROL TO FAMILY PLANNING

1. The quoted material is from Ettie Rout to M.S., Apr. 10, 1935, MS-SS; *American Medicine* 41 (1935), pp. 167–70 and *Journal of the American Medical Association* 106 (1936), both cited in David Kennedy, *Birth Control in America: The Career of Margaret Sanger,* (New Haven: 1970), p. 241. Also see "Summary of Polls on Birth Control," Dec. 8, 1936, MS-LC; Henry F. Pringle, "What do the Women of América Think?" *Ladies Home Journal* 55 (Mar. 1938), pp. 14–15 +, clipping in MS-SS, along with a press release from the BCCRB dated Feb. 17, 1938. Finally, Susan Ware, *Holding Their Own: American Women in the 1930s* (Boston: 1982), p. 7.

2. Margaret's comments are penciled over the Rout letter (see note 1). Subsequent events are recounted through "Summary of Legal References" in Guy Irving Burch (then helping Sanger at the NCFLBC) to C. C. Little, Mar. 23, 1936, MS-SS; Marguerite Benson (executive director of the ABCL) to Burch, Mar. 28, 1936; Benson to Charles Scribner (another of Sanger's lawyers), Mar. 30, 1936; and Scribner to Adelaide Pearson (also of the NCFLBC), Apr. 17, 1936, all in MS-LC. The Moore incident is recounted in Hazel Moore to Mrs. L. E. Goodisson, Apr. 29, 1935, MS-LC.

3. For a chronology of *U.S. v. One Package,* see M.S. to Dr. Sakao Koyama, Osaka, Japan, June 27, 1932, and Mar. 14, 1933, in the Japan file, MS-LC; M.S. to Morris Ernst, Mar. 30, 1932, in which, recognizing the potential historic nature of the case, she protests that her own name cannot go on it, says

that the clinic doctors get in trouble with the medical establishment for involving themselves in "propaganda," but then concedes the necessity of using a licensed physician; Florence Rose to Morris Ernst, Feb. 8, 1933, and Ernst to Rose, Feb. 10, 1933; Alexander Lindley of Ernst's firm to Rose, Oct. 3, 1935; Ernst to Dr. Robert L. Dickinson, Nov. 2, 1935, all in Ernst file, MS-LC. The material in quotation is from the decision rendered by Augustus Hand (U.S. v. One Package, 86 F. 2d 737 [1936]), pp. 5–6, copy found in Margaret Sanger Center of New York papers, now in MS-SS. Marquis James, "Morris L. Ernst," *Scribner's Magazine* 104:1 (July 1938), provides a charming profile, copy in MS-LC. Also see James Reed, *The Birth Control Movement and American Society: From Private Vice to Public Virture,* (Princeton: 1984), p. 121, and C. Thomas Dienes, *Law, Politics and Birth Control* (Urbana, Ill.: 1972), pp. 108–15.

Once again, this narrative departs significantly from *Birth Control,* Kennedy's biography of Sanger. Nowhere is Kennedy's bias against Sanger more evident than in his recounting of *U.S. v. One Package,* where he neglects even to mention her role in the litigation, positions her instead as resistant to all judicial initiatives, and even goes so far as to suggest that the case was carried to appeal because William J. McWilliams, counsel to the ABCL, brought the two birth control factions together by convincing them both "that judicial interpretation was a more profitable avenue of reform than legislative amendment." See, Kennedy, *idem,* pp. 240–43. Morris Ernst, in fact, consistently encouraged Sanger in her legislative work, though he always cautioned her to emphasize the import of recent court rulings in her lobbying. Nor did either of them need to be told to carry the Moscowitz decision through an appeal. They never considered not doing so. See Florence Rose, "Report of Interview with Morris Ernst," May 18, 1936, and Arthur Packard, "Birth Control Legislation and Agency Programs, Conversation with Morris Ernst," Jan. 23, 1936, Rocky-RG2. Kennedy's subsequent assertion, *idem,* p. 257, that the squabbles among the women of the movement were only resolved as a result of the intervention of male lawyers with "cooler heads" is untrue and offensive. Regrettably, he always seems to hold Sanger to a different standard of comportment than he does doctors, priests, lawyers, or anyone else with whom she had differences.

U.S. v. One Package was Harriet Pilpel's first major birth control assignment, and the occasion on which she met Sanger, who sent her flowers in thanks. See Florence Rose to H.P., Sept. 19, 1936, and H.P. to M.S., Dec. 7, 1936, MS-LC.

4. M.S., form letter to supporters, Dec. 14, 1936, MS-LC; *Life* Jan. 11, 1937, clipping in MS-SS. Actually, the *Life* piece was planned before the court decision. See Florence Rose to Stella Hanau, Oct. 12, 1936, MS-LC. Also see *Time,* Dec. 21, 1936, clipping in MS-LC; "Birth Control Today," *The Nation* 144:2, (Jan 9, 1937), p. 34; "Mrs. Sanger Gets Town Hall Medal," *The New York Times,* Jan. 16, 1937, 15:5. For Catholic attack when medal was announced in Dec., see "Town Hall Club Honors Dishonor," *Ave Maria* 44 (Dec, 19, 1936), pp. 791–92. And, finally, press release, "Birth Control Committee Disbands, Victorious," July 3, 1937, MS-SS; and *A New Day Dawns for Birth Control: Summary of Seven Years Which Led to Legislation and Cleared the Way for an Epoch-Making Advance,* NCFLBC pamphlet, July 1937, MS-LC.

5. "A.M.A. and Birth Control," *Birth Control Review* 16:6 (June 1932), p. 164; "Resolution House of Delegates, American Medical Association, 1933

Annual Session," copy in MS-SS; Ira S. Wile, M.D., "Critique of Commentary on 1937 AMA Resolutions," Jan. 1937, MS-SS. On the 1937 AMA report, see *JAMA* 108: 22 (June 1937), pp. 2217–18; and William Laurence, "Birth Control is Accepted by American Medical Body" *The New York Times,* June 9, 1937, 1:2–3.

6. Editorial, "Contraceptive Advice, Devices and Preparations Still Contraband," *JAMA* 108:14, (Apr. 1937), pp. 1179–80; reply by Morris L. Ernst, et al., "Correspondence: Contraceptive Advice, Devices and Preparations," *JAMA* 108:21 (May 1937), pp. 1819–20, copies also in Ernst file, MS-LC. The signatories were Frederick A. Ballard, Alexander C. Dick, Harrison Tweed, and Charles E. Scribner. For a concurring opinion, also see Charles Scribner, memorandum for the NCFLBC, Apr. 16, 1937, MS-LC. The Ernst quote is from Morris Ernst, "Public Health and Birth Control Laws," speech delivered Dec. 19, 1936, MS-LC. Also, see Hannah Stone, M.D., "Birth Control Wins," *The Nation,* Jan. 16, 1937, reprint in MS-SS; Margaret Sanger, "The Status of Birth Control: 1938," *The New Republic,* Apr. 20, 1938, clipping in MS-LC; and, finally, Kennedy, *Birth Control,* pp. 215–17 and 255–56, and Reed, *Birth Control Movement,* p. 190. Morris Ernst, *The Best Is Yet* (New York: 1945), a reminiscence, contains several favorable comments about Sanger.

7. United States v. One Package, 86 F 2d 737 (1936), concurring decision of Learned Hand, copy in MS-NYC papers, now in MS-SS. The legislative history is best summarized in C. Thomas Dienes, *Law, Politics and Birth Control,* pp. 188–93, 245–52.

8. "Contraceptive Caravans and More Clinics Urged by Mrs. Sanger," press release, BCCRB, July 19, 1937, MS-SS. "List of Contraceptive Centers in the United States, September, 1936," identifies the 300 facilities to which Sanger referred, many of them shoestring operations, and forty-four of them in New York State alone. A copy of the list is in the Morris Ernst Papers, Schlesinger Library, Radcliffe College. Also see, Arthur W. Packard to Rockefeller Files, "Memorandum of Conversation with Mrs. Sanger," Oct. 9, 1936, and A.W.P. to files, "Conversation with Margaret Sanger," June 15, 1937, both in Rocky-RG2.

9. Robert Hardie, U.S. Department of Agriculture, Farm Security Administration to Gladys Smith, Jan. 3, 1937, MS-LC. Reed, *Birth Control Movement,* p. 266, documents the FSA story from materials in the papers of Clarence Gamble, who funded it. On the distribution of contraception among migratory workers in California, see Grace Naismith, "The Birth Control Nurse," *Survey Graphic* 32:2 (June 1943), also cited in Reed, *idem.*

10. Edna McKinnon to M.S., memoranda dated Nov. 23/24, 1936, Jan. 12, 1937, Apr. 6, 1937, and Apr. 13, 1937, all in MS-LC; "Report of Marguerite Benson, Executive Director of the American Birth Control League," Sept., 1936, copy in PPFA-SS. An entire file on the Conference on Better Care for Mothers and Babies is in MS-LC, including a notation of the initial invitation that went to the ABCL; a copy of a letter from M.S. to Katherine Lenroot, Jan. 5, 1938, asking that she be invited as well, along with Lenroot's form response. M.S. to Fred Adair, M.D., Jan. 13, 1938, describes the situation regarding Hannah Stone. Hazel Moore, memorandum, "Special Interview with Mrs. Elwood Street," explains the exclusion from the planning committee. Sanger subsequently wrote letters to all the participants in the conference protesting the

exclusion and silencing of Stone. See M.S. to "Associations, Members of the National Conference on Better Care for Mothers and Babies," June 22, 1938. The recollections of Martha May Eliot, M.D., are in her interviews with Jeanette Cheek, November 1973 to May 1974, in the Oral History Project on Women in the Family Planning and Abortion Movements, Schlesinger Library, Radcliffe College, pp. 425–26.

11. Reed, *Birth Control Movement,* pp. 247-52. Also see speeches by Pascal K. Whelpton, Scripps Foundation for Research in Population Problems, and Ralph Chester Williams, M.D., medical director of the Farm Security Administration, at the Third South Conference on Tomorrow's Children, Oct. 31, 1941, Nashville, Tenn., copies in MS-SS.

12. See especially, Lydia A. DeVilbiss, M.D., to M.S., Oct. 20, 1933, May 21, 1934, Jan. 10, and Jan. 22, 1935, M.S. to L.D., Jan. 18, 1935, and M.S. to Dr. Wells P. Eagleton, May 12, 1937, all in MS-LC. Also see M.S. to L.D., Sept. 19, 1935, Nov. 2, 1936, a listing of the Florida clinics, a suggested program of operation, and a copy of the case records they used, dated July 17, 1936; a preliminary report on the use of rubber sponge pessary and Fem Foam, May 1, 1936; and "Dorothy" to Hazel Zborowski (a Sanger clinic administrator), Aug. 8, 1935, all in MS-SS. Hannah Stone to M.S., Oct. 9, 1936, MS-SS, suggests that she did not approve of the foam method, but Sanger overruled her, and let the trial go ahead. The American Birth Control League refused to work with DeVilbiss, not because she was a racist, but because it disapproved of her simple method. See Linda Gordon, *Woman's Body, Woman's Right: A Social History of Birth Control in America* (New York: 1976), p. 309.

13. Anthony R. Measham, M.D., *Family Planning in North Carolina: The Politics of a Lukewarm Issue* (Chapel Hill: 1972), pp.1-11; Wilma Dykeman, *Too Many People, Too Little Love, Edna Rankin McKinnon: Pioneer for Birth Control* (New York: 1974), pp. 45–87; Reed, *Birth Control Movement,* pp. 252–56, p. 268; Martha Eliot interview, pp. 427–28; Phyllis Tilson Piotrow, *World Population Crisis: The United States Response* (New York: 1973), pp. 141–42. Also see, Hazel Moore, Report, 1937, "Birth Control for the Negro," MS-LC; and Clarence J. Gamble, medical field director of the BCCRB, "An Outline of the Recent Field Work of the Birth Control Clinical Research Bureau," Jan. 1939, MS-SS.

14. "Committee on Public Progress" files in MS-LC and MS-SS include, for example, M.S. to "Dear Friend" forms for 1938 and 1939, pointing out the *One Package* decision and AMA endorsement and asking that individual letters be written to Roosevelt, Lenroot, and Parran, along with Francis Harrington, the new administrator of the WPA. Fact sheets accompanied these mailings. Letters were also solicited to be sent to various popular magazines and journals. A 1938 Public Progress Committee letter to the *Women's Home Companion* elicited a full-page editorial in support of birth control, see MS-LC. Florence Rose to Morris Ernst, Dec. 1, 1938; M.S. to Mary Woodard Reinhardt, Dec. 8, 1938; Hazel Moore to F. Rose, Dec. 16, 1938; Moore to Reinhardt, Jan. 6, 1939, and Reinhardt to M.S., Mar. 3, 1939, detail discussions with Senator Wagner, all in MS-LC. The league's activities are chronicled in Marguerite Benson, "A Public Trust," *Birth Control Review* 4:1 (Sept. 1936), p. 1; *The Most Important Thing in the World,* ABCL pamphlet, 1938; and "263,990 to be Sought for Birth Control Work," *New York Herald Tribune,* Mar. 24, 1938, clipping, all in

MS-SS. On Parran and the VD campaign, see Allan M. Brandt, *No Magic Bullet: A Social History of Venereal Disease in the United States Since 1880* (New York: 1985), pp. 143–47. The final quoted material is from the reference sheet attached to M.S. to "Dear Friend," asking for letters to Dr. Thomas Parran, Jr., n.d. (1938), MS-LC.

15. An extensive and highly personal correspondence between M.S. and Elizabeth Arden is at MS-SS. Also see Grant Sanger, Schlesinger Library interview; M.S. to Mabel Dodge Luhan, "Thursday," n.d. (1937) in MDL-Yale; *Tucson,* a 1953 pamphlet by Bernice Consulish, society editor of *The Arizona Daily Star,* copy in the archives of the library of the University of Arizona; and, finally, Blake Brophy, "Tucson's Arizona Inn, the Continuum of Style," *The Journal of Arizona History* 24:3 (Autumn 1983), reprint available at the inn. My thanks to Stuart Sanger for his lively tour of Tucson in March of 1986.

16. M.S., *Autobiography.* Stanley Rinehart to M.S., Apr. 12, 1935, tells of his inability to get *My Fight* reprinted. M.S. to Robert Parker, Nov. 5, 1939, says the book has not sold out its first printing of 5,000 copies. On the writing of *Autobiography,* also see M.S. to Juliet Rublee, Feb. 7 (1938), MS-DC, and M.S. to Mabel Dodge Luhan, Mar. 13, 1937, MDL-Yale. Additional information came from the author's 1985 telephone interview with Katherine Bredt of New Jersey, who acted as secretary to Heywood and Holt and transcribed the interviews. Clippings from the reviews are in MS-LC; see especially "Sanger Saga," *Time,* Nov. 14, 1938; "Personal History of a Pioneer," *Saturday Review of Literature,* Nov. 12, 1938; "Love for Children Tends to Grow," *Knoxville Tennessee Journal,* Oct. 30, 1938; "Margaret Sanger—An Autobiography," *Women's Press,* New York, Jan. 1939. Again, I am indebted to Carolyn Heilbrun's rich perspective on female autobiography in *Writing Women's Lives* (New York: 1988).

17. M.S. to Rabbi Sidney Goldstein, Jan. 16, 1941; Florence Rose to Goldstein, July 29, 1941, MS-LC.

18. M.S., Journal, "1938—Tucson"; June 30, 1938; and Jan. through Mar. 1939, MS-SS. Also see M.S. to H.E., Nov. 13, 1937, and M.S. to Françoise Cyon, Oct. 9, 1938, MS-SS; and M.S. to Juliet Rublee, Jan. 12, 1937, Jan. 30, 1938, MS-DC. References to awards, lectures, and local clinic visits are in the Arizona files at MS-SS. See especially "Notes on the Mother's Clinic," Tucson, July 11, 1935; "Margaret Sanger, Award Winner Here," clipping from *The Arizona Republic,* Feb. 19, 1937; and "Population Pressure," editorial, *Arizona Daily Star,* Mar. 16, 1938. The Sanger–Slee correspondence for these years in MS-SS gives a general flavor of their deteriorating relationship.

19. M.S., Journal, Feb. 3, 1938, Sept. 1, 1939.

20. Havelock Ellis, *My Life* (New York: 1940), pp. 629–34; H.E. to M.S., Feb. 16, 1939, MS-LC; M.S. to Françoise Cyon, Jan. 30, July 13, and July 18, Aug. 7, 1939, Dec. 14, 1940; Journal, Aug. 7, 1939, and undated reference to publication of Ellis's autobiography in 1940. Transcript of "Let's Talk It Over with Dorothy Gordon and Margaret Sanger," July 17, 1939, MS-SS.

21. The Sanger reference is in Ellis, *My Life,* p. 520, also see pp. 299–309, 458–59, 474–77, and Arthur Calder-Marshall, *A Life of Havelock Ellis* (New York: 1956), p. 226. Françoise Cyon to M.S., Oct. 29, 1946, MS-SS, is the first in a decade-long correspondence on the subject of the book, which upset Françoise as well, so much so that she wrote her own memoir to complement it. Also

see M.S. to Vincent Brome, Jan. 6, 1954, MS-SS. The final quote is from M.S. to H. de S., Mar. 18, 1948, MS-LC.

22. See George Perrott, secretary, Intergovernmental Committee, to Robert L. Dickinson, Jan. 10, 1939, Dickinson to Perrott, Jan. 12, 1939, and "Digest of Remarks" before the committee, including Margaret's quoted remarks, n.d. (1939), all in MS-LC. Telegram, M.S. to Eleanor Roosevelt, Jan. 11, 1939, ER papers.

23. Clippings from *The New York Times,* the *New York Herald Tribune,* the *Baltimore Sun,* and other papers, all dated Jan. 17, 1940; Eleanor Roosevelt to M.S., invitation for lunch on May 15, 1940; and M.S. to E.R., May 28, 1940, both in E.R. papers.

24. Kennedy, *Birth Control,* p. 263, citing "Opinion of the General Counsel, January 23, 1939," USPHS records, National Archives; M.S. to Mary Lasker, Nov. 12, 1939, and Sept. 18, 1940, MS-SS; Birth Control Federation of America, "Birth Control and the Negro: An Analysis and Program," July 1939; Albert Lasker to M.S., Feb. 9, 1940, and M.S. to Albert Lasker, July 9, 1942, all in MS-SS. Additional Lasker correspondence of a later date has been collected by Esther Katz of NYU, and overall impressions were refined in the author's interview with Mrs. Lasker at her home in New York on Jan. 31, 1989.

Margaret, in turn, was fiercely loyal to Lasker. When an irritable staff member complained about having to indulge Lasker, referring to her as another rich woman "who's made us her hobby," Sanger urged her to "curtail her frankness" until she'd had a rest or a vacation. See Cecil Damon to M.S., Feb. 1, 1941, MS-SS, and Sanger's reply.

On the problems of the Negro Project, also see M.S. to Clarence Gamble, Nov. 26, 1939, Dec. 10, 1939, and Feb. 4, 1940, MS-SS. Finally, the Vatican issue is in M.S. to Samuel McCrea Cavert, Esq., Jan. 5, 1940, MS-LC. Gordon in *Woman's Body,* pp. 332–33, selectively quotes racially insensitive language in the proposal that certainly cannot be condoned, but was regrettably typical of the times. For example: "The mass of Negroes, particularly in the South, still breed carelessly and disastrously, with the result that the increase among Negroes, even more than among whites, is from the portion of the population least intelligent and fit, and least able to rear children properly." Gordon's unqualified indictment of the project as elitist and racist has since been used to condemn Sanger on the same grounds, resulting in the need for repeated explanations from Planned Parenthood officials. See, for example, a memorandum from Planned Parenthood of Mid-Iowa to its board members, committees, and funders dated Jan. 27, 1989, enclosing a biographical statement dated May 30, 1986, prepared by the Planned Parenthood Federation of America. Again, my thanks to Molly Ivins for these documents.

Finally, for an unqualified endorsement of the project from a black woman, see Dorothy Boulding Ferebee, M.D., National Council of Negro Women, "Planned Parenthood as a Public Health Measure for the Negro Race," *Human Fertility* 7:1 (Feb. 1942), pp. 7–10.

25. "Report on Washington D.C. meeting, March 5, 1941," MS-SS; Eleanor Roosevelt to Mary Lasker, June 17, 1941, MS-LC; Kennedy, *Birth Control,* p. 264, citing "Eleanor Roosevelt to Dr. Parran, Aug. 16, 1941" and "Dr. Warren F. Draper to Mary Lasker, October 17, 1941," USPHS records, National Archives. "Report of Luncheon Meeting Held at The White House at the Invita-

tion of Mrs. Franklin Delano Roosevelt," Dec. 8, 1941, ER papers, which includes the material quoted. Another report on the meeting is in Edna McKinnon to Florence Rose, "Memorandum, Dec. 12., 1941," MS-LC. McKinnon's effectiveness as a lobbyist may have been compromised by the fact that her sister Jeanette was the only member of Congress to oppose American involvement in the war on pacifist grounds. Also see D. K. Rose to M.S., Dec. 12, 1941, MS-SS. Another interesting aside on Mrs. Roosevelt's personal education in birth control is in M.S. to William Meyer, M.D., of Poughkeepsie, N.Y., MS-LC enclosing foam powder for the wife of one of the Roosevelt gardeners who apparently was having trouble with a diaphragm. "What happens in these quarters carry a very important influence, not only in Washington, but also in the rest of the country," Margaret observed. Dykeman, *Too Many People,* has the White House story and many others.

26. Draft of revised U.S. Public Health Directive on the acceptability of Planned Parenthood programs, Feb. 1942, and "Summary of Conference . . . with Dr. Warren F. Draper, Mar. 12, 1942," both in MS-SS; Kennedy, *Birth Control,* pp. 266–67, citing "Memorandum, Warner W. Gardner, Solicitor of Labor, to Katherine Lenroot, June 1942, Children's Bureau Records, Central Files, Department of Health, Education and Welfare, Washington, D.C."; and "J. G. Townsend to C. C. Pierce, May 1, 1942, Population Council."

27. M.S. to Eleanor Roosevelt, Oct. 27, 1941, and receipt for contribution, Nov. 25, 1941; E.R. to Mary Lasker, Jan. 21, 1942, including material quoted; M.L. to E.R., May 12, 1942, Oct. 7, 1942, and Dec. 22, 1942, all in ER papers, Hyde Park. Margaret's personal correspondence with Eleanor Roosevelt is in MS-SS; see especially M.S. to E.R., May 28, 1940; invitation to the WH, Jan. 14, 1946; and M.S. to E.R., July 8, 1952, which is quoted. Also see "Statement by Mrs. Franklin D. Roosevelt," Jan. 27, 1943, and D. Kenneth Rose to M.S., Feb. 3, 1943, MS-SS. In our 1986 interview, Margaret Marston remembered her grandmother saying she'd been born a Socialist and would die a Republican—anyone sensible wouldn't be a Catholic or a Democrat."

28. On the military's VD campaign, see Allen M. Brandt, p. 164, and on discrimination against enlisted women, Susan M. Hartmann, *The Home Front and Beyond: American Women in the 1940s* (Boston: 1982), p. 39. Mildred Delp, R.N., memorandum, "My Days," California, Mar. 27–Apr. 15, 1944, recounts her activities among women war workers, MS-SS. Gertrude Bailey, "Birth Control Urged for WAAC," the *New York World-Telegram,* undated clipping in the Mary Compton correspondence, MS-SS.

29. On the merger, see "Birth control organizations of America will join forces," press release, Jan. 19, 1939, and for background: Arthur Packard to John D. Rockefeller III, Jan. 6, 1937; M.S. to Arthur Packard, July 11, Sept. 12, and Nov. 18, 1938, and Rockefeller funding memoranda on the ABCL, May 9, 1938, the BCCRB, Dec. 12, 1938, and the BCFA, Apr. 28, 1939, all in Rocky-RG2; also, memo to Mrs. Sanger from Mr. Hastings, May 24, 1938, on his meeting with Mrs. Diego Suarez, a board member of the ABCL and a past funder of the BCCRB who had become critical of Sanger's personal leadership style, MS-SS; ABCL Annual Report for 1938, copy in PPFA-SS; and, finally various letters between M.S. and George Aubrey Hastings, a public relations and fund-raising consultant for the BCCRB between 1935 and 1938, which details how tough it became to keep raising money, all in MS-SS. BCCRB papers

for 1935–38 in MS-LC document efforts by Margaret to compete with the league by opening clinics out west under its tutelage.

30. The quote is from M.S. to C. C. Little and to Mrs. Lewis L. Delafield, Dec. 30, 1937, MS-SS. Also see "Summary of Recommendations to Joint Committee of ABCL and BCCRB," Oct. 10, 1938; "Minutes of the Meeting of the Birth Control Council of America," June 22, 1937, and press release, Jan. 19, 1939, MS-SS. A withering attack on the John Price Jones report for its sleight of hand with respect to Margaret's accomplishments is in Penelope Huse to Paul Franklin, Jan. 25, 1938, FR-SS. A more balanced view, but one still sympathetic to Sanger no matter how difficult her personality, is in Mrs. Walter E. Campbell of Massachusetts to Marguerite Benson of the ABCL, Feb. 18, 1938, PPLM-SS. Dorothy Brush to M.S., Jan. 12, 1938, identifies the problem of no succession. M.S. to Edith How-Martyn, Feb. 1, 1938, has the lizard reference. The final quotes are from M.S. to D. K. Rose, Dec. 27, 1939, and M.S. to Cecil Damon, n.d. (responding to a Damon letter of Dec. 24, 1939), all in MS-SS. For newspaper coverage, see "Birth Control Rift Ended by Merger," *The New York Times,* Jan. 19, 1939, 15:5. Also see Reed, *Birth Control Movement,* p. 265, and Kennedy, *Birth Control,* pp. 256–57.

31. Kenneth Underwood, *Protestant and Catholic: Religious and Social Interaction in an Industrial Community* (Boston: 1957), esp. pp. 19–21, 31–38. Ruth Smith, ed., Planned Parenthood League of Massachusetts, *PPLM Reports* 24 (Spring 1974). PPLM, confidential memorandum "Re: Our Present Plight," Nov. 1953, MS-LC. Loraine Campbell, president of the Mother's Health League in Massachusetts, made a $10 contribution to the union in gratitude. See Campbell to Mrs. Anne Sullivan, PPLM-SS. Also see M.S. to Rabbi Sidney Goldstein, Jan. 16, 1941, and Richard H. Field, Esq., to Florence Rose (n.d.), 1941 or '42, both in MS-LC; and finally, Eugene L. Belisle, "Birth Control in Massachusetts," *The New Republic* 105:23 (Dec. 8, 1941), pp. 759–60; and Eugene L. Belisle, "Church Control vs. Birth Control," *The Nation,* Nov. 28, 1942, clipping in Florence Rose to Charles Scribner, Jan. 11, 1943, MS-LC.

32. The Rose quote is from the "Summary of Recommendations," Oct. 10, 1938, which he drafted for John Price Jones, MS-SS. Also see "National Referendum on the Name to be Adopted by State Leagues, Affiliated Committees and Federation, April 17, 1941," copy in Clarence Gamble's papers, cited by Reed, *Birth Control Movement,* p. 421; Margaret's objections are in Proceedings of BCFA, Conference on Plan for Framing a Public Health Program, June 30, 1941, MS-SS, and in M.S. to D. Kenneth Rose, Jan. 22, 1942, MS-SS. Her quotes are from M.S. to Thomas Parran, M.D., July 3, 1942, MS-SS, and from my interview with Olive Byrne Richard.

33. The funding history of the BCFA is in Arthur Packard, memoranda to files, Mar. 15, 1940, Jan. 6, 1941, May 13, 1941; D. Kenneth Rose to Packard, Feb. 12, 1941, and Rockefeller funding memoranda for the BCFA, Apr. 3, 1940, and May 20, 1941, all in Rocky-RG2. The one exception was Mrs. Diego Suarez, who contributed $10,000 per year for three years. Also see Albert Lasker to M.S., Feb. 9, 1940, and D. Kenneth Rose to Mary Lasker, Mar. 17, 1942, MS-SS. The Cromwell provision is in Marion Paschal to Mrs. Walter Stenson, n.d. (1940), MS-LC. The Packard quote is from A.W.P. to files, Oct. 29, 1941, Rocky-RG2.

34. D. Kenneth Rose, "Speech Delivered at the Annual Dinner, Jan. 28, 1942," and "Notes on Talks with Mrs. Sanger and Mrs. Lasker," n.d (1941) MS-SS. Rose's contrary point of view is in Rose to Mrs. Albert D. Lasker, Feb. 5, 1941, and Rose to M.S., Feb. 7, 1942, both in MS-SS. Also see M.S to Mary Lasker, Jan. 6, 1945, uncollected Lasker letters. J. H. J Upham, M.D. (board chairman), "Report on Planned Parenthood in Wartime," 1942; minutes of workshop sessions, Annual Meeting, June 15, 1942; "Suggested Policy on Planned Parenthood and Public Health," Apr. 6, 1943; "Suggested Policy on the Catholic Church, April, 1943," MS-SS; Richard N, Pierson, M.D. (chairman of PPFA Medical Committee and former U.S. Public Health Agency official), "Birth Control Comes of Age," in "Proceedings of the 24th Annual Dinner Meeting," Jan. 24, 1945; and Pascal K. Whelpton, "Population Forecasts and Problems in a Post-War World," BCFA Annual Meeting, Jan. 28, 1942, all in MS-SS. A cogent summary of Sanger's complaints is in the resignation submitted by her former secretary Florence Rose: F. Rose to K. Kenneth Rose, Sept. 10, 1943, MS-SS. Press coverage included "New Drive Planned for Birth Control, *The New York Times,* Jan. 31, 1941, 21:6; and for the Catholic angle, Edgar Schmiedeler, "Are American Women Shirkers?" *Catholic World* 153 (July 1941), pp. 426–29 and Edgar Schmiedeler, "Putting Birth Control Over," *Catholic Mind* 41 (Apr. 1943), pp. 34–44.

35. Birth Control Federation of America, "Memo to State and Local Affiliates from the National Clinic Service Department, Mar. 1, 1940," explains the difficulties first encountered in trying to maintain uniform standards for affiliated clinics. For an overall view of PPFA in this period, see Martin Rein, "An Organizational Analysis of a National Agency's Local Affiliates in Their Community Contexts," Planned Parenthood Federation of America, 1961, copy in PPFA-SS. Also see Piotrow, *World Population,* p. 16.

36. M.S. to George Plummer, Feb. 5, 1939, MS-LC.

19: INTERMEZZO

1. M.S. to Edith How-Martyn, June 16, 1940, MS-SS; M.S. to Lillian Hellman, July 19, 1941, and to H.G.W., Oct. 14, 1941, MS-LC; M.S. to Françoise Cyon, June 18, 1943, MS-SS; M.S. to H.G.W., May 31, 1943, MS-SS, and Feb. 8, 1944, Wells Papers, U. of Illinois, Champagne-Urbana; Juliet Rublee to M.S., passim, 1938–41, MS-SS; M.S. to William L. Holt, a Tucson doctor, Apr. 22, 1941, MS-LC; C. V. and Bessie Drysdale to M.S., Sept. 13, 1945, copy in Rosika Schwimmer papers, New York Public Library. The final quote is from the Sanger Journals, 1938–1941, MS-SS.

Sanger's pacifism and her sympathies for Indian independence, of course, came to the attention of the FBI, which tracked the activities of the American Round Table on India, to which she belonged, in a memorandum dated Mar. 6, 1943.

2. M.S., Journal, Aug. 11, 1940, MS-SS; Florence Kerr to M.S., Jan. 24, 1941, MS-LC; M.S. to Carrie Catt, Feb. 12, 1940, MS-LC; Alice Paul to Florence Rose, Nov. 12, 1941, and Rose memo to D. K. Rose, Mrs. Sanger et al., Nov. 17, 1941, MS-SS; M.S. to Nora Stanton Barney, Mar. 29, 1943, MS-LC, and June 14, 1943, MS-SS; N.S.B. to M.S., June 10, 1944, and M.S. to "Editor Saturday Evening Post," Dec. 4, 1942; M.S. manuscript, "Is This the Time to

Have a Child?" June 1942; M.S. *The Daily Worker* manuscript for article, "Women in War," n.d. (1942 or '43); M.S. to Marie Equi, Mar. 23, 1943, all in MS-SS. Finally, see D. Kenneth Rose to Clarence Gamble, Mar. 11, 1943, for his sense that neither American industry nor organized labor was interested in health programs for American workers, Gamble correspondence, MS-SS.

3. M.S. to H.G.W., May 31, 1943, MS-SS; M.S. to H.G.W., Feb. 9, 1944, and M.S. to Kip Wells, cablegram, Aug. 15, 1946, Wells Papers, U. of Illinois. David Smith, *H.G. Wells, Desperately Mortal, A Biography* (New Haven: 1986), pp. 457–8. *Crux Ansata* translates literally as "cross with a handle," presumably a reference to the cross born by the earliest Christian crusaders, whose motivation, in Wells's view, had been primarily economic and not religious.

4. Sanger Journal, Aug. 23, 1940, Mar. 15, 1941, Aug. 8, 1943, MS-SS; M.S. to George Ferguson, Aug. 31, 1942, MS-LC; M.S. to Lawrence Lader, April 2, 1953, MS-SS, has the final memory.

5. My warmest thanks to Leon Thikoll, Esq., of Tucson for uncovering Noah Slee's Last Will and Testament of Oct. 8, 1942, and an Affidavit and Petition for Administration of Estate Less Than $500.00, in the Superior Court of the State of Arizona, copies of which were submitted by Stuart Sanger for the probate of his mother's estate on Dec. 27, 1967. A "Statement of Securities" held by the Bank of New York & Trust Company as custodian for Margaret Sanger Slee, dated June 30, 1936, MS-SS, identifies hundreds of shares of stock in companies like Bethlehem Steel, Chrysler Corporation, GM, and various oils and minerals, showing some losses and some gains recorded in Slee's handwriting. There are no subsequent records until the 1950s, when her portfolio was valued at less than $200,000, but by that time she had already spent down or given away some of her principal. At her own death in 1966, Margaret's estate, consisting of cash, treasury bonds, stocks, and a $15,000 legacy from Juliet Rublee, was appraised at a total value of only $111,891.11, according to the Certificate of Appointment of Appraisers, In the Matter of the Estate of Margaret Sanger Slee, Superior Court of the State of Arizona, filed Sept. 12, 1967. Finally, see Anne Slee Willis to M.S., July 29, n.d. (1943), MS-LC.

6. M.S. to Dorothy Brush Dick, June 26, 1943, MS-SS; D.B.D., remarks at Slee Memorial Service, Sept. 1943, MS-LC. Also see M.S. to Elizabeth Arden, July 19, 1943, MS-LC; and "In Memoriam," July 1943, the obituary published by the Margaret Sanger Research Bureau, copy in AS-Countway. Finally, compare Sanger's nasty mention of Slee in *Autobiography,* p. 379, with quotes in Lawrence Lader, *The Margaret Sanger Story* (New York: 1955). Personal letterhead, newspaper articles, and some professional conference brochures from the 1950s use the Slee surname.

7. M.S. to Françoise Cyon, Aug. 14, 1943, MS-SS; quotes are in order from M.S., Journals, June 24, 1942, and Nov. 8, 1944. Also see entry for Sept. 1, 1942. An account of Nan's death is in the Van Voris interview with Olive Byrne Richard, p. 27. Margaret was so frantic when Nan refused medical care that she left Ethel in charge and went shopping, but then carried on when she was gone at the moment of Nan's death.

8. William Sanger to M.S., Sept. 18, "1942" (probably 1943, judging by the content), MS-SS.

9. The quote is from Stuart Sanger to J.N.H.S., Jan. 14, 1938, MS-SS.

10. Stuart Sanger to M.S., Oct. 27, 1939; Grant Sanger to M.S., n.d. (sometime during the war), concerning Stuart's behavior; Anna Werner to M.S., miscellaneous letters from 1931 and 1932 regarding Stuart's drinking and gambling; Sanger Journal, June 1941; all in MS-SS. Also see the Jacqueline Van Voris interview with Margaret Sanger Marston and Nancy Sanger Ivins, MS-SS, esp. pp. 1–11. Finally, I must again express thanks to Margaret Sanger Marston for the candor of our interview on Jan. 17, 1985, in Arlington, Va., and to Olive Byrne Richard for the same.

11. Morris Fishbein of the AMA to Grant Sanger (with Margaret's comments), Jan. 23, 1939, MS-LC; G.S. to M.S., correspondence passim, 1938–39; and Edwina Campbell Sanger to M.S., passim, with quotes from Aug. 2 and Nov. 18, 1939: M.S., Journal, n.d. (1944), all in MS-SS. Grant Sanger, in an interview of Nov. 16, 1984, also remarked on the similarities between Peter and Bob Higgins, the football player. In 1986, Peter Sanger was killed in a plane crash at Fishers Island, New York, where he ran a marina.

12. Sanger Journal, passim, Oct. 22, Nov. 8, 1944; April 17, April 18, and Dec. 25, 1945, MS-SS. Also see Pandit, Address to the Family Planning Association of Great Britain, June 2, 1956, MS-SS. "Woman of the Week," *The Arizona Daily Star,* Dec. 15, 1946, clipping in scrapbooks of Planned Parenthood of Tucson, shows Margaret pictured with her dog.

13. Edwina and Grant Sanger to M.S., n.d. (1945), MS-SS; M.S. to H.de S., Nov. 11, 1945, MS-LC; John Elliott of Scudder, Stevens & Clark, portfolio managers, to M.S., Nov. 30, 1948, says she loaned $20,000 to Grant; Elliott to M.S., Sept. 18, 1950, says she then purchased the mortgage. There is no record of a comparable amount to Stuart. Also see Grant Sanger to M.S., Dec. 16, 1948, all in MS-SS. Additional information came from my interviews with Grant Sanger on Nov. 16, 1984, and Dec. 18, 1987; my interview with Margaret Marston, Jan. 17, 1985, and various conversations with Alex Sanger.

14. An extensive correspondence with Leighton and Catherine Rollins is in MS-SS. Mention of a $1,000 loan to "Rawlins" is in Cele Damon Wright to M.S., Apr., 4, 1950, MS-SS. Also see Hobson Pittman to M.S., Sept. 17, 1946, Jan. 2, April 26, June 16, and Aug. 21, 1947, in MS-SS, which also includes a clipping of an article about Pittman from *American Artist,* 1945. Additional Pittman letters are in MS-LC. For recollections of Sanger's social life and her generosity to favored friends and causes, I am also grateful to Grace Sternberg, whom I interviewed in Tucson in March 1986. The material quoted is from M.S. to Dorothy Brush, Jan. 14, 1947; Anne Kennedy to M.S., Oct. 19, 1951, and M.S. to A. K., Oct, 29, 1951; and finally, D.B. to M.S., Mar. 24, 1949, MS-SS. Also see Brush to M.S., Aug. 25, 1949, MS-SS. Accounts of the Haiti holiday are in M.S. to Mary Lasker, Feb. 1 and 17, 1948, in the Lasker personal correspondence, Sanger Papers Project. Margaret wrote many letters during the summer of 1948 on letterhead from "Sailaway" in Bridgehampton.

During the 1930s Brush married Alexander Dick and had a daughter, now Sylvia Dick Karas. Her subsequent relationship with Lewis Walmsley lasted until the 1960s, when they finally married after the death of his wife. My thanks to Sylvia Karas for her reminiscences by phone in Bridgehampton, N.Y, 1988.

15. Eleanor Roosevelt to M.S. (on black-rimmed mourning stationery) accepting invitation to reception in Tucson, Mar. 3, 1946; M.S. to R. L. Dickinson, May 28, 1946, MS-SS, and M.S. to Rodger S. Callway, chairman, PPFA

executive committee, Jan. 6, 1947; D.K.R. to John D. Rockefeller III, July 2, 1948, and Arthur W. Packard to J.D.R. III, July 9, 1948, all in Rocky-RG2. Also see James Reed, *The Birth Control Movement and American Society: From Private Vice to Public Virtue* (Princeton: 1984), pp. 261–71.

16. M.S. to Julian Huxley, Aug. 5, 1946; M.S. to Lady Denman of the FPA, Sept. 11, 1947, and Denman to M.S., Aug. 18, 1947; Arthur W. Packard to "Files," Dec. 9, 1947. (Packard and John Rockefeller III first authorized only $2,500, but J.D.R. III then extended the amount.) Rocky-RG2. The Brush quote is from Lader, *Sanger Story,* p. 355. Also see "Mrs. Sanger to Sweden," *The New York Times,* Aug. 21, 1946, 24:4; "Mrs. Sanger's Plan Opposed by Britons," *NYT,* July 4, 1947, 3:4; and Grace Robinson, "10-Year Moratorium on Europe Babies Urged," clipping from the *New York Daily News,* July 1, 1947, in AS-Countway. Information on Ottesen-Jensen is from the author's interview with Frances Ferguson, PPFA president in the 1950s, June 1986.

17. Arthur W. Packard to Lewis H. Weed of the National Research Council, Dec. 12, 1947; M.S. to A.W.P, Mar. 13, 1948, and A.W.P. to M.S., Mar. 16, 1948; Mary Compton, secretary to M.S., to A.W.P. May 14; M.S. to A.W.P., May 17; A.W.P. to J.D.R. III, May 19, including a copy of the program, all in Rocky-RG2; M.S. to Gerda Guy, July 21, 1948; and M.S. to Dr. C. P. Blacker, Nov. 1, 1948, both in IPPF-Cardiff; transcript, Quincy Howe, "Frontiers of Science," CBS broadcasting from Cheltenham, Aug. 24, 1948, MS-SS. Sanger's speech is in International Congress on Population and World Resources in Relation to the Family, *Proceedings* (London: 1948), pp. 85–95, copy in MS-SS. The late Fred Jaffe mentioned the sexual tensions that informed contraceptive policy during this period in numerous conversations. The "unmanly" reference is from Peter Collier & David Horowitz, *The Rockefellers: An American Dynasty* (New York: 1976), p. 284. Frances Ferguson, former president of PPFA and IPPF, also refers to the gender issue at PPFA in the 1950s in her interview with James Reed, June 2, 1974, Schlesinger Library Oral History Project on Women in Family Planning. A good analysis of the history of demography in this period is in John Hajnal, "The Study of Fertility and Reproduction, a Survey of Thirty Years," in *Thirty Years of Research in Human Fertility: Retrospect and Prospect, Papers Presented at the 1958 Annual Conference of the Milbank Memorial Fund,* (New York: 1959), pp. 11–37. Also see Reed, *Birth Control Movement,* pp. 281–84; and Beryl Suitters, *Be Brave and Angry: Chronicles of the International Planned Parenthood Federation* (London:1971), pp. 4–5.

18. Helen Donington, executive secretary, to M.S., Nov. 16, 1948, Jan. 28, Mar. 25, 1949; M.S. to Donington, Jan. 13, Feb. 8, Feb. 18 (telegram), 1949; M.S. to Elise Ottesen-Jensen (spelled "Yenssen" in the first instance), Apr. 22, Aug. 2, 1949; M.S. to Helen Cohen (Donington was newly married), May 25, Sept. 14, 1949, all in IPPF-Cardiff.

19. Arthur W. Packard to "The Files," Mar. 30, 1949; Frank Lorimer to D. Frank Milam, PPFA, Apr. 11, 1949; Lorimer to Packard, enclosing a copy of Lorimer to M.S., both dated Apr. 11, 1949; Packard to "File," June 9, 1949, enclosing copy of Shidzue Kato to M.S., n.d. (1949), all in Rocky-RG2; Lorimer to M.S., Feb. 14, 1950, MS-SS. Also see William Vogt, *The Road to Survival* (New York: 1948), p. 280.

20. M.S. to Dr. Julian Huxley, June 7, 1949, MS-SS. The Smith citation is

quoted in a clipping from *The Churchman,* July 1949, also at MS-SS. M.S. to H.de S., Jan. 20, July 3, 1949, MS-LC. Finally, see "Life Congratulates Margaret Sanger," *Life* 26:26 (June 1949), p. 24.

21. Direct quotes are from M.S. to Françoise Cyon, Dec. 6, 1949, and Dorothy Brush to M.S., both at MS-SS. Also at Smith see M.S. to Cyon, Oct. 8, 1949, along with Sanger's typed responses to the correspondence decorating course, Jan. 31, 1949. Later correspondence with Frank Lloyd Wright from Mar. 1953 is in MS-LC.

Grant Sanger recalled his mother's desire to have Wright's blessing in his interview of Dec. 1986, and Stuart Sanger took me to see the house on Sierra Vista Drive in 1986, then owned by a University of Arizona professor and his wife, Keith and Adrian Lehrer. He remembered that his mother had insisted on leaving the hospital and driving over in an ambulance to inspect it during its construction.

20: LAST ACT

1. M.S. to Ray Jansen, Harrisburg, Pa., n.d. (1949–50), and M.S. to H. de S., Jan. 29, 1950, MS-LC; Edwina Sanger to M.S., Feb. 22, 1950, MS-SS, mentions the editorial in the *Washington Post.* Also see "Planned Parenthood Honors Its Pioneers," *The New York Times,* Feb. 2, 1950, 25:1.

2. Correspondence concerning Hannah Stone's death and Margaret's covering the expense of a memorial service are in Florence Rose to D. K. Rose, Oct. 28, 1941; and Abraham Stone to M.S., Oct. 15, 1941, both in MS-LC. Several boxes of correspondence with Mary Compton (Johnson), 1939–61 are also in MS-SS. See esp. M.C. to M.S., June 7 and Nov. 15, 1943, re: rubber diaphragm shortages, and June 27, 1943, re: staff bonuses; Feb. 5, 1947 and "Wed. the 14th, 1948," re: finding endowments for marriage counseling and sterility services. The findings of the Indianapolis Survey are reported in Pascal K. Whelpton and Clyde V. Kiser, "Social and Psychological Factors Affecting Fertility," *Milbank Memorial Fund Quarterly* 21: 3 (July 1943), pp. 221–80. Analyses of additional data by others who worked on the massive undertaking were published in subsequent volumes of the journal. Examples of Sanger clinic research projects are in Abraham Stone to M.S., June 21, 1943; B. J. Todd, vice president of Ortho Products, to Dr. Abraham Stone, Sept. 3, 1943; Stone to Dr. Douglas Forman, Christian Medical Council for Overseas Work, July 9, 1949, all in AS-Countway. On Sanger's search for a "spermatoxin," also see her correspondence with Stuart Mudd, M.D., MS-SS; a journal entry for Sept. 4, 1940, MS-SS; Robert L. Dickinson to M.S., Nov. 26, 1948, MS-SS; and Abraham Stone, M.D., "Current Research in Contraception in U.S.A.," *The International Journal of Sexology* 7:2 (Nov. 1953), pp. 77–80. On the sterility service inaugurated in 1945, see Lena Levine, "The Margaret Sanger Clinical Research Bureau, 1923–1955," Fifth International Conference on Family Planning, *Report of the Proceedings* (London: 1955), pp. 283–85, copy in MS-SS.

The success of the sterility service led to the registering of a complaint with the Grievance Committee of the New York County Medical Society by a physician claiming the Sanger Clinic had no right to practice medicine. See "A Physician" to Grievance Committee, Dec. 13, 1950; Abraham Stone, M.D. to William H. Lewis, Jr. M.D., Jan. 22, 1951; and Harriet F. Pilpel to Mrs. Maud

Rogers, Feb. 7, 1951, all in AS-Countway. On the wind-up of affairs at the clinic, see especially Abraham Stone to M.S., Apr. 4, 1947; Stone to Stephen Blodgett, Sept. 10, 1951; Stone to Saper & Rapaport, auditors, June 15, 1951, and M.S. to Stone, Jan. 9, 1951, among other relevant papers in AS-Countway. Also, Cecil Damon Wright to M.S., Apr. 14, 1950, Feb. 8 and Dec. 26, 1951, and M.S. to William Vogt, Jan. 16, 1952, all in MS-SS; and M.S. to Charles E. Scribner, Sept. 19, 1950, MS-LC.

3. A folder on the Nobel Prize is in MS-SS. See for example Mrs. G. J. Watumull to Dr. C. P. Blacker, Mar. 22, 1960, on "1960 Committee for Margaret Sanger" letterhead; also, Dorothy Brush to Margaret Grierson, Dec. 14, 1959, DB-SS. On the Lasker award, see M.S. to Mary Lasker, Feb. 16 and Mar. 14, 1950, uncollected Lasker Papers and miscellaneous Lasker correspondence from this period at MS-SS. A copy of the award address, dated Oct. 25, 1950, is in MS-SS, and reference to Grant's role is in Edwina Sanger to M.S., Nov. 5, 1950, also at Smith.

On the sterilization controversy, see Clarence Gamble to M.S., Nov. 1, 1950; H. Curtis Wood, Jr., M.D., president of Birthright, Inc., to M.S., Oct. 28, 1950; M.S. to the editor, *Coronet,* May 5, 1950, endorsing an article on sterilization, "Birth Control Is Not Enough"; and M.S. to David Loth, Apr. 12, 1951, all in MS-SS. The speech received press coverage. See especially: "1950 Planned Parenthood Awards to Go to Mrs. Sanger and Dr. Moses," *The New York Times,* Oct. 19, 1950, 14:4–5, and "Mrs. Sanger Urges U.S. Sterility Plan," *The New York Times,* Oct. 26, 1950, 26:3. Further background on Clarence Gamble's position on sterilization is in Clarence Gamble to the PPFA board of directors, Mar. 16, 1946, including clippings of Clarence Gamble, "Why Fear Sterilization," *Hygeia,* Jan., 1948, a magazine of the AMA, MS-SS. More recent perspectives are in Leslie Aldridge Westoff, "Sterilization, Why Six Million Have Deliberately Chosen an Ultimate Form of Contraception," *The New York Times Magazine,* Sept. 29, 1974, pp. 30–31, 80–89. Why Sanger was so blind to the racial implications of her remarks is impossible to explain. What is clear, however, is that she continued to think of herself as sympathetic to the cause of improved racial relations. See, for example, Mary McLeod Bethune to M.S., Mar. 17, 1952 and M.S. to M.M.B., Feb. 5, 1953, MS-SS. Finally, on Margaret's medical condition, see Margaret Sanger Marston and Nancy Sanger Ivins interview with Jacqueline Van Voris, p. 56, MS-SS. Additional perspective on her conditions comes from my own interviews with Margaret Marston, Grant and Stuart Sanger, and Grace Sternberg.

4. The Sanger-Rublee correspondence for this period is in MS-SS. Also see Rublee to Dorothy Brush, Aug. 19, 1953, DB-SS; Brush to M.S., July 16, 1953, and M.S. to Brush, July 21, 1953, both in MS-LC; Edith How-Martyn to M.S., Nov. 1, 1950, and Jan. 13, 1951, MS-SS; (M.S. to Vera Houghton, Feb. 18, 1954, acknowledging notice of How-Martyn's death, IPPF-Cardiff; Sanger Journal, 1951; Juliet Rublee to M.S., Aug. 2, 1951; George Rublee to M.S., Oct. 15, 1951, and Gladys Plummer to M.S., Sept. 25, 1951, all in MS-SS; Françoise Cyon to M.S., Feb. 8, 1951, and M.S. to F.C., Oct. 30, 1951, both in MS-LC.

I am also grateful to Lawrence Lader, Sanger's first biographer, who explained, in our interview of November 1986, the power she was able to derive from her spiritual beliefs, and to Olive Byrne Richard for her recollection of the movie incident and for a copy of the letter in her possession, dated Jan. 22, 1952. M.S.

to Wm. Sanger, Mar. 20, 1952, MS-SS, also requests permission to portray him in the movie, and in a touching gesture encloses an old tattered rug from their house in Hastings that had been one of his favorites.

5. Materials on Stone's WHO project include, Abraham Stone, "Abstract of Assignment to India"; "Press Conference by [Stone]," New Delhi, Dec. 15, 1951; and "For Fewer Indians," reprint of a *Newsweek* story of Jan. 28, 1952, all in AS-Countway. Also see Abraham Stone to M.S., n.d. (1951, from the India trip), and M.S. to "D. Lannanti" (actually "Dhanvanti") Rama Rau, Dec. 28, 1951, both in MS-SS; and, finally, David G. Mandelbaum, *Human Fertility in India: Social Components and Policy Perspectives* (Berkeley, Cal.: 1974), and Phyllis Tilson Piotrow, *World Population Crisis: The United States Response* (New York: 1973), p. 34. Data on the Brush Newsletter is in Mrs. Philip Pillsbury, "Report of the International Committee to the Membership," New York, May 1954, p. 4, IPPF-Cardiff. Also see "Report of Meeting of International Committee on Planned Parenthood," Aug. 29–30, 1951; Arthur Jones to files, memorandum on ICPP, Sept. 28, 1951, both in Rocky-RG 2; M.S. to Vera Houghton, Jan. 25 and Oct. 8, 1951; and M.S. to Claire Folsome, Ortho Products, Jan. 23, 1951, all in IPPF-Cardiff.

The Tisserant incident is in "Historical Interview," Sept. 18, 1951, MS-SS. There is no exact record of the conversation. Several years later, however, Angus MacDonald sent the Cardinal a copy of Lawrence Lader's biography, *The Margaret Sanger Story* (New York: 1955). See A.M. to His Eminence Eugene Cardinal Tisserant, Apr. 22, 1955, MS-SS.

6. M.S. to Dorothy Brush, Mar. 14, 1952, MS-SS. J. D. Rockefeller, Jr., to Dana Creel, Feb. 29, 1952, Rocky-RG 2, and M.S. to Vera Houghton, Apr. 22, 1952, IPPF-Cardiff, detail the economic transaction. On the organizational details see, Dhanvanthi Rama Rau to M.S., Sept. 5, 1951, MS-SS; M.S. to Vera Houghton, Mar. 19, 1952, enclosing copies of Dhanvanthi Rama Rau to Mrs. C. J. Watumull, Mar. 11, 1952, and Watumull to Rama Rau, Mar. 14, 1952; William Vogt to M.S., Mar. 21, 1952, and M.S. to Vogt, Mar. 26, 1952 (including quote about Mead); Vera Houghton to M.S., Mar. 31 and Apr. 18, 1952, and M.S. to Houghton, Apr. 22, 1952; Vogt to M.S., Apr. 1, 1952, all in IPPF-Cardiff; and Dhanvanthi Rama Rau to M.S., July 4, 1952, MS-SS.

On the endorsements, also see Vida Scudder to M.S., June 21, 1952 and M.S. to Scudder, July 13, 1952. When the aging social reformer and educator declined to endorse the birth-control effort on the grounds that, as "an old spinster," she did not want to sponsor "anything concerning which I should never say my prayers," Margaret responded firmly but kindly that "your education has been so deplorably neglected by me." Finally, see Albert Einstein to M.S., June 28, 1952 and M.S. to Einstein, July 11, 1952, all in MS-SS.

A charming recollection of the frenzied conference planning is in Ved Mehta, "Personal History: The Benefactress," *The New Yorker,* May 9, 1988, p. 79. Mehta's father, an Indian physician teaching in Los Angeles, came to Margaret's attention through a prize winning essay he wrote on population. Margaret put him in touch with her longtime supporter Ethel Clyde, who became something of a patron to the Mehta family, after he accompanied her to the conference in Bombay.

7. Kato, *A Fight for Women's Happiness: Pioneering the Family Planning Movement in Japan* (Tokyo: 1984), pp. 88–89; Malia Sedgewick Johnson,

"Margaret Sanger and the Birth Control Movement in Japan, 1921–1955," doctoral dissertation, University of Hawaii, 1987, pp. 93–94; author's interview with Taki Katoh, New York, 1988. The reference to Peggy is in Shidzue Kato to M.S., Dec. 14, 1949, MS-LC.

8. M.S., 1952 itinerary, MS-LC; M.S. to Gen. Douglas MacArthur, Oct. 25, 1945, MS-SS; Shidzue Kato to M.S., June 28, 1949, MS-SS; Tsunego Baba to M.S., July 21, 1949, MS-LC; Capt. George H. Hendricks to M.S., Aug. 30, 1949, and M.S. to Hendricks, Sept. 10, 1949; Charles E. Scribner, memorandum to presidents and executive secretaries, PPFA, Feb. 17, 1950, and Gen. Douglas MacArthur to Charles E. Scribner, Feb. 24, 1950, all in MS-SS. Many of these materials are well utilized in Johnson, "Birth Control Movement in Japan." Kato's observations on MacArthur are from a July 25, 1985 interview with Johnson, cited on p. 104. Shidzue Kato, *Fight for Women's Happiness,* provides a firsthand account of these events on pp. 87-98. Theodore Cohen, *Remaking Japan: The American Occupation as New Deal* (New York: 1988), provides an excellent summary of the reform initiatives of the Americans, especially on behalf of women and labor, and has many references to the cooperative efforts of Kanju and Shidzue Kato, though none specific to the Sanger controversy. See esp. pp. 306–12. Also see "Mrs. Sanger Barred by MacArthur from . . . Japan," *The New York Times,* Feb. 13, 1950, 1:2; and "Japan, Trouble Coming Up," clipping from *Newsweek* May 1950, MS-SS; and Piotrow, *World Population,* p. 32.

9. Shidzue Kato to M.S., Dec. 14, 1949, MS-LC, talks about the fundraising. On the Gamble support for the work of Dr. Yoshio Koya, see James Reed, *The Birth Control Movement and American Society: From Private Vice to Public Virtue* (Princeton: 1984), p. 297, and miscellaneous Sanger–Gamble correspondence from this period in MS-SS. M.S. to Dr. Abraham Stone, July 22, 1952, MS-SS, talks about the visa complications. Also see Sanger FBI file, Files of G-2, 1st Army, confidential dossier on Margaret Sanger Slee with a disposition form dated Mar. 13, 1952. This file was included in materials provided from the records of the Department of the Navy, Naval Investigative Service: A copy of Sanger's seven page "Greetings from Japan, Nov. 1952" (most likely written by Dorothy Brush), is in Rocky-RG 2. The final quote is from M.S., handwritten notes for speech, Tokyo, Japan, 1952, MS-SS, also cited in Johnson, "Birth Control Movement in Japan," p. 106. Finally, see "Mrs. Sanger's Visit Excites Japanese," *The New York Times,* Nov. 10, 1952, 10:1.

10. Material on the Bombay conference is in Margaret Sanger, "Newsletter, Greetings from India," Dec. 1952, copy in Rocky-RG2; "Awareness of Birth Control Growing World-Wide," undated clipping from *Arizona Daily Star,* including a photograph of Sanger presenting the Tucson check in India, copy in scrapbooks of Planned Parenthood in Tucson; Third International Conference on Planned Parenthood, *Report of the Proceedings, November 24–29 , 1952* (Bombay: 1952), copy in MS-SS; M.S. to Dhanvanthi Rama Rau, Jan. 5, 1953, and Rama Rau to M.S., Jan. 5 and Apr. 2, 1953, all in MS-SS. For additional biographical information, see Dhanvanthhi Rama Rau, *An Inheritance: The Memoirs of Dhanvanthi Rama Rau* (New York: 1977). The grants are mentioned in Ellen Watumull to Rufus S. Day, Jr., Aug. 14, 1958, IPPF-Cardiff.

11. Warren Weaver to John D. Rockefeller III, Jan. 8, 1952, sets forth their objectives as follows: Weaver, then director of the Rockefeller Foundation's

division of natural sciences, wrote: "The men should be of the highest calibre, should be dependable in some relevant discipline, should have imaginative and free-ranging minds, should have curiosity and openmindedness, and must be the sort of persons who can communicate in a small group discussion—this involves the capacity to listen, among other things!" Also see "Population Conference Invitation List and Draft Telegram," Apr. 9, 1952; Robert Bates to Lewis Strauss, memorandum on Population Conference, May 22, 1952; List of Acceptances to Conference on Population Problems, May 28, 1952; Conference on Population Problems, June 20–22, 1952, Summary Report; all in Rocky-RG 2. A transcript of the Williamsburg Conference, running more than 100 pages, is in Rocky, J.D.R. III papers. Collier and Horowitz, *The Rockefellers,* p. 284, addresses the issue of the Catholic influence on the basis of the authors' interviews with Donald McLean and Frank Notestein. Finally, see Reed, *Birth Control Movement,* p. 272.

12. Conference on Population Problems, Williamsburg, Va., June 20–22, 1953, "Resolution Adopted by the Members of the Conference; Draft Press Statement," Aug. 1, 1953, and "New Group Sets Up Population Study," clipping from *The New York Times,* Aug. 17, 1953; M.C. Balfour to Dr. Detlev Bronk of the National Academy of Sciences, July 15, 1942, and William Vogt to Detlev Bronk, July 8, 1952; Frederick Osborn to J.D.R. III, enclosing a draft of a report of grants for 1953–55, May 31, 1955; Dana S. Creel to J. D. R., Jr., "Planned Parenthood," Mar. 11, 1955, recounting the history of the family's contributions; all in Rocky-RG 2. A copy of the "Report of The Population Council, Inc., Nov. 5, 1952 to Dec. 31, 1955," is in AS-Countway. Also see Piotrow, *World Population,* pp. 13–15.

13. M.S. to Clarence Gamble, Dec. 1, 1953, MS-LC; M.S. to the Rockefeller Brothers Fund, n.d. (1953,) MS-SS; M.S. to Mr. and Mrs. J.D.R., Jr., Feb. 1953; Dana S. Creel to JDR, Jr., Feb. 23, 1954; J.D.R., Jr., to Dana S. Creel, Mar. 5, 1955; D.S.C.to J.D.R., Jr., Mar. 11, 1955; Mrs. J.D.R., Jr., to D.S.C., Mar. 22, 1955; D.S.C. to Tom O. Griessemer, IPPF, Mar. 28, 1955; D.S.C. to Mrs. J.D.R., Jr., Mar. 28, 1955; M.S. to D.S.C., Mar. 31, 1955; Robert C. Bates to General Files, Apr. 11, 1955; and "PPFA Agency Analyses" memoranda of Dec., 1953; May 1954; May 1955; June 1956; May 1957; Aug. 1958, all in Rocky-RG 2. J.D.R., Jr., died at the Arizona Inn in 1960.

14. Edwina Sanger to M.S., Mar. 12, Apr. 6, and Aug. 2, 1953, MS-LC, and M.S. to Vera Houghton, Mar. 12, 1954, MS-SS; Alex Sanger interview with the author.

15. M.S. to Robert Levy, Jan. 9, 1953, MS-LC; M.S. to Herbert and Betty Simonds, May 11, 1953, MS-LC, mentions "feeling better on new drug"; M.S. to *The New York Times* subscription department, Jan. 7, 1953, MS-LC. I am also grateful to Sumiko Ohmori for her engaging reminiscences of June, 1988, New York, N.Y.

16. Lawrence Lader, *The Margaret Sanger Story* (New York: 1955); Lader interview with the author, Nov. 1986, New York, N.Y. M.S. to Lawrence Lader, July 5, 1953, Nov. 6, 1953, Jan. 19, 1954, Mar. 2, 1954, Mar. 11, 1954, recently given to the Sanger Papers Project to be deposited in MS-SS. The Cyon quote is from F.C. to M.S., June 18, 1957, MS-SS. Dorothy Brush's comment is in D.B. to a "Mr. Barker," Feb. 22, 1955, DB-SS. The Sanger quotes are from M.S. to Abraham Stone, n.d., AS-Countway and M.S. to Harriet Pilpel, July 16,

1954; also see M.S. to H.P., Dec. 2, 1954, MS-SS. The Ellis distortions are acknowledged in M.S. to Françoise Cyon, Apr. 24, July 22, and Sept. 9, 1955, Jan. 25, May 2, and July 13, 1956, and F.C. to M.S., May 13, 1956, but Margaret refused to accept responsibility for them. Wm. Sanger to M.S., July 1, 1953, MS-LC, refuses to cooperate.

17. This dimension of the history of the pill's development is covered more extensively in Reed, *Birth Control Movement,* pp. 311–16, from which much of this narrative is taken. I am grateful to Jim Reed for sharing his research with me, including correspondence and other material from the papers of Gregory Pincus at the Library of Congress.

18. Reed, *Birth Control Movement,* pp. 317–39; Obituary for Katherine Dexter McCormick from the *Santa-Barbara News-Press,* Dec. 31, 1967, clipping in MS-SS; M.S. to K.M., June 10 and Sept. 17, 1938; K.M. to M.S., Aug. 15, 1938, MS-LC:

19. Reed, *Birth Control Movement,* pp. 339–45; M.S. to K.D.R., Nov. 28, 1948, and miscellaneous additional correspondence from that year; K.M. to M.S., Oct. 19, 1950 and M.S. to K.M., Oct. 27, 1950; K.M. to M.S., enclosing the $5,000 check for international work; M.S. to K.M., Jan. 8, 1951; K. M. to M.S., Mar. 30, 1952, all in MS-SS; M.S. to K.M., Feb. 24, Mar. 3, Mar. 27, Oct. 5, 1953, all in MS-LC. Copies of the correspondence detailing PPFA's early support for Pincus are in AS-Countway. See, for example, D. F. Milam, M.D. to G.P., Oct. 31, 1950. Gregory Pincus, "Report of Progress to PPFA," Jan. 24, 1952, is in MS-SS. Also see Gregory Pincus, *The Control of Fertility* (New York: 1965), p. 6.

20. Reed, *Birth Control Movement,* pp. 339–45. Reed determines the extent of McCormick's contribution from an interview with Hudson Hoagland. M.S. to Betty Simonds, June 2, 1953, MS-LC, mentions her appointment with McCormick and Pincus. The direct quote is from K.M. to M.S., Feb. 17, 1954, MS-SS.

21. M.S. to K.M., Feb. 23, 1954; G.P. to K.M., Mar. 5; G.P. to PPFA, Progress Report, Mar. 5; M.S. to K.M., Mar. 26; K.M. to G.P., Mar. 31; G.P. to M.S., Mar. 31; A. Stone to K.M., Apr. 22; K.M. to M.S. June 17, 1954, all in MS-SS; Reed, *Birth Control Movement,* pp. 348-58. Also see John D. Rock, M.D., and David Loth, *Voluntary Parenthood* (New York: 1949); John Rock, M.D., *The Time Has Come, A Catholic Doctor's Proposals to End the Battle over Birth Control* (New York: 1963); and on the Sanger clinic's role in testing: M.S. to Dr. Lena Levine, Feb. 20, 1956, MS-SS; and Drs. Herbert S. Kupperman and Abraham Stone, "Preliminary Report on Progesterone Studies," Mar. 1956, AS-Countway. "Conversation with Dr. Pincus, June 30, 1955," mentions the Worcester State Hospital sample. The final quotes are from K.M. to M.S., May 31, 1955, both in MS-SS; and M.S. to Gregory Pincus, Gregory Pincus Papers, Library of Congress, hereinafter, GP-LC.

22. M.S. to K. M., Dec. 12, 1956, and K.M. to M.S., June 3, 1957, MS-SS.

23. M.S. to Herbert and Betty Simonds, May 11, 1953, MS-LC; Stockholm Recording and "This I Believe," script by Margaret Sanger, Nov. 1953, MS-SS; M.S. to Lawrence Lader, Aug. 26, 1953, Sanger Papers Project, to be deposited in MS-SS; author's interviews with Harriet Pilpel, Feb. 11, 1986, and Frances Ferguson, June 9, 1986.

24. On Japan, see Shidzue Kato, *Fight for Women's Happiness,* p. 101. My

thanks to Taki Katoh for sending me a copy of the book. Johnson, "Birth Control Movement in Japan," translated the entire transcript of the committee session back into English and appended it to her dissertation, Appendix B., pp. 146–79. There are several references in the Q&A to Margaret's fatigue. Lady Rama Rau's disdain for the Japanese is in M.S. to Vera Houghton, Mar. 23, 1956, IPPF-Cardiff. T.O. Greïssemer to Mrs. J.D.R., Jr., Sept. 22, 1955, details the expenditures from her grant for the Tokyo conference, and Montgomery S. Bradley to "General Files," July 18, 1956, summarizes opinion about it, both in Rocky-RG 2. News articles on Margaret's trip were in the *Arizona Star,* in Sept. 1955, microfilm in the library of the University of Arizona in Tucson. On the U.N., see Piotrow, *World Population,* p. 13. On IPPF in general, see Mrs. Philip W. Pillsbury, May 1954 report, pp. 3–7; M.S. to Mrs. G. J. Watumull, Nov. 16, 1953, MS-LC, and re: reimbursements to Margaret, see M.S. to Vera Houghton, Mar. 26, July 13, Aug. 11, Aug. 17, 1954; M.S. to Jerome Fisher (treasurer), Mar. 26, 1954; Tom Greissemer to M.S., Aug. 11, 1954, all in IPPF-Cardiff; and Juliet Rublee to M.S., n.d. (1953), MS-LC. Also see Robert C. Bates, memorandum, "International Planned Parenthood Federation, Dec. 23, 1953," Rocky-RG 2; and Berryl Suitters, *Be Brave and Angry: Chronicles of the International Planned Parenthood Federation* (London: 1973), pp. 68–91. Finally, on Margaret's ill health, see news reports from the *Arizona Star* for Mar. 24, Mar. 25, June 27, July 28, and July 31, 1955, University of Arizona, Tucson.

25. About finding more money, see M.S. to Katherine McCormick, undated (1954); June 19, 1954, and Feb. 27, 1956, all in MS-SS. McCormick, in turn, sent money to cover expenses when Margaret returned to the hospital in October of 1954. See K.M. to M.S., Oct. 14, 1954, MS-SS. The quotes are respectively from Juliet Rublee to Dorothy Brush (Rublee comments on Brush's "bitchy" remark), Aug. 19, 1953, and M.S. to D.B., July 28, 1956, both in MS-SS. Additional discussion of internal IPPF problems is in the correspondence between M.S. and Eleanor Pillsbury during 1956, MS-SS, and in M.S. to Mrs. Raymond V. Ingersoll, July 22, 1959, MS-SS. M.S. to "Friends of Planned Parenthood" (in Massachusetts), Feb. 27, 1953, MS-LC, is one of many examples of how vituperative her criticisms could be. Also see Frances Ferguson's interview with James Reed, June 3, 1974, Schlesinger Library Oral History Project; my own interview with Mrs. Ferguson on June 9, 1986 in New York; and, finally, Suitters, *Be Brave and Angry,* pp. 184–86.

26. An extensive Gamble–Sanger correspondence from this period is in MS-SS. Also see M.S. to Dhanvanthi Rama Rau, June 25 and Sept. 2, 1954, MS-SS; M.S., to Vera Houghton, Nov. 4, 1953, Feb. 8 and April 8, 1955; C.P. Blacker to M.S., Aug. 8, 1955; V.H. to M.S., Aug. 27 and Dec. 30, 1954, Feb. 24 and June 29, 1955, all in IPPF-Cardiff.

27. Hugh Moore, Bruce Barton, and Will Clayton to Mrs. Walter E. Campbell, Nov. 13, 1956, enclosing a copy of *The Population Bomb*; Campbell to Moore, Nov. 30, 1956; Moore to Campbell, Jan 10, 1957; Campbell to Charles W. Morton, associate editor, *The Atlantic Monthly,* Nov. 8, 1957, all in PPLM-SS. The saga of the aborted Washington Conference and the alternative regional initiative in Jamaica, W.I., is in E. Weeks to Dana S. Creel and Montgomery Bradley, June 11, 1956; Montgomery S. Bradley to general files, June 14, 1956; D.S.C. to M.S., Sept. 28, 1956; D.S. C. to Mrs. J.D.R., Jr., Nov. 29, 1956; M.S.

to D.S.C., Dec. 12, 1956; D.S.C. to Mrs. J.D.R., Jr., May 1, 1957; D.S.C. to Laurance S. Rockefeller, Mar. 17, 1958, all in Rocky-RG 2. Also see M.S. to Gregory Pincus, Dec. 12, 1958, GP-LC. The Osborn quote is from F.O. to M.S., April 3, 1947, MS-SS. Finally, see Reed, *Birth Control Movement,* pp. 303-304, and Piotrow, *World Population,* pp. 18–19.

28. Examples of Sanger's declining health and increasing disenchantment are in M.S. to Dorothy Brush, Nov. 12, 1956, Apr. 11 and Nov. 11, 1957, DB-SS; M.S. to Vera Houghton, Aug. 30, 1956, May 21 and July 18, 1957; Mrs. G. J. Watumull to C. P. Blacker, Feb. 22, 1957; and ten "President's Memoranda" announced in a letter of Feb. 22, 1958, and first distributed on May 10 and July 18, 1958, all in IPPF-Cardiff. Indulgent responses include Vera Houghton to M.S., June 30, 1958. The material quoted is in "Margaret" (Margaret Pyke) to "Pip" (C. P. Blacker), Aug. 12, 1958, both in IPPF-Cardiff, and the overall impression was confirmed by my interview with Frances Ferguson, June 9, 1986. The final quotes are from M.S. to Dorothy Brush, Nov. 12, 1956, and D.B. to Margaret Grierson, Dec. 3, 1957, both in DB-SS. Finally, see Suitters, *Be Brave and Angry,* pp. 135.

29. A complete, fifteen-page transcript of the Mike Wallace interview is in MS-SS. (A brief excerpt, incorporating only the Sanger quote about celibate priests, was recently included in a retrospective on Wallace's career shown on CBS News, and I am grateful to Betsy Roistacher for calling my attention to it.) A clipping of the Jack Gould review from *The New York Times,* Sept. 23, 1957, is also at Smith, along with several folders of mail received in response to the interview, most of it from opponents, eager to chastize Margaret's views. Margaret Sanger Marston's recollections are from my interview with her in 1985, Joan Hoppe's, from a conversation with Peter Engelman. Margaret told Olive Richard not to be distressed over Wallace. "He was, of course, speaking for the R. C. 's as instructed," she wrote in M.S. to Olive Byrne Richard, Sanger Papers Project, to be deposited in MS-SS.

21: WOMAN OF THE CENTURY

1. Gregory Pincus to Katherine McCormick, Mar. 5, 1954; K.M. to M.S., July 19, 1954; and Pincus to K.M., July 27, 1957, details the Puerto Rico situation. Frederick Osborn to Vera Houghton, Apr. 22, 1957, IPPF-Cardiff, confirms Population Council interest in joint meetings. Gregory Pincus to M.S., July 22, 1957, GP-LC, reports on the pill and side-effects. On Puerto Rico, see Reuben J. Hill, J. Mayone Stycos, Kurt W. Beck, *The Family and Population Control: A Puerto Rican Experiment in Social Change* (Chapel Hill, N.C.: 1959), passim; Adaline Pendleton Satterthwaite, M.D., interview with James Reed, Schlesinger-Rockefeller Oral History Project, June 1974, pp. 13–32; and finally, Phyllis Tilson Piotrow, *World Population Crisis: The United States Response* (New York: 1973), pp. 31–32, and James Reed, *Birth Control Movement and American Society: From Private Vice to Public Virture* (Princeton: 1984), pp. 359–61.

2. PPFA's early reticence about the pill is in Carl Hartman, M.D. and Alan Guttmacher, M.D., July 10, 1957; and K.M. to M.S., Jan. 28, 1958, enclosing "Excerpt from Report of National Director," PPFA, Apr. 9, 1958 (with Margaret's margin comment), both in MS-SS. Hartman also expressed his reserva-

tions in "Plan for a Planet," his contribution to "Our Margaret Sanger," the collection of reminiscences and photographs prepared for her in 1959, pp. 102–107, also in MS-SS. Also see "Enovid Contraceptive Pill Is Cleared by FDA, But Not All the Questions Have Been Answered," *Science,* 14:8, (Aug. 16, 1963), pp. 621–22; and for more recent contrasting viewpoints, Paul Vaughan, "The Pill Turns Twenty," *The New York Times Magazine,* June 13, 1976, pp. 9, 61–75; Barbara Seaman, "The New Pill Scare," *Ms.* 3:12 (June 1975), pp. 61–64, 98–101; and Scientific Working Group on Oral Contraceptives and Neoplasia, The Pill—is there a cancer connection? Report of the World Health Organization (Geneva, Switzerland: 1990).

3. On the perceived failure of simple methods in India, see John E. Gordon and John B. Wyon, *The Khanna Study: Population Problems in the Rural Punjab* (New York: 1971), passim, and Reed, *Birth Control Movement,* pp. 300–302. The Population Council authorization of the NCMH to evaluate the effectiveness of contraceptive measures is detailed in Dana S. Creel to the Files July 11, 1957; D.S.C. to Laurance S. Rockefeller, July 16, 1957; and Randolph B. Marston to Arthur Jones, authorizing a $30,000 contribution, all in Rocky-RG 2. Frederick S. Jaffe, "Knowledge, Perception and Change: Notes on a Fragment of Social History," *The Mt. Sinai Journal of Medicine* 42:4 (July–Aug. 1975), pp. 286–99 underscores the effect of American fertility survey research, especially the work of Princeton University demographer Charles F. Westoff, on generating interest in new methods, as well as the caution of Planned Parenthood officials. On the development of the IUD, also see Piotrow, *World Population,* pp. 13–15, and Reed, *idem,* pp. 294–308. Finally, see R. A. Hatcher, F. Guest, F. Stewart, et al. *Contraceptive Technology: 1988–1989.* 14th rev. ed. (New York: 1988); and Wyeth Laboratories Inc., *Contraceptive Costs in the Nineties: A Comparative Cost-Benefit Study of the Norplant System* (Philadephia: 1990).

4. Joseph Kahn, *Birth Control: New York's Untold Story,* reprint from the *New York Post,* PPFA, 1958; Winfield Best, ed., *The Anatomy of a Victory: A Panel Discussion on a Public Controversy,* PPFA, 1959. Both pamphlets were distributed to affiliates nationwide, and copies are in MS-SS. Survey findings are from "Results of a Poll of 166 Catholic Laymen on Oct. 6, 1960," MS-SS. Also see Jaffe, "Knowledge, Perception," pp. 290–91, and Piotrow, *World Population,* pp. 16–17. The quotes are from James Finn, "Controversy in New York," *Commonweal* 68, Sept. 12, 1958, p. 586; and " 'Lawless' Birth Control," *Newsweek,* July 25, 1960 (citing *The Pilot*), clipping in Institute for Sex Research files, Bloomington, Ind.

5. M.S., "Special Poll of Opinions," Aug. 28, 1958; D. Rama Rau to M.S., Sept. 9, 1958 and M.S. to D.R.R., Sept. 17, 1958; M.S. to C.P. Blacker, Mar. 5, Sept. 12, Nov. 10, Dec. 3, 1958, Jan. 9, 1959; C.P B. to M.S., Mar. 29, 1958; Oct. 1, 1958; M.S. to C.P.B., July 16, 1959, has the news of Dr. Stone's death, all in IPPF-Cardiff. Olive Byrne Richard's interview with Jacqueline Van Voris, p. 24, discusses the succession problem, and Reed, *Birth Control Movement,* p. 293, discusses the Swedish initiative.

6. Interview with Grace Sternberg, Tucson, Ariz., Mar., 1986. Another recollection of the events in New Delhi is in my interview with Frances Ferguson, June 9, 1986. Sixth International Conference on Planned Parenthood, *Report of the Proceedings 14–21 February 1959* (London: n.d.), has Sanger's inaugural

speech on pp. 10–11, and the field reports of Gregory Pincus, John Rock, and Celso R. Garcia on pp. 212–30. M.S. to Mary Lasker, Mar. 20 and Apr. 1, 1959, uncollected Lasker correspondence, has a moving account and photographs of the events. Also see M.S. to M.L., Jan. 10, 1959, for a record of Lasker's contributions to enable Jonathan Schultz to attend the conference with Margaret. The original copy of "Our Margaret Sanger, by Many of Her Friends, Relatives and Comrades," Apr. 3, 1959 is in MS-SS. Finally, see Beryl Suitters, *Be Brave and Angry: Chronicles of the International Planned Parenthood Federation* (London: 1973), pp. 163–66.

7. Dudley S. Kirk, Sixth International Conference on Planned Parenthood, *Proceedings,* pp. 64–66. For the full flowering of these arguments, also see J. Mayone Stycos, "A Critique of the Traditional Planned Parenthood Approach in Underdeveloped Areas," in *Research in Family Planning,* edited by Clyde V. Kiser (Princeton: 1962), pp. 477–501; and J. Mayone Stycos, et al., *Clinics, Contraception and Communication: Evaluation Studies of Family Planning Programs in Four Latin American Countries* (New York: 1973). The McCormick material is from K.M. to M.S., June 15, 1960 and Feb. 20, 1961, MS-SS. Also see Suitters, *Be Brave and Angry,* p. 282. Current policy arguments from a feminist perspective are best presented by publications of the International Women's Health Coalition, a private, not-for-profit advocacy group. See, for example, *Reproductive Choice in Jeopardy: International Policy Perspectives, Presentations at the Biennial Conference of the Association for Women in Development, Washington, D.C., April, 1987* (New York: 1987); and *Population Control and Women's Health: Balancing the Scales* (New York: 1989).

8. Grace Sternberg interview, Mar., 1985; Jacqueline Van Voris interview with Margaret Marston and Nancy Ivins, p. 21; Sumiko Ohmori interview, June 1987; "Dr. Sanger Presented Key to Tokyo," undated clipping, *Japan Times,* MS-SS. M.S. to Mary Lasker, May 2, June 12, July 14, 1959, uncollected Lasker papers, Sanger Papers Project.

9. "Bishops on Birth Control," *Time,* Sept. 25, 1958, reports on the recent endorsement of contraception as "a valuable, liberating force in the family" by the Lambeth Conference of Anglican and Episcopal bishops. The conference also endorsed voluntary sterilization as a justified process, though a "morally grave" decision. Also see "The Birth Control Issue," *Time,* Dec. 2, 1959, both clippings in Institute for Sex Research Papers, Bloomington, Ind; Theodore C. Sorensen, *Kennedy* (New York: 1965), pp. 108–113; and Piotrow, *World Population,* pp. 36–47. Direct quotes are from the Reston interview in *The New York Times,* Nov. 28, 1959, p. 1; Eisenhower's press conference, Dec. 3, 1959, p. 1; and J. F. Kennedy again, Apr. 22, 1960, all quoted in Piotrow, *idem,* pp. 16–17. Eleanor Roosevelt's syndicated column of Dec. 1, 1959 is also quoted, p. 240.

10. "Says Ike 'Set Back' Birth Control," extract from *Japan Times,* Dec. 10, 1959, IPPF-Cardiff; M.S., "Population Planning: Program of Birth Control Viewed as Contributing to World Peace," *The New York Times,* Jan. 3, 1960, Sec. 4, p. 8:5–6; Norman Thomas to M.S., Jan. 5, 1960; M.S. to N.T., Jan. 11, 1960, and M.S. to Sen. John F. Kennedy, Jan. 11, 1960, all in MS-SS.

11. This analysis is from Piotrow, *World Population,* pp. 50–51, which cites Theodore C. Sorenson in *Kennedy* (New York: 1965), p. 209. Also see "Mrs. Sanger Staying: Anti-Kennedy Birth Control Leader Delays Moving," *The New*

York Times 39:6 (Nov. 10, 1960). The story ran on the international AP wire. Clippings, including one from a Nov. 14 story in *The Daily Gleaner* in Kingston, Jamaica, are in IPPF-Cardiff.

12. Materials on the CBS and NBC documentaries; reprint of the Newsweek special report, "A New Look at the Population Crisis," n.d. (1961); Frederick Osborn, "This Crowded World," Public Affairs Committee Inc., in cooperation with The Population Council, 1960; "Statement of Conviction About Overpopulation by Nobel Laureates and Others," PPFA, Nov. 17, 1960, all in MS-SS. Piotrow, *World Population*, pp. 50–52. Piotrow quotes Eisenhower, as his private conversation early in 1960 with Ambassador James Riddleberger, then director of the International Cooperation Administration, was reported to her by Riddleberger in an interview of Apr. 29, 1970, p. 46.

13. M.S. to Hugh Moore, Feb. 19, 1960; Lammot duP. Copeland to M.S., Mar. 20, 1960, and M.S. to Copeland, Apr. 5, 1960, all in MS-SS; M.S. to Mrs. J.D.R., III, Feb. 19, 1960; Mrs. J.D.R., Jr., to M.S., Feb. 26, 1960; Lammot duP. Copeland to J.D.R. III, Feb. 1, 1960; Dana S. Creel to Hugh Moore, Mar. 15, 1960; Frederick Osborn to J.D.R., III, Apr. 14, 1960; Robert C. Bates to J.D.R., Jr., Aug. 12, 1960, all in Rocky-RG 2. MS-SS also has a copy of the form letter, M.S. to "Dear Friend," Nov. 1, 1960; M.S. to "Dear Mr. Smith," May 13, 1960, enclosing the draft with Margaret's handwritten notations and excisions; responses to the letter, including H. V. Lang to M.S., Nov. 14, 1960, and Clara T. Warne to M.S., Dec. 26, 1961; and finally, a copy of the Dec. 6, 1960, ad in *The New York Times*. The Sanger FBI file has the memorandum from J. Edgar Hoover, with the notation of William Josephson, general counsel to the United States Peace Corps.

14. The quotes are from M.S. to Harold Oram, n.d. (1961), and M.S. to Harold L. Oram, Feb. 21, 1961, MS-SS. Also see Hugh Moore to M.S., Dec. 2, 1960, and M.S. to Moore, Dec. 30, 1960; Program, "World Tribute to Margaret Sanger," May 11–12, 1961, New York, N.Y, including lists of sponsors and patrons; and Lammot DuP. Copeland to C. P. Blacker, May 29, 1961, all in MS-SS. Montgomery S. Bradley to general files, Mar. 8, 1961, and April 6, 1961, discuss the event from the perspective of the Rockefeller staff and include a clipping of "Woman in the News, Birth-Control Pioneer Margaret Sanger," *The New York Times,* May 12, 1961, all in Rocky-RG 2. Finally, see "The Population Bomb," *America* 105:27 (May 1961), pp. 364–65. My thanks to Alex Sanger for a copy of William Sanger's death certificate. The 1919 letter from M.S. to W.S. remains at MS-SS in its original envelope with markings in Margaret's handwriting dated 1942 and 1952. Margaret Sanger Marston, Olive Byrne Richard, Stuart Sanger and Grace Sternberg variously recalled Margaret's condition during these years, including the treatment of the drug and alcohol problem, in their respective interviews. All agreed, however, on the liberating effect of getting off Demerol. Richard's specific recollections are from her interview with Jacqueline Van Voris.

15. Ellen Watumull to "Friends of Margaret Sanger," Oct. 20, 1961; J.D.R. III to M.S., Nov. 13, 1961, and M.S. to J.D.R. III, Nov. 21 and Nov. 25, 1961; J.D.R. III to Dana S. Creel, Nov. 30, 1961 and Montgomery Bradley to Dana S. Creel, Dec. 18, 1961; Montgomery Bradley to RBF files, May 9, 1961, all in Rocky-RG 2. Minutes of PPFA-World Population Executive Committee Meeting, Mar. 8, 1962, MS-SS, do address the need of a loan by the Margaret Sanger

Research Bureau. The loan was authorized with reluctance for one year only. Examples of other responses to Watumull's entreaty include John Rock, M.D. to M.S., Nov. 7, 1961, and R. C. Elstone, general secretary of IPPF to M.S., July 25 and Nov. 12, 1962, MS-SS.

16. Symposium program in MS-SS; "The Population Explosion," *The New York Times,* May 15, 1961, clipping enclosed in Cass Canfield to David Rockefeller, May 17, 1961, Rocky-RG 2; Piotrow, *World Population,* analyzes state department thinking and activity, pp. 55–62. Also see David S. Broder, "Government Quietly Buries NIH Birth Control Report," Washington *Evening Star,* Sept. 1962, clipping in Institute for Sex Research files.

17. Hugh Moore to M.S., Sept. 22, 1961, discusses the merger. Also see "Planned Parenthood Federation of America, Inc., Officers, 1960–1961," Nov. 1960; Alan Guttmacher, M.D., "The Challenge for Family Living," address to World Population Emergency Campaign dinner, San Francisco, May 15, 1962; and Alan Guttmacher, M.D., "PPFA-WPEC Program, 1963–1970," all in MS-SS. Montgomery S. Bradley to RBF files, "Planned Parenthood Federation of America," May 9, 1961, reports on a conversation with Canfield re: the organization's fund-raising and image problems, Rocky-RG 2. Jaffe, "Knowledge, Perception," explains how PPFA stepped in to fill the gap of a public health care system oriented only to acute episodic care.

18. John Rock, M.D., *The Time Has Come: A Catholic Doctor's Proposals to End the Battle over Birth Control* (New York: 1963), passim; John Rock, M.D., "It Is Time to End the Birth-Control Fight," *The Saturday Evening Post,* April 20, 1963, clipping in Insitute for Sex Research files, Bloomington, Ind. Richard Cardinal Cushing to Alan Guttmacher, M.D., Feb. 13, 1965. My thanks to William Josephson, Esq., counsel to the Alan Guttmacher Institute, for a copy of this letter. Additional correspondence is in the Alan Guttmacher papers, Countway Library of Medicine, Harvard University. For a skeptical commentary on the papal commission, see Garry Wills, *Bare Ruined Choirs: Doubt, Prophecy, and Radical Religion* (New York: 1972), pp. 174–87. Margaret's obituary, among other articles, mentioned the unconfirmed reports about the commission's findings, see "Margaret Sanger Is Dead at 82; Led Campaign for Birth Control," *The New York Times,* Sept. 7, 1966, clipping in MS-SS. The quoted excerpts from *Humanae Vitae,* (*Of Human Life*), were published in *The New York Times,* July 30, 1968.

19. Piotrow, *World Population,* pp. 70–79.

20. Lloyd Shearer, "Margaret Sanger, Fifty Years of Crusading," *Parade,* Dec. 1, 1963, clipping in MS-SS.

21. Interview with Stuart Sanger, Mar. 1986, Green Valley, Ariz., and with Margaret Marston, Jan. 1986, Arlington, Va. Margaret Marston and Nancy Ivins interview with Jacqueline Van Voris, pp. 33–34. Olive Byrne Richard never used the surname of her children's father. She had two boys.

22. Interview with Alex Sanger, April 1987, New York, N.Y.; interviews with Stuart Sanger, Grace Sternberg, and Greta Titche, a former Tucson Planned Parenthood board member, Tucson, Ariz., Mar. 1986. My thanks to Mrs. Titche as well for the many local newspaper clippings she gave me, including, "Birthday Party Set for Margaret Sanger," the *Tucson Daily Citizen,* Sept. 1965. Extensive correspondence in the Florence Rose papers at Smith College

chronicles the increasing acrimony between family and friends over placing Margaret in a nursing home, and gives a sense of her life there. See esp. M.S. and Grace Sternberg to Leighton Rollins, July 11 and July 21, 1963 and Florence Rose to M.S., May 31, 1964 and March 9, 1966, all in MS-SS; Dorothy McNamee to Dorothy Brush, May 23, 1963 and Christmas card, nd, probably 1964; and Dorothy Brush to Margaret Grierson, Jan. 3, 1964, all in DB-SS.

23. My thanks again to Greta Titche for a copy of the dinner invitation and program and for assorted newspaper clippings: "Dinner to Cite Mrs. Sanger," the *Tucson Daily Citizen,* Mar. 22, 1965; "Dinner Speakers Here Pay Tribute to Planned Parenthood Founder," the *Arizona Daily Star,* Mar. 23, 1965; "Margaret Sanger Hailed As Woman of Century," the *Tucson Daily Citizen,* Mar. 23, 1965. An article on the honorary doctorate also appeared in the *Tucson Daily Citizen,* May 8, 1965.

24. Lyndon B. Johnson to the Hon. L.W. Douglas, Mar. 31, 1965, Lyndon Baines Johnson Library, Austin, Tex., says the Douglas letter and endorsement were turned over to the Distinguished Civilian Service Awards Board. Also see John W. Macy, Jr., executive secretary, Distinguished Civilian Service Awards Board to Hon. Jacob J. Javits, Feb. 11, 1965, copy in L.B.J. Library; Mrs. Harold N. Wells to L.B.J., Dec. 8, 1964, L.B.J. Library.

25. Piotrow, *World Population,* pp. 88–92, 103–42. As U.S. representative to the United Nations in 1973, George H. Bush, Jr., also underscored the critical importance of family planning assistance in the foreword he wrote to Phyllis Piotrow's book. Also see Marybeth Albanese Petschek, MPH, "Leona Baumgartner, MD: Introducing Population to APHA and U.S.A.I.D.," unpublished paper presented to the American Public Health Association Annual Meeting, Anaheim, Cal., Nov. 11, 1984. L.B.J. to Hon. Lewis Douglas, Mar. 31, 1965, L.B.J. Library, also contains a dinner invitation with a handwritten notation: "This was not done. No further action necessary, 3/30/65)." Also see George Rosenberg, managing editor, the *Tucson Daily Citizen* to L.B.J., Jan. 20, 1966, and Jack Valenti, special assistant to the President, to George Rosenberg, Jan. 29, 1966, saying "The President has your letter about Mrs. Margaret Sanger and has asked me to thank you in writing. As you well know, no one in this government is unaware of the far reaching contributions of Mrs. Sanger." Harry C. McPherson, Jr. to Maj. Gen. William H. Draper, Jr., Feb. 9, 1966, L.B.J. Library, rejects a request for a White House reception for population activists, saying it was the unanimous view of his colleagues that the "resources of the Administration could best be used by increasing the efforts we are making, at home and abroad, to meet today's population problem in an effective way." Mrs. Lyndon B. Johnson to Winfield Best, Oct. 10, 1966, L.B.J. Library, says she and the President would be out of the country on the occasion of the PPFA dinner. Interior Secretary Willard Wirtz attended instead. Joseph A. Califano, Jr., *The Triumph & Tragedy of Lyndon Johnson: The White House Years* (New York: 1991), pp. 154–159, recounts his negotiations on Johnson's behalf with irate Catholic officials and praises Johnson for this courage in moving forward.

26. Mrs. Lyndon B. Johnson to M.S., Aug. 11, 1966; Douglas Cater, special assistant to the President, to Dr. Alan Guttmacher, Sept. 28, 1966, both in L.B.J. Library. Stuart Sanger and Margaret Marston interviews, 1987.

27. "Margaret Sanger is Dead at 82; Led Campaign for Birth Control," *The*

New York Times, Sept. 7, 1966, 1:2; Ernest Gruening, "Margaret Sanger," *Congressional Record* 112:150, 89th Cong., 2d sess., pp. 1–2; Grant Sanger, Schlesinger-Rockefeller interview, p. 45.

28. The Ferguson eulogy was reprinted as "Margaret Sanger, A Witty Friend & A Gracious Hostess," *Tucson Daily Citizen,* Sept. 8, 1966, along with an editorial of praise. Descriptions of the funeral and memorial service are from my interview with Grant Sanger of Dec. 1987 and from Florence Rose to Dorothy McNamee (a friend of Margaret's in Tucson), Sept. 25, 1966, MS-SS, which includes a clipping from the *Daily News* on the weather.

29. Margaret Marston's interview with Jacqueline Van Voris, p. 58, recalls the phrase, which she reiterated to me in our interview of 1987. Olive Byrne Richard, in her interview with Van Voris has almost the same words, p. 25, both in MS-SS.

Selected Bibliography

This book is based on intensive primary research in archival records and in books, periodicals, and newspapers. Most important were the hundreds of thousands of letters and documents in the Margaret Sanger Papers at the Library of Congress and at Smith College, but many additional collections were consulted to provide context for the viewpoints expressed by Sanger and her associates.

Archival research was then supplemented by personal interviews and by an extensive reading of secondary literature in American social and political history, women's history and women's studies, psychology, demography, family planning, and population policy.

ARCHIVAL COLLECTIONS:

British Museum, Manuscripts Division, London, England.
  Marie Stopes Papers
Cardiff University Library, Manuscripts Division, Cardiff, Wales
  International Planned Parenthood Federation Papers
Catholic University, Manuscripts Division, Washington, D.C.
  John A. Ryan Papers
  National Catholic Welfare Conference Papers
Countway Library of Medicine, Harvard University, Boston, Mass.
  Robert Latou Dickinson, M.D. Papers
  Abraham Stone, M.D. Papers
  Clarence Gamble, M.D. Papers
  Norman Himes, Ph.D. Papers
  Alan Guttmacher, M.D. Papers
Dartmouth College Library, Manuscripts Division, Hanover, New Hampshire
  Margaret Sanger correspondence with Juliet Rublee
Houghton Library, Harvard University, Cambridge, Mass.
  American Birth Control League Papers
Indiana University Institute for Sex Research, Bloomington, Indiana
  Alfred E. Kinsey, Ph.D. Papers
International Institute of Social History, Netlau and Freedom Collections, Amsterdam, The Netherlands (inquiry by mail).
Library of Congress, Washington, D.C.
  Congressional Hearings, 1931–1934
  Margaret Sanger Papers
  Gregory Pincus Papers
National Archives, Washington, D.C.

U.S. Senate Bill Records
U.S. Supreme Court Records
New York Public Library, Manuscripts Division, New York, N.Y.
Carlo Tresca Papers
Rosika Schwimmer Papers
New York University Bobst Library, Tamiment Institute, New York, N.Y.
Elizabeth Gurley Flynn Papers
Emma Goldman Papers
Eugene V. Debs Papers on University Microfilm
New York Local Socialist Party Letterbooks, 1910–12
New York State Legislature, Lusk Commission
Investigation of Radicals in New York State, 1917–18, on microfilm.
U.S. Military Intelligence Reports, Surveillance of Radicals in the United States, 1917–1941, on University Microfilm. Titles examined included *Socialist Activities in New York City,* 1918, and *Emma Goldman, Alexander Shapiro, and Alexander Berkman,* 1918
Rockefeller Archives, Pocantico Hills, New York
Bureau of Social Hygiene Papers
John D. Rockefeller, Jr. Papers
John D. Rockefeller III Papers
The Population Council Papers
Rutgers University Library, Manuscripts Division, New Brunswick, N.J.
Modern School Asssociation Papers
Arthur and Elizabeth Schlesinger Library, Radcliffe College, Cambridge, Mass.
Mary S. Calderone Papers
Morris Ernst Papers
Mary Ware Dennett Papers
Sophia Smith Collection, Smith College, Northampton, Mass.
Margaret Sanger Papers
Planned Parenthood Federation of America Papers
Planned Parenthood League of Massachusetts Papers
Dorothy Brush Papers
Florence Rose Papers
Blanche Ames Ames Papers
Florence Guertin Tuttle Papers
Wellcome Institute for the History of Medicine, London, England
Marie Stopes Papers
Yale University Beinecke Rare Book and Manuscripts Library, New Haven, Conn.
Mabel Dodge Luhan Papers
Yale University Sterling Library, Manuscripts Division, New Haven, Conn.
Rose Pastor Stokes Papers

UNCOLLECTED PAPERS:

Letters of Margaret Sanger to Françoise Lafitte Cyon in the possession of François Lafitte, Birmingham, England. (Recently given to the Sophia Smith Collection, Smith College.)

Margaret Sanger Center Collection, Planned Parenthood Federation of New

York City, New York, N.Y. (Also given to the Sophia Smith Collection, Smith College.)

Margaret Sanger Collection, Katharine Dexter McCormick Library, Planned Parenthood Federation of America, New York, N.Y.

New York Academy of Medicine, New York, N.Y.

Planned Parenthood Federation, Chicago Area, Chicago, Ill.

Planned Parenthood Association of San Francisco and Alameda County

Margaret Sanger's correspondence is currently being collected, organized, and microfilmed under the direction of Esther Katz, Ph.D., the Margaret Sanger Papers Project, Department of History, New York University, New York, N.Y.

PERSONAL INTERVIEWS:

Cheri Appel, M.D., New York, N.Y.
Rada Bercovici, New York, N.Y.
Katherine Bredt, New Jersey (by telephone)
Gerda Bruno, M.D., Lawrence, Kansas (with Regina Markell Morantz, 1976)
Charles and Ellen Brush, New York, N.Y.
Nelle Dick, Miami, Fla. (by phone)
Frances Ferguson, New York, N.Y.
Paula Gould, New York, N.Y.
Joan Sanger Hoppe, Great Barrington, Mass. (by phone)
Frederick Jaffe, New York, N.Y.
Sylvia Dick Karas, New York, N.Y. (by phone)
Taki Kato Katoh, Tokyo, Japan (by phone) and New York, N.Y.
Lawrence Lader, New York, N.Y.
François Lafitte, Ph.D., Birmingham, England
Mary Lasker, New York, N.Y.
Charlotte Levine, Brooklyn, N.Y.
Margaret Sanger Marston, Washington, D.C.
Sumiko Ohmori, New York, N.Y.
Harriet Pilpel, Esq., New York, N.Y.
Olive Byrne Richard, Indian Wells, Florida
Alexander Campbell Sanger, Esq., New York, N.Y.
Grant Sanger, M.D., New York, N.Y.
Stuart Sanger, M.D. and Barbara Sanger, Green Valley and Tucson, Ariz.
Grace Sternberg, Tucson, Ariz.
Greta Titche, Tucson, Ariz.
Anthony West, Fishers Island, N.Y. (by phone)
Joseph Wortis, M.D., Brooklyn, N.Y.

TRANSCRIBED INTERVIEWS:

Schlesinger Library Oral History Project on the History of Women in the Population Control and Abortion Movements

Elizabeth Arnold, R.N. (with James Reed)
Mary S. Calderone, M.D. (with James Reed)
Arlene Carmen (with Ellen Chesler)
Loraine Leeson Campbell (with James Reed)

Martha May Eliot, M.D. (with Jeanette Cheek)
Frances Hand Ferguson (with James Reed)
Estelle Griswold (with Jeanette Cheek)
Mrs. Alan F. Guttmacher (with James Reed)
Emily Mudd, M.D. (with James Reed)
Sarah Marcus, M.D. (with Ellen Chesler)
Lonny Myers, M.D. (with Ellen Chesler)
Grant Sanger, M.D. (with Ellen Chesler)
Sophia Smith Collection
Nancy Sanger Ivins and Margaret Sanger Marston (with Jacqueline Van Voris)
Olive Byrne Richard (with Jacqueline Van Voris)
Columbia University Oral History Project
Roger N. Baldwin (with Harlan B. Phillips and Thomas F. Hagan)
Jonah J. Goldstein (with Neil Newton Gold)
Mildred Gilman (with Pauline Madow)

MAJOR NEWSPAPERS AND PERIODICALS EXAMINED FOR ARTICLES BY AND ABOUT MARGARET SANGER AND THE BIRTH CONTROL MOVEMENT (IN CHRONOLOGICAL ORDER). FOR CITATIONS TO INDIVIDUAL ARTICLES IN THESE PUBLICATIONS AND OTHERS, PLEASE SEE THE ENDNOTES AND FOOTNOTES.

The Corning Democrat, 1878–1894.
The Call, 1911–1916.
The Masses, 1914–1917.
Mother Earth, 1910–1917.
The Woman Rebel, 1914.
Revolutionary Almanac, 1914.
The Blast, 1916.
The Modern School Magazine, 1914–1915.
Revolt, 1915–1916.
New York Medical Journal, 1917.
The New York Times, 1912–1966.
New York Herald, 1915–1917.
New York Herald Tribune, 1921–1940.
New York World, 1920s.
Brooklyn Daily Eagle, 1916–1917.
The New Republic, 1914–1945.
Ecclesiastical Review, 1915–1925.
Current Opinion, 1915–1922.
Survey, 1917–1925.
The Birth Control Review, 1917–1938.
The Nation, 1920–1950.
Harper's Weekly and Harper's Monthly Magazine, 1915–1930.
Metropolitan Magazine, 1917.
Eugenics Review, 1920s.

Woman Citizen, 1920s
The New Yorker, 1925–1940.
The Atlantic Monthly, 1920s.
Journal of the American Medical Association, 1920–1937.
Medical Journal and Record, 1920s.
American Journal of Obstetrics and Gynecology, 1920–1935.
American Journal of Public Health, 1920–30.
American Journal of Sociology, 1930s.
The Ladies' Home Journal, 1917–1940.
McCall's Monthly Magazine, 1920s–1930s.
Congressional Digest, 1931–1936.
The Milbank Memorial Fund Quarterly, 1923–1940.
The Annals of the American Academy of Political and Social Science, 1931–1932.
Catholic World, 1930s.
News-Week and Newsweek, 1930s.
Time, 1930s.
Fortune, 1930s.
Life, 1937–1960s.
Look, 1939.
Asia, 1936.
Journal of Contraception, 1935–1939.
Human Fertility, 1940–1948.
Ecclesiastical Review, 1916–1930s.
The Catholic Charities Review, 1920s–1930s.
Commonweal, 1930s, 1950s, early 1960s.
Catholic World, 1930s.
Science, 1955–1965.
Family Planning Perspectives, 1967–1978.
The Journal of American History, 1970s, 1980s.
The Journal of Social History, 1970s.
The New York Review of Books, 1970s, 1980s.
Signs, Journal of Women in Culture and Society, 1970s, 1980s.
American Quarterly, 1977.
Feminist Studies, 1970s, 1980s.
Journal of Women's History, 1989–1990.

Gloria Moore and Ronald Moore, *Margaret Sanger and the Birth Control Movement, A Bibliography, 1911–1984* (Metuchen, N. J. and London, 1986) provides an invaluable retrospective and chronologically ordered bibliography of books and articles by and about Margaret Sanger, which regrettably only came to my attention after much of the research for this study was complete.

PRINTED PRIMARY AND SECONDARY SOURCES:

Sophie D. Aberle and George W. Corner, *Twenty-Five Years of Sex Research: History of the National Research Council Committee for Research in Problems of Sex, 1922–1947* (Philadelphia: 1953).

M.J. Akbar, *Nehru: The Making of India* (New York: 1989).

Christopher Anderson, *Young Kate* (New York: 1988).
William Archer, *The Life, Trial and Death of Francisco Ferrer* (London: 1911).
Paul Avrich, *The Modern School Movement: Anarchism and Education in the United States* (Princeton: 1980).
J.A. and Olive Banks, *Feminism & Family Planning in Victorian England* (New York: 1972).
Alex Baskin, *Margaret Sanger,* The Woman Rebel *and the Rise of the Birth Control Movement in the United States* (Stonybrook, New York: 1976).
Mary Catherine Bateson, *With a Daughter's Eye: A Memoir of Margaret Mead and Gregory Bateson* (New York: 1984).
Rosalyn Fraad Baxandall, *Words on Fire: The Life and Writing of Elizabeth Gurley Flynn* (New Brunswick, New Jersey & London: 1987).
Mary R. Beard, *Woman as Force in History: A Study in Traditions and Realities* (New York & London: 1973). Originally published in 1946.
Mary R. Beard and Dorothy Brush, *The Force of Women in Japanese History* (New York: 1953).
August Bebel, *Woman and Socialism* (New York: 1910).
Gilbert W. Beebe, *Contraception and Fertility in the Southern Appalachians* (Baltimore, Md.: 1942).
Quentin Bell, *Virginia Woolf: A Biography* (New York: 1972).
Irving Bernstein, *Promises Kept: John F. Kennedy's New Frontier* (New York: 1991).
Annie Besant, *The Law of Population* (London: 1884).
Winfield Best and Frederick S. Jaffe, eds., *Simple Methods of Contraception: An Assessment of their Medical, Moral and Social Implications* (New York: 1958).
Dorothy Bocker, M.D., *Birth Control Methods* (New York: 1924).
Allan M. Brandt, *No Magic Bullet: A Social History of Venereal Disease in The United States Since 1880* (New York: 1985).
Edward Brecher, *The Sex Researchers* (New York: 1969).
Keith Briant, *Passionate Paradox: The Life of Marie Stopes* (New York: 1962).
Renate Bridenthal, Atina Grossmann, and Marion Kaplan, eds., *When Biology Became Destiny: Women in Weimar and Nazi Germany* (New York: 1984).
Alan Brinkley, *Voices of Protest: Huey Long, Father Coughlin and the Great Depression* (New York: 1983).
Francis Lyons Broderick, *Right Reverend New Dealer, John A. Ryan* (New York: 1963).
Dorothy Dunbar Bromley, *Birth Control: Its Use and Misuse* (New York: 1934).
Dorothy Dunbar Bromley, *Catholics and Birth Control: Contemporary Views on Doctrine* (New York: 1965).
Heywood Broun and Margaret Leech, *Anthony Comstock: Roundsman of the Lord* (New York: 1927).
Richard D. Brown, *Modernization: The Transformation of American Life, 1600–1865* (New York: 1976).
Pearl Buck, *To My Daughters With Love* (New York: 1967).
Mari Jo Buhle, *Women and American Socialism, 1870–1920* (Urbana, Ill.: 1983).

Elisabeth Bumiller, *May You Be The Mother of A Hundred Sons: A Journey Among The Women of India* (New York: 1990).

Arthur Calder-Marshall, *The Sage of Sex: A Life of Havelock Ellis* (New York: 1956).

Arlene Carmen and Howard Moody, *Abortion Counseling and Social Change: From Illegal Act to Medical Practice* (Valley Forge, Pa.: 1973).

Edward Carpenter, *Love's Coming of Age: A Series of Papers on the Relations of the Sexes* (Kansas: 1927).

William H. Chafe, *The American Woman: Her Changing Social, Economic, and Political Roles, 1920–1970* (New York: 1972).

Enid Charles, *The Twilight of Parenthood* (New York: 1934).

Harold Child, *Essays and Reflections* (Cambridge and New York: 1938).

Nancy Chodorow, *The Reproduction of Mothering: Psychoanalysis and the Sociology of Gender* (Berkeley, 1978).

R. Swinburne Clymer, M.D., *The Rosicrusians: Their Teaching, Their Manifestos* (Quakertown, Pa., 1941).

Peter Collier & David Horowitz, *The Rockefellers: An American Dynasty* (New York: 1976).

Ainsley J. Coale and Melvin Zelnick, *New Estimates of Fertility and Population in the United States* (Princeton: 1963).

Lizabeth Cohen, *Making a New Deal: Industrial Workers in Chicago, 1919–1939* (New York: 1990).

Theodore Cohen, *Remaking Japan: The American Occupation As New Deal* (New York: 1988).

Virginia Coigney, *Margaret Sanger: Rebel with a Cause* (Garden City, N.Y.: 1969). A biography for young adults.

Virginia MacMakin Collier, *Marriage and Careers, A Study of One Hundred Women Who Are Wives, Mothers, Homemakers and Professional Workers* (New York: 1926).

Anthony Comstock, *Traps for the Young* (New York: 1884).

Blanche W. Cook, ed., *Crystal Eastman on Women and Revolution* (New York: 1978).

James F. Cooper, M.D., *Technique of Contraception* (New York: 1928).

Nancy F. Cott, *The Grounding of Modern Feminism* (New Haven: 1987).

———, *The Bonds of Womanhood: Woman's Sphere in New England, 1780–1835* (New Haven: 1977).

Canon Valere Coucke and James J. Walsh, *The Sterile Period in Family Life* (New York: 1933).

James Gould Cozzens, *Ask Me Tomorrow* (New York: 1940).

Joan Dash, *A Life of One's Own: Three Gifted Women and the Men They Married* (New York: 1973).

Allen F. Davis, *American Heroine: The Life and Legend of Jane Addams* (New York: 1973).

Simone deBeauvoir, *The Second Sex* (New York: 1953).

Carl N. Degler, *In Search of Human Nature: The Decline and Revival of Darwinism in American Social Thought* (New York: 1991).

———, *At Odds: Women and the Family in America from the Revolution to the Present* (New York: 1980).

Françoise Delisle, *Friendship's Odyssey* (London: 1946).
Floyd Dell, *Love in Greenwich Village* (New York: 1923). *Love in the Machine Age* (New York: 1930).
John D'Emilio and Estelle B. Freedman, *Intimate Matters: A History of Sexuality in America* (New York: 1988).
Mary Ware Dennett, *BIRTH CONTROL LAWS: Shall We Keep Them, Change Them or Abolish Them?* (New York: 1926).
Hugh de Selincourt, *One Little Boy* (New York: 1922).
Robert L. Dickinson, M.D. and Louise S. Bryant, *Control of Conception* (Baltimore, Md.: 1931).
Robert L. Dickinson, M.D. and Lura Beam, *The Single Woman: A Medical Study in Sex Education* (Baltimore: 1934).
R. L. Dickinson, M.D. and Lura Beam, *A Thousand Marriages: A Medical Study of Sex Adjustment* (Baltimore: 1953).
C. Thomas Dienes, *Law, Politics and Birth Control* (Urbana, Ill.: 1972).
Hasia Diner, *Erin's Daughters in America: Irish Immigrant Women in the 19th Century* (Baltimore: 1923).
Dorothy Dinnerstein, *The Mermaid and the Minotaur: Sexual Arrangements and Human Social Malaise* (New York: 1976).
Lavinia Dock and Isabell Stewart, *A Short History of Nursing* (New York: 1931).
Emily Taft Douglas, *Margaret Sanger: Pioneer of the Future* (New York: 1970).
Ann Douglas, *The Feminization of American Culture* (New York: 1977).
Richard Drinnon, *Rebel in Paradise: A Biography of Emma Goldman* (Chicago: 1961).
Charles V. Drysdale, *The Small Family System, Is It Injurious or Immoral?* (New York: 1914).
Charles V. Drysdale et. al., *Small or Large Families: Birth Control from the Moral, Racial and Eugenic Standpoint* (New York: 1917).
George Drysdale, *The Elements of Social Science: An Exposition of Cause and Only Cure for the Three Primary Social Evils: Poverty, Prostitution and Celibacy* (London: 1886).
Louis I. Dublin, *A Family of 30 Million: The Story of the Metropolitan Life Insurance Company* (New York: 1943).
Melvyn Dubofsky, *We Shall Be All: A History of the Industrial Workers of the World* (Chicago: 1969).
Ellen Dubois, *Feminism and Suffrage: The Emergence of an Independent Women's Movement in America, 1848–1869* (Ithaca: 1978).
Will and Ariel Durant, *A Dual Autobiography* (New York: 1977).
Nancy Shrom Dye, *As Equals and As Sisters: Feminism, the Labor Movement, and the Women's Trade Union League of New York* (Columbia, Mo.: 1980).
Wilma Dykeman, *Too Many People, Too Little Love, Edna Rankin McKinnon: Pioneer for Birth Control* (New York: 1974).
Max Eastman, *Enjoyment of Living* (New York: 1948).
Barbara Ehrenreich, Elizabeth Hess, Gloria Jacobs, *Re-making Love: The Feminization of Sex* (New York: 1987).
Paul R. Ehrlich, *The Population Bomb* (New York: 1971), originally published in 1968.

Havelock Ellis, *Essays in Wartime: Further Studies in the Task of Social Hygiene* (Boston and New York: 1917).
———, *Little Essays of Love and Virtue* (New York: 1922).
———, *Man and Woman: A Study of Human Secondary Sexual Characteristics* (New York: 1904).
———, *My Life* (New York: 1940).
———, *Studies in the Psychology of Sex: Vols. I and II* (New York: 1936).
———, *The Dance of Life* (Cambridge: 1923).
———, *The Soul of Spain* (London: 1908).
———, *The Task of Social Hygiene* (Boston: 1914) reprinted with an introduction by Sheila M. Rothman (New York: 1978).
Mrs. Havelock Ellis, *Steve's Woman* (New York: 1909).
John Tracy Ellis, *American Catholicism* (Chicago: 1969).
Erik H. Erikson, *Childhood and Society* (New York: 1950).
Identity, Youth and Crisis (New York: 1968).
Young Man Luther: A Study in Psychoanalysis and History (New York: 1958).
———, *Gandhi's Truth* (New York: 1969).
Morris L. Ernst, *The Best Is Yet* (New York: 1945).
Candace Falk, *Love, Anarchy and Emma Goldman* (New York: 1985).
Family Planning Association of India, *The International Conference on Planned Parenthood, Report of the Proceedings. November 24–29, 1952* (Bombay, India: 1953).
Family Planning Association of Great Britain, *Proceedings of the International Congress on Population and World Resources in Relation to the Family* (London: 1948).
James Waldo Fawcett, *The Trial of William Sanger* (New York: 1915).
Peter Gabriel Filene, *Him/Her/Self: Sex Roles in Modern America* (New York & London: 1974).
Leslie Fishbein, *Rebels in Bohemia: The Radicals of the Masses, 1911–1917*, (Chapel Hill: 1982).
Eleanor Flexner, *Century of Struggle: The Woman's Rights Movement in the United States* (New York: 1973).
Elizabeth Gurley Flynn, *The Rebel Girl* (New York: 1973).
Elizabeth Frank, *Louise Bogan: A Portrait* (New York: 1985).
Ellen Frankfort, *Vaginal Politics* (New York: 1972).
Steve Fraser and Gary Gerstle, eds., *The Rise and Fall of the New Deal Order, 1930–1980* (New York: 1989)
Ronald Freedman, Pascal K. Whelpton, and Arthur K. Campbell, *Family Planning, Sterility and Population Growth* (New York: 1959).
Frank Freidel, ed., *The New Deal and the American People* (New York: 1964).
Sigmund Freud, *A General Introduction to Psychoanalysis*, translated by Joan Riviere (New York: 1960).
———, *Collected Papers* (London: 1940).
———, *The Interpretation of Dreams* (New York: 1965).
Betty Friedan, *The Feminine Mystique* (New York: 1963).
Peter Fryer, *The Birth Controllers* (New York: 1966).
Peter Gay, *The Bourgeois Experience: Victoria to Freud: Volume I: Education of the Senses* (New York: 1984).

Paul H. Gebhard et. al., *Pregnancy, Birth, and Abortion* (New York: 1958).
Henry George, *Progress and Poverty* (New York: 1879).
Carol Gilligan, *In a Different Voice: Psychological Theory and Women's Development* (Cambridge, Mass. and London: 1982).
Charlotte Perkins Gilman, *The Man-Made World* (New York: 1911).
———, *Women and Economics: A Study of the Relation Between Men and Women as a Factor in Social Evolution.* Edited with an introduction by Carl N. Degler. (New York: 1966), originally published in 1898.
———, *The Yellow Wallpaper* (New York: 1973), originally published in 1899.
Victoria Glendinning, *Rebecca West: A Life* (New York: 1987).
Vicki Goldberg, *Margaret Bourke-White* (New York: 1986).
Emma Goldman, *Anarchism and Other Essays* (New York: 1910).
———, *Living My Life* (New York: 1931).
William J. Goode, *World Revolution and Family Patterns* (New York & London: 1970), originally published in 1963.
Linda Gordon, *Woman's Body, Woman's Right: A Social History of Birth Control in America* (New York: 1976).
Michael Gordon, ed., *The American Family in Social and Economic Perspective* (New York: 1973).
George Grant, *The Legacy of Planned Parenthood* (Brentwood, Tenn.: 1988).
Madeline Gray, *Margaret Sanger: A Biography of the Champion of Birth Control* (New York: 1978).
Dorothy Green and Mary-Elizabeth Murdock, eds. *The Margaret Sanger Centennial Conference* (Northampton, Mass.: 1982).
Elizabeth Griffith, *In Her Own Right: The Life of Elizabeth Cady Stanton* (New York: 1984).
Phyllis Grosskurth, *Havelock Ellis: A Biography* (New York: 1980).
Ernest Gruening, *Many Battles: The Autobiography of Ernest Gruening* (New York: 1973).
Bernice J. Guthmann, *The Planned Parenthood Movement in Illinois, 1923–1965*, Pamphlet (Chicago, Ill.: 1965).
Alan F. Guttmacher, M.D., Winfield Best, Frederick S. Jaffe, *Birth Control and Love: The Complete Guide to Contraception and Fertility* (New York: 1969).
Alan Guttmacher Institute, *Abortions and the Poor: Private Morality, Public Responsibility* (New York: 1979).
Margaret J. Hagood, *Mothers of the South* (Chapel Hill, N.C., 1939).
Emily Hahn, *Mabel: A Biography of Mabel Dodge Luhan* (Boston: 1977).
Nathan G. Hale, Jr., *Freud and the Americans: The Beginnings of Psychoanalysis in the United States, 1876–1914* (New York: 1971).
Ruth Hall, *Passionate Crusader: The Life of Marie Stopes* (New York: 1977).
John S. Haller and Robin M. Haller, *The Physician and Sexuality in Victorian America* (New York & London: 1977).
Mark Haller, *Eugenics: Hereditarian Attitudes in American Thought* (New Brunswick, N.J.: 1963).
Robert W. Haney, *Comstockery in America: Patterns of Censorship and Control* (Boston: 1960).
Hutchins Hapgood, *A Victorian in the Modern World* (New York: 1939).

Susan M. Hartmann, *The Home Front and Beyond: American Women in the 1940s* (Boston: 1982).
William Haywood, *Bill Haywood's Book* (New York: 1929).
Carolyn Heilbrun, *Writing Women's Lives* (New York: 1988).
James M. Henslin, ed., *Studies in the Sociology of Sex* (New York: 1971)
Harold Hersey, *Margaret Sanger: The Biography of the Birth Control Pioneer* (New York: 1938).
Sylvia Ann Hewlett, *A Lesser Life: The Myth of Women's Liberation in America* (New York: 1985).
Granville Hicks, *James Gould Cozzens* (Minneapolis: 1966).
John Higham, *Strangers in the Land: Patterns of American Nativism 1860–1925* (New York: 1974).
Reuben J. Hill, J. Mayone Stycos, Kurt W. Beck, *The Family & Population Control: A Puerto Rican Experiment in Social Change* (Chapel Hill, N.C.: 1959).
Norman E. Himes, *Medical History of Contraception* (Baltimore: 1936).
Shere Hite, *The Hite Report: A Nationwide Study of Female Sexuality* (New York: 1976).
Karen Horney, M.D., *The Neurotic Personality of Our Time* (New York: 1937). *Self-Analysis* (New York: 1942).
———, *Feminine Psychology* (New York: 1967).
Jane Howard, *Margaret Mead: A Life* (New York: 1984).
Irving Howe, *Socialism in America* (New York: 1985).
Henrik Ibsen, *Four Great Plays* (New York: 1959), Introduction by John Gassner.
Harold L. Ickes, *The Secret Diary of Harold L. Ickes* (New York: 1953).
International Planned Parenthood Federation, *The Fifth International Conference on Planned Parenthood, Report of the Proceedings, Tokyo, Japan, 1959* (London: 1956).
———, *The Sixth International Conference on Planned Parenthood, Report of the Proceedings, February 14–21, 1959* (London: 1959).
International Women's Health Coalition, *Population Control and Women's Health: Balancing the Scales* (New York: 1989).
———, *Reproductive Choice in Jeopardy: International Policy Perspectives, Presentations at the Biennial Conference of the Association for Women in Development, Washington, D.C April, 1987* (New York: 1987).
Shidzue Ishimoto, *Facing Two Ways: The Story of My Life* with Introduction and Afterword by Barbara Molony (New York: 1925, reprint ed. California, 1984).
Frederick S. Jaffe, Barbara L. Lindheim, and Philip R. Lee, *Abortion Politics: Private Morality and Public Policy* (New York: 1981).
Janet and Edward James, eds., *Notable American Women, 1607–1950* (Cambridge, Mass.: 1971).
Julia E. Johnson, ed., *Selected Articles in Birth Control* (New York: 1925).
Paul E. Johnson, *A Shopkeeper's Millennium: Society and Revivals in Rochester, New York, 1815–1837* (New York: 1978).
Jacqueline Jones, *Labor of Love, Labor of Sorrow: Black Women, Work, and the Family from Slavery to the Present* (New York: 1986).

Shidzue Kato, *A Fight for Women's Happiness: Pioneering the Family Planning Movement in Japan* (Tokyo: 1984).
The Reverend George A. Kelley, *The Catholic Marriage Manual* (New York: 1959).
David M. Kennedy, *Birth Control in America: The Career of Margaret Sanger* (New Haven: 1970).
———, *Over Here: The First World War and American Society* (New York: 1980).
Linda Kerber, *Women of the Republic: Intellect and Ideology in Revolutionary America* (Chapel Hill: 1980).
Alice Kessler-Harris, *Out to Work: A History of Wage Earning Women in the United States* (New Brunswick, N.J.: 1982).
Daniel J. Kevles, *In the Name of Eugenics: Genetics and the Uses of Human Heredity* (New York: 1985).
Ellen Key, *Love and Marriage* (New York: 1911).
———, *The Century of the Child* (New York: 1909).
———, *The Renaissance of Motherhood* (New York and London: 1914).
Alfred C. Kinsey, Wardell B. Pomeroy, Clyde E. Martin, Paul H. Gebhard, *Sexual Behavior in the Human Female* (Philadelphia: 1953).
Alfred C. Kinsey, Wardell B. Pomeroy, Clyde E. Martin, *Sexual Behavior in the Human Male* (Philadelphia: 1948).
Freda Kirchwey, ed., *Our Changing Morality* (New York: 1924).
Clyde V. Kiser, ed., *Forty Years of Research in Human Fertility: Retrospect and Prospect* (New York: 1971).
Ethel Klein, *Gender Politics* (Cambridge, Mass. & London: 1984).
Heinz Kohut, M.D., *How Does Analysis Cure?* (Chicago: 1984).
Mirra Komarovsky, *Blue-Collar Marriage* (New York: 1967), originally published in 1962.
Antoinette F. Konikow, M.D., *Physician's Manual of Birth Control* (London: 1931).
———, *Voluntary Motherhood* (Boston: 1923).
Marie E. Kopp, Ph.D., *Birth Control in Practice: Analysis of 10,000 Cases and Stories of The Birth Control Clinical Research Bureau* (New York: 1934).
Aileen S. Kraditor, *The Ideas of the Woman Suffrage Movement, 1890–1920* (New York: 1971).
Lawrence Lader, *The Margaret Sanger Story and the Fight for Birth Control* (New York: 1955).
———, *Abortion* (Boston: 1966).
———, *Abortion II: Making the Revolution* (Boston: 1973).
Suzanne LaFollette, *Concerning Women* (New York: 1926).
B. Conliffe Lagemann, ed., *Nursing History: New Prospectives, New Possibilities* (New York: 1983).
Orvin Larson, *American Infidel: Robert G. Ingersoll* (New York: 1962).
Christopher Lasch, *Haven in a Heartless World: The Family Besieged* (New York: 1977).
———, *The New Radicalism in America: The Intellectual as a Social Type* (New York: 1965).
Joseph P. Lash, *Eleanor and Franklin* (New York: 1971).
———, *Eleanor: The Years Alone* (New York: 1972).

Leo J. Latz, *The Rhythm of Sterility and Fertility in Women* (Chicago: 1932). 17th printing, 1944.
William Leach, *True Love and Perfect Union: The Feminist Reform of Sex and Society* (New York: 1980).
Judith Walzer Leavitt, *Brought to Bed: A History of Childbirth in America 1750–1950* (New York: 1986).
Rosanna Ledbetter, *A History of the Malthusian League, 1877–1927* (Columbus, Ohio: 1976).
Herbert Leibowitz, *Fabricating Lives: Explorations in American Autobiography* (New York: 1989).
William E. Leuchtenburg, ed., *Franklin D. Roosevelt: A Profile* (New York: 1967).
Mary S. Lovell, *The Sound of Wings: The Life of Amelia Earhart* (New York: 1989).
Mabel Dodge Luhan, *Movers and Shakers* (New Mexico: 1985).
Robert and Helen Lynd, *Middletown* (New York: 1928).
Norman and Jeanne Mackenzie, *H.G. Wells, A Biography* (New York: 1973).
Janice R. and Stephen R. MacKinnon, *Agnes Smedley: The Life and Times of An American Radical* (Berkeley: 1988).
David. G. Mandelbaum, *Human Fertility in India: Social Components and Policy Perspectives* (Berkeley: 1974).
Steven Marcus, *The Other Victorians: A Study of Sexuality and Pornography in Mid-Nineteenth Century England* (New York: 1964).
John Marshall, *Catholics, Marriage & Contraception* (Baltimore, Md.: 1965).
William H. Masters, M.D. and Virginia E. Johnson, *Human Sexual Response* (New York: 1980), originally published in 1966.
Henry F. May, *The End of American Innocence: A Study of the First Years of Our Own Time* (New York: 1959).
Katherine Mayo, *Mother India: Slaves of the Gods* (New York: 1929).
Mary McCarthy, *The Group* (New York: 1954).
Margaret Mead, *Blackberry Winter: My Earlier Years* (New York: 1972).
———, *Male and Female: A Study of the Sexes in a Changing World* (New York: 1949).
Anthony R. Measham, M.D. *Family Planning in North Carolina: The Politics of a Lukewarm Issue* (Chapel Hill: 1972).
Barbara Melosh, *The Physician's Hand: Work, Culture and Conflict in American Nursing* (Philadelphia: 1982).
Jean Baker Miller, M.D. ed., *Psychoanalysis and Women* (Baltimore, Maryland and Middlesex, England: 1973).
Alice Miller, *The Drama of the Gifted Child: How Narcissistic Parents Form and Deform the Emotional Lives of Their Talented Children* (New York: 1981).
Gail Minault, ed., *The Extended Family: Women and Political Participation in India and Pakistan* (Columbia, Mo.: 1981).
Juliet Mitchell, *Psychoanalysis and Feminism: Freud, Reich, Laing and Women* (New York: 1974).
James C. Mohr, *Abortion in America: The Origins and Evolution of National Policy, 1800–1900* (New York: 1978).
David Montgomery, *Worker's Control in America* (Cambridge: 1979).

Regina Morantz-Sanchez, *Sympathy and Science: Women in American Medicine* (New York: 1985).
Bessie L. Moses, M.D., *Contraception as a Therapeutic Measure* (Baltimore: 1936).
Gunnar Myrdal, *Population: A Problem for Democracy* (Cambridge, Mass.: 1940).
George H. Naphys, M.D. *The Physical Life of Woman: Advice to the Maiden, Wife, and Mother* (Philadelphia: 1888).
National Committee on Maternal Health, Inc., *The Abortion Problem: Proceedings of the Conference Held Under the Auspices of the NCMN, Inc. at the New York Academy of Medicine, June 19, 1942* (Baltimore, Md.: 1944). *Selected Bibliography of Contraception, 1940–1960* (New York: 1960).
Scott Nearing, *The Super Race: An American Problem* (New York: 1912).
John T. Noonan, Jr., *Contraception: A History of Its Treatment by the Catholic Theologians and Canonists* (Cambridge: 1966). Reissued in an enlarged paperback edition, 1986.
Mary Beth Norton, *Liberty's Daughters: The Revolutionary Experience of American Women, 1750–1800* (New York: 1980).
Mary Adelaide Nutting, *A Sound Economic Basis for Schools of Nursing* (New York: 1926).
William L. O'Neill, *Divorce in the Progressive Era* (New Haven, Ct.: 1967).
———, *Everyone Was Brave: The Rise and Fall of Feminism in America* (Chicago: 1969).
Elaine Pagels, *Adam, Eve and the Serpent* (New York: 1988).
Elsie Clews Parsons, *Social Freedom* (New York: 1915).
Elizabeth Israels Perry, *Belle Moskowitz: Feminine Politics & the Exercise of Power in the Age of Alfred E. Smith* (New York: 1987).
A Physician, *Madame Restell: An Account of her Life and Horrible Practices Together with Prostitution in New York: Its Extent, Causes and Effects Upon Society* (New York: 1847).
Donald K. Pickens, *Eugenics and the Progressives* (Nashville, Tenn.: 1968).
Gregory Pincus, *The Control of Fertility* (New York: 1965).
Phyllis Tilson Piotrow, *World Population Crisis: The United States Response* (New York: 1973).
Planned Parenthood Federation of America, *A Tradition of Choice: Planned Parenthood at 75* (New York: 1991).
Pope Pius XI, *Casti Conubii: On Christian Marriage* (Washington, D.C.: 1931).
Pope Pius XII, *Moral Questions Affecting Married Life: The Apostolate of the Midwife* (New York: 1951).
David Pivar, *Purity Crusade* (New York: 1973).
Wardell B. Pomeroy, *Dr. Kinsey and the Institute for Sex Research* (New York: 1972).
Caroline Pratt, *I Learn From Children: An Adventure in Progressive Education* (New York: 1948).
President's Research Committee on Social Trends, *Recent Social Trends in the United States* (New York: 1933).
Lee Rainwater, *And the Poor Get Children* (Chicago: 1960).
———, *Family Design: Marital Sexuality, Family Size and Contraception* (Chicago: 1965).

Dhanvanthi Rama Rau, *An Inheritance: The Memoirs of Dhanvanthi Rama Rau* (New York: 1977).
Gordon N. Ray, *H.G. Wells and Rebecca West* (New Haven: 1974).
James Reed, *From Private Vice to Public Virtue: The Birth Control Movement and American Society Since 1830* (New York: 1978). Reissued in paperback as *The Birth Control Movement and American Society: From Private Vice to Public Virtue* (Princeton: 1984).
Ira L. Reiss, *Premarital Sexual Standards in America* (Illinois: 1953).
Report of the Fifth International Neo-Malthusian and Birth Control Conference, Kingsway Hall, London, July 11–14, 1922 (London: 1922).
Adrienne Rich, *Of Woman Born: Motherhood as Experience and Institution* (New York: 1976).
Herbert W. Richardson, *Nun, Witch, Playmate: The Americanization of Sex* (New York: 1971).
Caroline Hadley Robinson, *Seventy Birth Control Clinics: A Survey and Analysis Including the General Effects of Control on Size and Quality of Population* (Baltimore: 1930).
Paul Robinson, *The Modernization of Sex* (New York: 1976).
Victor Robinson, *Pioneers of Birth Control* (New York: 1919).
William J. Robinson, *Eugenics, Marriage and Birth Control* (New York: 1917).
John D. Rock, M.D. and David Loth, *Voluntary Parenthood* (New York: 1949).
John D. Rock, M.D., *The Time Has Come, A Catholic Doctor's Proposals to End the Battle Over Birth Control* (New York: 1963).
Eleanor Roosevelt, *This I Remember* (New York: 1949).
Michelle Zimbalist Rosaldo and Louise Lamphere, eds., *Woman, Culture, and Society* (Stanford, Ca.: 1974).
Phyllis Rose, *Parallel Lives: Five Victorian Marriages* (New York: 1984).
———, *Woman of Letters: A Life of Virginia Woolf* (New York: 1978).
Rosalind Rosenberg, *Beyond Separate Spheres: Intellectual Roots of Modern Feminism* (New Haven: 1982).
———, *Divided Lives: American Women in the 20th Century* (New York: 1992).
Barbara Gutman Rosenkrantz, *Public Health and the State: Changing Views in Massachusetts, 1842–1936* (Cambridge, Mass.: 1972).
Robert A. Rosenstone, *Romantic Revolutionary: A Biography of John Reed* (New York: 1975).
Ellen K. Rothman, *Hands and Hearts: A History of Courtship in America* (New York: 1984).
Sheila M. Rothman, *Woman's Proper Place: A History of Changing Ideals and Practices, 1870 to the Present* (New York: 1978).
Sheila Rowbotham, *Hidden from History: Rediscovering Women in History from the 17th Century to the Present* (London: 1976).
Sheila Rowbotham and Jeffrey Weeks, *Socialism and the New Life: The Personal and Sexual Politics of Edward Carpenter and Havelock Ellis* (London: 1977).
Louise Palken Rudnick, *Mabel Dodge Luhan: New Woman, New Worlds* (Albuquerque, New Mexico: 1984).
Mary P. Ryan, *Cradle of the Middle Class: The Family in Oneida County New York, 1790–1865* (Cambridge, Eng. and New York: 1981).

Margaret Sanger, *An Autobiography* (New York: 1938).
———, *Appeals from American Mothers* (New York: 1921)
———, *The Case for Birth Control: A Supplementary Brief and Statement of Fact* (New York: 1917).
———, *Family Limitation*, various editions. (New York: 1914–1919.)
———, *Happiness in Marriage* (Elmsford, New York: 1969). Reprinted from the original 1926 edition.
———, *Motherhood in Bondage* (New York: 1928).
———, *My Fight for Birth Control* (New York: 1931).
———, *The New Motherhood* (London: 1922).
———, *The Pivot of Civilization* (New York: 1922).
———, *Sayings of Others on Birth Control* (New York: 1921).
———, *What Every Girl Should Know* (New York: 1980). Reprint of the 1920 edition.
———, *What Every Boy and Girl Should Know* (New York, 1969). Reprint of the 1927 edition.
———, *Woman and the New Race* (New York: 1920).
Margaret Sanger, ed., *Proceedings of the World Population Conference* (London: 1927).
———, ed., *Proceedings of the American Conference on Birth Control and National Recovery, Jan. 15–17, 1934, Washington, D.C.* (Washington: 1934).
———, ed., *The Sixth International Neo-Malthusian and Birth Control Conference*, 4 vols. (New York: 1925–26).
Margaret Sanger and Hannah M. Stone, M.D., eds. *The Practice of Contraception: An Introductory Symposium and Survey. Proceedings of the Seventh International Birth Control Conference Zurich, Switzerland 1930* (Baltimore, Md.: 1931).
Arthur Schlesinger, Jr., *The Age of Roosevelt: The Crisis of the Old Order* (New York: 1957).
———, *The Coming of the New Deal* (New York: 1959).
———, *The Politics of Upheaval* (New York: 1960).
Arthur Schlesinger, Jr., ed., *Walter Lippmann: Early Writings* (New York: 1970).
Olive Schreiner, *Woman and Labor* (New York: 1911).
Judith Schwarz, *Radical Feminists of Heterodoxy, Greenwich Village, 1912–1940* (New Hampshire: 1982).
Richard Sennett and Jonathan Cobb, *The Hidden Injuries of Class* (New York: 1972).
Mary Jane Sherfey, *The Nature and Evolution of Female Sexuality* (New York: 1972).
Robert E. Sherwood, *Roosevelt and Hopkins: An Intimate History* (New York: 1948).
Richard Harrison Shyrock, *Medicine and Society in America: 1660–1860* (New York: 1960).
Barbara Sicherman, ed., *Alice Hamilton: A Life in Letters* (Cambridge, Mass.: 1984).
Barbara Sicherman and Carol Hurd Green, eds., *Notable American Women,*

The Modern Period, A Biographical Dictionary (Cambridge, Mass.: 1980).
Kate Simon, *Bronx Primitive* (New York: 1982).
Kathryn Kish Sklar, *Catherine Beecher: A Study in American Domesticity* (New Haven: 1973).
Agnes Smedley, *Daughter of Earth* (New York: 1928).
David C. Smith, *H.G. Wells, Desperately Mortal, A Biography* (New Haven: 1986).
June Sochen, *The New Woman: Feminism in Greenwich Village, 1910–1920* (New York: 1972).
Susan Sontag, *Illness as Metaphor* (New York: 1979).
Theodore C. Sorenson, *Kennedy* (New York: 1965).
John Spargo, *Socialism and Motherhood* (New York: 1914).
Christine Stansell, *City of Women: Sex and Class in New York, 1789–1860* (New York: 1986).
Paul Starr, *The Social Transformation of American Medicine* (New York: 1987).
Ronald Steel, *Walter Lippmann and the American Century* (New York: 1980).
Regine K. Stix and Frank W. Notestein, *Controlled Fertility* (Baltimore: 1940).
Lothrop Stoddard, *The Rising Tide of Color Against White World Supremacy* (New York: 1920).
Hannah Meyer Stone, M.D. and Abraham Stone, M.D., *A Marriage Manual: A Practical Guide Book to Sex and Marriage* (New York: 1935).
Marie C. Stopes, *Married Love* (London: 1927).
———, *Radiant Motherhood* (London: 1920).
Jean Strouse, *Alice James: A Biography* (Boston: 1980).
Jean Strouse, ed., *Women & Analysis: Dialogues on Psychoanalytic Views of Femininity* (New York: 1974).
J. Mayone Stycos, et al., *Clinics, Contraception and Communication: Evaluation Studies of Family Planning Programs in Four Latin American Countries* (New York: 1973).
Berryl Suitters, *Be Brave and Angry: Chronicles of the International Planned Parenthood Federation* (London: 1973).
Alvah Sulloway, *Birth Control and Catholic Doctrine* (New York: 1959).
Frederick J. Taussig, M.D., *Abortion: Spontaneous and Induced* (St. Louis, Mo.: 1936).
Meredith Tax, *The Rising of the Women: Feminist Solidarity and Class Conflict, 1810–1917* (New York: 1980).
Robert Taylor, *Saranac: America's Magic Mountain* (Boston: 1986).
Alfred Terhume, *The Life of Edward FitzGerald, Translator of The Rubaiyat of Omar Khayyam* (London: 1947).
Lewis M. Terman, *Psychological Factors in Marital Happiness* (New York: 1938).
Mary Lou Thompson, ed., *Voices of the New Feminism* (Boston, Mass.: 1970).
Warren S. Thompson and Pascal K. Whelpton, *Population Trends in the United States* (New York: 1933).
Judith Thurman, *Isak Dinesen: The Life of a Storyteller* (New York: 1982).
Anne Huber Tripp, *The I.W.W. and the Paterson Silk Strike of 1913* (Urbana, Illinois: 1987).

Kenneth Underwood, *Protestant and Catholic: Religious and Social Interaction in an Industrial Community* (Boston: 1957).

T.H. Van de Velde, M.D., *Ideal Marriage: Its Physiology and Technique* (New York: 1930).

Martha Vicinus, ed., *Suffer and Be Still: Women in the Victorian Age* (Bloomington, Indiana & London: 1973).

William Vogt, *The Road to Survival* (New York: 1948).

W. Warren Wager, ed., *H.G. Wells: Journalism and Prophecy 1893–1946* (Boston: 1964).

Susan Ware, *Beyond Suffrage: Women in the New Deal* (Cambridge, Mass.: 1981).

———, *Holding Their Own: American Women in the 1930s* (Boston: 1982).

John B. Watson, *The Psychological Care of Infant and Child* (New York: 1928).

H.G. Wells, *Ann Veronica* (London: 1909).

———, *Socialism and the Family* (London: 1908).

———, *The Secret Places of the Heart* (London, New York, Toronto and Melbourne: 1922).

Anthony West, *H.G. Wells: Aspects of a Life* (New York: 1984).

Charles F. Westoff, *Family Growth in Metropolitan America* (Princeton, N.J.: 1961).

Leslie Aldridge Westoff & Charles F. Westoff, *From Now to Zero: Fertility, Contraception and Abortion in America* (Boston: 1968).

Alice Wexler, *Emma Goldman: An Intimate Life* (New York: 1985).

———, *Emma Goldman in Exile: From the Russian Revolution to the Spanish Civil War* (Boston: 1989).

Edith Wharton, *The Age of Innocence* (New York: 1920).

Pascal K. Whelpton and Clyde V. Kiser, eds., *Social and Psychological Factors Affecting Fertility* (Princeton, N.J.: 1959).

Morton White, *Social Thought in America: The Revolt Against Formalism* 2d ed. (Boston: 1957).

Robert Wiebe, *The Search for Order 1877–1920* (New York: 1967).

Sean Wilentz, *Chants Democratic: New York City and the Rise of the American Working Class, 1788–1850* (New York: 1984).

John Whitridge Williams, M.D., *Obstetrics: A Textbook for Use of Students and Practitioners* (New York: 1909).

Garry Wills, *Bare Ruined Choirs: Doubt, Prophecy, and Radical Religion* (New York: 1972).

Richard and Dorothy Wirtz, *Lying In: A History of Childbirth in America* (New York: 1978).

Robert Woodbury, *Maternal Mortality: U.S Department of Labor, Children's Bureau Publication 158* (Washington, D.C.: 1926).

Virginia Woolf, *To the Lighthouse* (New York: 1927).

Joseph Wortis, M.D., *Fragments of an Analysis with Freud* (New York: 1954).

John E. Gordon and John B. Wyon, *The Khanna Study: Population Problems in the Rural Punjab* (New York: 1971).

Rachelle S. Yarros, *Modern Woman and Sex: A Feminist Physician Speaks* (New York: 1933).

William Butler Yeats, *Selected Poetry* (London: 1974).

DOCTORAL DISSERTATIONS AND UNPUBLISHED MANUSCRIPTS:

Janet F. Brodie, "Family Limitation in American Culture: 1830–1900." Doctoral Dissertation, University of Chicago, 1982

Harold Hersey, "Birth Control Pioneer," Unpublished Ms., 1938. Manuscript Division, New York Public Library.

Alexander Campbell Sanger, "Margaret Sanger, The Early Years, 1910–1917." Senior Thesis, Princeton University, 1969.

Malia Sedgewick Johnson, "Margaret Sanger and the Birth Control Movement in Japan, 1921–1955." Doctoral Dissertation, University of Hawaii, 1987.

William N. Morehouse, "The Speaking of Margaret Sanger in the Birth Control Movement from 1916 to 1937." Doctoral Dissertation, Purdue University, 1968.

Carlo Tresca, "Autobiography," Unpublished Ms., in the Carlo Tresca Papers, Manuscript Division, New York Public Library.

Maris A. Vinovskis, "Demographic Changes in America from the Revolution to the Civil War: An Analysis of the Socio-Economic Determinants of Fertility Differentials and Trends in Massachusetts from 1765 to 1860," Doctoral Dissertation, Harvard University, 1975.

Francis M. Vreeland, "The Process of Reform with Especial Reference to Reform Groups in the Field of Population." Doctoral Dissertation, University of Michigan, 1929.

Acknowledgments

My work on this book has spanned two decades, during which I have incurred many debts.

I am grateful first for financial support. I became interested in Margaret Sanger and the history of birth control in America years ago while a graduate student at Columbia University, where I was supported by a Faculty Fellowship. I was subsequently awarded a two-year grant from the Program for Population Research in the Social Sciences, sponsored jointly by the Ford and Rockefeller Foundations. The late Fred Jaffe, then of the Alan Guttmacher Institute, encouraged my application for that stipend because of his own affection for Sanger and his conviction that the past might inspire, and perhaps even enlighten, contemporary population policymakers. I hope that this book rewards his confidence, at long last.

I am grateful, second, to my uncommonly talented colleagues in the world of New York government, politics and civic affairs. In 1977, I set aside this project to join the campaign, and later the administration, of former New York City Council President Carol Bellamy. As chief of staff to the first woman ever elected to citywide office, I experienced the very special rewards of committing oneself to public service, and some of the hazards too, especially for women who dare to be outspoken. My own practical experience, then and since, invariably informs this book, as much as the more conventional archival research in which it is grounded.

My return to the project in 1985 was made possible by the generosity of David and Sheila Rothman, who found a temporary place for me at Columbia University's Center for the Study of Medicine and Society, where I could wend my way back into scholarship. For their support and friendship, and for David's careful and thoughtful reading of an earlier draft of this manuscript that I presented as a doctoral dissertation in American history, I am deeply indebted. No less is my debt to Rosalind Rosenberg, of Barnard and Columbia, and to Sylvia Law, of the New York University School of Law, who both also read and annotated the dissertation with great intelligence and sensitivity; to Atina Grossmann and Priscilla Wald of Columbia, who served on the committee; to James Reed of Rutgers and Gina Morantz-Sanchez of UCLA, whose fine scholarship in the history of medicine and of sexuality first inspired my own; and to Temma Kaplan, former director of the Barnard College Women's Center, where I read several chapters of this work in draft.

For research guidance I am indebted as well to the diligent and devoted archivists who have patiently assembled and organized the papers that Margaret Sanger and a large supporting cast of characters left behind. Special thanks are due Susan Grigg, the director of the Sophia Smith Collection at Smith College, and Susan Boone, Mary-Elizabeth Murdock, Eleanor Lewis and Dorothy Greene, all former staff members; Esther Katz and Peter Engelman, who both graciously read and commented on the manuscript, and Cathy Hajo and Anke Hubbard, all of the Margaret Sanger Papers Project at New York University and Smith College; Patricia King, Elizabeth Shenton, and Eva Moseley of the Schlesinger Library at Radcliffe College; Richard Wolfe of the Countway Library of Medicine at Harvard University; Peter Johnson, archivist for the Rockefeller family, who facilitated my use of the rich collections at the archives at Pocantico Hills; Claudia Anderson of the Lyndon Baines Johnson Library in Austin, Texas; the archivists of the Franklin Delano Roosevelt Library in Hyde Park, New York; Dr. Anthony Zito of Catholic University and, finally, the many cooperative staff members at the Library of Congress and the National Archives in Washington, D.C.

Countless Planned Parenthood personnel all over the country have also been responsive to my inquiries, especially, Gloria Roberts of the Planned Parenthood Federation of America; Elly Anderson of Planned Parenthood of Southern Arizona; Charlotte Levine, formerly of the Margaret Sanger Center of Planned Parenthood–New York City; and Steve Plevar, who is currently in charge of public relations there. Phyllis Martin of the Painted Post Historical Society helped me in Corning, New York. Paul Avrich helped locate anarchists. Taki Katoh sent materials from Japan, and Barbara Ramusack shared her research on India. Molly Ivins sent the latest in anti-Sanger propaganda. Joan Dunlop of the International Women's Health Coalition has educated me on contemporary issues in international family planning. Helene and Mark Kaplan graciously stored my early research files during the years when I was otherwise engaged, and they deserve a special benediction. Delores Jones has kept me well-organized ever since.

New York University's Biography Seminar, and more recently the distaff sessions on "Writing Women's Lives," have provided a most rewarding opportunity to share thoughts and concerns about craft. David Garrow, whose forthcoming study of the Supreme Court's decisions in the Griswold and Roe cases promises to pick up where this story leaves off, has offered fresh insights in the final stages of my work. Jane Alpert, who has been thinking about the history and the politics of family planning, also offered thoughtful comments.

In addition, many cherished friends have faithfully eyed pieces of the manuscript whenever I needed a new perspective or just a word of encouragement. My warmest thanks to Louise Burnham, Naomi Marks Cohan, Peggy Davis, Barry Ensminger, Jamie Fellner, Leslie Koch, Neal Johnston, William Josephson, Eden Lipson, Suzanne Slesin, Gillian Walker, and William Wilson. Still more friends and family have listened to me talk on and on about Margaret Sanger over the years. To all of them I am also grateful, and especially so to film critic, Joel Siegel, who unearthed an early edition of *Woman and the New Race.*

The one clear benefit of taking so many years to write this book has been the refinement in the interim of personal computers. For assistance in choosing hardware and in helping me realize WordPerfect's full potential, special blessings to Michael Kraft, Faried Abrahams, and Peter Lesser. My thanks as well to Charles Kaiser, Rich Meislin, Neal Johnston, Costa Rodis, Felicia Halpert, and especially to New York's only computer whiz by day and comedienne by night, Teri Coyne.

The extensive traveling I have done to track down Margaret Sanger has only been possible because of the friends and family who put me up at night in distant places: Alan and Betty Newmark in London, Jamie Fellner and Rick Cotton in Washington, Lois and Leon Thikoll in Tucson, Lewis Chesler in Los Angeles, Barbara Chesler in New Haven, Eleanor Lewis in Northampton, and Barbara Sicherman, lo, those many years ago in Cambridge.

The many generous individuals who made themselves available for interviews are acknowledged in the bibliography and notes, but special mention is again due the family of Margaret Sanger, especially the late Grant Sanger, M.D., and the late Olive Byrne Richard—who were my most devoted muses—Stuart and Barbara Sanger, Alexander Campbell Sanger, and Margaret Sanger Marston (now Margaret Marston Lampe). They have all been unusually gracious.

Robert Asahina has been an especially wise and judicious editor, and there is really no way to acknowledge my appreciation of his extensive contribution to this book, save to say that I hope we will do another together. The same must be said for my dear friend Arthur Klebanoff, who has been a wonderfully devoted and able agent. My thanks as well to Sarah Pinckney of Simon & Schuster and especially to Ann Finlayson and Florence Falkow, for saving me from embarrassment with their rigorous and intelligent copy editing of the manuscript.

The essential debts are of course the most personal and the hardest to acknowledge. My parents, Howard and Celia Chesler, taught me a long time ago about the importance of balancing love and work in my life. My children, Jonathan and Betsy Mallow—both uncannily wise and winning—refresh my determination to do so each time I set my eyes upon them. My exceptional husband, Matt Mallow, is my ballast. He has nurtured this book in all ways possible, and to him it is dedicated with love. He's certainly waited for it for a very long time.

New York, New York
January 1992

Index

Picture Credits

M. Heinaman. From the Sophia Smith Collection, Smith College. 1
From the Sophia Smith Collection, Smith College. 2, 3, 4, 5, 6, 7, 8, 12, 13, 14, 15, 17, 19, 20, 21, 23, 26, 27, 28, 31, 32, 35, 36, 37, 38, 41, 42, 43
From *Woman Rebel,* Alex Baskin, ed., New York: Archives of Social History, 1976. 9
UPI/Bettmann. 10, 16, 18, 22, 24, 30, 33
The Bettmann Archive. 11, 34
The Francis Countway Library of Medicine, Harvard University. 25
Planned Parenthood Federation of America, Inc. 29
Jay Sternberg. From the Sophia Smith Collection, Smith College. 39
M. L. Saigal/Planned Parenthood Federation of America. 40
Meljay Photographers, Inc./Planned Parenthood Federation of America. 44
© David Levine. Used by permission of the artist. 45, 46